10-

Burt Franklin: Research and Source Work Series #91

THE

HISTORY

OF

THE FACTORY MOVEMENT

IN TWO VOLUMES

VOL. I

THE

H I S T O R Y

OF

THE FACTORY MOVEMENT

FROM

THE YEAR 1802 TO THE ENACTMENT OF THE
TEN HOURS' BILL IN 1847

By **ALFRED KYDD**

IN TWO VOLUMES

VOL. I

Burt Franklin: Research and Source Work Series # 91

BURT FRANKLIN
NEW YORK

Published by BURT FRANKLIN
235 East 44th Street
New York, N.Y. 10017

First Published
LONDON
1857

Printed in U.S.A.

DEDICATION.

TO THE

RIGHT HON. LORD FEVERSHAM.

My Lord,

" The highest humanity is the soundest policy."
Your lordship, early in your political career, appreciated the truth and wisdom of this maxim. A
quarter of a century has elapsed since, at a county
meeting in the Castle-yard of York, by the bold
expression of your sense of the responsibilities of the
rich to the poor, and of the government to society,
your lordship linked yourself to the hearts of the
factory operatives. Your lordship has witnessed a
protracted conflict between the supporters and opponents of factory regulation,—you have taken therein
an important part; the social, moral, and educational
advantages which have followed the passing of the
Ten Hours' Bill, in 1847, cannot have failed to be
gratifying to your heart, and, in some degree, to
have rewarded you for your manifold exertions.

When friends to the oppressed factory workers were few, your lordship stepped boldly forth, and, by your example, contributed to bring about a salutary change in public opinion. When public opinion had undergone a desirable transition, and the mind of the legislature had become ripe for legislation; your lordship distinguished yourself by the earnestness with which, in your legislative capacity, you sealed the efforts of earlier years, with the approval of a majority of the House of Lords.

Because of early, consistent, and continuous exertions, on behalf of the interests of those engaged in factory labour, I esteem it a privilege to be allowed to dedicate " THE HISTORY OF THE FACTORY MOVEMENT," to your lordship.

I have the honour to be,

My Lord,

Your Lordship's humble and obedient servant,

ALFRED.

PREFACE.

CUSTOM has established the rule, that authors should state the reasons why they write books. Recent discussions in parliament, and the tone of a portion of the periodical literature of the time, have convinced the Author that the facts of the factories, as these existed prior to factory regulation by law, were either forgotten or misunderstood, and, that the means taken to change that condition have been frequently misapprehended; he, therefore, considers it to be a duty to present to the public and to statesmen a narrative, compiled from authentic sources, embodying these facts. The social condition of the working classes is a subject of growing influence; the number of persons, under the operation of the Factories' Regulation Acts, is, probably, not fewer than half a million, and is rapidly on the increase; the past history of the factory operatives, as a class, can scarcely fail to be of interest to many among themselves; the parliamentary records, of more than half a century, bear witness to the importance of the factory question in the eye of the legislature; as a subject of social and political moment, it is worthy of special study. The press, which in this country reflects and leads public opinion, and prepares the national mind for legislation, has long esteemed the factory question as one of high importance

The leaders of the factory movement, in comparatively recent times, have, by extraordinary exertions, forced on an unwilling government, a recognition of its duty, to protect by law the helpless; it was reserved for the promoters of the factory movement to break through the commercial materialism of their age, to compel society and the legislature to recognise every woman, young person, and child, employed in the textile branches of British manufacture, as a human creature, having a mind and body to be cared for, and, as being an object of higher regard than merely a piece of factory furniture, whose existence had no end to accomplish, beyond producing the greatest possible quantity of goods at the lowest possible cost.

To supply, in a condensed form, yet, with a fulness sufficient for the ordinary purposes of the practical student in history and politics, a narrative of these exertions, is, the Author trusts, a work not incompatible with the wants of the age. Many efforts are now being made on behalf of the social improvement of the working classes; a circumstance which renders a knowledge of the past more desirable than it, otherwise, would have been.

The subject of factory regulation has, for years, received a considerable share of the Author's attention; he believes that its importance, though generally recognized, is not so fully appreciated, as it deserves; he has been personally familiar with some among the principal leaders of the factory movement; from his own experience, he is certain that their labours have not hitherto been duly acknowledged. Historical justice, of which much has been recently said, requires, that all efforts, for or against the public good, should be registered; and, that every necessary means should be applied for the establishment and preservation of the whole truth, without regard to the prejudices or interests of parties or individuals.

The factory system is the result of a new power in modern civilization, unknown to ancient states, and having no parallel in the history of modern nations; its origin, progress, and effects, as manifested in society, consequently, claim close attention from all who are interested in the present and future well-being of those engaged in manufacturing industry.

The division of labour is an important condition of modern production; it is as applicable to the narration of events as to watchmaking, and will be found advantageous for purposes of information and reference.

The vague sense often attached to the word *constitutional*, induces the Author to observe that, when used by him, it is to be understood by the reader as meaning, *in concordance with the general spirit of the laws of this country.*

The Author has endeavoured to present facts and

documents in the words in which he found them, rather than in his own, but, he has not shrunk from an expression of his opinions; knowing, that every discriminating reader will separate the statement of things done, from the judgment expressed, and give unto each due consideration. The Author has often asked himself—"Why should the history of a movement which occupied many years of the lives of some self-sacrificing, strong-minded, persevering, and benevolent men, ultimately commanded an over-ruling share of public attention, and left the mark of its existence on the legislation of the country, be to society less interesting or valuable than the biography of an eminent statesmen or divine?"

The Author's desire to do justice to the services of some public men whose motives, intentions, and actions have, even in the highest places, been misunderstood and misrepresented, constitutes the warrant for the work on which he has entered.

LONDON, *October*, 1857.

CONTENTS.

a

THE

HISTORY OF THE FACTORY MOVEMENT.

————o————

CHAPTER I.

WILLIAM PITT, THE ENGLISH MANUFACTURERS, AND ENGLISH CHILDREN.
—PROMINENT FACTS ILLUSTRATING THE SOCIAL CONDITION OF
ENGLAND ANTERIOR TO THE INTRODUCTION OF THE FACTORY
SYSTEM.

THE history of the manufacturing industry of this country
has long been a subject of universal interest. The historians,
the social, political, and moral economists of France, have
devoted to the manufacturing industry of England a large
share of their attention. The proximity of the two nations,
the wide difference in their internal economy, in their industrial development, in the native bent of the genius of
their peoples, have opened to the thoughtful of each nation
a profitable and comprehensive range of inquiry and comparison in the study of the other. These circumstances
render it desirable that the information conveyed by the
authors of one nation regarding the industry of the other
should be trustworthy.

William Pitt was an eminent statesman. We esteem M.
Michelet, the French historian, as a man of genius and an
author of deservedly high reputation. For these reasons,

his words relating to a statesman whose name is representative of an important period of English history have an especial interest. In a translation of *The People*, there is the following statement:—"In the height of the great duel between England and France, when the English manufacturers represented to Mr Pitt that the rise in the rate of wages incapacitated them from paying the taxes, he pronounced the terrible words, 'Take the children.' Those words weigh heavily upon England as a curse. Ever since that hour the race of its men have been deteriorating. This people, heretofore so athletic, is growing nerveless and enfeebled. What has become of that vividness and freshness of complexion which was so great a charm of English youth?—Faded, sullied. They listened to Mr Pitt. *They took the children.*" Granting the truth, in all its fulness, of the effects of the factory system, as narrated by M. Michelet, the memory of so distinguished a statesman as William Pitt demands an examination into the part which he is represented to have taken.

In the absence of proof of the fact related, we cannot admit the reasonableness of charging so terrible a national calamity upon a statesman who, so far as his public acts and recorded declarations are representative of his opinions, would have been the last of English statesmen to have uttered a sentiment so unmanly — so unwise. On what occasion was it that William Pitt, having been confronted by the English manufacturers in distress, said to them, in order that they should have been enabled to pay their taxes, "Take the children"?

"In the height of the great duel between England and France" the manufacturers of England were, as a rule, eminently prosperous. That prosperity increased the cupidity of some, and laid the foundation of the colossal fortunes of others, whose benevolence in their own neighbourhoods was beneficially exerted. True, there were times of great distress, when, for a season, the manufacturing industry was prostrated ; the remedy was not found by William Pitt in the unnatural labour of children, but in financial changes, in issuing exchequer-bills, the suspension of cash payments, giving direct relief in money, and other measures of a like kind. There is a passage in a speech spoken by William Pitt on February 12th, 1796, which, by misapprehension, may have led to the French historian's assertion. Mr Whitbread having in the House of Commons moved the second reading of the Labourers' Wages Bill, William Pitt said—" Experience had already shown how much could be done by the industry of children, and the advantage of early employing them in such branches of manufacture as they were capable to execute. The extension of schools of industry was also an object of national importance. If any one would take the trouble to compute the amount of all the earnings of the children who are educated in this manner, he would be surprised, when he came to consider the weight which their support by their own labours took off the country, and the addition which, by the fruits of their toil, and the habits to which they were formed, was made to its internal opulence. The suggestion of these schools was originally drawn from Lord Hales and Mr Locke, and upon such authority he had no difficulty in recommending the plan to the encouragement of the Legislature. Much might be effected by a plan of the nature susceptible of constant improvement." It is possible that M. Michelet may have mistaken the industrial schools recommended by William Pitt, for the employment of children in factories. William Pitt stated on whose authority the industrial schools he approved were founded.

In 1697, the neglected state of the children of the poor attracted the attention of the Government. The Board of Trade was authorised by William III to inquire into the subject; the Commissioners appointed were Lord Hales and

John Locke. Their report, said to have been written by Locke, is the key to the objects contemplated by Pitt; these are faithfully conveyed in the following clause, extracted from the "Heads of a Bill for the better support and maintenance of the poor; prepared according to the plan opened by Mr Pitt to the House of Commons, in the present session of Parliament, 1796."

"That the persons appointed to the management of the poor of any parish or united parishes, shall from time to time provide, by all lawful means in their power, a proper stock of hemp, flax, silk, cotton, iron, leather, or other materials, and also proper tools and implements for the employment of the poor; and it shall be lawful for the said parish, or united parishes, and for the poor thereof, and the person, or persons appointed to the management of the said poor, respectively to carry on all or any trades, mysteries, or occupations whatever, within any school or schools of industry established by virtue of this Act, and the buildings thereunto belonging, or at the houses or habitations of the poor persons of such respective parishes; any law, usage, or custom to the contrary notwithstanding; and that all persons whatever, who shall be lawfully settled in any parish where he, she, or they, may reside, or in any parish united therewith; and also all other persons residing in any such parish, under the authority of the Act, who shall be willing to be employed in any trade, mystery, occupation, or employment, carried on in the school, or schools of industry there, shall for themselves, respectively, and such of their respective families who are able and willing to work, be entitled to be employed in such school, or schools of industry, and to be instructed in any such trade, mystery, occupation, or employment there carried on, as shall be suited to his, her, or their strength, or ability, at such wages, or recompense, as shall be settled and established to be paid or made for the work done or performed by him, her, or them, in such school, or schools of industry, according to the directions of this Act."

In the bill were provisions enabling the parish authorities to apprentice "to any respectable person in Great Britain," every male child of the age of fourteen, female child at twelve, or earlier if thought fit, for the purpose of being taught a useful handicraft. In 1817, the fundamental principle of the industrial training-schools projected by Hales and Locke, was approved by a Poor-Law Committee of the House of Commons. The pauperism and crime of the present century are in a great degree attributable to the neglect on the part of governments of the merciful and wise suggestions of Hales and Locke, supported by Pitt, but unfortunately not reduced to practice. The evil, as well as the good in society, bears witness to the truth of the words : " Train up a child in the way he should go, and when he is old he will not depart from it."

All who know the writings of Locke will remember how zealously, under all circumstances, he contended for health and recreation. Locke knew that the love of action was inseparable from childhood, and it was the constant aim of his practical philosophy to render the application of this instinctive desire healthful in mind and body to its possessor ; results incompatible with the unregulated factory system. Not any statesman, having read the writings of Locke, could fail to observe the importance he attaches to a full allowance of sleep, and exercise in the open air, and, having approved these writings, could name their author in support of any practice opposed to these essential requisites. William Pitt's known approval of the efforts of his friend, the first Sir Robert Peel, is in itself decided proof that the former could not have said to the manufacturers, in the sense conveyed by M. Michelet, " Take the children." The children were taken before " the great duel " was at its height, and William Pitt was no obstacle to their emancipation and improvement. The respect due to the memory and character of a departed statesman, a sense of the importance of the words of a living historian, full of sympathy for the oppressed of all nations, and the close connection of his statement with the subject under consideration, demand from us, thus early, the remarks we have made. In passing, we cannot avoid observing that all the conditions of health and strength associated with industry, contended for by Locke, were compatible with domestic manufacture as practised anterior to the introduction of complicated machinery and steam power as agents of production. Had British statesmen discovered and applied the means necessary for uniting health and labour under the changed conditions of productive industry, there would not now have existed the necessity for that history which it is our duty to narrate.

The affirmation which we have quoted from a translation of M. Michelet's book, has been adopted and repeated by other French authors of high reputation, and has, consequently, assumed the character of an established truth. Not any statesman ever maintained the industrial rights of the labourers of England more earnestly than did William Pitt; he distinguished himself by his defence of the Poor Law of Elizabeth. So far was William Pitt from saying to the manufacturers of England, " Take the children," that he, on the contrary, contended that every labouring man and his family had a right to be made comfortable in his own dwelling, and actually introduced into parliament a bill, intended to supply every labouring man and his family, when and where required, " with a cow or a, pig, or some other animal yielding profit." The industrial schools approved by William Pitt, were entirely opposed in principle and practice to the unregulated factory system. The schools were local and parochial, and in their management health was a principal consideration.

The French authors who have arraigned the character of William Pitt by so serious an imputation on his humanity, and his wisdom as a statesman, have not given their authorities for so grave a charge ; in the absence of those authorities the weight of their declaration is lessened. We have been unable to discover any grounds for the accusation, beyond those already named, the misinterpretation of which may possibly have misled M. Michelet and his followers.

A knowledge of the importance of the question of factory labour, and a due appreciation of the efforts to secure factory regulation under the law, require that some of the more prominent facts illustrating the industrial condition of this country anterior to the general introduction and development of the inventions of Watt, Hargraves, and Arkwright should be stated. An understanding of the past is the best key to an apprehension of the present. This maxim has been sanctioned by the experience and example of the wisest among political philosophers. "Antiquity," said Bacon, "deserveth that reverence that men should make a stand thereupon, and discover what is the best way; but when the discovery is well taken then to make progression." A course in itself so necessary and recommended by so great an authority will, we trust, be met by universal approval.

In the year 1764, James Watt, the Scottish machinist began his improvements of the steam engine. In 1767, James Hargraves, a Lancashire carpenter, invented the *spinning jenny*. These inventions were followed by that of the *spinning frame*, generally ascribed to Richard Arkwright, a native of Preston, and the *mule*, by Mr Crompton, of Bolton. The effects of these improvements in the means of production, by substituting inanimate for animate power, were immense; their social effects, rightly appreciated, were not less remarkable than their productive results. Within the brief period of twenty-one years, namely, from 1764, the date of the improvements of Watt, to 1785, the time of the introduction of the *mule* of Mr Crompton, the means were invented and applied, which, followed by others of a similar kind, accomplished what no conqueror by the power of armies and the force of decrees could have realized—they changed the personal and relative condition, and, consequently, the habits and character, of numerous sections of the people ; they aggregated into a few districts what was formerly a widely-spread cottage industry; they congregated in huge buildings, under no moral control, large numbers of persons of both sexes and of all ages (in the place of domestic cottage employment, under the control and superintendence of parents); in the train of these inventions, and their consequent changes, have followed others which have very materially affected not only the domestic condition of the manufacturing operatives, but the social condition of all engaged in manufacture, whether employers or employed; and also weakened the link which united the labouring population to the Church, and, further, interfered with the practical government of the country.

It is not an easy task for men living in the last half of the nineteenth century, to represent by the aid of knowledge and reflection, within their own minds, the actual circumstances existing in the last half of the eighteenth century. The present is to the majority all-engrossing, it is to them everything, the beginning, the middle, and the end. It is not possible to recall a complete picture of the past, we must be content to state a few prominent facts, and our authorities for the same.

Sir James Stewart, whose *Inquiry into the Principles of Political Economy* was published in the year 1767, has observed:—"Were the people of England to come more into the use of living upon bread, and give over consuming so much animal food, inhabitants would certainly increase, and many rich grass fields would be thrown into tillage.

Were the French to give over eating so much bread, the Dutch so much fish, the Flemish so much garden stuff, and the Germans so much sourkraut, and all take to the English diet of pork, beef, and mutton, their respective numbers would soon decay, let them improve their grounds to the utmost." It will be noted by the reader that Sir James Stewart has said that the diet of the people in England of his time consisted of "pork, beef, and mutton." A better informed, less prejudiced, and therefore more credible witness than Sir James Stewart it would be impossible to produce; he was a keen observer, a man well-travelled and well-read. Adam Smith, in his great work, *The Wealth of Nations*, has borne very ample evidence on what, in recent years, has been comprehensively called "The Condition of England Question." This author, writing antecedent to the year 1776, has said:—"The real recompense of labour, the real quantity of the necessaries and conveniences of life which it can procure to the labourer, has, during the course of the present century, increased perhaps in a still greater proportion than its money price. Not only grain has become somewhat cheaper, but many other things, from which the industrious poor derive an agreeable and wholesome variety of food, have become a great deal cheaper." "The common complaint, that luxury extends itself even to the lowest ranks of the people, and that the labouring poor will not now be content with the same food, clothing, and lodging which satisfied them in former times, may convince us that it is not the money price of labour only, but its real recompense, which has augmented." Adam Smith, after having referred to the seven years' war with France, which closed in 1763, has remarked that "though more than 100,000 men, all accustomed to the use of arms, and many of them to rapine and plunder," "were at once thrown out of their ordinary employment," "not only no great convulsion, but no sensible disorder, arose from so great a change." A circumstance which in itself attested a morally and socially healthful condition of society.

The evidence of Sir James Stewart as to the food of our forefathers in the last half of the eighteenth century is very decided; the evidence of Adam Smith as to their social condition is not less so. How our forefathers were clad and lodged are subjects of interest, and we cannot be justly charged with exaggeration when we state that their linen and woollen garments served to protect them efficiently from the inclemencies and through the changes of the seasons, and with these, as a rule, they were plentifully supplied; it was matter of complaint that luxury had extended "itself even to the lowest ranks of the people, and that the labouring poor would not be contented with the same food, clothing, and lodging which satisfied them in former times." With such testimony before us, we may safely affirm that convenient plenty was at that time the lot of the labouring population of England. Not any one who has profited by the conversations of the aged of both sexes, the latest living links in the chain of generations, serving to bind together the past and the present, will fail to recall the "Goodmen" and "Notable Housewives" as life-like as memory can do; the fathers and mothers of such, he will associate with thrift and comfort. "The spinning-wheel," which was forced from the cottages in all districts, because of the mechanical inventions referred to, was neither offensive to the eye nor the ear, its motion, when in use, was distinctly visible, and its sound not unpleasant. The employment of spinning with the wheel was not opposed to the agreeable exercise of conversation, it was not injurious to health; to the "housewife" it constituted a constant and profitable exercise. Such domestic employment was favourable to the promotion of parental authority and filial obedience, and to the growth of all the domestic sympathies. The gradual acquirement of habits of industry by children so situated was not inconsistent with the *healthful pleasures* of infancy and childhood. Under such social arrangements, the pastor had a ready access to his flock ; by his visits devotional feelings and moral habits were encouraged.

A tolerably just notion of the effects on the operative classes of the introduction of mechanical inventions in the practice of spinning, may be formed by reading the following resolutions, unanimously adopted at the quarter sessions held at Preston, for the county of Lancaster, on November the 11th, 1779 :—"Resolved that the sole cause of great riots was the new machines employed in the cotton manufacture ; that the county, notwithstanding, had greatly benefited by their erection ; that the destroying them in one county would only be the means of transferring them to another county ; and that, if a total stop were put by the Legislature to their erection in Britain, it would only tend to their establishment in foreign countries, to the detriment of the trade of Britain." The struggle, for such it must be called, indicated by these resolutions has been of long continuance; it has not even now closed, the competition of " the iron men " against the men of bone, flesh, and muscle is still a source of controversy and complaint; the claims of capital, real or supposed, and the claims of labour, real or supposed, are in frequent opposition, of which strife that same town of Preston, so late as 1853, afforded a mournful example.

Dr Aikin, in his description of the country round Manchester (published in 1795), has left on record a graphic and faithful delineation of the results of what is now known as " the factory system " on the health, morals, and character of the labouring population:—" The invention and improvement of machines to shorten labour have had a surprising influence to extend our trade, and also to call in hands from all parts, particularly children for the cotton-mills. It is the wise plan of Providence that in this life there shall be no good without its attendant inconvenience. There are many which are too obvious in these cotton-mills, and similar factories, which counteract that increase of population usually consequent on the improved facility of labour. In these, children of a very tender age are employed, many of them collected from the workhouses in London and Westminster, and transported in crowds as apprentices to masters resident many hundred miles distant, where they serve unknown, unprotected, and forgotten by those to whose care nature or the law had consigned them. These children are usually too long confined to work, in close rooms, often during the whole night. The air they breathe from the oil, &c., employed in the machinery, and other circumstances, is injurious; little attention is paid to their cleanliness; and frequent changes from a warm and dense to a cold and thin atmosphere are predisposing causes to sickness and debility, and particularly to the epidemic fever which is so generally to be met with in these factories. It is also much to be questioned if society does not receive detriment from the manner in which children are thus employed during their earlier years. They are not generally strong to labour, or capable of pursuing any other branch of business when the term of their apprenticeship expires. The females are wholly uninstructed in sewing, knitting, and other domestic affairs, requisite to make them notable and frugal wives and mothers. This is a very great misfortune to them and to the public, as is sadly proved by a comparison of the families of labourers in husbandry and those of manufacturers in general. In the former we meet with neatness, cleanliness, and comfort; in the latter with filth, rags, and poverty, although their wages may be nearly double those of the husbandman. It must be added, that the want of early religious instruction and example, and the numerous and

indiscriminate association in these buildings, are very unfavourable to their future conduct in life." In an earlier
part of the same book, Dr Aikin has observed:—" The
prevalence of fevers among persons employed in cotton-mills
might be lessened, by the attention on the part of the
overseers to the following circumstances. Besides a due
regard to ventilation, personal cleanliness should be strongly
recommended and encouraged ; and the parents of children
should be enjoined to wash them every morning and evening,
to keep their shoes and stockings in good condition, and
above all, never to send them to work early in the morning
without giving them food.

" It is greatly to be wished that the custom of working
all night could be avoided. The continuance of such a
practice cannot be consistent with health, and I am glad
to find that it does not prevail universally." The weighty
judgment of Dr Kay (now Sir James Kay Shuttleworth)
and Mr William Rathbone Greg, at a subsequent period,
fully verified the well-founded opinion of Dr Aikin.

It had appeared to the minds of some sincere and
able men, in various ranks, that it was possible to retain
all the " good " referred to by Dr Aikin, and, at least,
to mitigate in an important degree the " attendant inconveniences." It would be a fountain of never-ceasing sorrow,
if not any change and increase in the means and powers
of production could take place without an increase of human
suffering and depravity. If this were indeed an inevitable
law, then the genius of man would necessarily be his
enemy, for " inconveniences " of the nature and to the
extent named, with so much candour and mildness, by Dr
Aikin, would, in time, become evils of so great magnitude,
as to organically and progressively injure the whole frame-
work of the body politic. The promoters of factory
legislation acted under the conviction that the inventions of
man are useless, nay worse than useless, injurious, when,

without regard to their personal, domestic, social, political, moral, and religious effect on the people, those inventions are used only as means " to heap up riches," making many poor, that a few may become enormously rich. To enjoy the use, to avoid the abuse of all such improvements, were the objects of the promoters of factory legislation.

Full half a century elapsed between the description of the evils of " the factory system," as witnessed and narrated by Dr Aikin, and the passing of the Ten Hours' Bill in 1847. These were upwards of fifty years of efforts on the part of an energetic body of men, who endeavoured to bring factory labour under the control of Christian and constitutional principles. These efforts in the factories, on the platform, through the press, the pulpit, and the parliament, called into existence almost every shade of controversy, religious, moral, social, economical, political, philosophical, and parliamentary; and it is to the sayings and doings of the principal actors in so momentous a conflict, that we desire to devote the following pages.

CHAPTER II.

PARISH APPRENTICES UNDER "THE FACTORY SYSTEM."—ORIGIN OF
FACTORY REGULATION.—RESULTS ON HEALTH AND MORALS.—
PARLIAMENTARY EFFORTS OF THE FIRST SIR ROBERT PEEL.

IT has been held by the wisest and greatest of British
statesmen that the children of the poor have especial claims
on society; in the Church they are recognised as " God's
own poor." Under the constitution their rights in former
times were especially conserved, and made "part and
parcel" of the law of the land. Infancy is the period of
life which, because of its helplessness and hopefulness, has
especial claims on human sympathies—claims sanctified by the
words—" Suffer the little children to come unto me, and forbid
them not." There can be no injustice greater than,
under any pretext, the sacrifice of helpless infancy—the
tearing up of the roots of all the affections which, when
cherished, give unto life its dearest and most lasting ties,
thus robbing existence of its fairest fruits, forestalling the
strength of a state, and trampling under foot all the more
sacred duties of life. Man cannot present himself to the
consideration of his fellow-man in a more revolting character than when, breaking through all the ties of nature and
the most hallowed principles of religion, he ventures for
his own lucre's sake to become the ensnarer and oppressor
of " the little children." Yet all this was done, under the
assumed sanction of law, and by those who claimed for

themselves the protection of the avowedly Christian institutions of England.

When the first factories were erected, it was soon discovered that there was in the minds of the parents a strong
repugnance to the employment thus provided for children;
the native domestic labourers being then able amply to
provide for their children, rejected the tempting offers of
the millowners, the parents preferring to rear their children
in their own homes, and to train them to their own handi-
crafts. For a long period it was by the working people
themselves considered to be disgraceful to any father who
allowed his child to enter the factory,—nay, in the homely
words of that day, as will be remembered by the old men
of the present age,—" that parent made himself the town's
talk," and the unfortunate girl so given up by her parents,
in after life, found the door of household employment closed
against her—" Because she had been a factory girl." It
was not until the condition of portions of the working
classes had been reduced, that it became the custom with
working men to eke out the means of their subsistence by
sending their children to the mills. Until that sad, and
calamitous custom prevailed, the factories in England were
worked by " stranger-children," gathered together from
the workhouses.

Under the operation of the factories' apprentice system
parish apprentices were sent, without remorse or inquiry,
from the workhouses in England, and the public charities
of Scotland, to the factories, to be " used up " as the
" cheapest raw material in the market." This inhuman
conduct was systematically practised—the millowners communicated with the overseer of the poor, and when the
demand and supply had been arranged to the satisfaction
of both the contracting parties, a day was fixed for the
examination of " the little children," to be inspected by the
millowner, or his agent, previous to which the authorities

of the workhouse had filled the minds of their wards with the notion that, by entering the mills, they would become ladies and gentlemen. On the day appointed, the children were drawn up to be inspected and selected; those chosen were then conveyed by coach, by waggon, or boat, to their destination, and, as a rule, from that moment were lost to their parents and relatives. It sometimes happened that traffickers contracted with the overseers, removing their juvenile victims to Manchester, or other towns, on their arrival; if not previously assigned, they were deposited sometimes in dark cellars, where the merchant dealing in them brought his customers; the millowners, by the light of lanthorns, being enabled to examine the children, their limbs and stature having undergone the necessary scrutiny, the bargain was struck, and those poor "innocents" were conveyed to the mills. The general treatment of those apprentices depended entirely on the will of their masters; in very many instances their labour was limited only by exhaustion, after many modes of torture had been unavailingly applied to force continued action; their food was stinted, coarse, and unwholesome; in "brisk times," their beds (such as they were) were never cool, the mills were worked night and day, and as soon as one set of children rose for labour the other set retired for rest. Discrimination of sexes was not regarded, vice, disease, and death, luxuriated in those receptacles of human woe. We dare not trust ourselves to write all we know on this subject, much less all we feel, the cases stated hereafter are representative of the system. The moral nature of the traffic between parish authorities and the buyers of pauper children, may be judged from the fact that in some cases one idiot was accepted with twenty sane children. A question arises—what was the fate of these idiots?—that secret has not been revealed. " Prior to the show-day of the pauper children to the purveyor or cotton-master," says

the author of the *Memoir of Robert Blincoe*, " the most
illusive and artfully-contrived falsehoods were spread, to
fill the minds of the poor infants with the most absurd
and ridiculous errors as to the real nature of the servitude
to which they were to be consigned. It was gravely stated
to them, according to Blincoe's statement, made in the most
positive and solemn manner, that they were all, when they
arrived at the cotton-mill, to be transformed into ladies and
gentlemen: that they would be fed on roast beef and plum-
pudding—be allowed to ride their masters' horses, and
have silver watches, and plenty of cash in their pockets.
Nor was it the nurses, or other inferior persons of the
workhouse, with whom this vile deception originated, but
with parish officers themselves. From the statement of
the victims of cotton-mill bondage, it seems to have been
a constant rule with those who had the disposal of parish
children, prior to sending them off to cotton-mills, to fill
their minds with the same delusions."

We have said that such was the general aspect of the
factory system in those days,—there were exceptions; some
men there are who cannot rid themselves of natural feeling.
Of this class there were some factory masters; they had
respect to the defenceless state of their apprentices, and
signalised themselves by occasional acts of kindness, but
even in *their* mills the hours of labour were unnatural and
excessive. Cotton factories were established in England
towards the close of the eighteenth century, and were
rapidly spread over the counties of Lancaster, York, Derby,
Nottingham, and other districts; they were usually built
on mountain streams, in the more secluded parts of the
country. Several were also erected in Scotland, among
these was the factory of Mr Dale, of Glasgow. It is very
pleasing to know that there were exceptions to the cruelties
above referred to, and conspicuously among such must be
ranked the factory of Mr Dale.

About the year 1780, cotton factories were introduced into the west of Scotland. In 1784, Mr Dale, a Glasgow manufacturer, established a cotton-mill, near the falls of the Clyde, in the county of Lanark. To found a factory was then far from an easy task. The labouring population of Scotland having been accustomed to comfort, traditionally and by habit to personal freedom, refused to enter the cotton-mills. Close confinement, and long hours of labour, were by the vast majority of the working men and their families detested. Water power was in those days, to the founder of a factory, a condition of primary moment. The banks of the river Clyde, now constituting one of the most populous and best known districts in Scotland, contained in 1784 many a rugged path, seldom trod by the foot of a stranger, and leading to secluded nooks hidden from common gaze. In one of these retired corners was built Mr Dale's cotton factory. Mr Dale applied to the managers of charities, and the parish authorities of Edinburgh, for a supply of children. The application was successful, and the children under Mr Dale's control ultimately numbered five hundred. Mr Dale, in exchange for the services of these children, undertook to feed, lodge, and clothe them. It has been our lot to know two women, who, in early life, had been Mr Dale's apprentices. On the authority of these witnesses, Mr Dale was a man of benevolent disposition, seldom visited his factories; when he did visit them, it was remarked that " things were put in better order," and he sometimes brought the children little presents, and was at heart the friend of his work-people. By way of encouragement to settlers, Mr Dale caused houses to be built at New Lanark Mills, and let them at very low rents, but so great was the aversion of the Scotch peasantry to the then novel system of working in factories, that very few, not being homeless and friendless, would accept of house accommodation from Mr Dale on the lowest possible terms. The ages of the children when apprenticed to Mr Dale were from five to eight, the period of apprenticeship from seven to nine years, the hours of labour in the factory from six in the morning to seven in the evening. Mr Dale's was one of the most humanely conducted factories in the empire; he was known as one of the most spirited, enterprising, and benevolent men of his age. The following notice of his labours, and their effects, is copied from the *Annual Register*, of 1792: "New Lanark —Mr David Dale, of this place, in the course of six years has reared a village on the banks of the Clyde, containing 2,000 persons; and erected five cotton-mills, each of which contains 6,000 spindles. The various provisions which this extraordinary man has made for the health of the children employed by him are highly praiseworthy. They have every day some hours allotted to them for exercise in the fields, and their looks bespeak health and vigour. These hours of relaxation the boys enjoy in succession, their apartments are likewise cleaned and well aired, and ten schoolmasters are daily employed in their tuition."

These facts will enable the reader to judge of the operation of "the factory system" in Scotland, in its mildest and most attractive form.

On the 21st of May, 1816, the first Sir Robert Peel presented a paper to a Committee of the House of Commons, as "the substance of what he knew respecting the state and management of the cotton manufactories, within the scope of his acquaintance, which was not less than five-and-forty years." From a printed copy of that paper, we make the following extract:—"Mr Arkwright was the inventor of machinery, of great national importance, which was employed at a time when steam power was little known in large buildings, which were erected in situations commanding considerable water power, but generally in country places remote from inhabitants: to work these machines the surplus population of large towns was sought after, and many thousands of parish children were supplied from London, Birmingham, and other populous districts.

" The house in which I have a concern gave employment at one time to near one thousand children of this description. Having other pursuits it was not often in my power to visit the factories, but whenever such visits were made, I was struck with the uniform appearance of bad health, and in many cases stinted growth of the children ; the hours of labour were regulated by the interest of the overseer, whose remuneration depending on the quantity of work done, he was often induced to make the poor children work excessive hours and to stop their complaints by trifling bribes." This statement of the first Sir Robert Peel will enable the reader to judge of the nature and effects of " the factory system," as manifested under the authority of one of the most humane employers of parish apprentices in England.

In Scotland and in England there were factories, in comparison with which those of Dale and Peel were highly-favoured retreats, affording to their inmates very superior accommodation and unusual enjoyment. Waggon-loads of little boys and girls were sent by the parish authorities and from the principal towns of England and Scotland to the lonely banks of mountain streams and rivulets, there to undergo hardships and torture, the bare mention of which leaves a lasting impression of horror, and fills the soul with shame for the crimes man has committed against his fellows. Little children have been worked for sixteen hours and upwards, with few and trifling intermissions, day and night have been devoted to almost constant labour; a portion of the Sabbath has been for these helpless ones appropriated to toil. In stench, in heated rooms, amid the constant whirling of a thousand wheels, have little fingers and little feet been kept in ceaseless action, forced into unnatural activity by blows from the heavy hands and feet of the merciless overlooker, and the infliction of bodily pain by

instruments of punishment invented by the sharpened ingenuity of insatiable selfishness. Tens of thousands of
" the little children" in those mills have been destroyed
because of their owner's lust of gold. The necessaries and
decencies of life were but little cared for in some cases;
in many, fatally neglected. Education was, as a rule,
entirely unprovided for. Children have dropped down at
their frames exhausted, the fingers of little ones have been
snapped off instantly, their limbs have suffered in like
manner; there have been living bodies caught in the iron
gripe of machinery in rapid motion, and whirled in the
air, bones crushed, and blood cast copiously on the floor,
because of physical exhaustion. We know those who have
seen little children standing at their spindles asleep, their
little hands and fingers, like the mechanical hands of the
automaton, performing their accustomed evolutions among
the threads and spindles; it was at such times especially
that hands and fingers were lacerated. The factory apprentices have been sold by auction as " bankrupt's effects."
The scantiest share of coarsest food capable of sustaining
animal life has been day by day doled out to the parish
apprentices; in the bothies and outhouses of cotton factories
boys and girls, suffering from the unsatisfied cravings of
hunger, have watched for the swineherd, have stealthily
struggled with the pigs for food, and have been fed upon
the purloined contents of the pig-trough. The well-attested
memoir of Robert Blincoe contains a circumstantial account
which we prefer giving in almost the words of the author:—
" The store pigs and the apprentices used to fare very
much alike ; but when the swine were hungry, they used
to grunt so loud, they obtained the wash first to quiet them.
The apprentices could be intimidated, and made to keep
still. The fatting pigs fared luxuriously, compared with
the apprentices. They were often regaled with meal balls,
made into dough, and given in the shape of dumplings."

Blincoe and others, who worked in a part of the mill whence they could see the swine served, used to say to one another, ' *The pigs are served; it will be our turn next.*' "Those who were in a part of the building contiguous to the pig-sties used to keep a sharp eye upon the fatting pigs and their meal balls, and, as soon as the swineherd withdrew, Blincoe used to slip down stairs, and stealing slyly towards the pig-trough, plunge his hand in at the loop-holes, and steal as many dumplings as he could grasp. The food thus stealthily obtained from the pig-trough was exultingly conveyed to a hiding-place, and there greedily devoured. The pigs, though usually esteemed the most stupid of animals, learned from experience to guard their food by various expedients; made wise by repeated losses, they kept a keen look-out, and the moment they ascertained the approach of the half-famished apprentices they set up so loud a chorus of snorts and grunts, it was heard in the kitchen, when out rushed the swineherd, armed with a whip, from which combined means of protection for the swine this accidental source of obtaining a *good dinner* was soon lost! Such was the contest carried on for some time at Litton Mill between the half-famished apprentices and the well-fed swine."

Some of the helpless victims, though young in years, were old in suffering, and nightly prayed that death would come to their relief ; weary of prayer, some there were who deliberately accomplished their own destruction. The annals of Litton Mill afford an instance of an attempt of this kind—one of many, for they were of frequent occurrence:—"Palfrey, the smith, had the task of riveting irons upon any of the apprentices whom the master ordered, and those were much like the irons usually put upon felons. Even young women, if suspected of intending to run away, had irons riveted on their ankles, and reaching by long links and rings up to the hips, and in these they were

compelled to walk to and from the mill and to sleep.
Robert Blincoe asserts that he has known many girls served
in this manner. A handsome-looking girl, about the age of
twenty years, who came from the neighbourhood of Cromford, whose name was Phœbe Rag, being driven to despera-
tion by ill-treatment, took the opportunity one dinner-time,
when she was alone, and supposed no one saw her, to
take off her shoes, and throw herself into the dam at the
end of the bridge, next the apprentice-house. Some one
passing along, and seeing a pair of shoes, stopped. The
poor girl had sunk once, and just as she rose above the
water he seized her by the hair. Blincoe thinks it was
Thomas Fox, the governor, who succeeded Milner, who
rescued her. She was nearly gone, and it was with some
difficulty her life was saved. When Mr Needham heard
of this, and *being afraid the example might be contagious,*
he ordered James Durant, a journeyman spinner, who had
been apprenticed there, to take her away to her relations
at Cromford, and thus she escaped."

There are those still living who can point out the spots
where there were buried the remains of those who were
once their own fellow-companions in wretchedness, but over
whose bodies no voice hath said " Earth to earth, ashes to
ashes, dust to dust." Many having died in the night, their
bodies were stealthily removed, and were buried without
ceremony in graves unknown to their former comrades—
these bodies were cast into the earth and buried with "the
burial of an ass." A clergyman of the Church of England,
revered by all who know him, and who has devoted much
of his time and attention to a consideration of the condition
of the working classes, has favoured us with the following
important statement:—

" An instance still living, and of high respectability, may
illustrate the practice under the system of unprotected
' factory apprentices.'

"At one of the earliest establishments for spinning by water-power in Wharfdale, Yorkshire, the apprenticeship system had been carried out for some time, when A—— S——'s widowed mother was compelled by want to submit her daughter to the system. Disgraceful as the widowed mother felt it, at that time she had no alternative. The mill was not very far distant from her cottage, but very soon she was compelled to carry her little one to and from it, for it was not possible for the child, without assistance, to reach home in any reasonable time in heavy weather: she was only six years old. This difficulty led the Widow S—— to remove to a cheap tenement, next to one of the 'prentice houses, and there it was that A—— and her mother became fully acquainted with the horrors of that abominable system. One of A—— S——'s statements, confirmed frequently (many years after) by her mother, was, that these wretched victims of heartless avarice, the factory apprentices, were fed chiefly on porridge, which was seasoned with beef and pork *brine*, bought at the Government stores, or those of contractors—the ' bottoms ' of casks supplied to the navy. This nauseous mixture was sometimes so repulsive, even to hungry stomachs, that it was rejected. Whereupon, the overseer or overlooker was accustomed to stand over the apprentices with an instrument of punishment, a whip, or thong, or cow-hide, as the case might be, and compel them to swallow this disgusting diet. They were fed out of troughs, much resembling those used by pigs. There were among them delicate, intelligent young people, evidently off-casts and outcasts of genteel progenitors, but all wretched and reckless to the utmost degree.

"The deaths which occurred were not unfrequently from cruel punishment, at work, or in the 'prentice house, and were not always followed by any usual mode of burial. A plantation hard by was believed to be the resting-place from their sorrow of many who disappeared. A survivor

of this 'prentice band—'Old Nanny' was her only name
—was visited in September, 1833, by the writer, who had
been informed by a reputable person that 'Old Nanny'
could give information respecting those secret burials, she
having related them to him. She was a miserable-looking
creature, evidently deformed in the feet from mill work,
and when very quietly questioned about the plantation
burials, she became highly excited, and said, 'I won't tell
you—I can't. Who sent you here? I know nought about
it; don't ask me.' Her wild aspect was awful. But what
she chose to tell confirmed entirely the statement of A——
S——, who was found in a state of emaciated health by the
writer, whilst visiting some cottage neighbours in 1827.
She was then some thirty years old.   At her own request she was taken into the family of the writer to try
her ability in domestic service, to which she had been un-
accustomed, weaving having recently been her work. Her
health rallied a little, but she was never able to fulfil the
duties, to which she applied herself very diligently; she at
length married a respectable small tradesman, who had been
her companion as a child, and when last heard of was living
as 'Old A——' in her native village, a few miles from the
scene of her early sufferings. Her excellent character and
Christian deportment would not allow the writer to doubt
her statements. She never related the 'prentice house
tales without horror, and used to say that the cries of
the poor wretches under the lash of the overseer were
heart-rending. She and others had heard them often, es
pecially at feeding-time."

It has been customary to erect monuments for the good
and wise, whose memories the living desired should be
preserved for ages yet untold. The wicked and the foolish
have also their monuments. The greedy and negligent
men under whose rule the cruelties of " the factory system,"
and its worst horrors, were perpetrated, have had, and now

have, *their* monuments, not tall columns, and statues on pedestals, but stunted men and women, twisted spines, distorted limbs, increased crime, and decreased manliness. It was impossible that a system which jested with civilisation, laughed at humanity, and made a mockery of every law of physical and moral health, of the principles of natural and social order, could remain unchecked. It is in the nature of wrong and error to destroy the prey on which they feast, or oblige man to check their force through the operation of preventive laws: overseers, millowners, and statesmen, had failed to fulfil their duties, but disease and death were faithful to their functions. Fever, nourished in the crowded sleeping-rooms, and in the ill-ventilated factories, could not be confined to lonely dells and scattered villages. Fever, and its follower death, are stern messengers, and manifest a wondrous power of locomotion; the first steals along noiselessly and unseen, but in time both are felt. The fevers generated under " the factory system," necessarily caused throughout the districts in which factories were most common very considerable uneasiness, discussions in the newspapers followed, and complaints were made that the hospitals were crowded with factory patients. It is but reasonable to suppose that these discussions led to considerable alarm among the negligent and guilty millowners. Manchester and its district being then, as now, the centre of the cotton manufacture, suffered most from the evils of "the factory system;" there, fever was most common and malignant, not confined to the occupants of the mill, for it had invaded the mansions of the rich; there, consequently, complaints of those not engaged in factories were most frequent, and newspaper controversies most keen. In January 1796, a committee was appointed to superintend the health of the poor in the towns of Manchester and Salford, and commonly designated " The Manchester Board of Health." On the 25th of January, in the same year, Dr

Perceval, an eminent physician of that town, submitted for the consideration of the Board, the following heads of resolutions:—"It has already been stated that the objects of the present institution are to prevent the generation of diseases; to obviate the spreading of them by contagion, and to shorten the duration of those which exist, by affording the necessary aids and comforts to the sick. In the prosecution of this necessary undertaking, the Board have had their attention particularly directed to the large cotton factories established in the town and neighbourhood of Manchester; and they feel it a duty incumbent on them to lay before the public the result of their inquiries:—1st. It appears that the children, and others, who work in the large cotton factories, are peculiarly disposed to be affected by the contagion of fever, and that when the affection is received it is rapidly propagated, not only amongst those who are crowded together in the same apartments, but in the families and neighbourhoods to which they belong. 2nd. The large factories are generally injurious to the constitution of those employed in them, even where no particular diseases prevail, from the close confinement which is enjoined, from the debilitating effects of hot or impure air, and from the want of active exercises, which nature points out as essential in childhood and youth, to invigorate the system, and to fit our species for the duties of mankind. 3rd. The untimely labour of the night, and the protracted labour of the day, with respect to children, not only tends to diminish future expectations as to the general sum of life and industry, by impairing the strength and destroying the vital stamina of the rising generation, but it too often gives encouragement to idleness, extravagance, and profligacy of the parents, who, contrary to the order of nature, subsist by the oppression of their offspring. 4th. It appears that the children employed in factories are generally debarred from all opportunities of education, and from moral or religious instruction.

5th. From the excellent regulations which subsist in several cotton factories, it appears that many of these evils may, in a considerable degree, be obviated; and we are therefore warranted by experience, and are assured that we shall have the support of the liberal proprietors of these factories, in proposing an application for Parliamentary aid (if other methods appear not likely to effect the purpose) to establish a general system of laws for the wise, humane, and equal government of all such works."

These heads of resolutions are important, they are in themselves a condensation of the evils of "the factory system." The natural repugnance of the labouring population to factory labour, had in the cotton districts been partly overcome, and some of the more depraved among parents had begun to live on the wages of the labour of their offspring, an inversion of the order of family economy, which in time was followed by a fearful retribution. The question of factory regulation was thus fairly raised in the heart of Manchester; the conditions, too, under which factory regulation by Act of Parliament was rendered necessary, were in the resolutions of Dr Perceval clearly laid down. These facts scatter to the winds the hacknied, false, and silly charges of the opponents of factory regulation, that it had its origin in the sentimentality of "pseudo-philanthropy, sham humanity, and Samaritanism." They establish the fact that factory legislation had its origin in self-preservation; the enormities of the unregulated factory system having burst their boundaries were already spreading disease and death broadcast, their threatened victims were thereby forced to apply for a power stronger than the will of the factory occupiers. The evils of "the factory system" having become subjects of popular discussion, were from that time destined to command the attention of the Imperial Parliament. Mr Wilbraham Bootle was the first to moot the question in the House of Commons; his efforts, though they did not result in any practical measure, must have in some degree contributed to prepare the mind of the country and of Parliament for practical legislation. In 1802, the first Sir Robert Peel brought the questions of factory labour and factory legislation under the notice of the House of Commons. The first Sir Robert has left on record the circumstances which induced him to plead the cause of the factory child.

He found the mind of parliament fully prepared for the adoption of the provisions of his bill for "*the preservation of the health and morals of apprentices and others employed in cotton and other mills, and in cotton and other factories ;*" his difficulty was not in want of support, but in the urgency of those who supported his efforts. " I remember very well," said he (in 1816) "that in passing that bill (the Act of 1802) I had a great deal of care upon my hands to prevent the manufacturer suffering as well as the apprentice ; many gentlemen would have urged me in the most earnest manner to shorten the hours of labour, much below what I thought it proper to shorten them." "I was desired to let that bill operate through every cottage in the country ; I deemed that so unreasonable, that I was determined to give up all management of the measure if it was not left to me ; in consequence of that, the opposition which arose more from humanity than anything else was withdrawn, and I brought in the bill in the state in which it now appears, without any opposition of any consequence being stated."

There was, notwithstanding, some opposition to the proposed measure. On the third reading of the bill in the House of Commons, which took place on June the 2nd, 1802, some of the opponents of factory legislation having spoken against the measure, the first Sir Robert Peel replied :—" I am sorry to have to address the House again on this late stage of the bill, after so great a majority of the House and the country had declared in its favour. I confess it does not go to the extent that might be wished, but it is advisable to do as much as can be done in the present instance without venturing on anything like hazardous innovation. The great and first object I had in view in bringing in this bill was to promote the religious and moral education of the children ; and in my endeavours to accomplish this end, the measure I hope will prove free from harm, and productive of much real advantage. Without a measure like the present, no gentlemen of weight in the country could visit these mills, even though fever raged in them, or other kinds of misery and distress; so that there was no hope without it of introducing any system of wholesome regulations." It was in this spirit and for these objects that the power of parliament was first successfully invoked to protect the young and helpless in the mills. The exposure of the wrongs endured by factory children did much towards immediate improvement.

The bill passed into a law in 1802, and from that period was known as " *an Act for the preservation of the health and morals of apprentices and others employed in cotton and other mills, and in cotton and other factories.*" It enacted, that from and after the 2nd day of December, 1802, all such mills and factories within *Great Britain and Ireland*, wherein three or more apprentices, or twenty or more other persons shall at any time be employed, shall be subject to the several rules and regulations contained in the Act. The principal of these were as follow :—The hours of actual work were limited to twelve per day, reckoning from six o'clock in the morning to nine at night, as the portion of each day during which twelve hours actual labour might be lawfully taken ; the Act also provided for the gradual abolition of night work, and that night work in all mills should finally cease in June 1804. It provided for the instruction of all apprentices in reading, writing, and arithmetic, and that one complete suit of clothing shall be supplied to each apprentice once a year. That factories shall be whitewashed twice a year, and at all times properly ventilated; also for the separation of the sexes as regarded sleeping apartments. At the Midsummer session of each year, in districts in which factories were situated, the Justices of the Peace of these districts were enjoined to appoint two Factory Inspectors, one a Justice of the Peace, the other a Clergyman of the Established Church, the mills and factories under the Act were to be registered annually with the Clerk of the Peace ; the penalty following on the known violation of the Act was a fine not exceeding five pounds nor under forty shillings, at the discretion of the Justices before whom the offender shall be convicted. This Act of Parliament judged by the intention of its promoters deserved the title it assumed, and was designed to "preserve the health and morals" of factory workers.

The thought naturally suggests itself,—What was the cardinal principle which actuated the majority of the Members of the House of Commons, and made them so pressing in their desires to reduce humanity to practice ? The answer is important. It was then ruled by the judges that "Christianity is part and parcel of the Laws of England." It was then the current belief of our legislators that all their Acts should be based on Christianity, and consequently that all the arrangements of the internal industry of the country should be subjected to Christianity. Fixedness of purpose and resoluteness of will were then, more than now, the characteristics of British statesmen; the theory was then prevalent that circumstances must be made subservient to principle, it was left to later times to reduce to practice the opposite theory, namely, that principle must yield to circumstances.

The facts of the factories once made known to the

Legislature by an influential Member of Parliament, filled many minds with grief and shame for the past, and made them alive to their duties and responsibilities. They believed that according to the theory of the British constitution the state ought to be Christian; that the increase of knowledge, of science, of art could alone be truly beneficial for all, by being made subservient to the spirit of Christianity. The over-working and cruel treatment of children were opposed to the command "Love thy neighbour as thyself," and were felt to be antagonistic to Christian civilisation, and the majority of the Legislature desired the immediate removal of so grave a reproach. These statesmen did not hope for the regeneration of society by any new discovery of principles or plans; they were contented to travel in "the old paths," and to contemplate the probable future of their country while standing on the landmarks of the past. These convictions may by some among modern political economists be considered erroneous, and find a place in their list of "obsolete prejudices;" these convictions were conscientiously entertained, the efforts made to reduce them to practice were creditable to the actors, and deserve from all the respect due to practical sincerity.

CHAPTER III.

THE NEW LANARK MILLS. — MEETING OF SCOTTISH MANUFAC-
TURERS IN GLASGOW.—REPEAL OF THE IMPORT DUTY ON COT-
TON.—BEGINNING OF THE TEN HOURS' BILL MOVEMENT.

IN tracing the history of a nation's civilization, it is interesting
to observe the struggles between the acknowledgement of
sound maxims in theory and their violation in practice.
English literature is replete with the acknowledgement that
man considered physically, mentally, and morally, deserves
the constant watchfulness of philosophers and statesmen,
and that there is no surer or speedier road to national ruin
than the sacrifice of the physical strength and moral worth
of a population. This universal acknowledgement, notwithstanding, there has been in all ages a desire manifested for
an opposing practice, and on the balance existing between
the forces of truth and error depends the strength or weakness of a State. This view of a nation's interests commanded the attention of the supporters of factory regulation,
and was prominently set forth by the leaders of the question
in and out of Parliament.

Mr Dale, of Glasgow, sold the New Lanark Mills; Mr
Robert Owen and partners, of Chorlton Mills, Manchester,
were the buyers. Mr Owen, subsequently well-known as
"Owen of Lanark," entered in 1799 on his official duties
as Resident-Manager of the New Lanark Mills. Mr Owen
had not then in public denounced what he afterwards de-

clared to be " the errors of all the religions in the world."
Mr Owen was then known as an efficient and practical
Manager of Factories. He had not been long resident at
New Lanark when he introduced important changes, intended to improve, physically and morally, the condition
of those under his control. Mr Owen's experiments at the
New Lanark Mills were introduced and conducted with
the most scrupulous regard for the religious opinions of
all concerned; their success, together with Mr Owen's
writings in the Press, earned for him the sympathy and
approbation of many able and influential men without distinction of creed, rank, or party.

The kind of religious instruction imparted to the children
at the New Lanark Mills will be understood by the reading
of the following extract, from the evidence given by Mr
Owen before a Committee of the House of Commons, in
1816:—

" What religious instruction do you give the children ?
—They have the same religious instruction in the Schools
of New Lanark as in all the other schools in Scotland.

" Do they regularly attend Church on Sundays ?—
Those that are old enough and have accommodation in
the parish or other churches, which are all a mile distant,
very generally attend.

" What age do you think them old enough at ?—That
depends very much upon the opinion of the parents and
the inclination of the children; but there is a Sunday-
school also open three times a day; the young children
under ten years of age, who are considered too young to
go to church, and particularly to walk through snow and
bad weather in winter, attend the Sunday-schools for two
hours in the forenoon and two hours in the afternoon; the
young persons who are more advanced in life, and who
may not have accommodation in the parish church or in

the public chapels, have an opportunity of meeting on the Sundays.

" Are they examined as to their improvement in religious knowledge?—They are.

" By whom?—By the parish minister."

In 1813, Mr Owen addressed a letter to the owners and superintendents of manufactories, in which he with confidence and satisfaction referred to his own efforts to improve the workpeople of the New Lanark Mills. The spirit which pervaded and the objects contemplated by the publication of this remarkable letter may be understood by the reading of the following extracts :—" Shall, then," said Mr Owen, " large sums of money continue to be expended to procure the last devised mechanism of wood, brass, or iron; to retain it in perfect repair ; to provide the best substance for the prevention of necessary friction, and to save it from falling into premature decay? Shall years of intense application be devoted to understand the connection of the various parts of these lifeless machines, to improve their effective powers, and to calculate with mathematical precision all their minute and combined movements ? And (when in these transactions time is estimated by minutes, and the money expended for the chance of increased gain by fractions), shall not some attention be afforded to consider whether a portion of time and capital could not be more advantageously employed to improve the living machines?"
. . . . . " Since the general introduction of inanimate mechanism into British manufactories, man, with few exceptions, has been treated as a secondary and inferior machine; and far more attention has been given to perfect the raw materials of wood and metals than those of body and mind. Give but due reflection to the subject, and you will find that man, even as an instrument for the creation of wealth, may still be greatly improved." At a meeting of

the Scottish cotton-spinners, held in Glasgow in 1815, Mr Owen proposed that the cotton-spinners and manufacturers of Scotland should solicit the Government to repeal the import duty on cotton of fourpence and a fraction per pound, and, *as a contemporaneous measure*, enact a law limiting the ages at which children should be employed in factory labour, to reduce the working hours to ten per day, and to render instruction in reading, writing, and arithmetic compulsory; in fact, to establish an educational test as a condition to precede employment in factories. The resolution for the abolition of the import duty on raw cotton was unanimously adopted; that in favour of the limitation of the ages at which it should be lawful to employ children in factory labour, the limitation of the hours of labour, and the application of an educational test to those seeking employment in factories, was rejected. Mr Owen subsequently published a letter in the newspapers, addressed to the chairman of the meeting of the Scottish cotton-spinners and manufacturers, setting forth his reasons for both resolutions. The Government repealed the fourpence per pound import duty on cotton, and retained the fraction. Mr Owen resolved to persevere in his efforts to obtain, through the medium of parliament, a Ten Hours' Act. In pursuance of this object, he had interviews with the leading members of both houses of parliament. Through Mr Owen's exertions several meetings of the most active members of the House of Commons were held in London. The objects of these meetings were to consider the condition of factory workers, and the propriety of factory regulation by Act of Parliament. At one of these meetings the draft of a bill, prepared by Mr Owen, was adopted as the basis of future action. At the request of Mr Owen and others, the first Sir Robert Peel agreed to re-introduce the questions of factory labour and factory regulation to the notice of the Legislature. It was not remarkable that

the first Sir Robert Peel should have been chosen to lead
in parliament on the factory question. He was the most
prosperous and experienced cotton-spinner distinguished by
a seat in the House of Commons, a practical and clear-
headed speaker. His decided success as a cotton-spinner
gave to his words additional weight on all that related to
cotton manufacture ; the ease and satisfaction with which
he carried his Bill of 1802 through parliament warranted
the hope of speedy success. Between 1802 and 1815 a very
decided change had taken place as regarded the cotton
manufacture and those employed in mills. This change has
been very distinctly stated in the first Sir Robert Peel's
paper, "*the substance*" of his "*five-and-forty years'*" experience. "Large buildings," said the first Sir Robert, "are
now erected, not only as formerly on the banks of streams,
but in the midst of populous towns, and instead of parish
apprentices being sought after, the children of the surrounding poor are preferred, whose masters being free from the
operation of the former Act of Parliament are subjected
to no limitation of time in the prosecution of their business,
though children are frequently admitted there to work
thirteen or fourteen hours per day at the tender age of seven
years, and even in some cases still younger. I need not
ask the Committee to give an opinion of the consequence
of such a baneful practice upon the health and well-being
of these little creatures." . . . "I most anxiously press
upon the Committee that unless some parliamentary interference takes place, the benefits of the Apprentice Bill will
soon be entirely lost, the practice of employing parish apprentices will cease, their places will be wholly supplied by
other children, between whom and their master no permanent contract is likely to exist, and for whose good treatment there will not be the slightest security. Such indiscriminate and unlimited employment of the poor, consisting
of a great proportion of the inhabitants of trading districts,

will be attended with effects to the rising generation so serious and alarming, that I cannot contemplate them without dismay, and thus that great effort of British ingenuity, whereby the machinery of our manufactures has been brought to such perfection, instead of being a blessing to the nation will be converted into the bitterest curse." The deteriorated condition of the population of the factory districts was a fact within the experience of the first Sir Robert Peel, and, naturally, filled his mind with serious apprehensions. He had watched the downward progress; had witnessed the aversion of the working classes to send their children to the factories ; had marked that aversion yield, of necessity, to a forced compliance ; had observed the progress of a system which in practice supplanted the labour of parents by that of children ; his keen perception enabled him to apprehend that, eventually, the places of the factory apprentices would be taken by the children of the neighbouring working population; to such children he was anxious to extend the legal protection which had proved beneficial to the factory apprentices. The lesson is instructive, and deserves the attention of those statesmen who pretend to have discovered that unchecked and acknowledged evils contain within themselves their own remedies.

The actual change in the circumstances of the cotton manufacture, so simply and graphically stated in the expressive words of the first Sir Robert Peel, fully warranted the proposed change in the regulation of factories. The first Sir Robert Peel, and Mr Owen, were agreed on the desirableness of factory regulation, and the attention of both, though unknown each to the other, had been directed to the great fact that a new and great power had been introduced into the national economy, for whose entrance and development not any provision had been made. Both were conscious of the nature of the evils likely to flow from the unregulated introduction and development of

mechanical power. The first Sir Robert Peel was as ardent
an admirer of genius as any modern political economist,
but his vision was not darkened by the mechanical ingenuity
he observed and admired; and he rightly apprehended that
that which might under some circumstances be a great
and positive blessing, might under others be converted
into " the bitterest curse."

Under the force of these convictions, preparations were
entered into for bringing one of the most important and
most disputed questions of the past and present ages under
parliamentary discussion. It is not unreasonable to suggest
that neither the first Sir Robert Peel, nor any of his
supporters, foresaw the long and arduous struggle that
awaited their followers in and out of parliament. The actual
evils, as witnessed by themselves, the first Sir Robert Peel
and Mr Owen knew, and they hoped for the speedy success
of their remedial efforts. The extent and full force of
the evils of the factory system, in all their varied ramifications,
as subsequently made known by searching inquiry, certainly
few men could have conceived.

The recorded experience of the first Sir Robert Peel on
all that related to the past is invaluable; although even in
the past that experience was by himself declared to be
limited within a comparatively narrow range. If under
the benevolent rule of Mr Dale evils did exist, sufficient in
enormity and magnitude to quicken into active life the
naturally mechanical mind of Mr Owen, and force it to
search for a remedy, if that remedy readily recommended
itself to the wary and ripened judgment of the first Sir
Robert Peel, the mind accustomed to contemplate the proneness
of the human heart to become hardened by the constant
practice of cruelty and continuous association with misery,
may, by imagination and reasoning, be enabled to approach
the possibility of the horrors to which helpless children
enclosed within the walls of cotton factories were sometimes

subjected; but even these reasoners would fail fully to comprehend the reality, until made plain to the understanding by the penetrating force of untiring investigation. It will for ever remain creditable to the judgments of the first Sir Robert Peel and of Mr Owen, that they boldly raised the question,—Whether a system which sacrificed man to aggregated productive power, health and morals to mammon, ought, unimpeded, to establish its iron sway over hundreds of thousands of human beings? It is to the honour of the better qualities of the human heart, and may be, perhaps, profitably remembered in this age, when " the separation of classes " has, because of its prominence, become to the bench, the pulpit, and the press, subject of exposition, lamentation, and reproach, that a millowner and a capitalist was the projector of the Ten Hours' Act, and one of the same class its first leader in the House of Commons. These were followed by others, not less remarkable for their desires practically to benefit the whole factory population, cousistently with the interests of their country. The good services of all such ought assuredly to be placed on record.

Concurrently with the arrangements entered into with the leading members of the House of Commons, the first Sir Robert Peel, on June 6th, 1815, reintroduced the questions of factory labour and factory regulation to the notice of parliament. The following report of the speeches then delivered cannot now fail to be of interest to all whose duties or studies have led them to consider the past and present condition of the labouring population of this country.

" Apprentices in Cotton Mills.

" Sir Robert Peel called the attention of the house to the expediency of some legislative regulation, for the purpose of restricting the employment of young children in manufacturing labour. It was well known that a bad practice had prevailed, of condemning children, whose years and strength did not admit of it, to the drudgery of occupations often severe, and sometimes unhealthy. What he was disposed to recommend was, that no children should be so employed under the age of ten years, either as apprentices or otherwise, and the duration of their labour should be limited to twelve hours and a half per diem, including the time for education and meals, which would leave ten hours for laborious employment. The accounts he had recently seen, showed that it was not so much the hardship as the duration of the labour, which had produced mischievous effects on the health of the rising generation. It was to be lamented, however, that the inspectors, appointed under a late Act, had been very remiss in the performance of their duties. He should, in consequence of this misfortune, propose that proper persons be appointed at quarter sessions, and that they should be paid in due proportion for their trouble. It was gratifying, however, to learn, that the loss of life had been exceedingly small, not exceeding one per cent. per annum; a loss falling short of the average loss sustained in every other class of manufacturing industry. As he was desirous that the measure he was now suggesting should be put into the most perfect state that was attainable, he should submit that the bill for which he intended to move should be read a first time, and then printed. During the recess it might be circulated through the country, and receive the proper amendments. It could, if it should be found necessary to guard against the arts of designing men, be afterwards made a part of this bill,— that no engagement contracted after this period, in violation of the provisions of the bill, should be lawful. Under these considerations, he moved for leave to bring in a bill, 'to amend and extend an Act, made in the 42nd year of his present Majesty [George the Third], for the preservation of the health and morals of apprentices, and others employed in cotton and other mills, and cotton and other factories.'

" Mr W. Smith expressed his cordial approval of the bill, &c.

" Mr Horner observed, that the former measure, and even the present bill, as far as he could understand its object, fell far short of what parliament should do on the subject. The practice which was so prevalent of apprenticing parish children in distant manufactories, was as repugnant to humanity as any practice which had ever been suffered to exist by the negligence of the Legislature. These children were sent often one, two, or three hundred miles from the place of their birth, separated for life from all their relations, and deprived of the aid and instruction which in their humble and almost destitute situation they might derive from their friends. The practice was altogether objectionable on this ground, but even more so from the enormous abuses which had existed in it. It has been known that with a Bankrupt's effects, a gang, if he might use the word, of these children, had been put up to sale and were advertised publicly as part of the property. A most atrocious instance had been brought before the Court of King's Bench two years ago, in which a number of these boys, apprenticed by a parish in London to one manufacturer, had been transferred to another, and had been found by some benevolent persons in a state of absolute famine. Another case more horrible had come to his knowledge while on a Committee up-stairs; that not many years ago an agreement had been made between a London parish and a Lancashire manufacturer, by which it was stipulated that with every twenty sound children one idiot should be taken ! A practice in which there was a possibility that abuses of this kind might arise should not be suffered to exist, and now, or in the next

session when the bill should be discussed, should meet
with the most serious consideration.

" Leave was given, and the bill was afterwards brought
in and read a first time."

The renewed exertions of the first Sir Robert Peel, in
1815, called into existence the germs of what subsequently
became an active opposition. Those among the millowners
who were opposed to factory regulation, used their energies
to delay the passing of the Ten Hours' Bill, as introduced
to the House of Commons; their supporters in parliament
were successful in persuading the first Sir Robert to
abandon his design of immediate legislation, and to move
for a Committee of Inquiry. He was ever anxious to
conciliate his opponents, a desire very creditable to his
heart, but in the then existing state of parties by no
means favourable to the speedy success of the measure of
which he was the exponent. To the anxiety of the first
Sir Robert Peel to conciliate opposition, then comparatively
powerless in numbers and influence, may be attributed in
a great degree the protracted struggle for factory regulation.
He was conscious of the justness and practical utility of
the cause he advocated, and like many other men of good
intentions, gave to opponents credit for openness to conviction and conscientious candour not always well placed
Boldness and rashness in legislation have been the prolific
parents of many evils; some evils have been prolonged
from the want of steadfast energy in those who desired
their suppression. It is a misfortune greatly to be regretted, that men of enlarged experience and known
integrity, who have introduced to the notice of Parliament
necessary remedial measures for positive social evils, have
frequently increased their own labours and the labours of
others, from the fear of giving offence. This was the case
with the first Sir Robert Peel: he made concessions to

opponents who sought for and used those concessions, not to discover the truth, but as a means of delay necessary to enable them to organise and direct a previously-conceived scheme of opposition. The first Sir Robert Peel, having listened to the counsels of timid friends and the solicitations of known opponents, abandoned the thought of immediate legislation, and resolved on a motion for inquiry. On April the 3rd, 1816, he consequently moved for the appointment of a Committee to consider the state of the children employed in manufactories. The perusal of the debate that followed the motion in the House of Commons will unfold the growing importance of the question. Factory legislation, principally because of the rapid expansion of the interests thereby affected, had become a subject of national moment.

"STATE OF CHILDREN IN MANUFACTORIES.

" Sir Robert Peel rose, in pursuance of a previous notice, to submit a motion to the House respecting the state of children employed in cotton manufactories. The object of his motion was altogether national, as it affected the health and morals of the rising generation, and went to determine whether the introduction of machinery into our manufactories was really a benefit. The principal business in our cotton manufactories was now performed by machinery, and of course interrupted the division of work suitable to the respective ages, which formerly was practised in private houses. The consequence was that little children of very tender age were employed with grown persons at the machinery, and those poor little creatures, torn from their beds, were compelled to work, even at the age of six years, from early morn to late at night, a period of perhaps fifteen or sixteen hours ! He allowed that many masters had humanely turned their attention to the regulation of this practice; but too frequently the love of gain predominated, inducing them to employ all their hands to the greatest possible advantage. Some time ago he had introduced a bill into the House for regulating the work of apprentices, which was attended with the happiest results, and their time was limited; but children were still subjected to all the hardships to which carelessness or cupidity might expose them. The House were well aware of the many evils that resulted from the want of education in the lowest classes. One object of the present bill was to enable manufacturing children to devote some of their time to the acquirement of a little useful simple knowledge, such as plain reading and writing. He hoped those poor children would experience the protection of the House, for if it were not extended to them all our excellent machinery would be productive of injury. It might, perhaps, be said that free labour should not be subjected to any control ; but surely it could not be inconsistent with our constitution to protect the interests of those helpless children. The honourable Baronet concluded with moving that a Committee be appointed to take into consideration the state of the children employed in the different manufactories of the United Kingdom, and to report the same, together with their observations thereupon, to the House.

" Mr Finlay defended the character of the cotton manufacturers as a body. He would venture to affirm that the cotton mills of Glasgow were not only situated most advantageously for health, but were conducted on the most liberal plan.

" Lord Lyttleton said, he was persuaded it would be found impossible, when the committee went into the business, to apply such a bill as was brought forward last session to all the manufactories in the kingdom.

" Mr Curwen took that opportunity of protesting against the principle of legislation for the regulation of the authority

of parents over their children, who must be best aware
of the quantity of work those children were able to bear,
and who must undoubtedly feel most for their distresses.
Such a proceeding was a libel on the humanity of parents.
He had, however, no objections to a committee.

"Mr Gordon earnestly supported the motion.

"The motion was agreed to, and a committee appointed."

It is a law of nature that parents should love their own
children, but the perversion of that law is of frequent occurrence,
and confined to no race or country. Mr Curwen indicated
what parents ought to do, which was not a satisfactory
answer to the first Sir Robert Peel, he having rested his
efforts for compulsory regulation on an acknowledgement
of duty, and *his own knowledge of its non-fulfilment*: in
some cases the parents themselves were not free agents,
they having had the value of their own labour reduced by
the introduction of machinery, not a few having been forced
into unwilling idleness, sought for, and found a defence for
the cruel injustice done to their children, in the sense
of their own undeserved poverty. Mr Curwen, in common
with many others, failed to perceive that factory legislation
was necessary because of the palpable violation of the laws
of nature—a truth, the want of the perception of which
was a stumbling-block in the path of improvement.

CHAPTER IV.

NATURE OF THE EVIDENCE TAKEN BEFORE THE SELECT COMMITTEE
OF 1816.—CONDITION OF CHILDREN EMPLOYED IN FACTORIES.—
STATE OF THE QUESTION.

REASONABLE men habitually accept the judgment of those
who, from their special studies and experience, understand
special subjects. This is the homage which common sense
pays to scientific knowledge, and it may be ranked amongst
the "signs of the times" that this kind of homage is not
on the increase; Mammon-worship has usurped the place
of the respect due to solid acquirements and scientific
research. Unverified theory is frequently preferred to
the decided convictions of the ablest professional authorities,
and subjects of the most vital moment are viewed through
the lens of self-interest. The results are in keeping with
the process; the mystifications, incongruities, and contradictions consequent are appalling. It is not any longer
considered to be the duty of a statesman to understand
principles, or to endeavour to be guided by the voice of
experience; society pays heavy penalties for the empiricism
and inconsistencies of its chosen guides. The propounders
of factory legislation were not of this class; they knew
that safe action could only follow from sound judgment,
and they were guided by that knowledge:—"The wisdom
of the prudent is to understand his way;" the result of
extended experience; "but the folly of fools is deceit."

The principal members of the medical profession have rightly earned for themselves a distinguished post among the leaders of every social improvement. Quackery, it must be owned, is everywhere too common; it is an old disease, having its origin in audacity and ignorance, and is not by any means easily eradicated. The most intense study, the widest experience, and the closest observation of all that relates to life, health, and disease, are the requisites of an efficient physician. In proportion as the union of these requisites in the same person is rare, and when existing, important, so is the worth of his testimony. This being so, it was but reasonable that among the witnesses examined before the Select Committee of the House of Commons, appointed in 1816, to take evidence on the state of the children employed in the manufactories of the United Kingdom, should have been the most eminent medical men of the time. The importance of such evidence it is almost impossible to over-rate; from knowledge or experience, the witnesses were eminently qualified to give sound opinions on the subjects brought under their consideration by the members of the committee. These subjects having been life, health, disease, and their principal coincident conditions, have not, with the lapse of time, lost any portion of their value. We feel that it is due to the memories of medical authorities so distinguished, to give portions of their evidence in their own words.

" ASHLEY COOPER, Esq., called in and examined:

" You are by profession a surgeon?—Yes.

" You have had very great experience in your profession? —Yes.

" Has your attention been directed to children in the course of your practice?—Yes, certainly.

" At what age may children, without endangering their

health, be admitted to close labour for thirteen hours per day?
—I think at no age.

" What is the length of the day that you would
recommend?

" Upon a subject of this kind one must answer upon
general principles; for the preservation of health three
things are certainly necessary, air, exercise, and nourishment ; and I conceive that if a child has not a due proportion of exercise, if it is confined for a great number
of hours in air of a certain temperature, and if it has
not a proper proportion of nourishment, it cannot be in
health.

" Do you not think that the labour many children in
manufactories undergo is of itself sufficient exercise to
answer the purposes of health?—Not if it is in a confined
situation.

" Do you think that children, of from seven to ten
years of age, can be employed more than ten hours per
day without injury to their health?—I think not.

" What do you consider to be the effect upon the
development and growth of the bodies of children from
six to ten years of age, if so many hours of confinement
are imposed upon them?—The result of confinement,
commonly, is not only to stunt the growth, but to produce
deformity; and to that point I can answer, from a good
deal of experience, that deformity is a common consequence
of considerable confiement.

" What is your opinion as to the effect of confining
children of from six to seven years of age in manufactories,
with all the circumstances attendant, where they work,
chiefly standing, from fourteen to fifteen, and sixteen
hours a-day?—That it must be very injurious to general
health."

" Sir GILBERT BLANE, Baronet, M.D., called in and examined :—

" You are by profession a physician ?—I am.

" It is well known you have had much experience in your profession ?—I have.

" Supposing that children are employed in close rooms, regularly day by day, for thirteen hours and a half, one hour and a half being occupied in meals, is it your opinion that the children so employed at the early age of from six to twelve would receive no injury in their health ?—It is necessary I should premise, I have no experience as to manufactories, and, therefore, my answer must depend on general analogy. From what I have observed in the course of my experience, for the last three and thirty years, in all ranks, and from being twelve years physician to one of the largest hospitals in London, I certainly should say it was greatly too much for the health of children. My grounds of inference are founded on the natural appetency of all young creatures to locomotive exercise, and the open air ; from what I have witnessed in the lower orders, and particularly from the bills of mortality in this town, in which I have observed, in the course of the last century the mortality diminished from one in twenty to one in thirty-eight; and upon casting my eyes upon the different periods of life, I find that the great difference has arisen from the diminished mortality of children : and this diminished mortality has, I apprehend, arisen from children being brought up in purer air, with more cleanliness and greater warmth ; that cleanliness, warmth, and ventilation, are the great causes of the health of young persons, and to which the diminution of mortality, in this metropolis, has been chiefly owing. The diminution of mortality in grown persons has been owing chiefly to the same causes, preventing the generation and propagation of infectious fevers." Testimony to the same effect was given by Christopher Pemberton, Esq., M.D., and

George Leman Tuthill, Esq., M.D. The next important
portion of the inquiry was, in what degree do the necessary
conditions for health and strength exist? In a tabular
statement of the hours of labour in forty-three cotton factories
in Manchester and neighbourhood, made by the proprietors
of the factories referred to, the actual hours of work per day
were 12, 12½, 13, and 14,—one 14½, and one 10½. This
labour was performed in an atmosphere of from 70 to upwards
of 78 degrees, often in ill-ventilated rooms. These conditions
were incompatible with health, and there was no lack of
circumstantial evidence proving the soundness of the judgment expressed, from a knowledge of natural laws, by the
most eminent medical authorities of the age. Mr Kinderwood,
a surgeon, whose practice was confined exclusively to Oldham
and district, gave the following evidence :—" Have you
perceived any effect on the digestive organs from employment
in cotton factories?—The digestive organs become debilitated
with the other parts of the system: it is a function that is
easily injured; a child may eat a sufficient quantity of food,
and not turn it into nutrition. If there is not a digestive
power in the stomach, no matter what food he takes, the food
is not converted to nutrition, he does not get any flesh."
Mr Kinderwood also spoke as to the prevalence of scrofula
and consumption, to the frequent occurrence of serious and
fatal accidents from unfenced machinery and low-roofed mills.
The following extract of Mr Kinderwood's evidence is important, in so far as it relates to exercise, rest, and meals :—" As
far as you have had opportunities of observing, are the
children universally kept to their employment without
relaxation; during the hours of work before and after dinner?
—The most common thing is to have breakfast sent, during
which the machinery is working ; but I have stated, I think,
there is one mill where there is a recess from the mill for
breakfast, and they go out for twenty minutes, the same in
the afternoon for bagging (tea-drinking) as it is termed.

" You mean a sort of watering time, or for refreshment ?—Yes.

" Is that usual in other mills in that neighbourhood ? —I mention it as a singular instance.

" In those mills where the children are kept in to breakfast, and where no time is allowed in the afternoon, do you know whether the children are kept constantly at the employment between the meals ?—Certainly, they are kept constantly at the employment, for they eat the breakfast with the machinery employed which they are paid to look after ; perhaps one child may look after the machinery of another, and the compliment may be returned, I do not know how that is."

Mr Bill, a Manchester surgeon, of twenty years experience in the Manchester infirmary, had been long seriously impressed with a sense of the ill effect of spinning-factories, " both as to health and morals." " These works crowded the Infirmary with patients." — Mr Boutflower, a surgeon resident in Salford, forwarded a paper which was given in evidence as follows :—" That of seven or eight thousand patients who are annually admitted to the Manchester Infirmary, one half of the surgical complaints are scrofulous. A difference very striking occurs at Liverpool: in a report of 15,000, only 152 are marked as scrofulous." —Mr Simmons, senior surgeon of the Manchester Infirmary, having had in that capacity an experience of twenty-five years, also gave very decided testimony on the evil effects of factory labour on health.

Of late years Manchester has become celebrated for educational efforts ; public schools, rival schemes for educating the young, free libraries, lecture halls, and reading rooms, bear witness to the enterprise of rival sects and parties, and warrant the belief that many have found out " that the soul to be without knowledge it is not good." One of the effects of the factory system, as stated in

evidence before the committee of 1816, was, to lessen the
opportunities of education afforded to the young. Convenient schoolrooms had been erected for the instruction
of the children of the labouring population in reading,
writing, and arithmetic, but the forms were not half filled,
the Lancasterian and National schools of other towns in
which factories had not been erected commanded a much
better attendance. In Manchester the average time of
attendance at the Lancasterian school was about four
months, at Newcastle-on-Tyne four years; " the sole
reason of which was that the parents of the children in
Manchester were tempted to send the children to the
works at an early age (for there was no limitation by law),
and, on the contrary, there was no inducement at Newcastle for the employment of children under twelve,
thirteen, and fourteen, and therefore they remained during
that period, upon the average, in the school."—Before
the committee much evidence was given on the habits of
persons employed in factory labonr.—Mr Nathaniel Gould,
a Manchester merchant of great respectability, and who for
thirty years had attended to the religious, moral, and
social condition of his humbler fellow-citizens, made known
the results of his careful and lengthened observation. Mr
Gould, on being asked his opinion on the causes that
prevented children engaged in factory labour from attending Sunday schools, answered :—" There are two causes :
the one is, I think, that the parents of the children that
do not work in factories, are more attentive to their
children, than those whose children do work in factories ;
I am speaking generally on this. The other great cause,
in my mind, is, that the children having been confined
so very much in the factories all the week, have less
inclination to go to the Sunday schools, as well as their
parents to send them ; I think it is natural for many
parents to wish their children to be as much as may be

in the open air on the Sabbath-day, in order that they may get some strength against they begin the work next week, and recruit themselves a little.

" Have the children at Manchester, who work in factories, any means of instruction after they enter the factories, except what they derive from the Sunday schools?—The length of their time of labour in the week-days precludes all chances of any other opportunity than Saturday evenings, when it seems too much to expect or wish them to go to a school, and the only schools I have heard of for the occasion are two in connexion with Sunday schools, the scholars of which amount together only to about 170." Mr John Moss, who had been from February 1814, to March 1815, master of the apprentices at a cotton-mill— Backbarrow—had on one occasion known children work from eight on Saturday night to six on Sunday morning; the same children had resumed work at twelve o'clock on Sunday night, and worked until five in the morning. Every Sunday children were employed in cleaning the machinery; their orders were to work from six to twelve— had known children work for three weeks together, from five in the morning until nine or ten at night, with the exception of an hour for meals—had frequently found the children asleep upon the mill floors after the time they should have been in bed. Injuries from machinery often occurred—several of the children were deformed. The same causes which operated to prevent the attendance of children at Sunday schools contributed to prevent their attendance at churches and chapels." On the authority of Mr Nathaniel Gould, and other witnesses, a considerable proportion of the whole rising population of Manchester, and district, received but a very limited secular education, and were shut out from the force of religious influences conveyed through the means of Sunday school and pulpit. The witnesses stating these facts, reasonably therewith, con-

cluded that there were among the factory population
with whose circumstances they were familiar, an increased,
and increasing, depravity of character and morals.

Not any stronger proof could be given of an utter want
of common sense and self-reliance on the part of a nation,
of the power of money over the mind and morals, than
the fact that it was found necessary to examine medical
witnesses to prove that cleanliness, and exercise in the
open air, were necessary for the health of children. Any
cottager's wife could have settled the question. Who
that ever nursed a child could doubt that close confinement,
excessive labour, and a tainted atmosphere, were injurious
to health? Selfishness and obstinacy could alone require so
uncalled-for an exhibition of physiological knowledge—
instinct itself had, from the birth of the first living animal,
proved all that reason, humanity, and science, had contended
for. These circumstances notwithstanding, so darkened
and perverse were the minds of the opposing millowners,
that they hoped to shake the confidence of intelligent men
in the laws of nature, and to over-rule the force of the
highest authorities by an array of testimony opposed to
nature, facts, and reason. The evidence hitherto stated on
the evils of "the factory system" could, to a just and
comprehensive mind, lead to only one conclusion, namely,
the desirableness of improvement. Numerous sections of
the owners of factories had become alarmed, they conceived
that "their craft was in danger," had prepared for the
production of witnesses, intended to prove very different
results from those in the preceding pages. Mr William
Taylor, manager "of a considerable part of the spinning
concerns of Horrocks, Miller, and Co., of Preston," and
who represented before the committee twenty-four cotton-
factories (being, in fact, the deputy of the cotton-spinners
of Preston and neighbourhood, with two exceptions), was
opposed to all parliamentary interference, he thought it

would " create great misunderstandings and unhappiness in families." The firm with which Mr Taylor was connected at Preston, had factories in various towns of the county of Lancaster, and employed 7,000 persons, and his evidence had been prepared with much care, intended to prove that employment in cotton factories was not, more than other employments, injurious to health or morals, but on the contrary, individually and nationally advantageous.

Mr William Sandford, a Manchester cotton-spinner, produced before the Committee a tabular statement intended to prove the superiority of the health of children employed in factories over those employed in other trades. From the *data* on which Mr Sandford based his calculations, " the balance of health in favour of factories in money appeared to be as three shillings are to two shillings; the balance of health in favour of factories in number of persons, as five to four." Mr Sandford produced a document signed by the head master and principal visitor of a Sunday school in Manchester, showing that the children that work in factories were " equally *regular* (or more so) in their *attendance*, more clean in their *persons*, more *orderly* in their *conduct*, and better *clothed* than those who did not." Mr Hollis, a Nottinghamshire manufacturer, was of opinion " that the children employed in his own manufactory were in a trifling degree inferior in point of appearance to those children in the neighbourhood belonging to farmers and agriculturists, but they were equally healthy." Mr Hollis handed in documents signed by clergymen, magistrates, and others, setting forth the excellent condition of all employed in cotton factories in various parts of the counties of Nottingham and Derby.

Mr Augustus Lee, of the firm of Phillips and Lee, Manchester, was of opinion that the reduction of the hours of labour would be injurious to the morals of the factory workers of Manchester, and " perhaps injurious to the tranquillity of the town." Mr Augustus Lee, from "long experience and observation in cotton mills," was of opinion " that an attempt to regulate free labour by legislation would in its consequences inflict the severest injury upon the class of persons it was designed to serve; that the alleged evils principally arising from the difference of skill, care, and management, would have their best remedy in the direct interests of the parties concerned, which has been exemplified in the progressive and humane improvements of the most successful manufacturers; the circumstances of trade are so complicated and different, that no general rule can be devised without great unequal pressure; that restrictive regulations were no more applicable to the cotton, flax, or woollen manufacturers than to many others; therefore they appeared to him partial and unjust. The reasons for them were chiefly derived from speculative opinions in opposition to experience; and many of the reasons might be directed equally against manufactures altogether. The restrictive regulations must increase the enormous poor-rates, by lessening the quantity of industry from the same population and subsistence, as well as diminish the demand for its labour, by enhancing its price. They would give foreign countries in which there were no restrictions an advantage over our own, and at a crisis when we were still struggling for the existence of our manufactures under an enormous load of taxes; they would probably produce an emigration of workmen and a transfer of capital to foreign countries; by their operation an immense revenue is at stake; the safety of three manufactures, equal to more than sixty millions sterling per annum, may be hazarded, of which more than one-half, according to the official reports, is dependent upon foreign demand, and, of course, upon foreign competition."

Mr George Augustus Lee " had travelled on the continent and personally examined into the state of manufacture in France; at Rouen he had visited two cotton manufactories, each employing 1,000 people; the proprietor had been protected from conscription, encouraged, and decorated with the Legion of Honour by the first Napoleon. Mr Lee assured the committee that the progress of the cotton manufacture in France gave him great alarm." Mr Lee was evidently convinced that the only road open for the improvement of the health and morals of the population was through the increase of accumulated riches, and the extension of foreign trade. He stated facts, enunciated principles, and foretold results with that air of confidence which alone belongs to men who fancy that they know the whole truth.

The disagreement of the witnesses examined was distinct and irreconcilable. Men of the highest respectability gave evidence on the same subject, leading to opposite conclusions. The evidence was not, to many minds, conclusive for or against legislative interference. This perplexity was itself a result, evidence of an important change in the minds of legislators. One-tenth part of the medical testimony against over-work given in 1816, would, in 1802, have been considered irrefragable proof. The subject was still open for investigation and controversy, and the first Sir Robert Peel and his supporters could, at this time, only have anticipated that any renewed appeal to parliament for factory regulation would be met by an organised and energetic opposition.

CHAPTER V.

RENEWED EFFORTS OF THE SUPPORTERS OF FACTORY REGULATION.—
POWER, POSITION, AND ARGUMENTS OF OPPONENTS.—DEBATE IN
THE HOUSE OF COMMONS IN 1818.

WHEN a truth has once gained possession of the mind of
an earnest man who measures the fulfilment of his duties
by the sense he feels of his responsibilities, it will not be
allowed to slumber in indolent and fruitless inactivity.
Important truths take stronger root in the minds of sincere
men than with the majority of mankind. Such men cannot
be dismayed. Obstacles will arise, delays ensue, and sometimes doubts intervene to check the realisation of thoughts
in practice; good thoughts, seriously entertained, will live
on, and cannot possibly be neutralised by the existence
of difficulties. A strong sense of duty is proof against
obloquy and slander, and steadfast amidst the novelties and
exigencies of current times. The frivolous and the weak
are easily thwarted in their designs : in the understanding
of the frivolous, life has but few serious duties ; in the case
of the weak, timidity renders them impotent :—" A double-
minded man is unstable in all his ways."

The opponents of factory legislation were not slow to
profit from the contradictory nature of the evidence given
before the committee of the House of Commons in 1816.
The combined cotton-spinners opposed to factory regulation were rich and well-organised, advantages which their

energy and business habits enabled them to turn to account. They secured a widely-extended circulation to such portions of evidence as were favourable to their opinions, they omitted the portions opposed thereto. They were not sparing in their insinuations against the supporters of the Ten Hours' Bill. Slander is a very powerful weapon, and, like the assassin's dagger, wounds most fatally when the hand that strikes is hidden from the eye of the victim. This treacherous and dangerous weapon was often and powerfully used by some among the opponents of factory regulation. The motives of the first ⟨ Sir Robert Peel were misrepresented, the character of a truly good man— Mr Nathaniel Gould, traduced; others suffered in their degree.

Here we must pause: it has been the habit of the opponents of factory legislation, for want of better arguments, to represent its original supporters as men of little worth, of mediocre talent, as mere visionaries — speculative dreamers devoid of every quality calculated to give weight and force to their opinions. We have already spoken of the first Sir Robert Peel, and have given judgment on his talent and character as a parliamentary leader. We cannot, in justice to the memory of Nathaniel Gould, proceed without recording our testimony to his worth. Nathaniel Gould was a prosperous and universally respected Manchester merchant, faithful in the discharge of every duty ; his time, his talents, and his wealth were used in the service of his fellow-creatures ; his active benevolence called forth the admiration of his neighbours and the gratitude of the poor, his sympathies for their children led him to constant and active exertions in their schools, every measure calculated to improve their condition, religiously, mentally, and physically, found in him a willing supporter. In Manchester there was not a more respectable, there was not a more respected citizen than

Nathaniel Gould; he became the out-of doors leader in the great question which now engages onr attention. With the self-sacrifice of a Christian indeed, he threw himself into the gap between the oppressor and the oppressed, his days and nights, his physical and mental energies, his great influence and wealth, were all willingly devoted to the cause he had resolved conscientiously to maintain. Until then his name had been without reproach, all admired his benevolence, his perseverance, his self-sacrifice, but now the anger of the oppressors of the factory children was kindled against him, their malice dared to impugn his motives ; slander was their weapon, tales, malicious as they were false, were spread to his disparagement, one of the best men in Manchester was represented to have been one of the worst; even then, he was true to the cause he had espoused, and he defended it as a duty he owed to God and man.

Conscious of the frail tenure of human life, but firm and sincere in purpose, before the passing of Peel's Bill in 1819, Nathaniel Gould allotted in his will the sum of 5,000l. for the realisation of the good work in which he had engaged. He lived to see that work accomplished, and spent not less than twenty thousand pounds in the expenses attendant on the passing of what is called "Peel's Bill," but which, in its labour and expense, was eminently "Gould's Bill." During one of Nathaniel Gould's visits to London, he took lodgings in Dover street, Piccadilly, purposely to be "in the track of members of both Houses." One evening, when busily engaged writing notes to members of parliament, on the necessity of supporting the first Sir Robert Peel in the House of Commons, his bill for factory regulation then being before parliament, there entered a neatly-dressed, sedate, pleasant-looking young man:—"Well, Mr Gould, how are you getting on, do you see much ground for hope yet?"—"Aye, Robert," said Mr Gould, "it is hard work, but we shall succeed, depend upon it."—"Well, Mr Gould, I have told you that you have much to contend with in the House, and many that won't offend you, you will find voting against the bill in the House."—"No doubt, Robert, but our cause is good, and must succeed ; a matter of time and a matter of money, but, Robert, it is *a righteous cause,* and must succeed." After a few more words, this gentlemanly. looking young man walked up to Mr Gould; a slight interruption followed. Mr Gould said, " Aye, Robert, thou art a good fellow—good night," and familiarly patted his youthful friend on the shoulder as he retired. Nathaniel Gould's assistant, whom he loved and trusted, now a most reputable London merchant, said,—" Well, Sir, what was all that about ? "—" We'll see," said Nathaniel Gould, stepping near to a candle, and opening his hand, which contained a fifty-pounds bank note; he then observed—" Robert is a good fellow, he little knows what I am spending in this business, but he means well, and I will not offend him." That young man was the second Sir Robert Peel ; his donation was a proof of his desire to serve the cause which his father and he had in parliament supported. While living (apart from personal exertions, which were incessant), Nathaniel Gould contributed munificently to the principal public charities in Manchester ; in justice to the memory of this truly pious and christian man, we append a list of some of the sums set apart in his will for public purposes; it is not for the world's benefit that the good which men have done should be forgotten in the grave.

Legacies for charitable purposes bequeathed by the late Nathaniel Gould, of Manchester.

		£
To the Public Infirmary of Manchester		200
„ House of Recovery	. .	500
„ Lying-in Hospital	. .	200
„ Jubilee Charity	. .	200

£

To the Lancasterian School   . 100
  „   Sunday School   . 500
  „   Auxiliary Society for Education . 500
  „   Auxiliary Bible Society   . 500
  „   Christian Knowledge Society   . 500
  „   British and Foreign Bible Society 500
  „   National School   .   . 500
  „   Poor pious Clergy   .   . 100
  „   Misses Young (two daughters of
         a recruiting officer at Man-
         chester, who died there, leaving
         his children destitute)   . 500

At the meeting called to establish " the Town Wards and Infirmary," since called, "The House of Recovery," Mr Gould contributed 300*l.* ; the subscription not equalling on the whole his expectation, he contributed anonymously an additional 200*l.*, making with the legacy named above 1,000*l.* It was his desire that " the Gospel should be preached to the poor ;" as a means to this end he bought the galleries of St Stephen's Church, Manchester, intending these to be free sittings. This purchase, notwithstanding, he was compelled to pay an assessment on the value. When the property came into the hands of the Reverend Joseph Gould, nephew of the late Nathaniel Gould, he too was charged the assessment ; by legal advice, he let the front seats, and eventually conveyed the whole to the poor for ever,—thus realising the intention of his uncle, of whom it may be truly said:—" He loved his God, and served his kind."

Much has been said and written about the power of the feudal barons over their dependants, in ages long past ; the theme has been a favourite one with those who prefer the palliation of the crimes of their own age by a comparison with extreme cases in other ages. The power of punishment, reduced to practice, by barons in feudal times, was unequal to the searching and direct despotism frequently manifested by the unscrupulous owners of some cotton manufactories over their infant labourers. True, the unscrupulous factory-owner could not with impunity hang a refractory servant by the neck until life was extinct, a power which the ancient barons possessed, but then the baron's means of knowing those among his vassals who dared to think differently from himself were few, in comparison with those at the command of the factory-owner; the serfs of the soil, spread over a wide domain, except in times of war, the toils and excitement of which they courted rather than feared, were seldom interfered with; it was in the very nature of feudalism to depend more upon attachment than terror, the love of the chief and the honour of the clan were more potent influences in securing servitude than the dread of personal punishment. A few hundreds of individuals, cooped up within the walls of a cotton manufactory, were well known to the owner, under the immediate inspection of himself, any one of whom was easily singled out for punishment. This was frequently done; an operative who dared to give evidence on the factory system, to tell others what he had himself endured, or known others endure, was a marked man, and his name once in the "black book," he and his were objects of relentless persecution. What persecution? The persecution of being refused to "earn his bread by the sweat of his face:"—think of it, for there is none greater.

The opponents of factory legislation were unceasing in their efforts to make popular the doctrine that it was not consonant with the duties of an "enlightened government," in any way to interfere with the relations of capitalists and labourers. In the estimation of these millowners, the beginning and the end of the duties of a government consisted in protecting their property, and allowing them to treat all those under their control as to themselves seemed best. "Let all things alone," is the approved maxim of indolent statesmen and satisfied capitalists, but though supported by much plausible reasoning, did not meet with the approval of the factory operatives, or the more humane among their employers. It is deserving of remark, that the popular doctrine of "letting all things alone," has grown up in this country at the very period of her history when the old moorings of society have been sundered. In any country which, like England, had risen to influence through the slow growth and gradual evolutions of many ages, a country in which security of person and property had from habit and law been firmly established, so long as agriculture and manufacture remained nearly in their relative proportion, one to another, "letting all things alone" would, in all that related to industry, have been, if not a safe, at least not a suddenly dangerous course. A people wedded to the soil, attached to family, property, and country, required but little attention from statesmen ; their industry, thrift, and patriotism, were the sources of national strength, and bonds of health, comfort, and order. To such a people, the modern maxim of "do nothing" would have had the negative merit of saving their interests from the blight of official incapacity, and its result—ill-judged intermeddling. When numerous sections of the population forsake the parishes of their forefathers, and all the associations which connect the cordings of society (binding men and women to home and duty), and are concentrated in indiscriminate masses, subject to conditions which they every day feel to be injurious to health and virtue, but which, by their own confession, they are unable to change, to preach to such a population, " Let all things alone," is to hand them over defenceless to the cruelties attendant on graduated death, to prepare for future generations an incalculable increase of misery and crime. The primary distinction between a wisely adjusted system of national economy, and "letting all things alone," is, that in the former, all known, serious, and dangerous evils are restricted in their operation by law; in the latter, they are left to the full force of their unrestrained action, to become in time deeply seated organic diseases; in the one case social despotism is bridled, in the other, it may kill its victims by tens of thousands, none daring to make it afraid. Of all kinds of absolutism, no matter by what name known, the most destructive and relentless is the absolutism of Mammon over human sinews. Such was the conscientious conviction of the most active among the principal supporters of factory regulation, and although they, because of circumstances already named, were delayed in the labour in which they had engaged, they were far from being disheartened or doubtful of ultimate success. These untoward circumstances, united with the failing health of their parliamentary leader in the House of Commons, prevented for a season the re-introduction of the Factories' Regulation Bill as originally intended.

Early in 1818, the supporters of factory regulation were active in their operations, resolved that not any further delay should take place on their part. In the hope of disarming opposition, they, chiefly through the solicitation of the first Sir Robert Peel, had agreed in their bill to lengthen the restricted hours from ten to eleven per day. The opponents of the measure were equally active, and took the lead in parliament. On February the 18th, 1818, Lord Stanley presented a petition from the owners and occupiers of cotton mills in Manchester and vicinity. The petitioners condemned the evidence given before the committee of 1816, and prayed, "that if the House required further information upon the subject, they would be pleased to appoint a special commission of its own members for the purpose of examining upon the spot into the actual condition of persons employed in the various cotton and other manufactories." The question was now fairly before the House of Commons; on February the 19th, the first Sir Robert Peel introduced to the notice of the House his promised motion; " the importance of which increased more and more on every consideration of it." . . . . " In Manchester alone, about 20,000 persons were employed in the cotton manufactories, and in the whole of England about three times that number." . . . . " It was notorious that children of a very tender age were dragged from their beds some hours before daylight, and confined in the factories not less than fifteen hours ; and it was also notoriously the opinion of the faculty that no children of eight or nine years of age could bear that degree of hardship with impunity to their health and constitution." . . . . " Those who were employers of the children, seeing them from day to day, were not so sensible of the injury that they sustained from this practice as strangers who were strongly impressed by it. In fact, they were prevented from growing to their full size. In consequence, Manchester, which used to furnish numerous recruits for the army, was now wholly unproductive in that respect." The honourable baronet concluded, by moving " that leave be given to bring in a bill to amend and extend an Act made in the forty-second year of his present Majesty, for the preservation of the health and morals of apprentices and others employed in cotton and other mills, and cotton and other factories." A debate ensued, Mr Peel (the second Sir Robert) spoke with much point and force in favour of the motion. The principal opponent was Mr Finlay; he said, " that excepting in one instance, in the county of Lancaster, there was no proof of the existence of any evils which could justify legislative interference."

The bill was brought in and read a first time.

The second reading of the bill took place on February

23rd, 1818 ; Sir Robert Peel said, "In the bill brought in in 1815, the age at which the children might be employed was fixed at ten. He now proposed the age of nine years, and that the powers of the Act should terminate when the child reached the age of sixteen, and could be considered a free agent. He, therefore, now recommended that children employed in cotton factories should from nine to sixteen be under the protection of parliament, and before nine that they should not be admitted ; that they should be employed in working eleven hours, which with one hour and a half for meals made in the whole twelve hours and a half. It was his intention, if possible, to prevent the recurrence of such a misfortune as that which had lately taken place— he alluded to the fourteen poor children who were lately burnt in the night in a cotton factory. [At Colne bridge, near Huddersfield.] He knew that the iniquitous practice of working children at a time when their masters were in bed, too often took place. He was ashamed to own that he had himself been concerned where that proceeding had been suffered ; but he hoped the house would interfere and prevent it for the future. It was his wish to have no night work at all in the factories." The honourable baronet concluded by moving " that the bill be read a second time." The debate which followed, though conducted with earnestness on both sides, elicited not any new facts or views on the subject. The principal speakers for the bill were the first Sir Robert Peel and Mr Peel (the second Sir Robert) ; against the bill, Mr Philips and Mr Finlay. The bill was read a second time and committed, the report received and ordered to be taken into consideration on the 6th of April. On April the 10th, the first Sir Robert Peel presented a petition from all the cotton-spinning factories in Stockport, in favour of the Cotton Factories' Bill. To this petition Sir Robert attached the greatest importance. Sir James Graham, on the contrary, assured the house "that these petitioners were no other than a set of idle, discontented, discarded, and good-for-nothing workmen, who conceived that they did too much when in employment for the wages which they received. He knew them to be of the description which he had stated, and he had no doubt, if the bill before the house were carried in the present session, these men would endeavour next year to have a bill carried to limit their hours of employment to a much smaller number than those which were fixed by the bill."

The first Sir Robert Peel defended the character of the petitioners against the charges of Sir James Graham. The petition was ordered to lie on the table.

Between the second reading and the time appointed for the third reading, petitions for and against the bill were presented from various towns and villages in the factory districts of the United Kingdom.

The discussion on the Factories' Regulation Bill in the House of Commons on April 27th, 1818, was, in all important respects, a repetition of leading portions of the evidence given before the Committee of the House of Commons in 1816. The first Sir Robert Peel stated at length his motives for introducing the bill, and explained its provisions. The principal speakers in opposition were Lord Stanley, Mr Philips, and Mr Finlay. The ablest speech in support of the bill was that of Mr Peel (the second Sir Robert). He denied that either parents or children were free agents. Referring to the nature of the evidence against the bill, he said, — "Indeed, if all that the honourable members had said of the healthiness of cotton mills were true, application ought to be made to the Legislature for the erection of cotton mills, for the purpose of further and more effectually providing for the health of his Majesty's liege subjects. The instances produced from the evidence were certainly strong enough to support the most unqualified of the assertions which had been made as to the healthiness of cotton mills. One of the instances was that of a mill at Glasgow, in which he believed an honourable gentleman opposite was concerned. It was given in evidence that in this mill 873 children were employed in 1811, 871 in 1812, and 891 in 1813. Among the 873 there were only three deaths; among the 871 two deaths; among the 891 two deaths; being in the proportion of one death in 445 persons. So very extraordinary a small proportion had naturally excited the astonishment of the Committee [1816], and therefore, as was to be expected, they questioned medical gentlemen as to the proportion of deaths in different parts of the kingdom. When this statement was shown to Sir Gilbert Blane, he expressed his surprise, and observed, if the fact was not asserted by respectable persons he should not believe it; and being asked ' why he distrusted it ? ' he said that ' the average number of deaths in England and Wales was 1 in 50 (in 1801 there had been 1 in 44). There were favoured spots, certainly — Cardigan, in which the deaths were as 1 in 74; Monmouth, in which there was 1 in 68; Cornwall, 1 in 62 ; and Gloucester, 1 in 61 ;' yet in the cotton factories they were stated to be as one in 445 ! In one of Warton's beautiful poems which begun with these lines—

> ' Within what mountain's craggy cell
> Delights the Goddess, Health, to dwell.'

After asking where the abode of this coy goddess was to be found, whether on ' the tufted rocks,' and ' fringed declivities ' of Matlock, near the springs of Bath or Buxton, among woods and streams, or on the sea-shore, it would certainly have been an extraordinary solution of the perplexity of the poet, if, when he inquired—

> ' In what dim and dark retreat
> The coy nymph fixed her fav'rite seat?' —

it had been answered, that it was in the cotton mills of

Messrs Finlay and Co., at Glasgow; yet such was the evidence respecting this mill, that its salubrity appeared six times as great as that of the most healthy part of the kingdom. This was the sort of evidence which had been brought to disprove the evidence of disinterested persons, of medical men, and even of persons who had an interest opposed to the measure before the house." The house divided—Ayes, 91; noes, 26.

The opponents of factory laws have ever been ready with their demand for renewed investigation, and each fresh inquiry has closed by strengthening the cause of factory legislation. "The reason why" is obvious; the evils of the factory system were real, deeply rooted, and widely spread; as light was reflected on the system, its hideousness became the more apparent. Yet there were method and policy in the cry for "more light." Those from whose lips the cry issued did not desire "more light," but more opportunities for delay; they cherished the hope that they would weary their opponents and force them to capitulate or compromise. Nor were these hopes always without foundation. The policy was, to a limited extent, successful; the first Sir Robert Peel did make concessions; he departed from the original proposition of ten hours per day as the working hours in factories, and he reduced the age of admission from ten to nine years, but he did not thereby conciliate his opponents. On the contrary, he increased their determination and increased their hopes of success. After so memorable an illustration of the undesirable results of concession and compromise, only ignorance and weakness could at any future time be urged in excuse for the repetition of so dangerous a lesson. The experience thus gained was not lost on the active leaders of the factory regulation movement, who, at a subsequent period, nailed their banner aloft, and on that banner inscribed their motto, "The Ten Hours' Bill, and no surrender."

CHAPTER VI.

PROCEEDINGS IN THE HOUSE OF LORDS.—APPOINTMENT OF A COM-
MITTEE.—NATURE OF THE EVIDENCE. — ARGUMENTS FOR AND
AGAINST STATED.

WHENEVER one portion of society, either from an ignorance
of the conditions necessary for healthful, physical, mental,
and moral action, or from self-interest, have resolved to perpetuate an existing order of things injurious to the interest
of their fellow-men, the supporters of the predominant conditions find many plausible reasons of defence; among these
is frequently an appeal to some popular sentiment. One of
the chief sources of delusion in all ages has been the use
of the words freedom and liberty: these words are responded
to by a deeply seated hatred to restraint implanted in the
heart of man, and their studied and crafty application has
oftentimes done more to continue positive slavery, and to
prevent the formation of requisite conditions for rational
freedom, than the united action of all other agencies. It
was, therefore, not surprising that the opponents of factory
regulation should have claimed for themselves the proud, and,
when justly used, honourable distinction of being "the advocates of liberty and freedom," arrayed in opposition to men
whom they by inference, and sometimes openly, condemned
as the enemies of both. It had probably occurred to but
few among the influential opponents of all legislative interference between capitalists and labourers, that the limits of

justifiable interference depended at all times upon the reasonable control manifested by man over his desires and in his conduct towards his fellow-man, and that he cannot be called free whose wants oblige him unwillingly to submit to conditions of existence positively injurious to his own health and morals, nay, even, if man, from ignorance and long habits of subjection, should without murmur or complaint toil for his daily bread to the certain injury of body and mind, and against the interests of those dependant on him, such a one is not a free man, but a being sunk even beneath the meanest conditions of ordinary serfdom, and any interference by law to check the operation of the power that forces man into such degrading and undesirable submission, whether willing or unwilling, is an interference on the side of true freedom, and a preliminary step towards the establishment of rational liberty. The force of these truths, with their practical operations in his father's mills, no doubt, led the second Sir Robert Peel to deny "that either parents or children were free agents." It has been one of the misfortunes of the present century to hear too much about capitalists and labourers and too little about man and his duties, a misfortune that repeated discussions on factory regulation were destined in some degree to modify. It sounds exceedingly well to say to a working man—"You are sixteen years of age, you are an adult, you are a free agent, at perfect liberty to work on the conditions offered, or, to refuse those conditions, as you please;" but if the working man has not any other property than his labour, and the capitalist offering these conditions has means of support greater than the working man, the choice open to the latter, no matter of what age, in ninety-nine cases out of a hundred is between submission and starvation. Shakespeare most expressively puts into the mouth of Shylock the words—

"You take my life
When you do take the means whereby I live."

The working man's "means" of living are the wages of his labour; the moment he ceases to labour his "means" are at an end; a circumstance which to him makes almost constant daily employment an indispensable condition of honest and honourable existence.

These conditions being so with the adult factory operative, he felt that all appeals made to him by the owners of factories against shortening the hours of the labour of his children, when employed in factory labour, though conveyed to him in honeyed words about "freedom and liberty," were unfitted to his wants, and, with few exceptions, fell barren to the ground. All that gold and energy could do to enlist the working men of the factory districts on the side of the opponents of regulation was done between the sitting of the first Sir Robert Peel's committee, in 1816, and the committee of the Lords, presided over by Lord Kenyon, in 1819. The agencies, however, which were comparatively fruitless when applied to working men, were more successful among a few whose opinions oscillated on the pendulum of personal interest, and on others whose judgments were fashioned by abstract theories of political economy, apart from the consideration of the actual facts of life.

The Cotton Factories' Bill was formally introduced to the House of Lords on May 7th, 1818, by Lord Kenyon, and read a second time on the 8th. On the first and second readings the Earl of Liverpool expressed strong and decided opinions in favour of the bill, declaring that "it was part of the common law of the land that children should not be over-worked, and that if all the medical staff of Manchester were brought to the bar of the house to prove that children worked more than fifteen hours a day without being thereby injured, he would not believe them." Lord Kenyon was equally decided. The Earl of Lauderdale and the Lord Chancellor were strenuously opposed to the bill, complained of the want of evidence, and condemned the evidence given before the committee of the House of Commons in 1816. The debate on the second reading closed with an understanding that counsel and evidence should be heard against the bill before a committee of the whole House. On May the 19th the subject was again brought before the House of Lords ; an animated debate followed, in which the Bishop of Chester [George Henry Law, D.D.] declared that " parliament was the natural guardian of the unprotected." He "felt it due to the situation he held, to his acquaintance with the situation of the children employed in factories throughout his diocess, to state these sentiments to their lordships, and to call upon them to assert the cause of defenceless and suffering youth, more especially since, by doing so, their lordships would support the interests of society at large." In the committee Messrs Warren, Scarlett, Harrison, and Evans were counsel for the petitioners against the bill. It was at the close of the debate, which followed on the speech of Mr Warren, agreed that counsel should be further heard before a committee to-morrow. On the 5th of June it was, by the consent of the supporters and opponents of the bill, agreed to postpone the further consideration of the question for the session. Lord Kenyon pledged himself to bring the subject before their lordships on an early day of the ensuing session. The subject was consequently brought under the consideration of the House of Lords on February 4th and 8th, 1819. On February 25th Lord Kenyon moved " That a committee be appointed to inquire into the state and condition of the children employed in cotton factories, and to report thereon to the House," which motion was, after a debate, carried by a majority. The Lord Chancellor (Lord Eldon), in the course of the debate in the Lords, stated his opinion " that the offence of over-working children was one indictable at common law." He " saw no reason why the master cotton-spinners, manufacturers, and master chimney-sweepers, should have different principles applied to them than were applied to other trades." " A general law ought to be passed, if necessary, for the regulation of manufacturers of all kinds ; but it might happen that a particular law, applicable only to children in one trade, might expose them to greater evils than those from which it was intended to protect them." These observations prove that the Earl of Eldon was not opposed in principle to regulation, but to its partial application.

All the leading features of the evidence given before the committee of the Commons in 1816, were repeated before the committee of the Lords in 1819 ; these, however, were brought out in bolder relief, of which we will supply a few examples, on the examination by counsel before the Lords in 1818. Mr Thomas Wilson, a surgeon and apothecary, of Bingley, in Yorkshire, on being asked the question, " Is it not, in your judgment as a medical man, necessary that young persons should have a little recreation or amusement during the day ? is it not contributory to their health ? " answered, " I do not see it is necessary." The same witness "was of opinion that the employment in cotton factories was as healthful as employment in agriculture ; an opinion fortified by twelve and a half years experience as a surgeon and apothecary."

" Mr Edward Holmes, M.D., of Manchester, had been in practice in Manchester twenty-four years, and had during that period been connected with the Manchester Infirmary, Dispensary and Lunatic Asylum, and from 1796 with the House of Recovery," was examined by the committee.—" As you doubted," said the committee to Mr Holmes, " whether a child could work for twenty-three hours without suffering, would you extend your doubt to twenty-four hours ?"— answered, " that was put as an extreme case, my answer only went to this effect, that it was not in my power to assign any limit."—" Not even twenty-four hours ? "—" I should think that extremely improbable : I have no doubt

at all. All I wished to say was, I could not, if your lordships were to assign to me any portion below twenty-four, say
whether it was above or under the line, for so extraordinary
have the facts appeared that have come out on the investigation of these factories, that I begin to doubt many of
the common-place opinions that have been entertained upon
that subject."

The reader may be astonished at such extraordinary
medical evidence; it is, however, a specimen of a large
stock, and the only key we can supply to understanding
why some medical men discovered that "recreation" was not
necessary to the health of young persons, and their possible
ability to work incessantly any number of hours below twenty-
four, even "twenty-three," without physical injury, is afforded
in the course of the evidence itself:—Mr Edward Carbutt
informed the committee of the Lords that "a committee of
Master Cotton-spinners in Manchester, opposed to factory
legislation, employed himself and other members of the medical
profession to examine the health of children employed in
factories." We adduce the facts as stated in evidence:—
The Committee: "You were applied to professionally?" *Mr
Carbutt:* "Yes, I was." *Committee:* "And paid professionally
as any other gentleman would be." *Mr Carbutt:* "At the
time I examined the Ancoats-twist mill, I had no expectation of payment, I have not yet received any; but it *is
probable I shall,* when examining the others; *I perceived
there was an intention of paying me professionally.*"

Before the committee of 1819, evidence of an entirely
opposite nature, and corroborative of the opinions of Ashley
Cooper, Esq., Sir Gilbert Blane, Christopher Pemberton, Esq.,
and Sir George Leman Tuthill, was given by Mr William
Simmons, M.D., Mr Michael Ward, M.D., Mr Wistanely,
M.D., gentlemen whose experience in factory districts, and
high professional reputation gave their evidence increased
importance.

"Mr George Paxton, a Manchester factory operative employed in the Albion Mills, examined :—

"What are your hours of working? — From six to half-past nine in the evening, and half an hour for dinner.

"Are all the hands allowed that half hour to quit the mill?—They cannot do their duty; they can scarcely clean what they have to clean in the time, and oil it.

"How often are they kept to clean and oil?—Every day.

"The children?—Yes.

"Are their present hours of work longer than they used to be?—Yes.

"Since when?—Since this day fortnight: we had a report that the Time Bill was thrown out of the House, and on the Tuesday following the hours were lengthened from six to half-past nine, and half an hour for dinner: and before that it was from six to half-past seven, and an hour for dinner.

"Do the work-people complain of the hours being lengthened?—Yes: we opposed it, and gave over that evening: when the master came the next morning he went to the manager, and I believe he swore, at least he told me so, that those men who did not choose to work the hours might go about their business. We told him the children could not stand the hours.

"What is the name of the manager?—James Stanfield.

"Has he been long manager?—Yes, ever since I have been there.

"Were you afterwards required to work those lengthened hours?—Yes, and we have done it ever since.

"Is the meat liable to be covered with dust from the cotton in the mill?—Yes, it cannot avoid it.

"Do children often leave their meat?—Often: my children have left it : when they get home at night they cannot eat : I got a strap to awaken my own children, my feelings got the better of my passion, and I did not beat them: and what was the more impeaching to my feelings was, they could not eat their supper when they got home: I reflected upon it, and in vexation of spirit I could not eat my own supper: we all went to bed crying."

"Mr John Farebrother, thirty-one years of age, a working spinner from Bolton, in Lancashire, examined:

"Were the children as ill-used while you were overlooker, as when you worked as a boy?—We were worse used; the mill was worked by steam, and my master had another to join him, and the hours were lengthened; they were more ill-used than they were before.

"Were they ill-used besides the number of hours being lengthened?—They have been very much beaten for not being there in time of a morning: they began at five o'clock.

"Who used to beat them?—When I was an overlooker I used to beat them myself, and sometimes the master.

"Was it your duty to beat them, if you could not get them to do their work?—Yes.

"Did your master tell you to do so?—Yes, and he used bad language to me for not doing it.

"Were you forced to see a certain quantity of work produced?—Yes, I was.

"Which master was this?—Mr Luke Taylor: I have seen him, with a horsewhip under his coat, waiting at the top of the place, and when the children have come up, he has lashed them all the way into the mill if they were too late; and the children had half a mile to come, and be at the mill at five o'clock."

"Mr Jeremiah Turner, of Portwood, in Cheshire, stated that "accidents of a serious and fatal nature were of frequent occurrence."

James Watkins, Esq., a magistrate for the district of Bolton-le-Moors, Lancaster, "had devoted much attention to the condition of factories," and gave most important evidence, a portion of which was as follows:—"It is an unquestionable truth that children employed in cotton factories that have fallen under my observation are generally puny and squalid, especially those who work at mills where steam-engines are used: but in establishments where the machinery is worked by water-wheels, the climate of the rooms is more wholesome, and the appearance of the children better; still, a great inconvenience presents itself where power is drawn from a source which occasionally fails. It happens that in dry, as well as in rainy seasons, the power is suspended by a want, as by an excess, of rain; and to bring up the time so lost, children are unmercifully kept at their work sixteen hours in twenty-four. The pernicious custom, too, which generally prevails, of these little workers being constrained to eat their breakfasts in the mill, and no relaxation out of it, except half an hour to three-quarters of an hour (seldom longer) will truly account for the peculiar sickness which seems to fasten upon the whole race. It was not known scarcely by any one proprietor or occupier of factories, where apprentices are not employed, that they were subject to any legislative restrictions, and this explains why the Act of Parliament was not provided in any one of them. In several instances it was found very difficult to arrive at genuine information as to the general treatment of children, and the ordinary discipline in mills; and it is to be regretted that deception in some cases was practised by wealthy proprietors of large establishments. It might be deemed invidious to mention names. Children working in woollen mills are universally healthier and more robust, though those buildings are filthy; it is, however, represented as an impossibility to keep them clean, from the quantity of animal oil that escapes from the wool in the various processes it undergoes. Hours of work are shorter than in cotton factories, and the climate of these mills is comparatively salubrious. The smaller cotton establishments (and they are numerous) which do not contain 'three or more apprentices, or twenty or more other persons,' but which contain 'an average of fifteen persons,' were also visited by me, and, admitting of no exception, they were thought to be *worst of all*, in the fullest meaning of the words; similar to these are some large mills, whose respective stories are let off to different occupiers; it is thence hoped that any future enactment will extend *to all factories whatever*. An invincible jealousy regarding the hours of work pervades the whole race of cotton spinners (Messrs Calrow's and Messrs Grant's are certainly exceptions), each competing with the other as to the greatest quantity of yarn to be turned off, pending the protracted hours of labour, and yet, collectively and individually, a strong wish is expressed for such legislative restrictions as will apportion the hours of confinement, labour, and refreshment, to the age and strength of the juvenile class of our fellow-creatures. Mistaken, too, on the score of individual interest is this excessive confinement; because, by correct calculations, it is ascertained, that where establishments are conducted upon the humane principle that they ought to be, that where the health and comfort are primary duties, as much yarn is spun, and *better* spun, in twelve hours than in fifteen; in the one instance human life is happily prolonged; in the other, misery, disease, and sorrow are identified with a short existence."

A full review of the evidence, as given before the committee presided over by Lord Kenyon, and also the "out-of-doors" proceedings of the opponents and supporters of the bill, will show that the separate parties entertained and advocated opinions decidedly opposed, each to the other. The opponents of all factory legislation contended that the necessity for regulation by law had not been made out; that the proposed factory bill struck at the very root of family order by interfering with parental authority; that it indirectly opposed the free labour of adults, and was opposed to individual liberty; that the adoption of the bill as law would ruin the manufactures to which its operation was to be applied; that a restriction on the hours of labour would, in effect, be equivalent to a bounty paid to rival manufacturers on the continent; that if parliament passed a bill to restrict the hours of labour in factories, parliament could not refuse to pass bills to regulate the hours of labour in all other trades; that under the operation of such a law the employment of children would decrease, that adults would be preferred, that this result would be injurious to the interests of all concerned; that the existing system of labour promoted industry and good order among the work-people, both children and adults; that, on the other hand, shortening the hours of labour, as proposed in the factory-workers' bill, would promote indolence and profligacy in affording time to go to public-houses at night, and to be otherwise disorderly; that very desirable and necessary improvement would result from the free action of the mill-owners themselves; that they were the best judges of their own interests, and that whatever was to them most advantageous, must necessarily be most advantageous to all employed by them; that all interference by government with capitalists, in the use of their capital, was wrong in principle, and must ever prove injurious in practice.

The supporters of factory legislation maintained that the necessity for interference by law had been fully made out; that one effect of the proposed bill would be to strengthen family order; that parents who sacrificed the health of their offspring to their own sensuality were not fit guardians of their own children; that such cases of parental cruelty were comparatively few; that the vast majority of the parents of children employed in factories desired a reduction of the hours of labour; in the absence of the authority of law, parents were unable to enforce their own desires; that a reduction of the hours of labour in factories would contribute towards the improvement of the health and morals of all persons employed in factory labour; that the enactment of the proposed bill would not prove ruinous, or even injurious, to the success of British manufacture; that man, not money, was the primary consideration; that the limit of interference by law with labour and capital must at all times depend upon the ability of men to control their own habits and desires; that the very existence of the evils complained of was evidence that " the factory system " did not contain within itself the means of correcting those evils; that every seeming profit to individuals or the nation was more than counterbalanced by its consequent loss; that as the laws of England were avowedly founded on the laws of nature and the laws of God, not any practices should be allowed in the social condition of England opposed to Christianity and the Constitution; that "the factory system," as then conducted, with few exceptions, outraged nature and violated Christianity.

The parliamentary struggle was drawing to a close. It is due to the contending parties to say, that each was energetic in the advocacy of its own views, and that the subject caused the liveliest interest throughout the country. On June the 14th, 1819, Lord Kenyon introduced to the House of Lords the bill, as it had been finally agreed to in the House of Commons. He " rested his support of the bill upon the facts proved in evidence, contended that this was not in any manner a speculative question, but a question of practical humanity, arising out of the actual sufferings of the children employed in the cotton factories, for which no relief was to be found in any of the provisions of the common law, and therefore it became necessary to resort to a special legislative measure." The opposition in the Lords, though influential, was ineffective ; the bill passed through the various stages, and became law. This result was satisfactory to the country, and was accepted throughout as " a triumph of the Christian feeling of the Legislature over the selfishness of a limited section of factory owners." The substance of the Act was as follows:—A.D. 1819. 59 George III: An Act to make further provisions for the regulation of cotton mills and factories, and for the better preservation of the health of young persons employed therein. It enacted that, from and after the first day of January 1820, no child shall be employed in cotton-spinning under nine years of age. No person under sixteen years of age to be employed more than twelve hours per day. To every such person in the course of the day not less than half an hour shall be allowed to breakfast and not less than one full hour for dinner ; such hour for dinner to be between the hours of eleven o'clock in the forenoon and two o'clock in the afternoon. Time lost by accidental intermission to be made up after the rate of an additional hour per day. Ceilings and interior walls to be washed with quicklime and water twice a year. The Act, or a faithful abstract, to be hung up in a conspicuous part of the factory. Penalties for violation of the Act to be not less than 10*l.*, nor more than 20*l.* for each offence. " That this Act shall be deemed and taken to be a public Act, and shall be judicially taken notice of as such by all judges, justices, and others, without specially pleading the same."

The Factories' Regulation Act, when obeyed, was most salutary and beneficial, disproving in practice every argument which had been urged in opposition. The bill, as originally introduced, was intended to be applied to *all mills ;* the operation of the Act was limited to *cotton manufactories,* a circumstance to be regretted; the result also of an injudicious concession to opponents. Though the Act was in practice beneficial to the operatives engaged in factory labour, yet, the spirit and letter of the law were frequently evaded. The law was by some influential owners of cotton factories viewed as a standing grievance and "a stain on their humanity." The weakness of such an objection is self-evident. Laws are "the application of man's wisdom to his wants," and have their origin not in his perfection, but imperfection; obedience to a necessary law is the primary requisite of good citizenship. "Knowing this, that the law is not made for a righteous man, but for the lawless and disobedient." Man's independent free will is a very good topic for clap-trap declamation, but it is, in society, practically impossible. The Factories' Regulation Act, though in practice satisfactory, met with the opposition and condemnation of that tribe of self-sufficient theorists to whose abstract dogmas it was in principle opposed. The opponents of factory legislation, whose minds were wedded to a theory opposed to all interference by law, continued their opposition unabated and uninfluenced by experience, and pointed out the violations of the law as proofs of its failure. The Factories' Regulation Act remained on the statute-book in defiance of such opposition; although very inadequate to the accomplishment of all it was designed to realise in practice, it was decidedly an important step in what future years proved to be the right direction.

The two fundamental propositions on which opposition to parliamentary interference was based were the following:—"Whatever is most profitable for the individual is most profitable for all those with whom he is connected"— a rule the universal application of which was manifestly absurd. 'Whatever is advantageous to an individual in practice, is advantageous to a nation considered as an indi-vidual state in the society of nations." It appears never to have occurred to the minds of modern writers on political economy that the wealth of an individual and the wealth of a nation are, in some important respects, different in their sources and effects; the wealth of a nation is intrinsic and internal, that of an individual extrinsic and external; the wealth of an individual does not spring, alone, from within himself, it is purchased and owned as property existing apart from himself, and may be wholly lost so as never to be recovered. The wealth of a nation is not necessarily in all respects of this character, it is not purchased by an operation of exchanges, but, in its origin, flows from the earth and the labour of the people; it is perennial, and if from any cause its operations are suspended, there is a fundamental law in nature which, unless the community itself be destroyed, insures the renewal of those operations, and, as an inevitable result, the return of national wealth. There is no such law invariably applicable to individual wealth. Assuredly the application of principles profitable for individuals may be advantageously applied to nations, but not necsssarily so; there cannot be proved to exist any invariable law of this kind : as Locke has very judiciously observed, "the merchant may grow rich by that which makes the nation poor," and on the contrary, a nation may be rich while its merchants, individually considered, are not wealthy. The *doctrinaires* of the modern schools of political economists have been useful in directing the attention of mankind to a more systematic study of the origin of national wealth than was formerly practised, but they have been, like most "schools," too fond of generalities, and have overlooked many important particulars necessary to be remembered by statesmen, and the neglect of which has led to undesirable results.

CHAPTER VII.

ANTI-SLAVERY FEELING IN YORKSHIRE.—RICHARD OASTLER'S PRIN-
CIPLES DEFINED—HIS LETTER ON "YORKSHIRE SLAVERY."—
DISCUSSION IN THE PRESS.—MEETING OF BRADFORD MILLOWNERS,
FAVOURABLE TO FACTORY REGULATION.—OPPOSITION MEETING AT
HALIFAX.

IT is a weakness of human nature, not admitting of a valid
defence, that at times the majority of men are prone to
forget their immediate social duties, those duties which
concern most closely their own neighbours, to content
themselves with a retrospective patriotism, related to past
ages, or a geographical humanity, remote in its main results
from their own interests, and not requiring any immediate
change in their own practices. This weakness is confined
to no age or country, its theory and practice correspond,
both are eminently latitudinarian. It is, therefore, not
remarkable, that in the years 1829 and 1830, this delusive
failing should have been prominently manifested in the
West Riding of the County of York. When England was
moved, from centre to circumference, with appeals on
behalf of the liberation of West Indian slaves, when the
West Riding of the County of York was aroused to action
by the eloquence of Henry Brougham, when, without
exception, in Yorkshire, church, chapel, and newspaper, were
organs of appeal for "liberty and right," when charity

children were singing in the streets the winning words of
the Christian poet, Cowper:—

" Still in thought as free as ever,
Where are England's rights, I ask,
Me from my delight to sever,
Me to torture, me to task ?
Fleecy locks and black complexion,
Cannot forfeit nature's claim,
Skins may differ, but affection
Dwells in black and white the same.
* * * *
Slaves of gold, whose sordid feelings
Tarnish all your boasted powers,
Prove that you have human feelings,
Ere you proudly question ours !"

When sentiments akin to these words, strengthened by
the oft-repeated cry of "Britons never shall be slaves,"
were ringing in the ears of every one, and the highly
nervous had their nightly sleep disturbed by hideous
visions of kidnapping, murder, the crack of the lash, the
clanking of chains, the writhings and groans of victims,—
some among the most prominent of these sympathizers were
rapidly growing rich on the profits of the labour of the
little children, worked excessive and unnatural hours in
the woollen and worsted factories of the West Riding,
that same West Riding, whose voice, like "the sound of
many waters," cried aloud " Slaves, be free;" but in the
multitude of whose voices not one had been raised for
the helpless factory child, who was "tortured" and
"tasked" with impunity at the thresholds of the doors
of women and men, filled with what they themselves
declared to be " a sublime enthusiasm" for the wrongs
of injured negroes. Though this neglect of home duties,
and habit of building up a reputation, and satisfying
conscience by a distant philanthropy, is common to a
proverb, there have been some notable and noble exceptions. Fortunately there have existed, in all ages, fearless

and bold men, who have observed the evils of their own times, who have dared to denounce wrong and error, to bring the professions and practices of their own neighbours into striking contrast; these men have been the salt of the earth, without whose savour the world would have become a barren waste. The actions of such men are not the results of convenience; a faithful conscience is their constant monitor, the impulse of their deeds has its origin in their keen sense of duty, there is a wholeness and simplicity in their moral nature, which impart to all their acts consistency and force; when checked by opposition, they rise with their necessities, feel themselves strengthened by the conscious-ness of their own rectitude; they, to a considerable extent, direct and control circumstances, leave the print of their footmarks on the habits of their fellow men, and, when successful, register their existence in the laws of their country. Among this class of the world's benefactors must be ranked Richard Oastler.

The prominent part which Mr Oastler has taken in the internal politics of this country, and more especially in the factory question, renders it necessary, at this time, to state the leading principles which moved and guided him in action :—This course will enable the reader to comprehend his proceedings. The foundation of Mr Oastler's social and political system is Christianity. He maintains that as Christianity is the avowed theory of the British Con-stitution, Christianity ought also to be the rule for the practice of British society; that the acts of avowedly Christian men are to be measured by their professed duty to and reverence for GOD, and their obligation to obey his Laws : that professions and forms, unsupported by corresponding acts, are evidences of hypocrisy deserving direct condemnation; that the poor and the oppressed have special claims on the consideration of Christian men and Christian governments; that cruelty, oppression, and tyranny, by whatever names veiled, are unchristian, and in an avowedly Christian state, unconstitutional; that reason and all the fruits of genius should be subjected to the Laws of GOD; that the great error committed by modern British statesmen has been their adoption of the theories of men, in preference to the Christian groundwork of the ancient common law of England; that the important problem for British statesmen to solve was, How to reconcile the principles of the ancient constitution of the country to the changed wants and phases of society; that as the Christian faith is derived from the living God, and is itself His own revelation, every doctrine issuing from this source must in practice be for the positive advantage of men, temporal as well as spiritual; that Christianity is the only vital principle of all permanent good to men and nations; that it is the incumbent duty of every sincere Christian to sacrifice his own physical comfort, personal riches, and if needful, his own existence, in the cause of religious duty, social order, and justice. Mr Oastler, consistently with these convictions, has taken for his motto— "The Altar, the Throne, and the Cottage," and through good and evil report has maintained the reasonableness of, and the advantages to be derived from, a social system, in which the temporal and moral condition of society is made subservient, so far as may be possible, to the Law of GOD. These fundamental propositions were not preserved in the mind of Mr Oastler,—for purposes of occasional show,—to be paraded by way of holiday amusement; in his understanding and practice they constituted the every-day rule of practical utility; thus having taken his stand on the Bible as the acknowledged standard of truth in the Church and the State; to the people of England, he spoke in the words of Holy Writ:—"If ye will fear the Lord, and serve Him, and obey His voice, and not rebel against the commandment of the Lord, then shall both ye, and also the King that reigneth over you, continue following the Lord your God. But if ye will not obey the voice of the Lord, but rebel against the commandment of the Lord, then shall the hand of the Lord be against you, as it was against your fathers." " Counsel is Mine and sound wisdom. I am understanding ; I have strength. By Me kings reign, and princes decree justice. By Me princes rule and nobles, even all the judges of the earth."

Mr Oastler entertains peculiar views on the question of machinery. He maintains " that the true friend of science and of inventions is he—and he only—who would limit their exercise to the improvement and benefit of the condition of the thinking, consuming, sentient being, created in the image of God—man. Hitherto we have been drunk with the worship of our own inventions; we have laid ourselves down and let them ride over us. It is high time that we raised ourselves from the dust—turned ourselves round, not in revenge, but in the thoughtfulness of manhood, resolved that henceforward the creatures of our own imagination should be regulated by the law of God; that they should ' work ill' to no man, curbed by the law of the land, rendering compensation for the labour withdrawn." He maintains, that not any invention should be introduced and applied, without a compensation having been awarded to those workmen the value of whose labour would in consequence be reduced; and he asks, in one of his letters addressed to *the working men,* from which the extracts quoted are taken, " Ought any improvement to be adopted in a rational society which cannot provide for the wants of those whose labour it supersedes? Is it indeed a law of necessity that hundreds of thousands of human beings should be subjected, year after year, age after age, to penury and destitution, because one of their fellow-men has been more cunning than themselves — that they, their wives, and their children, should be robbed of every domestic and social comfort, and be doomed by 'science,' from childhood to old age, to agonise in 'hopeless competition' against a power invented by man and wielded by wealth." On the "evils" which have followed from the unregulated introduction and use of machinery he has often expressed decided opinions.

Mr Oastler's political opponents have always admitted him to be a man of eminent ability and undoubted benevolence. Among his personal friends and political opponents was the late Mr Edward Baines, of Leeds. In 1831, at a public meeting in Leeds, at a time when political controversy was keen, and Mr Oastler and Mr Baines in opposition, each to the other, the latter frankly acknowledged Mr Oastler's claims to attention. Mr Baines observed "that whatever might have been said about Mr Oastler's brimstone speeches, he (Mr Baines) must say that there had been no brimstone that night. A speech which was in its nature so impressive, and uttered with such a seeming intention to produce conviction, rather by the force of argument than declamation, he thought he had seldom heard; and he was glad to be able to express to Mr Oastler his very warm satisfaction at the tone and manner he had adopted. * * * Mr Oastler had said, very truly, that they were old acquaintances; he believed their acquaintance was of thirty years' standing, and therefore they ought not to discuss any subject in bad feeling. He (Mr Baines) had the honour of knowing Mr Oastler's father ; a more benevolent and excellent man he believed this country had not produced ; and if the great pains taken by that deceased, and he might then say his much lamented, friend to stem the horrors of war, and prevent the shameful expenditure of public money, which led to the imposition of the burden under which they now laboured, had been successful, they might have obviated the necessity for that discussion. He (Mr Baines) was an humble instrument in the late Mr Oastler's hands on that occasion, but they were not supported as they ought to have been by the manufacturers. If their efforts had been successful, he believed that a great deal of the calamity and distress under which the country was labouring, and the wretchedly long hours would have been prevented. So that Mr Oastler was a kind of hereditary supporter of benevolence, because he inherited it from his father." Mr Oastler thus had, from his father, a reputation for generous sympathies and an active interest in public affairs. Mr Oastler is well known as an apt, ready, and powerful political writer, having in a remarkable degree the faculty of expressing his opinions, with clearness and force, on any subject to which he has directed his attention ; his experience of English society has been varied and extensive ; his public letters and essays are more remarkable for keen observation and prescience of mind, than for book learning and scholarly polish. He is a bold, correct, and eloquent speaker, and was by the late Sir Francis Burdett justly designated " a natural and gifted orator." His appearance is manly and commanding, his voice powerful, his enunciation distinct, his matter and manner English throughout. Mr Oastler's success as an orator has not been effected by startling contrasts or exciting novelties ; it is his rule to speak right on the things which his hearers themselves do know ; few have equalled him in a statement of facts in plain words, appealing directly to the understanding, or, in giving home thrusts by the daring use of an opponent's admissions in argument Mr Oastler has oftentimes made thousands of men, women, and children to glow, tremble, and weep, because of the force of homely words, expressed with feeling and earnestness. When assailed by formidable opposition, he rises to the highest pitch of kindled energy, there is then in his manner a " touch-me-not " air, which has often proved appalling to men not deficient in moral courage. He is a man of keen sensibilities, generous sympathies, strong attachments, and untiring perseverance. When he entered the field of religious, social, and political controversy, as the advocate of the claims of the factory workers to legislative protection, he was in the prime of manhood, a respected, honoured, and influential citizen of the West Riding of his own native Yorkshire. He is remarkable for simple habits, and his fondness of little children whose society he cultivates and enjoys. His pleasures are those of the fireside and the garden, and in the home-circle of every house he visits, his name is a household word.

Though Mr Oastler had lived for many years in the heart of the manufacturing district of Yorkshire, had often visited the poor, had in their own cottages and in the Leeds Infirmary seen many sickly factory children and factory cripples,—the causes of their sickness, deformity, and lameness were unknown to him. Mr Oastler had often expressed his opinion that the working men of the manufacturing districts suffered, physically, from various causes ; that it would be consistent with the professions of those who advocated negro emancipation (with whom he in principle cordially agreed, and actively co-operated), to endeavour to discover those causes, and to apply remedial measures; in his own words—" to apply their avowed principles to the wants of their own neighbours." Of the actual facts of the factories he was then ignorant. When he returned from the various towns of the West Riding to his home, and saw the factories lighted up at night, he accepted of " these sights as signs of prosperity."

In 1830 Mr Oastler was on a visit to his friend, Mr John Wood, of Horton Hall (now of Thedden Grange, Hampshire), a very kind-hearted man, and, at the time referred to, an extensive manufacturer in the town of Bradford, Yorkshire. Mr Wood was wealthy and generous; moved by a sense of duty, he had in vain endeavoured by his own private influence to reform the factory system. Mr Wood knew Mr Oastler well ; in the course of conversation one

evening Mr Wood said: " Mr Oastler, I wonder you have
never turned your attention to the factory system."
"Why should I ? I have nothing to do with factories,"
was Mr Oastler's reply. "That may be," rejoined Mr
Wood, "you are, however, very enthusiastic against
slavery in the West Indies ; and, I assure you, there
are cruelties daily practised in our mills on little children, which, if you knew, I am sure you would strive
to prevent." " Cruelties in mills ? " exclaimed Mr Oastler,
" I do not understand you ; tell me." Mr Wood then
informed Mr Oastler of much that Mr Wood knew ;
among other things, that in " his own mill, little children
were worked from six o'clock in the morning to seven
o'clock in the evening, and that the only break off they
had was forty minutes at noon ; which break was ten
minutes more than any other millowner allowed. While
in some mills in the neighbourhood the poor children
were worked all that time without one minute of rest." Mr
Oastler was astonished, and to his horror discovered " that
little children were worked 14, 15, 16, and even 18 hours a
day, in some mills, without a single minute having been
set apart for meals, and that implements of cruelty were
used to goad them on to this excessive labour. Besides all
this, in many mills they were cheated out of portions of
their scanty wages by fines and other means of fraud.
Worse still, they were often subjected to shocking inde-
cencies, and they were brought up in total ignorance of
their duties to God and to man." Mr Oastler was deeply
impressed with all he had heard. Mr Wood was fully sensible of the horrors and vices of the factory system, and
solicited from Mr Oastler a pledge that he would use all
his influence in an endeavour to remove from the factory
system the cruelties which were regularly practised in
the mills. Mr Oastler has, in *The Home* (1851), a periodical
of which he was the editor, narrated a circumstance which
very clearly indicates the state of his own mind and that

of Mr Wood :—"You will, Edwin, remember," wrote Mr Oastler, "that I was on a visit at the house of a dear friend, a millowner, and that he, to my great surprise, had informed me that I lived not far from a town where human beings—little children, boys and girls—were daily sacrificed for gold. I told you how much I was horrified at his recital. With feelings which I will not attempt to describe, I went to bed. I had requested the servant to call me at four in the morning, having occasion to ride some miles to an early appointment. When my friend's valet aroused me, he said,—'My master wishes to see you, Sir, before you leave ;' he afterwards showed me into his master's bedroom. My friend was in bed, but he was not asleep; he was leaning upon a table beside his bed. On that table were placed two candles, between them was the Holy Bible. On my advancing towards the side of his bed, he turned towards me, reached out his hand, and, in the most impressive and affectionate manner, pressing my hand in his, he said, 'I have had no sleep to-night. I have been reading this book, and in every page I have read my own condemnation. I cannot allow you to leave me without a pledge, that you will use all your influence in endeavouring to remove, from our factory system, the cruelties which are regularly practised in our mills. . . . . . I promised my friend that I would do what I could. I felt, Edwin, that we were, each of us, in the presence of the Highest. I knew that that vow was recorded in Heaven. I have kept it, Edwin, the grace of God having upholden me; I have been faithful. Trusting in the same power, old and feeble as I am, I hope to be faithful even unto death.' "

In the morning of the next day after the conversation with Mr Wood, Mr Oastler adopted the first step towards the fulfilment of his promise; he wrote a letter narrating the results of his experience at Bradford, and addressed the same to the Editors of the *Leeds Mercury*, then, as now, one of the most influential journals in Yorkshire. This letter was after publication subjected to severe and protracted criticism. In a historical sense, this letter is valuable, as being the foundation of what might not improperly be called, "the active Ten Hours' Bill movement;" the first Sir Robert Peel, as has been shown, had, in the vain hope of conciliating opposition, abandoned the Ten Hours' limit as the rule for factory labour, no legal regulation was then applicable to other than cotton factories. When Mr Oastler addressed the Editors of the *Leeds Mercury*, on the condition of children employed in woollen and worsted factories, he was unacquainted with the labours of Gould, Peel, and their coadjutors; he had resolved to light a flame which should be seen throughout England, and the burning of which was subsequently watched with interest throughout Europe and the American Union. Mr Oastler's first letter on the factory question deserves attention for the facts it contains, and the key which it affords to the state of the mind of the writer, when he entered on what has proved, to him and to his country, a momentous labour:—

"YORKSHIRE SLAVERY.

" *To the Editors of the Leeds Mercury.*

" 'It is the pride of Britain that a slave cannot exist on her soil; and if I read the genius of her constitution aright, I find that slavery is most abhorrent to it—that the air which Britons breathe is free—the ground on which they tread is sacred to liberty.'—*Rev. R. W. Hamilton's Speech at the Meeting held in the Cloth-hall Yard, Sept. 22nd, 1830.*

" Gentlemen,—No heart responded with truer accents to the sounds of liberty which were heard in the Leeds Cloth-hall yard, on the 22nd instant, than did mine, and from none could more sincere and earnest prayers arise to the throne of Heaven, that hereafter slavery might only be known to Britain in the pages of her history. One shade alone obscured my pleasure, arising not from any difference in principle, but from the want of application of the general principle *to the whole empire.* The pious and able champions of *negro* liberty and *colonial* rights should, if I mistake not, have gone farther than they did; or perhaps, to speak more correctly, before they had travelled so far as the West Indies, should, at least for a few moments, have sojourned in our own immediate neighbourhood, and have directed the attention of the meeting to scenes of misery, acts of oppression, and victims of slavery, even on the threshold of our homes.

"Let truth speak out, appalling as the statement may appear. The fact is true. Thousands of our fellow-creatures and fellow-subjects, both male and female, the miserable inhabitants of a *Yorkshire town,* (Yorkshire now represented in parliament by the giant of anti-slavery principles,) are this very moment existing in a state of slavery, *more horrid* than are the victims of that hellish system—'*colonial slavery.*' These innocent creatures drawl out, unpitied, their short but miserable existence, in a place famed for its profession of religious zeal, whose inhabitants are ever foremost in *professing* 'temperance' and 'reformation,' and are striving to outrun their neighbours in missionary exertions, and would fain send the Bible to the farthest corner of the globe—ay, in the very place where the anti-slavery fever rages most furiously, her *apparent charity*, is not more admired on earth, than her *real cruelty* is abhorred in heaven. The very streets which receive the droppings of an 'Anti-slavery Society' are every morning wet by the tears of innocent victims at the accursed shrine of avarice, who are *compelled* (not by the cart-whip of the negro slave-driver) but by the dread of the equally-appalling thong or strap of the overlooker, to hasten, half-dressed, *but not half-fed*, to those magazines of British infantile slavery—*the worsted mills in the town and neighbourhood of Bradford ! ! !*

"Would that I had Brougham's eloquence, that I might rouse the hearts of the nation, and make every Briton swear, 'These innocents shall be free!'

"Thousands of little children, both male and female, *but principally female*, from seven to fourteen years of age, are daily *compelled* to *labour* from six o'clock in the morning to seven in the evening, with only—Britons, blush while you read it!—*with only thirty minutes allowed for eating and recreation.* Poor infants! ye are indeed sacrificed at the shrine of avarice, *without even the solace of the negro slave;* ye are no more than he is, *free agents;* ye are compelled to work as long as the *necessity* of your needy parents may require, or the cold-blooded avarice of your worse than barbarian masters *may demand!* Ye live in the boasted land of freedom, and *feel* and mourn that *ye are slaves*, and slaves without the only comfort which the negro has. He knows it is his sordid, mercenary master's interest that he should *live*, be *strong* and *healthy*. *Not so with you.* Ye are doomed to labour from morning to night for one who cares not how soon your weak and tender frames are stretched to breaking! You are not mercifully valued at so much per head; this would assure you at least (even with the worst and most cruel masters) of the mercy shown to their own labouring beasts. No, no! your soft and delicate limbs are tired and fagged, and jaded, at only *so much per week*, and when your joints can act no longer, your emaciated frames are cast aside, the boards on which you lately toiled and wasted life away, are instantly supplied with other victims, who in this boasted land of liberty are HIRED—not sold—as slaves, and daily forced to *hear* that they are free. Oh! Duncombe! Thou hatest slavery—I know thou dost resolve that 'Yorkshire children shall no

more be slaves.' And Morpeth! who justly gloriest in the
Christian faith—Oh, Morpeth! listen to the cries and count
the tears of these poor babes, and let St Stephen's hear thee
swear 'they shall no longer groan in slavery!' And Bethell,
too! who swears eternal hatred to the name of slave, when-
e'er thy manly voice is heard in Britain's senate, assert the
rights and liberty of Yorkshire youths. And Brougham!
thou who art the chosen champion of liberty in every
clime! oh bend thy giant's mind, and listen to the sorrowing accents of these poor Yorkshire little ones, and note
their tears; then let thy voice rehearse their woes, and
touch the chord thou only holdest—the chord that sounds
above the silvery notes in praise of heavenly liberty, and
down descending at thy will, groans in the horrid caverns
of the deep in muttering sounds of misery accursed to
hellish bondage; and as thou sound'st these notes, let Yorkshire hear thee swear, 'Her *children* shall be free!' Yes,
all ye four protectors of our rights, chosen by freemen to
destroy oppression's rod,

> ' Vow one by one, vow altogether, vow
> With heart and voice, eternal enmity
> Against oppression by your brethren's hands ;
> Till man nor woman under Britain's laws,
> Nor son nor daughter born within her empire,
> Shall buy, or sell, or HIRE, or BE A SLAVE !'

"The nation is now most resolutely determined that
negroes shall be free. Let them, however, not forget that
Britons have common rights with Afric's sons.

"The blacks may be fairly compared to beasts of burden,
kept for their master's use; the whites, to those *which others
keep and let for hire.* If I have succeeded in calling the
attention of your readers to the horrid and abominable
system on which the worsted mills in and near Bradford
is conducted, I have done some good. Why should not
children working in them be protected by legislative enact-

ments, as well as those who work in cotton mills? Christians should feel and act for those whom Christ so eminently loved, and declared that ' of such is the kingdom of Heaven.'—I remain, yours, &c.,

"RICHARD OASTLER.

" Fixby Hall, near Huddersfield, Sept. 29, 1830."

The reading of Mr Oastler's letter caused much excitement. As originally written, it was signed " A Briton," Mr Oastler was wishful not to be known as the author, but the senior editor of the *Mercury* insisted on having a real name attached, Mr Oastler consequently appended his signature. Many there were filled with astonishment, some denied the existence of the evils complained of, others affirmed that if Mr Oastler's signature had not been appended to the letter in the *Leeds Mercury*, they could not have believed that such things were, the late Mr Baines (senior editor of the *Leeds Mercury*) admitted that the evils stated therein, if true, constituted a real grievance. A keen controversy followed in the Leeds press, chiefly in the columns of the *Leeds Mercury* and *Leeds Intelligencer*. In this warfare, Mr Oastler was completely triumphant ; like a strong and practised wrestler, he closed upon his opponents, and cast them from his arms on the ground. Every fact relating to the labour of children in factories, stated in Mr Oastler's first letter, was proved to be correct ; the complaints of his opponents were ultimately confined to the tone and manner of the writer; the intense and protracted interest caused by the letter being a very satisfactory reply to such objections. The cruelties in the mills were proved not to be confined to Bradford, they extended throughout the woollen, flax, and worsted districts. A correspondent of the *Leeds Mercury*, Mr R. Webster, in a letter dated " Halifax, 8th November, 1830," wrote: " There is not a mill in the whole town of Halifax which

allows a single moment either for breakfast or tea,—and
the time for dinner is much the same as those in Bradford.
But I believe the hours of labour to be longer than those
at Bradford. None of the mills in this town stop sooner
than half-past seven, and some of them not before half-
past eight or nine o'clock,—and the attendance of the
children is required at six in the morning." . . . . . " Let
any one walk through the mills at the time of breakfast,
and see the poor children eating their coarse fare, whilst
at the same time they must attend to the respective
machines at which they are employed—like beasts of
burden, they must eat and work,—and I am sure that an
individual, after seeing this, if he were a Christian—if he
were a man, he would blush to see the degradation to
which those children were brought by the avarice of their
employers. I do not, however, mean to charge this
epithet upon all the manufacturers of this town—quite
the reverse, I know there are honourable exceptions;
but at the same time there are individuals who would
not care to exact labour from them both day and night,
consequently, those who are possessed of more humanity
are obliged, however reluctantly, to follow the same rule."
On November 11th, 1830, the editor of the *Leeds Intelligencer* wrote :—" It is generally allowed that the *principle* of Mr Oastler's statement is right and commendable;
but that he has somewhat sinned in his manner of laying
it down. If we may presume to offer advice, we would
recommend an immediate meeting of the Bradford spinners ;
let them begin by a proper understanding amongst each
other, and we are sure that they will end as they ought
to do—by a change of plan, by allowing proper hours
for refreshment and relaxation ; and certain we are that
they will not thereby lose in pocket, while they will
gain in character and inward satisfaction. If they neglect
to do something of this sort, the public will probably take

the matter up, and parliament may be called upon to
protect the children by a legislative enactment, similar
to that which applies to the cotton manufactories. But we
know the Bradford manufacturers too well to suppose that
an act of parliament is necessary to induce them to act
with common humanity." From the publication of Mr
Oastler's original letter, which, though dated September
29th, 1830, was not published in the *Leeds Mercury* until
October 16th of the same year,—from this date until
November 22nd, a keen newspaper controversy was waged
on the condition of children employed in factories, the
greatest interest prevailed, the working men were so
gratified with Mr Oastler's exertions on their behalf, that
though, in most cases, radicals of the Cobbett and Hunt
schools, they openly expressed their approval of Mr Oastler's
proceedings, knowing him to be a "Church and King tory
of the old sort;" at one of their Huddersfield public
meetings, they unanimously adopted the following resolution : "That the thanks of this meeting are eminently
due, and are hereby given, to Richard Oastler, Esq., for
his able and manly letters to expose the conduct of those
pretended philanthropists and canting hypocrites who travel
to the West Indies in search of slavery, forgetting that
there is a more abominable and degrading system of slavery at
home." It was evident that the discussion had reached a
point at which it could not rest, the public mind had been
thoroughly awakened, not a few of the millowners of the West
Riding of Yorkshire felt their humanity and consistency
at stake : to quote the words of one of themselves, " Mr
Oastler's facts were so strong and so often repeated that
I felt my honour impugned ; to move in the matter was
a necessity."

The author of this discussion stated his whole views on
the factory question, briefly, but strongly; those views were
in advance of the mind of the age. We repeat them in

his own words:—"The factory system, as at present conducted, is, in every sense of the word, the worst that can be; with proper arrangements it might be made the best. The skill and ingenuity of man is now made to destroy the happiness and comfort of many, merely for the gain of a few: it might be made instrumental to every man's increase in comfort and happiness. The factory system is necessary, but it is not necessarily an evil; it is conducive to the misery of many—it might be made advantageous to all. It is a system which drags in the train of the remorseless tyrant the man of benevolent mind; it compels the kind-hearted master either to relinquish business altogether, or in some measure to copy the cruelty of the oppressor. The system which impoverishes, enslaves, and brutalises the labourer can never be advantageous to any country. The nation's strength and stability is built, if built for perpetuity, on the solid basis of a contented and happy population. The constitution of this country and the present [unregulated] factory system cannot long exist together; their principles are as opposite as light and darkness." Those who for thirty years have watched the social condition of England will be enabled to weigh the justness of these observations, published under the signature of Richard Oastler in 1830.

On November the 22nd, in the words of the *Leeds Mercury*, "A numerous and highly respectable meeting of the worsted spinners of Bradford, and of the trade generally, convened by twenty-three of the principal firms in that town, was held at the Talbot Inn, for the purpose of promoting a legislative enactment to diminish and limit the hours of labour in worsted mills, and to effect other regulations connected therewith."

The gentlemen who constituted this most influential meeting were unanimous in their condemnation of long hours in factories—all admitted the evils of the unregulated

factory system; owned that the competition of rival manufacturers had been so great that in self-preservation they
were forced to follow the custom of the trade, in order
to be enabled to meet their competitors in the market; that
it was desirable that the system should be changed; that
children employed in factories should not be overworked;
that time should be allowed for rest and recreation; that
those desirable results could only be secured by a legislative
enactment, binding on all. The services of Mr Oastler were
duly acknowledged. These proceedings were hailed with
satisfaction by the operatives, and approved by the press.
The spirit of the principal local journals may be inferred by
the perusal of the following paragraph, published in the
Leeds Mercury of November 27th, 1830:—

" We refer with great satisfaction to what may be called
the practical result of the discussions which have taken
place in this paper on the hours of labour for children in
the worsted manufactories. Without in any degree altering
the opinion we expressed at the time of Mr Oastler's first
letter, we feel that it is due to that gentleman to say that
the public are indebted to him in a high degree for his
humane exertions in favour of those who, by reason of their
tender age and dependent situation, could not speak for
themselves. The most appropriate reward he can receive
will be that meed of gratitude to which he is entitled. The
manufacturers of Bradford are also doing themselves great
honour, and we trust that their laudable example will be
generally followed. It will be seen that the Bradford petition is
to be presented by Lord Morpeth [now the Earl of Carlisle], who
interested himself to complete the regulations in cotton mills,
moved by Mr Hobhouse in May 1829, and whose disposition
and information so well qualify him for the task."

The editor of the *Leeds Intelligencer* expressed his satisfaction in terms not less distinct than those we have quoted
from the columns of the *Leeds Mercury*.

Simultaneously with the Yorkshire movement for regulating the hours of labour in factories, a movement for a similar purpose was proceeding in Lancashire. The evasions of the Act applicable to cotton factories, and the growing evils of the factory system, had induced some Lancashire millowners to consider the propriety of appealing to parliament for a more efficient measure of regulation than the then existing law. These Lancashire millowners had in their contemplated measure resolved to apply to parliament for a general law applicable to cotton, worsted, linen, silk, flax factories, &c. A correspondence between the Lancashire and Yorkshire millowners, favourable to a restriction of the hours of factory labour, followed, the result of which was the introduction into parliament, by Sir John Hobhouse (now Lord Broughton) and Lord Morpeth, of a bill, the provisions of which, as originally introduced, applied to cotton, woollen, worsted, linen, and silk factories. In it was proposed the restriction of working hours to "not more than eleven and a half on any one day, nor more than eight and a half hours on a Saturday," with an allowance to each person in the course of every day, of "not less than one half hour to breakfast, and not less than one hour to dinner;" that no person under eighteen years of age shall be allowed to work beyond those hours; that no child shall be employed in any description of factory labour under nine years of age,—the provisions of the bill to be in force on and after the first day of August, 1831. Mr Hobhouse's bill, as originally suggested, met with the entire approval of the owners of factories in favour of regulation. The operatives were unanimous and enthusiastic in its support; they believed that their hour for deliverance from bondage was at hand; they held many meetings, and forwarded to parliament many petitions.

In order to convey a sense of the feeling which then

pervaded the minds of the operatives, we extract from the reports of their meetings the following resolutions:—

" That the operatives, as individuals employed in the woollen, flax, linen, worsted, cotton, and silk mills and factories, have long entertained a deep conviction of the necessity of a legislative enactment, to protect from the baneful effects of the present long hours of working the children engaged therein ; and have learnt with heartfelt satisfaction of the introduction into the Commons' House of Parliament of a bill for that purpose.

" That it is the opinion of this meeting, that such bill will produce the beneficial results required, and likewise tend to ameliorate the condition of the labouring classes in general.

" That our best and warmest thanks are due to J. C. Hobhouse, Esq., as the mover, and Lord Morpeth as the seconder, of this bill, for the manly, independent, and humane manner in which they have come forward to propose so just, so humane a law."

A feeling for a public measure so unanimous and powerful bade fair for success; all who desired an improved factory system were hopeful. A dark cloud was gathering, unseen and unexpected. A body of influential mill-owners, chiefly resident in the neighbourhood of Halifax, had resolved to oppose the bill. The first alarming sign of this formidable opposition appeared in the form of a *leader* in the columns of the *Leeds Mercury*, avowedly the condensation of the opinions of " practical men " on the question. A meeting of the millowners opposed to factory legislation was subsequently held at Halifax, at which a series of resolutions were passed, setting forth the views of those present. These resolutions deserve especial attention, containing, as they do, the opinions of their supporters on subjects of social interest beyond the question of factory labour.

They may safely be accepted as the political and economical creed of the majority of the millowners opposed to factory legislation, and as an epitome of their principles and desires. The meeting was convened on the 5th of March, 1831. Mr James Akroyd, of Halifax, in the chair, on which occasion it was unanimously resolved:—

"1st. That this meeting views with alarm the measures proposed in the House of Commons, to curtail the hours of labour in mills and factories, and to limit the ages of children employed in the same.

"2nd. That the condition of those employed in worsted mills does not warrant the conclusion that the present usages of the trade are injurious to the health and comforts of this class of operatives ; and that the present term of labour (viz., twelve hours per day) is not attended with any consequences injurious to those employed, and is not more than adequate and necessary to provide for their livelihood.

" 3rd. That an enactment which will abridge the hours of labour, or limit the age of children employed in worsted mills, will produce the following effect:—1st. It will cause a proportionate reduction of the wages of this class. 2nd. It will materially cripple the means of those who have large and young families, who, in many instances, are the main support of their parents. 3rd. It will raise the price of goods to the consumers, which will affect the home trade considerably, and will produce the most serious effects upon the prosperity of this district, by tending to foster the manufactures of foreign nations, our trade with whom depends upon the cheap and advantageous terms on which we now supply them with goods, and whose manufacturers would be enabled by an advance of price successfully to compete with the British merchant. 4th. It will throw out of employment and the means of existence numbers of children now beneficially engaged in worsted mills, and a corresponding proportion of wool-sorters, combers, weavers, and all those other classes necessary to produce the present supply of goods. 5th. The agriculturists will also feel the effects of the diminished consumption of wool in no slight degree.

" 4th. That the manufacture of worsted yarn is a much more healthy and wholesome employment than the preparing and spinning of cotton or flax, both as regards the material employed, and the temperature requisite for its advantageous manufacture, and that experience proves that the health and general comfort of the population employed in worsted mills is equal, if not superior, to that of any other extensive class of operatives.

" 5th. That the age to which it is proposed to limit those employed in worsted mills will be inefficient in securing the advantages which are desired, in as much as the period between fourteen and twenty-one is the most critical period in the life of those employed, and that those of the ages between seven and fourteen are more capable of undergoing long continued labour, than those of the ages before named. For confirmation of this opinion, we would appeal to all medical men of the district.

" 6th. That the character of the generality of master worsted spinners in respect to humanity, kindness, and considerate attention to those in their employ is unimpeachable, but that though there may be exceptions to this general and well-known fact, which this meeting is unacquainted with, yet that no legislative enactment can effectually protect innocence and poverty from the fraud and tyranny of the unprincipled, and from those evils inseparably connected with, and incidental to, all manufactures in the present state of society.

" 7th. That this meeting is impressed with a sense of the numerous hardships to which the labouring classes are subject, and that it declares it to be the bounden duty of all intrusted with the superintendence of mills and manufactories, to adopt every means by which the health and comfort of these classes may be best secured; but that so far from being justly charge-able with being the authors of the present protracted hours of labour, this meeting cannot submit to the imputation of ava-rice and injustice, and tyrannous conduct, whilst the fact is so notorious that it is the *actual necessity* for voluntary and daily labour, to which the operative classes are subjected by the political and domestic circumstances of this country, *which alone* call for and demand the present long hours of applica-tion and labour.

" 8th. That until the burthens which now press upon the labouring classes are removed, all measures which tend to narrow the resources, obstruct or confine the industry, or reduce the rate of wages of the labouring classes have a posi-tively injurious character, and ought to be deprecated and opposed by every humane and considerate individual.

" 9th. That when this meeting consider the present state and future prospects of trade at home and abroad, when it con-templates the rapid steps of foreign competitors in the various markets of the world towards perfection in manufactures—when it considers the condition of the people of this country, whose means to purchase worsted fabrics are most seriously diminished in consequence of the oppressive nature of taxes, monopolies, and restraints upon capital and industry, it cannot but feel convinced that every new impediment to the free exercise of industry and labour will be an additional grievance and hardship on their lot, and will be not less detrimental to the comforts and interests of the poor than to the enter-prise and energies of their employers.

" 10th. That the British manufacturer is subject to a tax on corn, which operates as a heavy tax on labour, whilst rival manufacturing nations are exempt from this impost on trade; and that in addition to direct taxes on oil and soap, which are articles essential to the existence of the worsted ma-nufacture, he is subject to the unjust influence of a monopoly, which denies him free access to our possessions in India, where there are millions of subjects who might rapidly become consumers of worsted fabrics.

" 11th. That such being the difficulties with which the manufacturer has to contend, it would be inflicting the most injurious effects upon this branch of industry (effects which are totally unwarrantable on the grounds of humanity and kindness to the labouring classes), to curtail the hours of labour, and limit the ages of children employed in worsted mills, unless the legislature shall at the same time fix the amount and rate of wages. That the impossibility of any legislative enactment to regulate these details is obvious, and that it cannot secure the labouring classes from the inevitable reduction in wages, which will be the consequence of shorter hours of labour, and of fluctuations of trade, whilst it will fetter their hands in times of brisk demand.

" 12th. That there are many worsted spinners in this district, whose manufactories are dependent upon a due, and not excessive, supply of water, and that they have considerable interruptions to their trade in seasons of flood and drought, and that any restrictions upon the privilege hitherto enjoyed of working such mills in the wet season of the year, certain extra hours to compensate for the loss of time occasioned by the above casualties, would materially depreciate the value of such factories, and would be very injurious to the working classes, inasmuch as the proprietors would be unable to pay their operatives full wages, when the circumstances enumerated compel them to suspend their labour.

" 13th. That this meeting is convinced of the pernicious tendency and effects of all *legislative enactments*, whether protective or restrictive, which propose to regulate the details of trade and manufactures:—1st. Because they cannot equitably proportion the restrictions on industry to the circumstances of every individual case to which they apply, &c. 2nd. Because the consequences which they produce on the general interests of the trades affected by them, are more detrimental than the evils which they are intended to remedy.

" 14th. That a petition to both Houses of Parliament be drawn up, embodying those resolutions, and praying, that if on the balance of evidence tendered before a committee of the House of Commons, and on consideration of all the effects such an enactment will produce, it shall seem necessary to their honourable house to resort to interference with present established custom and usage in the worsted trade, that their honourable house would be pleased to adopt twelve hours per day, or seventy-two hours per week, as most fit, and least injurious term of labour, under present circumstances, to those employed."

The publication of these resolutions caused, in the minds of the operatives, very considerable alarm, but contributed to increase, rather than to diminish, their exertions. Mr Oastler, in a letter of remarkable energy and acuteness, examined these resolutions in their order. As was customary, he made good his positions on scriptural grounds, and after reviewing the arguments of his opponents, much to their annoyance, he presented to them, the following synopsis of their principles:—

" 1st. God's laws must bend and break at the call of avarice and self-interest!

" 2nd. Money is of more value than principle, morality, and religion!

" 3rd. Government is no longer of any use, because it is unable to protect the innocent and weak against the rapacity of the guilty and strong!

" 4th. The state of the trade of this country is really such, that its very existence depends upon excessive application and overworking on the part of the operatives!

" 5th. It is better that the labouring classes should live by the excessive and overpowering toil of their infants, than that the parents should labour for the support of their offspring!

" 6th. The exorbitant taxes which we are obliged to pay, the loss we sustain by the East India monopoly, the corn laws, and every other abuse, as a matter of clear right and justice, must and ought to be paid and borne out of the blood, bones, and sinews of our infantile population ! "

Mr Oastler's letter was read with avidity by all classes, its arguments became in the hands of the operatives, weapons of attack on, and defence against, the opposing millowners. The question increased in interest in the mind of the public in the manufacturing districts. Crowded meetings of operatives were often held, speeches were made, petitions signed and forwarded to parliament. Meantime the opposing millowners were also active, their influence united with that of others, principally Scotch millowners, was brought to bear on the minds of the members of the House of Commons. Mr Hobhouse's bill underwent many modifications; he finally consented to a measure applicable to cotton mills only, rendering it unlawful to work any child in a cotton Factory, who should be under eighteen years of age, more than sixty-nine hours per week.

The disappointment and regret at the fate of Mr Hobhouse's bill, throughout the manufacturing districts, particularly the West Riding of Yorkshire, was great. The factory operatives of the West Riding felt that their fondest hopes had been blighted, that the relief of their little ones from excessive toil was still distant, they, however, did not yield to despair, they turned their eyes by common consent to Fixby Hall; they were confident that they had in Mr Oastler a bold and faithful friend. They *trusted* not in vain.

There was evidently awakened in the very heart of England a home war against the unregulated factory system. Its supporters, however, had increased in strength. It was impossible to defend the cruelties of the Factory system, when and where acknowledged, but the nature of the remedy was a fertile source of discussion. There had arisen in this country a school of political economists, who professedly pointed to *The Wealth of Nations* as the text-book of their practical philosophy, though they, as a rule, omitted to state that that celebrated book contained contradictory doctrines ; they preferred popularizing the portions of Adam Smith's great work, which supported what they believed to be their own interests, failing to take any notice of portions of the same book fundamentally opposed to their favourite dogmas. These political economists were " on principle " opposed to all state interference between labourers and capitalists; they assumed that they were in possession of treasures of wisdom unknown to their opponents, that the principles of the ancient policy of England were erroneous, and in practice, ruinous to the interests of a nation; they were powerfully represented in the press, and exercised a very considerable share of influence through the pulpit; they assumed to themselves the distinction of being in favour of " the greatest happiness to the greatest number;" they maintained that each man in all his actions pursued his own pleasure, and that as a rule the happiness of the whole community would be most surely promoted, by allowing each individual member to work out his own ends in his own way, without restraint or control. This body of political economists possessed great talents and wealth, united with untiring industry, and were very ably represented in the legislature by a rising school of statesmen, of which Mr (now Lord) Brougham was the active leader. Circumstances had very materially changed since the first Sir Robert Peel had found it necessary, in defence of the interests of the manufacturers, to check the humanity of the House of Commons. We have noted the discrepancy which existed between Adam Smith and his influential disciples, the inconsistency belonged to the master, the followers were consistent and faithful to that portion of his doctrines which they had adopted, and therefore, unsparingly condemned Poor Laws, Usury Laws, and Factory Laws as evils not to be tolerated. The intellectual vigour and mental resources of the political economists, backed by the wealth, influence, and business talent of the millowners opposed to regulation, increased the difficulties in the path of Factory Legislation to an incalculable extent.

CHAPTER VIII.

THE PRINCIPLE OF FACTORY REGULATION CONSONANT WITH THE SPIRIT
OF THE LAWS OF ENGLAND—MR OASTLER'S APPEAL TO THE WORK-
ING CLASSES—THE FIXBY COMPACT—CHOICE BY THE SUPPORTERS
OF FACTORY LEGISLATION OF MICHAEL THOMAS SADLER, ESQ., M.P.,
AS PARLIAMENTAEY LEADER—SUMMARY OF HIS PRINCIPLES.

FACTORY Regulation, considered apart from all extraneous
subjects, was simple and easy of comprehension—here was
excessive and unnatural labour, confessedly, existing in open
defiance of the laws of health; that it was desirable to check
such a practice, was a truth which not any reasonable man
could doubt. It was not unreasonable, that as the persuasion
and endeavours of the benevolent had failed to introduce the
required rules favourable to health, those anxious for their
establishment should ask for the force of Law. They had by
the highest authorities been taught, that all human laws must
concord in spirit with the law of nature, and the law of revelation, they knew that it was a part of the common law of
England to protect the health of the nation, and if necessary,
that it was the duty of the legislature by statute law, to put
down all practices injurious to the health of the public. The
supporters of Factory regulation were conscious that the
unregulated Factory system was opposed to the laws of nature
and revelation, injurious to the public health and morals; they
were assured that it was the duty of all the individuals in a
state, to conform to the rules of propriety and good neigh-

bourhood; that property itself was the creature of society, and could only exist rightfully and permanently on conditions consistent with the welfare of the whole community; that the very existence of society depended upon its right to restrain by human laws, all the practices of individuals opposed to its welfare. Knowing these things, and having had their attention directed to the enormous and growing evils of the unregulated Factory system, Mr Wood and his coadjutors at Bradford were not disposed to sit quietly down under the horrors of Yorkshire slavery, because Sir John Hobhouse had failed to legislate for woollen, worsted, flax, and silk mills.

Mr Oastler's opinion on the course proper to be pursued was soon made known. In the *Leeds Intelligencer*, of October 20th, 1831, he published the following letter; it tells its own tale, and deserves especial attention; it is redolent with facts from the factories, and indicates, on the part of the writer, energy, decision, and foresight:

" SLAVERY IN YORKSHIRE.

"TO THE WORKING CLASSES OF THE WEST RIDING OF THE COUNTY OF YORK.

" My Friends,—Sir J. C. Hobhouse's bill for shortening the hours of labour in ALL factories is lost! Yes, the bill, on which you had fixed your fondest hopes, is vanished! Aye, my friends, that bill which had enlivened the hearts of your poor Factory children, which had for once implanted the gleam of hope in *their* hearts, and taught *them* to chaunt in songs of praise the name of Hobhouse—is abandoned by its author! Your hopes—your infants' hopes, are suddenly blighted! Your fond anticipations of your children's happiness and liberty are for a season blasted. The harps which your little ones had prepared to attune in grateful strains to the songs of liberty, must now be hung upon the willows—for how can they sing the song of freedom in the land of tyranny? Bend not, however, to dispair—but trust in God, and in yourselves—

the God of justice, of mercy, and of truth, still reigns—and he will plead your cause, and make the unfeeling iron-hearted masters, erewhile, relent; but if they still resist, and steel themselves against his laws, in anger he will speak, and make the oppressors quake.

* * * * *

"After all, we are told that we live in the land of liberty; and if we attempt to rescue British infants from slavery, we are, forsooth, the friends of the slave trade, and are only raising the hue and cry to turn the attention of the nation from West Indian slavery. Yes, my fellow-country-men, this has been said a thousand times since the factory system was exposed. The real friends of tyranny have put on the mask of philanthropy, and, with the cry of 'no slavery,' would rivet the chains upon *your* children, all the time persuading you they are the only 'Liberals' of the day. From such turn away! And be ye assured that no man, be his pretensions what they may, can really wish to emancipate the poor black slave in the West Indies, who refuses you his aid and assistance in emancipating *your* children from a state of slavery more horrid than that by which the infants of the slaves in the West Indies are cursed. Be duped no longer! Willingly lend your assistance to emancipate black slaves; but *imperatively* require from those members of parliament, ministers of religion and its pro-fessors, as well as the '*factory masters*' who solicit your aid in favour of the blacks, that they shall prove their sincerity, and that they really do hate slavery, by encouraging and signing petitions in favour of 'ten hours a day' as the limit of your children's work. If they refuse this, you will need no further proof that they are no real friends of liberty, however 'liberal' they may profess themselves to be, bring them to this touchstone, and you will then either tear off their 'liberal' mask, or compel them to join you in emanci-pating your little ones. It is your bounden duty, my countrymen, as it is your interest, no longer to be supine. I do not say you have been deceived by any of those persons who pledged themselves; but I do say you have a right to know why the bill, after having passed in the committee, was altered when it came into the House. For the future your path is plain. Let no promises of support from any quarter sink you to inactivity. *Consider that you must manage this cause yourselves,* nor think a single step is taken so long as any constitutional effort is left untried. Establish, instantly establish, committees in every manufacturing town and village, to collect information *and publish facts.* The public, generally, do not know what it is; then tell them how it has gone on destroying the health and morals of the people; how it operates in families by preventing the growth of those parental and filial affections which nature has implanted in every breast, but which this hateful system habitually eradicates. Show also how the baneful effects of the destruction of these feelings, afterwards, operate on society! Tell, how the factory system beggars the industrious domestic manufacturer! *Count, if you can, the hundreds of respectable families who have been driven from comfort and independence by the all-powerful operation of this monopolising system!* Point to the poor rates, and show how it has filled the ranks of the paupers; and never forget that these 'liberal factory masters' are not quite so 'liberal' as the tyrannical slaveholder! The latter provides for his slaves when they are weak, or maimed, or sick, or aged, and when they can no longer work. But the former, with a 'liberality' unknown in the West Indies, after they have maimed or weakened their work-people, or when they have worked them till they can work no more, turn them out, *for you who can work to support,* thus swelling the poor rates and lessening your earnings. Tell the shopkeeper, the butcher, the farmer, and the artisan, how this destructive system curtails the income of his customers, and increases the demand upon his funds. Yes, yes! bring all these facts before the public, and show the hideous monster in his native glare. Then ask, shall he go on conquering and to conquer, *until the manufacture of the empire is concentrated under one large roof, and the world is supplied by one gigantic firm?* Till human nature is almost physically and morally destroyed, *and all the inhabitants of this land shall be the slaves of one great manufacting nabob.* Let your committees call on every Christian, and particularly on every Christian minister, and respectively solicit their aid. Surely no follower of Christ can withhold his assistance. In due time call public meetings, and there plead the cause of the poor infant sufferers, and expose the horrors of the factory system; then prepare petitions to parliament, praying it to interfere in the sacred cause of suffering humanity; and, on every election for members of parliament, use your influence throughout the empire to prevent any man being returned who will not *distinctly and unequivocally pledge himself to support a 'Ten Hours a day and a Time-book Bill.'* If you will instantly begin to work on this plan, and *steadily pursue it*, you are sure of success. It is impossible that a system so cruel, so injurious, so unjust, so unchristian, can stand in a Christian country when once the eyes of the public are open to its horrors. *Your present failure points the road to your certain success!* Ye were lulled to drowsiness, and rested in false security, because ye trusted in the *nerve* of your friends and the *goodness* of your cause. But *now* you have plainly proved that you must win the day yourselves—that the little knot of cruel and oppressive spinners has more *powerful influence* than has that host of kind and tender-hearted masters who are your and your children's friends. Can it be believed that in England, in the nineteenth century, in a 'reforming' House of Commons, a bill limiting the hours of labour for children of nine years of age in ALL factories to twelve per day, should have been refused, because it was 'too liberal!' Kind Heaven! and do we live in a Christian country? *And will not the ministers of Jesus interfere?* Every man who really and truly hates and abhors slavery must and will 'come over and help us' to destroy this horrid system of slavery in Yorkshire. Oh! be no longer led astray by any foolish cry got up for political purposes, but resolve, until you gain your prayer, your voice shall always be against the man who would perpetuate the present 'factory system.' Let your politics be 'TEN HOURS A DAY, AND A TIME-BOOK;' and whoever offers himself as a candidate at any future election, unless he will *solemnly pledge* himself to these two points, REFUSE HIM YOUR SUPPORT! Don't be deceived: you will hear the cries of—'No slavery'—'Reform'— 'Liberal principles'—'No monopoly,' &c. But let your cries be—'No Yorkshire slavery'—'No slavery in any part of the empire'—'No factorymongers'—'No factory mono- polists.' If you are determined, rest assured you will suc- ceed. Your children will be liberated from a bondage greater than they would have inherited had they been born of negro slaves. Once more—be not led astray by the perpetual cry of 'liberal principles.' Depend upon it, the man who will refuse to 'liberate' your children is neither 'liberal' nor a 'hater of slavery.' Now then, my friends, for 'a long pull, a strong pull, and a pull altogether!' Victory is yours, if you are true to yourselves! *Let the tyrants know that you have sworn,* 'OUR CHILDREN SHALL BE FREE!'—I am, my friends, a sincere enemy to slavery in every form, in every part of the world, and your sincere well-wisher,

"RICHARD OASTLER.

"Fixby Hall, near Huddersfield, Oct. 10th, 1831"

Not any great object requiring the sanction of the legisla- ture, can be accomplished, except through the concentrated force of public opinion; the first requisite for success is to acquire the confidence of the people. Mr Oastler's letter was admirably adapted for that end; it stimulated all the sympathies of the human heart favourable to humanity; it aroused in the mind of every Christian a sense of duty; it was bold, and, in politics, boldness is often a source of strength; it was decided in tone, and left nothing to chance, but clearly outlined a plan of operation. The weight of Mr Oastler's letter was increased, because of a compact which had been entered into between himself and the leaders of the working men. A portion of the working men of Huddersfield, who took an active public interest in the politics of their time, appointed a deputation from their body to confer with Mr Oastler on the factory question. Mr Oastler's account of his interview with the working men, as published in the columns of *The Home*, is graphic and interesting. "One Sunday morning," wrote Mr Oastler, "when we were all preparing to go to church, about half-a-dozen working men, from Huddersfield, called upon me. They had read my letters in the newspapers about 'Yorkshire Slavery;' they informed me that they wished to converse with me about those letters of mine, and that they came on behalf of the factory-workers of Huddersfield, to thank me for them, and to offer their best assistance to me. I told them that 'I was going to church, that on any other day I should be glad to see them.' They replied, 'Sunday, Sir, is the only day on which we can come; we are in the mills all the rest of the week, from early in the morning till late at night.' This information brought home most forcibly to my mind, that the factory system and the fourth commandment could not work together. I thought the matter over, consulted with Mrs Oastler, and, seeing that it was clearly a work of charity, remained with them; the rest of the family went to church. Those men being factory-workers, gave me much useful information, invited me to communicate freely with them, and offered, cordially, to co-operate with me, in striving to obtain a change in the factory system. I heard all they had to say with great interest. I was struck with their intelligence and civility. I had seen much of the poor when in sickness and distress, at their homes, in the workhouse, and the infirmary; but, until that day, I had never entered into communion with working men, on matters relating to themselves as a class, connected with their employers. A new field seemed to be opened unto me ; these working men surprised me by the knowledge which they communicated, and the sensible manner in which they conveyed that knowledge to me. Still I thought there were hindrances to our working together, I being a tory and a churchman, they radicals and dissenters; therefore, after thanking them, I said, ' It will be better that we work separately, you taking your course, I taking mine.' They thought differently. After a good deal of conversation, we agreed to work together, with the understanding, that parties in politics, and sects in religion, should not be allowed to interfere between us. That agreement has never been broken."

The compact entered into between the working men and Mr Oastler had a very solid foundation, both were of opinion that labour was property, and entitled to the protection of the law. Every one acquainted with the late Mr Cobbett's *Legacy to Labourers*, a most able production, and with the opinions of the late Earl of Eldon on the Poor Laws, will not have much difficulty in apprehending why radicals and tories could unite on questions of industry. The Yorkshire radicals, at the time referred to by Mr Oastler, were readers of the works of Cobbett, and opposed to Brougham, on all the principal questions connected with the social arrangements of a state. Because of the organised correspondence of the radical committees of Yorkshire, the Huddersfield and Fixby compact was to Mr Oastler a lever of power, which to his honour he has never used for any other purpose than that for which it was entered into,—"to lift the oppressed out of the mire into which, by those who preferred mammon to righteousness, they had been cast."

Mr Oastler's letter to the working men of the West Riding was read, approved, and the advice therein contained acted upon in a solid and efficient manner ; seed was then sown, destined to bear important fruit, nor was there wanting one able and willing to lead the question in parliament.

In the year 1829, the late Michael Thomas Sadler, published his celebrated work on *Ireland; its evils, and their remedies.* Mr Sadler's book having contained the synopsis of a reply to *Malthus* on *Population,* and having been written with ability on a subject of pressing interest, commanded considerable attention among those interested in social and economical theories; it contained the following exposition of the author's views on the factory question :—" Most writers and travellers have hitherto held it an unequivocal mark of barbarism, wherever the female sex has been degraded into common drudges; this, however, our present civilised system has long had the gallantry of doing in England, the effects of which, in a moral point of view, are too well-known to need pointing out or proving ; and not only so, but even children are, by a solecism of speech, now become workmen, our language not having as yet accommodated us with an appropriate word for the occasion. The morning of life, which GOD and nature intended as a time of mirth and pleasure, is made that of imprisoning, unhealthful, and demoralising labour; and our political philanthropists wished to extend this system, instead of encouraging cultivation, though, no doubt, their feelings would be severely shocked at seeing such treatment transferred to the brute creation ; as, for instance, were the farmer providing himself with gearing and implements for the purpose daily to labour a yearling foal at the

plough, aye, and nightly, if it suited his interests. Cruelty
like this to animals would excite universal sympathy and
abhorrence, and probably travel the nation in ten thousand
paragraphs : it is thus our delicate susceptibilities find
vent ! It is rather a melancholy task to trace the progress
of the new system; to anticipate the ultimate consequence, if
every other interest amongst us must give way to it, is
most appalling. In the times of ignorance, 'man went
forth to his work in the morning,' he was the labourer
of the family, and it sufficed ; but now his INFANT
CHILDREN are demanded to make up his necessary means
of subsistence, and too often become, not his assistants,
but his rivals in the market of labour, to use the phrase
of the times, so that himself is often now found there "all
the day idle, because no man hath hired him," when the
fashionable system of policy coolly recommends his deser-
tion. In good times as they are called, he sees his children go forth to their work in the *evening* (to save the
capital of the machine owners) when the benevolent law
of nature universally obeyed throughout animated life, is
reversed as it regards those to whom it is the most essential.
To be sure, he has ever been informed, and assured that
these things were all for his advantage, especially when
he has thought otherwise, and been turbulently disposed ;
but he has been the truer prophet and political economist ;
his labour has become less and less valuable, till he is at
length pronounced, on high authority, to be redundant ;
and measures are at this instant being projected to send
him out of his country. Inventions which retain the
pleasing appelation of 'machines for shortening human
labour,' are to all intents and purposes, become machines
for supplanting it as far as possible; in one sense, indeed,
they are appropriately named, for they have the effect
of shortening life. Contrivances to dispense with this
labour almost altogether are hailed as public benefits and

eagerly adopted. On this subject I shall not further express myself, but conclude with the language of an able article on politically economy in the 'Edinburgh Encyclopædia:'—'All the workmen of England would be turned into the street, if the manufacturers could employ steam engines in their place at a saving of five per cent.'"

Mr Sadler entered parliament, as representative of the Borough of Newark in 1829, and had by word and vote supported Mr Hobhouse in all his parliamentary efforts in support of Factory Regulation. Mr Sadler had been for many years, a resident in the town of Leeds, had taken an active interest in the affairs of the Borough, and had been treasurer of the Board of Management of the Poor, he was practically familiar with the evils of unregulated factory labour. Among Mr Sadler's early and most intimate personal friends in Yorkshire was Mr Oastler, a close correspondence was kept up between these gentlemen on subjects of public interest, a glance at a portion of this correspondence will manifest the interest Mr Sadler felt on the factory question. The following are extracts from the letters of Mr Sadler to Mr Oastler :—

"London, September 1st, 1831.

"I need not inform you, that I not only concur with Mr Hobhouse's factory bill ; but, as I have expressed to him over and over again, I go much beyond it. Had he not taken it up this session, I should have done so, as my views and feelings are very strong upon that subject, and I have made calculations and published them in my book upon Ireland, showing the excessive mortality, &c., that the infamous and unnatural factory system occasions.

"I have been, within these few days past, urging a provision for the poor of Ireland, and was beaten by twelve only—which, even the ministers themselves, acknowledge to be a defeat. I hope, and indeed feel sure, that you will be with me upon this point. On this day fortnight, I hope to lay before parliament, a long considered plan, for the bettering the condition of the labouring poor of this country : on which I think, also, we should agree. My greatest loss is, that I have no energetic friend like yourself, at my elbow, to prompt and encourage me in these endeavours."

"London, September 20th, 1831.

" I cannot refrain from thanking you most deeply for the kind interest you take in a subject just started in Leeds, relating to so humble an individual as myself. [This refers to Mr Oastler's suggestion, that arrangements should be begun among the factory workmen to forward Mr Sadler's election for Leeds.]

"No man living can be more conscious, how humble are his claims to any distinction of the nature contemplated; indeed, I am distressedly conscious of that fact, and am only cheered by the thought, that my earnest wish is, *to better the condition of the oppressed and degraded part of my fellow creatures, and especially those* whose cause you have so generously and painfully advocated."

"London, September 22nd, 1831.

"I am entirely with you on all the important topics you mention—and they are the most important to the country, of any that can be mooted ; and I take up not one of them from personal considerations,—for the first time, or for electioneering purposes,—a course which I am sure you would despise me, if you thought me capable of adopting. Being in some measure however 'embarked,' I must go forwards; but I do so with the deep (I must say distressing) conviction of my own weakness and un-worthiness, which are not words of course with me, but which I feel deeply, and yet know that I do not feel enough.

" Accept my best thanks for your kindness, and for that energetic friendship which you, I know, are exercising in my behalf. I have very few recommendations in my favour, and those are simply, an earnest wish to better the condition of the industrious classes (who, between ourselves, have been *shamefully neglected* and in some cases *cruelly depressed*), joined with a full determination to attempt the task.

"I thank you most deeply for your concluding advice—I need it greatly. May my motives be kept single, and my conduct upright and humble! Indeed, I have more temptations arising from despondency and want of confidence, at this moment, than vanity or pride, which would ill become me; having no pretensions whatever to anything that could make me proud. The happy medium, is, what religion alone can give: I have of this, a little—may God increase it; that is His gift, and the most precious one He bestows.

" The millowners, I am aware, are very powerful in Leeds. I meditate nothing but what I think would be for *their* interest, properly understood, if carried into full effect; nothing that I would not gladly submit to, were I one of them. Adieu.

" Our objects are the same, and I hope I shall live to see some of them realized. In the meantime, allow me, in great haste, to subscribe myself, my dear Sir, your affectionate friend and fellow labourer,

"M. T. SADLER."

"Leeds, Nov. 2, 1831.

" My dear Sir,—A succession of gentlemen have been with me this day, leaving me, till this moment, no time whatever to draw up the ————; I regret this much, but not so deeply as I should have done, had you not said you intended to be here on Friday evening, when what I shall pen will be submitted to your inspection, and so modified as to meet your views, which, I am sure, are more enlarged than my own on the point at issue; as you are so well aware what would least alarm the millowners. I have principally attended to what it was right to propose in behalf of those employed: you have attended to both considerations.

"I shall, therefore, be entirely governed by you in this important matter. In the course of conversation with those who have been with me to-day, I find that the public are ripe for our attempt in behalf of the poor friendless factory victims. If it conduce to a satisfactory issue, the chief merit is yours—for your zeal in their behalf has not been a hatred of slavery in the abstract, but you have manfully come forward, and have unceasingly advocated the cause of the most degraded and abused class of beings existing."

"Leeds, Nov. 20th, 1831.

"My dear Friend,—The question of factory labour never has been taken up with sufficient energy in parliament; and the law, as at present carried, is not only nothing, but actually worse than nothing: I will mention why I think that the twelve hours' labour, assigned to young children, under a bill professedly passed for their protection, is worse than if no bill had passed; as I find, that even in the flax mills here, they NOW work little more than that time, in several instances not any more, not so much: still their health fails, and all the pernicious consequences you so much deplore ensue.

"Perhaps there may be many millowners (if left to themselves), who would NOT work so long as that; several have not, even in more barbarous times, if possible, than these, worked their children more than TEN hours,—DALE OF LANARK, for instance. But if parliament deliberately takes the thing up, and settles twelve hours, or even eleven hours per day, labour for children, the private individual responsibility of the employers seems done away with in a great measure: they will argue, and feel, and act under the impression that, if those who seek only to serve the children prescribe those hours, it would be worse than folly not to abide by them; deliberately considered, as they must have been. On the other hand, I am persuaded, and all I hear and read confirms me in my conviction, that TEN hours can never be receded from by those who love children, or who wish to obtain the approbation of Him who was indeed their friend and lover. I am sorry, therefore, to see that Sir John Hobhouse has not only conceded his bill, but his very views and judgment to the political economists, who in this, as in many other things, are the pests of society and the persecutors of the poor—unknowingly I hope—but whether they are so ignorantly or wilfully, makes no difference as regards their miserable victims. Their principles and schemes have led to the degradation, misery, and destruction of the working classes.

"*I had rather have no bill, than one that would legalize and warrant their excessive labour.*"

Mr Sadler had, during the progress of Sir John Cam Hobhouse's bill, been solicited by the Short-time Committee of Huddersfield to give to that bill his support. Mr Sadler was very energetic, and in his correspondence with the Huddersfield Short-time Committee he pointed out to them the high position they had gained through Mr Oastler's exertions, and strenuously urged them not to be contented with any measure short of a ten hours' limitation, and very freely expressed his dissatisfaction with the result of Sir John Cam Hobhouse's parliamentary exertions on behalf of the factory operatives. Sir John Cam Hobhouse considered any effort for a Ten Hours' Bill in parliament utopian. Mr Sadler ascertained from Sir John what his opinions were on the subject, and it was mutually agreed that if Mr Sadler desired further legislation, and to the extent indicated by the

Huddersfield Short time Committee, then Mr Sadler must, himself, lead the question in the House of Commons.

The working men, and those of their employers favourable to factory regulation, by common consent selected Mr Sadler as their future leader in parliament; they found in him an able and faithful champion of their cause. He was one of the few who preferred the path of difficulty to the easy roadway of the merely partisan politician. Sadler did not follow the crowd; he exercised his mental faculties on the most abstruse and difficult questions; he strove, by the solitary force of his own intelligence, to illuminate the social and political atmosphere of his age. His genius was luminous; it penetrated the centre of the social system by the fulness of its own light, and balanced the good against the evil of every proposed or realized change. Sadler had a great object in view—the upraising of the whole labouring population; his mind was sufficiently practical to formulate measures, and possessed, in a rare degree, the faculties requisite for the just apprehension of principles. Familiar, through the aid of studious investigation, with the practical tenour of the legislation of centuries—deeply versed in the writings of the earlier English authors, from Alfred the Great to Lord Chancellor Bacon, he approved their leading principles, and was opposed to the monopoly of riches; he desired the distribution, rather than the heaping-up of the products of labour and land, and devoted his energies to that end. Sadler's soul, like that of his friend Oastler, was dead to class or party interests, as understood by the leading political writers and legislators of his time; his sympathies were on the side of the injured and oppressed. He firmly believed it to be an ordination of Providence, that the poor shall never cease out of the land; that religion, justice, and humanity concorded in enforcing the necessity and wisdom of a permanent, legal, and ample provision for their wants. In the estimation of Sadler, to labour was the law of life, and the business of philosophers, mechanicians, and statesmen, was to discover how life's burthens should be lightened, and its enjoyments increased for *all*, in proportion as man's control over the materials of the earth increased; that the nearest approach to the *Millennium* was to be found in the elevation of the labouring portions of the community. In him a love of the truth was paramount to every other consideration— he never feared to tread wherever his principles might direct. Such a leader in parliament could not fail to give moral weight and dignity to any cause with which his heart was identified. He might not, like Brougham, defy a senate with a sneer; nor, like O'Connell, frown with contempt on an opposition; nor, like Peel, win by strategy what could not be gained by openness. Like many men of genius, Sadler was sensitive to excess, his gentle nature but ill fitted him to withstand the ridicule and buffoonery unhappily associated with political strife (and with which he, more than any other public man, was assailed). He was too candid to be crafty; more a student than a party politician; though called a Tory, he was, properly speaking, of no party—he was of the nation. His courage was the result of a union of head and heart; he was not led from without by the applause of multitudes; was invariably anxious to be true to himself. At all times controlled by conscience, whatever cause he espoused he persevered in to the end. His knowledge was comprehensive, extending from ancient rule to modern experience; he enriched the principles he advocated with a copious learning, hallowed by religious devotion, and strengthened by an undeviating faith in the supreme wisdom of God's laws, as known and practised under the Jewish theocracy. The laws of the Hebrews, relating to the poor, were the constant themes of Mr Sadler's admiration. Under the Mosaic economy, to relieve the distressed, and aid the poor, were acts of justice, not depending on the promptings of humanity, but, as understood by Mr Sadler, these deeds were commanded by GOD, and were the indispensable conditions on which property could be owned; and that, in any state of society, the abrogation of like practices could not fail to produce the saddest possible results. The factory question was only an important step in the ladder of Sadler's social system; his pleadings were as earnest for the downcast agricultural labourer as for the depressed factory child; a circumstance which strengthened him at every step, for the mind of Sadler concentrated diversities of knowledge, and directed these to the speciality on which his intellectual force was applied. The subserviency of the factory question to Sadler's own views was a valid security for a faithful protection of the interests confided to his care. In the hands of Sadler, the cause of the factory operatives was not, as the exigencies of party required, cast into the scale of time-serving faction. Factory regulation was by him maintained as a national necessity, and sealed with the maxim—"The safety of the people is the highest law."

CHAPTER IX.

MECHANICAL, SOCIAL, AND MORAL PROGRESS.—LETTER OF SIR JOHN
CAM HOBHOUSE, BART., M.P., ON THE DIFFICULTY OF FURTHER
LEGISLATION.—MR OASTLER'S REPLY.—OPINIONS AND LETTER OF
THE RIGHT HON. T. B. MACAULAY ON THE FACTORY QUESTION.
—SPEECH OF MR SADLER ON INTRODUCING THE TEN HOURS' BILL
TO THE HOUSE OF COMMONS.—APPOINTMENT OF A PARLIAMENTARY
COMMITTEE.

THERE cannot be any doubt entertained of the increase of
scientific, chemical, and mechanical knowledge ; during the
three past ages man's control over inanimate matter has rapidly increased ; mechanicians and engineers are capable of
producing in a few days, what, a century ago, would have
been the work of years. Scientific knowledge, and the division of labour, have multiplied the powers of production with
a rapidity beyond the means of calculation. While this great
fact of material progress is prominent and undeniable, the
social and moral progress of the majority of English society is
not by any means an undisputed question. Some among the
most thoughtful of our time have doubted if all our scientific,
chemical, and mechanical skill, have lightened the day's toil of
any human being ; others have declared that at no period of
the nation's history has it been more difficult for a labouring
man to earn his bread by the sweat of his brow than in these
latter days. It cannot be reasonably contended that the bitter
fruit of man's first disobedience, as represented in the newly-
born infant, weighs more heavily on the present than it did in
past generations. " Original sin " is, in its own nature, un-

changed, yet crime increases with frightful celerity, and the
statute book is swelled to inordinate size with criminal laws,
some of these for crimes of the most odious kinds ; and the
question is still asked, with more and more urgency, from
bench and pulpit, " What can be done with our criminals ?"
The progress of industrial development has increased, manifold,
the means of supplying the wants of man ; universal equality
may be, only, the benevolent vision of utopian dreamers ; the
distribution of the products of industry may be, for the wisest
of purposes, unequal; it may be an eternal law that some
shall be rich and others poor. But that state of society has not
any just claim to wear the honourable distinction of civilization in name, under the rule of which, in fact, it is for the
comforts of the many not to increase in something like a due
proportion to the increase of man's control over the raw material of the earth, and whose moral condition is either doubtful or retrograding. There is no lack of men, and clever men
too, disposed at all times to eulogise modern industrialism.
There never was any want of men, in any age, to chime in
with the fashionable chorus of their own time. When Moses
came down from the Mount, carrying in his hand the tables of
the testimony, the voices he heard were not those who shouted
for mastery, or those who cried for being overcome ; they
were the voices of those who were making merry, singing and
dancing round the golden calf. So far as we apprehend the
superiority of the present over past ages, its existence is
acknowledged without reserve. To " take stock " of material progress is very desirable ; it is a proper employment for
a nation proud of its business talent. The social and moral
economist must study social and moral progress; he who
assumes to legislate, and fails to estimate these, is, at best, to
borrow a phrase from Adam Smith, " That insidious and
crafty animal, vulgarly called a statesman." All political
economy that has not for its object, and fails in its practice, to
increase the command of the labourers over the necessaries,

conveniences, and comforts of life, is, for all the purposes of desirable civilization, a delusion. It would be difficult to conceive a more dangerous heresy than that contained in the maxim :—" A measure may be morally right and politically wrong." Whatever measure is morally right, will in practice. be found politically and socially right, so far as the interests of a nation are concerned ; as for the real or supposed interests of party politicians, these are unworthy of a moment's consideration, beyond the knots of crafty tricksters who are mean enough to entertain them.

The principal exponent of the factory question, and the parliamentary leader thereof, had observed, in their own time, a considerable change for the worse in the condition of the agricultural and manufacturing population. The enclosure of commons, and their appropriation by a few landowners (without regard to the immemorial rights and usages of the peasantry, to whom, with very rare exceptions, not any "allotments" were made)—the pulling down of cottages, which followed the cry of " a redundant population," and other acts of social oppression, had, to a great extent, injured the condition and prospects of the agricultural labourers, and forced very many families from their once comfortable rural homes (the homes of their forefathers) into the manufacturing districts The unregulated introduction and use of machinery had operated injuriously on the value of the labour of 840,000 hand-loom weavers ; small manufacturers had in most cases been reduced from comfort to penury ; the horrors of the factory system had pierced the souls of Oastler and Sadler, and made them earnest, bold, and eloquent in its denunciation. The progress of agitation in Yorkshire had been rapid and successful; it had crossed the borders of Yorkshire into Lancashire and Cheshire. Men so impressed, and so hopeful, could not entertain doubts as regarded success ; they had resolved to gain their avowed object, and neither feared nor cared for obstacles.

In few assemblies has enthusiasm less influence than in the

British House of Commons ; in its collective capacity it is
not disposed, readily, to concede any demand ; it prides itself
on a kind of stoical indifference to recently-organised movements, and waits for " the pressure from without." A manifestation of this feeling the supporters of factory regulation
were destined to endure. Mr Oastler had opened a correspondence with several members of both Houses of Parliament, necessarily, with various results, the general feeling of
the House of Commons was very candidly expressed by a not
unfriendly pen. In consequence of a statement made on the
authority of Sir John Cam Hobhouse, and published in the
Leeds Mercury, Mr Oastler wrote to him, and was answered
in the following letter ; it contained the convictions of the
honourable baronet, on the probable success of Mr Sadler's
contemplated bill in the House of Commons. It is the
judgment of a mind endowed with keen perceptions, by habit
and experience ; accustomed to estimate the legislative action
of the House of Commons; undoubtedly, well versed in the
state of the factory question.

"Hastings, November 16, 1831.

" Sir,—I beg to acknowledge the receipt of your letter, and
of the *Leeds Intelligencer*, of Thursday, Nov. 10. Of my
letter to Mr Baines I have no copy; otherwise I would, with
pleasure, send it to you—at the same time I think it right
to inform you, that if the extracts published in the
Mercury are not satisfactory, neither the whole letter, nor
anything I have it in my power to say, would be found
more acceptable.

" I regret very much to perceive that the discussion on
the factory system is mixed up with the party politics of
Yorkshire, and more especially of the town of Leeds—still
more do I regret that the good operatives should have been
so much deluded, either by very ignorant or designing men,
as to promise themselves the accomplishment of what can
never be realized. Those acquainted with the real state of

the question, so far as parliament is concerned, know very well that nothing can be more idle than to talk of the possibility of limiting the hours of daily labour to *ten* for five days, and to eight on the Saturday—and I was, and am surprised to find, by Mr Sadler's answer to the Huddersfield deputies, that the worthy member for Aldborough should appear to concur in views so extravagant, and which can only end in disappointment.

" The deputies of the operatives who attended me during the passing of the bill, and who, indeed, framed the Act, have it in their power to lay before their constituents such information as would at once convince them how groundless, and how prejudicial to their own interests, are all such expectations; and I can assure you, Sir, that the sooner the delusion is dispelled, the more likely will the reasonable wishes of the parties concerned be fulfilled. The censures which, it seems, are passed upon those concerned in the recent Act, and more especially on myself, can proceed only from those altogether unacquainted with the circumstances of the case, and from those who know nothing of the difficulty of carrying a controverted measure through parliament. It would doubtless have been very easy to have prepared a plan which would have pleased all the operatives for the moment, and have gained much applause from their inconsiderate friends, and which would have been rejected at the very first mention of the proposal in the House of Commons. But a man who has higher objects than immediate praise, would have been highly culpable in pursuing such a course, and sacrificing an attainable good for a fleeting popularity. Certainly the present Act is far from being so extensive, either in its operation or in its restrictions, as I could wish, but it was the opinion of the deputies of the operatives, that it secured many advantages, and was a decided improvement of the former legislation on the subject. I had therefore no choice left to me, except of two modes of procedure, namely, to attempt to pass my original bill in the face of all the opposition arrayed against me, and at a time when even the very forms and delays of parliament would have defeated me ; or to secure so much of the Act as I could pass without opposition of any kind. I did so by waiting day after day for a favourable moment, and at last got through the stages of it at *half-past three in* the morning!! I will leave you to judge what would have been the result, if I had attempted to force any controverted clause upon the House, any single antagonist would have objected to the *time* of the discussion, and that obstacle alone would have been quite sufficient to postpone the question from day to day, until the end of the session.

" My principal opponents are the Scotch flax-factors, and the West of England woollen-factors. The latter I think I might have managed to conciliate. The former gave me no hopes of a compromise, and they sent down so numerous and influential a body of members to the House against me, that resistance was hopeless; at least, as I before said, at that period of the session, and in the then state of public business. If I should be induced to make an attempt to bring back my bill to its original shape, I shall have to encounter the same difficulties, and without appointing a select committee to examine evidence, I fear that even the very introduction of the measure would be opposed with success. Should Mr Sadler make the effort which he seems to contemplate, of limiting the hours of labour to *ten*, you may depend upon it he will not be allowed to proceed a single stage with any such enactment, and, so far from producing any beneficial effects, he will only throw an air of ridicule and extravagance over the whole of this kind of legislation. I trust that, on mature reflection, that very respectable gentleman will adopt a more useful course of conduct, and in that case he may depend upon my exertions, such as they are, to second and encourage his honourable labour. You are welcome to give any publicity which you may think desirable to this communication, and I cannot conclude without hoping that what I have thought right to impress upon your consideration may alter in some degree the opinions you have hitherto entertained as to the best mode of promoting the object which we have, I believe, mutually at heart.—I have the honour to remain, Sir,

      " Your very obedient and humble servant,

                  " JOHN C. HOBHOUSE.

" Richard Oastler, Esq."

To this letter Mr Oastler replied as follows:—

      " To Sir John Cam Hobhouse, Bart., M.P.

        " Fixby Hall, near Huddersfield, Nov. 19th, 1831.

" Sir,—Accept my most respectful thanks for your letter of the 16th inst., and believe me when I assure you I feel grateful to you for the exertions you have made in behalf of poor innocent and defenceless factory children; but allow me also to state, that I exceedingly regret you felt yourself obliged to yield the sacred cause of the poor to the " cold, calculating, but mistaken Scotch philosophers," who seem, very unfortunately, to have an overwhelming influence over the government of this country. Yes, Sir, although I cannot feel otherwise than grateful to you for what you have done, I wish you had manfully met those unfeeling misanthropes (whose God is money, and whose policy is the ruin, degradation, and banishment of the poor) by sound, philosophical and Christian argument, on the arena of the House of Commons, rather than have succumbed between the Committee and the House ; then I am sure the laws of this country would never more have been disgraced by a statute *legalising* the working of poor little children nine years old, for twelve hours per day ! Say what we may, this is disgusting tyranny, practised under the name of freedom, on the weakest, most innocent, and most abject slaves. In this part of the country very great anxiety is felt on the subject, and the friends of the children are exceedingly wishful *to know who are their enemies.* From the general tenour of your letter to Mr Baines (so far as he

thought proper to publish it,) we were led to believe the
' quarter' to which you were ' obliged to listen,' must have
been the government ; and yet Mr Baines says, ' the government are not to be charged with the defeat of the measure.'
Then again Mr Baines says, ' the Board of Trade was
inclined to support *you* until embarrassed by the members of
the north.' And you say they (*i. e.* the Scotch members)
' were *supported* by the Board of Trade.' Mr Baines afterwards adds, ' It is to the credit of Yorkshire, that none of
the opposition given to the bill proceeded from either of its
members or manufacturers.' Now if you did not inform him
that this was the fact, he ought not to have assumed it, and I
fancy you could not have told him so, because I happen to
know that petitions were sent against it by *some* of the
manufacturers of Huddersfield, Halifax, and Bradford; and I
think Mr Baines will not dispute that these places are in
Yorkshire. Then, again, I was informed, by a most respectable and humane manufacturer, who *supported* the bill with
very great zeal and perseverance, and at considerable expense,
that Mr Marshall, of Leeds, opposed the bill. Now I fancy,
that Mr Baines himself will admit that Leeds is in Yorkshire,
and that Mr Marshall is a Yorkshire manufacturer. It was in
consequence of these positive contradictions in Mr Baines's
report, that I was induced to trouble you, finding that many
persons were puzzled, and did not know whether Mr Baines or
yourself might have made these irreconcilable statements,
which you must agree with me, no rational person could comprehend. I regret exceedingly you have no copy of the
letter, but I feel satisfied you could not have authorised Mr
Baines to print such nonsense. I have asked Mr Baines for
an explanation ; he has not favoured me with one. It appears
to the friends of the measure essentially necessary, that they
should actually *know* their opponents, otherwise they should
never know where to direct their energies. If these men *did*
oppose the operatives, they have a right to be informed of it;

they would then be able to assist in sending *up* to parliament *interest* and *argument* as strong as theirs.

" That the Factories' Bill should now be made a political electioneering question cannot be matter of *surprise,* and, I think, is not one of *regret.* We have witnessed a friend of emancipation (yourself) defeated by a certain kind of *influence,* exercised over the feelings and judgment of the representatives of the people—' the Scotch flax-spinners' for instance, who ' sent *down* so numerous and influential a body of members ' to the House *against* you. It is very plain that, if the friends of the measure are not determined, when an election takes place, to send up ' as numerous and influential a body of members' in favour of the measure, there can be no hopes of any relief. I am not aware that the question is intended to be mixed up with *general* politics, but merely so far as to *secure* votes in its favour from the new members; and I sincerely hope that no members will be returned (where the operatives have any influence, or where the hateful factory system is known) but those who are *known* to be friendly to a Ten Hours' Bill. I hope the workmen will have the wisdom not to be gulled by the terms whig, tory, or radical, but be *determined to support men who will support this bill.* I really think the ' good operatives' are quite as able to exercise a correct judgment on this question as they are on the very complicated one of ' parliamentary reform ;' and you know the King himself and the government made that an '*electioneering question.*' We are exhorted, I see, by Mr Baines, to 'petition parliament.' This may be very right *when we have secured good members;* but if we are to have our petitions presented to a body of representatives, governed by ' the cold, calculating, but mistaken *Scotch* philosophers,' then I fancy we might as well save ourselves the trouble and expense ; and I think it is very plain, from the concluding part of your letter to Mr Baines (if he quotes correctly), that we have no chance of 'conciliating' the Scotch members with-

out a 'numerous and influential body of members,' who will
be resolved to do an act of justice to our cruelly insulted and
degraded infants.   I hope also the landowner, the farmer, the
little millowner, the domestic manufacturer, the little tradesman, the shopkeeper, the mechanic, and the artisan, will ALL
join us in this struggle against 'Scotch philosophy;' or they
may be assured, EVERY ONE OF THEM, that the system of
infantile slavery is a system of UNIVERSAL PAUPERISM ; nay,
thousands of them have already proved this awful truth.

"I am truly sorry you despair of ever carrying a bill for
'*ten* hours for five days, and *eight* on the Saturday.'   You
have certainly had much experience how the '*influence*' is
got up 'so far as parliament is concerned;' but we know
that hitherto the operatives have *neglected* to use *their* influence, *and we think we are their friends when we advise them
to use it*.   The 'Scotch philosophers' have hitherto had ALL
the influence, and the poor children have only had the support of disinterested philanthropists like yourself; and besides,
we are told that, in a reformed parliament, the people will have
a more direct influence.   I think, then, the friends of the
measure should rejoice that the people are *determined* to make
this a political (electioneering) question.

"I hope the limits sought for by the operatives may in the
end be realised; nay, in such a case I cannot doubt, till I am
informed upon what principle of religion, nature, law, or
policy, a child ought to be subject to two hours' *longer* work
per day than a full-grown man.   When I am made wise on
this point, I may perhaps doubt.   But *all* the 'Scotch philosophy' can never make me *fear* the success of this measure until that question be answered, and even when that
point is solved, two others will arise—*viz.*, If it be beneficial ?
If it be magnanimous and worthy of the bravest nation in the
world ?

"I am not altogether ignorant of the kind of parliamentary
influence which makes you doubt the *possibility* of carrying

even your original measure; and I know something of the
difficulties you have to encounter, yet, I have no doubt that a
much more extensive measure will be adopted before many
years are passed; and although, at present, the idea of working infants ONLY ten hours a day may appear ignorant,
ridiculous, extravagant, idle, delusive, and impossible to the
legislators of this country, I cannot doubt that, in a very
short time, our legislators will hardly believe it was *ever*
possible for a Christian parliament to *refuse* such an act. I
anticipate with gladness the day when yourself, Mr Sadler,
and Mr Strickland (for he is *now*, I am happy to say,
a TEN hours' man), will be exerting your mighty powers
of eloquence for the liberation of the most oppressed beings
under the sun. The alteration would at once prevent the
unnatural effect of *increasing* human labour with the *increase*
of machinery; it is this circumstance, proceeding not from
the *nature* of machinery, *but from the avarice of man*, which
makes machinery often *appear* to be a curse. The *natural*
effect of machinery must be to lessen human labour; the
actual effect, *under the present system*, is to increase it.

"I rejoice that Mr Sadler has declared himself a legislator on this subject, *in accordance with the principles of his
whole life;* the declaration is founded on justice, the principles are those of truth, and *must* ultimately prevail. I am
at a loss to conceive how a Ten Hours' a Day Bill can be
' prejudicial to the operatives,' or how such a desire can be
called ' extravagant and unreasonable.' If this measure is
' rejected at the very mention of the proposition in the
House of Commons,' none will regret it more than myself;
but that unfortunate circumstance would not dishearten its
friends. It would only spur them on to greater exertions,
and would undoubtedly lead to certain success. ' Immediate
praise ' and ' fleeting popularity ' are, indeed, unworthy motives, and particularly in a legislator. So far as I have
experienced, they are the *last things* a man will be troubled

with, *if he pursue a straightforward course, and act upon principle.*

"Your 'Cotton Act' is, I believe, an improvement, and I thank you for it; but I do wish you had debated the question in the House. I think, with Mr Strickland, that it would have been better 'that the abandonment of the bill should have been caused by an open division.'

"I must apologise for the freedom and length of this epistle, and cannot conclude without thanking you most sincerely for your kind attention to my letter, and assuring you that I feel unfeignedly grateful for the exertions you have already made, and still hope that you will, on full consideration, support the principle of limiting the labour of your children to *ten hours* a day, that being as much as they can or ought to endure. As you say that I may give any publicity I may think advisable to your communication, I shall give it, along with mine, to the editors of the newspapers. I feel there ought to be no secrets on the subject.

"I have the honour to remain, Sir,

"Your most obedient, humble servant,

"RICHARD OASTLER."

Mr Sadler, encouraged by the favourable and enthusiastic feeling in Yorkshire, and neighbouring counties of Lancashire and Cheshire, introduced his projected Ten Hours' Bill to the House of Commons early in 1831. He was energetically supported by his friends not in parliament, and strengthened by numerous petitions. Notwithstanding the efforts of a very powerful opposition, the feeling in favour of factory interference was decidedly on the increase. The readers of *Reviews* will recal the "Let all things alone" doctrine which pervaded the essays in the *Edinburgh*, among these the brilliant critical productions from the pen of Mr T. B. Macaulay. By way of example, take Macaulay's review of *Southey's Colloquies on Society;* it contains the following paragraph:—" As to the effect of the manufacturing system on the bodily health, we must beg leave to estimate it by a standard far too low and vulgar for a mind so imaginative as that of Mr Southey, the proportion of births and deaths. We know that, during the growth of this atrocious system, this new misery, to use the phrases of Mr Southey, this new enormity, this birth of a portentous age, this pest which no man can approve whose heart is not seared or whose understanding has not been darkened, there has been a great diminution of mortality, and that this diminution has been greater in the manufacturing towns than anywhere else. The mortality still is, as it always was, greater in towns than in the country. But the difference has diminished in an extraordinary degree. There is the best reason to believe that the annual mortality of Manchester, about the middle of the last century, was one in twenty-eight. It is now reckoned at one in forty-five. In Glasgow and Leeds, a similar improvement has taken place. Nay, the rate of mortality in those three great capitals of the manufacturing districts, is now considerably less than it was fifty years ago, over England and Wales, taken together, open country and all. We might, with some plausibility, maintain that the people live longer because they are better fed, better lodged, better clothed, and better attended in sickness, and that these improvements are owing to that increase of national wealth which the manufacturing system has produced." In the same essay, Mr Macaulay condemned the " intermeddling" of government, and expressed his opinions on the duties of rulers in very decided words:—" It is not," wrote the *Edinburgh Reviewer*, in 1830, " by the intermeddling of Mr Southey's idol, the omniscient and omnipotent state, but by the prudence and energy of the people, that England has hitherto been carried forward in civilization ; and it is to the same prudence and the same energy that we now look with comfort and good hope. Our rulers will best promote the improvement of the nation by strictly confining themselves to their own legitimate duties, by leaving capital to find its most lucrative course, commodities their fair price, industry and intelligence their natural reward, idleness and folly their natural punishment, by maintaining peace, by defending property, by diminishing the price of law, and by observing strict economy in every department of the state. Let the government do this ; the people will assuredly do the rest." It would be irrational to suppose that any man of Mr Macaulay's standing, as a gentleman and an author, so thoroughly convinced of the advantages associated with our modern manufacturing system, so decided and emphatic against "intermeddling," and so assured of the advantages arising "by leaving capital to find its most lucrative course," could have conceived the necessity for interference by law in the regulation of factories. The proposition requires no defence, for had Mr Macaulay been correct in his statements, not any interference could have been advantageous. The mind of Mr Macaulay had evidently undergone a considerable change between the years 1830 and 1832, as the subjoined letter, addressed to Mr Ralph Taylor, Secretary of the Leeds Short-time Committee, will prove:—

"London, March 16th, 1832.

" Sir,—I am decidedly favourable to the principle of Mr Sadler's bill. That is to say, I think that the hours of labour of children ought to be regulated. But I see, I confess, some strong objections to the machinery by which Mr Sadler proposes to effect this object; and I know that some of the most zealous and intelligent friends of the working classes, both in and out of parliament, agree with me in thinking, that if the bill now before us should pass into a law without great modifications, its effect would be most seriously to injure the labourers of our manufacturing districts. There is a strong and general feeling in the House of Commons, that something ought to be speedily done for the protection of the children.

There is also, I think, a general feeling that the details of Mr Sadler's bill have not been well considered. The government will, I believe, take the question up: and I hope and trust, that before the end of this session, we shall have a law which will accomplish your object in an unexceptionable manner. Permit me to add one word on the subject of the Order in Council, which has been sent to St Lucie. That Order, as you justly say, has provided that a slave shall be forced to work only nine hours a day, and only five days a week. But you forget, I think, that the slave has to find his own subsistence besides. The time which is secured to him is not holiday time. He must cultivate his own provision-ground during the hours when he is absent from his master's sugar planta-tion. The labour of the slave which the Order in Council limits, is a forced labour, and an unpaid labour. He may work eighteen hours a day voluntarily, and for hire if he pleases. The Order does not in the least restrict him from performing any quantity of work which it may be his own pleasure to perform. There is, therefore, not the slightest analogy between the case of a freeman of mature years. The law ought to limit the hours of forced labour of the slave:—and why? Because he is a slave. Because he has no power to help himself. But the freeman cannot be forced to work to the ruin of his health. If he works over hours, it is because it is his own choice to do so. The law ought not to protect him; for he can protect himself.

" The case of a child bears a nearer analogy to the case of a slave. The child may have cruel parents, or may be in the power of those who are not his parents. It is therefore just and reasonable, that the law should extend to the child a pro-tection similar to that which it extends to the slave. But the reason for this protection ceases as soon as the child becomes his own master, and is capable of contracting on his own behalf. The Order in Council to which you refer, limits the hours during which free negroes are to work. And in the

same manner I would limit the hours of labour for a child of
thirteen or fourteen.   But why the hours of labour of a youth
in his twentieth year should be limited, as proposed by Mr
Sadler's bill, I cannot understand.

"I earnestly hope that we may be able to come to a
speedy and satisfactory adjustment of this question.

"I have the honour to be, Sir,

"Your most obedient servant,

"T. B. MACAULAY."

Mr Macaulay's letter is evidence of a change in his mind;
though distinctions are carefully made between slaves and
freemen, adults and children; yet the question presses for an
answer, What was the physical and moral condition of those,
designated adult free men and women, resident in the factory
districts, who habitually allowed their children to work under
conditions which called for interference by the state?   The
answer is necessarily the converse of Mr Macaulay's eulogium of
the manufacturing system, as expressed in 1830. The judgment
of the statesman of 1832, was ripened by increased knowledge, beyond that of the *Reviewer* of 1830. While standing
fast by the rule of 1830, the force of evidence, and a
growing public opinion, had caused a recognition of an
opposing principle, as regarded children employed in
factory labour.

Mr Macaulay's letter of March, 1832, was, to the supporters of factory legislation, more encouraging and hopeful
than the letter of Sir John Cam Hobhouse, to Mr Oastler, on
the same subject, in November, 1831. Mr Macaulay's
sources of information were excellent; the progress of the
question, among those in high quarters, in and out of office,
was owing to increased knowledge, and the untiring and
energetic labours of its supporters in the country, and in London.

On December the 15th, 1831, Mr Sadler obtained leave to
bring into parliament a bill " for regulating the labour of

children and young persons in the mills and factories of this country." Mr Sadler consequently framed his bill, had it printed and circulated among the members of the House of Commons, and moved its second reading, on the 16th of March, 1832. As a valuable contribution to the historical and social literature of the country, Mr Sadler's speech on that occasion deserves to take high rank; as an exposition of the wrongs endured by the operatives engaged in factory labour, and an answer to the opponents of his measure, it has not been surpassed; its worth is permanent, its contents eminently deserve the close study of those who feel an interest in the improvement of the labouring portions of the commonwealth. Mr Sadler said:—

" Sir,—In rising to move the second reading of the bill, which I have had the honour of introducing into parliament, for regulating the labour of children and young persons, not being free agents, employed in the mills and factories of the country, of whatever description, I shall, as far as is consistent with the high importance of the subject, and the great and general interest which it has excited throughout the entire community, compress the arguments and facts upon which I found the necessity of this measure ; and I shall not misapply many moments of the time which I must still occupy by allusions personal to myself, however much I may have been provoked to such a course. I will merely say, that in bringing forward this measure, I make no pretensions to a degree of humanity beyond that which I share with the people at large; still less am I influenced by any views adverse to the prosperity and extension of our manufactures and commerce: least of all can I be governed by feelings otherwise than cordial to those embarked in these great concerns. On the contrary, in pursuing this course, I am acting under the impression, at least, that the measure which I propose will advance the true and permanent interests of the manufacturers, the cordial encouragement and support of many of the most humane and best-informed of whom I regard as the strongest proof of the necessity of the measure, and the surest presage of its success. As to the imputation cast upon me by others of a different description, who wish to defeat this attempt, as they have hitherto done preceding ones of a like nature, not only by thwarting the designs, but by maligning the motives, of those who make them ; and who, therefore, accuse me of being instigated by a mean desire of popularity, in now undertaking a cause which, nevertheless, some of them know well enough, I advocated as strongly long before I was in parliament, as I can do on the present occasion : I say, as to this imputation, I should have passed it over in silence, only that it affords me an opportunity, which I will not neglect, of proving, even from the mouths of its opponents, that the measure is popular—popular in the fullest and best sense of the term,—and the House, I think, has seen, from the petitions which have already loaded its table, signed by magistrates, clergy, and professional men, as well as by immense numbers of the operative classes, that its popularity is founded upon the principles, the intellect, and the feelings of the British community, and that those who resist it must reckon on contempt and indignation.

"The bill which I now implore the House to sanction with its authority, has for its object the liberation of children and other young persons employed in the mills and factories of the United Kingdom, from that over-exertion and long confinement, which common sense, as well as experience, has shown to be utterly inconsistent with the improvement of their minds, the preservation of their morals, and the maintenance of their health ;—in a word, to rescue them from a state of suffering and degradation, which it is conceived the children of the industrious classes in hardly any other country have ever endured.

" I am aware that some gentlemen profess, upon principle, a great reluctance to legislate upon these matters, holding such interference to be an evil. So, I reply, is all legislation,—upon whatever subject,—and an evil only to be tolerated for the purpose of preventing some greater one ; I shall therefore content myself with meeting this objection, common as it is, by simply challenging those who urge it to show us a case which has stronger claims for the interposition of the law, whether we regard the nature of the evil to be abated, as affecting the individuals, society at large, and posterity ; or the utter helplessness of those on whose behalf we are called on to interfere ; or, lastly, the fact—which experience has left no longer in doubt, that, if the law does not, there is no other power that can or will adequately protect them.

" But, I apprehend, the strongest objections that will be offered on this occasion, will be grounded upon the pretence that the very principle of the bill is an improper interference between the employer and the employed, and an attempt to regulate by law the market of labour. Were that market supplied by free agents, properly so denominated, I should fully participate in these objections. Theoretically, indeed, such is the case, but practically I fear the fact is far otherwise, even regarding those who are of mature age ; and the boasted freedom of our labourers in many pursuits will, on a just view of their condition, be found little more than a name. Those who argue the question upon mere abstract principles seem, in my apprehension, too much to forget the condition of society : the unequal division of property, or rather its total monopoly by the few, leaving the many nothing but what they can obtain by their daily labour ; which very labour cannot become available for the purposes of daily subsistence, without the consent of those who own the property of the community,—all the materials, elements, call them what you please, on which labour can be bestowed, being in their possession. Hence it is clear that, excepting in a state of things where the demand for labour fully equals the supply (which it would be absurdly false to say exists in this country), the employer and the employed do not meet on equal terms in the market of labour; on the contrary, the latter, whatever be his age, and call him as free as you please, is often almost entirely at the mercy of the former;—he would be wholly so were it not for the operation of the poor-laws, which are a palpable interference with the market of labour, and condemned as such by their opponents. Hence is it that labour is so imperfectly distributed, and so inadequately remunerated ; that one part of the population is over-worked, while another is wholly without employment ; evils which operate reciprocally upon each other, till a community which might afford a sufficiency of moderate employ¯ment for all, exhibits at one and the same time part of its members reduced to the condition of slaves by over-exertion, and another part to that of paupers by involuntary idleness. In a word, wealth, still more than knowledge, is power; and power, liable to abuse wherever vested, is least of all free from tyrannical exercise, when it owes its existence to a sordid source. Hence have all laws, human or divine, attempted to protect the labourer from the injustice and cruelty which are too often practised upon him. Our statute-book contains many proofs of this, and especially in its provision for the poor. The Anti-Truck Bill of last year is an instance of this benevolent kind of interposition ; and that sacred institution which has been adopted and legally enforced, as far as the limits of civilization extend, and which justifies its claim to divine origin by its humanity and mercy—the institution of the Sabbath—is a constantly-recurring example of interference between the employer and the employed, solely and avowedly in favour of the latter : and I cannot help regretting, that almost every other red-letter day has been long ago blotted out from the dark calendar of labouring poverty, whose holidays are now too 'few and far between' to cheer the spirits or recruit the health of our industrious

population. It was promised, indeed, and might have been
expected, that the great inventions of recent times would
have restored a few of these ;—would have somewhat
abridged human labour in its duration, and abated its intensity : and it is only by effecting this that machinery can
justify its very definition, as consisting of inventions to
shorten human labour. I look forward to the period when
machinery will fully vindicate its pretensions, and surpass,
in its beneficial effects, all that its most sanguine advocates
have anticipated : when those inventions, whether so complicate and minute as almost to supplant the human hand,
or so stupendous as to tame the very elements, and yoke
them to the triumphal car of human industry, shall outstrip
our boldest expectations, not so much, indeed, by still further
augmenting the superfluities of the rich, as by increasing
the comforts and diminishing the labour of the poor; thereby
restoring to the mass of our fellow-beings those physical
enjoyments, that degree of leisure, those means of moral
and mental improvement, which alone can advance them to
that state of happiness and dignity to which, I trust, it is
their destiny to attain. Hitherto, however, I repeat, the
effect has been far different. The condition of the operative
manufacturers has been rendered more and more dependent
and precarious : their labour, when employed, is in many
cases so increased as to be utterly irreconcilable with the
preservation of health or even life ; infancy itself is forced
into the market of labour, where it becomes the unresisting
victim of cruelty and oppression ; while, as might be expected
from such an unnatural state of things, the remuneration for
this increasing and excessive toil is regularly diminishing,
till at length multitudes among us are reduced, in their physical condition at least, below the level of the slave or the
brute. In proof that this is no singular or overcharged
view of the present effect, or at all events of the ultimate
consequences, of this dreadful system, I shall appeal to the

language of a benevolent and enlightened individual, formerly a member of this House, and an ornament to it and the country—I mean the late Sir Robert Peel. His deliberate judgment upon this important subject is thus recorded in a document which he delivered to the committee on the bill he introduced in 1816 :—

" ' Such indiscriminate and unlimited employment of the poor, consisting of a great proportion of the inhabitants of the trading districts, will be attended with effects to the rising generation so serious and alarming, that I cannot contemplate them without dismay; and thus that great effort of British ingenuity, whereby the machinery of our manufacturers has been brought to such perfection, instead of being a blessing, will be converted into its bitterest curse.'

" Neither in quoting this passage, nor in making the observations which introduced it, would I be understood to recommend any interference with the efforts of human ingenuity, or with the market of labour, as supplied by free agents. But in showing how far even adults are from being free agents, in the proper meaning of the term, and, on the contrary, how dependent for their employment, and consequently their daily bread, upon the will of others, I have prepared the way for the conclusion, that children, at all events, are not to be regarded as free labourers; and that it is the duty of this House to protect them from that system of cruelty and oppression to which I shall presently advert. The common-place objection, that the parents are free agents, and that the children therefore ought to be regarded as such, I apprehend has but little force. It is, however, so often and so confidently urged, that I shall be excused for giving it some attention.

" The parents who surrender their children to this infantile slavery may be separated into two classes. The first, and I trust by far the most numerous one, consists of those who are obliged, by extreme indigence, so to act, but who do it with great reluctance and bitter regret; themselves perhaps out of employment, or working at very low wages, and their families in a state of great destitution. What can they do ? The overseer, as is in evidence, refuses relief if they have children capable of working in factories whom they object to send thither. They choose, therefore, what they probably deem the lesser evil, and reluctantly resign their offspring to the captivity and pollution of the mill: they rouse them in the winter morning, which, as a poor father says before the Lords' Committee, they ' feel very sorry ' to do;—they receive them fatigued and exhausted, many a weary hour after the day has closed;—they see them droop and sicken, and in many cases become cripples and die, before they reach their prime : and they do all this because they must otherwise suffer unrelieved, and starve, like Ugolino, amidst their starving children. It is mockery to contend that these parents have a choice ; that they can dictate to, or even parley with, the employer as to the number of hours their child shall be worked, or the treatment it shall be subject to in his mill; and it is an insult to the parental heart to say that they resign it voluntary;—no, ' Their poverty, and not their will, consents.' —Consents, indeed ! but often with tears, as Dr Ashton, a physician familiar with the whole system, informed the committee, a noble member of which, indeed, observed to one of the poor parents then examined, who was speaking of the successive fate of several of his children, whom he had been obliged to send to the factory—' You can hardly speak of them without crying ? ' The answer was 'No !' and few, I should suppose, refrain from sympathising with him, who heard his simple but melancholy story. Free agents ! To suppose that parents are free agents while dooming their own flesh and blood to this fate, is to believe them monsters.

" But, Sir, there are such monsters : unknown indeed in the brute creation, they belong to our own kind, and are found in our own country; and they are generated by the very system which I am attacking. They have been long known, and often described, as constituting the remaining class of parents to which I have adverted. Dead to the instincts of nature, and reversing the order of society, instead of providing for their offspring, they make their offspring provide for them : not only for their necessities, but for their intemperance and profligacy. They purchase idleness by the sweat of their infants, the price of whose happiness, health, and existence, they spend in the haunts of dissipation and vice. Thus, at the very same hour of night that the father is at his guilty orgies, the child is panting at the factory. Such wretches count upon their children as upon their cattle; —nay, to so disgusting a state of degradation does the system lead, that they make the certainty of having offspring the indispensable condition of marriage, that they may breed a generation of slaves. These, then, are some of the free agents, without the *storgè* of the beast, or the feelings of the man, to whom the advocates of the present system assure us we ought to entrust the labouring of little children. One of these 'free agents,' a witness against Sir Robert Peel's bill, confessed that he had pushed his own child down and broken her arm, because she did not do as he thought proper, while in the mill. The Lords' Committee refused to hear him another word. And shall we listen to those who urge us to commit little children to such guardianship? We have heard, in a late memorable case, a *dictum*, uncontradicted I believe in any quarter, stating that, by the constitution of England, the first law officer of the crown, representing the sovereign, is the guardian of all children, of whatever rank, improperly treated by their parents; but that that court is limited in its interference by the circumstance of there being property under its control. Will it be contended, then, that in these extreme cases of cruelty and oppression (for such I shall call them), where protection is far more imperatively demanded, that poverty should be a bar against the course of British justice? If so, let us boast no longer of the impartiality of our laws! Why, if in a solitary instance a parent were to confine his child, or a master his apprentice, in a heated room, and knowingly keep him at his labour more hours than nature could sustain, and at length the victim were to die under the tyrannous oppression, and a coroner's inquest were to return a true and just verdict upon the occasion, what would be the result? .... And are the multiplication of such gradual murders, and the effrontery with which they are perpetrated, to become their expiation? If not, it is high time that the legislature should interfere and rescue from the conspiracy of such fathers and such masters, instigated by kindred feelings, these innocent victims of cruelty and oppression.

" There are other descriptions of children, also, whom I should be glad to know how the objectors to whom I am alluding, make out to be free agents. I mean, first, poor orphan children—a class which the system is a very efficient instrument in multiplying : very few adult spinners, as it is often alleged, and as I shall prove, surviving forty; in many instances, therefore, leaving their children fatherless at a very early period of life : indeed, so numerous are these, that a physician, examined on the occasion to which I have so often alluded, was painfully struck with the proportion. Are these orphans free agents?—Again, there is in all manufacturing towns, a great number of illegitimate children, and these also are very much increased by the system in question. I am aware that a celebrated authority has said, these are, ' comparatively speaking, of no value to society;—others would supply their place,'—yet still I cannot but regard these as objects of the deepest compassion. To this list of free agents I might also add the little children who are still apprenticed out in considerable numbers, often I fear by the too ready sanction of the magistrates—whose hard, and sometimes fatal,

treatment has been the subject of many recent communications
which I have received from individuals of the highest credit
and respectability. But, as the objectors to legislative protection for the factory children can make it out to be unnecessary, because their parents are 'free agents' for them,
when they have any surviving, so also it is quite as clear,
probably, in their apprehension, that the parish officer is as
good a free agent for the poor orphan, the illegitimate, or the
friendless little apprentice, who may be under his special
protection.

"But I will proceed no further with these objections.
The idea of treating children, and especially the children
of the poor—and, above all, the children of the poor imprisoned in factories—as free agents, is too absurd to justify
the attention I have already paid to it. The protection of
poor children and young persons from those hardships and
cruelties to which their age and condition have always rendered them peculiarly liable, has ever been held one of the
first and most important duties of every Christian legislature.
Our own has not been unmindful in this respect; and it is
mainly owing to the change of circumstances that many of
its humane provisions have been rendered inoperative, and
that the present measure has become the more necessary. I
had meant to take a short review of these various efforts
down to the time of the benevolent Hanway; but, interesting
as the subject is, and applicable to the present discussion, I
must forbear, in respect to the time it would occupy, to do so.
It was the introduction of Sir Richard Arkwright's invention
that revolutionised the entire system of our national industry.
Previously to that period, the incipient manufactures of the
country were carried on in the villages and around the
domestic hearth: that invention transferred them principally
to the great towns, and almost confined them to what are now
called factories. Thus, children became the principal operatives; and they no longer performed their tasks, as before,

under the parental eye, and had them affectionately and considerately apportioned, according to their health and capacities, but one universal rule of labour was prescribed to all ages, to both sexes, and to every state and constitution. Such a regulation, therefore, it might have been expected, would have been adapted to the different degrees of physical strength in the young, the delicate, and especially the female sex. But no!—I speak it with shame, with horror—it was stretched, in many cases—I had almost said in nearly all—beyond what the most athletic and robust of our own sex, in the prime and vigour of life, can with impunity sustain;—to the ultimate destruction, in a vast majority of instances, of the health, the happiness, and the very life, of the miserable victims. Our ancestors could not have supposed it possible—posterity will not believe it true—it will be placed among the historic doubts of some future antiquary—that a generation of Englishmen could exist, or had existed, that would labour lisping infancy, of a few summers old, regardless alike of its smiles or tears, and unmoved by its unresisting weakness, eleven, twelve, thirteen, fourteen, sixteen hours a day, and through the weary night also, till, in the dewy morn of existence, the bud of youth faded, and fell ere it was unfolded. ' Oh, cursed lust of gold!' Oh, the guilt which England was contracting in the kindling eye of Heaven, when nothing but exultations were heard about the perfection of her machinery, the march of her manufactures, and the rapid increase of her wealth and prosperity!

" Early, however, in this century, the late Sir Robert Peel, knowing well the enormities of the factory system, and finding, from his own experience, that nothing but a legislative enactment could remove them, obtained the first Act for the protection of poor children employed in cotton factories. About fifteen or sixteen years afterwards, he carried another measure, of a similar, but more comprehensive nature. Lastly, the right honourable member for Westminster obtained another Act, last session, having the same benevolent object in view. But, on all these occasions, the attempt, by whomsoever made, or whatever was its character, was met with the same strenuous, or, as I might well call it, vehement opposition. Whether it was proposed to limit the labour of infants and young persons, beside the time necessary for their meals and refreshment, to ten, eleven, or even twelve hours a-day, it was all one ; the proposal was scouted and resisted. The motives and conduct of those engaged in attempting to obtain this protection, were maligned. The universal humanity of all those in every pursuit, whose power over these children was unrestrained, was boldly asserted; the superior health, happiness, and even longevity, of those employed were always maintained. Whatever was the nature or duration of the employment which these young persons, whether daily or nightly, pursued, it was contended that no injury, but abundance of good, was done to them. On every occasion this opposition has virtually succeeded, so as to defeat the original intentions of those who have successively proposed these measures. It has succeeded in lengthening the term of infantile labour, in limiting every act to one particular branch of business, in introducing provisions which have rendered them liable to constant evasions, and it is well known that the whole of them are evaded, and rendered little better than a dead letter.

"The very same opposition that has so long and so often triumphed over justice and humanity, is again organized, and actively at work, and will proceed as before. Every branch of manufacture proposed to be regulated claims in turn to be excepted; a committee of inquiry is again demanded, and, I fear, in order to postpone, if not finally to defeat, the present measure. The nature of the evidence that will be brought forward is perfectly familiar to those acquainted at all with the subject. Certificates and declarations will be obtained in abundance, from divines and doctors, as to the morality and

health which the present system promotes and secures. I
cannot refrain from giving a sample of what may be expected
in this line, and I think it will prepare us for, and arm us
against, whatever may be advanced in favour of so unnatural
and oppressive a system. I mean not to impeach the inten-
tional veracity or the learning of the witnesses who appeared
in its favour, and whose evidence cuts a very conspicuous
figure in these ponderous reports ; it furnishes, however,
another proof of the strange things that may be, perhaps
conscientiously believed and asserted when the mind or
conduct is under a particular bias. They have said that the
children who were worked without any regulation, and
consequently according to their employers' sole will and
pleasure, were not only equally, but more healthy, and better
instructed than those not so occupied ; that night-labour was
in no way prejudicial, but actually preferred ; that the
artificial heat of the rooms was really advantageous, and quite
pleasant; and that nothing could equal the reluctance of the
children to have it abated. That so far from being fatigued
with, for example, twelve hours' labour, the children performed even the last hour's work with greater interest and
spirit than any of the rest. What a pity the term was not
lengthened ! in a few more hours they would have been
worked into a perfect ecstasy of delight. We had been
indeed informed that the women and children often cried
with fatigue, but their tears were doubtless tears of rapture.
A doctor is produced, who will not pronounce, without
examination, to what extent this luxury of excessive labour
might be carried without being prejudicial. I must quote a
few of his answers to certain queries. 'Should you not
think (he is asked) that, generally speaking, a child eight
years old standing twelve hours in the day would be
injurious ?' The doctor reverses, perhaps by mistake, the
figures, but his answer concludes,—'I believe it is not.'
'Supposing (it was again demanded) I were to ask you

whether you thought it injurious to a child to be kept standing three-and-twenty hours out of the four-and-twenty, should you not think it must be necessarily injurious to the health ; without any fact to rest upon, as a simple proposition put to a gentleman of the medical profession?' ' Before I answer that question,' the doctor replies, 'I should wish to have an examination, to see how the case stood; and if there were such an extravagant thing to take place, and it should appear that the person was not injured by having stood three-and-twenty hours, I should then say it was not inconsistent with the health of the person so employed.' ' As you doubted,' said a noble Lord, ' whether a child could work for twenty-three hours, without suffering, would you extend your doubts to twenty-four hours?'—'That was put to me as an extreme case,' says the doctor : ' my answer only went to this effect, that it was not in my power to assign any limits.' This same authority will not take upon himself to say whether it would be injurious to a child to be kept working during the time it gets its meals. Another medical gentleman is ' totally unable to give an answer' whether ' children from six to twelve years of age, being employed from thirteen to fifteen hours in a cotton factory, in an erect position, and in a temperature of about eighty degrees, is consistent with safety to their constitution.' Another boldly asserts that he does not see it necessary that young persons should have any recreation or amusement ; nor that the constant inspiration of particles of cotton is at all injurious to the lungs. Reports of the state of particular mills are also given on medical authority, but the reporters seem to have totally forgotten that they had examined a body of persons constantly recruited, from which the severely sick, and those ' who had retired to die,' were necessarily absent; and not to have suspected that many of these mills were also previously and carefully prepared for such inspection. Still, I observe, it is allowed that ' many of them (the children) were pale, and apparently of a delicate complexion;' but 'without any decided symptoms of disease.' What did that paleness and delicacy, in the rosy morning of life, indicate? Why, that disease, though not decided as to its symptoms, was fastening, with mortal grasp, upon its victims; that already early labour and confinement had, 'like a worm i'the bud, fed on their damask cheek;' that the murderous system was then about its secret, but certain and deadly, work. In corroboration, however, of all that these learned persons have advanced, and in full proof of the excellency of the entire system, bills of mortality of certain places and works were adduced, in some of which it was made to appear that, in a mean number of 888 persons employed, the annual mortality had, during eight years, averaged $3\frac{875}{1000}$, or 1 in 229 only! This sort of evidence suggests many ludicrous ideas, which, however, I shall suppress as unsuitable to the subject : it will, doubtless, be again adduced in great abundance before another select committee. Physicians, divines, and others, will be still found to testify to the same effect. But I will take the liberty of showing, before I sit down, the true value of all such certificates. The Parliament, indeed, did not much regard these champions of the factory-system on a former occasion; and, after what I shall advance, I hope the House will not trouble them again.

"I shall now proceed to show the necessity of a general measure for regulating the labour of children and young persons employed in mills and factories, of whatever description, the protective acts already obtained having been confined in their operation to one branch of manufacture only, and in that almost entirely defeated as to their original intention and design.

"I need not inform the House that the great invention of Sir Richard Arkwright, originally used for the spinning of cotton, has at length been applied, with the necessary adaptations, to a similar process in almost all our manufactures.

Now the fact that parliament has several times, notwithstanding the severest opposition, seen it necessary to regulate
the labour of children in the former pursuit, proves the same
necessity to exist regarding those other factories, now so
numerous, which have been hitherto entirely exempted from
all such control. It would be the grossest injustice, as well
as insult, to argue that those engaged in the cotton-trade
were one whit less humane and considerate, and consequently
required legislative interference one whit more, than those
engaged in spinning any other material; and if it be contended
that the labour of the latter is, in many cases, either less
unhealthy or less immoderate than that of the former, I meet
the assertion with a direct negative. Nor, in contending for
the necessity of this measure, do I implicate the conduct of
the millowners generally, many of whom, I am well convinced, are among the most humane and considerate of
employers; on the contrary, the interests of these, as well
as the welfare of the children, equally demand legislative
protection.

"And, first, in reference to one description of spinners,
from some of whom I am now meeting with opposition of
every kind,—I mean the spinners of flax,—I would seriously
ask any gentleman, who has himself gone through a modern
flax-mill, whether he can entertain the slightest doubt that
the occupation, as now pursued, must, in too many cases,
be injurious to health and destructive of life. In many departments of these mills, the dust is great, and known to be highly
injurious. In those in which fine spinning has been introduced,
the air has to be heated, as in some of the cotton mills; the flax
has also, in one of the processes, to be passed through water
heated to a high temperature, into which the children have
constantly to plunge their arms, while the steam and the spray
from the bobbins wet their clothes, especially about their
middle, till the water might be wrung from them, in which
condition they have during the winter months, to pass nightly

into the inclement air, and to shiver and freeze on their return home. In the heckling-rooms, in which children are now principally employed, the dust is excessive. The rooms are generally low, lighted by gas, and sometimes heated by steam; altogether exhibiting a state of human suffering, the effects of which I will not trust myself to describe, but appeal to higher authority.

"I hold in my hand a treatise by a medical gentleman of great intelligence, Mr Thackrah, of Leeds, who, in his work, ' On the Effects of Arts and Trades on Health and Longevity,' thus speaks of this pursuit—' A large proportion of men in this department die young. We find, indeed, comparatively speaking, few old persons in any of the departments of the flax-mills.'—' On inquiry at one of the largest establishments in this neighbourhood, we found that of 1,079 persons employed, there are only nine who had attained the age of fifty; and besides these, only twenty-two who have reached forty.'

"It may, perhaps, be here remarked, that this factory-census does not indicate the rate of mortality, but merely shows that few adults are required in these establishments. If so, then another enormous abuse comes into view; namely, that this unregulated system over-labours the child, and deserts the adult; thus reversing the natural period of toil, and leaving numbers without employment, or the knowledge how to pursue it, if they could obtain any, just at the period when the active exertions of life ought to commence. Why, this is to realize, in regard of these victims of premature labour, the fate of the poor little chimney-sweeper, whose lot, once commiserated so deeply, is now, I think, too much forgotten, and whose principal hardship is not that he is of a degraded class, but that when he has learnt his business, he has outgrown it, and is turned upon society too late to learn any other occupation, and has, therefore, to seek an employment for which he is unqualified. So far, then, this unrestricted factory system perpetrates the deepest injury, not only upon individuals, but upon society at large.

" But to return to Mr Thackrah. He says, that 'a visitor cannot remain many minutes in certain rooms without being sensibly affected in his respiration.' Also, that ' a suffocating sensation is often produced by the tubes which convey steam for heating the rooms.' He examined, by the stethoscope, several individuals so employed, and found, in all of them, ' the lungs or air-tube considerably diseased.' He adds, that ' the coughs of the persons waiting to be examined, were so troublesome as continually to interrupt and confuse the exploration by that instrument' He says, ' that though the wages for this labour are by no means great, still the time of labour in the flax-mills is excessive. The people are now (November 1830) working from half-past six in the morning till eight at night, and are allowed only an interval of forty minutes in all that time. Thus human beings are kept in an atmosphere of flax-dust nearly thirteen hours in the day, and this not one but six days in the week.' ' No man of humanity,' he observes, ' can reflect, without distress, on the state of thousands of children,—roused from their beds at an early hour, hurried to the mills, and kept there, with an interval of only forty minutes, till a late hour of night—kept, moreover, in an atmosphere loaded with noxious dust.' ' Health,' he exclaims, ' cleanliness, mental improvement—how are they regarded ? Recreation is out of the question. There is scarcely time for meals. The ɪ y period of sleep, so necessary to the young, is too often abridged Nay, children are sometimes worked even in the night ! Human beings thus decay before they arrive at the term of maturity.' He observes elsewhere, ' that this system has grown up by a series of encroachments upon the poor children ; that the benevolent masters are not able to rectify these abuses. A legislative enactment is, alone, the remedy for this as well as the other great opprobrium of our manufactures—the improper employment of children.' Such are the opinions of this medical gentleman upon this subject, written long before the present bill was before the House; and founded upon daily observation and experience.

"I might add the opinion of another very excellent practitioner of the same place, Mr Smith, respecting the cruelty of the present system, and the misery and decrepitude which it inflicts upon its victims; but his opinions, given with great force and ability, have, I think, been already widely disseminated by means of the press. The other surgeons of the Leeds infirmary—all men of great professional eminence — entertain, I believe, precisely similar opinions. One of them, Mr Hey, a name that at once commands the highest respect in every medical society of this country, or indeed of Europe, presided, as mayor of Leeds, at an immensely numerous meeting of the inhabitants of that borough, when a petition from that place, in favour of the bill, was unanimously agreed to; and afterwards received the signatures of between 18,000 and 20,000 persons.

"In silk and worsted mills, and especially in the former, the nature of the employment may be less prejudicial in itself; but then its duration is often more protracted, and it falls in a larger proportion upon females and young children. In many spun-silk mills, in which a different operation from that of silk-throwing—and one conducted upon Arkwright's principle—is carried on, the practice of working children at a very tender age, and often all night, prevails. In some of these, I am informed, they commence at one o'clock on the Monday morning, and leave off at eleven on Saturday night; thus delicately avoiding the Sabbath, indeed, but rendering its profitable observance, either for improvement, instruction, or worship, an utter impossibility.

"In the worsted mills, the greatest irregularities, as to the hours of working, have existed, and therefore, occasional oppression in these departments has long prevailed. Let the following extract suffice, from a document drawn up by a gentleman in this branch of business, Mr Wood,—to mention whose name is to kindle at once the most enthusiastic feelings in the bosoms of the honest operatives of the north, and to whom is due the honour of originating and supporting this attempt to regulate the labour of children; and who, while he has conducted his own manufacture with the greatest humanity and kindness, has still earnestly sought to ameliorate the general condition of the labouring poor. This gentleman gives the ages of 475 persons, principally females, employed at a worsted-mill, which, it appears, average about the age of thirteen; and adds—

" ' Children of these years are obliged to be at the factories, winter and summer, by six in the morning, and to remain there till seven in the evening, with but one brief interval of thirty minutes, every day except Saturday, ceasing work on that day, in some factories, at half-past five, in others, at six or seven p.m. Not unfrequently this labour is extended till eight or nine at night—fifteen hours—having but the same interval for meals, rest, or recreation : nay, such is the steady growth of this over-working system, that children have been confined in the factory from six in the morning till eight at night—fourteen hours continuously, without any time being allowed for meals, rest, or recreation;—the meals to be taken while attending the machines; and this the practice of years.'

" This picture, sufficiently appalling, has also to be darkened by the addition of frequent night-labour. Such is the practice at Bradford and the neighbourhood. But to show that the evils are not confined to any particular neighbourhood, and that they prevail wherever unprotected children are the principal labourers of the community, I shall next advert to their treatment in the flannel manufactories in the Principality of Wales. I quote the following account which I have received from the most respectable quarter :—

" ' With certain fluctuations in the degree of labour, resulting from the difference in the demand of manufactured goods, the children here work twenty-four hours every other day, out of which they are allowed three hours only for meals, &c.   When trade is particularly brisk, the elder children work from six in the morning till seven in the evening, two hours being allowed for meals, &c., and every other night they work all night, which is a still more severe case ; for this additional night labour they receive five-pence. There is another lamentable circumstance attending the employment of these poor children, which is, that they are left the whole of the night alone ; the sexes indiscriminately mixed together ; consequently you may imagine that the depravity of our work people is indeed very great.   The adults are employed in feeding the engines.   Independent of moral considerations, the accidents that occur to these poor little creatures are really dreadful ; the numbers of persons to be seen with mutilated and amputated limbs are quite distressing, and this will ever be the case till some better regulation is carried into effect.   There is not a single place of charitable education for a population of about 8,000 souls beyond a Sunday-school.'

" As to woollen mills, they are not, generally speaking, injurious to health, though such is the case in certain departments of them, especially since the introduction of the rotatory machines.   Here I might argue that the lightness of the labour, which is the reason usually urged against an interference with excessive hours, no longer applies, as in woollen mills the labour is, in general, much more strenuous than that in most of the before-mentioned factories.   But I disdain to avail myself of an argument, however plausible, which I believe to be fallacious, and I will here observe, once for all, that it is not so much the degree of labour which is injurious to these work-children (how revolting the compound sounds!—it is not yet admitted, I think, into our language ; I trust it will never be familiarised to our feelings);

—I say, it is not so much the degree, as the duration of their labour, that is so cruel and destructive to these poor work-children. It is the wearisome uniformity of the employment, —the constrained positions in which it is pursued—and, above all, the constant and close confinement, which are more fatiguing to the body as well as mind, than more varied and voluntary, though far stronger, exertion. I dwell upon this point, because it is the sole possible plea for the long and imprisoning hours of the present laborious system : though when properly considered, it is one of the most powerful arguments against it. Light labour ! Is the labour of holding this pen and of writing with it strenuous? And yet, ask a clerk in any of the public offices, or in any private counting-house, when he has been at his employment some half-dozen hours in the day less than one of these children, whether he does not think that he has had enough of this light labour— to say nothing of the holidays, of which he has many, and the child none. Ask the recruit recent from the plough, whether an hour of his light exertion is not more fatiguing than any three he ever endured in the fields. Ask his experienced officer how long he can subject even the veteran to this sort of slight but constrained exertion, though in the open air, with impunity. I might appeal to the chair, whether the lingering hours which have to be endured here, though unaccompanied with any bodily exertion whatever, are not ' weariness to the flesh.' But what would be the feelings of the youngest and most active individual amongst us, if, for example, he were compelled to pace that table, engaged in some constant and anxious employment, stunned with the noise of revolving wheels, suffocated with the heat and stench of a low, crowded, and gas lighted apartment, bathed in sweat, and stimulated by the scourge of an inexorable task-master? I say, what would be his ideas of the light labour of twelve or fourteen hours in such a pursuit, and when, once or twice in every week, the night also was added to such a day? And how would he feel, if long years of such light labour lay before him? If he be a parent, let him imagine the child of his bosom in that situation, and then judge of the children of thousands who are as dear to the Universal Parent as are his own to him! Let him think of his own childhood, and he will then remember that this light labour is the fatigue of youth, and that strenuous exertion, when the buoyant spirit exercises the entire frame, is its sport. I might quote authorities on this subject; but it is unnecessary. Common sense and common feeling at once decide the point, and confute this disgusting plea of tyranny for the captivity of youth. Hence the late Sir Robert Peel, in bringing forward his last measure, emphatically observed, that ' it was not so much the hardship as the duration of labour, which had caused the mischievous effects on the rising generation.' But if, after all, honourable members choose to argue the question on different grounds, and wish to establish a variation in the duration of the labour of children in mills and factories, in reference to the nature of the employment,—be it so. Confident in my own mind that the bill proposes the utmost limit which the youthful constitution can safely bear, in any pursuit, or under any circumstances, I can have no objection to that period being abridged in the more pernicious and strenuous employments of the country.

"I shall not attempt at present to give any precise account of the length of labour generally borne in different mills and factories; it varies according to the humanity of the employer, and the demand for his goods at particular seasons. But let me here remark, that these variations constitute one of the main reasons for a legislative protection; otherwise the humane masters will be driven out of the trade : for these, it is quite clear, cannot control others less feelingly disposed. They are, indeed, in the present state of things, as little free agents as the children whom they employ ; and, moreover, the want of a due regulation throws the effects of those fluctuations to which trade and manufactures are subject. in an undue and distressing degree upon those who are the least able to sustain their effects. Thus, if the demand and profit of the employer increase, the labour of the operatives, most of whom are children, augments, till many of them are literally worked to death; if that demand diminish, the children are thrown partially or wholly out of work, and left to beggary and the parish. So that their labour, averaged throughout the year, as some millowners I perceive have calculated its duration, does not appear so excessive. For, at the very moment that a strenuous opposition is being made against the curtailment of infantile labour, the masters themselves, in certain flax-mills in the North, have curtailed it to some purpose—having, if I am not misinformed, diminished the employment in some mills, and shut up others entirely. And I have no doubt but that, at this particular moment, abundance of evidence might be adduced before a select committee to show that the hours mentioned in the bill are observed, and indeed a much stricter limitation enforced. But then, if it be right that the owners should be allowed to throw out of employment all these children at a few days' notice, is it proper that they should be permitted to work them for an unlimited number of hours, the moment it suits their purpose? If the effect of this bill were, in some measure to equalize the labour of these poor children, and thereby prevent those fluctuations which are so distressing to them in both its extremes, it would so far accomplish a most beneficent object. It might, I think, transfer a little of the fluctuation from the factory to the stock-room, with great advantage to the operatives, and, consequently, to the public at large.

"It is impossible to furnish any uniform account of the hours of labour endured by children in these factories, and I am unwilling to represent extreme cases as general ones, although it is the bounden duty of Parliament to provide against such, as it does, for example, with respect to atrocious crimes, which are extreme cases in civilized society. I shall therefore only give one or two instances of the extent of oppression to which the system is occasionally carried. The following were the hours of labour imposed upon the children employed in a factory at Leeds last summer :—On Monday morning, work commenced at six o'clock ; at nine, half an hour for breakfast ; from half-past nine till twelve, work. Dinner, one hour; from one till half-past four, work. Afternoon meal, half an hour ; from five till eight, work : rest for half an hour. From half-past eight till twelve (midnight), work : an hour's rest. From one in the morning till five, work : half an hour's rest. From half-past five till nine, work : breakfast. From half-past nine till twelve, work; dinner; from one till half-past four, work. Rest half an hour; and work again from five till nine o'clock on Tuesday evening, when the labour terminated, and the gang of adult and infant slaves was dismissed for the night, after having toiled thirty-nine hours, with brief intervals (amounting to only six hours in the whole) for refreshment, but none for sleep. On Wednesday and Thursday, day work only. From Friday morning till Saturday night, the same prolonged labour repeated, with intermissions as on Monday, Monday night, and Tuesday; except that the labour of the last day closed at five.—The ensuing day, Sunday, must, under such circumstances, be a day of stupor ; to rouse the children from which would only be to continue their physical sufferings, without the possibility of compensating them with any moral good. Clergymen, Sunday school-masters, and other benevolent persons, are beginning to feel this to be the case; physicians, I find, have long observed it; and parents, wishful as they are that their offspring should have some little instruction, are yet more anxious that they should have rest. Sunday schools have long been rendered appendages to the manufacturing system, which has necessarily emptied the day schools of the poor wherever that system prevails: not content with monopolizing the whole week with protracted labour, the Sabbath itself is thus rendered a day of languor and exhaustion, in which it is impossible that due instruction can be received, or the solemn duties which religion enjoins duly performed; in fact, it is a mere fallow for the worn-out frame, in order that it may be able to produce another series of exhausting crops of human labour. If some limits, therefore, are not prescribed to these constant and cruel encroachments, our labouring population will become, ere long, imbruted with ignorance, as well as enslaved by excessive toil.

"I now proceed to show the physical and moral consequences of this dreadful system; and on this important part of the subject, as I am aware that I shall be at issue with its supporters and apologists, I shall appeal to authorities which none will be disposed lightly to dispute; and to facts—decisive, as I think, of the whole question—facts which I challenge them to controvert or evade. The authorities to which I allude, are such as the late Dr Baillie, Sir Astley Cooper, Sir Gilbert Blaine, Doctor Pemberton, Sir Anthony Carlisle, Sir George Tuthill, and many other physicians and surgeons of the highest eminence and celebrity throughout the profession, especially for their physiological science. The deliberate opinions of these distinguished persons on the subject under our consideration are contained in these volumes (minutes of evidence before former parliamentary committees). Time would fail were I now to read them, or even to make selections. They ought, however, to have been carefully consulted by certain hon. members before they had cried out for another select committee; ignorant I would fain hope, of the affecting evidence published by preceding ones. Let it suffice that these high authorities are strong and unanimous against the system of early and protracted labour for children and young persons. I appeal to the whole of them in favour of this bill, or rather, indeed, of far more binding limitations than it proposes; for when I

advert to their deliberate declarations, I feel a growing dissatisfaction at its provisions. Other medical authorities of
great eminence have since then appeared, whose views, I
know, in many instances, to be, if possible, still more marked
and decided upon this important point ; and can it, I would
ask the House, be a question whether we should tolerate a
degree of infantile labour, which our highest medical authorities assure us the human frame is utterly incapable of
sustaining with impunity ?

"If it be objected that these individuals, however great
and distinguished, had no practical knowledge of the factory
system and its effects, I will turn to another description of
evidence—namely, to that of professional gentlemen practically
acquainted with it, and long residing in its very seat and
centre—Manchester. The first is a name equally dear to
philosophy and philanthropy,—long at the head of the profession in that part of the empire—Dr Perceval. He saw
the rise, progress, and effects of the system, and closely
connected as he was with many who were making rapid
fortunes by it, still he expressed himself upon the subject, as
a professional man and a patriot, in terms of the strongest
indignation. He says, even of the large factories, which
some suppose need little regulation, that they ' are generally
injurious to the constitution of those employed in them, even
when no particular diseases prevail, from the close confinement
which is enjoined, from the debilitating effects of hot or
impure air, and from the want of the active exercises which
nature points out as essential to childhood and youth, to
invigorate the system, and to fit our species for the employment and the duties of manhood. The untimely labour of
the night, and the protracted labour of the day, with respect
to children, not only tend to diminish future expectation as
to the general sum of life and industry, by impairing the
strength and destroying the vital stamina of the rising generation, but it too often gives encouragement to idleness,

extravagance, and profligacy, in the parents, who, contrary to the order of nature, subsist by the oppression of their offspring.' He goes on to deplore the impediments which the system throws in the way of education, and asserts the necessity of establishing ' *a general system of laws for the wise, humane, and equal government of all such works.*' I regret that time will not permit me to quote him more at large; but who that is acquainted with general literature or philosophy, can be ignorant of the writings of Perceval of Manchester?

" I will refer the House to another authority, belonging to a different branch of the same profession, and scarcely a less celebrated one,—I mean the late Mr Simmons. After nearly thirty years' experience in the General Infirmary of Manchester, and being also at the head of other charitable institutions in that town connected with his profession, few men, I should conceive, were more competent to speak as to the effects produced by the factory system than himself. I must again deeply regret that I cannot quote his opinions at length. His description of the consequences of this species of over-exertion is most appalling; and he adds these emphatic words:—'I am convinced that the hours of employment are too long to endure at *any age.*' Speaking of the evils of the system, he says, ' I shudder at contemplating them !'

" I might multiply these authentic and affecting testimonies to almost any extent. I will, however, present, in as few words as possible, the effects, as described by medical men, of these long hours of confinement, without sufficient intervals for meals, recreation, and rest, and continued often through the night, in rooms artificially heated, and lit by gas ; the atmosphere being otherwise so polluted and offensive as to render respiration painful, even for a few minutes. They describe the consequences to be in many cases, languor and debility, sickness, loss of appetite, pulmonary complaints, such as difficulty of breathing, coughs, asthmas, and consumptions ; struma, the endemia of the factory, and other chronic diseases;—while, if these more distressing effects are not produced, the muscular power is enfeebled, the growth impeded, and life greatly abridged Deformity is also a common and distressing result of this over-strained and too early labour. The bones, in which the animal, in contra-distinction to the earthy, matter is known to prevail in early life, are then pliable, and often cannot sustain the super-incumbent weight of the body for so many hours without injury. Hence, those of the leg become bent ; the arch of the foot, which is composed of several bones of a wedge-like form, is pressed down and its elasticity destroyed, from which arises that disease in the foot only lately described, but common in factory districts. The spine is often greatly affected, and its processes irregularly protruded, by which great deformity is occasioned. The ligaments also fail by over-pressure and tension. Hence the hinge-joints, of which they are the main support, such as those of the knee and the ancle, are over-strained, producing the deformity called knock-knees and lame ancles, so exceedingly common in mills. Thus are numbers of children distorted and crippled in early life, and frequently rendered incapable of any active exertion during the rest of their days. To this catalogue of sufferings must be added, mutilation of limbs or loss of life, by frequent accidents. The overworking of these children occasions a weariness and lethargy which it is impossible always to resist: hence, drowsy and exhausted, the poor creatures fall too often among the machinery, which is not in many instances sufficiently sheathed, when their muscles are lacerated, their bones broken, or their limbs torn off, in which cases they are constantly sent to the infirmaries to be cured, and if crippled for life, they are turned out and maintained at the public cost; or they are sometimes killed upon the spot. I have myself known, in more instances than one, the arm torn off,—in one horrible case, both; and a poor girl now exists upon a charitable subscription who met with that dreadful accident at one of the flax mills in my neighbourhood. In another factory, and that recently, the mangled limbs of a boy were sent home to his mother, unprepared for the appalling spectacle: I will not describe the result. It is true that a great majority of these accidents are of a less serious nature, but the admission-books of the infirmaries in any manufacturing district will show the number; and their accounts of the expense of buying irons to support the bending legs of the young children who become crippled by long standing in the mills, will also prove the tendency of over-confinement and early labour to produce deformity. Dr Ashton and Surgeon Graham, who examined six mills in Stockport, in which 824 persons were employed, principally children, have reported the result individually, and the list seems rather that of an hospital than a workshop. The particulars are deeply affecting, but I must only give the totals. Of 824 persons, 183 only were pronounced healthy; 240 were stated to be delicate; 258 unhealthy; 43 very much stunted; 100 with enlarged ancles and knees; and among the whole there were 37 cases of distortion. The accidents by machinery are not, I think, noticed; but I find that Dr Winstanley, one of the physicians of the Manchester Infirmary, on examining 106 children in a Sunday school, discovered that no less than 47 of them had suffered accidents from this one cause. I have this morning received, from one of the most eminent surgeons of this metropolis, a letter, in which he informs me, that on making a tour through the manufacturing districts some years ago, he was painfully struck with the numerous cases of mutilation which he observed, and which he attributed to this long and wearying system of labour in mills and factories. Of the mortality which this system occasions, I shall speak hereafter.

"Can anything, then, darken the picture which I have hastily drawn, or, rather, which others, infinitely more competent to the task, have strikingly portrayed? Yes, Sir, and that remains to be added which renders it the most disgusting as well as distressing system which ever put human feelings to the utmost test of endurance. It has the universally recognised brand and test of barbarism as well as cruelty upon it. It is the feebler sex principally on which this enormous wrong is perpetrated. Female children must be laboured to the utmost extent of their physical powers, and, indeed, frequently far beyond them. Need I state the peculiar hardships, the disgusting cruelty which this involves? I speak not, poor things, of the loss of their beauty,—of the greater physical sufferings to which their sex exposes them. But, again taking with me the highest medical authorities, I refer to the consequences of early and immoderate labour; especially at the period when the system rapidly attains its full development, and is peculiarly susceptible of permanent injury. Still more are the effects felt when they become mothers, for which, I fear, their previous pursuits have little qualified them. It is in evidence, that long standing has a known tendency—how shall I express it?—*contrahere et minuere pelvem,*—and thereby to increase greatly the danger and difficulty of parturition, rendering embryotomy—one of the most distressing operations which a surgeon ever has to perform—occasionally necessary. I have communications upon this subject from persons of great professional experience; but still I prefer to appeal to evidence before the public; and one reference shall suffice. Dr Jones, who had practised in the neighbourhood of certain mills, in favour of which much evidence was adduced, which indeed it is rarely difficult to procure, states, that in the 'eight or ten years during which he was an accoucheur, he met with more cases requiring the aid of instruments (that circumstance showing them to be bad ones) than a gentleman of great practice in Birmingham, to whom he was previously a pupil, had met with in the whole course of his life.' Abundance of evidence to the same effect is before me. But I forbear. I confess, therefore, that I feel my indignation roused when I see papers put forth in which it is stated, as a recommendation forsooth of the present system, and as a reason why it should by no means be regulated, that in certain mills girls are principally employed. This a matter of exultation! I would ask those who so regard it, in the language of the poet, ' Art thou of woman born, and feel'st no shame ?'

" Nor are the mental, any more than the physical, sufferings of these poor young creatures to be overlooked. In the very morning of life, when their little hearts yearn within them for some relaxation and amusement, to be thus taken captive, and debarred the sports of youth, is almost as great, nay, a greater cruelty than to inflict upon them thus early the toil of an advanced life. Their fate, alas! reverses the patriarch's pathetic exclamation, and their infant days are labour and sorrow. I perceive that I excite the risibility of an honourable gentleman opposite. What there is to smile at in these just representations of infantile sufferings, I am really at a loss to imagine. I will venture, however, to give him and the House a few more of these amusing facts before I have done with the subject.

" It may be thought almost impossible that children should be assembled so early, and dismissed so late, and still kept through the whole period in a state of active exertion. I will attempt to explain this. First, then, their early and punctual attendance is enforced by fines, as are many other regulations of a very severe character; so that a child may lose a considerable part of its wages by being a few minutes too late in the morning. That they should not leave too soon is very sufficiently provided against. Now, this extreme punctuality is no slight aggravation of the sufferings of the child. It is not in one case out of ten, perhaps, that the parent has a clock; and, as nature is not very wakeful in a short night's rest after a long day's labour, the child, to ensure punctuality, must be often roused much too early. Whoever has lived in a manufacturing town must have heard, if he happened to be awake many hours before light on a winter's morning, the patter of little pattens on the pavement, continued, perhaps, for half an hour together, though the time appointed for assembling was the same. Even then the child is not always safe, however punctual, for in some mills two descriptions of clocks are kept, and it is easy to guess how they are occasionally managed. So much for the system of fines, by which, I am told, some millowners have boasted that they have made large sums annually.

"Then, in order to keep the children awake, and to stimulate their exertions, means are made use of, to which I shall now advert, as a last instance of the degradation to which this system has reduced the manufacturing operatives of this country. Sir, children are beaten with thongs, prepared for the purpose. Yes, the females of this country, no matter whether children or grown up—I hardly know which is the more disgusting outrage—are beaten upon the face, arms, and bosom—beaten in your free market of labour, as you term it, like slaves. These are the instruments. [*Here the honourable member exhibited some black, heavy, leathern thongs, one of them fixed in a sort of handle, the smack of which, when struck upon the table, resounded through the House.*] They are quite equal to breaking an arm, but that the bones of the young are, as I have before said, pliant. The marks, however, of the thong are long visible, and the poor wretch is flogged before its companions—flogged, I say, like a dog, by the tyrant overlooker. We speak with execration of the cart-whip of the West Indies, but let us see this night an equal feeling rise against the factory-thong of England. Is it necessary that we should inquire, by means of a select committee, whether this practice is to be put down, and whether females in England shall be still flogged to their labour? Sir, I should wish to propose an additional clause to this bill, enacting that the overseer who dares to lay the lash on the almost naked body of the child shall be sentenced to the tread-wheel for a month, and it would be but right if the master who knowingly tolerates the infliction of this cruelty on abused infancy, this insult upon parental feeling, this disgrace upon the national character, should bear him company, though he roll to the house of correction in his chariot.

" But the entire system, as now conducted, has not merely its defenders, but its eulogists. Hence, in a celebrated *Review*, in which its rise and progress are discussed, we find this opinion delivered with the utmost confidence:— ' We scruple not to say that the health, morals, and intelligence of the population have all gained by the establishment of the present system ' That this improvement ought to have been the result, I have already said: that it will be so, I confidently hope; but it can only be the case by adopting regulations of the nature now proposed. Health, morals, and mental improvement can never consist with constant confinement and excessive labour imposed upon any class of the community, especially upon its youth. That the general intelligence, however, has increased, I fully believe; so it would have done under any system—so it has in almost every country, whether manufacturing or otherwise : and I claim this increasing intelligence in favour of the regulation which I propose, for it has declared in behalf of this measure with a force and unanimity rarely known on any other subject. But as to public morals, alas! what has been gained by this excessive slavery of the juvenile part of the manufacturing population? It is during the present century, as the article in question shows, that the system has so greatly increased. The number of criminal committals has been furnished since the year 1805; let us, then, advert to those important returns for proof upon this subject. In the metropolitan county, including London, in which, if anywhere, the number is likely to be excessive, and the increase great, the average of the first three years was 1,192, that of the three last, 3,491, nearly three-fold!   But in Lancashire (including its rural hundreds) the average of the same period had increased from 369 to 2,088, nearly six-fold!   The mean proportion of the committals of England, exclusive of these two counties, being now about 1 in 1,255—that of Lancashire as 1 in about 550 annually. Where is this to end?

" As to that species of immorality not cognizable by law, there are no means of obtaining equally precise information, otherwise I fear there would be found in this respect as little ground for exultation.   Not to mention minor offences, the practice of tippling and drunkenness has astonishingly increased, and has been accompanied by a revolting indecency not formerly known among us: women and children now publicly indulging in this vice; such are the degrading effects of this system.   The great increase of debauchery of another kind, it would be absurd to deny; I never did hear it denied, that many of the mills, at least those in which night-working is pursued, are, in this respect, *little better than brothels.* The science of human physiology has been, I may say, disgustingly advanced, having been able to demonstrate how extremely near the confines of actual childhood the human female may become an unhappy mother, from the disgraceful scenes which have occurred in some of these mills and factories. Indeed, it is in evidence, on the authority of medical men conversant with that state of society, that the period of puberty is unnaturally anticipated.   But not to dwell upon the effects of this precocity, I will proceed to consider the alleged improvement in health.   I shall determine this important point, by referring to the place selected by the strenuous advocates of the system, and its principal seat, Manchester: the surprising longevity of that town having been over and over again asserted in proof of the incalculable advantages of the factory-system, as now conducted.

" Speaking of the general health of that town, I of course refer to that of the operatives, and not to that of the higher and more opulent ranks: and, in determining this, I shall still refer to medical authority and statistical facts, and not to loose and unfounded opinions, by which the public has been too long imposed upon and misled. I take, then, a tract just published, entitled ' Remarks on the Health of English Manufacturers, and on the Need which Exists for Establishing for them Convalescent Retreats.' It is written by Mr Roberton, a gentleman well known in the medical world, and author of previous works of deserved celebrity. He rebuts Mr Senior's assumption, founded on a series of gross mistakes, as to the great improvement which has taken place in our manufacturing population, and says of these so-much-improved operatives, that ' the nature of their present employment renders existence itself in thousands of instances, in every great town, one long disease.' He states, regarding Manchester, that ' during the last year, 1830, the patients admitted at the four great dispensaries amounted to 22,626,' independently of those assisted by other charitable institutions, such as the infirmary, &c., amounting in all to at least 10,000 more. To this he adds other calculations, which brings him to the conclusion that ' not fewer, perhaps, than three-fourths of the inhabitants of Manchester annually are, or fancy they are, under the necessity of submitting to medical treatment.' He describes at some length, and with great force and feeling, the evils of the factory system, and attributes to it, to use his own words, ' the astounding inebriety' of the population, many of whom have recourse, after long and exhausting toil, to that means of kindling a temporary sense of vigour and comfort. He states the lamentable effects, in other points of view, which are thus produced, and the want of moral and mental improvement with which they are necessarily accompanied. He says, that the present manufacturing system ' has not produced a healthy population,—neither one well-instructed and provident, but one, on the contrary, where there exists always considerable, and sometimes general poverty, and an extraordinary amount of petty crime,—that, in several respects, they are in a less healthy and a worse condition than at any period within the last two centuries.'

"I will give an appalling proof of this general misery and degradation. It appears, that during the last year, there were delivered by the lying-in charity of Manchester, no less than 4,562 poor married women; far more than half, therefore, of the mothers of Manchester are assisted by public charity,— in a word, nearly three-fifths of the children of that town are branded with the stigma of pauperism at their very birth.

"If it be argued that this institution is too indiscriminate in its charity, and consequently that its operations afford no just indication of the extent of the distress actually endured, I will again quote, in reply, the authority of Mr Roberton:— 'An overwhelming majority of the persons so relieved, are in a state of incredible destitution!' I proceed to prove his assertions by still stronger facts.

"The main, and, as it has been hitherto held, triumphant defence of the present system of excessive infantile labour, has been placed upon the assumed longevity of Manchester: and had what has been asserted in this respect been true, or at all approaching to the truth, the argument would have been doubtless settled in its favour. Thus we find it stated, over and over again, that the mortality which had kept diminishing for half a century, had, in 1811, fallen as low as one in seventy-four ; and that the proportion in 1821 was still smaller. It is asserted, I see, in a petition from the mill-owners of Keighley against this bill, that this proportion is one in fifty-eight, while that of Middlesex is one in twenty-six. I am glad the opponents of the bill have given this sample of their intelligence. But to return. It has been long remarked by statistical writers, that every community to which large numbers of immigrants, principally in the active period of

life, are constantly added, will exhibit a corresponding
diminution in the proportion of deaths, without that circumstance at all proving any real increase in the general health
and longevity of the place. But the above proportions were,
nevertheless, so extravagant, and the argument founded upon
them so important, that I determined to give the subject the
most careful and impartial examination. I have done so;
and these are the results. Taking the whole parish of Manchester,—and so far, therefore, doing great injustice to my
argument, as that parish contains I think nearly thirty townships and chapelries, some of which are principally agricultural,
—but, taking the whole parish, I find that, in the collegiate
church there, and in six other churches,—in the two churches
of Salford, in those of Charlton-row, now part of the town,
and in the eleven chapelries, including the Roman Catholic
and other dissenting burial-grounds, there were interred
between the years 1821 and 1830 inclusive, 59,377 individuals. The mean population of the whole parish (*i. e.* the
geometric mean, in order to be as exact as possible) was,
during the same period, 228,951. Now, the number of
burials is defective, one church (that of Peter's) being
omitted, and I think other burial-grounds also ; but does the
number actually returned give a proportion of 1 in 74 ? or
even as the Keighley petitioners reckon, 1 in 58 ? No, Sir,
it gives a proportion of 1 in $37\frac{9}{10}$ths, as the annual mortality
of the extended district included in the entire parish of
Manchester ! In Salford the number of deaths during the
same term was 996, the mean population having been 32,421,
or 1 death in every $32\frac{1}{2}$; and this in a population, let me
again repeat, increasing immensely by immigration.

" But a further calculation has to be made before the
subject under consideration can be properly understood. A
vast excess of this mortality, we may be assured, rests upon
the poor ; for nobody disputes that the longevity of the
wealthier classes has, in the meantime, greatly improved.

Thus, in Paris, a large and unhealthy city, where the mortality, however, is, I think, less than 1 in 42, Dr Villermé found, that in the first arrondissement, where the wealthier inhabitants principally reside, only 1 in 50 died annually; while, in the twelfth, principally inhabited by the poor, the proportion was as great as 1 in 24. Apply this to the mortality of Manchester, and then let us hear what can be said respecting the longevity of the poor manufacturers of that place. It proves all that has been advanced concerning the effects of infantile and long-protracted labour, which not only enfeebles, but sweeps to their untimely fate, so vast a proportion of the population.

" But on a point of such paramount importance, and so entirely decisive of the argument, no species of evidence ought to be wanting. I have, therefore, examined the last census of Manchester with great care,—I mean that part of it in which the registered burials are given, together with the ages of the interred ; and I have compared the proportion of those buried under the age of forty, and those buried above that age, with the corresponding interments of the immensely larger cities of London and Paris, taking the last ten years in the former instance, and one intermediate year in the two latter, without any selection whatsoever: these are the results: —to every 100,000 interments in each of these places under forty, there would be above that age, in London, 63,666; in Paris, 65,109; in Manchester, 47,291 only; in other words, 16,375 fewer would have survived that period in Manchester than in London, and 17,818 fewer than in Paris. Can anything, then, be more true than the complaint of the operative spinners, that few of them survive forty ; and where is the man that dares to oppose the effectual regulation of so murderous a system ?

" In the census of 1821, the population of England was generally given according to the different ages of the people. Manchester, however, furnished no such information ; otherwise, I am persuaded another argument might have been adduced demonstrative of the same melancholy fact. But I have examined the census of the hundred of Salford and of Macclesfield, which includes the towns of Macclesfield and Stockport, containing a great number of mills, and I have compared them with other places ; and taking the number of children under five, and the numbers which arrived at the different divisions, and especially at the more advanced periods of life, I find that wherever the present system prevails, the most melancholy waste of human existence is clearly demonstrable. I may also observe, that calculating the mean duration of life from mortuary registers, it is, in the metropolis of England, about 32 years ; in Paris, 31 ; in Manchester, $24\frac{7}{10}$ years only ! In other towns, where the same system prevails, it is still less: thus, in Stockport it is 22 years only, that town not having increased by immigration quite so rapidly as Manchester. A comparison with Liverpool in this respect would be manifestly inconclusive, so large a number of the adult inhabitants of that great sea-port being constantly absent on maritime pursuits.

" Other calculations I hold in my hand, but I will not weary the House with giving them in detail. I cannot, however, refrain from presenting the results of one of· them, as it disposes of the confident assertion of the improvement of the manufacturing community. In 1780, the celebrated Dr Heysham enumerated the population of Carlisle with great care, and separated the individuals into classes according to their ages. In 1821, a similar enumeration took place. In the meantime, the great discovery of vaccination had been made,—of such immense importance in these calculations : but it will be seen that even that, and all the acknowledged improvements in medical science, fail to compensate, in the amount of human lives, for the baneful effects of our manufacturing system as at present pursued. Calculating on the first division of the population, namely, the children under five years of age, and assuming them to be 1,000, there were, in 1780, from five years old to twenty, 2,229; in 1821, 2,107; between twenty and forty, in the former period, 2,143; in the latter, 1,904; above forty, in 1780, 2,084; but, in 1821, 1,455 only!

"Again, between the years 1779 and 1787 inclusive, Dr Heysham gives the number of interments in Carlisle; they amounted to 1,840, of which 1,164 were of persons under forty years of age, and the remaining 676 above that period of life. On examining the census, I find that between the years 1821 and 1830 inclusive, there have been buried in the same place 3,025 under forty, and 1,273 above that age. In the former period, therefore, there would be to every 10,000 deaths under the age of forty, 5,808 above that age; whereas, in the latter the proportion has been 4,208 only; showing how much smaller a number survives that age than formerly. The only way to evade this conclusion, is to suppose that the population has advanced with far greater rapidity since the former period; but this supposition would imply gross ignorance of the facts. The population of Carlisle was enumerated in 1764, and it is clear that it had been increasing even more rapidly before 1780 than it has done since. But in Carlisle, as everywhere else, the greatest proportion of mortality falls upon the poor; the expectation of life, as far as regards the upper classes of society, having evidently increased. What then becomes of the statements of the great improvement among our manufacturing poor, with facts like these before our eyes?

"I could multiply these proofs of the effects of the system to a great extent; but time will not permit, nor can it be necessary. I have taken up the challenge regarding the effects of the system as now pursued, given by its eulogists, and have contested the cause of humanity—as I trust I may call it—in the very arena, and with the weapons which themselves have chosen,—the prosperity, health, and longevity of the operatives of Manchester. I have shown that the same results accompany the same system, wherever pursued, namely, — slavery, profligacy, crime, disease, and death. Transfer the system to the whole country, and then contemplate its effects ; those effects are seen rapidly developing themselves as it advances. Infantile labour leads to premature marriage, which crowds the generations upon each other, and this circumstance, together with the great discoveries in medicine, may have increased the numbers of the people ; but, as far as the system has prevailed, it has diminished the relative number of the athletic and active, and given us in their stead a weak, stunted, and degenerate race ; and thus lessened the proportion of those who have to bear the burdens and fight the battles of the country. On this latter point I am furnished with some striking facts, and among the rest, the comparative difficulty of passing recruits wherever this system prevails, but such evidence is unnecessary ; I would rather point to its more obvious and general effects. Look, then, I say, at the miserable condition of the feeble beings which are at once its instruments and its victims. Supposing that it has augmented our numbers, 'It has,' in the emphatic language of the Sacred Volume, 'multiplied the people, and not increased the joy.' I invoke, therefore, the justice, the humanity, and the patriotism, of this House : the feelings of the country are already roused. I call upon parliament to assist, by this measure, to lighten the load of an oppressed people, which bows them and their very children to the dust ;—I call upon it to snatch the scourge from the task-masters of the country, and to break the bonds of infant slavery.

"The principal features of this bill for regulating the labour of children and other young persons in mills and factories, are these :—First, to prohibit the labour of infants therein under the age of nine years ; to limit the actual work, from nine to eighteen years of age, to ten hours daily, exclusive of the time allowed for meals and refreshment, with an abatement of two hours on the Saturday, as a necessary preparation for the Sabbath; and to forbid all night-work under the age of twenty-one.

"In this bill I have omitted many important provisions which I had intended to insert, in order to obviate, if possible, multiplied objections, and to secure the attainment of its main object. Thus, I had drawn up a clause subjecting the mill-owner or occupier to a heavy fine when any serious accident occurred, in consequence of any negligence in not properly sheathing or defending the machinery. I had intended to propose a remission of an hour from each day's labour for children under fourteen, or otherwise of six hours on one day in every week, for the purpose of affording those who are thus early and unnaturally forced into the market of labour, some opportunity of receiving the rudiments of instruction and education, the expense of which, upon the modern system, would have been comparatively nothing, especially if shared between the millowner and the public. Above all, I had contemplated a clause putting down night labour altogether. None of these propositions, I think, are half so extravagant, if duly considered, as the demands now made upon infantile labour, involving, as they too often do, the sacrifice of happiness, health, improvement—nay, life itself. But not to endanger the principal object which I have in view, and regarding the present attempt as the commencement only of a series of measures in behalf of the industrious classes, all I propose to the House on the present occasion is, the remission of labour to the extent already explained.

"And, first, as to the period of life at which this bill permits children to be worked in factories—namely, nine years old. I will only observe that our ancient statutes—not always peculiarly favouring the condition of poverty—have not been neglectful of this matter. The 23rd of Edward III, if I mistake not, assumes that a male child under fourteen is *non potens in corpore;* and the same of a female child under twelve. In the 5th of Elizabeth, however, I think that period was fixed at twelve years for both sexes; previously to which they were deemed *non potentes in corpore:* and I may further observe, that another humane provision of certain of these statutes, was the hiring of these young persons by the year, so that they might not be turned adrift on every fluctuation in the demand for their labour, nor even discharged in sickness, at the pleasure or convenience of their employers. The late Sir Robert Peel's bill originally fixed upon the age of ten, which was ultimately reduced to that of nine, where the present measure leaves it. Where is the individual, if disinterested and humane, that will contend that this is not early enough for these poor creatures to commence their career of labour and sorrow? Then, as to the daily duration of their labour before they arrive at years of discretion— namely, these ten long hours, which, with the necessary intervals, stretch the term to at least twelve; is not this sufficiently severe? And at a period when the professions of humanity are so much louder than formerly—when the penal code of crime has been revised so much, and mitigated so often—that there should be no amelioration proposed in the penal code (for such I am sure I may term it) of infantile labour, seems indeed strange. The term proposed is that fixed upon by that truly benevolent and enlightened individual just alluded to. His opinion on introducing his last measure in 1815 I quote from the *Parliamentary Register* of that period:—

" 'What he (Sir Robert Peel) was disposed to recommend was, that no child should be so employed under the age of ten years, and the duration of their labour to be limited to twelve hours and a half *per diem*, including the time for recreation and meals, which would leave TEN HOURS for laborious employment.'

" I think it would be almost an insult to the House to

appeal to authorities in proof that this is labour enough for any age to endure; abundantly sufficient for infancy and youth. A few medical authorities, however, I will quote, who delivered their opinions before Sir Robert Peel's committee. Dr Jones, a physician of much experience, asserts that ' *eight* or *nine* hours are the longest period which he could sanction.' Dr Winstanley, physician of the Manchester Infirmary, affirms that ' *eleven* hours *could not be endured without injury.*' Mr Boutflower, an eminent surgeon of the same place, says that ' *ten* hours are amply sufficient.' Mr Ogle, another experienced individual of the same profession, says that ' *eight* or *nine* hours are sufficient.' Mr Simmons, the senior surgeon of the Manchester Infirmary, declares that the hours of working of a person under sixteen, exclusive of the time allowed for meals, ought not to exceed ' *nine* hours in winter, and *ten* in summer ;' and he adds that to which I particularly call the attention of the House: ' It may become a question,' says this eminent and experienced person, ' whether with impunity the *strength of adults is capable of much longer exertion than this.*' Sir Gilbert Blaine says, that under ten, he ' should have no objection to sanction *five* or *six* hours, and at a more mature age *ten* hours, if not sedentary.' I might multiply these authorities at pleasure, but I will close them with the opinion of a physician, after whom I conceive few could be quoted with advantage—I mean the late Dr Baillie. He says, beyond *ten* hours a day there ought to be *no increase* of labour. ' I think,' says he, ' *ten* hours of confinement to labour, as far as I can judge, is as much as is compatible with the perfect well-being of *any constitution.*'

" These appeals are to me most affecting. Is there not, Sir, something inexpressibly cruel,—most disgustingly selfish, in thus attempting to ascertain the utmost limits to which infant labour and fatigue may be carried, without their certainly occasioning misery and destruction;—the full extent of profitable torture that may be safely inflicted, and in appealing to learned and experienced doctors to fix the precise point beyond which it would be murder to proceed? Are we to treat innocent infants, then, like the criminal soldier, who receives his punishment under the eye of the regimental surgeon, lest he should expire beneath the lash? But, horrible to relate, these eminent men *have* stood over fainting infancy, and long since *have* forbade the infliction; yet it has been continued till thousands have expired under it. They discharged their duty; they said ten hours were fully sufficient. That term has been exceeded; and I have shown the fatal consequences.

" But if it be still necessary to sanction the term of labour they have fixed, I will appeal to general experience, which, after all, is, on a point like this, better than all authority. In every other description of labour, twelve hours a day, deducting at least the intervals which this bill also prescribes, is the utmost duration of labour that the master thinks of demanding, or the workmen of enduring. Such is the case in agriculture. Look at the county reports, and you will find that these are the utmost limits in summer, except during a few weeks in harvest, and that they are diminished in winter, so as to correspond with the days as they become shorter; averaging, perhaps, throughout the year, not more than eight or nine hours of actual work. The same rule obtains among all those workmen and artisans whose pursuits are most essential to human existence, such as masons, bricklayers, carpenters, and others. Nor is it either humane or patriotic, as an eminent medical writer has remarked, to tempt them to those protracted exertions, which are often endured at the expense of health, and bring on premature decay.

" This natural regulation prevails everywhere, and has been observed in all ages. Thus, if we open the most ancient of volumes, we shall find that twelve hours, including the necessary intervals, constitute the longest day of human labour, which is still curtailed as the natural day shortens.

And as this limitation is dictated by the law of nature, so also is it affirmed by the law of God. Hear, then, the divine institution in this matter:—' Thou shalt not oppress an hired servant that is poor and needy, whether he be of thy brethren or of the stranger that is in thy land within thy gates. At his day thou shalt give him his hire; neither shall *the sun go down* upon it; for he is poor, and setteth his heart upon it; lest he cry against thee to the Lord, and it be sin unto thee.' ' Are there not twelve hours in the day ?' is reiterated by still higher authority. ' The night cometh when no man can work.' Yet, though man cannot—will not;—yet, says this system, children SHALL. I ask, whether it be right to work weak and helpless children in England, longer than adult labourers and artizans in the prime of their days have consented to toil in any age or country.

" I make another appeal in behalf of these children. I appeal to the utmost labour imposed upon criminals and felons, sentenced to expiate their offences, often of an atrocious character, and almost always perpetrated by the daring and powerful, in the vigour of life,—in the jails, houses of correction, bridewells, or other places of confinement and punishment in this kingdom. The law, even regarding these, ' in wrath remembereth mercy,' and after the fullest investigation, doubtless lest justice should degenerate into cruelty, limits the powers of its own ministers, thus:—' Every prisoner sentenced to hard labour, shall, unless prevented by sickness, be employed so many hours a-day, NOT EXCEEDING TEN, exclusive of the time allowed for meals; as shall be directed by the rules and regulations to be made under this Act, excepting on Sundays and other holidays.' I have examined the whole of these regulations, as established in every prison in England, and I find that the average labour imposed falls far short of the limits prescribed by this bill. Even the convicts at the hulks, I am informed, are only worked in winter from eight o'clock in the morning as long as daylight lasts; and in summer, from seven in the morning till six in the evening, from which time is deducted, in both seasons, about one hour and a-half for meals ; making, therefore, the duration of their actual labour, in summer, nine hours and a-half, and in winter, perhaps, about two hours less. I ask, then, whether it is right, or even politic, thus to give a premium to crime,—to protect guilt and persecute innocence : to work unoffending children longer than the law permits in the case of adult criminals and felons, whose labour constitutes their punishment ?

"Lastly, I appeal, in behalf of these children, to the protection afforded to the slaves of our West Indian colonies. By the Orders in Council, bearing date the 2nd of November last, the labour of the slaves, in all the crown colonies of England, is regulated as follows:—By section 90 of those Orders, no slave, of whatever age, is to be worked in any agricultural or manufacturing labour in the night, but only between six o'clock in the morning and six o'clock in the evening. By section 91, all such slaves are 'entitled to an entire intermission and cessation of every description of work and labour from the hour of eight till the hour of nine in the morning, and from the hour of twelve till the hour of two in the afternoon, of each and every day throughout the year.' Hence no slave can be worked more than nine hours in any one day. So much for the adult slaves. But by the succeeding section (92) it is ordered that 'no slave under the age of fourteen, or above the age of sixty, shall be compelled or required to engage in, or perform, any agricultural work or labour, in any of the said colonies, during more than six hours in the whole, in any one day.' Passing over many other beneficent regulations, such as allowing forty holidays annually, exclusive of Sundays, and the prohibition of the labouring of pregnant females, although I see witnesses for the factory system assert, that to work white females up to the period of their confinement is not at all improper or injurious.—I say, passing over every minor consideration, I can hardly restrain my indignation within due bounds, while

I appeal to the regulations regarding these slaves, and see that those proposed in favour of British children are so vehemently opposed. I compare not the English child with the African child; but I ask this House, and his Majesty's Government, whether it would not be right and becoming to consider the English child as favourably as the African adult? You have limited the labour of the robust negro to nine hours; but when I propose that the labour of the young white slave shall not exceed ten, the proposition is deemed extravagant. I might further appeal to our treatment of the brute creation. Acts of Parliament have protected these from cruelty infinitely less than that which this system tolerates. And yet the selfishness of man acts as the guardian of his cattle, and renders such laws almost unnecessary. The gentleman will not ride his hunter before he is full grown, nor does the farmer yoke his yearling foal to the plough, and scourge it forward as many hours, and even more, than the full-grown colt could bear. No! it is the factory child alone that is thus treated. By what term shall we designate that state of the law which permits the labour of the helpless infant, hours after it would have interposed in behalf of the panting brute,—hours after the driver has released his youthful slave?

" But I contend that, even as regards the poor factory child, a being esteemed so utterly worthless, it is detrimental to the mere interests of the employer to pursue so cruel a course. Beyond certain limits, human industry and attention cannot be profitably stimulated. When those limits are passed, what remains but that imperfect service, equally distressing to the employed and unprofitable to the employer; and the oppressor may be well addressed in the words of the poet,—

'Thou canst not take what nature will not yield,
Nor reap the harvest tho' thou spoil the field.'

" This fact is already in evidence, in the sober language of prose: manufacturers have confessed, that this excessive labour has been rarely profitable, though they have been urged to such a course by the rivalry and competition which the system both creates and continues. But were it ever so profitable, no gains, however ample, no prosperity, however permanent, could justify a practice so cruel and destructive.

"I have not time to enter upon the arguments which the advocates of the present system advance in its favour, nor to refute the objections which they perpetually urge against its proper regulation. They are precisely the same as those put forth by the planters in the crown colonies, against the amelioration, to which I have already referred, of the condition of the blacks and their children. The capital engaged,—the competition to be feared,—the irritation which will be produced,—the superior condition of those to be protected, are in both cases strenuously urged. The capability of children above a certain age to endure long labour, as well as adults, is equally asserted; and, above all, the coincidence of the request from both quarters, for a select committee, is also remarkable. But how different have Government met this proposition in each case? As regards the slave, they have declared that inquiries have been pursued long enough, and that they need no further information to enable them to legislate on 'the eternal obligation which religion founds upon the law of God.' Such are the words of the noble Secretary for the Colonies. Would that this reasoning and this feeling were transferred to these poor, oppressed children, slaves in all but name, who now demand our protection! I conceive that then 'the eternal obligation which religion founds upon the law of God,' would suffice to teach us our duty, without confiding our consciences to the keeping of a select committee. We can hardly be sincere in making this solemn appeal, if after having determined that six hours' labour are enough for a negro child, we doubt whether ten are fully sufficient for a British one.

"Another objection of some of the opposing millowners

I will briefly notice. They cannot consent, forsooth, to an abridgment of the long and slavish hours of infant labour because of the corn-laws. Why, these individuals—some of them not originally, perhaps, of the most opulent class of the community—have, during the operation of these laws, rapidly amassed enormous fortunes; yet, during the whole period, they could seldom afford either to increase the wages or diminish the toil of these little labourers. to whom, however forgetful they may be of the fact, many of them owe every farthing they possess: they have generally done the reverse. And they talk of corn-laws as their apology! 'This is too bad.' Can any man be fool enough to suppose that, were the corn-laws abolished to-morrow, and every grain we consume grown and ground in foreign parts, such individuals would cease to 'grind the faces of the poor?'

" But their opposition to this measure, it seems, is grounded on philanthropic considerations alone. The loss, say they, would fall upon the poor, whose wages would be diminished just in proportion as their extravagant labour was moderated. I rather doubt this conclusion; indeed I think we are warranted, not only by the dictates of common sense, but also by the principles of political economy, in denying it altogether. Nothing can be clearer, as a general axiom, than that the wages of labour are necessarily affected by the quantity of its products in the market. Thus a great authority in that science says, 'When the demand is given, prices and values,' consequently wages, 'vary inversely as the supply.' In full conformity with this doctrine, we have constantly heard the great and frequently-recurring distresses of the operatives, in certain branches of our manufactures, attributed to *over-production*. This was asserted, again and again, by the late Mr Huskisson, and repeated, I think, on a very recent occasion by the present Vice President of the Board of Trade. How then can it be, that if over-production has the effect of lowering wages, the moderating of this over-production could have any other effect than that of raising wages; and if so, how, I would ask, can that over-production be so well moderated as by regulating the excessive labour of infant hands? If it be said in reply, that the employment of many of our mills and factories depends on a demand that is governed by foreign competition, I fearlessly reply that this is not the fact. First, as to every free market in the world, I maintain that the most formidable competition is not that between British and foreign spinners, but between rival British ones only, which, when traced to its ultimate consequences, will be too often found a competition in cruelty and oppression, of which these innocent little labourers are the victims. Then, as to other and restricted markets, and particularly those for our cotton-yarns, the competition is not, as is too often stated, between British labour and foreign labour, but between British labour and foreign imposts; which, as our goods have progressively cheapened, have, upon the protective principle, been proportionally advanced, and would be still further raised were we, under the sanction of the learned doubts already quoted, to work our unprotected children for three-and-twenty hours out of the four-and-twenty. Thus our cotton-twist is subjected to enormous duties in Russia, Austria, the United States, and elsewhere; while in France and Spain it is prohibited altogether. Now I would seriously ask those who raise this outcry regarding foreign competition, whether these heavy duties and prohibitions are not of themselves a sufficient answer to their entire argument. As to the idea of regulating the labour of our infants and children according to the fluctuations of foreign tariffs, which we may rest assured will be still fixed on the protective principle, it is as ridiculously absurd as it is infamously cruel. A very little attention, however, to this part of the argument of our opponents will show its utter fallacy. The cry concerning competition was as loudly raised against the bill of the late Sir Robert Peel as it can be against the present measure; and the ruin of the spinning trade was as confidently pronounced if it were carried. It passed, and what has been the result? Why, the export of our yarns has nearly quintupled since he brought in that bill, while the trade of our then greatest competitors in that branch of manufacture, the French, has hardly kept pace even with the slow increase of their population. But the idea of French competition in cotton-spinning is a farce; their machinery, exceedingly inferior to ours, is also dearer to at least an equal degree; which circumstances, with many other obvious disadvantages, far more than counterbalance their supposed advantages in some other respects. Still more ludicrous is the novel assumption as to the rivalry of the United States in this respect. The country beyond all others where labour is dear and land is cheap, and where the mass of the population is so thinly scattered, turning cotton-spinner to any extent is too absurd for a moment's consideration. Let our import duty on the raw material, and theirs on the spun yarn, amounting together to perhaps 40 per cent., dispose at once of this plea of tyranny and oppression.

" But the whole argument, or rather objection, as applied to many other branches of spinning, equally fails. The export of worsted yarns, for instance, is small. In silk spinning (not meaning by that term silk throwing) I believe the competition with foreigners is not felt; and yet, in many of the mills of this description, the shameful practice of working young and helpless children by night, and within an hour of the Sabbath morning, is unblushingly pursued. But I shall discuss the point no further. The same argument, I have already said, was urged against Sir Robert Peel's bill, to which he replied, that 'no foreigners were then known to work the same number of hours' even as he proposed. Nor do I believe that they then consented, if they do now, to labour their children in the heated atmosphere in which so many of ours sicken and perish. If they have commenced the practice of long hours and excessive labour, it is our competition, and not theirs, that stands chargeable

with these evils ; nor will I be too confident that our cruelty
has not been contagious. Let us, then, enter into another
competition with them — a competition of humanity and
justice, and I firmly believe that they will still be our rivals.
At all events, let us, as was strongly urged at the introduction
of the free-trade system so called, set them the example.

" In corroboration of the views I have taken, that excessive labour has a tendency the reverse of increasing its
remuneration, I might appeal to the great and constant
declension in the declared or real, as compared with the official
or assumed and stationary value, of our exported goods, of
almost every description; especially of those more particularly
alluded to.   Thus, since the peace (1815), though our exports
of cotton yarns have increased in quantity nearly five-fold,
their real value has advanced little more than one-third ; a fact
which, together with many others of a similar nature, indicates but too clearly the increasing labour and diminishing
remuneration of our industrious and over-laboured population.
But this subject would carry me into too wide a field ; and
one, moreover, on which it is unnecessary for me, on this
occasion, to expatiate.   There are few operatives of this
country, I fear, who are not made aware of this fact by the
most infallible of all teachers—bitter experience.   Those who
contend that the amount of wages follows the degree of
labour, however great or protracted, seem, in my apprehension, totally to lose sight of one of the most simple and
beautiful provisions in the economy of nature—that whereby
human wants and necessities are nicely and beneficently
balanced by the means of supplying them: but in this
striking adjustment neither infant nor excessive labour is contemplated, and where it is called forth, it will sooner or later
derange the whole frame of society.   Finally, I would ask
those who are still disposed to hold a contrary notion, and
who therefore calculate with such arithmetical precision the
exact loss that the operatives will sustain if their labour or

that of their children were to be properly regulated, whether, upon their principles, the Sabbath is not a public nuisance and private injury, especially to the labouring poor. According to their views it must certainly have the direct effect of diminishing the wages of the industrious classes just one-sixth, and of reducing their comforts therefore in the same proportion. Dr Paley has argued to the contrary, and shown, that in the present state of society the labourers of the community receive as much for their six days' toil as they would for the seven. I think he might have said more, for reasons obvious enough, but upon which I shall not now enter. He has thus demonstrated that sacred institution to be one in all respects favourable to humanity. The entire question is, I think, too plain to require this attempt at elucidation, and its final solution appears to be this:—that degree of labour will be ultimately most profitable to mankind which is dictated by their necessities, proportioned to their strength, and consistent with their welfare and happiness. In concluding these remarks, I cannot refrain from observing how uncandidly the very same set of reasoners deal on these occasions with the labouring poor. Over-production is to account for their low wages and consequent distress; diminished production, on the other hand, is to produce the very same effect, and still further lessen their means of subsistence. These arguments, or rather excuses, remind one of the poor lamb in the ancient fable, which found it impossible to satisfy the wolf, whether it drank above or below at the same stream: it was equally in fault, and suffered accordingly

" I might here notice that an entire series of advantages which would incidentally result from this measure for shortening undue labour, is overlooked by its opponents ; for instance, the giving of employment to idle hands, and the affording of additional activity to many industrious pursuits; but I shall pass these entirely by; nor shall I even insist upon the validity of the argument I have been just urging; on the contrary, admitting all that has been said as to the fall in the wages of these children and young persons, and assuming the accuracy of the computations so confidently put forth on the subject, still, I say, the question stands upon other and more sacred grounds. It is one which the public will no longer permit the interested parties to decide by mere pecuniary calculations. And were the work-people threatened (as indeed they now are) that their wages would be diminished, and their means of subsistence still more abridged ;—that severe as are their present distresses, the furnace of their affliction would be ' heated one seven times more than it is wont to be heated,'—they have taken their firm resolve: they will not bow down to the golden image,—they will not sacrifice their children to Moloch ;—and where is the father, the patriot, the Christian, that does not glory in that resolve?

" I must now apologise to this House for having so long occupied its time and attention. I owe, however, a deeper apology to those whose cause I have attempted to advocate, for having, after all, left untouched many important claims which they have earnestly pressed upon my notice. But if honourable members will consult their own bosoms, they will find them there. We are about to deal with the strongest instinct and the holiest feelings of the human heart. The happiness and tranquillity of the present generation, and the hopes of futurity, depend, in no slight degree, on our resolves. The industrious classes are looking with intense interest to the proceedings of this night, and are demanding protection for themselves and their children. Thousands of maternal bosoms are beating with the deepest anxiety for the future fate of their long-oppressed and degraded offspring. Nay, the children themselves are made aware of the importance of your present decision, and look towards this House for succour. I wish I could bring a group of these little ones to that bar,—I am sure their silent appearance would plead more forcibly in their behalf than the loudest eloquence. I shall not soon forget their affecting presence on a recent occasion, when many thousands of the people of the north were assembled in their cause,—when in the intervals of those loud and general acclamations which rent the air, while their great and unrivalled champion, Richard Oastler (whose name is now lisped by thousands of these infants, and will be transmitted to posterity with undiminished gratitude and affection);—when this friend of the factory children was pleading their cause as he alone can plead it, the repeated cheers of a number of shrill voices were heard, which sounded like echoes to our own ; and on looking around, we saw several groups of little children, amidst the crowd, who raised their voices in the fervour of hope and exultation, while they heard their sufferings commiserated, and, as they believed, about to be redressed. Sir, I still hope, as I did then, that their righteous cause will prevail. But I have seen enough to mingle apprehension with my hopes. I perceive the rich and the powerful once more leaguing against them, and wielding that wealth which these children, or such as they, have created, against their cause. I have long seen the mighty efforts that are made to keep them in bondage, and have been deeply affected at their continued success ; so that I can hardly refrain from exclaiming with one of old, ' I returned, and considered all the oppressions that are done under the sun, and beheld the tears of such as were oppressed, and on the side of the oppressors there was power, but they had no comforter !'

" I trust, however, that this House, whose peculiar duty it is to defend the weak and redress the injured, will interpose and extend that protection to these defenceless childen, which is equally demanded by the principles of justice, mercy, and policy. Many have been the struggles made in their behalf, but hitherto they have been defeated ; the laws passed for their protection have been avowedly and shamefully evaded, and have therefore had little practical effect but to legalize cruelty and suffering. Hence at this

late hour, while I am thus feebly, but earnestly, pleading
the cause of these oppressed children, what numbers of them
are still tethered to their toil, confined in heated rooms, bathed
in perspiration, stunned with the roar of revolving wheels,
poisoned with the noxious effluvia of grease and gas, till, at
last, weary and exhausted, they turn out, almost naked, into
the inclement air, and creep, shivering, to beds, from which a
relay of their young work-fellows have just risen. Such, at
the best, is the fate of many of them, while, in numerous
instances, they are diseased, stunted, crippled, depraved, and
destroyed. Sir, let that pestilence, which no longer walketh
in darkness among us, but destroyeth at noon-day, once seize
upon our manufacturing population, and dreadful will be the
consequences. A national fast has been appointed on this
solemn occasion; and it is well:—let it be one which the Deity
himself has chosen,—let us undo the heavy burdens, and let
the oppressed go free.

" Sir, I have shown the suffering,—the crime,—the mortality, attendant upon this system ;—consequences which, I
trust, parliament will at length arrest. Earnestly do I wish
that I could have prevailed upon this House and his Majesty's
government to adopt the proposed measure, without the delay
which will attend a further and, as I shall ever maintain, an
unnecessary inquiry. Would that we might have come to a
resolution as to the hours that innocent and helpless children
are henceforth to be worked in these pursuits, so as to render
the preservation of their health and life probable, and the due
improvement of their minds and morals possible ! Would
that we had at once decided, as we could wish others to
decide regarding our own children, under like circumstances, or
as we shall wish that we had done, when the Universal Parent
shall call us to a strict account for our conduct to one of the
least of these little ones ! As the case, however, is otherwise,—as we are, it seems, still to inquire and delay, I will
now move the second reading of the bill ; and afterwards

propose such a committee as, I hope, will assist in carrying into effect the principle of a measure so important to the prosperity, character, and happiness of the British people."

The opposition to Mr Sadler's measure was such as to force him, though with great unwillingness, to agree to the appointment of a parliamentary committee, a source of great but, under the circumstances, unavoidable delay. This inquiry caused Mr Sadler great anxiety and labour. It was urged in reply, that Mr Sadler's statements were exaggerated, that the health and morals of young persons, and others engaged in factory labour, were satisfactory, that the manufacturers would, before a committee, entirely rebut the facts stated in Mr Sadler's speech, that legislation would prove injurious to the interests of the children, that the honourable member was a mistaken, though well-intentioned friend of the working classes. The general feeling of the House of Commons was favourable to inquiry, but opposed to immediate legislation. The Chancellor of the Exchequer (Lord Althorp), on behalf of the ministry, charged Mr Sadler with having stated only one side of the question, condemned the measure as hasty and ill-advised, admitted that some regulation was required to prevent cases of extreme hardship and oppression, and recommended " that the House should proceed in this matter with the utmost caution." The Chancellor of the Exchequer concluded his speech in the following words, which convey a sense of the position of the question, and the feeling of the majority of the House of Commons thereon: "I am not prepared to pledge myself in any way with respect to the measure. Even if the committee should report favourably of the bill, I will not pledge myself before the report be made to support a measure of such vast importance. I do not feel justified in saying, that whatever the opinion of the committee may be, I will abide by their decision. The honourable gentleman (Mr Sadler) has, I think, done perfectly right in referring this measure to a select committee.

Although he seems to think that a more public investigation would be desirable, I am inclined to believe that the examination of a select committee is more likely to elicit the truth than an examination at the bar of this House. I hope that, by the exertions of the committee, the whole question will be fairly brought under the consideration of the House."

The bill was read a second time, and, on the motion of Mr Sadler, was ordered to be committed to the following members:—Mr Sadler, Lord Viscount Morpeth, Mr Strickland, Mr Heywood, Mr Wilbraham, Mr George Vernon, Mr Benett, Sir Henry Bunbury, Mr Poulet Thomson, Mr Dixon, Sir John Cam Hobhouse, Mr Horatio Ross, Mr Robinson, Mr Meynell, Mr Percival, Mr Boldero, Lord Nugent, Mr Shiel, Sir George Rose, Mr Attwood, Mr Ridley Colborne, Mr Kenyon, Mr Fowell Buxton, Mr Estcourt (Oxford), Mr John Smith, Mr John Weyland, Lord Viscount Lowther, Mr Hope, Mr Moreton, Mr Lennard. To which were afterwards added the names of Mr Bainbridge, Sir Robert Peel, Bart., Mr Gisborne, Lord Viscount Sandon, Sir Robert Harry Inglis, Bart., Sir Henry Willoughby, Bart., and Mr Mackinnon.

CHAPTER X.

MERCY A LEADING FEATURE IN FACTORY AGITATION—PUBLIC MEETINGS
IN YORKSHIRE—COUNTY MEETING AT YORK—PROCESSION AND
PUBLIC ENTRY OF MR SADLER AND MR OASTLER INTO MANCHESTER.

NOTWITHSTANDING all the denunciations which have been
uttered against unjust gains, they have found many admirers;
but few have stopped to inquire the cost—to sum up how
many have been made wretched that one may live in a large
mansion and fare sumptuously every day. The sympathy of
the multitude with an emperor on a barren rock, is creditable
to them: it speaks of their perception of the vicissitudes of
life; misfortune has won upon their natures, and they would
compassionately relieve the oppressed; they would forgive his
crimes, because of pity for his fate. Who would dare to
blame them; who to regret the exercise of their mercy?
Better that they should be moved to tears for one, than that
their souls should become parched, and their hearts never
know the sense of sympathy. "The quality of mercy is
not strained; it droppeth as the gentle rain from Heaven
upon the place beneath. It is twice blessed: it blesseth him
that gives, and him that takes." Mercy is in its quality the
same to the ore as to the many; to fallen greatness as to
subdued lowliness; but, like " the gentle rain from Heaven,"
its usefulness must be measured by the extent of ground on
which it drops, and its blessings by the wants of the earth.
It is a feature of modern civilization that it begets within

its heart a numerous body of human beings, endowed with every natural capacity for mental and physical enjoyments, but who have throughout life no mental enjoyments, and whose animal existence is a daily returning round of physical suffering, and for whom society has no sympathy. The life of such has only a relief in sleep, and a glimmering hope in death. These unfortunate human beings are not reached by any of the pompous philanthropies, which manifest their existence in outward and visible signs, having engraven on their fronts names and dates, which, on behalf of the donors, sometimes seem to say, " pause, stranger, pause—admire my generous goodness; see what a pattern I am of what you should be." These observations may be, to men of naturally weak morality, unpleasant—men too who pride themselves upon the exact-ness of their views, and measure their "donations" by the figures in the subscription list of their rivals in the social scale; as the phrase has it, " respectable men," who look for a defence of all the suffering of the unfortunate in denunciations of their improvidence, and justify these by a list of the *liberal* institutions to which those self-satisfied eulogists have subscribed, without their having asked themselves whether the means to enjoy these institutions are within the reach of the majority of those for whom they are avowedly intended, or asked " What is the balance between my own efforts to relieve the wretched and the results of the practices which sustain me, in causing poverty, suffering, and crime? " Such home questionings might disturb the serenity of some who move through their duties with a mechanical regularity, enlivened with occasional manifestations of zeal for what they modestly designate " enlightened views and a liberal policy," sometimes, nay frequently, ending in social darkness and positive punishment to the majority of those whose misfortunes deserve relief, and their failings pity. It is within the moral ability of but few men to feel for misery—they have not themselves suffered—and extend mercy to those whose misfortunes have been uniform and constant, and who consequently have not experienced the momentous changes which startle the beholder, and force the most careless to gaze on the illustrious victims of misfortune in wonder mellowed with pity. Mercy for the lowly is the spring rain of Heaven ; the agitation of the elements is sometimes necessary to prepare for its reception, to render its droppings fertilizing and the earth fruitful.

There are but few who dare to refuse a nominal acknowledgment of the blessings of mercy, or of advantages arising from the practice of moral virtues, but there is unfortunately a kind of implied contract among men, that they shall not be called upon to perform moral duties when the exercise of these would interfere with the acquisition of riches. There is consequently practised a general toleration of positive evil, under the pretext of what is designated " aknowledge of the world:" it is sceptical of the sincerity of every act which is not a source of personal gain; it considers the expression of generous sentiment as at best " an amiable weakness;" it sneers at enthusiasm for good, and esteems self-sacrifice as akin to madness; all its maxims and its practices are opposed to the exercise of virtue for its own sake; all unite to harden the heart and cause the understanding to prefer property to truth, profit to justice, and selfishness to charity. So systematic is this conventional hypocrisy, that weak men, of even good intentions, are afraid to condemn it in tones louder than a confidential whisper: it is only the few whose keen sensibilities have been too strong to be subdued by the force of example; these draw their conclusions from their own experience, become laden with a sense of the duties due from themselves to others; they yield to the irresistible impulses of their sensitive natures, and, at all risks, break through the trammels of social usages, and boldly proclaim to the world the faith that is within them. It is to the courage and indomitable spirit of a few such men that England is indebted for the Ten Hours' Bill movement of 1831 and 1832,—a movement in its origin and objects allied to mercy and consistent with justice.

The agitation for shortening the hours of labour in factories was renewed in the West Riding of the county of York in a period of extraordinary political excitement. The mind of the country was then firmly resolved to obtain a reform in parliament; the House of Lords, with the late Duke of Wellington at their head, seemed resolved to oppose the Reform Bill. From London to the most remote village of the three kingdoms there were political clubs. Birmingham and Nottingham threatened; the press teemed with inflammatory speeches, letters, and *leaders*. It is a feature of every such crisis not only to absorb public sympathy, but to put down all efforts intended to establish other movements. Meetings for the Ten Hours' Bill were held in rapid succession at Heckmondwike, Bradford, Huddersfield, Dewsbury, Keighley, Halifax, Leeds, Holmfirth, and many other places, and lastly at York. These meetings were numerously attended, presided over by the regularly-constituted authorities—the mayor of Leeds, the high sheriff of the county of York; in all cases by the principal local authority. At these meetings, when the then popular cry of "Reform" was raised, the response, spoken in a manner not to be misunderstood, was :—" We are here about this question of Ten Hours' labour, and will not allow it to be mixed up with any other." The opponents of factory regulation made many efforts to drown the cry of "Ten Hours a day," with the popular shouts of " Reform," " No Corn laws." These efforts signally failed, a circumstance which proves how thoroughly the desire for restricting the hours of factory labour had seated itself in the minds of the operative classes, and how resolutely resolved they were to succeed in accomplishing their object. As the movement continued, it gradually acquired importance. At the Bradford meeting, held on December 27th, 1831, the Rev. G. S. Bull, a clergyman who to the Church of England has been a support and an ornament, joined the Ten Hours' Bill cause; then followed, at the same meeting, the adhesion of Mr Rand, an extensive millowner.

Within a brief period afterwards, the Ten Hours' Bill movement ranked amongst its foremost supporters the names of Oastler, Sadler, Col. Murgatroyd, Tempest, Wood, Bull, Pollard, Ferrand, Fielden, Rand, Condy, Fletcher, Smith, Thackerah, Hanson, Perring, Foster, Schofield, Capt. Wood, Stocks, Halliley, Kay, Pitkethly, Leach, Hall, Osborne, Cook, Tweedale, Richardson, Albutt, and many others. These names represented much talent and experience. Messrs Wood, Rand, and Fielden (head of the firm of Fielden and Brothers) were influential and successful mill-owners; Mr Condy, a literary barrister of high reputation; Mr Fletcher, an eminent surgeon in Bury, Lancashire; Mr C. Turner Thackerah, and Mr Samuel Smith, of Leeds, medical men uniting in a high degree observation, experience, and science; Mr Bull, a popular and honoured Church parson; Messrs Perring and Foster, editors of newspapers; Mr John Hanson, one of the most intelligent and able working men of Huddersfield. These "leaders" were supported by committees, consisting of the principal operatives of their districts; they were supported by the body of the beneficed clergy, by ministers of various other religious denominations, most of the respectable medical practitioners, and other influential gentlemen. All efforts at out-of-doors opposition were fruitless.

It is interesting and instructive to observe how the evils of the factory system had become apparent to the minds of the thoughtful among the various classes. By way of example, at the Leeds meeting, Mr John Marshall, jun., of the firm of

Marshall and Co., argued against parliamentary interference as a general principle, but considered that the legislature ought to protect the health of children. Mr Marshall said :

"I must confess that I cannot admit that the children in our manufactory are suffering materially in their health from the hours which we work at present." Mr Samuel Smith answered : "Gentlemen—As one of the surgeons of the Infirmary of this town, I have had extensive opportunities of witnessing the baneful effects produced upon the health and limbs of children by too long work, and too short intervals for rest and relaxation. I have seen limbs which have been beautifully formed, in a short time, from the operation of these causes, reduced to the lowest state of deformity; and individuals who, but for these causes, would have been models of beauty and manhood, doomed to remain through life deformed dwarfs. It is now about twelve years since my attention was first directed to this subject, in consequence of seeing an unusual number of cases of deformity of the lower extremities, sent (to the Leeds Infirmary) from a neighbouring manufacturing town (Bradford). The surprise, however, at this circumstance ceased, when it was ascertained that at that period the children were worked much longer hours in the factories of that town than in this.

"The supports for bent bones, from those causes, soon after this period, became an item of such importance in the yearly expenses of the institution, that the weekly board very properly thought it their duty to pass a resolution, taking from the surgeon the power of ordering machines costing beyond a certain sum, without first obtaining the consent of the board, and we have now frequently to compound the matter, by getting the parish from which the poor patient comes to pay one-half the expense and the Infirmary the other. Mr Marshall has stated to you that he is not aware the children in his factory suffer in their health, in consequence of the length of time they worked. I give Mr Marshall credit for being sincere in this expression. I sincerely believe that he is not aware of it, but every one to his own business—*I am aware of it*, and, accordingly, I may state, that the very last case of the kind I have alluded to which I have investigated was from that gentleman's factory. It was only on Friday afternoon last that a beautiful girl, of fifteen years of age, presented herself at my table at the Infirmary, being my admission week; she had a recommendation, signed 'Marshall and Co.' Her spine was bent into the form of the letter S. As I always wish to investigate the causes of disease, in order that I may be the better able to effect a cure, I ascertained that she had been several years at Mr Marshall's factory, that she had been worked fourteen hours a day, with what intervals do you think for rest and refreshment?—why, ten minutes for drinking, fifteen minutes for breakfast, and forty minutes for dinner. This poor girl, but for these causes, would have been as handsome a woman as there is in the town of Leeds ; she must, however, now remain deformed for life. She may be seen by any one; and I hesitate not to say that it was by these causes that the deformity was produced, and I believe that the persons under whom she has worked are aware of it. I understand she was a *line-spreader* ; I do not know the nature of it—but I believe it is an occupation in which only one hand is used. I find that a short time ago her occupation was changed.

" The number and the serious nature of the machinery accidents admitted into the Infirmary is quite frightful to contemplate. I feel confident the proportion of these accidents will be materially diminished by the Ten Hours' Bill, not in the proportion of the one, two, or three hours, which may be deducted from the hours of labour, but in a much larger proportion; for I have long entertained a suspicion that many of these poor children get their fingers and hands involved in the machinery while in that state of listlessness and apathy, produced by fatigue. I have it in confession from an over-looker, that it is often necessary, towards the latter part of the day, to shake poor factory-children by the shoulders to keep them awake while standing at their work. Is it proper—is it right, that poor children who, even when standing upon their legs, cannot keep their eyes open, should be placed almost in immediate contact with all kinds of dreadful machinery, with cog wheels, and things which are emphatically called ' devils !' ? "

At the Bradford meeting (Dec. 27, 1831), the Rev. George Stringer Bull stated briefly the circumstances which induced him, in his capacity of a Christian clergyman, to take an inte-rest in the factory question. Medical men, as represented by Mr Smith, of Leeds, were influenced by their experience of the effects of the factory system on the body ; ministers of the Gospel, as represented by the Rev. G. S. Bull, were influ-enced by their sense of the effects of the factory system on mind and morals. Mr Bull, addressing the Bradford meeting, said : "As I entered this room I heard a person ask, ' What have the parsons to do with it ? ' Mr Chairman, the parsons have a great deal to do with it ; and I conceive that a most fearful responsibility rests upon those ministers of the Gospel who fail to oppose all the influence they possess against anything which tends to prevent the moral improvement and religious advancement of the people. I have not been invited to take part in the proceedings of this day, but I did not need any invitation. As an inhabitant of the neighbourhood, I claim my right to deliver my sentiments upon this subject. Since I have dwelt in this part of the country, I have been frequently struck with the evils of this system. I have noticed the many obstacles in the way of the moral and religious improvement of young persons, and the consequent moral evil entailed upon them when they become parents and heads of families, and their children after them, has caused me to experience pain every day of my life. Now, sir, I happen to be connected with about five hundred Sunday scholars in our district, and I assure you I feel my very heart smart within me when I am scolding these poor little children for coming too late to school, and consider the amount of labour exacted from them during the week. It is not at all extraordinary that they should take an extra nap on Sunday morning, when they have been compelled to get up at five o'clock, and sometimes earlier, on the other days of the week ; and though I have felt it a matter of duty to scold them for coming late to school, I have thought within myself that somebody else was to blame besides them. And if, after they have been stoved up during the week, we stove them up in the Sunday schools, where are they to get a breath of fresh air, or anything that will administer to health ? They cannot find it in the mills, nor when they have been to their work in the morning; they cannot find it when returning home at night, after a fatiguing day's labour, exposed to rain and the inclemency of the weather. It is impossible they can find it in the mills six days in the week, nor on the seventh in our Sunday schools, for, you know, our school-rooms are crowded to excess. Then, where are they to get a single draught of health, and where are they to obtain anything like moral improvement ? It is said that some of the most strenuous supporters of Sunday schools are to be found amongst those who employ the children. I acknowledge that it is so ; but I would ask those gentlemen, what can we do for the instruction of these children on the Lord's day ?— that is, perhaps, two or three hours, for by the time the names are called over, the absentees inquired after, and the other little matters arranged, pray what time is left to teach them

A B C? Besides, what business have you to teach them A B C on Sundays? They ought to learn that on the week days, and a great deal more besides, and be exercised in purely religious instruction on Sundays. I consider it a sort of desecration of the Lord's day; and that it is not warranted without the most rigorous necessity. I trust we shall give impartial attention to the arguments which may be advanced to-day, and not suffer our feelings to warp our judgment in any part of this discussion. With regard to the gentlemen who are exerting themselves in promoting the emancipation of these poor children—of Mr Sadler I can say, and I am most conscientiously speaking when I state that in all our private communications this has been the subject, ever since I knew him in 1823, that has laid nearest his heart. The first time I ever saw him was in Hull : we happened to talk upon Sunday schools, and he called my attention to the very system we are now met to consider, and he denounced it with all those feelings which a man of humanity and consideration would do. I do declare, without any reference to political partialities, but most conscientiously, and upon the word of a Christian, that I believe the poor of this country have not a more firm and unflinching friend than Michael Thomas Sadler." The interest which working men felt in the question, and the importance of the facts they stated, may be judged by the following observations spoken at the Huddersfield meeting (Dec. 26, 1831), Mr George Beaumont said: "Mr Chairman, I should wish to make one or two observations. I went into a factory at seven years of age, and worked till I was fourteen, and I worked from six in the morning till eight in the evening, with only forty minutes' intermission. I had my meals brought into the work-room, and after biting once I followed my work at the machine, but before I could bite again I had to pick the lint off. And what has been the result? Look at me now: (*Mr Beaumont alluded to his diminutive stature.*) At that manufactory it was usual to keep a tally in the rooms, so that if there were two hundred persons in one apartment, only one person was allowed to go out at a time. But these are only part of the evils which these little sufferers have to endure. Look at the time they have to go to the mills, and the risks they have to brave. I have assisted in carrying a little sister, not six years old, to the mill, at six o'clock in the morning, through frost and snow ; and I have seen an instance of a boy, who had not been a quarter of an hour in the mill, being caught by a strap, dragged into the machinery, and his head severed from his body. I say, further, that those who advocate the abolition of colonial slavery ought not to be considered as sincere unless they advocate the extinction of slavery in factories. If ten hours a day be the utmost extent allowed by law for culprits or transports to labour, should children be worked fourteen or sixteen hours a day, merely because their parents are poor ? A factory in this town, last week, worked from six in the morning to nine at night, with only an hour for meals."

The Yorkshire meetings were addressed at great length by Mr Oastler. At Huddersfield (Dec. 26, 1831), he spoke as follows :—

" Gentlemen, you shall have no party politics from me, 'but ten hours for five days and eight for Saturdays.' I feel most happy to meet you upon that question, and upon that question I shall always be ready to join you with heart and hand. If we differ about other things, let us take care that we do not lose *that point ;* let it be our care to relieve our children from the slavery under which they now labour, and can scarcely be said to exist. Let no feelings of animosity, as politicians, ever interfere in that question ; but let us be resolved, as tories, as radicals, as whigs, to join hand and heart till British infants are free. I beg leave to congratulate you, Mr Chairman, upon your having been the first proper officer of his Majesty to constitute a regularly-organised meeting for considering the propriety of making infants free, and I feel happy that I have lived to take part in such a meeting as this, and I rejoice exceedingly that the silvery notes of a Minister of the Gospel have been heard amongst us; having been born, as my friend Mr Baines has told you, of a very benevolent parent, and having been for many years in the habit of attending and supporting benevolent institutions. I have been an old soldier in the cause of negro emancipation, although, since I began to write and talk against 'Yorkshire Slavery,' my enemies, or rather the enemies of the children, have had the audacity to say that I did it for the purpose of withdrawing the attention of Englishmen from negro thraldom. I will yield to no man in hatred of slavery. When I was a youth, and when the name of Wilberforce was hissed at for political purposes, though only in my teens, I undertook a paper war for him, and fought as manfully against his opponents as I now fight against the opponents of the freedom of infants. Some persons have said to me, 'What business is it of yours? What have you to do with factories? You have got a good place up at Fixby, yonder; *you* are right, be thankful.' My answer was this, ' I am one of the human race; and I see these infants in misery, and so long as I live will I exert my powers to relieve them from their bondage.' Yes, yes, I know that the God who made me, never made a human being to be miserable; I know that it is the design of the Divine Being that all the sons and daughters of Adam should be happy. Do I then say that there should be no grades in society; that there are not to be servants and masters? No; but I do say that servitude and labour ought not to be oppressive. I know from my own experience, for I am but a servant, that I have as much pleasure in serving my master, as my master can have in receiving my services. No master has a right to demand the services of any human being unless the reward of those services will be a comfortable living, and that is, I verily believe, all the working classes want. But I have been charged with being an enemy to the factory-masters. Those who have said so do not know me; nor do they know the factory-masters. Let me set you right upon that point; I know more about it than you do, but I will tell you nothing but truth. I hold in my hand some letters from factory-masters, not many miles distant from my own house, and I will read them to you in order that I may set the question right between yourselves and your employers. That man, in my opinion, does the poor most good who corrects them if mistaken with regard to the character of those who employ them. Providence has placed me in a situation between the infants and their masters, and that very position has made me the medium of their information: I have in my hand a letter from one of the principal millowners in the West Riding of the County of York, and he is a Radical. He says, 'I admire, exceedingly, your labours to effect an amelioration in the condition of children employed in factories; you have my hearty good wishes for your success, but you have a mass of stupidity to struggle with. I wish the humanity of some of the friends of liberal measures were not so diffusive, nor of so itinerant a character, that it might become a little more localised, and that it might be allowed to visit our *own neighbourhood.*' So says the Radical. I will give you a short but comprehensive extract of a letter from another large factory-holder, who is a Whig, for I have them from all sorts. He says, ' How can I assist you in the cause of the factory children? You may command my best energies.' Now, there's for you! What could he say more? Well done Mr Whig millowner. I have not done yet, gentlemen. I hold in my hand a communication from a Tory millowner. He thus concludes his letter, in which he has authorised me to give money to committees in case they cannot raise sufficient themselves. I have not yet had occasion to give any; though I lent some the other day, but they would not keep it, because they said they could get enough in their own town, and would repay me. But what says the Tory gentleman? You shall hear; ' Let us all pray, as with one mind, to God, that he may be pleased to bless us by allowing us to have the wish of our hearts gratified.' This is in one letter, and he concludes another in a somewhat similar manner—' And with my sincere prayer that we may be the honoured instruments in the hands of God to diminish this worst of all slavery, I am, &c.' Now these are letters I have received from three of the most respectable and three of the largest millowners in the West Riding of Yorkshire, radical, whig, and tory though they be. Believe it not, then, that Richard Oastler is an enemy to the factory-masters, for they it is that are enabling him to stand against all the rebuffs and abuse of his opponents. And I will tell you more—I was supported by these three men before I knew that a single operative had taken the field. Let it then be understood that the cause stands better than it did. They are not all against you. I said at Leeds, and I believed it, and I believe it now, that three-fourths of the manufacturers of the West Riding of the County of York are with me upon this question. But it is stated in a Saturday paper that that is not credited. Be it so. What will it prove? That ' the greatest enemy the factory-masters are said to have' has too good an opinion of them. I firmly believe I am correct, though I know that in certain quarters great efforts are making to destroy the effect. I should now like to talk to you a little about the factory system; I have said enough about myself. It was a factory-master that first called my attention to it. I had often heard of the evils in factories, but I take shame to myself that I did not examine into them sooner; it was a factory-master who asked me to come forward because I had a bold heart and feared nobody. I gave him my word that I would not rest till I had conquered, or sunk into my grave; and I never will. Gentlemen, I am old enough to remember that there were thousands of respectable domestic manufacturers worth their 50*l.*, or 100*l.*, or 200*l.*, who were able to make their cloth at home and go to sell it in the market; but they are now reduced almost to pauperism, or to the class of common labourers. They were the best masters the workmen ever had—these were the strongest bulwarks of the state—but they are now mixed amongst the paupers and labourers in one common mass. I remember the time when there were happy companies upon the village green, as blithesome and as gay as lambs, and I have gambolled with them—but they are now all gone and disappeared; we see nothing of the sort now! We scarcely see the complexion of a boy or girl in a country place, but they are black, blue, or brown. I remember the time when it was not so, but now they are locked up the live-long day in a loathsome factory; and when I know that the Almighty Creator of the Universe never intended them to be sent there, I feel that I am doing the work of God when I require the doors to be opened, and that these little ones should once more see the rising and setting of the sun. It is, in my opinion, the factory system which has caused a great deal of the distress at the present time—a great deal of the immorality at the present time—a great deal of the weakness of men's constitutions at the present time. It is, then, against that baneful system I have lifted up my arm, and I ask you, not to help me to pull it down, but to correct its errors, and to keep it from falling. When I contemplate the life of a factory-child, my heart is filled with horror to think that human nature is so corrupt that any individual, calling himself a man, would live a day under that load of guilt which he ought to feel as a man who is causing such dreadful misery. Take a little child, for it is in units we must deal; the whole mass of factory woes would cloud your understandings and make you like myself, as I have by my opponents been described—'mad.' Take, then, a little captive, and I will not picture 'fiction' to you, but I will tell you what I have seen. Take a little female captive, six or seven years old; she shall rise from her bed at four in the morning of a cold winter's day; but before she rises she wakes perhaps half-a dozen times, and says, 'Father is it time? Father is it time?' And at last when she gets up she feels about in the dark for her clothes, and puts her little bits of rags upon her weary limbs—weary with the last day's work ; she leaves her parents in their bed, their labour (if they have any) is not required so early; she trudges onward all alone through rain and snow, and mire and darkness, to the mill, perhaps two miles, or at least one mile; and there for thirteen, fourteen, fifteen, sixteen, seventeen, or even eighteen hours is she obliged to work, with only thirty minutes interval for meals and play ! ! Homewards again at night she would go, all in the dark and wet, when she was able, but many a time she hid herself in the wool in the mill, as she had not strength to go. The girl I am speaking of died; but she dragged on that dreadful existence for several years. But this is not an isolated case. I wish it were. I could not bring you hundreds of such cases exactly, because I have mentioned eighteen hours, but if I had said sixteen hours, I could have brought hundreds. And if the little dear were one moment behind the appointed time; if ' the Bell ' had ceased to ring when she arrived, with trembling, shivering, weary limbs, at the factory door, there stood a monster in human form before her, and as she passed he lashed her ! ! (*Here Mr Oastler struck the front of the platform with a long heavy strap.*) This (holding up the ' strap ') is no '*fiction.*' It was hard at work in this town last week, and I have seen the effects of such instruments in black marks from the neck to the seat of children. This system ought to be exposed, to be corrected. What I am going to tell you is a fact, and it was committed in Christendom. A little boy ran away, for about three-quarters of an hour, out of a factory, and when he returned he was taken into a room by the overlooker, a quantity of tow was tied over his mouth, and he was stripped and flogged with a hazel stick till every bit of the skin was flayed off from the back of his head to the bottom of his back, and so tight had the tow been tied round his head, the black marks occasioned thereby remained many days. For weeks the poor sufferer was unable to go to his work. Had he been my child he should have gone to his grave rather than to such a place of torture. This was not done in the West Indies, neither was it done in this immediate neighbourhood; this horrifying case of cruelty occurred, however, not very many miles from this place. And should I be called ' mad' because I endeavoured to expose this system? I think there are many men more mad than I am who have not joined hand and heart in the cause years and years ago. I am glad, however, that we have got a public meeting on the subject; I am glad we have got friend Booth (the chairman) to lead the van. I trust we shall crush the anti-christian, anti-social system, and that children will be allowed to leave their work when they have been employed ten hours. It was my intention to have adverted to the general effects of this system, but that has been done already. Allow me, however, to occupy your time a few moments while I take notice of the remarks in last Saturday's paper respecting the working of children eleven hours a day. The question now occupies a very different position from what it did when Sir John Hobhouse's bill was introduced. Then the workmen asked for a limitation to twelve hours a day, and a great many persons opposed it, and now you have found many of them are opposed to a ten hours' bill. And how? By proposing one for eleven hours! I want you to be careful on this point, for I am positively sure that an eleven hours' bill means *no bill at all.* They tell you that if you get a ten hours' bill you will petition for it to be done away with next year. They say also that you will have lower wages. I do not think they know what you will have; it is speculation; but I will tell you

I think you will have better wages, and I think the manufacturers will have better profits, and the shopkeepers better customers, and all will go on well. The reason why I think you will have better wages is, the market of labour will be more circumscribed, and therefore you will have it more within your own power. Now, the labour of children is co-extensive with your own, it may be demanded for the whole twenty-four hours; but if it were less, you would both get better wages; and a manufacturer told me, for I have it all from them, that they will get a better profit out of your better wages, and when you get more money, you will be better customers to the shopkeeper. I am absolutely shocked that Christians who are very anxious to do away with slavery in the West Indies can endeavour to bribe the worst feelings in parents to sell the labour of children for a shilling a week extra, and to lend their support to an eleven hours' bill. What is the most debasing principle of human nature, nurtured by 'African Slavery?' That a parent is so dreadfully demoralized as to sell his child for gold!! Yes, this is the most hateful part of that most hateful system! And I remember to have seen those very persons hold up to execration an African father or mother, because they would sell their child, who are now asking you to do what is the very same in principle, namely, to consign your child to excessive labour, under the idea of receiving more money for the same. It is the system of slavery in factories which destroys all parental feeling, and they think that it has gone on so far that you are now so unfeeling as to support the cruel oppression of your children from the hope of receiving more wages; but I hope that you will tell them, if your children do run the risk of getting less wages, they shall not any longer be slaves. It now becomes my duty to beg for these poor slaves. You know these things can't be done without money. I have spent a little; but we think the people of Huddersfield would like to put their mites into this Gospel Treasury of our Lord. It is the intention of the Committee to go round from house to house, to collect subscriptions to support a delegate to London, in order that the poor children may not be trampled on by forty delegates from other places. Let me remind every person who may be afraid that other institutions will suffer from this, that the tree of benevolence has taken deep root and is widely spreading ; water it well then at the roots, and it will still spread more luxuriantly, until it cover the whole earth. If the factory system were corrected and its mischiefs curtailed, I believe that England would outstrip all her former doings, and become the guardian angel of the world— which, that she may be, is my most earnest wish and desire."

Mr Oastler's speech at Huddersfield possesses a historical and social interest ; he described what he himself had seen of the social condition of the manufacturing population of Yorkshire before the introduction of the centralised, unregulated factory system. The annexed extract will, however, better enable the reader to judge of the force of the words which, when spoken in the ears of Englishmen, aroused them to a sense of their wrongs and duties :—

Mr Oastler, while addressing a crowded meeting at Keighley (Jan. 30th, 1832), said :

" What ! shall that being which nature in its infancy has made perfectly helpless, with all its sinews and fibres as weak as possible, shall that being be compelled by the hand of avarice, and the hand of tyranny, to be worked to death before it arrives at maturity, although we farmers, for our own sakes, take care of our horses when young in order that we may work them to our profit when they are old ? What ! shall those individuals who entertain the horrid Malthusian doctrine, and suppose that the Creator sends beings into the world without being able to provide food for them, shall they lay their savage paws upon them and work them to death, calling them redundant and superfluous ? In the name of Christianity, in the name of Britain, I say ' No,' and I hope that very shortly we shall hear the same negative responded from St Stephen's. Yes, I have no doubt when our legislators are informed of the actual evils which exist, when they perceive how the factory system demoralises and debases society, notwithstanding that an interested faction may go up to London to oppose us, our legislators will assert that it ought no longer to be tolerated, and declare that the children shall hereafter be protected by the law of the land, and that they shall be sealed from slavery by the seal of the King of England. But supposing, gentlemen, that their health were not injured, are they brutes ? No, no. If they had been whelped by the lioness, no man dare have seized them to oppress them. She would have risen in all her mighty power and bade defiance to the oppressor of her young. And think you not that English Christian mothers feel as fondly for their young as the lioness ? Ah, yes, they do, yet they have not the power of the lioness, but in solitude and confinement are condemned to mourn over the helpless fate of their offspring, and it is on that account they now take a part in our meeting, while we are attempting that which the order of society prevents them from doing—publicly pleading the cause of their infant children. But, as I said, if they were brutes the tyrant dare not seize them. They are not brutes. The whole of these little ones which it pleases Almighty God of his infinite mercy to commit to your care, fathers and mothers, have to perform their duties in this world as members of society, and members of social government. Yes, they have to be taught that they themselves must learn to be good ; and how can they learn the principles of morality, when, from the dawning of the morning almost to the midnight hour, they are shut up in the fumes of a factory, engaged in twisting, and twining, and joining together threads, as though that were the only duty for which they were created into the world ? I say this, that we ought to assert that it is improper that a child in its youth should work longer than ten hours a day, if it is expected that that child shall be a good subject under the Government. The law of the land expects us all, even the factory children, to understand our duty as good subjects when we arrive at full age; but how in the name of common sense can a young factory child, that is torn from its bed in a morning, and goes home to bed with aching legs at night, and too often cannot reach it, but slumbers on its way, how is it possible such a child can know the law which is made for its own government ? It is absolutely impossible. But, gentlemen, these little children are not brutes ; they have not only to learn their duty to man, they have not only to live upon the earth a few years, but there is a wide extending eternity opening before them, and we know, as Christians, that in that eternity they must occupy either a place of misery or a place of happiness. They have to learn their duty to God ; and if it be impossible that they should be able to learn their duty to man, it is absolutely impossible that they should learn their duty to God. Then, woe be to that man, wherever he is and whoever he is, who, in the search of gain, prevents those employed under him from having the opportunity of preparing to meet their God. Woe be to him, whether he be rich or whether he be poor. There is a dread responsibility attaches to every human being who employs little children under such circumstances, for which he will have to account at the day of judgment ; and although some of their employers may laugh at us for saying so now, the day will come when they will tremble. Yes, my friends, these little children are brought into the world thus to perform their duty ; but how does this horrid system prevent them ? The moment a child is able to creep from its mother's lap, almost—for I have known them taken at six years old—and from morning till night, from week to week, and from year to year, if their health permit, are they compelled to labour and toil. And is this a state of things that can be approved of by any person calling himself a Briton or a Christian ? Is this really what

was intended for an immortal soul that is put into the casket
of a beautiful child ?   Is it thus that children should be led to
Jesus, who said ' Suffer little children to come unto me, and
forbid them not, for of such is the kingdom of heaven ?'   Oh,
no, benevolence has endeavoured, but in vain, to make up for
the evils that the factory system has brought upon our
juvenile population.   Benevolent individuals, who have seen
how morally impossible it is for children under the factory
system, as it is now and has been for some time practised, to
be educated properly, have designed, superintended, and promoted Sunday schools.   Benevolence has waited upon the
children, and has been compelled against its better feeling to
make that day which every Christian acknowledges to be a
sabbath and day of rest, into another day of labour for the
children, and of labour for the teachers.   Think not that I
am speaking against Sunday schools.   No; I am endeavouring
to uphold the individuals who have promoted them, and who
have spent their days in endeavouring to teach children that
which in my conscience I believe they have a right to be
taught on the week day.   Yes, yes, benevolence has
endeavoured, but as I before said has endeavoured in vain, to
make up for the dreadful evils which this horrid system produces.   You see your infirmaries erected by kind and benevolent individuals, and in those places where factories
predominate you will find them occupied, in a majority of
cases, by persons who have received their diseases from the
factory system.   Within a very few years, benevolence,
finding that still the avaricious and haughty tyrant seized its
prey, and rendered it incapable of receiving instructions on the
sabbath—for I know many that are prevented, being compelled by the fatigue of the week's labour to spend their
Sundays in bed — benevolence has designed another plan ;
infant schools have been established, in order that they may
receive some little instruction before they are consigned to the
demon of the factory system ; and so avaricious, so malignant,

so blood-thirsty — I mean of the blood of their souls — have some factory-masters become, that they have given this as a reason in a petition to the House of Commons why children eight years old ought not to be protected. Seeing, then, that benevolence, with its outstretched arm, has been overmatched, and that the abettors of the factory system have determined to make it only subservient to their own interests, is it not high time that Britons should speak out, and that at all events those who are not blinded by this accursed system should raise their voices and petition loudly, and frequently, and continually, that British children may be free. I say it is high time."

These speeches were spoken in the presence of those who were capable of judging of the truth of every fact stated; in this consisted their principal value, for the factory system, as then existing, was attacked in the stronghold of its supporters.

The exuberant fulness of Mr Oastler's sympathies, his disregard for personal consequences, and his strong hatred of oppression, have sometimes caused him in public controversy to use expressions which, to others less moved and more under the control of conventional propriety, have appeared extreme. These expressions Mr Oastler's opponents have not failed to make the most of ; in council no man is more calm and careful, in action he is dauntless and brave. No words can equal his own, published in 1850, as a description of his state of mind in the early stages of the factory movement, as begun by himself :—" Those who blame me," said Mr Oastler, " for having been violent in this cause, should consider the deep, the solemn, the overwhelming conviction, on my mind, of its vast importance; they should never forget that there were external circumstances surrounding me, calculated to awaken my sym-pathies and to arouse my indignation. I saw my young and helpless neighbours dying excruciatingly by inches under the lash and toil of the factory monster ; I heard their groans, I watched their tears; I knew they had relied on me, they told me so. I was visited by their weeping mothers, who, sorrowing, showed me their children's bleeding wounds, and in accents which such mothers alone could speak, asked : 'Is this fair, sir? Is it not enough that these poor things should be killed by labour, while doomed to earn our bread; and *must* they also be kicked, and lashed, and struck in this fashion?' Then, gazing in maddened anguish, and lifting their tearful eyes to heaven, they have said: 'There is a God, and he will recompense.' I saw full-grown athletic men, whose only labour was to carry their little ones to the mill long before the sun was risen, and bring them home at night long after he had set. I heard the curses of these broken-hearted fathers! They were loud and deep, but registered—never to be forgotten.

" To have been cool, calm, and unmoved, when surrounded by such circumstances, would have required a colder heart than mine; to have expected me to address, in drawing-room language, the oppressors of the helpless, men whose whole souls were absorbed in the one thought of coining gold out of tears and suffering, would have been to have supposed me something more, or something less, than a man."

There was between Mr Oastler and his hearers a bond of sympathy; he appealed to the love they bore their offspring, to the sense of the degradation they endured; he warmed within them the consciousness of duty, the responsibility thereto attached; he awakened their hope by pledging himself to secure their release, or, perish in the attempt; he strengthened their patriotism by exhorting them to care for their country as became Englishmen; he entreated them, for mercy's sake, to grant unto him their approval and support. Who could deny the facts stated by Mr Smith, of Leeds, by the Rev. Mr Bull, by the factory operatives, of what they themselves had endured? Those who eagerly listened, carried with them to their own homes the glad tidings that sincere and bold men were pledged to secure the emancipation of little children from the slavery in the mills. Yorkshire, through the force of such speeches as have been quoted, and the aid of the printing press, was excited through controversy; and the operatives, being hopeful, were full of enthusiasm. The question was a home one, felt and known by all who suffered; they, in the simplicity of their hearts, had not their virtuous resolutions deadened by the chill damp of economical theories. These were the weapons of the opponents of factory legislation.

The Yorkshire meetings had features peculiarly their own. The tears, the smiles, the songs, the vows of the women and children, the sense of indignation which now and again shot from the eyes of *all* when the nobler feelings of their hearts were appealed to, will, by those who witnessed those scenes, never be forgotten. As the cruelties endured were named, women, men, and children wept; as hope was appealed to, they cheered; the children and girls, in shrill notes, sang their simple chaunt,—" We will have the Ten Hours' Bill, that we will." Here and there, a mother clasping an infant to her breast, kissing it, and exclaiming: " Factory slave thou shalt never be," gave to the proceedings a dramatic interest, remarkable, intense, and exciting.

There has not been held, in the whole course of English agitations, a more remarkable gathering than that which met in the Castle Yard of York, on April 24, 1832, to demonstrate to Parliament that Yorkshire was in earnest for a Ten Hours' Bill. The nearest factory town to York was Leeds, a distance of twenty-four miles; many of the outlying districts were from forty to fifty miles from the place of meeting The air was cold, the rain during the previous night fell in torrents, the weather was described in the Castle Yard to be " the most inclement within memory." Leeds, Bradford, Bingley, Keighley, Dewsbury, Heckmondwicke, Batley, Huddersfield, Honley Holmfirth, Marsden, Meltham, Elland, Hebdenbridge, Pudsey, Rawden, Otley, and other towns and villages were that day represented in the Castle Yard. Thousands of men foot-sore, but not faint of heart, who had walked from twenty-four to fifty miles, blessed God when their eyes that morning saw York Minster. Not only men, but factory boys and girls, mothers with infants in their arms, fifty miles from their own homes, were there to hold up their hands to heaven as an earnest of their desire to be freed from a worse than an Egyptian bondage. It was a sight to have made a man love his kind; to have seen how the stronger helped the weaker along the road to York, and from York home again ; to mark them share each others' food, to behold the noble spirit of self-sacrifice which made those in front wait for and often return to help onward those in the rear. Oastler and Bull were everywhere cheering and encouraging the straggling bands. Fatigue, hunger, and thirst, were borne with courage and self-denial; property of all kinds was safe as if all had been in their own parishes. The meeting was most numerously attended, the Castle Yard, which was then of very large area, having been three parts full. The estimated numbers varied, all admitted there were many thousands. We are indebted to a friend for a personal narrative of this most interesting assemblage ; his recital contains points of special interest, which could not be ascertained from the usual sources of information. The author of the narrative was a zealous supporter of the factory movement, and wrote with all the warmth of an earnest man. He published his description of the York meeting shortly after its occurrence, and when the incidents were fresh in his memory. He was assisted by facts communicated by several friends, who described what they saw. The whole comes therefore stamped with authority, and we shall quote freely from the account so rendered.

" A numerously signed Requisition had been accepted by the High Sheriff of Yorkshire for a County Meeting on the Factory Bill.

" The largest and most populous county in England was, by the far-famed Reform Bill, partitioned into North, East, and West Divisions. In its undivided state it was a little kingdom of itself, and its public gatherings were often noble exhibitions of old English feeling.

" We were starting for York. The West Riding was up for one grand effort in favour of the *White* Slave's emancipation, and every village, town, and hamlet in the province, at all contiguous to the manufacturing districts, was in a stir. It was not the war-whoop of revenge that rent the air, but it was the loud voice of parental sympathy, and of Christian solicitude for the lives, the morals, and the domestic as well as religious and educational rights of the poor and honest workers of Yorkshire. ' For God and our Children ' was the motto on many a rude and homely banner, that was floating out of the windows of the manufacturing towns and hamlets of the crowded West—' To York! to York ! ' was the word ; and the resistless ' King Richard' Oastler had issued his manifesto requiring all his subjects to attend.

" The preparations for this great gathering were on a splendid scale. It was a great undertaking to conduct so many thousands to York.

" Let the people of the more favoured and quieter counties, where the tall murky chimney was never seen, and the ' many-windowed pile,' so feelingly described by Wordsworth, rears not the roof beneath which infancy and childhood have so long groaned under the direst slavery that ever defiled the earth—let the quiet farmers and shopkeepers of the non-manufacturing counties imagine a vast population, chiefly lying at an average of thirty-five miles at least from the county town, resolving upon a *Pilgrimage of mercy* to liberate their own children from the thraldom they had long endured unpitied because unknown.

" The preparations for this meeting alarmed even Mammon himself. His votaries dreamed of, and cried ' Treasons, stratagems, and spoils.' York would be sacked—the farmers on their way would be plundered—their ricks fired—their flocks slaughtered, and then, what waste of time!—the factories must be stopped, for even children and young persons resolved to go—women were determined to be at the place of concourse —and such was the stir among the 'monied interest' that a great talk was heard of an application to the Executive to forbid the meeting. But the High Sheriff's precept was now out—he had accepted as security the word of 'King Richard' that the King's peace should not be broken; and a powerful impetus had been given to the Christian and humane feeling of the county.

"In some villages and scattered patches of houses, contributions of bread and other provisions were amply raised by the poor for the pilgrims—but the great want of all was, shoes. These were lent; and whilst some had the ill-fitting and grotesque coats of their neighbours, others were content with a portion of a well-greased wool sheet: and at the appointed hour, which varied as the distance might be, the confluent streams of animated beings began to move.

"Leeds was the first halt. On the evening before the meeting, Leeds was crowded with the people (young and old) of Dewsbury, Bradford, Halifax, Birstal, and Huddersfield, and far beyond these and their numerous surrounding townships— of Keighley and Sutton—of Holmfirth, and even Chapel le Firth on the bare moors—in fact from that range of hills rising in Derbyshire, and running down into Scotland's border, called 'the back bone of England,' to the centre of the city of the North, the swarming thousands poured down on that occasion. Their progress was peaceable, and in every way orderly.

"Large masses went on in rustic order, singing Jehovah's praises, and imploring, in verse perhaps rudely composed for the occasion, His never failing compassion for themselves and their little ones.

" As a sample of these productions of the poetic rangers of our Northern moors and hills, the following (from the pen of a hand-loom weaver) may be given, which was composed on that occasion.

" ' How wretched is thy fate—to be
    Shut up in early years,
From light, and life, and liberty,
    And all that life endears.
No moral lesson taught to learn,
    Thy manners all defiled,
Thou still must pass unheeded on,
    Poor little Factory Child.

" ' No pure domestic bliss is thine,
    Which others seem to share ;
'Tis thine to labour—or to pine
    'Mid want, distress, and care :
Thou'st no protection from the great—
    Thou must be reconcil'd
To pass thy days unheeded on,
    Poor little Factory Child.

" ' No youthful pastimes are thy lot,
    Which youthful minds require ;
Thou liv'st and linger'st on the spot,
    Which quenches all thy fire :
Thy bosom never felt the sweets
    Of treatment kind and mild ;
But hard fatigue and harsh commands,
    Poor little Factory Child.

" ' Thy future years will bear the gloom
    Thy tender age has known ;
Restriction wears the mental bloom—
    Confinement keeps it down.
Thy body, too, alike must feel
    The ills upon it piled—
Thou still must pass unheeded on,
    Poor little Factory Child.'

" The banners were in many cases very strikingly expressive. Most of them had a Scriptural phrase or allusion. Some were painted by the rude artist to represent the

' horrors' of the mill system—such as a father carrying his little girl through a pelting storm of sleet and snow to a noted flax mill near Leeds, at five in the morning, himself in tatters, and having taken off his own remnant of what was once a coat, to cover his hapless babe, who was doomed to earn its parent's living, as well as its own, at the certain destruction of its own health and morals, and probably its very life—doomed to lie in a premature grave.

" Others had inscribed ' Father, is it time ?' a cry which is often heard the night through in the crowded and wretched dormitory of the factory working-people, and which little children, more asleep than awake (dreading the consequences of being late), were often heard to utter.

" In reference to this, one incident in particular had about then become generally known, which made this motto on the banners of the York pilgrims very heart-stirring. A little white slave, whose weary labours were kindly consummated by the friendly hand of death—who had been used to work incredibly long hours, and was now stretched upon the bed from whence she rose no more—in the last struggle of nature waking from one of those interrupted slumbers that often precede the last pang of death, as her fond parents stood watching with many tears the exit of the worn-out infant slave to her long home, she (so true yet so outraged was nature) suddenly started from this closing sleep, and exclaiming ' Father, is it time ?' sunk back into that father's arms, and escaped to where tyranny could not reach her.

" We have stated, that these advocates of their own cause and their children's first rested at Leeds.

" Warehouses were there provided for each party that came in, and a good litter of straw ' long feathers ' was spread for them to lie upon, until, after a few hours' rest, they should resume their work. For such as had need, some bread was provided, at these stations, and a limited quantity of beer. The masses moved out of Leeds all that tempestuous night.

Many could not proceed in consequence of the weather, thousands proceeded, mostly on foot, but some in carts and waggons, which they provided for themselves. The next station of the *Pilgrims* was *Cross Roads*, on a Heath, half way between Leeds and York.

"Here a little refreshment awaited them, and then 'Onward' was the cry. But a darker night never shrouded the sky.

"The appearance of the road was novel and impressive; it resounded with cheers, which were uttered by the *Pilgrims* at those who passed them in carriages of various sorts. In some groups there were torches, composed of old ropes, and the undulations of the road afforded many views of illuminated groups, successively rising over the hills and disappearing the next instant, leaving a loud, long cheer behind, as they sank out of view. It was indeed a moving scene.

"With the early dawn, the Race-course at York began to teem with multitudes. The Grand Stand was the rendezvous. There, the poor fellows were promised a little cheer, (who had need and were unprovided), of the plainest sort—bread, cheese, and small beer. And here the hand of Providence is to be admired! By some accident the bread had been mis sent to another place—It was by many believed to have been a foul plot to cause disaster—the beer was there without the bread, and the hungry and the drenched to the skin were there, disappointment and anger were there ; but for a good Providence and the magnanimity of 'King Richard,' there might have been havoc that day.

"Oastler soon heard of the sad dilemma, and no sooner heard, than, with quick and steady step, he was met by one of his warmest friends, then just arrived, pacing toward the Grand Stand. Arriving there, he was greeted with 'a three times three' that rent the air. His own account, (in a letter to a friend), of that critical moment is this:

"'When I left the George Inn, to meet the hungry and exasperated people, I saw John Wood, (a principal mill-owner at that time, and a liberal friend of the factory bill), who asked me, " Well, how are you getting on?" I knew that his nerves would not bear the shock, so I said, " Oh, cleverly ; I am going to Knavesmire to lead the people to the meeting." Near Micklegate Bar, I met my own parson—parson Bull. I told him all about it, " that I expected the people would be so enraged that they would murder me ; but my duty called me, and, at all hazards, I must do my best to quiet them." He, like a brave fellow as he is—(he is both good and brave) —pressed me " to allow him to accompany me and share my fate." " No," said I, " my friend, when they have killed me, they will rush to the city for bread and revenge, and you must remain here, meet them at the Bar, and try to appease them. May-be, they will kill you also, but we must do our duty, and leave the event with God." " I will obey your orders," cried Bull, " and the Lord be with you."

"'In a short time I was in sight of the crowd, on Knavesmire. I commended myself to God—and advanced. Judge of my surprise when I saw them, they did not rush on me in anger as I expected—my faithful friend, Pitkethly, was striving to appease them—he soon saw me, and shouting, " the King, the King!" he cleared a passage for me to the centre of the assembled multitude. I mounted a table, and, as soon as I spoke, they cheered most lustily. I said a few words to console and animate them, and then marched off to the Castle Yard—thanking God, who had thus preserved my life, and given me the hearts of " my people." Poor lads! they were hungry, but how patient.'

" Arrived in the Castle Yard, and orderly arranged, to the number of many thousands, around the hustings, the business proceeded. They had walked through a tempest many weary miles—they were generally *drenched* to the skin, they had now to stand about five hours, whilst the various speakers stated to the undivided county of York, duly convened and assembled, the object of the meeting, and the merits of the case to be discussed.

" The writer of this imperfect sketch saw numbers, whose footsteps were traced in their own blood *into* the Castle Yard, and *out of it* homewards, occasioned by the length and wetness of the journey, and the badness of their shoes and *clogs,* in which many had walked from thirty to forty, and some fifty miles.

" That meeting was an impressive one, and was so felt. Many good English yeomen were there. Though the meeting was principally composed of the ' mill-hands,' they were not without much sympathy from the honest farmers and rural gentry of the county.

" The clergy too felt their case ; they were headed by the benevolent John Graham, Rector of St Saviour's, York. Some other clergymen of York were there—several clergymen from the West Riding were present, and forcibly advocated the cause of their suffering flocks. The Rev. J. C. Boddington, of Horton, near Bradford, made a most forcible appeal, and gave plain facts and arguments in favour of a Ten Hours' Bill. The Rev. George S. Bull was at his post, and in short, but expressive terms, recorded his claims, as pastor of his flock, for legislative protection. Captain Wood, of Sandal, was urgent for the bill, and the Honourable William Duncombe, who had been a successful candidate in that yard for the suffrage of the county, now did his duty nobly, and spoke out in honest Christian eloquence, for the children of the oppressed, from whose cause he never flinched.

" And ' King Richard ' was there, moving his audience into tears, into ecstasy, and into the firmness of immovable determination by his eloquence. And there was Sadler, beyond all the rest—he on whose most worthy shoulders the burden and heat of the work had so lately fallen.

" Much enfeebled and exhausted in body, his spirit bounded over all the snares and stumbling-blocks of the enemies of humanity, his close and fervent arguments put all their sophistry to the blush; and he that day, and many days before and after it, proved that he was a special instrument in God's hand to break the hateful yoke from the necks of British childhood and youth, and to set the innocent captives free.

" There stood his friend and supporter with heart and purse, John Wood, of Bradford, than whom no one did more for this cause; and he did more, perhaps, by his frequent public declarations of his own past *error* as a supporter of the white slavery system in factories, than by the thousands of pounds which he freely disbursed in promoting this cause."

The proceedings of this county meeting lasted five hours: there stood (after their exhausting march) that dense mass of human beings, as if rooted to the earth. The meeting was addressed by clergymen, physicians, and influential county gentlemen. Mr Smith, of Leeds, made a clear and simple statement of the evils of the factory system, which admitted of no contradiction; Michael Thomas Sadler, Esq., M.P., renewed his pledges to mercy against Mammon; George Strickland, Esq., M.P., (now Sir George), assured his constituents, and others, of his determination to be faithful to the cause of the factory children. A Yorkshire nobleman, the Honourable William Duncombe, now Lord Feversham, cheered the hearts of all by assuring his hearers that he considered the factory question as of the highest importance, and judiciously observed:—" After all, highly important, and deeply interesting as this question is, I consider it but a branch of a question, which will ere long force itself upon the attention of parliament and the executive government— I mean the whole condition and circumstances of the industrious and labouring classes. Not that I contemplate the possibility of being enabled, by any human law or enactment,

to secure to all the various classes and interests of this empire
an uninterrupted quantum of happiness; I believe it has been
decreed otherwise ; that as it has been ordained by the
Almighty Creator of the Universe, that the rays of the sun
shall not always shine upon us, but that night shall follow
day, and winter succeed the summer, so has it been decreed
in His inscrutable wisdom that we should experience a season
of adversity as well as prosperity, that we may learn how to
enjoy the one, and learn, also, how to appreciate the other.
But I nevertheless hold it to be the bounden and indispensable duty of every man who has the safety, honour, and
welfare of the country at heart, to direct his most anxious
attention to the state and circumstances of the industrious
and working classes, with the view, and in the hope of
being enabled to ameliorate their condition, to alleviate their
burthens, and to mitigate their distress.   This is no new
doctrine of mine; this is no opinion taken up yesterday, or
to-day, for the purpose of obtaining any momentary applause,
or any ephemeral popularity—it is one which I have long
entertained, and which, when the opportunity presented
itself, I have endeavoured to enforce.   But not to trespass
farther upon your indulgence on the present occasion, I
will only repeat my most cordial assent and unequivocal
approbation of the object for which you are assembled here
to-day, and should there be any individuals who are still
doubting, and wavering in doubt as to the course they
should pursue, or who are determined, if they interfere at
all, to oppose the bill, from anything like party feeling
and political bias, I would entreat them to dismiss all such
considerstions from their minds; I would implore them to
weigh the matter with that impartiality and that earnestness
which its importance demands; I would ask them to recollect
that this is not the cause of party, that it is the cause of
justice—that it is the cause of real humanity, of Christian
benevolence—that it is the cause of those who, from their
earliest youth and their tenderest years, contribute by their

labour and their industry to form the source of our country's
wealth and our country's greatness, the remedy for whose
grievances is not in their own hands—that it is the cause
of the oppressed and the industrious poor:—

> ' Let not ambition mock their useful toil,
> Their homely joys, and destiny obscure ;
> Nor grandeur hear, with a disdainful smile,
> The short and simple annals of the poor.' "

These generous and manly words, from the lips of the
heir of a noble house, and the representative of the
county of York, had great weight with all classes, they
strengthened in the breasts of the operatives their cherished hopes of final release, they felt in their oppression that
their woes had reached the ears of some among the great
and honoured of the land, that the wrongs of the cottage had
been met by sympathy in the mansion.

Joseph Yorke, Esq., the High Sheriff, when he closed the
business of the meeting, said :—" Gentlemen, I cannot let
this opportunity pass without remarking upon the good conduct you have observed during the course of this day ; a
conduct which reflects credit upon yourselves, which should
be held up as an example for the imitation of others, and
which is worthy of the great county to which you belong.
The business of the day is concluded."

The friend whose communication we have already quoted
continues his graphic description of what he and others saw,
as follows :

" ' Three cheers for the High Sheriff' made the welkin ring ;
and a clergyman on the platform, whose heart was in the
right place, demanded one cheer more ' for the Factory
Children and their Mothers,' and this was louder still—this
struck another chord in the brave hearts of the now receding
multitude, who thought next of ' home,' and, though dreary,
yet dear. With the ' King' at their head they quietly and
orderly departed, and ' To Tadcaster,' was the cry in that
heart-moving host.

" Such a one never visited York before—no such purpose
had ever brought so many thousands of poor men to that city,
at their own charge, unpaid and poorly provided for—not to
shout for blue, yellow, or pink ; not to cram public houses,
and fill the streets with victims of inebriety ; but a host upon
whose faces were imprinted the deep lines of care, and yet the
sure marks of tender affection for their hapless babes, their
heart-sick wives, their degraded sisters and relations, on whose
behalf they had come ; and having recorded their protest
against the tyranny that crushed and cankered all the ' sweets '
of ' home,' and demanded in firm but respectful terms the
justice of their country, they now peacefully retired, foot-sore
and weary, and many of them very hungry, yet they shouted,
' Oastler and our Children,' and set their faces homeward
once more.

" ' Do you think,' said a Dignitary on that day, to a
country clergyman from the west, whom he met at the Castle
Yard gates, ' Do you think that these men are to be trusted—
would it be well to have the military ready ? ' ' What makes
you fear ? ' said the other. ' Why, really, they look a stern,
determined set of men—there is something very alarming in
their appearance. Do you suppose they will stop in York
to-night ? ' ' Not a dozen of them,' was the reply. ' And as
to your fears, give them to the winds : these are not the men
to sack York or do mischief. They have come at the bidding
of their wives and children to ask for justice, not mercy.'
The West Riding clergyman proceeded to explain to the
Prebendary the state of the case, and he declared that the
visit and the visitors were both unparalleled in the annals, not
of York only, but of the civilised world ; and parted, much
affected with the subject.

" The weather continued boisterous and wet—torrents
poured down—bread was scarce—and where to rest that night
many knew not. Stables, barns, school rooms, and out-houses
had been engaged at Tadcaster, and well strewn with ' long

feathers ; ' but there were many who could not reach so far—
it was nine long miles, and their feet were bare—blistered—
bleeding, some profusely, and far short of Tadcaster, some
hundreds implored a resting-place at inns of various grades,
or wherever they could get a roof to cover them. The
inhabitants were truly kind, and the poor befriended the
poor.

"The principal leaders of this affecting group had
occasion, for the sake of business as well as refreshment, to
wait a few hours at York. Sadler was nearly exhausted.
His friend John Wood, with his accustomed benignity,
provided at his hotel every refreshment, restorative, and
comfort, that York afforded, for the benevolent Parliamentary
Champion and his attendant friends ; but the comforts of a
fireside and 'good beds' at York were no entertainment to
those who had followed in spirit, and some in person, on their
weary way, the Pilgrims who were pacing the road homewards amid storms of rain.

"The thought that some might perish from destitution or
exhaustion, was no sooner suggested by the Rev. G. S. Bull
to the party at the George, in Coney street, than the cry went
round, 'What can be done ?' Mr Bull then proposed that
the most ample covered waggons that York could afford, with
a store of bread and restoratives, should at once start and
bring up the rear ; he offered to take the command of the
hospital train ; but he was not allowed to perform this
work of mercy alone. Messrs Robert Hall and William
Osborn, jun., (to whose able and indefatigable, and
peculiarly disinterested labours, the Factory workers owed
then, and must continue to owe, a lasting and yet unpaid debt
of gratitude), at a moment's notice of the plan proposed,
insisted upon being upon the staff, alleging that they had
been comfortably bedded the night before, while their
reverend coadjutor had been all the rainy night previous with
the Pilgrims upon the road.

"The waggons were procured, ample means for defraying the expenses were instantly afforded by Mr Wood, and after a search in the streets of York for stragglers, which brought only three persons to the waggons, the party started, provided with lanterns to inspect the roadside, or the ditches if requisite. At the first public house that came in view after leaving the city, search was made for the disabled. The landlord was sitting up at his fire—the kitchen floor was strewed with those who were 'fair *done*,' (to use their own term)—the outbuildings and stables were equally well furnished, and presented a singular spectacle. The reverend 'King of the Cripples,' as the chief of this staff humorously designated himself, went into these places to ask for bad cases, of lame Pilgrims who would not be able to proceed, and some bad ones soon presented themselves.

"The first that was awakened from his sound sleep, and lifted his head from a blanket of straw, was an old Waterloo veteran, whose medal gave him at once a noble distinction. 'What's your errand,' said he, 'is there ought amiss?' 'Nothing, my lads, except, as I suspect, with your heels. Have you any cripples here? for I am come, by order of the Committee, to seek them up, and have a comfortable covered waggon to take them on in.' The soldier rubbed his eyes, to take a full view of his unexpected visitor. and then shedding some honest tears, he said, 'God bless you, friend—you are a Christian! And now,' says he, 'where's that lad that I dragged in?' and he groped for him among the straw, and soon produced a poor Factory Boy, long a victim of the system—lean, withered, and wan—whose feet were literally raw; he had wrapped them in part of what had been a shirt, and seemed unwilling to move, overpowered as he was with fatigue. His comrades and townsmen, of whom two or three were in company, designated him by the curious and abbreviated name of 'Pick Butt.'

"Several more, with their feet bleeding profusely, and in

wretched plight, were also found, and removed to the hospital waggons, where they were warmly covered and well disposed of. The Waterloo veteran, though nearly as bad as the rest, with the true magnanimity of his ' order,' refused to go, and gave place in favour of those who should yet be found on the road, as he said, ' quite mashed up.' The joy and gratitude of many of these disabled Pilgrims—several of them twenty, and some forty miles from home, when thus overtaken and aided, was admirable and very gratifying.

" At Tadcaster, a very full load was completed, and, attended by their chaplain, the waggons went out of Tadcaster at an early hour, with ' King Richard ' and his men, who had halted there for the night, and, after a very frugal breakfast, at martial summons, prepared to renew their journey. The care of the Committee in sending waggons for the disabled seemed to inspirit the whole company ; and as a dense mass emerged from that peaceful town on the Leeds road, the company in the waggon unexpectedly struck up, as a morning song, the venerated doxology of ' Praise God, from whom all blessings flow ; ' the rear and van caught the strain, and a more solemn and affecting anthem never echoed on the blue vault of heaven ; many a silent tear commended it to the Intercessor above. There were men on that road who had an interest in Heaven, though their lot on earth was poor indeed.

"The weather now cleared a little, the march was more cheerful, and home began to draw nearer. The district and the moor over which this multitude traversed, presented a singular, interesting, and animated appearance. Since the days of Julius Cæsar such a company had not traversed those hills. The receding and pursuing hosts in earlier days shouted for the battle as they caught sight of each other. Those fields and wilds had been dyed with the blood of feudal chieftains and their trains, and the hardy sons of ' the far North ' had bled there, too; but now the earth was scalded by the tears of British parents who were returning to comfortless homes, the scenes of wasting and excessive toil, in which, too often. *they* were to live, involuntarily idle, by the deathly labours of their hapless babes. Yes, they wept as they returned, and God has registered those tears. There was hope, indeed, but it was faint; and there was the sympathy that they had witnessed at York which abated the smart.

" The last battalion had passed the Cross Roads, and about two miles from Leeds the ' King ' called for a halt, till the rear should come up.

" Oastler had headed his 'subjects' on foot through the entire journey. He was importuned to ride, but would not; he even refused the shelter of an umbrella, because others were destitute of that cover. He refused refreshment because there was too little for all. His hardy endurance of more than his full share of fatigue was the means of inspiriting the vast mass, who sacrificed and endured so much on this occasion.

" One incident will not be forgotten. There was a place on the road where a footpath, through the fields, shortened the distance. Oastler, with a few friends, took that path, upon which they had not proceeded far when a boy, of about ten years, was discovered lying in a furrow, in the last stage of exhaustion, benumbed with wet and cold, and literally perishing. The poor child was carried to the turnpike road, and there mounted on horseback, before a kind friend, who took the straggler on his lap. The boy was thus brought under the special conduct of ' his Majesty ' to the hospital van, when every attention was promptly given to his case, and he soon revived. The hand of a kind Providence was thus manifested, and was acknowledged with thanksgiving. Not a life was lost !

" The ' Crusaders ' now poured into Leeds, and they were greeted by thousands. Here and there a diabolical spirit of disappointment was seen at the safe conclusion of this unparalleled enterprise, and some even ventured to exult over the sorry plight of that yet undaunted and cheerful body, who had endured so much with such exemplary fortitude from the adverse elements. Many had yet twenty or nearly thirty miles to go, and after a short halt and refreshment, and a visit in the White Cloth Hall Yard from Sadler, who came to cheer and to be cheered, ' the King's own,' the Huddersfield division started again, and arrived at home, amid the greetings, cheers, and tears, of wives and children, who came out to welcome them *to the best they had left*.

" It will seem incredible that, after all this fatigue, the Huddersfield men that same evening held a public meeting, and kept up their recital of the Pilgrimage to a vast auditory until a late hour: finishing that day's work by a dance in the market place ! That night, when Oastler undressed, the skin of the soles of his feet peeled off with his stockings. The remoter effects of this mighty effort are still in operation. The journey, its objects, its circumstances, will never be forgotten ; and generations yet unborn will learn with wonder, that, in a professedly Christian land, such a cause should exist for such a demonstration of patriotic sympathy and parental affection.

" The happier firesides, it may be hoped, of our distant successors on the theatre of life, will be entertained with the legend of ' The Pilgrimage of Mercy,' and England's hearths and Altars shall yet, we hope, record the downfal of infant slavery in every part of our island, and the triumph of Christian love."

In the factory agitation science was brought out of her recesses, and exhibited to the popular gaze; the science of the physical organization of man and the science of life were made plain to the common understanding; drawings of factory operatives, whose limbs had been distorted and sources of life weakened by excessive labour, were unrolled and explained before aggregated masses, in public meetings. The effect was extraordinary. Men who had hitherto thought but little on life, health, and disease, were astounded at what they beheld, and ashamed that they had allowed the oppression, the hideous results of which they for the first time contemplated. Mr Smith, Infirmary Surgeon, of Leeds, lecturing in the Castle Yard of York, on the beautiful arch of bone in the human foot, formed so as to sustain the whole weight of the human frame, uniting grace, strength, and elasticity, fitted for rest and motion; and showing his auditors how young children, who in factories were kept standing fourteen or sixteen hours of the day, had the arch of bone pressed down, the bones having fallen in, these children, so injured, being, in consequence, deformed for life, was a novelty in agitation, the necessity for which made good men blush. Such an exhibition of science, side by side with the injuries of the helpless, did much towards convincing the learned of the evils of the factory system. The simple-minded see, hear, and believe. The learned ask for analysis and proof,—they are "slow of heart to believe." It was so of old, the unlettered fisherman heard and had faith; a vision from heaven was required to convince the learned tent-maker, but when convinced, who ever preached as did Paul? The journey of these drenched and weary travellers to York appealed to the hearts of all; each man, woman, and child, though silent, yet, in person, asked for pity and redress. The inspiring eloquence of Oastler, and the Christian tone of his supporters, filled the minds of their hearers with the noblest of sentiments, and a strong sense of duty, as standards by which they might judge their own actions and those of others. These things were necessary for acquiring the desired end; for opposition and interest were powerful; custom had enslaved the moral sentiments in many, and made others blind to their own guilt. Indolence, the shield of error, had to be shaken off, and conscience, the sentinel of truth, to be quickened into activity. A task, the end of which was noble, but the path to which was strewn with thistles and briers. Courage in a good cause is the right arm of strength, and elevation of soul, the living principle of a nation's greatness. " Never," said Edmund Burke ; and none knew better than he—" Never," said the political philosopher, " was there a jar or discord between genuine sentiment and sound policy. Never, no, never did nature say one thing and wisdom say another. Nor are sentiments of elevation in themselves turgid and unnatural. Nature is never more truly herself than in her grandest forms." Few spectacles can, in moral grandeur, excel the noble determination of a numerous body of men, resolved that mercy shall temper a nation's rule, and Mammon be muzzled by law.

The parliamentary exertions of Mr Sadler on behalf of the industrious classes, and especially those engaged in factory labour, were acknowledged by the almost simultaneous greeting of tens of thousands of the working classes. In the autumn of 1832, when on a visit to his friend Mr Oastler at Fixby Hall, sixteen thousand persons, chiefly from Huddersfield and district, assembled in Fixby Park to do him honour, and thank him for his efforts on behalf of the oppressed. At Manchester, Mr Sadler and Mr Oastler were welcomed by a public procession and dinner. The reporter for the *Leeds Intelligencer* thus described the scene he witnessed: " Soon after five (in the afternoon of Saturday the 23rd of August, 1832) Mr Sadler and Mr Oastler left the Shakespeare, and entered an open carriage prepared for them by the Committee, amidst the most enthusiastic cheering; the bands saluting and the flags waving. They were accompanied by Mr John Wood of Bradford, the Rev. Mr Bull, and Mr Perring. Amidst this almost hurricane of applause the word was given to move forward for the place of meeting—Camp Field.

" The procession was headed by two men, bearing a flag with the representation of a deformed man, inscribed—' Am I not a man and a brother?' underneath, ' No White Slavery.' Then came a band of music ; then the Committee and their friends; then a long line of Factory children bearing a great variety of banners, decorated mops, brushes, and other utensils connected with their employment, hundreds of them singing, ' Sadler for ever, Oastler for ever; six in the morning, six in the evening.'

" One of the children carried a whip, and a strap made into thongs, with the inscription, ' Behold and weep.' Next to this immense multitude of ' little victims,' as they were aptly designated, came the carriage with the visitors. A countless number of men followed, five or six deep, all staunch friends of the Ten Hours' Bill, having at short intervals bands of music, banners, &c., with mottos expressive of some sentiment, opinion, or fact connected with the great cause. We cannot pretend to give a tithe of these inscriptions. We observed, ' Cursed are they that oppress the poor ;' ' Let us unite and gain by strength our right ;' ' Sadler and Oastler for ever;' ' Welcome to Sadler;' ' Oastler our Champion;' ' Sadler our advocate;' ' Let us unite in laying the axe to the root of infant slavery;' ' No White Slavery ;' ' Death to infant oppression;' a figure of a deformed man exclaiming, ' Excessive toil is the burden of my soul ' One person carried a very neat model of a cotton-factory, inscribed, ' The infant's Bastile.' On other banners we remarked, ' Revere Oastler, the children's friend;' ' The Factory system is the bane of health, the source of ignorance and vice; ' ' The enactment of a Ten Hours' Bill will be attended with beneficent results to both master and man.' Many of these flags and banners were of costly materials, and the devices skilfully executed; some of them were of more homely materials, but all were showy, and the effect to the eye cannot be conveyed in the most eloquent description. There were seventeen bands of music, and several hundred flags.

" In this order did the procession move through the principal streets of Manchester. The applause which greeted Mr Sadler and Mr Oastler was both enthusiastic and continuous. The men shouted; the women clapped their hands, or held up

their infant children, and screamed ' God bless Mr Sadler,'
' God bless Mr Oastler;' and thousands, we repeat, thousands,
crowded round the carriage as it proceeded, and insisted upon
shaking their benefactors by the hands, and all cried ' *Welcome to Manchester.*' Nor were the greetings confined to the
crowds in the streets. The windows were filled with spectators; even the house-tops in many instances were occupied.
As to Mr Sadler, his name was in every mouth.

> ' He comes—Sinope's streets are filled with such
> A glut of people, you would think some God
> Had conquered in their cause, and them thus ranked,
> That he might make his entrance on their heads.
> Mothers did rob the crying infants of the breast,
> Pointing Ziphares out to make them smile;
> And climbing boys stood on their fathers' shoulders,
> Answering their shouting sires with tender cries,
> To make the concert up of general joy.'

" This is poetry, but if applied to the scene in the streets of
Manchester on Saturday evening, no fiction—it describes
only that which really took place. It is to the honour of the
females of the capital of Lancashire, that they seem most
anxious to give their offspring the benefit of a more humane
system, without reference to the question which avarice has
raised in Yorkshire as a decoy—an asserted diminution of
wages."

Another witness thus expressed his opinion. " The Manchester meeting has passed off in a most gratifying manner.
It is acknowledged on all hands, that such an assembly,
together, as to numbers, good feeling, and good order, never
yet took place at Manchester. The procession was headed by
thousands of poor factory children. It is calculated that at
least one hundred thousand persons were present in the streets
and Camp field. Mr Sadler and Mr Oastler were received
with the greatest enthusiasm, and the vast multitude separated
in the most perfect good order. Mr Sadler is on his way with

his true yoke-fellow, 'King Richard,' to Bradford, on Monday. This meeting will surely have due weight *in high places.* Will they say *now,* that the operatives do not care about the Ten Hours' Bill."

The Bradford procession and meeting were imposing and successful. It was apparent, beyond possible contradiction, that the factory operatives and their leaders were thoroughly in earnest, and that all efforts to neutralize their energy and resolution had proved fruitless.

Important services were rendered in 1832, by the publication of a small weekly periodical, *The British Labourer's Protector and Factory Child's Friend.* It was edited by the Rev. G. S. Bull, and Mr Charles Walker, of Bradford, Yorkshire. Its pages were devoted to an exposition of the evils of the unregulated factory system. Its circulation was very great, and the gratuitous services of the editors and their correspondents, for the labour was one of love, instructed the public mind to a very considerable extent.

Mr Oastler's exertions on behalf of the factory children brought down on his head much abuse and vituperation. In the manufacturing districts of the north, he is familiarly spoken of as " the King," a name given to him in contempt, but now considered a title of honour; how acquired, the following extract from *The Fleet Papers,* for January, 1841, will explain. In a letter addressed to Mr Thornhill, Mr Oastler wrote:—" Why, sir, you know what little school-boys do when the big ones have grieved them—they call names. It was just so with my rich and powerful enemies—nickname after nickname was given to me—and now I come to my title of ' King.' As these opprobrious terms were attached to my name by my antagonists, it was my habit to adopt them, and thus deprive them of their sting. So, whatever epithet they added to ' Oastler,' I claimed it as my own. If they said ' fool,' I rejoined ' so be it, but your tyranny shall cease.' When they denounced me as ' a madman,' my answer was

' be it so; but the monster shall fall.' Thus they attacked, and thus I repelled their intended insults, through a long list of terms of contempt and derision, which to recount would only weary you. At length I was tired of change, when, in an unlucky moment for themselves, in burlesque, they called me ' King.' For why or for wherefore, is best known to them. I at once adopted the nickname of ' King ' as I had done the others; but I added, I will change no more. There was an end of their insulting vocabulary—there was the beginning of my style and title of ' King.' My efforts in the factory question, as you know, obtained me some notoriety; and in proportion to the *hate* of the tyrants, was the *love* of the slaves. The people everywhere clung to the last nickname given to me by my foes; and when I appeared amongst them, I was greeted by no other name. The habit of calling me ' King,' in a while grieved none but those who gave me that title. I soon found that there was power even in the name of ' King.' On some occasions, when I have had to stem the angry torrent of revenge, the authority of that title has had its use. My opponents would gladly have recalled that nickname, but in a while they used it also, until the habit became universal, and is so now in Yorkshire and in Lancashire; when speaking to me, or speaking of me, both friends and foes say ' King.' "

CHAPTER XI.

THE SOCIAL AND MORAL CONDITION OF MANCHESTER AND DISTRICT IN 1831 AND 1832, AS DESCRIBED BY MR WILLIAM RATHBONE GREG, OF BURY, LANCASHIRE, AND DR KAY (NOW SIR JAMES KAY SHUTTLEWORTH).

NOT any subject of great public interest can fail in this country of being thoroughly discussed. Sooner or later writers having knowledge and superior talent will take sides, and thus an important public question will be sifted to the bottom; impartiality, indeed, is rarely to be expected, but from the force of controversy the principal facts will be cast on the surface. This is one of the advantages which flow from free speaking and free printing, the benefit of which it is the happiness of this country to enjoy. It was earnestly maintained by the free-trade school of political economists that Mr Sadler's bill did not strike at the root of any of the social evils operating on the working classes, that the true remedies were a repeal of the corn laws, an extended electoral suffrage, an increase of education, a thorough revision of the laws of trade, thereby enabling the British manufacturer successfully to conduct his business without the necessity of making demands on the labours of the working classes inconsistent with their permanent well-being. In the absence of these changes it was maintained that shortening the hours of factory labour would be a national calamity. Among the disciples of this school were two classes: the ultra free-traders affirmed that these changes once accomplished, not any factory regulation would be required; others, more familiar with the state of the manufacturing districts, considered that those measures should be preliminary to factory legislation. To the last-named class belonged William Rathbone Greg, Esq., of Bury, Lancashire, and James Phillips Kay, Esq., M.D., two gentlemen whose pamphlets, the first published in 1831, the second in 1832, both devoted to a consideration of the physical and moral condition of those engaged in factory labour, conveyed to the reading public a more detailed, graphic, faithful, but deplorable account of the condition of the population of Manchester and district, than was elsewhere to be found. The publication of these pamphlets accelerated the growth of public opinion in favour of factory legislation ; it was the custom of Mr Oastler and others to read extracts therefrom, corroborating the parliamentary evidence on the question, and either leaving out or replying to the educational and economical theories of the authors. This mode of reasoning had weight on public opinion ; it proved the evils complained of to be real, and prepared the way for the proposed remedy. From these pamphlets we will select a few passages,— they will enable the reader to judge of the past and to compare it with the present of Manchester and neighbourhood.

Mr Greg, for confirmation of his " views on the *present* (1831) unwholesomeness of large manufactories," appealed "to any one who has been long and intimately connected with the interior of these establishments; who has seen children enter them at ten or twelve years of age, with the beaming eye, and the rosy cheek, and the elastic step of youth; and who has seen them gradually lose the gaiety and light-heartedness of early existence, and the colour and complexion of health, and the vivacity of intellect, and the insensibility to care, which are the natural characteristics of that tender age, under the withering influence of laborious confinement, ill oxygenated air, and a meagre and unwholesome diet." Mr Greg had "witnessed all this repeatedly, and found it impossible to resist the obvious conclusion—a conclusion which cannot be gainsaid by any man of experience and observation."

Among the causes producing "this unhealthiness among the people employed in large manufactories, and the peculiar class of diseases which prevail among them, viz., general lassitude and debility, dyspepsia, and gastralgia," Mr Greg enumerated unwholesome and inadequate diet, " potatoes, butter, sometimes pastry, sometimes bread, often oatcake, and *occasionally, though rarely,* a small sprinkling of bacon, or other meat, constitute their dinner six days out of the seven. For breakfast and supper they take sometimes fruit-pies, sometimes coffee (or what they call such), but far more generally tea, diluted till it is little else than warm water, and the materials of which never came from China, but are the production of one of those in-numerable frauds which are practised upon those of the poor who are desirous to imitate the rich." " At first they make use of tea as a stimulant, to relieve the internal languor and depression which always accompanies an unhealthy and ill-regulated digestion; it affords a temporary relief at the expense of a subsequent reaction, which in its turn calls for another and stronger stimulus; and it is generally the case, that those among the work-people, who have been long habituated to the use of tea as a frequent meal, are at length reduced to mix a large proportion of spirits in every cup they take. This pernicious practice prevails to an incon-ceivable extent among our manufacturing population, at every age, and in both sexes.

" From the long hours of labour, and the warm and often close atmosphere in which they are confined, a very large proportion of our manufacturing labourers feel the necessity of some artificial stimulus ; and we regret to say, that many of them, especially those which receive the highest wages, are in the habit of spending a portion of their leisure, after working hours, more particularly on a Saturday evening, and during the Sunday, in besotting themselves with ale and beer; and, still oftener, with the more efficient stimulus of gin. It is customary for them in many of the towns to stop at the gin-shops, and take a dram as they go to their work in the morning, and another as they return at night; and where, as is frequently the case, the houses of the work-people lie in a cluster round the factory, it is not uncommon for a wholesale vendor of spirits to leave two gallons (the smallest quantity which can be sold without a licence) at one of the houses, which is distributed in small quantities to the others, and payment is made to the merchant through the original receiver. The quantity of gin drunk in this way is enormous; and it is painful to know, that children, and even girls, are initiated into this fatal practice at a very early age. . . . . . Ardent spirits are not the only stimulus which this class of people indulge in. Many of them take large quantities of opium in one form or another; sometimes in pills, sometimes as laudanum, sometimes in what they call an *anodyne* draft, which is a narcotic of the same kind. They find that this is a cheaper stimulus than gin, and many of them prefer it. It has been in vogue among them for many years when wages were low, and the use of it is now continued when there is no longer this excuse."

"The work of spinners and stretchers," Mr Greg considered to be "among the most laborious that exist, and is exceeded, perhaps, by that of mowing alone; and few mowers think of continuing their labour for twelve hours without intermission. Add to this that these men never rest for an instant during the hours of working, except while their *mules* are *doffing*, in which process they also assist; and it must be obvious to every one, that it is next to impossible for any human being, however hardy or robust, to sustain this exertion, for any length of time, without permanently injuring his constitution.

" The air in almost all factories is more or less unwholesome. Many of the rooms are obliged to be kept at a certain temperature (say 65 degrees Fahrenheit) for the purpose of manufacture, and from the speed of the machinery, the general want of direct communication with the external atmosphere, and from artificial heat, they often exceed this temperature. This of itself is sufficient to enervate and destroy all energy of frame. . . . The hands employed in these large manufactories breathe foul air for twelve hours out of the twenty-four; and we know that few things have so specific and injurious an action on the digestive organs, as the inhalation of impure air.

" Women are often employed in factories some years after their marriage, and during their pregnancy, and up to the very period of their confinement; which, all who have attended to the physiology of this subject know, must send their offspring into the world with a debilitated and unhealthy frame, which the circumstances of their infancy are ill-calculated to renovate; and hence, when these children begin to work themselves, they are prepared at once to succumb to the evil influences by which they are surrounded.

" In consequence, also, of the mother's being employed from home, their children are entrusted, in a vast majority of cases, to the care of others, often of elderly females, who have no infant family of their own, having in their youth had their children nursed by others, have never formed those habits of attachment, and of assiduous attention to their offspring, which could alone afford a probability of a proper care of the children committed to their charge. These women often undertake the care of several infants at the same time; their habits are generally indolent and gossiping; the children are restless and irritable, from being deprived of a supply of their natural food; (as when the mothers suckle them, they can only perform that duty in the intervals of labour; and the almost universal practice among them is to still the cries of the infant by administering opiates, which are sold for this purpose under several well-known forms. The quantity of opium which, from habit, some children become capable of taking, is almost incredible, and the effects are correspondingly destructive. Even when the infants have a healthy appearance at birth, they almost, uniformly, become, in a few months, puny and sickly in their aspect, and a very large proportion fall victims to bronchitis, hydrocephalus, and other diseases produced by want of care, and the pernicious habits detailed. Spirits, particularly gin, are frequently given when the infants appear to suffer from pain in the bowels, which, from injurious diet, is very common among them.

" The licentiousness which prevails among the dense population of manufacturing towns, is carried to a degree which it is appalling to contemplate, which baffles all statistical inquiries, and which can be learned only from the testimony of personal observers. And, in addition to overt acts of vice, there is a coarseness and grossness of feeling, and an habitual indecency of conversation, which we would fain hope and believe are not the prevailing characteristics of our country. The effect of this upon the mind of the young will readily be conceived; and is it likely that any instruction, or education, or Sunday schools, or sermons, can counteract the baleful influence, the insinuating virus, the putrefaction, the contagion of this moral depravity which reigns around them?

' Nil dictu fœdum visuque hæc limina tangat,
Intra quæ puer est.'—*Juvenal.*
[Let nothing foul, either to the eye or the ear, be seen or heard within those doors which enclose a boy.]

" After all, what motive has either sex, in the class and situation to which we allude, for being virtuous and chaste? Where they are unshackled by religious principle, as is too generally the case, they have no delicate sentiments of morality and taste to restrain them from gratifying every passion; they have few or no pleasures beyond those which arise from sensual indulgence, and they have no motive for refraining from this indulgence ; it involves no loss of character, for their companions are as reckless as themselves ; it brings no risk of losing their employment, for their employers know that it would be unsafe to inquire into those matters. It is often a cause of no pecuniary loss, for in many cases the poor laws provide against this; and, all these circumstances considered, the licentiousness of the manufacturing population is a source of bitter lamentation to us, but of no astonishment whatever."

This is indeed a dark picture—a state of existence more degraded it is impossible to conceive: the miserable condition of the operatives is hardly more to be lamented than the utter disregard of their employers, for the fulfilment of moral duties towards the employed. Such a state of society could not have existed, had the owners of factories, as a rule, not been dead to every interest but that of money-getting.

Dr Kay thus describes the condition of the operatives of Manchester (1832) :—" Instructed in the fatal secret of sub-sisting on what is barely necessary to life, the labouring classes have ceased to entertain a laudable pride in furnishing their houses, and in multiplying the decent comforts which minister to happiness. . . . They are engaged in an employment which absorbs their attention, and unremittingly employs their physical energies. They are drudges who watch the movements and assist the operations of a mighty material force, which toils with an energy ever unconscious of fatigue. The persevering labour of the operative must rival the mathematical precision, the incessant motion, and the exhaustless power of the machine.

" Hence, besides the negative results, the total abstraction of every moral and intellectual stimulus ; the absence of variety, banishment from the grateful air, and the cheering influences of light, the physical energies are exhausted by incessant toil and imperfect nutrition. Having been subjected to the prolonged toil of an animal, his physical energy wasted—his mind in supine inaction—the artizan has neither moral dignity, nor intellectual nor organic strength to resist the seductions of appetite. His wife and children, too frequently subjected to the same process, are unable to cheer his remaining moments of leisure. Domestic economy is neglected, domestic comforts are unknown; a meal of the coarsest food is prepared with heedless haste, and devoured with equal precipitation. Home has no other relation to him than that of shelter—few pleasures are there—it chiefly presents to him a scene of physical exhaustion, from which he is glad to escape. Himself impotent of all the distinguishing aims of his species, he sinks into sensual sloth, or revels in more degrading licentiousness. His house is ill-furnished, uncleanly, often ill-ventilated, perhaps damp; his food, from want of forethought and domestic economy, is meagre and innutritious; he is debilitated and hypochondriacal, and falls the victim of dissipation.

"The average annual number of births (deduced from a comparison of the last four years), attended by the officers of the Lying-in Charity, is four thousand three hundred ; and the number of births to the population may be assumed as one in twenty-eight inhabitants. This annual average of births, therefore, represents a population of 124,400, and assuming that of Manchester and environs to be 230,000, more than one-half of its inhabitants are therefore either so destitute or so degraded, as to require the assistance of public charity, in bringing their offspring into the world. . . . . Visiting Manchester, the metropolis of the commercial system, a stranger regards with wonder the ingenuity and comprehensive capacity, which, in the short space of half-a-century, have here established the staple manufacture of this kingdom. He beholds with astonishment the establishments of its merchants—monuments of fertile genius and successful design ; the masses of capital which have been accumulated by those who crowd upon its mart, and the restless but sagacious spirit which has made every part of the known world the scene of their enterprise. The sudden creation of the mighty system of commercial organization, which covers this country, and stretches its arms to the most distant seas, attests the power and the dignity of man. Commerce, it appears to such a spectator, here gathers in her storehouses the productions of every clime, that she may minister to the happiness of a favoured race.

" When he turns from the great capitalists, he contemplates the fearful strength only of that multitude of the labouring population, which lies like a slumbering giant at their feet. He has heard of the turbulent riots of the people—of machine-breaking—of the secret and sullen organization which has suddenly lit the torch of incendiarism, or well nigh uplifted the arm of rebellion in the land. He remembers that political desperadoes have ever loved to tempt the population to the hazards of the swindling game of revolution, and have scarcely failed. In the midst of so much opulence, however, he has disbelieved the cry of need."

Dr Kay's acknowledgment of the deterioration in the domestic circumstances of the working classes of Manchester is striking and emphatic; they had so far sunk beneath their former state as to care little for the present and less for the future, to again quote the Doctor's compendious description of their moral and social state:—" The labouring classes had *ceased* to entertain a laudable pride in furnishing their houses, and in multiplying the decent comforts which minister to happiness." These pitiable outcasts of modern civilization had fallen from comparative comfort into the lowest depths of helpless and hopeless recklessness and misery. Who could describe the suffering which must have been endured, as step by step this melancholy descent had taken place ? The result was known, but the agony of human feeling which was suffered by tens of thousands of human beings in their down-ward course, and formed its prelude, was hidden. It may be thought of, but cannot be named. A population who had *ceased* to desire improvement when left to themselves, when unaided and uninfluenced by external circumstances, had become an ulcer in the heart of the state, the poisonous humours of which, had they continued unchecked, would not have failed to have vitiated the whole vital system. Delay in such a case would have been madness, and that too of the most dangerous kind.

The statements of Dr Kay, like those of Mr Greg, were the results of close inquiry and minute investigation. The opposition of both to a reduction of the hours of labour unaccompanied by other measures was decided and per-severing. "Those political speculators," said the Doctor, " who propose a serious reduction of the hours of labour, un-preceded by the relief of commercial burdens, and unaccom-panied by the introduction of a *general system of education*, appear to us to be deluded by a theoretical chimera. The time thus bestowed would be wasted or misused—would be spent in sloth, in dissipation, or in listening with eager wonder to the declamatory dogmatism of political dema-gogues." These observations of Dr Kay are a striking illustration of what Bacon has happily called, "Idols of the tribe." Here is a man of a high order of intelligence wedded to certain general principles ; he thinks it im-possible that good can follow from the adoption of any other measures than those approved by him. Rest of body is the first requisite for one who is habitually over-worked ; no evil can flow from this requirement being reduced to practice, experience has proved that factory regulation has been beneficial in body, mind, and morals to those for whose good it was intended, its promoters have not been deluded theorists, they have been practical statesmen. It is deserving of attention that while Dr Kay maintained that long hours of labour were required to compensate the millowners for the payment of fiscal burden, he was eloquent on the riches of the few and the misery of the many, thus proving that the industry of the many had aided in the production of wealth which the few enjoyed. So true it is that " the mind," as Bacon has observed, "is not like a plain mirror, which reflects the image of things exactly as they are ; it is like a mirror of uneven surface, which combines its own figure with the figures of the objects it represents." Dr Kay conceived that each part of the system was, as it existed in 1832, " necessary to the preservation of the whole." In the absence of other changes he inferred that : "Whatever time was subtracted from the hours of labour must be accompanied with an equivalent deduction from its rewards." Mr Greg, who, as a cotton spinner, had practically observed the effects of long and short hours, was of a different opinion ; he prognosticated that the reduction in the quantity produced in ten hours would not be equal to the reduction of from twelve to ten. Arithmetic was on the side of Dr Kay, but human nature, which cannot always be calculated by the rule of three, was on that of Mr Greg. Virtue and intelligence are, or ought to be, the great aims of civilised communities, these cannot be realised in the absence of conditions indispensable to health of body and mind. The evils and horrors of " the factory system " had grown up observed by few; when examined in all its hideousness it presented a picture which overwhelmed weak minds with sorrow and shame; men of cultivated understanding and resolute will were necessary for its amendment. Though Mr Greg and Dr Kay would probably have felt shocked at being associated with Mr Oastler and Mr Bull, yet the labours of the former contributed practically toward the same end as the latter—the physical, moral, and mental elevation of those employed in factory labour. A population so sunk in the slough of human, or rather inhuman, misery, could not be easily or rapidly improved: their industry had enriched a few millowners, but had lowered the standard of humanity.

What would have been the fate of these unfortunate factory operatives had the factory system never existed? They would have slumbered on in ignorance and comparative plenty, enjoying many natural comforts of which changed circumstances had deprived them; manufacture had indeed produced a change, it had lowered its victims beneath the level of brutes in their habits, and perverted the superior reason of living women and men from an appreciation of the homely virtues of domestic life to an admiration of that which was sensual and vicious. These things it had done, but it had failed to add one atom of moral good to society, or to have made even those who pocketed its money-gains wiser or happier.

Appropriately to Mr Greg's pamphlet, it is due to the author to say that subsequent experience caused, avowedly, a change in his opinions, the extent of which we cannot define. In a tract published by Mr Robert Hyde Greg (brother to Mr Wm. Rathbone Greg) on the factory question, an apology for the pamphlet quoted, is set forth, on the grounds of the author's youth and inexperience, and that he had "imprudently adopted as facts, the misrepresentations of a heated partisan of the Ten Hours' Bill." Mr Fletcher, the eminent surgeon of Bury, in Lancashire, is the individual referred to; he, in a letter published in the London *Times*, for June the 8th, 1837, animadverted on the apology of Mr R. H. Greg, and challenged him to refute any fact or argument in the obnoxious pamphlet, an important portion of the materials of which had been supplied by Mr Fletcher, and hitherto unacknowledged by Mr William Rathbone Greg. The challenge was not accepted. Not any man was better able to judge of the condition of the working classes of Lancashire than was Mr Fletcher; we willingly give our testimony to his virtues and services.

He was among the earliest supporters of a Ten Hours'

Bill; he has from the first been an able and persevering advocate of the claims of factory children to the protection of the law ; his experience of the effects of factory labour on health and morals was, because of his extensive professional practice as surgeon in a factory district, of necessity, great ; his talent and moral courage marked him out as an able auxiliary of any cause he might espouse. It was Mr Fletcher's habit for years to lecture in the towns and villages of his own neighbourhood on the factory system, and its injurious effects on health. His benevolence won for him the respect of the poor; his high professional knowledge, while it failed to disarm the prejudice of opponents, forced even from them an acknowledgment of his talent and sincerity. Mr Fletcher has been throughout life an observer of facts ; the fruits of his experience have been freely communicated to others, who, in and out of parliament, have turned those to good account, so far as Mr Fletcher's desires and the interests of the factory operatives were concerned. Mr Fletcher has been at all times an arduous, if not always a conspicuous worker, for the elevation of the working classes; so long as probity, superior talent, and energy shall command respect, he will not fail to enjoy the good opinion of his fellow-citizens; when the solid and superficial have been separated, and each has received his due, the name of Mr Fletcher will stand high among the moral and social reformers of his generation.

CHAPTER XII.

EVIDENCE BEFORE THE SADLER COMMITTEE.—MR SADLER'S EXTRA-
ORDINARY EXERTIONS.—PRECARIOUS STATE OF HIS HEALTH.—
GROWTH OF PUBLIC OPINION.—PRESENTATION OF THE GREAT
YORKSHIRE PETITION.—" THE DUKE OF SUSSEX AND THE FACTORY
BILL."—PERSECUTION OF WORKING-MEN WITNESSES BY THEIR
EMPLOYERS.

IT is difficult to form just conceptions of the force of habit;
fully to apprehend its influence on the actions of men is
perhaps beyond the range of the human intellect. A
comparison between the duties and acts of men, as these
are understood in an avowedly Christian community, will
assist in the estimating of the direct result flowing from
the daily practices of life. "The law," says Dr Brown,
" on which right and wrong depend, did not begin to
be law when it was written; it is older than the
ages of nations and cities, and contemporary with the very
eternity of God. There is indeed, to borrow Cicero's
noble description, one true and original law, conformable to
reason and to nature; diffused over all, invariable, eternal;
which calls to the fulfilment of duty and to abstinence
from injustice, and, which calls with irresistible voice, which
is felt in all its authority, wherever it is heard. This law
cannot be abolished or controlled, nor affected in its sanctions
by any law of man. A whole senate, a whole people cannot
dispense from its paramount obligation. It requires no

commentator to render it distinctly intelligible ; nor is it different at Rome, at Athens now, and in the ages before and after; but in all ages, and in all nations, it is, and has been, and will be, one and everlasting; one, as that God, its great author and promulgator, who is the common Sovereign of all mankind, is himself one. Man is truly man as he yields to this divine influence. He cannot resist it, but by flying, as it were, from his own bosom, and laying aside the feelings of humanity, by which very act he must already have inflicted on himself the severest of punishments, even though he were to avoid what is usually accounted punishment. We feel that the laws of nature are laws which no lapse of ages can render obsolete, because they are every moment operating on every heart, and which, for the same reason, never can be repealed till man shall have ceased to be man." This law, inherent in the heart of man, pregnant with the feelings of humanity, sanctioned by the command—" Do unto others as you would they should do unto you," is constantly violated. The world is saturated with crimes, because of the violation of the laws of nature and the dictates of conscience. We are unable to account for the systematic violation of known and acknowledged duties, but by the consciousness of natural depravity and a reference to the force of habit. The majority of the millowners and their servants were professing Christians, members of some one or other of the various religious denominations, agreeing in common on the fulfilment of the duties of life, thus adding the obliga- tion of revealed to natural law, and being, therefore, bound in reverence and duty to do justly and love mercy. Yet many of these millowners, and their principal servants, violated almost unceasingly the promptings of humanity and the revealed Law of God, as avowed by their own professions. Strange, and, at first sight, apparently unaccountable inconsistency. How to be accounted for, otherwise than by an acknowledgement of natural depravity, and a consideration of the power of habit over the deeds of men, we know not. These violators of natural and revealed laws had allowed their minds to become impressed with the desirableness of one object, all others were lost in its contemplation—that object was the manufacture and sale of a commodity at such prices as to the manufacturers should be profitable. The sufferings endured by those engaged in the process of manufacture, either escaped observation, or were allowed, as necessary for the realization of the desired end. The effects of habit were not less strikingly illustrated, in the case of some statesmen. If the actual suffering of those engaged in the working departments of cotton-mills, had been placed side by side with the actual profits, and the only alternative have been the total acceptance or rejection of both, few members of the legislature would have hesitated. To reject both would have been the rule, but legislators had, in their own minds, been accustomed to associate factories with national wealth; national wealth, they maintained, was a necessity, and they failed in most instances to bestow more than a passing thought on the national evils paid as the purchase-money of the wealth they admired. They everywhere beheld the physical results of mechanical and concentrated power applied to manufacture, but seldom cast even a passing glance on the sources of widely-spread wealth, dried up in consequence. Dazzled by the prospect of present gain, they failed to have regard to the inevitable penalty which nature invariably levies upon all who fail to respect her laws. They imagined that the sufferings to which we have alluded were themselves alone to be weighed in the balance against the profits of the system ; nature, however, cannot thus be defrauded; her laws are inexorable, and the price which she demands for the infringement thereof, she has the power to enforce. In the train of those sufferings followed the sustenance of that poverty, the punishment of those crimes, which the factory system generated—the price in money of that penalty in itself being incalculable.

It was reserved for the committee, presided over by Mr Sadler, fully to establish the *data* from which the evils of the factory system could be more completely than hitherto estimated. It would be impossible to over-rate the practical utility of the evidence given before Mr Sadler's committee. Eighty-nine witnesses were examined, there were asked eleven thousand, six hundred, and eighteen questions; not one of these questions, or answers thereto, could be justly considered irrelevant, all bore directly on the main subject of the enquiry, and opened out a more complete picture of the social condition of those employed in the principal branches of manufacture, than any other on record. We select from this body of evidence, the principal facts elicited during the examination of factory operatives; the evidence of these witnesses, in all its main points, was corroborated by many others, and it may be accepted as a fair specimen of the kind of evidence given by that class of witnesses.

We, for brevity's sake, have condensed the facts stated before the Sadler committee, by several important witnesses, into narrative form, but have preserved, as far as convenient, the words in the questions asked, and the answers given.

Abraham Whitehead :—

" I am a clothier, and reside at Scholes, near Holmfirth, which is the centre of very considerable woollen mills for three or four miles ; I live near the centre of thirty or forty of them, and have had constant opportunity of observing the manner in which these mills are regulated and conducted, and I have observed them for at least the last twenty years. The youngest age at which children are employed is never under five, some are employed between five and six as pieceners. In the summer time I have frequently seen these children going to their work as early as five or six in the morning, and I know the general practice is for them to go as early to all the mills, with one or two exceptions ; I have seen them at work in the summer season between nine and ten in the evening; they continue to work as long as they can see, and they can see to work as long in these mills as you could see to read. In winter there is a variation; some of the mills begin to work at six o'clock, and some only begin so soon as they can see to work in the morning, but many of them begin by six, or between five and six in winter time. I live near to parents who have been sending their children to mills for a great number of years, and I know positively that these children are every morning in the winter season called out of bed between five and six, and in some instances between four and five. My business as a clothier has frequently led me into these mills, to carry work to or from them. I have for the last twenty years constantly made observations on these mills, having seldom missed a week going to some of them, and sometimes two or three times a day. I cannot say that I ever saw these mills actually at work later than ten ; I do not say they have not been at work later; I have seen them as late as ten in the winter season—children of tender years were employed. I have been in mills at all hours, and I never in my life saw the machinery stopped at breakfast time at any of the mills. The children get their breakfast as they can; they eat and work ; there is generally a pot of water-porridge, with a little treacle in it, placed at the end of the machine, and when they have exerted themselves to get a little forward with their work, they take a few spoonfuls for a minute or two, and then to work again, and continue to do so until they have finished their breakfast. This is the general practice not only of the children, but of the men, in the woollen mills in the district. There is not any allowance for the afternoon refreshment, called ' drinking,' more than for breakfast. In summer, some of the mills allow an hour for dinner, and others, forty minutes. There is no time allowed in winter, only just sufficient to eat their dinner; perhaps ten minutes or a quarter of an hour; and in some cases, they manage the same at noon as they do at breakfast and drinking. The children are employed as pieceners; they, when at work, are always on their feet—they cannot sit and piece. The only interval the children have for rest, is the very short time allowed for dinner, except it may sometimes happen that they may be out of what we call 'jummed wool,' and then the children have a short opportunity to rest themselves, and even then they are frequently employed in cleaning the cording machine.

"I have seen children during the last winter (1832) coming from work on cold dark nights between ten and eleven o'clock, although trade has been so bad with some of the mills that they have had nothing to do ; others have been working seventeen or seventeen and a-half hours per day. This requires that the children should be awakened very early in the morning. I can tell you what a neighbour told me six weeks ago—she is the wife of Jonas Barrowcliffe, near Scholes ; her child works at a mill nearly two miles from home, and I have seen that child coming from its work this winter between ten and eleven in the evening ; and the mother told me, that one morning this winter, the child had been up by two o'clock in the morning, when it had only arrived from work at eleven ; it then had to go nearly two miles to the mill, where it had to stay at the door till the overlooker came to open it. This family had no clock ; and the mother believed, from what she afterwards learnt from the neighbours, that it was only two o'clock when the child was called up and went to work; but this has only generally happened when it has been moonlight, thinking the morning was approaching. It is the general practice in the neighbourhood—and any fact that I state here can be borne out by particular evidence that, if required, I can point out.

" The children are generally cruelly treated ; so cruelly treated, that they dare not hardly for their lives be too late at their work in a morning. When I have been at the mills in the winter season, when the children are at work in the evening, the very first thing they inquire is, 'what o'clock is it?' if I should answer 'seven,' they say, 'Only seven? it is a great while to ten, but we must not give up to ten o'clock or past!' They look so anxious to know what o'clock it is, that I am convinced the children are fatigued, and think even at seven that they have worked too long. My heart has been ready to bleed for them when I have seen them so fatigued, for they appear in such a state of apathy and insensibility, as really not to know whether they are doing their work or not : they usually throw a bunch of ten or twelve cordings across the hand, and take one off at a time ; but I have seen the bunch entirely finished, and they have attempted to take off another when they have not had a cording at all; they have been so fatigued as not to know whether they were at work or not. The errors which they make when thus fatigued are, that instead of placing the cordings in this way [describing it], they are apt to place them obliquely, and that causes a flying, which makes bad yarn ; and when the billy-spinner sees that, he takes his strap or the billy-roller, and says, ' D——n thee, close it—little devil, close it,' and he smites the child with the strap or the billy-roller. It is a very difficult thing to go into a mill in the latter part of the day, particularly in winter, and not to hear some of the children crying for being beaten for this very fault. How they are beaten depends upon the humanity of the hubber or billy-spinner ; some have been beaten so violently that they have lost their lives in consequence ;

and even a young woman had the end of a billy-roller jammed through her cheek. The billy-roller is a heavy rod of from two to three yards long, and of two inches in diameter, and with an iron pivot at each end; it runs on the tops of the cordings over the feeding cloth. I have seen the billy-spinner take the billy-roller and rap children on the head, making their heads crack, so that you might have heard the blow at the distance of from six to eight yards, in spite of the din and rolling of the machinery; many have been knocked down by the instrument. I knew a boy very well, of the name of Senior, with whom I went to school; he was struck with a billy-roller on the elbow, it occasioned a swelling, he was not able to work more than three or four weeks after the blow, and he died in consequence. There was a woman in Holmfirth who was beaten very much with a billy-roller. This which is produced (*showing one*) is not the largest size, there are some a foot longer than that; it is the most common instrument with which these poor little pieceners are beaten—more commonly than with either a stick or a strap. It is detached from the machinery in the following manner:—Supposing this to be the billy-frame (*describing it*), at each end there is a socket open, the cording runs underneath here, just in this way, and when the billy-spinner is angry, and sees the little piecener has done wrong, he takes off this and says 'D——n thee, close it.' I have seen them frequently struck with the billy-roller; I never saw one so struck as to occasion its death, but I once saw a piecener struck on the face by a billy-spinner with his hand, until its nose bled very much; and when I said 'Oh, dear, I would not suffer a child of mine to be treated thus,' the man has said, 'How the devil do you know but what he deserved it.'

" With regard to the morals of the children who work in mills, we cannot expect that they can be so strict as children who are generally under the care of their parents. I have seen a little boy, only this winter, who works at a mill, and who lives within two hundred or three hundred yards of my door ; he is not six years old, and I have seen him, when he had a few coppers in his pocket, go to a beer shop, call for a glass of ale, and drink as boldly as any full-grown man, cursing and swearing, and saying he should be a man as soon as some of them. I do not know that there are many such boys, but the expressions of children in mills very much accord. You cannot go into a mill where even the most wealthy master clothier is called Sir or Master ; they call them all ' Old Tom,' or ' Young Tom,' &c. They call their employers so.

" There is not any possibility of children employed in this way obtaining any instruction from day-schools ; but since this factory bill was agitated, when I have been at mills, the children have gathered round me for a minute or two as I passed along, and have said, ' When shall we have to work ten hours a day ? Will you get the Ten Hours' Bill ? We shall have a rare time then ; surely some-body will set up a neet (night) school ; I will learn to write, that I will.' The opinion of the inhabitants of my neighbour-hood is, that if a Ten Hours' Bill be passed, it will be the greatest advantage that they could possibly enjoy. They are of opinion that the more hours they work, the less they receive for it. They say that the markets are overstocked by overworking, and the men are overworked. When a master gets an order for a certain quantity of goods, he sets all his men to work night and day until it is completed. It is the general opinion that if a stop is not put to this excessive and increasing labour, there will never be an end to the reduction of wages; but whether the wages will be reduced or not, they are convinced it will be a benefit ; and they are anxious that the bill should be passed into a law. I live six or seven miles from Huddersfield—there is a mill at Smithy Place, three miles and a-half from Huddersfield; and that mill worked so long about two years ago, that a boy at that mill actually hanged himself, because he said he would sooner do it than work so many hours a day as he had done. I had a brother-in-law working at the mill at the time, and sufficient evidence can be produced before this Committee, to prove that the boy destroyed himself rather than be so overworked. From what I have observed, I do not believe that so beneficial an alteration in the hours of labour as would follow the enactment of the Ten Hours' Bill, could be brought about except by a legislative enactment; for the parents who send their children to the mills are generally those who could not provide for them by any other means, and they have no alternative but to send them. But the masters as well as the men generally in the neighbourhood of Holmfirth, are disgusted with the overworking of children, and they say that it ought to be remedied. But it cannot be remedied unless every one is compelled to do as others do. We understand by the Ten Hours' Bill, a bill that will not allow children of a certain age to be actively employed more than ten hours per day, which will be twelve, leaving two hours for rest and refreshment. I have never seen the harsh treatment I have described, exercised upon persons of fifteen or sixteen years of age; persons of these ages are generally employed in some other business than piecening. It appears to me that parliamentary interference is necessary to protect the parents as well as the children. The children have excited commiseration by being overworked. It is also injurious to the parents, because the masters or millowners who have no conscience or feeling, do not care what length of time they run their mills. When one takes the lead, another must follow, and then all continue to work long hours : although the first might feel some advantage, yet when all come to that point, the advantage is lost, and they must strain another point or there is no advantage in it; by doing so, they lower the wages more and more—and the more they work, the less wages are obtained. If protection were afforded by law to children up to the age of fifteen, those above that age would then suffer; and why should they continue to work seventeen or eighteen hours per day? It seems to me that youths ought to have some opportunity of learning to read and write, and other domestic duties. For instance, when females who were brought up in mills get married, they know not how to conduct a family, how to purchase household things, or how to manage their children; it is even a proverb in the neighbourhood of Holmfirth, that the man who would have a good wife must take care not to marry 'a factory doll,' as she will not know how to manage a family. I think all ought to be protected by law until they be twenty-one years of age . . . . . . I know, from my own knowledge, that children of the age of from six to twelve have really been working from sixteen and seventeen hours per day—I know it by seeing them going to their work and coming from their work, the same children."

James Paterson:—

"I reside at Dundee, am twenty-eight years of age, and by business a mill-overseer. I have been acquainted with the mill system in Dundee and neighbourhood for a long time. At ten years of age I entered a mill; it was Mr Proctor's, of Glammis. I worked in the carding-room, which was very dusty. There were fourteen hours' actual work, and fifteen hours a-day confinement, including meals. I suffered from shortness and stoppage at the breast, and was forced to leave in consequence. I was nearly three years at Mr Proctor's. Other children were similarly affected; I had a brother who was at that work too, and he was compelled to leave for bad health, and was laid up and died of consumption. The doctor said it was occasioned by being confined at that work. My brother died at eighteen years of age; he had originally a good constitution.

*　　*　　*　　*　　*　　*　　*

" I worked at Mr Braid's mill, of Duntruin; there we worked as long as we could see in summer time, and I could not say at what hour it was we stopped. There was nobody but the master, and the master's son, had a watch, and we did not know the time. The operatives were not permitted to have a watch. There was one man that had a watch, I believe it was a friend who gave it him ; it was taken from him and given into the master's custody, because he had told the men the time of the day. There was no clock at that mill. There were a great many children in pro-portion to the number of adults, most of them were orphans. There was a part of them that came from Edinburgh, and a part of them from Perth. There were some of the orphan children from Edinburgh who had been in the mill, I believe, from four to five years. The children were incapable of performing their day's labour well towards the termination of the day; their fate was to be awoke by being beaten, and to be kept awake by the same method. They were under that mode of treatment, kept on the premises by being locked up, while at work ; they were guarded up to their bothies to take their meals, they were locked up in the bothies at night, and the master took the key away with him to his own bed-room ; they were guarded to their work, and they were guarded back again, and they were guarded while they were taking their meat, and then they were locked up for rest. The windows of the bothies where they slept had all iron stanchions on the outside, so that they could not escape. They were not allowed to go to a place of worship on the Sunday ; they were guarded on the premises by the master or his son. There were twenty-five or twenty-six of us together. There was one bothy for the boys, but that did not hold them all, and there were some of them put into the other bothy along with the girls. The ages of the boys that were put into the girls' bothy might be, I should suppose, from ten to fourteen, the ages of the girls, perhaps, from twelve to eighteen.

"The children and young persons were sometimes successful in their attempts to escape from labour and confinement. I have gone after them on horseback and brought them back myself. Those brought back were taken into the mill, and got a severe beating with a strap; sometimes the master kicked them on the floor, and struck them with both his hands and his feet. Those who had made engagements for any length of time, when they ran away, the master, if he could not find them before they got home to their relations, if they had any, he sent after them and put them in gaol. I knew a woman put in gaol, and brought back after a twelvemonth, and worked for her meat; and she had to pay the expenses that were incurred. There were some engaged for two years, and some as far on as three years, and some of those girls sent from Edinburgh, I heard them say, were engaged for five years. That girl that was sent to prison worked two years for nothing, to indemnify her master for the loss of her time while she was in the course of punishment, but there was a sister who came to work nine months or so to help her to perform the two years.

"When the hands worked those long hours, the master came himself and roused them in the morning, and those that would not rise, I have seen him take a pail of water and throw it upon them, to make them rise. One of the means taken to secure those children and young persons from running away was that their clothes, if they had any not in use, were kept locked up, so that if they ran away they could only run away with what was on their backs. Those children were at times beaten very violently."

Joseph Habergam:—

" I reside at North gate, Huddersfield, in Yorkshire—I was seventeen years of age on the 21st of April. I have been without a father six years on the 8th of August—my mother survives. I was seven years of age when I began to work at George Addison's, Bradley Mill, near Huddersfield; the employment was worsted spinning; the hours of labour at that mill were from five in the morning till eight at night, with an interval for rest and refreshment of thirty minutes, at noon; there was no time for rest or refreshment in the afternoon; we had to eat our meals as we could, standing or otherwise. I had fourteen-and-a-half hours' actual labour when seven years of age, the wages I then received was two shillings and sixpence per week. I attended to what are called the throstle machines; this I did for two years and a half, and then I went to the steam looms for half-a-year. In that mill there were about fifty children, of about the same age that I was. These children were often sick and poorly; there were always, perhaps, half-a-dozen regularly that were ill because of excessive labour. The work was not very hard, but having to work so very many hours made it worse; it was rather hard of itself, but it would have been better if we had not had so long to stand. We began to grow drowsy and sleepy about three o'clock, and grew worse and worse, and it came to be very bad towards six or seven, I had still to labour on. There were three overlookers; there was a head overlooker, and then there was one man kept to grease the machines, and then there was one kept on purpose to strap. Strapping was the means by which the children were kept at work. It was the main business of one of the overlookers to strap the children up to this excessive labour,— the same as strapping an old restiff horse, that has fallen down and will not get up. This was the practice day by day. The overlooker is continually walking up and down with the strap in his hand, and his office is to strap the children on to their labour. The children could not be kept so long to their labour, if they were not so treated. It was reckoned by the children to be very bad usage; towards the end of the day the flies of the machines would burst their knuckles. Accidents were frequent. The children were not capable of performing the amount of labour that was exacted from them, without perpetual cruelty. I had at that time similarly occupied a brother and a sister, his name was John, and her name was Charlotte. I cannot say how old my sister was, when she began to work in the mill, but my brother John was seven. They were often sick; my brother John died three years ago—he was then sixteen years and eight months old. My mother and the medical attendants were of opinion that my brother died from working such long hours, and that it had been brought about by the factory. They have to stop the flies with their knees, because they go so swift they cannot stop them with their hands; he got a bruise on the shin by a spindle-board, and it went on to that degree that it burst; the surgeon cured that, then my brother was better. He went to work again, but when he had worked about two months more his spine became affected, and he died. His medical attendants state that that spinal affection was owing to his having been so over-laboured at the mill; and that he died in consequence.

" Mill labour has had a great deal of effect on my own health, I have had to drop it several times in the year. When I had worked about half a year, a weakness fell into my knees and ankles; it continued, and it has got worse and worse. It was attended with very great pain, and the sense of extreme fatigue. Under these circumstances I had to work as often as I could, otherwise not any allowance would have been made to me by the occupier of the mill. I live a good mile from the mill; it was very painful for me to move; in the morning I could not walk, and my brother and sister used out of kindness to take me under each arm, and run with me to the mill, and my legs dragged on the ground in consequence of the pain; I could not walk, and if we were five minutes too late, the overlooker would take a strap, and beat us till we were black and blue. The overlooker knew the occasion of our being a little too late; we have stated to him the reason, but he never minded that, he used to watch us out of the windows. The pain and weakness in my legs increased.

[The witness, by request, stood up and showed the committee his limbs.]

"I was as straight and healthful as any one when I was seven years old. There were other children at the mill who became deformed in like manner. There were some very often sick, and some were deformed; but the parents who were able to support their children took them away; in consequence of seeing that they would be deformed if they did not take them away. My mother being a widow, and having but little, could not afford to take me away. The parish would not have relieved me if my mother had taken me away. She has frequently been to the parish authorities, but she was no better for it. I have seen my mother weep oftentimes, and I have asked her why she was weeping, but she would not tell me then, but she has told me since. She was so affected by seeing my limbs give way by working such long hours.

*　　*　　*　　*　　*

"The overlookers, under whom I have hitherto worked, have been in the habit of strapping and cruelly beating the children for very little faults; for being late in the morning, and for letting the ends run down. One part of the discipline of those mills is profound silence; they will not allow the children to speak: if two are seen speaking, they are beaten with the strap. The masters encourage the overlooker to treat the children in that manner. I have seen them when the master has been standing at one end of the room, and two of the overlookers speaking to him, and if he has chanced to see two girls speaking to each other, he has said, 'Look yonder at those two girls talking,' and he has run and beat them the same as they beat soldiers in the barrack-yard for deserting. The strapping was principally going on in the morning, from half past five to six ; for if there were twenty that were too late, they would all be beaten. There was strapping in the after part of the day also ; it began about three o'clock, and continued then till the time that they dropped their work—very cruel strapping. If they had not strapped the children they would have fallen asleep.

"Out of the thirty minutes allowed for dinner, five minutes and sometimes ten were occupied in cleaning the spindles. On Saturday night we gave over at six o'clock, after which time we used to be made to fettle the machines, which took an hour and a-half. Sometimes, during the time I worked at Bradley mill, the clock was a quarter of an hour too soon in the meal-time; we had just done fettling, and we had but half got our dinners, and the overlooker put the clock forward to one, and he rang the bell, and we were obliged to run back to our work. This was not an uncommon practice. During the two years and a-half I was at that mill, there were about a dozen of the children who died. The owner of the mill did not send after these children to inquire after them, or to relieve them when they were disabled by their long-continued labour—they lived sometimes for two or three months after they left. If any one had taken an account of the deaths at the mill, the deaths of those children would not have been included in that statement. They did not die in the mill; but I knew one boy who died when he had been out of the mill only two days ; he was stuffed up by the dust. There is considerable dust in that employment; you cannot take the food out of your basket or handkerchief but what it is covered with dust directly. This circumstance renders the more necessary that we, the children, should have

time to eat our breakfast and 'drinking,' which are brought
to us, but they will allow us no time, and we have to bite
our food as we can; it is laid up on the board—sometimes
the 'flue' gets into it, so that we cannot eat it. The children
are frequently sick because of the dust and dirt they eat
with their meat. If they were allowed a little time to get
their breakfast and 'drinking' in, they could then go out of
doors and get the meat clean and comfortable, and the dust
would not get into it. The children ate their dinner on the
boiler-house thatch or anywhere, as they could not go home.
I lived a good mile off. In winter we, the children, ate
our dinner sometimes out of doors, and sometimes in the
mill.

"When I gave over attending the 'throstles,' I worked
at 'bobbin winding' at the steam looms. The labour was
continued the same length of time, from five in the morning
to eight at night. When trade was brisk, I have worked
from five in the morning to nine at night. For this additional
hour's labour each working day I received, for the whole
six months, tenpence halfpenny. This was the sum received
by each, big and little, for the whole time. This was when
I worked at the throstles. I was forced to work the additional
hour. When we, the children, worked at the 'bobbin work,'
we were not used so cruelly: there was no strap, only the
overlooker was a very savage man, and he used to strike
the children under the ribs, till it took their wind away,
and they fell on the floor, and perhaps lay there for two
minutes. All the overlookers are in the habit of treating
the children with severity; the masters put them up to
it, because they could not get the quantity of work done
they wanted, unless they were to beat them.

"When I left Mr Addison's, Bradley mill, I went to
Mr Brooks's upper mill, Huddersfield. At Mr Brooks's the
usual time of labour for the children was twelve hours per
day. We worked from six in the morning till eight at

night; we had half an hour to breakfast, an hour at noon, and half an hour at drinking time, making altogether twelve hours of actual labour. The hours were too long, we could not stand them. I was ten years of age when I went there first; I remained nearly four years; I worked at Lewis's machine in the dressing department. I have stated the regular hours of working; when trade was particularly brisk I was obliged to work from five in the morning till half-past ten, sometimes till eleven, for four months together, and once all night. My regular wages was five shillings a week, and they gave a shilling extra for over-hours. I must either have worked those over-hours or left my place. It was the same in other places when trade was good. It is not easy to get a place, because there are so many boys; there is always somebody out of work. I found that labour to be very distressing to me, and it increased the pain in my limbs. It also increased the deformity which came upon me, and I have had to drop it several times for a fortnight together. They did not use the strap there, they used to strike with the fist and kick with the foot. During the time I worked there, I wished many times they would have sent me for a West India slave. I had heard the condition of the West India slaves described. I felt myself very much overworked, with insufficient rest, and very much injured by that length of labour. This rendered me very miserable in my mind, and I thought there could be nothing worse, and that there could not be worse slaves than those who worked in factories. On one occasion, I worked all Friday, Friday night, and Saturday.

"I left that situation. One morning I was between ten minutes and a quarter of an hour too late; the overlooker met me, he gave me a knock on the head against a step, and caused a great lump to rise; he said he would turn me off—'a young devil for being too late;' he followed me up the steps, but he could not catch me; I ran round the steps to get away from him, and I left that place. I was then fourteen years of age. I was beat and kicked in the way I have described for having been too late. It is customary in some places to abate the wages; I do not think they did so at Mr Brooks's. I left that mill, and I went to Mr William Firth's, Greenhead, Huddersfield, and they began this rule. They bated the boys 1½d. for six minutes, and a man 3d.; and when it got to sixteen minutes, they doubled it—6d. for a man and 3d. for a boy—and it was doubled again when it got up to thirty-one minutes; then the forfeiture for a boy was 4½d.—and a boy's daily wages was 10d., 1s., and so on. I do not know whether the overlooker kept the fines or not; he used to take them when he paid the wages. I was beaten as well as fined for being too late. It was the general system in that mill, at times, to beat the children as well as stop their wages. They did not beat them so cruelly—they did not beat them with straps, but with their fists. The practice of stopping wages for being too late does not do away with beating, but they were beat most, where they did not pay the fines. The longest hours I worked at Mr Firth's were from five in the morning till nine at night. Two hours were allowed for refreshment—there were fourteen hours of actual labour. I left that employment, because I could stand it no longer; the weakness was so bad in my knees and ankles. I was obliged totally to give up work. I believe I should have died if I had not given up— the doctors have nearly cured me. I was placed by my mother under the medical treatment of Dr Walker, of the Huddersfield Infirmary. In that Infirmary they can only take into the house twenty at once, because there are not subscribers enough to enable them to take more, and there are so many accidents that they are obliged to take in; they would have taken me in if they could; they have twenty-two in sometimes, but twenty is the regular rule. It is a new place. My mother got a recommendation from Mr Bradley Clay. It is nearly eleven weeks since I dropped work. Mr Oastler got me into the Leeds Infirmary as an in-patient, under the care of Mr Hey. He examined me, and said that my deformity was caused by the factory system. He said he thought he could have done me good if he had had me a few years ago ; there would have been means of bringing me straight. He said it was all from the factory system—working so long and standing so many hours. Mr Hey said, there were but poor hopes of me. Dr Walker says I never shall be right any more. The cause of my illness has been going on all along, but I have got rather worse since I was fourteen years of age. I cannot walk above thirty yards before my legs begin aching very bad, and then I cannot walk at all.

" When at the factory, I had not any opportunity of learning to read and write—only a little, on the Sabbath-day. I have tried to learn to write within these last ten or eleven weeks. I do not think that there is above one in a hundred in the factories that can write.

" I am now an in-patient in the Leeds Infirmary. There are cases similar to mine. There is one boy; he is weak in the knees, the same as I am, but not quite so far gone ; he is under Mr Smith, I think, a surgeon; and there is another boy in the same ward as I am, he was struck on the hip, by a slubber, with a billy-roller. There is another boy who was kicked by an overlooker with his foot, and his body was the same as if it was taken off, and set on behind him ; his body is twisted, and he goes upon crutches. I have been in the Leeds Infirmary a week last Saturday night; if I had been this week at Leeds, I should have been a fortnight next Saturday. Last Tuesday but one there was a boy brought in about five or six o'clock in the evening from a mill. He had been catched with the shaft, and he had both his thighs broke, and from his knee to his hip the flesh was ripped up the same as if it had been cut by a knife, his head was bruised, his eyes were nearly torn out, and his arms broken. His sister, who ran to pull him off, got both her arms broke and her head bruised, and she is bruised all over her body. The boy died last Thursday night but one, about eight o'clock ; I do not know whether the girl is dead, but she was not expected to live. That accident occurred in consequence of the shaft not being sheathed.

    *   *   *   *   *   *

" Dr Walker ordered me to wear irons from the ankle to the thigh; my mother was not able to get them, and he said he would write a note, and she might go to some gentlemen in the town and give them that note, and see if they would not give her something towards them ; and so she did, and I got the bare irons made, and I was coming into the yard where I live, and there was a man who worked at the same place that I did asked me to let him look at them ; I told him I could not get money to line them with, and he said, 'I will tell you where there is a gentleman who will give you the money;' he told me of Mr Oastler, and he said, 'I will go and see if he is at home, that you may not lose your trouble.' Mr Oastler was at home, and said I was to be there at eight o'clock in the morning, because he wanted to go off on a journey; I got there about half-past eight. Mr Wood of Bradford gave me a sovereign. Mr Oastler asked me what my lameness came on with, I told him, and he happened to mention it at the county meeting at York. My master saw it in the newspaper, and he sent the foreman to our house where I lived; he had not patience to read it, and he said to my mother, 'I suppose it is owing to our place that your Joseph got the use of his limbs taken away,' and my mother said he was informed wrong, that I had my lameness before I went to that factory ; but he said, 'If Joseph has said anything about our factory we shall certainly turn him off, and both his brothers.' I have two little brothers working at the same place. He said he did not know exactly how it was, but he would go back and see the paper himself, and if he found out that I had said anything about the factory system, *we* should be turned off. I have not been turned off, but my master will not speak to me or look at me; I do not know whether he will let me start again or not. My brothers have not been turned off.

*   *   *   *   *   *

" I had one of my arms broke. I was working at what is called a brushing-mill; there is a pin they put into the roller to make it run round, and the pin catched my sleeve, and twisted my arm round and broke it, and another boy has had his arm broken in the same way. At Mr Brooks's mill they cannot break their arms by that part of the machine, owing to a different arrangement. There was a boy who, to 'fettle' the machine, was kneeling down, and a strap catched him about his ankles, and carried him round the wheel, and dashed his brains out on the floor. These accidents usually happen at the latter end of the day; the children get tired— that boy got killed at a quarter-past seven at night. I have worked ten years in mills, and have in all cases been required to labour longer than my strength could bear. I have been rendered ill, deformed, and miserable by the factory system, as at present pursued. Oh! if I had a thousand pounds I would give them to have the use of my limbs again."

Benjamin Gummersil:—

" I reside in Bowling Lane, Bradford, in Yorkshire, and am now sixteen years of age. I have been employed in piecening at a worsted mill. I have worked at Mr Cozen's mill ; the hours of labour were from six in the morning to seven, and half-past seven and eight at night; half an hour was allowed at noon for dinner—not any time was allowed for breakfast or ‘drinking.’ As a child, I found the employment hard and laborious. I entered the mill at nine years of age; my father was obliged to send me to the mill in order to keep me. If we are higher than the frames, we have to bend our bodies and our legs, so. [Here the witness showed the position in which he worked.] I was a healthy and strong boy before I went to the mill. When eight years old, I could walk from Leeds to Bradford without any pain or difficulty, and did not in consequence feel much fatigue. I had worked about a year at Mr Cozen’s mill for those long hours, before I found my limbs begin to fail. The failing came on with great pain in my legs and knees; I felt very much fatigued towards the end of those days—then the overlooker beat me up to my work. I have been beaten till I was black and blue in my face, and have had my ears torn. I have been cruelly chastised—once I was very ill with it. I was beaten because I had mixed a few empty bobbins, having not any place to put them into separate. I was generally beaten most at the end of the day, when I grew tired and fatigued. In the morning I felt stiff, very stark indeed ; I was beaten in the morning as well, but not so much as towards the latter end of the day. I continued to attend the mill after my limbs began to fail. After I became deformed, I did not get on so well with my work as I could before. I got less in height, I cannot exactly say how tall I am now, I have fallen several inches in height. I had to stand thirteen or fourteen hours a day frequently, and was constantly engaged as I have described. [The witness, at the request of the Committee, exhibited his limbs, ‘and they appeared to be exceedingly crooked.’] I was perfectly straight before I entered upon this labour. There were other boys deformed in the same way. There was another boy going in the same way that I am, and there was another with one leg out and another in. A good many other boys suffered in their health, in consequence of the severity of their work. Other children have suffered, though not to the great extent that I have done. I have two brothers and two sisters who work in Mr Cozen's mill. They have not suffered in the same way that I have done. I have a brother that was working at a mill that was going the same way, but he recovered after he left. I have not any other brothers and sisters who are unhealthy—they are all straight besides myself. I cannot recollect my mother— my father is not deformed. I cannot write, I have not had any opportunity of learning. I can read some little, but very poorly. I am now supported by helping my sister to knit heels to weave with. I have sometimes pains in my limbs now; when I stand I have very much pain. I was working long hours when this deformity came on : when my legs got bad, I worked all the same hours, they were not shortened; sometimes I was bad and was forced to go home. The master nor the overlooker never sent the doctor to me, nor do they make me any allowance now. I went once to the doctor, Mr Blakey, to see if he could do me any good, or give me a recommendation to the Dispensary ; and he said they had called a committee for a boy like me before, but they could not do him any good. My father sent me to the doctor—Mr Blakey is one of the doctors of the Dispensary. I have been seen by Dr Beaumont, at Bradford; he looked at me, he said that he could not do me any good. I am quite sure that this pain in my limbs and this grievous deformity have resulted from long labour ; that is the opinion of my father and all my friends, and of all the medical men that have seen me.

"I have two sisters who worked the same hours at the

same mill, they have not suffered in their health. They did not do the same kind of work ; the one was a warper and the other a reeler. They had not to stoop so much as I had. I was a strong boy when I went to work, and I am sure ten hours a day labour was enough for me as a strong boy. I had five shillings and sixpence a week wages, and then I left and went again, and they gave me four shillings and sixpence, because I had got worse in my limbs. When I was nine years old, I first went into the mill. I got two shillings the first week when I was learning, and then I kept getting raised as I could work better. I worked as long for my four and sixpence as I did for my five and sixpence. When I began to be deformed and crooked, they gave me a stool to sit on, to enable me to reach my work. I could not work now while sitting. When we had all our ends up, there was a stool at top, and I went to sit me down there . . . . I cannot now stand without crutches or a stick, or something to lean against. I cannot walk at all. I cannot get up stairs except I creep up upon my hands and knees, or backwards way, which I do every night."

Elizabeth Bentley :—

" I am twenty-three years of age, and live at Leeds. I began to work at Mr Busk's flax mill when I was six years old. I was then a little ' doffer.' In that mill we worked from five in the morning till nine at night, when they were ' throng;' when they were not so ' throng,' the usual hours of labour were from six in the morning till seven at night. The time allowed for our meals was forty minutes at noon ; not any time was allowed for breakfast or ' drinking:' these we got as we could. When our work was bad, we had hardly any time to eat them at all : we were obliged to leave them or take them home. When we did not take our uneaten food home, the overlooker took it and gave it to his pigs. I consider 'doffing' to be a laborious employment. When the frames are full, the 'doffers' have to stop them, and take the 'flyers' off, and take the full bobbins off, and carry them to the roller, and then put empty ones on, and set the frame going again. I was kept constantly on my feet; there were so many frames, and they run so quick, the labour was excessive, there was not time for anything. When the 'doffers' flagged a little, or were too late, they were strapped. Those who were last in 'doffing' were constantly strapped— girls as well as boys. I have been strapped severely, and have been hurt by the strap excessively. The overlooker I was under was a very severe man. When I and others have been fatigued and worn out, and had not baskets enough to put the bobbins in, we used to put them in the window bottoms, and that broke the panes sometimes; and I broke one one time, and the overlooker strapped me on the arm, and it rose a blister, and I ran home to my mother. I worked at Mr Busk's factory three or four years.

"When I left Mr Busk's, I then went to Benyon's factory; I was about ten years of age, and was employed as a weigher in the card-room. At Benyon's factory we worked from half-past five till eight at night, when they were 'throng' until nine. The spinners at that mill were allowed forty minutes at noon for meals ; no more time throughout the day was allowed. Those employed in the card-rooms had, in addition to the forty minutes at noon, a quarter of an hour allowed for their breakfast, and a quarter of an hour for their 'drinking.' The carding-room is more oppressive than the spinning department : those at work cannot see each other for dust. The 'cards' get so soon filled up with waste and dirt, they must be stopped or they would take fire : the stoppages are as much for the benefit of the employer as for the working people. The children at Benyon's factory were beat up to their labour with a strap. I have seen the over-looker go to the top end of the room, where the little girls 'hug' the can to the 'backminsters;' he has taken a strap, and a whistle in his mouth, and sometimes he has got a chain and chained them, and strapped them all down the room. This was done to those children who were 'hugging' the cans. It was in the afternoon; the children were excessively fatigued: they were too slow, and the overlooker was angry with them. The girls have many times had black marks upon their skins. Had the parents complained of this excessive ill-usage, the probable consequence would have been the loss of the employment of the child. Of this result the parents were afraid.

"I worked in the card-room; it was so dusty that the dust got upon my lungs, and the work was so hard. I was middling strong when I went there, but the work was so bad; I got so bad in health, that when I pulled the baskets down, I pulled my bones out of their places. The basket I pulled was a very large one; that was full of weights, upheaped, and pulling the basket, pulled my shoulder out of its place, and my ribs have grown over it. That hard work is generally done by women: it is not fit for children. There was no spinning for me, and I therefore did that work. They gave me five shillings a week, the women had six shillings and sixpence. As a spinner, I had got six shillings. The hands were constantly leaving, because of the unhealthy nature of their employment, and the excessive labour they had to endure. The employment made us very thirsty: we drank a deal of water in the room. It was not so very hot as in the summer time. In the winter it was necessary to have the windows open; it made no matter what the weather was, and sometimes we got very severe colds in frost and snow. We were constantly exposed to colds, and were made ill by that cause also. Then I had not much food to eat, and the little I had I could not eat it, my appetite was so poor. My food being covered with dust, it was no use to take it home. I could not eat it, and the overlooker took it, and gave it to his pigs. I am speaking of the breakfast. I could not go home to dinner.

"I lived two miles from the mill. We had no clock. If I had been too late at the mill, I would have been 'quartered.' I mean that if I had been a quarter of an hour too late, a half an hour would have been taken off. I only got a penny an hour, and they would have taken a halfpenny more. I was never beaten myself. I have seen the boys beaten for being too late. I was generally at the factory in time. My mother has been up at two o'clock and at four o'clock in the morning. The colliers used to go to their work about three or four o'clock, and when she heard them stirring, she has got up out of her warm bed, and gone out and asked them the time ; and I have sometimes been at Hunslet Car at two o'clock in the morning, when it was streaming down with rain, and we have had to stay till the mill was opened. Had the hours of labour been moderate, I could have awoke regularly. It was a matter of anxiety and difficulty for me to arouse myself early enough for those hours of labour.

"I am considerably deformed in person in consequence of this labour. I was about thirteen years old when my deformity began to come on, and it has got worse since. It is five years since my mother died, and she was never able to get me a pair of good stays to hold me up; and when my mother died I had to do for myself, and got me a pair. Before I worked at a mill I was as straight a little girl as ever went up and down town. I was straight until I was thirteen. I have been attended by a medical gentleman, Mr Hare. He said it was owing to hard labour, and working in the factories. He told me so. I was coming from Leeds, and he asked a good many questions. He asked me if I had a father and mother? I said, no. He said if I had no objection he would take me in hand. I said I was much obliged to him. He told me to come to his house that night; and I went to the mill, and told them I was going to stop away.

I stopped at home ten weeks, and my cousins, that I was living with, had to maintain me, and they told me they were sure he would not do me any good, and they could not find me with support ; and Mr Hare told me it would be a year before I should be straight again. I was obliged to return to my work. It was two years ago that Mr Hare saw me; I was then twenty-one. I cannot express the pain I had all the time that the deformity was coming upon me.

"I next began to work at Tatham and Walker's flax-mill. I went into the spinning room. When they were busy, the hours of labour there were from half-past five in the morning to eight and half-past eight. I have seen the children strapped in that mill, the 'doffers' as well as others The children could not be kept up to their work unless they were beaten. The period allotted for refreshment at that mill, and at the time to which I allude, was forty minutes at noon in winter, and half an hour in summer. Since the factory agitation began, time has been allowed for breakfast and 'drinking.' When they were much thronged in winter, the hours of work were from six in the morning to seven or eight at night. The children were occasionally brought in from their meals before the time was up ; they were sometimes whipped in out of the mill yard ; the overlooker has got a strap, and gone out and strapped them in before their time, that they might come in and get on with their work.

" I have had the misfortune, from being a straight and healthful girl, to become very much otherwise in person. I do not know of any other girls that have become weak and de-formed in like manner. I have known others who have been similarly injured in health. I am deformed in the shoulders ; it is very common indeed to have weak ankles and crooked knees, that is brought on by stopping the spindle.

" I have had experience in wet spinning—it is very uncom-fortable. I have stood before the frames till I have been wet through to my skin ; and in winter-time, when myself and others have gone home, our clothes have been frozen, and we have nearly caught our death from cold. We have stopped at home one or two days, just as we were situated in our health; had we stopped away any length of time we should have found it difficult to keep our situations.

" I am now in the poor-house at Hunslet. Not any of my former employers come to see me. When I was at home, Mr Walker made me a present of 1s. or 2s., but since I left my work and have gone to the poor-house, no one has come nigh me. I was very willing to have worked as long as I was able, and to have supported my widowed mother. I am utterly incapable now of any exertion of that sort, and am supported by the parish."

Mr Gillett Sharpe, Keighley, examined:—

The witness having detailed the results of excessive labour on members of his own family, was asked:

" Have you reason to think that any of the children lose their lives in consequence of this excessive degree of exertion? —I have no doubt in my mind that such has been the case, and I may mention one instance of the kind. Four or five months back there was a girl of a poor man's that I was called to visit; it was poorly; it had attended a mill, and I was obliged to relieve the father in the course of my office (assistant-overseer), in consequence of the bad health of the child; by-and-by it went back to its work again, and one day he came to me with tears in his eyes : I said, ' What is the matter, Thomas ? He said, ' My little girl is dead.' I said, ' When did she die ?' He said, ' In the night; and what breaks my heart is this, she went to the mill in the morning, she was not able to do her work, and a little boy said he would assist her if she would give him a halfpenny on Saturday; I said I would give him a penny,' but at night when the child went home, perhaps about a quarter of a mile, in going home she fell down several times on the road through exhaustion, till at length she reached her father's door with difficulty, and she never spoke audibly afterwards; she died in the night.

" What was the illness of the child when you saw it at the parent's house ?—It seemed to be exhaustion, general debility, and weakness of body.

" Was there any medical person called in to visit her ?— Yes ; he asked me to send a doctor to visit her, and give her what he thought proper.

" What was the doctor's opinion ?—I do not know, I never spoke to the doctor; he gave her something, and she got better then.

" You cannot say what was the matter with her ?—No, but I could not help noticing, and it brought tears to my eyes, though the child did not belong to me, to think that she should have to work the last day of her life under such circumstances.

" Do you believe her indisposition was caused by working in the factories?—If she had been at home, instead of being confined in the factory, she would have been in a different situation.

" How old was the little girl ?—I cannot speak exactly to her age, I judged she might be ten years old.

" How long was this mill working in the day ?—I cannot speak to that ; I have no doubt it worked from six to seven.

" Had the child any specific disease that you know of ?— No, I do not know that she had."

Among the more systematic modes adopted to procure the greatest quantity of labour from the exercise of the faculties of little children, the following deserve special attention. In their own horrible way, they have a claim to be considered " improvements " upon the vulgar and common practices of beatings with leather straps, blows with billy-rollers, and like means of punishment. Mr James Turner, from Manchester, in the course of his examination by the Committee, stated that it was well known that other means than beating were adopted " to get as much work out of the little infants as possible," a statement which gave rise to the following questions and answers:—"What do you mean by other means ?—Other means besides coercive means. It is quite common in the mill, for instance, to give prizes to those that can do the most work in a fortnight or so. Last Saturday three weeks, two of these boys had been striving, for three pounds of bacon and three score of potatoes, which could do the most work for a fortnight; the prize was decided on that day, and the little boy that had won it had often complained, when he got home, that he could hardly get to bed. Then when the two boys have done this quantity of work, the overlookers almost insist that others should do the same. The girls they will give dolls to : they get two dolls, a big one and a little one, and hang them up on the frame, and those that do the most work get one of these dolls. This boy that I named, his name is Griffiths, that had won the bacon, he also had won on a former occasion half a peck of meal and some sugar. This is done to get as much work out of the little children as ever they can, and then when part have done it, they consider that all can do alike ; and they almost insist on their doing so, and use them harshly if they do not do so much work as those have done for their prizes.

" So that the children are on the one hand coerced, and on the other hand tempted, to perform more labour than is consistent with their health ?—Most certainly they tempt one, and then coerce the rest; this is a general practice at Longworthy and Co.'s, a large silk mill that we have in Mosley street.

" Is it so in the cotton mills ?—No, it is not; I never knew it done in the cotton."

Jonathan Downe examined:—
"When you worked in mills, what methods were taken

to rouse the children from drowsiness ?—It is a very frequent
thing at Mr Marshall's, where the least children are employed
(for there were plenty working at six years of age). It has
been the regular practice of late years for Mr Horseman to
start the mill earlier in the morning than he formerly did ;
and provided a child should be drowsy, the overlooker walks
round the room with a stick in his hand, and he touches
that child on the shoulder, and says, 'Come here.' In the
corner of the room there is an iron cistern; it is filled with
water, so that if any fire should occur in the room, they
could quench it with that water : he takes this boy, and
holding him up by the legs, dips him over head in the
cistern, and sends him to his work for the remainder of
the day; and that boy is to stand dripping as he is at
his work—he has no chance of drying himself. Such, at
least, was the case when I was there.

"In addition to the beating, have you known any other
methods of punishment resorted to for presumed offences ?—
Yes, that first is for drowsiness, the second is for any other
offence that may occur in any other room in that mill ; I never
saw it in any other place; it is just according to their crime,
great or small.   There is a stool fixed up at one end of the room,
the boy who offends is put to stand on this stool, sometimes on
both legs, and sometimes on one of his legs, with the other up,
and he has a lever to bear in his arms, thus [here the witness
exhibited the position by elevating his arms above his head],
and there he is to stand for ten minutes, or a quarter of an
hour, or half an hour, just according as the overlooker
chooses; and provided he should lower his arms, and it is a
great weight to bear for a quarter of an hour, I have seen the
overlooker come this way and say, 'Hold up,' and sometimes
the boy will strive to hold it up and not have strength to
raise it, and the overlooker has a stick or strap, and cuts
him till he does actually get it up, and the tears will run
down his face when he is there standing. I have seen it

there frequently, and it is the regular practice.—In what mills have you seen it?—At Mr Marshall's, of Shrewsbury; frequently in that mill."

Children so excessively worked were, in consequence, subjected to increased risks from machinery. It was proved in evidence that limbs would be sometimes caught by wheels in motion; that these were frequently torn to pieces. William Swithinbank, a cloth-dresser from Leeds, was asked, "Have you had any children in your family that have met with accidents at their work?—Yes, I have one boy that met with a very serious accident; it was at a machine called a crab, that the stuff goods go through; it pulled him in and caught his arm, and it tore it all to bits; it tore the veins from the arteries, and tore the muscles from the arm out; it was all torn. Have any other accidents of that sort happened there?—Yes; another boy, at the same crab, got killed, and another got his arm torn off."

A question naturally suggests itself,—Was the supply of labour so much below the demand as to render this excessive labour necessary for the purposes of manufacture and commerce? The reverse was the fact; the supply of labour was, under the arrangements then common, greater than the demand, a circumstance quite in keeping with the results. Eleven hours was the usual day's work in the woollen factories of Leeds; to this rule there were exceptions. It was the custom, with few exceptions, in Bradford, to work on Good Friday and on Christmas-day, a circumstance which, perhaps, as much as any other, proves how thoroughly the whole of life, in the case of the factory children, was devoted to labour.

It was amply proved before the committee, that the treatment of those engaged in factory labour was not improving. William Kershaw, of Gomersal, whose experience ranged over a period of half a century, was on this head very decided; the same witness declared that he was not "in any

point of view a free agent," that he had " no alternative but
of submitting " to allow his children to work " long and pernicious hours of labour, or allowing them to starve for want
of necessary subsistence,"—an affirmation strictly reasonable.
It is impossible to conceive a free agent, endowed with
moral sense, capable of allowing his offspring to be ruined
physically, morally, and mentally for any consideration. It
must have been with no ordinary feelings of anguish that
William Kershaw informed the committee that the " conduct
of his daughters was far from satisfactory; impudence and
immorality of every description appeared to be their growing
characteristics." Many witnesses gave painful testimony, the
result of personal observation, to the factory system being
a prolific and an increasing source of drunkenness, prostitution,
and indecency. These evils existed side by side with a rapid
increase of scientific, chemical, and mechanical knowledge
applied to the purposes of production.

The Rev. G. S. Bull and Mr Richard Oastler were
examined at great length; their evidence, as an exposition
of the evils of the factory system, was comprehensive and
complete. Before the Committee were presented a number
of documents from Scotland, signed by the resident ministers
of the gospel and the principal medical men of the districts
to which these documents referred. The Rev. A. L. Gordon,
of Aberdeen, had closely attended to the development of
the factory system in Aberdeen, and gave very decided evidence on its injurious effects. As an example of the contents
of the documents bearing the signatures of clergymen in
Scotland, we select the following because of its brevity.

" Arbroath, 2nd May, 1832. The undersigned have no
hesitation in offering it as their decided opinion, that the
present extended hours of labour in the flax mills of this
place have a most pernicious effect, both in a physical and
moral point of view, upon the young persons employed
in them. They have uniformly observed, that such young

persons want the healthful aspects of children not similarly confined. In respect of education, they are far behind what used to be the average advancement of the same class of children in this part of the country, and that their moral and religious condition is such as was to be expected in the case of persons who are removed from school to the unwholesome air and dangerous companionship of a manufactory, at the age which is most available for the formation either of virtuous or vicious habits. Although the practice of employing a great number of children in the mills is, in this place, only of recent date, yet enough has already appeared to prove that the tendency of such an unnatural system is to effect a rapid and certain deterioration of the race. And there is nothing of which the undersigned are more firmly persuaded than this, that if something is not speedily done to enable parents to resist the temptation or dispense with the necessity of sending their children to work in mills for a longer period than is consistent with the preservation of their health and the improvement of their minds, Parliament will have, at no distant day, to legislate for a population tenfold more ignorant, improvident, pauperized, and immoral than the present."

To this document was appended the names of the recognized heads of the Christian congregations of the town of Arbroath, churchmen and dissenters. Every one acquainted with Scotland will appreciate the worth of such evidence. The intimate connexion existing between the ministers of the gospel and the population of Scotland, enables the former to judge correctly of the actual position of the latter. It is well known that the question of education has, in Scotland, for ages, been a subject of the closest scrutiny; and the falling off in education, consequent on the increase of the factory system, was a serious and an appalling fact which christian ministers could not silently overlook.

The feeling of the operatives on the question may be

inferred from the statements of Mr James M'Nish, of Glasgow:
" Are the operatives of the city of Glasgow generally considered favourable to a regulation and limitation of the hours
of labour for children and young persons employed in the
mills and factories of the place?—Yes; and to do justice
to the cause, and to put on record what has actually taken
place, and what would hereafter take place, I will state
what would have occurred if Mr Sadler had not previously
adopted some means, and moved for this Bill in the House
of Commons. It was proposed by a great number of
individuals in the various manufacturing districts ; they had
even brought forward plans to form extensive combinations
to limit, on their own behalf, the labour to ten hours per
day. Circulars were printed, and about to be distributed ;
but when it was seen that he had moved for such a measure
in the House of Commons, they considered that they had
better turn their attention to assist him in this measure,
than attempt to legislate for themselves. The principal
reasons that the agitators of the self-legislation had for
coming before their fellow-operatives were, as they stated,
that the slave population were legislated for and protected,
that they had not to work more than ten hours per day,
and that the children had not to work at all till they were
fourteen years of age, and then only six hours a day; and
they likewise showed their fellow-operatives the future state
into which their children were springing up,—that they were
left completely exposed ; that their labour, which forms their
principal property, was left completely open to be trampled
upon by every avaricious employer as he chose; they were
therefore determined to form as extensive a combination
as they possibly could to reduce those hours of labour, for
the benefit of themselves and their children. The tendency
of those combinations I was opposed to as one of the
individuals of the association ; for I considered that the
result of those associations would be a great evil to the

country. In the first place, they would cause considerable irritation between the labourers and the employers, and ultimately, I believe, lead to bloodshed; and indeed those combinations can never extend beyond the circle of the large manufacturing towns; they can never reach the master in the country. I have no doubt that they would have succeeded in reducing the hours of labour in towns, and brought the town manufacturers to the brink of ruin, and I believe it would have obliged the town manufacturers to have petitioned for this legislative measure at some period themselves, perhaps at no distant period after those town manufacturers had starved a great number of their operatives; and, perhaps, in return for this starvation, got some of themselves murdered for starving those men. For although such acts are frequently thrown upon combinations, they generally proceed from individual want; for a man with a starving family will stop, I believe, at nothing. We have had instances of this; therefore I am of opinion, that if this Bill does not pass, the town manufacturers will have to petition for such a legislative measure; but I believe pride will not allow them to petition until they are brought to the brink of ruin themselves, and the commerce of the country is likewise endangered. I have also to state, that it is my opinion that these combinations would be very hurtful to the country: they might be a ready tool in the hands of any demagogue for a political purpose, who had a few hundred pounds to distribute amongst them, and might endanger the government; and, therefore, in my humble opinion, it will be the interest of the government, the employers, and the operatives, that this measure should be carried into effect at as early a period as possible."

The question of the preservation of the health of the manufacturing population was necessarily a subject of the highest importance. In a national as in an individual sense, health of body ought to be a primary consideration. In

so far as machinery and manufactories contributed to national
wealth, corresponding with the health and improved circumstances of those engaged in factory labour, machinery and
manufactories were blessings, but on no account could the
gain of riches to a few, be a compensation for the loss
of health to the many. In considering manufacturing or
any other kind of industry, the labourers employed should
not be considered only as a means to an end ; they are
human beings, endowed with faculties and feelings, and no
branch of national industry can be, in a national sense,
advantageous which does not directly contribute to their
elevation. The upraising of the industrious ought to be the
end of industry ; and that system of national economy in
which riches are everything and man nothing, is, in its
foundations, the contradictory of civilization, and in practice
a violation of the doctrine that "Love worketh no ill," and
opposed in spirit and deed to the truly wise philosophy
expressed in the words, "But now are they many, yet but
one body. And the eye cannot say to the hand, I have
no need of thee ; nor, again, the head to the feet, I have
no need of you." It is impossible to conceive a greater
national curse than a system of industry under whose
operation human beings are called into existence, reared
into premature puberty, worked excessive hours, in circumstances opposed to health of body and mind, and the whole
aim and end of their being tried by the one calculation
of upon how little can life and the motion of a pair of hands
be supported. The depression of living human beings to
the material level of the lowest kind of factory furniture,
is an act of the grossest blasphemy. It is the pride of
a few persons in the vain conceit of their own inflated
self-sufficiency, saying to many of their fellow-creatures,
"God made us a little lower than the angels, and so far
as we can, we will make you much lower than the beasts that
perish." Among the most desirable objects of civilization

is the increase of the consciousness of the moral responsibility of man, of his dignity as man, the enrichment of his birthright as a responsible, rational creature, born into the world possessing properties capable of improvement. When these results are not realized, to talk of civilization is an absurdity; under the unregulated factory system, men, women and children were degraded to the level of means and things, the personal *chattels* of a favoured few.

The evidence of the medical men examined before the Sadler committee of 1832, constitutes a cyclopædia of physiological, social, and moral knowledge, by the most eminent professional men of their age in the departments of anatomy and medicine. All were unanimous in their condemnation of the factory system—all agreed that factories were " nurseries of feeble bodies and fretful minds." This invaluable evidence does not allow of condensation, it is a monument of the extraordinary knowledge and intelligence of the highest order of scientific physiologists and anatomists, and we will not venture to separate the stones of the structure. Mr Sadler has often said, " To have succeeded in collecting that body of medical evidence is worth all my labour, anxiety, and sacrifice."

The following placard was widely circulated; its contents prove the conclusiveness of the highest medical opinions on the subject of the hours of labour, and shows the use made of the medical evidence by the supporters of factory regulation:—

"TABLE OF MEDICAL OPINIONS AND TESTIMONY before the Select Committee on the Ten Hours' Bill.

" Sir Anthony Carlile, F.R.S., principal Surgeon of Westminster Hospital forty years: 'More than ten hours is quite incompatible with health and moral propriety.' . . ' Every succeeding generation will be progressively deteriorated if you do not stop these sins against nature and humanity.'

"Sir William Blizzard, F.R.S., Surgeon to the London Hospital fifty years : Pronounces the present system of thirteen or more hours (including meals) to be 'horrible.'

"Sir Charles Bell, K.G.H., F.R.S., Surgeon to Middlesex Hospital: 'More than ten hours is painful in idea.'

"Sir George L. Tuthill, F.R.S., Physician to Westminster Hospital twenty years: Doubts very much whether ten hours will not be injurious to children under twelve years.

"Joseph H. Green, Esq., Surgeon to St Thomas's Hospital, Professor K.C.: 'I fear this country will have much to answer for in permitting the growth of the system of employing children in factories.' . . 'From nine years to twelve not more than six hours should be allowed. Twelve is the utmost adults should labour.'

"James Blundell, Esq., M.D., Physician to Guy's Hospital, Lecturer, &c.: 'I look upon factory towns as nurseries for feeble bodies and fretful minds. Ten hours are enough for human beings.'

"Thomas Hodgkin, Esq., M.D. (of the Society of Friends), Physician to the London Dispensary: 'Ten hours appears to be a proper time.'

"John Morgan, Esq., Surgeon to Guy's Hospital: 'Ten hours are injurious to young children of nine years.'

"Benjamin Brodie, Esq., F.R.S., Surgeon of St George's Hospital: 'I think ten hours too much for children of ten years of age, and twelve too much for all.'

"William Lutener, Esq., Surgeon: 'Will sanction eight or nine hours.'

"Samuel Smith, Esq., Surgeon to the Infirmary, Leeds: 'Ten hours are too long, many will suffer under it.'

"William Sharp, jun., Esq., Surgeon to the Dispensary, Bradford: 'I think it (ten hours) as long and perhaps longer than is consistent with their general health.'

"C. Turner Thackrah, Esq., Surgeon to the Infirmary, Leeds: 'I should be very ill content with an Eleven Hours'

Bill. Children should not work at all—the least time the best.'

" J. Malyn, Esq., Surgeon: ' Ten hours enough for those who are eighteen years old—too much for children of nine years.'

" P. M. Roget, Esq., F.R.S., late a Physician of Manchester Infirmary: ' I should think that a child under nine years of age ought not to be subject to the labour of a mill or factory. Ten hours sufficient for any age.'

" John Elliotson, Esq., F.R.S., Physician to St Thomas's Hospital: ' Ten hours are as much as can be endured with impunity.'

" C. A. Key, Esq., Surgeon of Guy's Hospital: ' I should say ten hours is even more than they could sustain with impunity.'

" G. J. Guthrie, Esq., F.R.S., Surgeon and Vice-President of the Royal College: ' Ten hours far too much.' Testifies that the factory children are worked on an average longer than soldiers !

" John R. Farre, Esq., M.D., a Physician of forty-two years' standing : ' I think that to secure a vigorous manhood nine years of age is too early.' . . . ' In English factories everything valuable in manhood is sacrificed to an inferior advantage in childhood.'

" Thomas Young, Esq., M.D., Physician: ' I think that ten hours is the extreme limit that ought to be allowed; it is quite enough for the healthy and robust, and too much for the feeble and delicate.'

" Benjamin Travers, F.R.S., Senior Surgeon of St Thomas's Hospital : ' I think it wonderful that ten hours can be endured.' . . . ' The bill would be advantageous to society at large.' "

The following address accompanied the placard:—

" Christians and Englishmen ! Read, and be convinced, that a Ten Hours' Bill must pass. Remember, besides the above testimony, admitting of ten hours as the smallest limitation which can be sanctioned, there is the written testimony of nineteen medical men in Scotland, of the highest class, and of thirteen clergymen, besides that of many physicians, surgeons, ministers of the gospel, and humane factory masters, who have raised their voices for the bill at public meetings. There is also the evidence, given before the committee, of two clergymen, two gentlemen, forty-one Yorkshire operatives, seven from Lancashire, seven from Scotland, and five others, including three females, in all one hundred and seventeen witnesses, against the present factory system.

" Men of Great Britain! Here is the four-fold voice of science, humanity, Christianity, and bitter experience, in favour of a Ten Hours' Bill. Will you suffer it to be drowned by the clamorous howl of avarice and selfishness? And will you suffer those who wish to represent you in parliament, to evade the question of a Ten Hours' Bill? First, ask them, whether Christianity and humanity demand it; and then ask them, whether they will support it, or whether they will allow the influence of wealth to triumph over the highest sanctions which God or his creatures can give. After such testimony as the above (not to mention that which bears on the daily working of the system,—without producing aggravated and extreme cases), surely henceforth opposition must be utterly inexcusable. Christians! fathers! mothers! will you support the Ten Hours' Bill, or renounce your religion and your names?"

The labour of Mr Sadler during the conduct of this enquiry was extraordinary; his days and nights were devoted, with but few and irregular intermissions, to incessant mental exertion. During the sittings of the committee, he was engaged in the trying process of constant investigation; when not so engaged, he was answering letters, giving audiences to deputations, often devoting whole nights to the correction of the notes of the short-hand writers engaged in reporting the evidence of witnesses. Physiologists have affirmed that those engaged in willing labour, are strengthened by the emission from the brain of increased muscular volition, and are, in consequence, enabled to perform herculean tasks with comparative impunity. These efforts, however, we are assured, must be only occasional; they were in Mr Sadler's case, at the time referred to, habitual; his nervous system suffered irreparable injury. Though conscious of the injuries so sustained, often naming them in his correspondence with confidential friends, occasionally forced to call in his physician, at times so seriously indisposed as to alarm his medical attendant, and necessitate consultation, yet so intense was the ardour of this truly good man, so resolute of purpose was he, so alive to the importance of the work in which he was engaged, that he persevered to the last, always affirming, "This is God's work in which I am engaged, and therefore it must be done." The work was done as no similar labour before or since has been ; its author, unfortunately, because of his zeal and perseverance in its execution, sapped the foundations of his physical strength. The change in Mr Sadler's appearance, consequent on the impaired state of his health, was painfully evident to his most intimate friends; of him it may be justly said, that he shortened his own days to lengthen those of others; that he worked excessive and unnatural hours, that others should have their hours of labour regulated to a reasonable limit. In this he may not have been personally wise, but the course of action was noble and selfsacrificing; nor was it labour in vain, for tried by the severest canon of the utilitarians, with whom he was in perpetual conflict, few men have, in their day and generation, been more useful than Michael Thomas Sadler;—"though dead he speaketh." Time has not blotted from the things that be, the records of the revelations of the cruelties, crimes, and horrors, which his patient industry brought to light, as contained in the evidence taken before the committee on the Factories' Bill, which he originated; cruelties, crimes, and horrors, which his courage, talent, and determination, contributed in a great degree, most happily, to banish from the daily practice of some among the leading branches of England's manufacturing industry.

The opponents of factory legislation had promised to rebut Mr Sadler's statements, contained in his speech on the second reading of the bill. They did not even attempt to fulfil their pledge; the weight of evidence was so great as to paralyze opposition, by counter-evidence on the part of those engaged in manufacture. The opponents of the measure resorted to personal persecution of witnesses. The nature of this persecution will be understood by the following extracts from the reports of the proceedings in parliament. On the 30th of July, 1832, Mr Sadler, addressing the House of Commons, said :—

"I hold in my hands two petitions from individuals of the humbler ranks of society. These petitioners complain of dismissal from their employment, in consequence of having been summoned to give evidence before the committee on the bill for regulating the hours of labour of children employed in factories, and pray for some compensation. I want to know from honourable gentlemen, who may laugh, what course these men are to take to obtain redress who are summoned before parliament to declare the truth ? I ask whether the summons is not imperative ? I ask whether it is fitting that these individuals should be exposed to suffering and ruin without any indemnification being offered them ?

"The first petition I shall present—and it is, perhaps, the first only of a series on the same subject—is from a person named Charles Stewart. It was suggested that this person should give evidence before the committee. He was a reluctant witness, but, nevertheless, conducted himself in a most becoming manner; and, though absent from his work only so long as was required, found himself, on his return home, supplanted in his situation. This has been the case, too, with several others. This petitioner casts himself upon the mercy of the house. He states that he was called before the committee of this house, and upon the authority of the house—a summons which he could not evade—but that, in consequence of having given evidence conscientiously, he is deprived of his bread, and therefore prays the house to grant him some compensation.

"I hold in my hand a similar petition, of another individual, named Alexander Deans. I beg to say that this individual, without being a voluntary witness, was pointed out to me as a person whose evidence was desirable; and his name having been transmitted to me, which was without his knowledge, he was accordingly summoned. Having given his evidence he returned home as expeditiously as he possibly could, and now finds himself dismissed from his employment.

"I have several similar representations to those made in these petitions regarding other parties brought before the committee on this subject; and, so convinced am I of the accuracy of the circumstances stated, that I have declined bringing forward many important witnesses, under the apprehension of their being ruined for giving evidence before the committee now sitting.

"I beg leave to say that nothing could be more respectful than the manner in which the testimony of these witnesses was given in regard to their employers; and I may mention one instance, in particular, in which the witness said, 'With regard to my employer, he is one of the best and kindest masters known in the business, and I hope that my testimony will not influence his mind against me.' But it did so influence his master's mind that he discharged him from his employ!"

Because of the resolution of Mr Sadler not further to expose the operatives to the risk of being deprived of the means of earning their bread for telling the truth, for *that* was the offence, the labours of the committee closed with the medical evidence. This attempt on the part of the master manufacturers opposed to factory legislation to stifle the truth by the persecution of witnesses, was to its authors disgraceful. Mr Sadler's case was more than proved ; every statement made by him in parliament, was more than borne out from the lips of living witnesses. It is almost impossible to overrate the difficulty or the importance of discovering the truth on all questions in which the interests of the working classes are concerned. In the absence of trustworthy knowledge, remedial measures must be necessarily imperfect, probably inoperative or even mischievous. Citizens are apt to forget their duties to the State, in the excess of the love they have for themselves. Had the factory witnesses deceived the committee with glowing panegyrics on the comfort and harmony of the factory system, their own interest with their employers would not have been injured—on the contrary, they would probably have been improved. Of these persecuting factory owners it may be truly said, " They loved darkness rather than light, because their deeds were evil." That light which they feared and hated was found, and though not so full a flame, as in the absence of their coercive repression would have been kindled, yet it was clear and full enough to let all England see factory-made cripples, paupers, and criminals, and invigorating enough to stimulate the sympathies of a large proportion of the British public to energetic action, in support of a wise humanity, and the lasting interests of a desirable civilization. The Sadler Report is a becoming monument to the memory of its author: the tact and knowledge manifested by him in conducting the enquiry were very great, and not any work known to us on the social condition of those engaged in factory labour, approaches to its value in point of information.

During the progress of Mr Sadler's parliamentary enquiry, the question was rapidly gaining ground out of doors. A society was established in London for the purpose of aiding the active friends of factory regulation, in the distribution of tracts and the concentration of public opinion. " The Metropolitan Society for the improvement of the condition of Factory Children" was honoured with the Duke of Sussex as patron, and William Allen, a distinguished member of the Society of Friends, and a man justly remarkable for his active benevolence, was president. On the 27th of June, 1832, Lord Morpeth presented a petition from the county of York, in favour of the Factories' Regulation Bill. His Lordship said, " This petition was of such an extent, and signed by so many thousands, that he could not say, in the ordinary language used in the presentation of petitions, that he now had a petition in his hand to which he requested the attention of the House. The petition was an immense roll, and lay on the floor, the noble lord holding the top of it only in his hand. The petition was signed by 138,652 names, and he knew by laborious experience that it measured 2,322 feet in length. The petitioners complained against the system of over-working children, and prayed for an immediate measure of relief. He had been convinced, from what had already occurred before the committee, that humanity demanded a speedy corrective of the evils to which the petition referred."

Mr George Strickland, M.P. for Yorkshire, declared "that he felt it as a reproach to this county that its children were not treated with kindness." A similar petition was intended for presentation to the Lords, and for that purpose was entrusted to his Royal Highness the Duke of Sussex. The history of the Yorkshire petition to the House of Lords is far from satisfactory. On the

6th of February, 1832, Mr Sadler had an interview with his Royal Highness the Duke of Sussex, on which occasion he avowed his desire to serve the cause of the factory workers, as advocated by Mr Sadler. His Royal Highness the Duke expressed "the most lively interest in the cause, and the strongest feeling of sympathy for the poor children," assuring Mr Sadler " that he felt it a great honour to have such a petition entrusted to him, and he should be proud to present it to their lordships, and to give it all the support of his influence." The operatives of the North appointed a deputation to wait on his Royal Highness. Mr Sadler corresponded with the Duke. It was finally arranged that the Duke should receive the deputation on the 7th of July, 1832. The following paragraphs, from the newspapers of that month, refer to the interview of the deputation with the Duke:—

" THE DUKE OF SUSSEX AND THE FACTORY BILL.— On Saturday, the 7th instant, the undersigned members of the Short Time Central Committee, of Leeds, waited upon his Royal Highness the Duke of Sussex, at Kensington Palace, to request his Royal Highness to present the great petition of the county of York, in favour of Mr Sadler's Factories' Bill, and to entreat his Royal Highness to support the prayer of the same in the House of Lords.

" Mr Oastler having stated to his Royal Highness the object which the deputation had in view, his Royal Highness, in a very complaisant and affectionate manner, replied as follows:—' I shall be exceedingly happy to support the prayer of the petition—it is a measure which I have very much at heart. I have several other petitions, which I delayed to present, as I thought they might have interfered with the Reform Bill; but as that is now settled, I shall take the earliest opportunity of presenting them, when I shall give the preference to the great petition from Yorkshire, and support it in the best manner I am able.'

THE HISTORY OF

"His Royal Highness then enquired 'into the state of trade, and the condition of the working classes;' to which Mr Oastler replied, 'that trade was not much better, but it was his (Mr Oastler's) opinion, that Mr Sadler's bill was a measure calculated to lay a foundation for improvement.'

"His Royal Highness then kindly dismissed the deputation, who were very much delighted to find that royalty could feel for poverty.

"RICHARD OASTLER.

"WILLIAM OSBURN.

"DANIEL FRASER.

"JOHN HANSON."

The Yorkshire petition was not presented to the House of Lords : " the reasons why " were not communicated. The petition was deposited in the Robing Room of the House of Lords, whither it had been conveyed by his Royal Highness's express orders. The consistent benevolence of the late Duke of Sussex is beyond doubt ; his conduct in the case referred to it is not in our power to account for.

CHAPTER XIII.

REJECTION OF MR SADLER, BY LEEDS AND HUDDERSFIELD, UNDER
THE REFORM ACT.—THE LATE MR JOHN FIELDEN, M.P. FOR
OLDHAM, HIS PRINCIPLES AND CHARACTER.—THE REV. G. S.
BULL, HIS PREACHING AND PRACTICE.—LORD ASHLEY AS THE
PARLIAMENTARY SUCCESSOR OF MR SADLER.—RENEWAL OF THE
FACTORY QUESTION IN THE HOUSE OF COMMONS.

THE author of the Reform Bill aimed at the accomplishment
of an important organic change in the constitution of the
country.   Party interests and party influences were busily at
work, and under the popular cry of " The bill, the whole bill,
and nothing but the bill," was hidden the determination of the
principal Whig families to secure for themselves ascendancy in
the future government of England.   It is natural for politicians
of the highest order to desire the opportunity of practically
applying their own cherished theories.   The desire is honourable to those who entertain it ; politicians of the lowest order
(the species is very numerous, and confined to no class or
party) look for personal gain, no matter how acquired; they
are ready on the shortest notice to do the meanest work, for
what is mildly called " a consideration."   The Reform Bill
received the royal assent on the 7th of June, 1832; in December, parliament was dissolved, and with the dissolution closed
the parliamentary career of Mr Sadler.   In parliament, Mr
Sadler advocated a representation of industrial interests
through the medium of varied qualifications, in opposition to

the ascendancy of any one class or rank of the people over the
others. He opposed the Roman Catholic Relief Bill, from a
belief that its operation would be dangerous to religious freedom; he maintained that that bill was opposed to a protestant
constitution. In his speech on the condition of the agricultural labourers he had boldly told the landowners of their
duties, and the failure of many in their fulfilment. His motion
for the establishment of a poor law in Ireland had brought
down on his head the ridicule of the self-styled " practical
statesmen " of the time. The free-trading manufacturers of
England, with few exceptions, treated Mr Sadler, because of
his determination to bridle their ill-considered avarice by law,
as an open enemy. Mr Sadler's efforts to be returned to the
first reformed parliament, for Leeds and Huddersfield, were
unsuccessful; he was in these towns ably supported, but the
combined interests of the millowners opposed to factory regulation, the Ultra-Dissenters, and Roman Catholics, were greater
than the support on the side of Mr Sadler. When in parliament he represented Newark, with the approval of the late
Duke of Newcastle. Mr Sadler had many friends, and had his
health been restored he would probably have resumed his parliamentary career at no very distant period; his absence from
parliament was a subject of deep and continuous regret, he
was the only able representative among known statesmen of a
class of industrial questions, the discussion of which, in the
House of Commons, was a public necessity. Not any more
striking proof of the public interest felt in Mr Sadler's position
as a " public man " could be named, than the fact, that a petition containing 40,000 signatures, addressed to the electors of
Leeds, was sent from Manchester to Leeds during the election
contest, praying for his return by that borough. The friends
of the Ten Hours' Bill felt Mr Sadler's rejection by Leeds
and Huddersfield to be a serious discouragement; they were,
however, in some degree comforted by the return to the House
of Commons, by the newly-created boroughs of Salford,

Oldham, and Ashton, of four staunch supporters of their cause: the late Mr William Cobbett, the late Mr John Fielden, of Todmorden, Mr Joseph Brotherton, and Mr Charles Hindley. The important services rendered by Mr Fielden to the Ten Hours' Bill cause, in and out of the House of Commons, demand a brief summary of his character and principles. The late Mr John Fielden, was the third of five sons of Mr Joshua Fielden, of Edge End, in the township of Todmorden and Walsden. The father was a member of the Society of Friends (of whom there were many in that part of the country), and brought up his family in his own religious opinions. He was himself what was called " a strong tory " in politics, but as the sons grew up in the midst of the political turmoil caused by the French Revolution of 1789, he found them one by one showing symptoms of opinions contrary to his own; and though he adhered to his own principles, he is said to have acknow- ledged towards the close of his life, " that his five sons, Samuel, Joshua, John, James, and Thomas, were as arrant Jacobins as any in the kingdom." About the year 1784, Mr Joshua Fielden began the manufacture of cotton; and the commencement of that vast pile of buildings, now known as *Waterside*, was three cottages, in one of which the elder Fielden began the business of cotton-spinning, which gradually increased to one of the largest concerns in the operation of cotton-spinning and manu- facturing in England. Mr Sadler was a churchman and a tory, Mr Fielden was a dissenter and a radical. It was a feature of the factory movement, that party politics were for- gotten in the desire for the public weal: this was the primary principle of "the Fixby compact," a principle at all times recognised as sacred and inviolable.

The late Mr John Fielden combined and represented in his own history two kinds of experience, he had worked as a factory operative, in his father's mill, and, therefore, in a limited degree, knew from personal trials, the sufferings endured by others. Many years of successful energy had raised him to the highest position as a cotton manufacturer; he was shrewd and far-sighted on the exchange, had a quick and safe eye for business; among manufacturers and merchants, his words and deeds commanded attention and respect; among his own work-people at Todmorden, he was sympathising, friendly, and easy of access to all who had grievances or remonstrances to communicate; he felt that he was the trustee of the interests of those he employed, and was unceasingly watchful for their welfare. This two-fold knowledge of workman and manufacturer, enabled its possessor to judge of the feelings of employers and employed. Every important act in the life of the late Mr Fielden, was settled in the region of the understanding; fancy and inclination were at all times under salutary control; his intellect was cool, clear, and capable of great decision; his mind was stored with facts, these he applied to special purposes by the force of the will; few men had less of show, possessing so much of substance, intellectual and worldly; he united in a remarkable degree caution and boldness, never allured into speculation in the anxious hope of acquiring sudden riches; he seldom missed a favourable opportunity of profiting by the state of the market; he never desired to astonish, with boasting of the extent of his commercial transactions, and was never anxious to speak in tones of conciliation for the mere sake of pleasing others. Has England ever asked herself how much she is indebted to the class of men of whom the late Mr John Fielden, of Todmorden, was a type? This man, with small extrinsic aid, untiring energy, industrious habits, and sterling integrity, raised himself from obscurity to eminence as a manufacturer and merchant. In every market of the world where cotton or cotton fabrics were bought and sold, the name of Fielden was known; it was synonymous with probity and confidence, it was England representing honest dealing and courageous enterprise. Maybe, as the eye glances over the *Gazette*, and conscience feels ashamed at the frauds disclosed in the columns of the

daily press—not petty, vulgar thefts, but transactions by men
of education and rank, compromising the commercial character of a nation,—perhaps the reader will pause to pay a
tribute of respect to the merchant princes of the present
generation, and to the memories of those in the past, who, like
the late Mr John Fielden, of Todmorden, never promised what
they failed to fulfil, who have distinguished between legitimate
trading and commercial gambling, and who have brought
into the marts of commerce the rectifying influences of
duty and honour. Mr Fielden's principles of economical
and commercial policy were the results of his own experience formulated into a system; that experience enabled
him to construct authentic tables of that branch of manufacture with which he was connected; from details he
ascended to principles, and was, in consequence of sincere convictions, a strenuous advocate for shortening the
hours of labour in factories, a measure alike favourable,
in his judgment, to the interests of the employers and
the employed. Mr Fielden contended that a reduction of
the working hours in factories was an indispensable condition
of the future success of the cotton trade. In a letter, addressed
to Mr Fitton by Mr Fielden, his views are very distinctly
stated; to this letter we are indebted for the following
extracts:—" Whether we look to the products of manual
labour, as instanced in the case of the handloom weavers, or of
manual labour aided by the most improved machinery employed
in the cotton trade, we find that for a nearly three-fold quantity produced in 1832, the manufacturers, and their work-
people, had a much less command over the first necessary of
life (wheat), than they had in 1815, for little more than one-
third of the quantity. Truly, it may be said, 'We labour for
that which is not bread, and spend our strength for nought;'
while those who tax us, and those who live on fixed incomes,
get an additional increase of the fruits of our labours, more
than correspondent with the increase of our production, and
for which we receive no equivalent whatever. And can this

course of proceeding continue? No, it cannot. The manufacturers cannot go on in this course much further, however
disposed they might be to do so; seventy parts out of one
hundred, constituting the whole for labour, expenses, and
profits, have departed between 1815 and 1832, both years
inclusive, and many parts more will be found to have fled in
1833. . . . Providence designed that the gifts she has
bestowed on man for increasing his supply of the necessaries
and comforts of life (by the invention and aid of machinery, or
otherwise), should not be abused; and so surely as we take
improperly from those who labour, and give it to those who do
not labour, so sure will a day of retribution and vengeance
overtake the oppressors."

Mr Fielden contended that an excess of production over
demand was the great cause of low prices, low profits, low
wages, that the home trade of the country was injured by
the inability of the operatives to consume a reasonable proportion of the products of the industry of the working
population; that no foreign trade was desirable beyond the
exchange of the surplus articles produced by Englishmen,
over and above the full supply of their own wants, for
those other useful articles, of which the foreigner had too
many; that a foreign trade, the basis of which was unlimited
cheapness, could only be extended by an increase of the
sufferings of the working classes; that " to place ourselves
in a state of dependence on foreigners for articles of the
first necessity, such as corn, to the injury of the home
grower, and without any permanent advantage to the manufacturer, who by such a course would only exchange his
home customer for a foreign customer; and as the former
is more certain, and, in every sense, more to be relied on
than the latter, to distress those engaged in agriculture and
manufactures in this country, by an increase of such foreign
trade to accomplish such an object, is to be guilty of the
grossest folly imaginable. . . . . What becomes of our
host of new acquisitions in mechanical skill, great improve-

ments in machinery, and unprecedented increase in production —all excellent things when rightly directed, if the result which has hitherto followed be to continue, namely, the withdrawal of work altogether from some, and their degradation into paupers. The reduction of wages visited on those who are left to compete with the improved mode of production, consequent upon the adoption of the new machines, from which, lessened wages, starvation, misery, and crime, ensue ; and the increase of labour, without any increase of remuneration of those comparatively few in number who are fortunate enough to get work on the new machines. If such consequences cannot be avoided, then of one thing I am certain, that all our boastful improvements in machinery are not a blessing, but a curse to the productive classes, whose work is being constantly increased in intensity, and deteriorated in value, by the changes arising from these improvements. But a right direction may and ought to be given to those invaluable improvements, and the masters and workmen, by cultivating a good understanding with each other, and by union of effort, ought to do it for themselves, without seeking for legislative interference on the subject." It was a maxim of Mr Fielden, " That what society ought to do and failed in doing, it was the duty of government to realize if possible by law." He did not allow his regard for voluntary action to neutralize his legislative efforts. Mr Fielden had consequently supported all the endeavours for the restriction of the hours of factory labour by law, from the time of Nathaniel Gould. He was not a hasty convert to any cause, but once resolved, his support was certain and energetic. In 1836, writing of his earlier years, he said, " As I have been personally engaged in the operations connected with factory labour, that is to say, for about forty years, a short account of my own experience may not be useless in this place, as it is this experience which teaches me to scoff at the representations of those who speak of the labour of factories as 'very light, and so easy as to require no muscular exertion.' I well remember being set to work in my father's mill when I was little more than ten years old; my associates, too, in labour and in recreation, are fresh in my memory. Only a few of them are now alive—some dying very young, others living to become men and women; but many have died off before they had attained the age of fifty years, having the appearance of being much older—a premature appearance of age which I verily believe was caused by the nature of the employment in which they had been brought up. For several years after I had been to work in the mill, the hours of labour at our works did not exceed *ten* in the day, winter and summer, and even with the labour of those hours, I shall never forget the fatigue I often felt before the day ended, and the anxiety of us all to be relieved from the unvarying and irksome toil we had gone through before we could obtain relief by such play and amusement as we resorted to when liberated from our work. I allude to this fact, because it is not uncommon for persons to infer, that because the children who work in factories are seen to play like other children when they have time to do so, the labour is therefore light and does not fatigue them. The reverse of this conclusion I know to be the truth. I know the effects which ten hours' labour had upon myself; I, who had the attention of parents better able than those of my companions to allow me extraordinary occasional indulgence. And he knows very little of human nature who does not know, that, to a child, diversion is so essential, that it will undergo even exhaustion in its amusements. I protest, therefore, against the reasoning, that because a child is not brought so low in spirit as to be incapable of enjoying the diversions of a child, it is not worked to the utmost that its feeble frame and constitution will bear." Mr Fielden could express his views on public questions in writing with force, as his published letters, and his work, entitled *The Curse of the Factory System*, testify. His common sense, a full share of which is far from a common possession, enabled him to apprehend the merits of public measures with a safe judgment. On the factory question his knowledge was so great and his earnestness so intense, as to raise his intellect to the level of genius. As a speaker, he was ignorant of the arts of rhetoric, but he could make himself understood ; was listened to with attention in the House of Commons ; his speeches when reported read agreeably, and were replete with facts, the weight of which was increased by his reputation for truthfulness and honesty of purpose. All parties agreed in aptly designating him, " Honest John Fielden, the radical member for Oldham." Mr Fielden's return to parliament was, by the factory operatives of the North, considered to be a most desirable result. In him they had implicit confidence ; his name was in their homes a household word, he was, from first to last, to them a judicious counsellor and faithful friend. In his own family circle, it was Mr Fielden's habit to cast aside the cares of the world, and enter heartily into the conversation of the hour. He would listen with delight to the prattle of his children—to amuse and instruct them was his most cherished enjoyment. As a husband, father, and friend, he was considerate, affectionate, and kindly in a remarkable degree.

It was the current opinion among the factory operatives of Yorkshire that the operation of the Reform Bill would not be favourable to their objects. They said,—" Experience has taught us that manufacturing capitalists, with some exceptions, are our opponents ; the Reform Bill will increase the influence of that body as a power in the state, and, therefore, prove injurious to our interests." This opinion, however, did not produce lethargy : the operatives availed themselves of every possible opportunity to question candidates on their intentions as regarded the Ten Hours' Bill. At every hustings in the manufacturing districts the Ten Hours' Bill was, by its supporters, made a cardinal question. This course contributed much to popularize the factory movement. It became apparent to every observer that Oastler and Bull were men who would be heard, and who when heard could make themselves understood. At this time Mr Bull was exceedingly active, and we feel bound to place on record our estimate of his character, principles, and labours, in so far as these are connected with the subject under consideration. The Rev. George Stringer Bull has devoted a large proportion of the active years of his manhood to the promotion of the interests of the working classes : the advocacy of no man could have been more disinterested than was the reverend gentleman's support of the short-time question. In the pulpit, in the press, or on the platform, few have, in the propagation of their opinions, been more successful. The heart of Mr Bull was in youth trained to feel for the poor, and his hand to administer relief, in his native parish, and under the paternal eye. When a boy he was a Sunday-school teacher, and was a connecting link between the pastor and the youth of the parish. When separated by the ocean from his own home, it was the custom of his former pupils and early friends, always to particularly desire his father to remember them most kindly to " Mr George," a circumstance which proves how thoroughly he commanded the affections of those with whom he was associated—a power, in his case, for good, which years have strengthened. The son of a rector in the Church of England, reared in an agricultural parish, near Ipswich, Mr Bull was early in life familiar with parochial duties. For several years the minister of an agricultural parish, Hessle, near Hull, before he removed to Hanging Heaton, near Dewsbury, and afterwards to Bierly, near Bradford, in Yorkshire, Mr Bull began his personal acquaintance of a manufacturing district with a matured mind and the possession of a considerable experience of agricultural districts in all that come within the sphere of the duties of a Christian minister. This experience, united to trained habits of discrimination, enabled Mr Bull, from observation, to judge of the condition of the agricultural and manufacturing districts. He believed it to be the especial duty of a Christian minister to attend to the interests of the labouring population and to care for the poor. Mr Bull's openness of manner and strong sympathy with suffering at once wins and retains the confidence of working men. He possesses in a remarkable degree the power of illustrating his meaning by a constant reference to simple objects and the occurrences of every-day life ; has a rare gift of narrative ; his short tales are always interesting and instructive ; few men can equal him in original anecdote, or excel him in giving force to the strong points of his stories, which appear endless, and are authenticated with names, dates, and places, and bring forth the lights and shades of character with a wonderful felicity. Mr Bull is one of the most agreeable of companions, and when relating an anecdote his countenance has a particularly pleasant expression. He is a man of vigorous mind, united to physical energy and power of personal endurance. In summer, when pressed with work, he rises with the lark, and retires to rest late at night; in winter, he is frequently in his study by four or five in the morning ; every hour of the day he is engaged reading, writing, visiting, relieving, teaching, preaching, or in the fulfilment of some other parochial duties. A quarter of a century back no man in England worked harder or more continuously than did " parson Bull, of Bierly." Few ministers of the gospel, in any age, have proclaimed the message of God to labouring men with more of earnestness than has Mr Bull. He is a bold man, and condemns all quacks, quackeries, and shams ; is prone, as he thinks it desirable, to tell the rich and poor, plainly and fully, of their faults and shortcomings; he hates compromises and concessions in politics, pretext and hypocrisy in religion. He maintains that it is the duty of good men to make all measures, which in themselves are just and necessary, practical and efficacious ; that a sincere belief in the truth of the Christian religion cannot fail to manifest itself in the performance of good deeds. It is but of little avail that political or religious opponents heap obloquy on the efforts of Mr Bull ; he answers their attacks forthwith, and continues his course with unabated zeal. Few clergymen have been more virulently attacked than was Mr Bull during his residence in Yorkshire ; no man ever suffered less in reputation from the pens of hostile critics. Mr Bull's political and religious opponents were the supporters of the unregulated factory system, or political economists of the Malthusian school. As to serve the cause of the factory children was, in his judgment, to serve the cause of God, Mr Bull felt, in conscience, bound to persevere; he was, consequently, an invaluable associate of Oastler and Sadler in their struggle for the relief of the factory operatives from oppressive labour.

From 1830 to 1841, the principal coadjutor of Mr Bull was Mr William Walker; their joint efforts in the press, and at public meetings, were of the highest value to the cause they desired to serve; not any two men could possibly be more distinct in mind—this was a source of strength to both. Mr Walker's methodical correctness, when united to Mr Bull's forcible expositions of factory wrongs, produced the most desirable results, namely, trustworthy statements supported with animation and power—necessary requisites to the formation of an intelligent public opinion.

It cannot be out of place to notice briefly the leading points of Mr Bull's observations on the condition of the agricultural and manufacturing population. In his time, the comforts of the agricultural labourers had been lessened, the decrease of wages had been greater in proportion than the decrease in the price of the necessaries of life. The farm-houses had been pulled down in many cases, or turned into cottages, " in very many cases the cottages had been pulled down." During seven years' experience in Bradford, York-shire, comforts had decreased, indecency and profanity were common. As regarded education, the comparison between the agricultural and manufacturing population was "incom-parably in favour of the agricultural." " The circumstances of the agriculturist were far more favourable, in all the principal points of comparison, than those of the manufacturer; his rent was less, his expenses were less in respect to the value of food generally, which was always greater in densely-populated districts. With regard to milk, particularly in the agricultural districts, a man might procure the same quantity of milk, for the sustenance of his family, for one-half the price at which it could be procured in the manufacturing districts, and of much better quality; and this is a very great assistance to the family of the cottager. Then, again, the hours of labour in the agricultural districts, both for the adult labourer and for the juvenile labourer, were considerably less, and the hours of leisure and refreshment greater. They had, therefore, less to pay to a doctor, and they required proportionately less clothes, and they were altogether far more comfortable, even in the depressed state of agricultural wages, than the labourers of the manufacturing districts." " The residence of the agricultural labourer was, as a rule, incom-parably more healthy and more comfortable than that of the manufacturing labourer."

When under examination before the Sadler committee, Mr Bull expressed his opinions on the factory system as follows: " I think there is a great deal of miscalculation with regard to the advantages of the manufacturing system to the poor, as at present carried on. Persons are apt to form their estimate from the amount of wages received by the children of a particular family; and when I have been accustomed to apply, as I sometimes do, and feel it my duty to do, to the overseer of the poor, or to some influential inhabitant of any parish, for relief or consideration towards any particular family, I have found that even they were not aware of the difference between an income derived from factory labour and an income derived from many other sources of employment. A factory child's income is subject to amazing diminution and deduction. I am accustomed to observe these things; being frequently intrusted with the distribution of charitable funds, my inquiries are necessarily very minute, and I have found that the washing, the mending, the wear and tear, the shoes, and the different articles of wearing-apparel, connected with the employment of a factory child, form very heavy items indeed; I have frequently calculated them, and compared my estimate of the expense with the parents of the children themselves; and I believe that, taking the average of twelve years of age, the extra expenses of a factory child, beyond that of a child engaged in many other employments, will be very nearly two shillings per head a week; and if the committee will permit me, as it is a matter of some importance perhaps, at least I presume to think it so, I would just say that with regard to these extra expenses, there is one particular point which ought to be considered, and that is the waste of the family meal; in that it is not, in most cases, an united but a divided meal. In some cases it may be united; where the children live very near the mill, they may go home and take it with the rest of the family; but in by far the greater number of cases, the children take their meals to the mill, their breakfasts, their dinner, and their drinking, or else they are sent to them; at all events the family meal is divided; and those who are accustomed to estimate pence and half-pence in a meal, know very well that the division of a family meal is an expensive system in a cottage. If the children all sit round a table, one may be more hungry than another; one may be supplied out of the deficiency of the appetite of another ; but when a separate portion is sent to each child in a mill, it very frequently happens that that portion is the best that can be obtained in the cottage, and a great part of it after all is frequently wasted. I have been informed of some places where the overlooker keeps a tub for waste bread and victuals which the children bring to the mill, and supplies one or two pigs with the wasted meals. Now this, I presume, is all a dead loss to the cottage ; and then another circumstance connected with divided meals, and which is a great source of expense and trouble, is the taking of those meals to the mill, the breakfast, the dinner, and the drinking; in fact almost every family is obliged to keep a messenger, if I may so speak, for that purpose ; at all events, whoever takes the meals, that person is in so doing, a source of expense to the family; and taking all these circumstances into consideration, the wear and tear of clothes, the expense of divided meals, and the sending them to the mills, I conceive that factory labour is far less profitable to a family than any other labour ; but if a remission of the hours of labour to ten hours a day can be obtained, then in very many cases, and in most cases, I believe, the children will be enabled to obtain their meals at home ; many will be able to get their breakfast before they go; and an hour being allowed for dinner, the greater number will be inclined to go home to dinner, and will also defer their afternoon meal till they get home, so, hereby, there will be a considerable gain, or saving of expenditure, which is the same thing in the family economy."

On the question being put by the Chairman of the Committee to Mr Bull—" What effect do you think this system has in forming that character so important in every sphere of life, but to the poor man more especially essential, either with a view to his own comforts, or to the proper bringing up of a family in the humbler circumstances of life—I mean that of the females who become wives at a subsequent period ?" Mr Bull replied, "I understand that I am asked what sort of a wife the factory child will make in process of time; in answer to which I wish to say that I should do injustice to many young persons who are brought up in the factory system, if I did not say that their industry, neatness, and disposition to improve themselves, are beyond the power of my commendation. I know several such, I have some such females employed for whom I do and ought to entertain the greatest respect ; but I would say that these are exceptions to the generality of young persons brought up in factories; I would say that the generality of them are as unfit as they possibly can be to fill the important station of a cottager's wife. How should they, considering the length of labour to which they are now subjected, from the youth up, until the time of their marriage, be able to learn the duties of the cottage ? I am acquainted with many that can scarcely mend a hole in their garments. I have heard it from their mothers and their relations, that they scarcely know how to darn a stocking ; and I beg to state that I know a case in which the father of a child (to illustrate the system) was so anxious that his little girl should acquire the use of the needle, that during a considerable period, when he was confined at home himself by a lameness, he sat over her after her return from her work, with a little rod in his hand, and insisted upon her mending her stockings, although she was falling asleep continually, and when she nodded over it, he gave her a very gentle tap upon the head with the rod. Although this incident may appear trifling to some, which, however, I trust it will not to the committee, yet it is a just picture of the effects of the system upon the domestic habits of the poor. I would also state that it is an important fact, with which I am well acquainted, that in many cases the young women

employed in factories do not make their own clothes at all ;
their working clothes they obtain at the slop shops which
abound in the manufacturing districts, where ready-made
clothes are to be had, and their Sunday dress is of course
of a very smart description wherever they can afford it,
and is manufactured by some notable milliner, who knows
how to set those matters off to the best advantage. Thus
they neither know how to make or mend a working dress,
or to supply the wants of a family when they become the
mothers of children."

Minuteness of detail is characteristic of Mr Bull, and
gave to his speeches, lectures, and letters, on the factory
question, real interest and value. By the opponents of
factory regulation he was feared and abused—by its supporters, respected and beloved. The factory operatives placed
implicit confidence in Mr Bull ; his services were called into
requisition on all important occasions. After parties had
been settled in the first reformed House of Commons, and
public business had resumed its usual course, it was felt to
be desirable to find a parliamentary leader of the factory
question in the Commons. The late Mr Fielden was new
to Parliament ; his known honesty and knowledge of the
question were strong recommendations ; he desired to support
rather than to lead, and was anxious that the subject should
be renewed under the most favourable circumstances that
were possible. To find a successor to Sadler was felt to
be a difficult task, yet the necessity of finding a parliamentary
leader was self-evident to all interested in the question.

The importance of the Factory question had gradually
increased its proportions ; among scientific physiologists and
statesmen in every civilized country, the subject received attention. Every country which had a national practice to palliate
when by an Englishman charged with the crime, retorted
by pointing to the English factory system. This kind of
defence was very weak and reprehensible, but it was to

Englishmen vexatious, and contributed to force the minds of many to desire a change. National jealousies have caused much bloodshed ; they have also done some good ; they have sometimes obliged nations, for shame's sake, to amend their morals. John Bull is prone to talk against slavery, and in the reform times, was very full of patriotism, and, like a person proud of his reputation, John felt that the door must somehow or other be closed against reproach. Statements of cruelties which from the lips of Mr Oastler had been designated "visionary," had now been verified by indisputable evidence, though it was customary by the opponents of factory regulation, in the hope of destroying Mr Oastler's usefulness to charge him with recklessness and exaggeration. The fact was that not any man could have been more careful in ascertaining the opinions of the highest authorities on the subject which engaged his attention. Not any fact he ever stated on the factory question has been proved untrue. In the subjoined document, privately acquired by Mr Oastler, the names were not signed, a circumstance which alone proved how powerful opposition was in the early part of the short-time movement in Yorkshire :—

" That we are the surgeons of the General Infirmary at Leeds, an institution which annually admits about five thousand patients.

" That although it is very certain scrofulous diseases are greatly aggravated by overworking, and that the tendency to scrofula itself may probably be produced by it, yet we can speak with greater confidence respecting its effects in producing distortion of the knees, ankles, and feet, many of which cases have been brought to the Infirmary in so aggravated a degree as to be incurable.

" That upon investigating these cases, we have been led to attribute them to the circumstance of the patients having been kept too many hours in the day upon their legs, at a period of life when the bones and ligaments have not attained sufficient firmness to sustain the superincumbent weight of the body for so long a time.

" We are decidedly of opinion, that working in the night is more injurious to the health of children than working by day; and, further, that the age of nine years is the earliest period at which they ought to be put to work."

Signed by the three surgeons of the Leeds Infirmary, March 22nd, 1831.

It was Mr Oastler's possession of such documents as the above, and he had several, which constituted his warrant for much of what he said, and enabled him ultimately to triumph over opposition.

It is very creditable to Mr Oastler's character as a public man, that statements originally denied when made by him were verified by undeniable authority. We append an example by way of illustration :—

" Mr John Baldwin, Halifax, thought there was great credit due to Mr Oastler, for drawing the attention of the public to the factory system. He at one time thought Mr Oastler in error, but after hearing him at a public meeting which was held in the Cloth Hall Yard, Halifax, where he stated that the children had eaten their meals as they worked, he thought Mr Oastler was telling falsehoods, and from such observations was induced to go into his own factory next morning at breakfast time, and then found what Mr Oastler had said was perfectly correct. He then put it to his conscience, and conscience told him that it was wrong. He then stopped the engine at once, and gave them half an hour to eat their breakfasts, and has done so ever since."

During the progress of the factory agitation the child from the field and the factory had been measured and weighed each against the other, and the last found wanting. The homes of the factory children had been visited, and the children watched as they, after a long day's work, sunk to sleep, unable to masticate the food they had intended to eat, sleeping with the food in their mouths. The infirmaries and streets told of cripples, the parish authorities of increased poor rates. Machinery had rapidly increased, giving millions of pounds sterling to a few persons, and in its unregulated course causing misery and death to immense numbers of human beings : the yielding up of the human frames of the many, as a means of accumulating riches alone, had been stigmatised as a national crime. Christianity, civilization, and great riches, had been spoken of in the same breath with the horrible facts of the factories, as narrated before a committee of the House of Commons. The comparison, thus instituted, carried in its wake a condemnation more terrible than an avowedly Christian and civilized nation could continue willingly to bear. The supporters of factory regulation were told that the nation's greatness depended upon the existing system of production. They denied the assertion, and to their denial added,—"If a nation's greatness required such cruelties, that greatness was an abomination, and ought not to exist." They were assured that a reduction of taxes and a repeal of the corn laws would remedy the evils complained of : they answered these assurances by pointing out that the system, the evils of which they complained, had its origin and growth when taxation was comparatively limited, and the corn laws, as enacted in 1815, unknown. The Sadler report placed in the hands of the Short Time Committees of the United Kingdom weapons which they, under the tutelage of Oastler, Sadler, Bull, Fielden, and others, were soon well instructed how to wield. A love of home was formerly among the working men of this country a trait of national character ; under the rule of the factory system this strong bond of order and happiness had been loosened. The leaders of the factory agitation appealed to the better sympathies of their countrymen to use their influence to renew this bond : home was with Oastler and Bull a theme of constant discourse, and their example was followed by many others. The factory system, as reflected in the Sadler report, was a fathomless source of illustration on the evils arising from a neglect of home duties. To restore the working man once more to his rightful place as the head and provider for his own household was a noble aspiration, and the unceasing desire of Mr Sadler : all his efforts, in and out of parliament, were directed to that end ; and when no longer enabled to serve the working men in the House of Commons, he counselled them not to delay their efforts to find another to represent in that assembly their feelings, desires, and objects.

The avowedly philosophical politician has usually a strong sense of contempt for enthusiasm, whether political, social, or religious. In his mind enthusiasm is closely allied to temporary insanity, and he hopes time will prove a remedy for the original disease. There were not wanting stoical philosophers of this order, who treated the strong desire of the operative classes as an evanescent feeling, and considered Mr Sadler's exclusion from parliament as a favourable circumstance, calculated to hasten the breaking up of the factory movement. Enthusiasm in a good cause does not readily die out among men seriously affected by real evils ; regret for disappointment in such cases is apt to sober the judgment, and in consequence to strengthen the resolve for resolute action. The loss consequent on Mr Sadler's rejection by Leeds and Huddersfield, as a candidate for a seat in parliament, was deeply deplored, but the circumstance did not unnerve either the factory operatives or their influential supporters. A meeting of delegates was held, to consider what, under the circumstances, ought to be done ; and, after long and anxious deliberation, it was resolved that the Rev. G. S. Bull should forthwith proceed to London, for the purpose of endeavouring to find an appropriate parliamentary leader. The mission was most important : the selection of Mr Bull was a proof of the great confidence reposed in him by the factory operatives and their friends— a well-merited acknowledgment of his sincerity, discretion, and judgment. The result of Mr Bull's mission was conveyed to the secretaries of the various short-time committees, and to others therein interested, by a letter, of which the following is a copy:—

" Dear Sir,—I have to inform you that, in furtherance of the object of the delegates' meeting, I have succeeded, under Mr Sadler's sanction, in prevailing upon Lord Ashley to renew *his* (Mr Sadler's) bill.

" Lord Ashley gave notice yesterday afternoon, at half-past two, of a motion on the 5th of March, for leave ' to renew the bill, brought in by Mr Sadler last session, to regulate the labour of children in the mills and factories of the United Kingdom, with such amendments and additions as appear necessary from the evidence given before the select committee of this house.'

" This notice, I am very happy to say (for I was present), was received with hearty and unusual cheers from all parts of a house of more than 300. No other notice was so cheered; and more than forty, some of them very popular, were given at the same time.

" I am informed that Lord Ashley received many unexpected assurances of support immediately after his notice, and has had more since.

" Pray call your committee together directly, and read this to them. As to Lord Ashley, he is noble, benevolent, and resolute in mind, as he is manly in person. I have been favoured with several interviews, and all of the most satisfactory kind. On one occasion his lordship said, ' I have only zeal and good intentions to bring to this work ; I can have no merit in it, that must all belong to Mr Sadler. It seems no one else will undertake it, so I will ; and, without cant or hypocrisy, which I hate, I assure you I dare not refuse the request you have so earnestly pressed. I believe it is my duty to God and to the poor, and I trust He will support me. Talk of trouble! what do we come to parliament for?'

"In a letter he writes, 'To me it appeared an affair less of policy than of religion, and I determined, therefore, at all hazards to myself, to do what I could in furtherance of the views of that virtuous and amiable man (meaning Mr Sadler).

"I have just left his lordship, and find him more determined than ever. He says, it is your cause ; if you support him he will never flinch.

"Yours, most faithfully,

"G. S. BULL.

"London, Feb. 6, 1833.
"To Mr ——, Secretary of the Short-time Committee, ——."

Lord Ashley's acceptance of leadership was known to the country, through the medium of the daily press, as the following extract from the *Times* of February the 7th, 1833, will prove. The remarks of the *Times* indicate the great interest the question had excited; it had grown from the obscurity of Fixby Hall and Huddersfield, Mr Oastler, and a few operatives, to be considered a subject of high national importance:—"The renewal of Mr Sadler's benevolent measure, the Ten Hours' Bill, was undertaken on Tuesday evening by Lord Ashley, who feels a deep interest in this afflicting subject. Lord Ashley gave notice, immediately on the return of the Speaker from the Lords, and that notice was received with unusual and very hearty approbation from all parts of a house of upwards of 300 members. His lordship has been requested by the official organ of the delegates' meeting, whose address was recently agreed to, to undertake this charitable work. It seems, however, that the millowners, unable to resist the strong tide of public opinion which the force of the evidence before the select committee, the result of Mr Sadler's indefatigable labours, has set in motion, have resolved to dole out some niggardly measure of relief to the poor children by the hand of Lord Morpeth, one of the members for the West Riding of Yorkshire. His lordship must have been somewhat forgetful of parliamentary courtesy when, after midnight on Tuesday, and when the house was all bustle, he announced his intention to bring in his, or rather the masters' bill, and, in so doing, dated his motion for the 27th of February, although Lord Ashley's was previously given for the 5th of March."

These remarks from the pages of the *Times* reflect much light on the position of the question at the time to which they refer. The opponents of the measure, unable longer to remain in successful opposition, hoped, by dividing the supporters of the Ten Hours' bill, to pass a measure through parliament, more satisfactory to themselves and yet sufficient to allay the public feeling which had been awakened, and to neutralize all future efforts on the part of the operatives, Mr Oastler and others. The opposition tactics were very readily appreciated by the operatives of the North, who resolved that in their cause the crafty maxim of " Divide and conquer," should not be practicable, with their consent.

Lord Ashley's adoption of the factory question, on the part of the operatives, was to them a source of congratulation and hope—a rising and Christian nobleman and statesman, who, avowedly, from a love of God, had resolved to serve the interests of man, was esteemed as a pearl of great value. His lordship's avowal that he had taken up the factory question as a duty he owed to " God and to the poor," and his declaration that if by the factory operatives supported, he would never flinch, were welcomed in tens of thousands of cellars, garrets, and cottages in the manufacturing districts. His lordship's letter, containing these words, having been

read to the local committees, and by them published, its contents were soon and widely known. The organization of the factory movement was so complete, that intelligence circulated with extraordinary rapidity. The main requisite for success in a movement involving humanity as a primary element, is an aknowledgment of the truth of a principle, he who asserts a broad principle, adheres to it, acts up to it, rests upon a rock which the waves of faction may beat against, surround, or sweep over, but it remains firm, hard, impenetrable, and is a safe and sure foundation on which to stand. Of all pitiable and fruitless things in existence, a statesman begging for his political bread from day to day, by the aid of mere expedients, is the most lamentable, humiliating, and wretched. He who faithfully believed he was bound to serve "God and the poor," was far removed from the mendicant politicians who lived upon the crumbs of accident, doled out by the hand of a treacherous and momentary popularity. At the request of Mr Bull, Mr Oastler addressed to Lord Ashley a letter of encouragement. His lordship's reply conveys very fully the state of mind of the writer as expressed by himself. His lordship's letter is as follows :—
" London, February 16th, 1833. I am much obliged to you for your kind and energetic letter ; much, very much, is owing to your humanity and zeal, and though I cannot reckon deeply on the gratitude of multitudes, yet I will hope that your name will for years to come, be blessed by those children who have suffered, or would have suffered the tortures of a factory. It is very cruel upon Mr Sadler that he is debarred from the joy of putting the crown upon his beloved measure ; however, his *must* be the honour, though another may complete it ; and for my part, I feel that if I were to believe that my exertions ought to detract the *millionth* part from his merits, I should be one of the most unprincipled and contemptible of mankind. Ask the question, simply,—*Who has* borne the real toil, who has

encountered the real opposition, who roused the sluggish public to sentiments of honour and pity ? Why, Mr Sadler, and I come in (supposing I succeed) to terminate in the twelfth hour his labour of the eleven." The appreciation of the labour of Sadler was just—time proved that the end to be obtained was more difficult than his lordship, when entering on his labours, anticipated; he had, however, resolved on the work to be done. In the same letter he continued : "I greatly fear my ability to carry on this measure. I wish, most ardently I wish, that some other had been found to undertake the cause; nothing but the apprehension of its being lost, induced me to acquiesce in Mr Bull's request. I entertain such strong opinions on the matter, that I did not *dare*, as a Christian, to let my diffidence, or love of ease, prevail over the demands of morality and religion." Under any possible circumstances, there could not have been a more lasting basis for permanent action than "morality and religion."

END OF VOL. I.

Burt Franklin: Research and Source Work Series # 91

THE

HISTORY

OF

THE FACTORY MOVEMENT

IN TWO VOLUMES

VOL. II

THE

H I S T O R Y

OF

THE FACTORY MOVEMENT

FROM

THE YEAR 1802 TO THE ENACTMENT OF THE
TEN HOURS' BILL IN 1847

By ALFRED KYDD

IN TWO VOLUMES

VOL. II

Burt Franklin: Research and Source Work Series # 91

BURT FRANKLIN
NEW YORK

Published by BURT FRANKLIN
235 East 44th Street
New York, N.Y. 10017

First Published
LONDON
1857

CONTENTS.

b

CHAPTER V.

CHAPTER VI.

CHAPTER VII.

CHAPTER VIII.

CHAPTER IX.

CHAPTER X.

CHAPTER XI.

THE

HISTORY OF THE FACTORY MOVEMENT.

———o———

CHAPTER I.

IMPORTANT MEETING AT THE LONDON TAVERN, IN 1833.—SPEECHES
OF DUNCOMBE, O'CONNELL, OASTLER, SADLER, AND LORD ASHLEY.

THE adoption by Lord Ashley of Mr Sadler's factory bill
was, to his lordship, and to the factory operatives, a step of
importance. The success of a movement must, to a great
extent, depend upon the judgment of the leader, his constancy
of purpose, and the confidence reposed in him by those he
undertakes to represent. "Divide and conquer," is the
favourite maxim of politicians, and they are ever in search
of some weakness or contradiction, real or apparent, in the
camp of their opponents. Those who had distinguished
themselves against Mr Sadler in parliament, knew how
thoroughly he possessed the confidence of the factory
operatives; they fondly hoped that his successor would have
less support in the country, and, consequently, less influence
in the House of Commons. There were those also, who
conceived it possible that Mr Sadler would not, under his
changed circumstances, continue to feel the same intense
interest in the factory question, which had hitherto animated

B

his whole soul ; that the want of position in parliament, as the leader of a great social question, would cool his ardour, and make him jealous of the honour conferred on his successor. The majority of politicians, distinguished as members of the legislature, are disposed to measure their duties by their appreciation of honours enjoyed; with Mr Sadler this was not the case ; he was moved to action by his sense of duty to God, and he accepted of honour or censure as they might occur, regardless of neither, but never allowing his own desires to form the rule of his practice, except in so far as these corresponded with the dictates of conscience. Mr Sadler's most intimate coadjutors fully appreciated his noble qualities of heart and head, these were not however understood by those who only knew him as an opponent in parliament, they hoped to gain strength by his exclusion.

The London Society for the Improvement of the Condition of Factory Children, acting under the patronage of his Royal Highness the Duke of Sussex, resolved to convene a meeting in the City of London Tavern, Bishopsgate street, of the friends of the society, on the 23rd of February, 1833. The meeting was most influentially attended; it served the threefold purpose, of bringing the condition of those employed in factory labour, under the consideration of the London public and press, to petition parliament for the restriction of the labour to ten hours per day, and to publicly inaugurate Lord Ashley, as the adopted parliamentary leader of the question. Sir Peter Laurie, Lord Mayor, occupied the chair. In the words of the morning newspapers, "The meeting was graced by a numerous and highly-respectable assemblage of ladies, who appeared to take a deep interest in the proceedings. Among the gentlemen who appeared on the platform, we observed: Lord Teynham, Lord Ashley, Hon. Wm. Duncombe, M.P., Colonel Torrens, M.P., Colonel Williams, M.P., Mr Robinson, M.P., Mr O'Connell, M.P., Mr Sadler, late M.P., Mr Wilks, M.P., Sir

William Blizard, Mr Lyall, Mr Alderman Venables, Mr
R. Peek, Sheriff, Hon. Mr Frazer, Sir Edward Knatch-
bull, M.P., Sir Andrew Agnew, M.P., Mr Owen, of
Lanark, Captain Brenton, R.N., Mr William Smith, late
M.P., Mr Carruthers, Mr Helps, Mr Freeze, Mr Nathaniel
Gould, Mr Labouchere, Rev. Dr Russell, Rev. Daniel
Wilson, &c." Mr Oastler and the Rev. Mr Bull attended,
by invitation, to address the meeting.

In the annals of factory agitation not any meeting, considered in all its bearings, moral, social, political, and in
connection with time and circumstance, could have been
more important. It was the first public meeting on the
factory question since the passing of the Reform Bill, at
which men of all shades of politics and religion had met
for the accomplishment of one common end. It was the
first public meeting on the question in London—it was the
first popular sign of renewed life and energy on the part of
the " Ten Hour Bill-men," since the rejection of their former
leader by constituencies rioting under the Reform Act—it
was the first time Lord Ashley had met in public the
founders and principal supporters of that cause, which he
had resolved to lead in parliament. The meeting was
addressed by the Lord Mayor, the Hon. Wm. Duncombe
[Lord Feversham], Rev. G. S. Bull, Mr O'Connell, M.P., Mr
T. W. Helps, Col. Williams, M.P., Mr G. Lyall, Mr Oastler,
Mr H. Pownall, Mr J. H. Freeze, Mr M. T. Sadler, and
Lord Ashley.

The following resolutions were unanimously adopted:—

" 1st. That it appears to this meeting, from the evidence
before the select committee on Mr Sadler's Factories' Regulation Bill, and from the testimony of many highly respectable persons well and practically acquainted with the factory
system, that it is the ordinary practice to work the children
of the poor, chiefly females, in the manufacturing districts
(who must either submit to that system or starve), from

six o'clock in the morning, or before, to seven, eight, or nine o'clock at night, in a standing position. and in a vitiated atmosphere, with very insufficient intervals for meals and recreation ; and that in time of brisk trade these evils are greatly aggravated.

"2nd. That this great city, the metropolis of a Christian and commercial empire, and justly famed for its institutions of mercy, is bound to express its conviction that ' the gains of oppression are a national loss,' and to declare its deep sympathy towards factory children of this empire, whose sufferings under the present system have been fully developed in the evidence before the select committee on Mr Sadler's bill, and for whose protection as well as for the general good of society, an effective legislative enactment is imperatively called for.

" That this meeting rejoices to perceive that the bill introduced by Mr Sadler, during the last session of parliament, and supported by the evidence collected by his indefatigable exertions, is taken up by the Right Honourable Lord Ashley ; and that his lordship is supported by the zealous cooperation of the operatives of the empire, for the protection of whose children that bill is designed."

The following petition was unanimously adopted :

" To the Honourable the Commons of the United Kingdom of Great Britain and Ireland in parliament assembled.

" The humble petition of the undersigned friends of the society for improving the condition of factory children, unanimously agreed to at a meeting convened by public advertisement, at the City of London Tavern, Bishopsgate Street, on Saturday the 23rd day of February, 1833, for the purpose of requesting your honourable house to take into consideration the condition of the children and young persons employed in the cotton, flax, silk, woollen, and worsted mills and factories, of the United Kingdom of Great Britain and Ireland.

" Humbly showeth,

" That your petitioners feel that the disgraceful and heart-rending disclosures which have from time to time been made by select committees of your honourable house, more especially by that held during the last session of the late parliament, relative to the undue and excessive working of children and young persons in the cotton, flax, silk, woollen, and worsted mills and factories of the United Kingdom, render it the bounden duty of your petitioners to press upon your honourable house the redress of wrongs, which, as affecting the infantile and youthful portion of the population, your petitioners are persuaded have no parallel in any age or country.

" That your petitioners are deeply impressed with the conviction that the interposition of the legislature to regulate the factory system, is called for, not only by the principles of humanity and justice, but by those of sound commercial policy; and that the lasting wealth, strength, and happiness, of a nation are incompatible with a system which is not only destructive of the health, the morals, and the social and domestic comforts of the manufacturing classes in general, but essentially ruinous to the physical and mental powers of the rising generation.

" That while your petitioners feel it to be a barbarous and revolting feature of the present factory system, that the injuries which it inflicts fall with peculiar severity on children of the weaker sex, occasioning, as they advance in years, a recklessness of character which renders them a prey to the seductions by which they are surrounded, your petitioners are convinced that its evils are not confined to any age or sex, but that morals, social order, and Christianity, are deeply outraged by their continuance; and that unless they are arrested by the strong arm of the legislature, the community at large must, at no distant period, participate in the fatal results.

"That your petitioners implore your honourable house to recognise and acknowledge, on behalf of the poor, that principle upon which our courts of equity have long acted where property is concerned ; that while protection and guardianship are extended to the orphan children of the rich for their security, it may not be deemed beneath the dignity of parliament to interfere to protect the helpless children of the poor, but industrious, classes in that which too often constitutes their sole property—their power and capacity to labour; and that with reference to this consideration, your honourable house will allow the medical evidence which was taken before the late select committee, and, above all, the comparative statement of mortality which is thereto appended, to have their due weight in your decision.

"Your petitioners entreat your honourable house, that for this purpose you will be pleased to adopt the bill of which Lord Ashley has given notice that he will move the introduction, being a measure similar to that proposed by Mr Sadler in the last session of parliament, with such alterations and additions as may be found expedient; limiting the time of working children and young persons employed in the cotton, flax, silk, woollen, and worsted mills and other factories of the United Kingdom to ten hours per day for five days of the week, and eight hours on the Saturday; and excluding children under nine years of age from being so employed under any circumstances whatsoever. And your petitioners also humbly entreat your honourable house that you will be pleased to direct that the working of children and young persons in the cases aforesaid, shall be comprised within twelve continuous hours, and arranged so as most to subserve their comfort and improvement; and lastly, that your honourable house will be pleased to enforce the provisions of the said bill by such degrees and descriptions of punishment as to your wisdom shall appear most likely to secure and compel their observance.

" And your petitioners, as in duty bound, will ever pray, &c."

These resolutions and the petition indicate a new phase in the progress of the factory movement : they are founded upon the evidence of the Sadler committee. The statements contained in that report were of so strong and decided a kind, as, if once admitted, to force restrictive legislation. The truthfulness of these statements was maintained by every speaker competent, from experience, to pronounce a judgment. At few public meetings have speeches more remarkable for practical knowledge or eloquence been delivered. The late Mr O'Connell was, beyond all doubt, essentially an orator : his speech at the London Tavern is an excellent specimen of eloquence; it is full of condensed feeling and stimulating thought. Few indeed could have concentrated more matter and sympathy into so few words, or met the strong points urged in opposition with so masterly a skill. Mr O'Connell said—" The resolution, in which he warmly and heartily concurred, was to the effect that ' the meeting were convinced that the gains of oppression were a national loss, and that legislative interference on the subject of the condition of factory children was imperatively called for,' and he was determined to support it with all his energies. He (Mr O'Connell) was a father, and could, therefore, feel an individual sympathy for these poor children. Who would not promote infant enjoyment ? With what feelings, then, could he regard that abominable system which changed the brightest period of human life into a frightful desert, and which deprived those wretched beings of the enjoyment of that part of human existence in which nature indemnifies herself by anticipation for all the after miseries of life? With this feeling he had often asked how parents could be induced to rend asunder the dearest strings of life : how the mother could forget the pangs which she had endured for the safety and happiness of her little ones, and consent to sacrifice them on the altar of the factory Moloch? The answer which he had received on these occasions terrified him; it was, want—wretchedness—misery—starvation. Nothing but starvation could ever interfere between the mother and the protection of her infants: nothing but actual want and the fear of their starvation could induce such a violation of all the maternal feelings. Good God! that such a system should exist in a Christian country; that poor infants should be condemned to the deprivation of sleep, the inhalation of poison, and the endurance of the extremes of human anguish, to obtain a miserable pittance to save themselves and their parents, perhaps, from starvation. The question was a question of blood, and those who should stand by and acquiesce in the continuance of such a system, after the facts which had been stated, would be guilty of murder. He (Mr O'Connell) knew that it was wrong in principle to interfere between the master and the labourer in questions of political economy; but, was this a question of political economy? His heart told him it was not, and that where the parental feelings are in question political economy itself must give way. The King, as the father of the orphans in his empire, has a power to protect them. This power he delegates to the Lord Chancellor in the cases of the children of the rich, and as soon as any pounds, shillings, and pence, are discovered to attach to those children, that legal functionary interferes to protect them. Why should not the poor children of the empire be protected in the same manner? Why should not they have a Lord Chancellor to watch over them? The answer would be, that those children have no property; but was not the labour of those children their property, and ought not they to be protected and provided with the means of properly exercising it? It had been said that the evidence given before the parliamentary committee, had been got up for the occasion, and that the promoters of it were a set of enthusiasts, whose judgment was swallowed up by their feelings. But this was a public committee, and evidence in contradiction could have been openly given ; nor were the scenes of those atrocities closed from the public eye—on the contrary, every manufactory was open to be viewed, and was proved, by concurrent testimony, to be a hive of swarming misery. The miserable creatures themselves, too, were brought before the committee, and their sunken eyes, hectic cheeks, emaciated limbs, on which was stamped the decrepitude of premature old age, spoke for them and gave a fearful corroboration to their testimony. He (Mr. O'Connell), notwithstanding the arguments which had been urged in its support, could not believe that such a system of cruelty was necessary for the commercial prosperity of the country ; it made the few rich rapidly, but if the same riches could be obtained at the expense of a little delay, could it be questioned that it would be preferable? He trusted that he should not be mistaken in supporting the cause—the cause of those who had no protector, no voice but the voice of humanity ; and that it should have the support of all his energies, humble as they were, he pledged himself. It was said that the number of hours to which it was proposed to reduce the labour of these children was too small, but he was surprised that human nature could bear, under such circumstances, to work even that number of hours. He, for himself, considered that ten hours were too many, but as medical men, and men of experience had decided that labour during that period could be borne, he should go along with them to that extent, but he would not consent to the addition of one half-hour, nay, not one minute, beyond the time so decided to be capable of being endured. He had heard that there would be much opposition to this proposed reduction, but he trusted that public feeling would render such opposition fruitless, and as he did not wish to introduce any remarks of a political tendency, although his breast was swelling and his mind tortured by such questions, he would confine himself to proposing the resolution." The speech of Mr Oastler is not less remarkable than that of Mr O'Connell. It is not less eloquent, its value is increased by an array of facts, such only as a man of Mr Oastler's close habits of observation could narrate; his speech contained the kernel of the question, and exhibited to the mind of England, at one view, the strong points of the case in favour of factory regulation, and much additional evidence on the cruelties practised in the district of Yorkshire with which he was intimately acquainted.   Mr Oastler said:—

"I will not enter into the evidence given before the House of Commons, but will state what I, an impartial witness, have seen.   In my district little children under seven years of age are sometimes made to work for eighteen, and in some cases for twenty hours out of the twenty-four.   It is impossible that the factory children could exist under such labour, and the churchyards had proved that they were not long able to do so.   I assure you, it is no uncommon thing that a child should be beaten with a heavy strap, laid on by a heavy hand, till its back and its breast are black.   I have seen a little child, not more than ten years of age, who, being tired, had spoiled a piece of yarn three inches long, (the value of which there is no coin low enough to express), was dreadfully beaten.   That child lived within a mile of my house, and I have counted thirty-three cuts on its back.   In a mill at Wigan, the children, for any slight neglect, are loaded with weights of twenty pounds, placed over their shoulders, and hanging behind their backs.   Then there is a murderous instrument, called a billy-roller, about eight feet long, and one inch and a half in diameter, with which many children have been knocked down, and in some instances, I believe, murdered.   In cotton mills the labour is restricted to twelve hours by Act of Parliament; but that is too long for any child to labour in this country, or in any part of the globe. The factory children, rising in the morning long before the rise of the sun or the dawn of day, some without shoes or stockings, might be seen dragging their weary bodies through the rain and snow along the streets of Christian Manchester; long before the shops were open, long before any one was stirring, except the scavengers, these little children may be seen in the streets of that great town. The parents are during this time in bed, and in hundreds of instances they have no other means of subsistence than the wages of their children's death. The little creatures thus bred up, when they do not fall into crime and come to an ignominious end, drag on a short life of misery and degradation. Thus it is that these sons and daughters of the heroes of Waterloo and Trafalgar are rewarded. Is this state of things to be endured? I doubt not that the humanity of the country will shout forth an answer in the negative. If England refuse to interfere in this matter, the God of little children will strike her, powerful as she is, and make her tremble. This is not, I know it is not, a meeting where politics should be alluded to—but I hope I may be allowed to mention one fact, which strikingly develops the misery occasioned by the factory system. No one here will deny that there is misery in Ireland, that there is poverty in Ireland, or that Ireland has suffered wrongs. At Manchester the other day, I heard the Rev. Mr Haines, Roman Catholic priest, exclaim, after eight years' residence in Manchester, and after fully considering the wretchedness of his native country—'Ireland, with all thy poverty and all thy wrongs, rather than Manchester with all thy wealth and thy factory system!' It has been asserted, that the volume which lies before you is a volume of ex-parte evidence. Surely enough has been said this day, and surely the character of the medical profession alone is enough to satisfy the public that that evidence could not have been taken ex parte. The committee had the opportunity of cross-examining the witnesses. I myself underwent a cross-examination, and, at all events, they had an opportunity of shaking the evidence that was given, if it had been in their power. The evidence of the medical gentlemen was founded on an experience, some of them of forty to sixty years; and, as the engineers of the human body—men who must know whether the steam-engine of the human body was of a ten or of a twelve-hours power—they unanimously decided, that it was scarcely of a ten-hours' power. Next came the testimony of the operatives. Now he had no doubt it would be very convenient to some to prevent the testimony of the operatives being taken at all, but that day had not arrived, and, he trusted, never would come. When we sent up operatives—friends, of course, to the cause—to be examined in London, headed by their worthy champion, Sadler, they were selected with the greatest care. Many who would have been sent up were left at home, lest they might be discharged by their respective employers. A great many of those who did come, were discharged on their return. Talk of tyranny, he knew nothing to equal that amongst any of the heathen nations—a man to be punished by a petty tyrant, for obeying the law of the land, is a new thing under the sun! There was a boy whose case was certainly deserving of being brought before their notice—a boy who, when seven years of age, had actually to be 'trailed' (the Yorkshire phrase), a couple of miles to perform twelve or fourteen hours' work every day. He was 'trailed' to his work by an elder brother and sister holding him up under the arms. That boy was well formed originally, and was now deformed in every limb, though only seventeen years of age. Thank God, his mind has not been contaminated—his character was good. He was charged by his master—Addison, of Bradford—with having come to London, and there told the grossest falsehoods. That same Addison, of Bradford, distinctly stated in the newspapers, that words

had been put into his mouth, and alluded to the Rev. Mr
Bull as the prompter of the boy. He also alleged that
the poor boy was in concealment lest he should turn traitor.
Addison thought the orphan was friendless, but it soon
appeared that he was no longer under the tyrant's rod;
that he had friends to assist him if he spoke the truth,
and those who would condemn him, if he resorted to subter-
fuge. The poor boy was not in concealment, though Addison
himself once was. The orphan was put to the Leeds
Lancastrian school. The Short Time Committee of Huddersfield procured a copy of his evidence given in the House
of Commons; they found that it was substantially true
in every respect, and Mr Osborn, of Leeds, who acted
as his foster-father, and myself, offered to enter into a public
examination of the circumstances ; the short-time committee
undertook to pay half the expenses of publishing the examination, and thus leave the public to judge whether the boy
were correct or not ; but the accuser has concealed himself
from us ever since. There were some other matters ventured
to be put forth in the public papers, equally without foundation ; and here I must say that the newspapers have always
been ready, at least, to give poverty fair play. I publicly,
humbly, but sincerely thank the press for the way they
have taken up the sacred, the holy, and the righteous cause
of these helpless individuals. To return to the subject of
the witnesses who had been examined before the committee.
A man of the name of Brown, of Leeds, charged a witness
of the name of Drake with falsehood. Drake told him,
in the public paper, that he had not even told all he knew,
and Brown was silent. As far as I know—and I have good
reason to know much—that book of evidence, filled as it is
with mourning, lamentation, and woe, is true; but does
not, cannot, contain the whole truth. One-tenth of the
miseries of the little children can never be revealed on
earth ; that exposure must be reserved for the great day

of account. There are cruelties of such an indecent nature committed, that if they were told they would scarcely be credited. We have to understate, rather than overpaint the picture; but if those monsters persist, we shall be compelled to outrage the lines of decency, and tell the world what tyrants—what monsters they are. There had been many difficulties raised in our path, as we travelled onwards in Yorkshire and Lancashire. I have been myself charged, over and over again, with being a great enemy to the emancipation of the blacks. But I deny that charge, having, even in my teens, under Mr Wilberforce, fought to obtain negro emancipation. I remember the time when the cry for negro emancipation was not so fashionable in Yorkshire as it is at this moment; and the very persons who were formerly disposed to hoot and to hiss me for advocating the emancipation of the blacks, are now disposed to treat me in the same way, for coming forward to support the emancipation of the white slaves. They are anxious in every way to burke the question. That question, like many others, had cost a great deal of money. There is one individual who is in the room at this moment, who has himself expended thousands of pounds upon it. I have often had occasion to go to that fountain of benevolence, but I can go no more—not that I have ever been sent empty away, (I have always been more than amply replenished), but it is impossible for any person to expect that one individual only is to bear all the expense. For my own part, my little all is gone. It has been but little—I wished it well. The battle is now for the emancipation of British children. The question is, whether British children should be murdered or not murdered, whether the bill, which is to impose eleven or twelve hours' work on delicate and half-starved children, is to receive the sanction of the law—or whether the measure entrusted to Lord Ashley is to pass into a law. The battle will have to be fought against a powerful, a malicious, a wealthy foe. The operatives are subscribing—nay, the very children, out of their miserable pittance, were subscribing to carry forward their measure of emancipation ; and surely, when British fathers and British mothers have heard of the deplorable state in which these helpless children are placed, it will not be considered too much to ask for a mite from them, in aid of this great work of reform. I conclude by seconding the resolution."

A very considerable number of mill-owners were anxious for a compromise, and their desires found a response in the House of Commons, a circumstance which gave to the London Tavern meeting additional importance. It was this fear of compromise, united with a determination not to make any concession, which caused the various speakers to refer especially to the question of time ; in no speech was this one point made more prominent, than in that of the Hon. William Duncombe, who was always understood to be a principal representative of the opinions of the operatives of Yorkshire on the Factory question, and was honoured by them as " a nobleman" in the literal sense of the word, as well as a mark of social distinction.

" The Hon. William Duncombe, M.P. for the North Riding of Yorkshire, begged to assure the respectable meeting which he saw then assembled, that his most strenuous efforts in parliament should be directed to the great object of protecting that helpless and hitherto unprotected class of young creatures employed in the factories of this great, wealthy, and commercial country. Feeling, as he did, the deepest anxiety for the success of the great object which they all pursued, he would still take the liberty of suggesting to them, to pursue that object with the greatest caution, for they were sure to encounter the most formidable enemies in their honourable, he might say glorious attempt of establishing the ten hours' system. He entirely concurred with the honourable and learned member for Dublin, that they should not abate a single moment of the proposed exemption ; to one second beyond the ten hours' labour he would not agree. He was aware it might be said, that the evidence in the book which then lay on their table (the Sadler report,) was ' got up,' was ' partial,' and therefore in no respect deserving of the credence which the society were disposed to bestow upon it. But could they remain insensible to the evidence given by the medical gentlemen, whose impartiality could not for a moment be questioned—he meant the medical men,—and they were nanimous in the opinion that more than ten hours' labour the human constitution could not endure ? When he represented the whole county of York, he had often presented petitions for the abolition of both negro and infant slavery, and a pleasing duty it was. He need scarcely say, that if any more petitions were sent to him upon the subject, they should have his most strenuous support. He would only further say, as had been expressed by Mr O'Connell, that to no other bill would he give his support, unless the time was shortened in place of being extended. To no bill with a moment more than ten hours would he ever agree."

Mr Sadler's speech was remarkably comprehensive, indicating a grasp of mind and a warmth of heart never more thoroughly united than in the public life of this benevolent statesman. Mr Sadler assured that assembly "That he felt no regret whatever in having been excluded from the House of Commons, but what resulted from a wish to have brought to a successful issue that and other measures, which he thought were also alluded to in the terms of the very flattering resolution which the meeting had kindly adopted; and, indeed, that regret respecting the factory bill entirely gave way, when he reflected that his noble friend, who was coupled with him in the vote of thanks, succeeded to his labours, escaping all the odium which he should have had to encounter for his advocacy of that and similar measures, as well as for other reasons, and bringing as his noble friend did, to the sacred task, the advantages of exalted rank and great attainments, and above all, a firm and religious determination never to abandon that cause which he had undertaken,—undertaken he could assure that meeting, with a reluctance which nothing but a high sense of duty, and an irresistible impulse of benevolence could have subdued. For himself he (Mr Sadler) felt it to have been enough for him, in the construction of this temple of mercy, to have laboured at the foundation ; he trusted and confidently hoped, that it was reserved for another and happier hand, erelong to lay the top stone, amidst the joyful congratulations of the entire country, in which none would join more enthusiastically than himself. In the meantime, however, he begged to observe, that his noble friend would, in the arduous task in which he had engaged need all their support. . . . . . . The apologists of the system, the pamphlets of one of whom he held in his hand, had said that ' the necessity for the long and destructive hours of labour imposed upon the poor children of this country, had to be traced to the imperfect political institutions, the heavy taxes, the immense debt of this country.' Vain excuses, indeed, while it was seen at the same time that the employed were thus maltreated, outraged, and over-laboured, for very inadequate wages, the employers, often from the lower ranks of the community, became suddenly and immensely rich. But to pass by these, it was well known that the factory system, as far as it had been established in America, was accompanied by precisely the same atrocity : indeed, he could assure the meeting, that he had had many American newspapers sent to him since he had agitated the question, in which it was stated, that a similar provision to that which he had endeavoured to obtain, was fully as necessary in America as in England. To what, then, could those long imprison-

ing and destructive hours of labour be attributed? Not
to high taxation, that was moderate—not to an immense
debt, there was none. To nothing but to the tyranny
and domination of the capitalists, spurred on by the lust
of gain, who had ever pursued that course, and would
still do so, till the strong arm of the law arrested their
guilty career in both countries, and which the journalist
in question asserted, was as necessary in the *new* world
as in the *old*. Away, then, with these apologies for the
tyranny of exorbitant wealth (as bad as that of unlimited
power), and let the law protect and preserve those helpless
beings who will never otherwise be defended, whatever be
the wealth of the institutions of the country tolerating them.
He might proceed to notice the other excuses put forth
by the willing panders of wealth and power, such as the
want of education and of character in the lower classes,
as originating this state of things. Education! He would
be glad to know how these poor little beings were to obtain
education? After a day's toil like that at present tolerated,
the idea of adding mental labour to the bodily labour
already endured, and additional confinement to what had
been already so oppressive, was to inflict additional physical
evils without the chance of adequately compensating them
by any moral advantage to be so derived. Much was said
about 'the schoolmaster being abroad'—he would ask, how
and when he was to find 'at home' these his oppressed
pupils? The talk of providing for the education of the
children of the poor in our populous districts, without
commencing with abridging their hours of labour, was mere
cant and hypocrisy."

The spirit which animated Lord Ashley, on entering
upon the footprints of Sadler, has been distinctly stated
in his Lordship's own words. His speech at the London
Tavern contains a full declaration of his state of mind,
and an unreserved acknowledgment of the services of his

parliamentary predecessor. Lord Ashley said " he could never be indifferent to the approbation of his fellow-country-men ; if he were so, he would distrust himself, feeling, as he did, that a disregard of honest fame is almost invariably accompanied by a disregard of virtue; but he did most solemnly assure the meeting that he did not take up this affair from motives of ambition. Strong and deep sentiments impelled him to that course; there were some there who could testify it; for when he found (and he had but few hours to make up his mind) that upon him depended the furtherance or the loss of Mr Sadler's bill, he did not (he used the word deliberately) dare to refuse. The confidence they reposed in him was a generous anticipation, but as to the thanks they had given him, he did not deserve them. It was by the voice of Mr Sadler that the people of England had been aroused from their apathy, and he in return had been assailed with obloquy, insult, and reproach, after collecting an amount of evidence which for its importance and accuracy, had rarely been equalled and never surpassed ; and yet that was the man who, to the great loss of the country, had been rejected from that house which he had adorned, and excluded from the representation of that people whom he had so materially served. It was, therefore, with the utmost regret, that he found himself called upon to take up the bill which had been introduced originally by their excellent friend, Mr Sadler ; that virtuous and amiable man had borne all the burden and heat of the day, and now he (Lord Ashley) came in to reap the abundant harvest that Mr Sadler had sown ; but he should most unwillingly find himself in the situation in which Louis the XIV always endeavoured to stand. That contemptible monarch desired great military reputation without having any military talents. When the siege of a town was going forward, he waited till the town was on the point of surrendering ;

he immediately took care to come to the spot, receive
the keys, and carry off, on his unworthy brow, all the laurels
which courage and ability had won. However, upon reflection,
he did not much fear but that the people of England would
do ample justice to such a man as Mr Sadler. They would
feel that by whomsoever the work might be nominally conducted to its conclusion, its real completion would have been
owing to him, and to him alone. Remote posterity would
bless his labours, and the enduring gratitude of millions would
inseparably associate his name with that great measure. He
most sincerely wished that some one of capacious mind and
profound knowledge, had undertaken this task ; so deep and
so various were the objects to be considered. It was a
great political, moral, and religious question ; it was political
because we should herein decide whether thousands should be
left in perpetual discontent, aye, and just discontent; it was
moral, because we must decide whether the rising generation
should learn to distinguish between good and evil—be
raised above the enjoyment of brutal sensualities, and be
no longer, as now they are, degraded from the dignity of
thinking beings. It was a great religious question ; for it
involved the means to thousands and tens of thousands of
beings brought up in the faith and fear of the God that
created them. He remembered in the days of his boyhood,
to have read of those who sacrificed their children to Moloch,
but they were a merciful people compared with Englishmen
in the nineteenth century. He had heard of the infanticide
of the Indians, but they too were a merciful people compared
with Englishmen in the nineteenth century. For these
nations destroyed at once their wretched offspring, and
prevented a long career of sorrowing and crime ; but we,
having sucked out every energy of body and of soul, toss
them upon the world a mass of skin and bone, incapable of
exertion, brutalised in their understandings, and disqualified
for immortality. He feared that in the House of Commons

they would have to encounter great and formidable opposition, but it was gratifying to think that all the masters were not against them, neither were they without numerous and cordial supporters in the house ; but it behoved those who were out of doors to use their best and most strenuous exertions to guard against the possible failure of the bill. There was but one consideration to which he particularly wished to call their attention, namely, that before the publication of the evidence, the people of England had nothing like the responsibility which since rested upon their heads. So long as these horrid truths remained unknown, the guilt attached to the perpetrators only ; but if we now permit this terrible system to be any longer continued, the guilt will descend upon the whole nation. Before he sat down he begged to assure them that he should not give way a single moment on the question of the ten hours. He assured the meeting that he should persevere in the cause he had commenced. He had taken up the measure as a matter of conscience, and as such he was determined to carry it through. If the house would not adopt the bill, they must drive him from it, as he would not concede a single step. He most positively declared, that as long as he had a seat in that house, and God gave him health and a sound mind, no efforts, no exertion, should be wanted on his part to establish the success of the measure. If defeated in the present session, he would bring it forward in the next, and so on in every succeeding session till his success was complete."

The proceedings of this meeting received all the publicity usually accorded to important public gatherings, to consider questions of great and vital importance. Oastler, Sadler, and O'Connell were names of great weight ; the interest inseparable from their speeches was increased by the nature of the subject discussed. No orator ever possessed a more thorough mastery over a people than did Mr O'Connell over the Irish. In politics he was the idol of their adoration and the director of their actions. He was said to be a descendant from the kings of Ireland; he was absolute monarch of the Irish population of the Roman Catholic Church. Every city, town, and village in the manufacturing districts of England and Scotland has its " little Ireland," as a district in Manchester is aptly named. Every " little Ireland " had its spiritual ruler, who acted in obedience to his superiors in the Church. The adoption of the factory question by Mr O'Connell was an event of great moment. He brought to the cause which he espoused not only personal talent and energy of the highest order, but talent and energy backed by the organized authority of the Roman Catholic Church. The late Mr O'Connell was essentially an apostle of the Papacy ; and within these islands, on all secular questions, the leader of the Roman Catholic clergy: his voluntary union with Oastler and Sadler in their crusade against the unregulated factory system, was, consequently, in the eyes of all concerned, an act of importance. The London Tavern meeting showed to the country and to parliament, that Mr Sadler's absence from the House of Commons was not the means of destroying interest in the factory question. In all great questions, men are the representatives of interests rather than their originators. A great cause may suffer, but cannot possibly be lost, because of the position of its advocates. This truth was illustrated in the factory agitation ; it had found root in the heart of the British nation, and was destined to increase in interest and power, in defiance of all losses and the most persevering opposition. Mr Sadler's zeal and resolution on behalf of the factory operatives were unabated: with him it could not be otherwise ; his policy rested upon what he devoutly believed to be the Rock of Truth, and for that reason knew no change. He cast the shadow of his approval over the adoption of the factory question by Lord Ashley, and side by side with Oastler and Bull, Michael Thomas Sadler felt as resolute of purpose as when he first resolved to present to an unwilling Legislature a full-length portrait of the miseries endured by the helpless victims of an insatiable thirst for gold.

The citizens of London, in the daily intercourse of their lives, were remote from the ocular observation of the effects of unregulated factory labour on health. To awaken a portion of them to a sense of their duty on a question of national interest, was not an easy task. The London Committee and their active friends were assiduous in their efforts, and conspicuously so was Mr Underwood, a London tradesman, for many years an active member of the Marylebone vestry, and in a parochial capacity distinguished for his advocacy of the interests of the poor. Mr Underwood was an energetic promoter of factory regulation, and enjoyed the confidence and friendship of Mr Sadler and Mr Oastler. As a tradesman, his character for probity was deservedly high; his well-known philanthropy won for him the regard of many who were his opponents on social and political questions ; the influence of his example and the value of his support were consequently enhanced. It is upwards of twenty-three years since his soul yearned to serve the cause of the workers in factories; it is now his privilege in an honourable old age to reflect on the results of his labours combined with those of others. Such reflection cannot be otherwise than pleasing, for his efforts were at all times well-intended and perseveringly pursued, and were eminently effective, in common with those of the Committee of the London Society for the improvement of the condition of factory children, in making known in London and its neighbourhood the grievous evils of the unregulated factory system.

Those proceedings in London caused much excitement throughout the country, and contributed to renew the hope and increase the vigour of all the leading supporters of the factory movement. Many meetings were held in Yorkshire and Lancashire; one of the most important was in the Manor Court House, Manchester, in April, 1833; it was addressed by Mr Oastler, Mr John Wood, and the Rev. G. S. Bull. The last-named gentleman's address was specially illustrative of what he, as a Christian minister, believed to be the duty of the ministers of the gospel of Christ in their recognized capacity as the instructors and guides of a Christian people. The reverend gentleman said :—

" I am intrusted by the Manchester Short Time Committee with a resolution.

" Approving, as I do, of the assertion made in the last sentence of this resolution, referring to the demoralizing effects of the factory system, I stand here for the first time in this metropolis of the factory world, to demand, not for the first, nor for the hundredth time, nor yet I trust for the last time, that infant slavery shall be abolished.

" It were easy, sir, for me to show that legislators and factory proprietors are ' verily guilty concerning this thing,' and that the system has indurated or petrified in many cases the parental heart itself, so that even ' the mother ' has sometimes ' forgotten ' to love and pity her own — her all but ' sucking child.' But, leaving the senator, the capitalist, and the monster, for others to deal with, I shall direct my respectful and earnest appeal to those who, like myself, profess to be the ministers of that Divine Redeemer who went about doing good, and to whom the speaking countenance of infancy and the imploring eye of misery were never lifted in vain. My object, sir, in selecting for observation the conduct of the Manchester ministers respecting the Ten Hours' Bill is not to exalt myself in the comparison: Sincerely do I assure you that I am, or have been, most deservedly in the same condemnation.

" And if, since I awoke from my lethargy, my pillow has been robbed of rest and my days of comfort, even then I have expiated (as far as my fellow man is concerned) but a small part of the guilt and of past neglect. But, sir, I want to learn how it is, that in this dense population, among whom, perhaps, nearly seventy stated ministers of various denominations reside, only two should have appeared as public advocates of this most humane and righteous cause.

"It cannot be because, like Moses, they are 'slow of speech,' for I myself have heard, seen, or read the fervid eloquence of your Stowells, your Newtons, and your McAlls, at Bible, missionary, tract, and anti-slavery meetings, to all of which I wish most heartily, God speed.

"It cannot be from want of example. The clergy of the Church of England might be edified by the noble and virtuous example of the venerable Archbishops of Canterbury and York, who are, and have been from the first, hearty friends of this cause, and the former of whom lately told me that I was quite in my duty as a clergyman to stand in the gap for the poor factory children. The Wesleyans have the edifying pattern of William Dawson, that plain honest Christian; and surely the Dissenters might safely copy Hamilton, of Leeds, and John Wilks, of London, who are both our friends.

"It cannot be from ignorance of the destructive and baneful effects of the present system of factory labour. They learn that daily and nightly. The Sunday school declares it,—the sick and dying bed reveals it,—the churchyard witnesses it,—each funeral knell proclaims it, and multiplied insults to morality, sobriety, and to the Almighty God himself, confirm it in every street of your city.

"It cannot be from ignorance of Scripture example. They know that Abraham, the father of the faithful, was thus commended of his God, 'I know him that he will command his children, and his household after him, and they shall keep the way of the Lord, to do judgment and justice.' And the ministers of Manchester know that avarice denies to poverty and industry the time necessary for domestic intercourse and family religion ; so that your Godless system of getting riches, or trying to get them, by long hours of machinery labour, stamps the master as the opposite to Abraham by guilt, whilst the operative's family is rendered so by dire necessity. The ministers of Manchester know that when Jacob, on his return to the land of his fathers, was urged by his appeased brother Esau to hasten his company forward, he said, ' Let my lord pass on before, I will lead on softly, according as the children shall be able to endure,' but they know that the possessors of wealth, too often unlike the patriarch, disregard what ' the children can endure,' and only calculate what the spindle can produce. [A voice from the crowd, ' Thou'll never be a bishop.'] Your boasted mechanical prosperity has taken you into deep waters, until Mr Gisborne, the apologist of the masters, tells you, in his place in parliament, that a Christian nation— a land of unparalleled plenty, of unexampled industry, of unrivalled splendour,—' whose merchants are princes ' and dwell in palaces, ' ceiled with cedar and painted with vermillion,'—that this land, the queen of nations and the perfection of beauty, has now, in the nineteenth century of the Christian era, to legislate ' between too much work and too little to eat,' whilst he, forsooth, is selling black diamonds [Mr G. had large collieries at or near Duckenfield]—with very small profits, no doubt, to the lords of the steam engine and the spindle and the loom.

" The ministers of Manchester know that when the political economists of Egypt consulted to deal wisely and à la Malthus with the ' superabundant ' and ' redundant ' Israelites, by throwing the babes into the Nile, and working the adults to death, Jehovah himself demanded satisfaction for their wrongs, and taught Egypt's scornful despot at length to set the captive free. Moses and Aaron, their great examples, braved all the frowns of Egypt's tyrants, and delivered their message without regard to earthly station or sordid respectability. When that great legislator, appointed by his God, had led that remarkable and favoured people to the wilderness, he gave them statutes and judgments, and a very considerable and most important part of them had direct reference to the care of the poor and the defence of the helpless. One of these remarkable precepts was this:—'Thou shalt not oppress the hireling in his wages, but thou shalt fear thy God.' David, too, had crowded his inspired verse with many a precept for the care of the poor, and many a promise to those who love them, like unto this—'Blessed is the man that considereth the poor. The Lord shall deliver him in the time of trouble—the Lord shall preserve him and keep him alive, and he shall be blessed in the earth.' Had not Solomon, too, given us all a warning in his Proverbs, xxiv, 11, 12 : ' If thou forbear to deliver them that are drawn unto death, and those that are ready to be slain—If thou sayest, ' behold we knew it not,' Doth not he that pondereth the heart consider it, and he that keepeth thy soul doth not he know it, and shall not he render to every man according to his works ?' and may we especially who are ministers, hear it and attend. What did Isaiah say to the oppressors of Israel ? ' Wash you and make you clean—put away the evil of your doings from before mine eyes, cease to do evil, learn to do well—seek judgment, relieve the oppressed, judge the fatherless, plead for the widow,' and on no less than these conditions would he make to that favoured nation the proposals of reconciliation. Were not all the prophets persecuted for their fidelity in rebuking the oppressor ? and did not the apostles of that Divine Saviour, whom the Manchester ministers profess to serve, cry aloud against the heartless avarice of the ' respectable ' of their generation ? What said the undaunted James ? ' Behold, the hire of the labourers which have reaped down your fields (had he lived now he would have said, 'worked so long in your factories for so little') —which is from you kept back by fraud—crieth—and the cries of the reapers (he might have said the poor factory children) have entered into the ears of the Lord God of Sabaoth.' But above all, the Lord of Glory Himself made it the chief part of his employment while dwelling among us in our flesh, to unmask the hypocritical Pharisee, whose garments were phylacteried with the oracles of God— who fasted and who prayed in the corners of the market, but whose hands were full of blood—doomed were they to the 'greater damnation.' And I now tell the ministers of Manchester, and I tell the religious people, that God abhors robbery for burnt offering, and that the rich would do better to give the hireling his due wages than to adorn the subscription list of fifty excellent institutions with large sums of money wrung from the sinews of tender infancy worn down with protracted and unwholesome toil. Why then do not the ministers of Manchester come forward to the help of the factory child ? Surely there is poverty enough to attract their notice in the midst of all this dazzling wealth. Your numerous institutions for the relief of the indigent, clearly prove the existence of a vicious system. Great and noble as is the purpose of your public charities, in a world where misery, the offspring of sin, must always be found, I hold that the best charity of all is to put the labourer in a condition to help himself, and to excite him to honest industry by a due reward. Let him have too, time to rest, to cultivate his mind, to instruct his family and to worship his God ; of all which blessings, thousands are utterly deprived by your present system. Do not the ministers of this town feel that your system in factories obstructs them in their holy office and invades their province? I met one of them but yesterday, who lamented this fact : I lamented too. I live amidst factories, and I say to the legislature :—

' Either declare my office useless and abolish it at once, or else give me at least the Ten Hours' Bill.'

" Let us trifle no longer. The love of their country should excite all professed ministers of the gospel to help us. They see a population, the alternate sport of exhaustion and excitement ; how can such a state of things issue, but in the very dissolution of society ? Their peace of conscience is surely involved in the part they take in the cause of degraded infancy and childhood. They are the servants of him, who though rich, yet for our sakes became poor—of him who rebuked those who would have kept the children from him, and who, had he sojourned in proud commercial Manchester, would have denounced her, though ' exalted to heaven,' as the seat of a system that will bring her ' down to hell,' unless she repents.

" Your ministers, sir, must stand too one day before a dread tribunal, where it will be as with the servant so with his master, as with the rich so with the poor. What then will become of worldly respectability ? Will it shield from an omniscient and impartial judge the man who sought his gains in the destruction of his fellow, or the minister who stood by and reproved them not ? There, sir, the thin disguise of worldly influence will be torn away, and there the wrongs of infancy shall be avenged. (The cheers here continued for several minutes.)

" I am not insensible, fellow-countrymen, to your approbation, but I would speak the truth if you were to hiss instead of cheer. I can reprove the sins of the poor, and I do it ; they too need it very greatly indeed. But I will deal fairly, and I never found the poor to hate me for being faithful, if I did not smooth over the sins of the rich." Mr Bull then referred to the present position of the Ten Hours' Bill, and stated that measures to defeat its subtle and cowardly foes, had been taken by a numerous meeting of the delegates of the operatives of England and

Scotland, then sitting in Manchester, and which he had been invited to attend. "And when (said Mr Bull) we can no longer sustain the struggle for the Ten Hours' Bill, we will turn it over to that sex (pointing to a group of females who were present) who will never be content with any place but the front rank in benevolence, and then who shall be able to resist? I for one, am settled never to flinch, never to cease, till our object is attained. And I hold this to be my duty to my country, to my office, and to my God. The firmer the foundation the better and the broader, the more sure will be the stability and prosperity of the superstructure, and that foundation, now so decayed, is to be found in the industrious and productive classes of society."

CHAPTER II.

APPOINTMENT OF A ROYAL COMMISSION OF INQUIRY—OBJECTS OF
THE COMMISSIONERS—OPPOSITION IN THE COUNTRY—PROCESSIONS
OF FACTORY CHILDREN IN MANCHESTER AND LEEDS—REPORT OF
THE COMMISSION—THE LATE MR GEORGE CONDY, OF MANCHESTER
—HIS SERVICES ON BEHALF OF THE FACTORY CHILDREN.

THE importance which the question of factory labour had
assumed in the eye of the country, and the untiring perseverance manifested by its leaders, could leave no doubt on
the mind of any reasonable observer of the "signs of the
times," that further legislation was imperative. Early in
the session of 1833, Mr Wilson Patten made known his
intention of moving,—"That an humble address be presented
to his Majesty, praying that he will be graciously pleased
to appoint a commission to collect information in the manufacturing districts with respect to the employment of children
in factories, and to devise the best means for the curtailment
of their labours." Mr Wilson Patten was strengthened in
his claims on the attention of the House of Commons by
Lord Morpeth, who assured the house that the agreement
between Mr Sadler and the opponents of his bill was, "That
Mr Sadler should first call his evidence and go through
his case, and then that the opponents of the bill should
call and go through theirs, and when the last session ended,
his opponents had not commenced." Lord Morpeth was

in favour of immediate legislation, and hoped by the bill which he intended to introduce "To reconcile all the leading parties, and bring this afflicting subject to a close." Mr Wilson Patten professed his anxiety not to delay legislation ; he wished the "subject to be better understood," and desired further inquiry, "also for the purpose of clearing the characters of the masters from those imputations which seemed to be cast upon them by the friends of Mr Sadler's measure, but which further evidence would prove to be utterly unjustifiable." Petitions were presented from Stockport and Lancaster, praying for a commission, for the purposes stated by Mr Wilson Patten.

On April the 3rd, 1833, he brought his motion for the appointment of a Commission before the House. An animated debate followed. Lord Ashley and his supporters opposed the motion of Mr Wilson Patten. In consequence of this discussion, Mr Wilson Patten added to his original proposition a clause to the effect, that the suggested inquiry should be so conducted "as to enable the house to legislate upon the subject during the present session." Mr Wilson Patten was supported by the government, and his motion carried by a majority of one. The Ayes were 74—the Noes 73.

Mr Spring Rice (now Lord Monteagle) on behalf of the government, "did not think that any persons would refuse to answer questions put to them by the Commissioners ; but if any person did refuse, there could be no doubt that the house would immediately pass a short bill to compel them to answer, and even upon oath, if required." The government pledged itself to lay the names of the Commissioners and their instructions on the table of the house—a promise which was not fulfilled. On the 3rd of June, Lord Ashley complained of "bad faith" on the part of the government. Lord Althorp answered Lord Ashley by saying that he had "forgot to lay the instructions before the house, but they were very full and consistent with what had been the understanding of the house. It was the wish of ministers that the examination should be a fair *bona-fide* examination."

The commission having been appointed, proceeded without delay with its labours. The following are the names of the Commissioners :—Francis Bisset Hawkins, Thomas Southwood Smith, Sir David Barry, Thomas Tooke, Leonard Horner, John Elliot Drinkwater, Robert Mackintosh, James Stewart, John Welsford Cowell, Edward Carleton Tuffnell, Alfred Power, Edwin Chadwick, Stephen Woolriche, John Spencer and Charles Lowdon. John Wilson, Esq., was Secretary to the commission.

The instructions issued by the Central Board of Factory Commissioners to District Civil and Medical Commissioners, were of the most minute and searching kind, embracing the most secret as well as the most common practices of life. The inquiry professed to be thoroughly impartial and comprehensive, so that any measures founded upon information acquired should be as "complete and satisfactory as possible." The Central Board of Factory Commissioners, in their anxiety to acquire complete knowledge, wrote down so many heads of inquiry, as to warrant the inference that they had not formed just notions of the time necessary for proper answers to be given; medical practitioners, particularly, complained of their inability to give the answers required in the time allotted. The first loud note of alarm and condemnation against the instructions of the central board to the district commissioners, appeared in the columns of the *Times*, for June the 3rd, 1833:— "We have looked," said the editor, "into the instructions issued by the central board to the subordinate commissioners, and we are bound to acknowledge that they have puzzled us as completely as they could have done those for whose especial embarrassment they were no doubt intended. Such a mass of impotent and stupid verbiage it has seldom been our fortune to face, or so

much pomp and pretension, combined with such vague-
ness and apparent insincerity of purpose. The whole
composition is on stilts; it is, besides, enveloped in in-
numerable folds of slip-slop phraseology, as if the entire
object of the author, or authors, had been to complicate
and mystify the simple question under examination, and
to defeat, by artificial difficulties, the ostensible end of
their own appointments.

"The instructions contain a diversity of plans for inquiring into questions but remotely connected with that
from which the establishment of the commission had
arisen, and, indeed, not entirely compatible with that
wholesome dread of ridicule, and anxious love of decency,
which ought to characterize the proceedings of such a
body. We subjoin as a curiosity, some of the queries
to be made of married women:—

"'Was your first child born within one year of your
marriage?'

"'How many children have you had still-born?'

"'How many miscarriages?—In the first three months;
in the next three months; in the last three months of
pregnancy?'

"'How many of the births were difficult cases; requiring instruments; not requiring instruments?'

"The central board ought to be ashamed of itself;
but boards are insensible to all such laudable emotions."

It is apparent that the instructions issued by the central
board, were drawn up upon the perusal of, and intended
to meet, the strong points of evidence given before the
Sadler committee. The use of instruments at childbirth,
was frequently named, by the medical witnesses whose
practice was confined to factory districts, and no doubt
suggested the rather indelicate queries copied by the
Times. The Factory Commission aimed at accomplishing
so much, that it knew the means directly at its command

were inadequate to the proposed ends ; it, consequently, looked for assistance from medical students, and the teachers of medical schools, in the larger cities and towns; also to the secretaries of benefit societies, and others familiar with the condition and practices of the factory population. The central board proceeded upon the assumption that every one would be able and anxious to facilitate the labours of the district commissioners, and that most well-informed persons would be prepared and willing to answer all the questions they were instructed to ask. An assumption without the shadow of a foundation, for those best able to answer the questions suggested were disgusted with the mere name of further inquiry, which they considered unnecessary and vexatious ; the operatives, too, had learned from experience, that to speak the whole truth was to them dangerous.

The appointment of this commission, and the objects of its inquiry, were, to the factory operatives and their friends, decidedly objectionable. They maintained that on all the points of inquiry full evidence had been given, that the object of the government in appointing the commission, was to prepare for the House of Commons only such evidence as would warrant a departure from Mr Sadler's Bill. They also maintained, that under any circumstances, a royal commission ought not to have been appointed—because that every enquiry ought to be open, and the evidence taken subject to cross-examination. A course of proceeding which the appointment of a select committee would have allowed, but that of a royal commission precluded. The weight of the medical evidence before the Sadler committee was so great, and so decisive, as to force either immediate legislation, or an excuse for the delay on the part of the government. Two classes of opponents were anxious for delay. Those who opposed factory legislation, from a sincere conviction of the truth of certain principles of political economy, felt that the force of facts was against their opinions (or, as they preferred calling them—"principles"); under the operation of "non-interference," so dear to the Benthamites, there existed, on the authority of the Sadler report, the greatest misery; they, consequently, sued for delay, in the hope that the result, in the shape of a report from a royal commission, would be more in accordance with "the greatest happiness" theory. True, there were, among the Benthamites, those who reasoned to the effect that the balance of riches was more than an equivalent for the misery endured, that the factory system was on the whole beneficial, and if allowed to work out its own destiny, would be to England an enduring blessing. Such reasoning, however, was not appreciated by the hearers at anything like the value claimed for it on the part of the professors; they, therefore, urged delay and inquiry. Those who opposed factory legislation from a conviction that their capital and profits would be thereby endangered, were clamorous for inquiry. They had forced on Mr Sadler the appointment of a select committee, under the pledge that they would disprove the statements contained in his speech; they now raised a cry, that the evidence given before the committee was one-sided, and, that the true state of those employed in factories could not be ascertained by the personal inquiry of commissioners. The operatives and their friends viewed the commission as an unnecessary and hostile proceeding, and resolved on opposition. The policy of the supporters of factory regulation will be best understood by some examples of their proceedings.

The following document represented the feelings of the factory operatives on the factory commission, it also illustrates the use they made of the evidence given before the Sadler committee:—

" The ADDRESS of the operatives of England and Scotland, to all ranks and classes of the land.

" Fellow Countrymen—We appeal to you on behalf of the Ten Hours Bill, now before the House of Commons, and under Lord Ashley's care. Whatever may be the manifold causes of national distress, and of that poverty, in most cases, or that profligacy in some, which induces parents to submit their offspring to such ruinous toil, and whatever remedies it may be considered proper to apply, still, in the name of justice, let the law of England protect children without further delay from lawless and heartless avarice. We, who now address you, are operatives ourselves ; we have heard and read discussion upon discussion on this humane and righteous measure, and after calm and deliberate reflection, we unanimously conclude that, it will be favourable to commerce in general, to the honest master, and the industrious man, and to the moral and political health of society. At this moment we are called upon by the unjust and mercenary influence of the mill-owners in Parliament, to submit the case of the factory child to the investigation of a commission. Eighteen hundred pages of evidence have been collected from masters and men, the medical and clerical profession, and especially from the poor hapless victims of this cruel, money-getting system. But this suffices not. By a table appended to the evidence before the select committee, it is demonstrated, that more have died before their twentieth year, where the factory system extensively prevails, than have died at their fortieth year elsewhere. But this suffices not. Insatiable as death, the rich oppressor still asserts his right, to add to his blood-guilty store, by working the British Infant beyond the time of the soldier, the farmer, nay the adult felon, and the more fortunate child of British colonial slavery.

" Fellow countrymen—This sort of oppression is not confined to our own generation, or our own country. It has been attributed to the corn laws : but when this system was yet in its infancy, and no corn law existed, the hours of labour exacted from children, were as bad or worse than now. It has been traced to taxation, which we feel to bear heavily and most unequally upon us. But in America, this, at all events, is not the cause of over-labour in factories, and there they work children in many cases longer than we do here. In fact, it is avarice which is the root of the evil—avarice which has not been content to supplant human labour by machinery, but now asserts, with bloody arrogance, its right to grind to the dust the helpless child, which it has obliged to take her father's place. Will you stand by and view this with cool indifference ? Will you not unite your energies with ours, to protect the weak against the strong, and the indigent against the rich oppressor ? See your country languishing—drooping its head under the chilly blasts of political economy—of grasping monopolies—of heartless calculation, which have blighted its fairest prospect. We know our agricultural brethren are sufferers from its horrid and pestilential breath as well as ourselves. The Ten Hours Bill is a sample in legislation favourable to us all. Sadler, than whom no man has been more beloved or hated, has stood like another Aaron between the dead and the living, with the fragrant incense of justice and benevolence in his hand, to stay the plague of political economy and all-engrossing covetousness. His senatorial mantle has fallen on a noble and illustrious successor, who fears God and regards man, but defies the scorn of the proud.

" Let Lord Ashley's name be dear to Britain's honest labourers and oppressed factory children. Let his factory bill have your support. Our request is that you will use every lawful and constitutional means to promote its legislative adoption this session. Give them no rest—pour out your petitions for us and our children at the foot of the throne, and into both Houses of Parliament. Protest, as we do, against the mill-owners' commission. We will not, except by legal obligation, try our cause before it. We challenge such a jury, appointed as it is by those who have been arraigned at the bar of their country to try their own cause, or rather to cover their guilt from public view. Our gracious sovereign has been imposed upon; we acknowledge and revere his Majesty's authority, but we condemn unmeasurably the act of his advisers. Is it thus that justice can be attained, when the cause of the poor is tried in open court, and that of the rich in the secret chambers of guilt? We leave our cause in your hands, and implore our fellow-countrymen of every rank, to petition without delay for the Ten Hours Bill, and that it may be passed without reference to a partial, unjust, unnecessary, and delusive parliamentary commission, sued out on false pretences, to the abuse of his Majesty's royal prerogative, and to the hurt and grief of his loving and loyal subjects.

" We address you as those who revere the constitution of our country. We honour the King—we respect the House of Commons; but we firmly believe that in the matter to which our present appeal refers, the influence of the interested and heartless mill-owners has misled the House of Commons, who were induced, by gross misrepresentation, to sanction the Commission by a majority of one !

" Surely so important a question, decided only by a majority of one, might have caused his Majesty's confidential advisers to pause.

" We believe his gracious Majesty has been imposed upon; and we have ventured to represent the same to our sovereign. We therefore protest—not against the exercise of his Majesty's royal prerogative, nor the authority of parliament—but we protest against the sordid influence by which both the one and the other have been so grossly imposed upon; and which influence seeks to rivet upon us and our children the chains of factory bondage.

" Signed on behalf of the operatives of England and
Scotland, in the manufacturing districts,
                    " GEO. HIGGINBOTTOM, Chairman.
" Manchester, April 25, 1833."

When the Commissioners arrived in Manchester, there
was handed to them, as had been arranged a fortnight before,
at a general meeting of factory delegates, the following
protest :—

" To the Commissioners appointed by the House to
inquire into the condition and sufferings of the Factory
Labourers.

" Gentlemen,—We, the undersigned, acting under the
direction, and on behalf of the great body of factory labourers, in the town of Manchester, beg leave to present this
our respectful remonstrance. First, however, we would
declare our unfeigned loyalty and attachment to the King
and constitution as by law established ; next, we would
express our no less sincere respect for yourselves, as well
as for the authority under which you appear amongst us.
Having premised thus much, we make bold to declare
our unconquerable aversion to, and suspicion of, the effects
of any inquiry so instituted; and our reasons are these
which follow :—The evidence obtained before the committee
on Mr Sadler's bill, was called for on the suggestion of
those factory masters, and their friends and dependants,
who have avowed their heedlessness of the waste of infant
life and strength, and the degradation in every way of the
factory population, when put in competition with the profits
of capital invested in steam mills. That evidence is now
admitted, by the intelligent part of the public, to be conclusive proof of the fact that the factory system, as at
present worked, does tend to deprave and degrade the
labourers employed in it; and, what is our most especial
cause of grief and despair, that it shuts out infancy from

any chance of human instruction, dwarfs their bodies, twists and bends their tender bones, and deforms their figures. The numerical statements of deaths, deformities, and disease, furnished to parliament, leave no room for doubt upon these heads. That evidence taken before a competent and ordinary court of inquiry, is violently and without reason put aside, to make way for a mode of inquiry chosen by those whose interests are openly opposed to the physical and moral well-being of the factory labourers; and those very parties, as we perceive by the series of questions issued to them, are, in their own counting-houses, without the responsibility of an oath, or the restraint which would be imposed by a face-to-face examination, and the chance of a cross-examination, to give such answers as they think fit, which answers, as we cannot but suppose, are to be placed in opposition to the unanswerable body of evidence alluded to above. On the other hand, what are the labourers to do ? Past experience has proved to them that there is no danger more directly threatening the very means of their existence than giving evidence of the facts as they exist. The minds of the masters must have undergone a complete revolution, if any such attempt on the part of the labourers will not only cause the loss of their places, but also the posting of their names in the entrance-hall of every mill far and near, for the purpose of insuring their exclusion from any such employment in any other place. For these reasons,—because the mode of inquiry is useless, its effects inevitably partial, its course unusual and unsatisfactory to the ends of justice ; and one side of the evidence cut off by intimidation, expressed or implied, and in any case not to be given with impunity. We respectfully take leave to protest against any proceedings which may be taken in the course of your inquiries being used as counterevidence to that taken before the committee on Mr Sadler's bill."

The operatives by this protest had debarred themselves from giving evidence ; it was resolved, notwithstanding, to give the commissioners an external view of the actual appearance of factory-workers. On Saturday, the 4th of May, 1833, the children engaged in the factories met on the field, called Peterloo,—unhappily memorable from the collision between the yeoman cavalry and the supporters of Mr Henry Hunt, in 1819. Here the children formed into a procession, having their usual banners. On these were the names of Sadler, Oastler, Bull, Fielden, and Ashley. Some banners had mottoes such as " A muzzle for the steam giant " —"Manufactures without child-slaying, &c." On reaching the York Hotel, in which the commissioners occupied apartments, a deputy from the children presented the following memorial :—

" To the Commissioners appointed by the King to inquire into the state of Factory Labour.

" Gentlemen,—We, children employed in the factories of Manchester, beg leave to present to you this our humble and respectful memorial. We implore your pity and compassion for our sufferings, for the great weight of labour thrown on our young limbs,—for the long duration of that labour daily, mostly in the close air of a heated room,—for the weakness it brings upon us while we are little, and the sickness and deformity which fall upon many of us,— for the overwhelming fatigue which benumbs our senses, and for the shutting out of any chance of learning to read and write like children of our age in other employments.

" We respect our masters, and are willing to work for our support, and that of our parents and brothers and sisters ; but we want time for more rest, a little play, and to learn to read and write. Young as we are, we find that we could do our work better if we were to work less time, and were not so weighed down by the long continuance of our daily toil.

" We do not think it right that we should know nothing but work and suffering, from Monday morning to Saturday night, to make others rich.

" Do, good gentlemen, inquire carefully into our condition. Let not a respect for wealth disguise from your view our severe wrongs, nor restrain you from declaring what measure of justice is due to us. Indeed, we tell you no lies, when, we say that our bodies are wasted, and our strength sinking, under our daily tasks ; and that we are without any time for amusement or learning. Surely the King does not intend that his youngest subjects should be worked the hardest, and suffer the most. We throw ourselves upon your mercy and justice. Look at us, and say if it is possible that we can be disbelieved ! Do your duty faithfully to us. Tell the King the actual state in which you find us. So shall you cause relief to come from our rulers ; and you will be repaid by good wishes from the grateful hearts of thousands of little children like ourselves."

At Bradford, the indignation of the operatives against the commissioners was intense. The evidence given before the Sadler committee was known to be correct, and further enquiry was considered to be an insult; the commissioners, however, had ample means afforded them to judge of the evil effects of unregulated factory labour. Hundreds of factory-made cripples were exhibited before them,—they had thus ocular corroboration of the truth of that evidence, the weight of which on the mind of parliament and the country they, it was popularly assumed, had been appointed to destroy.

The following account of the proceedings at Leeds, is copied from a pamphlet published at the time to which it refers ; it is a strictly correct narrative.—" Great Meeting in Leeds, on Thursday, the 16th of May, 1833, of the factory children. The commissioners appointed to report from this district arrived at Leeds on Monday, the 13th inst.

So soon as their arrival was announced, the Short-Time Committee assembled, and at seven o'clock, accompanied by about 1,000 operatives, proceeded to deliver the protest of the committee to the commissioners ; describing the object of their visit as an expensive plot to delay the passing of the great measure introduced into parliament by M. T. Sadler, Esq., and now advocated therein by Lord Ashley. On the Wednesday evening, however, their retreat was discovered, and considerable numbers assembled in front of the hotel. On Thursday the excitement was very great, as it was publicly announced that on the evening the factory children would assemble at seven o'clock in the Free Market, and proceed from thence to the hotel, to present their protest against the visit of the commissioners."

An eye-witness of the proceedings writes as follows :—

" During the whole of the day, boys were coming to the Union Inn, head-quarters of the Short-time Committee, from the different flax and woollen mills, for slips to bind round their hats, having printed thereon ' The Ten Hours Bill.' From the feeling which they manifested in favour of that measure, it appeared unnecessary for the committee to incur much expense, or make any extraordinary efforts to collect the children together. No band was engaged, and only two flags taken out, one of which was the famous one representing the scene in Water Lane (Marshall's Mills) at five o'clock in the morning, as it was thought prudent not to make much display, lest the children should be injured by the pressure of the crowd. At half-past seven the committee, &c., repaired to the Free Market, but soon after their arrival the meeting became so dense, that it was considered dangerous to keep the children long in that situation ; therefore Mr Cavie Richardson, whom the children had applied to, read their protest, to which they gave their assent by three cheers, and then proceeded to Scarborough's Hotel with an immense multitude, when six of the poor children, headed by Mr Richardson and other friends of the Ten Hours Bill, were introduced to the commissioners.

" Mr Richardson then advanced a few paces towards the commission, and delivered an address."

The commissioners listened to Mr Richardson with great attention, when that gentleman delivered into their hands the following protest of the children:—

" To the Commissioners appointed by the King to inquire into the state of Factory labour.

" Gentlemen,—We, children employed in the mills and factories of Leeds, feeling the intolerable burdens which are heaped upon us, and the manifold sufferings to which we are unfortunately subjected, cannot but express our anxiety to be delivered from those grievances which we are unhappily compelled to endure. We have rejoiced, and still rejoice, that our situation has attracted the attention of thousands and tens of thousands of kind-hearted individuals —of men who have hearts to feel for the defenceless victims of avarice. And we are glad to find that those who thus pity our hapless condition, are men who are determined to battle our enemies until victory is obtained, and our deliverance is complete. But these feelings of joy and gladness which have been created in our minds by the prospect of a speedy termination of our misery, have been greatly marred on learning that a commission of inquiry had been appointed to gratify our task-masters. The object of which commission we verily believe to be not to obtain correct information, but to clear our guilty tyrants from those charges which are founded on the most undeniable evidence, of the truth of which we ourselves can bear testimony. We are confident of its being unnecessary to give further evidence of the evils of the system under which we suffer; and, further, we know that should we declare the real nature of the treatment which we endure, and the dangers to which we are constantly exposed, our employers would not only dismiss us, but continue to display their base tyranny, by hunting us from place to place, and depriving us of every possibility of procuring an honest livelihood.

" But we are, moreover, given to understand that you have refused all inquiry in a fair and open manner, while, at the same time, you have been in secret with our masters, from which conduct we see that your object is not to do justice, or faithfully to search into the situation in which we are placed.

" Under such circumstances we protest against this commission, as being founded in injustice, inhumanity, and fraud, and as carrying with it consequences the most fatal to the interests and well-being, not only of us, but of society in general, except it be those who seek to continue slavery and its attendant evils, that they may riot in plenty and pride at the expense of the sweat, the blood, and the life of toil-worn childhood and insulted poverty.

" And, while we thus protest against the commission, we must say to you individually, ' Better would it have been had a millstone been tied about your necks and ye cast into the depths of the sea, rather than have been appointed to dishonour God, and wound the objects of his care, by offending one of the little ones.'

" At this stage of the proceedings never surely was so interesting an exhibition witnessed : not less than 3,000 ragged, wretched little ones, attended by at least 15,000 spectators. The commissioners had a full opportunity offered them of witnessing the disgusting effects of slavery in factories, and an unanswerable argument that employment, such as their dress and dirt exhibited they had been engaged in, ought not to be prolonged to longer hours than the felon is condemned or the black slave constrained to labour." The children retired, singing in unison their factory song :

" We will have the Ten Hours Bill,
That we will—that we will;
Or the land shall ne'er be still,
We will have the Ten Hours Bill."

After the presentation of the address an important conversation followed between Mr Oastler and Mr Drinkwater, one of the commissioners. "Mr Commissioner Drinkwater expressed his great regret that any objection should exist in furnishing the commission with every information sought for, and was replied to by Mr Oastler, that the country possessed every evidence it was possible to require, and that the proceedings originated out of the minds of the enemies of the bill. Mr Drinkwater rejoined that they bore the King's commission, and it was, therefore, incorrect to say it proceeded from the enemies of the bill. Mr Oastler then observed, we know all that very well—we know the ministers sent you, and we know that Lord Althorp is our enemy—that he has declared that to pass the bill will ruin the country, and that you have constant communication with, and all things are submitted to, the millowners, before they meet the public eye. Mr Drinkwater then assured Mr Oastler that their only object was to ascertain the truth. Mr Oastler observed, then your object has already been obtained, and any old washerwoman could tell you that ten hours a day was too long for any child to labour.

Mr Drinkwater then again pressed Mr Oastler to assist in getting information. Mr Oastler said, in his individual capacity he should give none, and asked if the commissioners were ready to indemnify such of the operatives and their families as would give evidence, as many of them had lost their employment in consequence of giving evidence before the committee of the House of Commons. Mr Drinkwater admitted that "this was a point of great importance to be got over." Mr Oastler added—" As the King's commissioners, unauthorised by the legislature, I do not recognise your authority, on the contrary, I protest against it, and I believe that the ministers are attempting to exercise a power which the constitution of England does not warrant; but if you will divest yourself of your assumed authority, and meet me in the capacity of private gentlemen, I will most willingly tell you all that I know, and put you into the way of obtaining the fullest possible information of all that is going on in the factories ; but as an Englishman, knowing my constitutional privileges, I cannot be a party to the violation, even in the most remote degree, of any principle of the British consti- tution." The commissioners declined to accept Mr Oastler's offer.

A protracted correspondence took place between Mr Sadler and the commissioners as to the mode of taking evidence. Mr Sadler desired that the examination of wit- nesses should be conducted openly, and their evidence reported fully, conditions to which the commissioners did not assent. This correspondence was conducted with eminent ability on both sides. The feelings which guided Mr Sadler in his conduct towards the factory commissioners may be apprehended by the perusal of the following passage of one of his letters, addressed to Messrs Drinkwater and Power, factory commissioners :—" I expressed, in my last address to you, my apprehension that an eleven hours bill might be attempted as the result of this inquiry ; if, however, the enemies of the measure are driven from that project, they are not without other expedients, in pressing which they will not fail to represent themselves as the best friends of those, the amelioration of whose condition they have con- stantly opposed. Another and a very favourite plan of certain opposing millowners, and one which was proposed to myself, will, perhaps, be next suggested, namely, to carry the protection required only to a certain age—say, twelve or fourteen years, which regulation it is calculated would well enough suit the purposes of certain employers, as in some pur- suits, the very little living machines it is found are hardly so profitable to work as the rather bigger ones. Hence the very same people who could not determine, in thirty years' time, that fifteen hours labour and confinement daily, in a cotton or flax mill, was at all injurious (rather the contrary), will all at once outbid the oldest and most zealous friends of the factory children, at the period of life which best suits the purpose, to the tender mercies of their unmitigated system, deprived of the nation's sympathies, and, consequently, without either relief or hope; the age in question being, nevertheless, that of their rapid physical development, when if the slightest reliance can be placed upon the unanimous opinion of the heads of the medical profession, the human constitution, and especially that of the female, demands the greatest care and attention, and when excessive labour and cruel treatment would be the most seriously injurious. Recommend, gentlemen, as strongly as you please, the remission of the hours of labour in early childhood, propose eight, six, or four hours if you see good, and let that portion of the press (thank God it is but a miserable part of that mighty engine, which has done so nobly in this righteous cause), which but a very short time ago could see no evil in working children eleven hours a day, now suddenly turn round and plead for six or eight only; thus, though varying the means, still steadily and consistently labouring to serve the same end, the cause of the *prominently interested!* But still *we* shall continue to demand that the young and rising generation beyond that age, shall not be required to labour longer than the adult artizan consents, or the felon and the slave is compelled to toil; in short, that no manufacturer shall be permitted to do what I rejoice to think what many of them would shudder to contemplate,—work the children of the poor of any age, or of either sex, to death. That constant and sufficient protection which selfishness itself affords to the labouring animals during the period of their growth, humanity will surely not deny to the unprotected youth of the country. The Ten Hours' Bill is, I repeat, at the very best, a twelve hours' bill, including necessary refreshment; and an act

that would consign the tender youth of the country to
thirteen or fourteen hours of labour and confinement would,
to all intents and purposes, be the opposing millowners', and
not the operatives' bill; and I think it would be hardly
proper to take lessons of humanity at least on this subject,
and on this occasion, from their school. Certain of your
instructions, I see, indicate the idea of a system of infant
' relays.' Relays ! The very term is disgusting ; the comparison between the management of human creatures and
that of cattle is, as Hume says, ' shocking ! ' But even in
any such comparison, the physical condition of the infantile
labourer, under the ' relay' system, would sink infinitely
below that of the brute. Besides, were such a plan even
proper or practicable in itself, it would open a door to those
perpetual and cruel evasions of the law, whether on the
part of masters or of parents, against which no enactment
could effectually guard ; so that the ' last state' of the poor
factory child would be ' worse than the first.' Lastly, a bill
founded on any such principle would operate practically as
the heaviest curse upon the adults, who would then have
to work against two or more ' relays,' rendering their
condition absolutely intolerable." In the course of this
correspondence the commissioners expressed themselves in
not very respectful terms regarding Mr Oastler, a circumstance which he turned to good account, at the various
public meetings, which he attended on the factory question.
The task which the factory commissioners had undertaken
was the most difficult possible. The government were
determined that the commission should report, the Ten
Hours' bill committee had declared war against the commission, they were therefore opposed with a most obstinate
and determinate spirit, they were watched morn, noon, and
night, and every available obstacle raised against them.
There is a latent feeling in the minds of Englishmen against
royal commissions and commissioners, there is a pre-dis-

position to treat them as the agencies of despotism. This state of mind was strengthened because of the same persons, in some cases, having been appointed factory commissioners who had, previously, been employed on the Poor-law commission. The grounds of opposition against the factory commissioners were twofold—first, a general feeling against royal commissions, a feeling which was traditional and considered patriotic and constitutional; second, a decided conviction that the factory commissioners had favourable opinions of the millowners, and were appointed to report in their favour. This second ground of objection was increased in force by the commissioners having partaken frequently of the hospitality of mill-owners opposed to factory legislation. A circumstance which, in the then excited state of the factory districts, gave potency to the current belief among the operatives, that the commissioners were unfriendly towards them, and favourable towards their employers.

The report of the commission of inquiry was laid on the table of the House of Commons on the 28th of June, 1833. It corroborated the evidence given before the Sadler committee in all its principal features; it was impossible that any credible report could do otherwise, so decided and universal was the evidence against the unregulated factory system. The commissioners declared:—

" From the whole of the evidence laid before us, of which we have thus endeavoured to exhibit the material points, we find:—

" 1st. That the children employed in all the principal branches of manufacture throughout the kingdom, work during the same number of hours as the adults.

" 2nd. That the effects of labour during such hours are, in a great number of cases, permanent deterioration of the physical constitution ; the production of disease wholly irremediable ; and the partial or entire exclusion (by reason of excessive fatigue) from the means of obtaining adequate education and acquiring useful habits, or of profiting by those means when afforded.

" 3rd. That at the age when children suffer these injuries from the labour they undergo, they are not free agents, but are let out to hire, the wages they earn being received and appropriated by their parents and guardians.

" We are therefore of opinion that a case is made out for the interference of the legislature in behalf of the children employed in factories."

Among the most resolute, and because of his superior intellect and knowledge, one of the most powerful opponents of the factory commission was the late George Condy, Esq., of Manchester. Mr Condy was in all senses a remarkable man; we conceive it to be consistent with our duty to take note of the more prominent points of his life and character. By his own industry and talent, in the capacity of a reporter for the *Times*, George Condy had been enabled to obtain the requisite knowledge for and to be called to the bar (in this respect resembling the late amiable and much-regretted Mr Justice Talfourd). The influence of his connection with the London press on his own mind was very marked and distinct; it taught him to take enlarged views of public measures. Few barristers apprehended more thoroughly the principles of the English law ; his knowledge was not that of a skilful attorney initiated into the secrets of sharp practice; his rule was to consider the spirit of the laws, and to frame his judgment in accordance therewith. This habit often led him to adopt and express opinions which to others appeared novel and startling, but which, on examination, were frequently discovered to be old and constitutional ; his literary productions were numerous and spread over a wide surface, in the columns of newspapers, magazines, and pamphlets. He was for some time editor and joint proprietor of the *Manchester Advertiser*. His writings are remarkable for terseness, vigour, boldness, and a dry sarcastic humour, which justifies the belief that his copy of Dean Swift's works was frequently read. The following brief extracts from letters addressed to Mr Oastler by Mr Condy, contain a glimpse of his creed on questions of social and political interest, and show the inner impulses which moved him to action :—

" My dear Oastler,—Your letter had the effect of a thunderbolt upon my ruminations. To such conclusions do we all come by attending to the wants and miseries of the multitude: yet, what is to be done by any man who knows the evil, loves the right, and has too good a conscience to keep silence? It is certainly more fortunate in regard to personal interests not to possess any such discernment. But I must believe that the impulses of a generous and feeling mind are imparted by a great moral power which puts upon us the sacrifice whether we will or not. It is an everlasting necessity to do the bidding of the Father of the universe. I am certain, from my own love of ease and books, that I have been roused and stimulated by no other force to take upon myself the trouble and obloquy, the loss of friends and professional profits—both necessary to my narrow means of existence, which have been my fate for the last five years. All this, if I did not foresee, I distinctly apprehended, or past experience would have been lost upon me . . . . . . Now for more general subjects, on which I feel it pleasant to unfold my mind to you. I agree with you in all your views, except the political union of the church with the state. Upon that point I am heterodox—or, rather, I am for pure orthodoxy. I hold the older doctrine that the Church should govern herself, as she is supposed to do by the very principle of her constitution, and as she did from the time of the apostles until the first act of English supremacy. But I will not dispute with you upon this point, when we agree upon some that are among the most essential.

" The winds of political controversy and change at present blow bleakly upon your clients, the labourers. The nation is infected with a monstrous, a portentous greediness of gain, which it seeks at the cost of the hunger and sufferings of the industrious classes. This leads to the wasting of the nation's resources, in seeking to check misery and crime, and all kinds of mad expedients are on trial to qualify industry to live without bread. Can anything in Old Testament history and prophecy equal the blindness of statesmen who uphold and propagate a system which costs more in military, police, criminal justice, punishment, and pauper management than the wages divided among all the manufacturing labourers. 'Take note, my son, how little wisdom serves to govern mankind.' The dying chancellor who spoke this left half the subject veiled. Take note, he should have added, what havoc wealth and power make of the bodies and necessary provision of the poor, and how cunningly they contrive to miss the secret even in hunting their darling riches. Queen Elizabeth reckoned her state rich in proportion to the abundance enjoyed by her people. Her whole reign, and especially her astonishing independence in money affairs, gave that maxim a glorious illustration. Could any man who lived to the close of it have believed that we should live to see a state of society seeking to found itself in permanent security by reducing the labour of the country to the lowest possible pittance ? And yet it is a horrible truth, which is enough to inspire another anti-Babylon prophet, that all the upper ranks in this country are infected with that belief, and that the laws are rapidly forming themselves into an entire conformity with it. Witness the detestable Poor Laws Act, which, against all sense of honour, manhood, justice, or common honesty, puts a premium upon the pursuit of male lust, at the cost and suffering of the other sex. What is there in the older superstitions more filthy than a statute which takes off the bridle upon masculine lust and fits it with a new coil upon the female and her relations ? I am tempted to believe in the transmigration of souls, and that the villain who contrived this is he between whom and the woman there is put inseparable enmity, by effect of . the primary curse." The writer of these plainly-expressed opinions rendered important services to the factory movement, and never more conspicuously than in publishing two pamphlets in 1833. The first intended to prove the constitutional illegality of the proceedings of the factory commission ; the second " An Argument for placing Factory Children within the pale of the Law." As a piece of controversial writing, the last has been seldom equalled ; it may now be read with profit and advantage. The publication of this pamphlet increased its author's reputation among the highest legal authorities; it was then, and long after, a text-book among the advocates of the short-time question. As a public speaker, Mr Condy's success was more a triumph of wit, sarcasm, humour, and ridicule, than of facts and argument. Those who were favoured with Mr Condy's society "in the social hour," will not, in fitting moments, fail to recall past scenes with delight. He was gifted with rare powers of conversation, " a fellow of infinite jest, of most excellent fancy ;" his satire could pierce without seeming to be intended to wound : in the overflowing of his wit, without effort, it was his habit to " set the table in a roar." These wonderful exhibitions of wit, fancy, and intellectual power were never enjoyed more thoroughly than within the hospitable home of Mr Oastler, at Fixby Hall. As the struggle of years began to ripen into prosperity, this gifted man died in the very meridian of life, having enjoyed for a brief period the income of a Commissioner of Bankruptcy in the borough of Manchester. The factory children have had few supporters of their cause more richly endowed, or more disinterested and sincere, than was the late George Condy.

CHAPTER III.

PARLIAMENTARY EFFORTS TO OBTAIN A TEN HOURS' ACT IN 1833.—
DIFFERENCE OF OPINION AS TO PENAL LEGISLATION.—GREAT
MEETING AT WIBSEY LOW MOOR, IN FAVOUR OF THE PERSONAL
PUNISHMENT OF HARDENED OFFENDERS AGAINST THE LAW.—
PASSING OF THE GOVERNMENT FACTORIES' ACT, FOUNDED ON THE
REPORT OF THE ROYAL COMMISSION.

ONE of the prominent mistakes of modern statesmen has
been to devote their attention to things rather than to human
beings,—hence the popular belief that cheapness must be
nationally advantageous. The interest of the consumer
seems at first sight to be inseparable from cheapness,
but the closest investigation will show that cheapness, the
result of long hours of labour and low wages, is invariably injurious to the labouring portions of a community;
the happiness and comfort of these is a subject of infinitely greater moment than the merely aggregated mass
of material products offered for sale at low prices in home
and foreign markets. The supporters of factory regulation had the honourable merit of beginning with the
consideration of human beings; there was, therefore, between
them and their opponents an impassable gulf. True, the
avowed end of both was the same, namely, the improvement of *all*, but the means leading to the end were
opposed: the free school of economists said—"All inter-
erence is wrong, get cheapness, and whatever else is

needful will follow in its train." The supporters of factory regulation said—" Check excessive and unnatural labour, care for health and morals, and whatever else is needful will follow in their train." In the discussion of the question between the opposing parties, which naturally took a wide range, a good deal of personal feeling was manifested. The weight of facts had been so decidedly in favour of the supporters of factory regulation, that the government was obliged to take sides. On June the 17th, 1833, Mr Sadler's bill, as amended by Lord Ashley, was read a second time in the House of Commons. The amended bill limited the hours of labour for women and young persons to ten per day, and contained a clause intended to secure personal punishment for the third offence in violation of the projected law, which, with a clause requiring a surgeon's certificate as to the age of children, were very offensive to the millowners, but very popular with the operatives. It was foreseen that this clause would be met by an organised and determined opposition by the millowners, and their friends, opposed to factory legislation ; in order to strengthen the hands of Lord Ashley, public meetings were held in the principal manufacturing towns of Yorkshire and Lancashire, and also an aggregate meeting in the West Riding, at which meeting " the personal punishment clause" formed the principal subject of discussion, and was universally adopted. Those among the millowners opposed to all regulation, when they found some measure of regulation inevitable, naturally desired that it should be as limited and loose as their opposition, in and out of parliament, could make it. The operatives, on the other hand, were desirous that the law should be binding and restrictive. They watched every step in the proceedings of parliament with intense interest, and were resolutely resolved on having the Ten Hours' Bill, with the personal punishment clause included. Experience has convinced most observers that it is easier to plant an idea in the mind than to eradicate it. The political atmosphere of the House of Commons, and of the factory districts of the north, were very different ; in the first, questions were looked at by many very much with the feeling with which a servant regards an unpleasant but indispensable duty; by the last, enthusiasm and resolution forced the mind onward, obstacles were either unseen or disregarded. The recently awakened intelligence of the operative classes was rigorous and energetic, it longed for a practical realization of its own power.

Lord Ashley, Mr Sadler and Mr Wood, in their anxiety to conciliate opposition, and in the expectation of gaining a few doubtful votes, had resolved to abandon the certificate and personal punishment clauses, in the hope of securing the acknowledgment by the House of Commons of the Ten Hours' limitation clause. Beyond all doubt, the thought of personal punishment was very odious and repulsive to the minds of the mill-owners, the very naming of "the House of Correction" was felt by them to be a degradation, it was very decided evidence on the part of the operatives and their supporters, of distrust in the honour of their opponents. The operatives knew from experience that fines to almost any amount could be levied in the factories, and they contemplated the probability of offenders against the law indemnifying themselves out of the earnings of those they employed in overtime; they also knew that money and the means of association were at the command of the factory owners; the operatives conceived the possibility of a wealthy millowner opposed to factory legislation, and not troubled with conscientious scruples about the sacredness of law, indulging in the cheap amusement of breaking the law, when convenient, and paying from the profits of his crime, the pecuniary fines imposed. Lord Ashley had by his written authority approved of personal punishment. His lordship, Mr Sadler, and Mr Wood, were not on principle opposed to Mr Oastler and Mr Bull, the question was one of time and degree; certainly Mr Oastler and Mr Bull were in no humour for concessions, and they had at their command the hearts and hands of the operatives of the north. Of all social and political movements on record, none has equalled in unanimity and energy the factory movement when in the strength of its vigour. Mr Oastler, its founder and apostle, had been, in the House of Commons, by Mr Gisborne, somewhat sneeringly, likened to "Peter the Hermit," certainly Peter never preached up the crusades more effectually than did Mr Oastler the claims of his juvenile clients. Not any words at our command can convey an adequate sense of the state of popular feeling at the time referred to. It is just possible that the principal actors in the stirring scenes of these times were they now to read their own speeches, as then reported, would do so with astonishment. Mr Oastler issued a placard which was marked by the impress of what was then called "the royal style,"—a bold and striking address intended to arouse the working men of Yorkshire to a sense of their duty. The sensation caused thereby was immense, and it contributed in a marked manner to give importance to the occasion. Mr Stocks, of Huddersfield, Mr Lawrence Pitkethly, and Mr John Leech, were exceedingly active—as they indeed always were in the interests of the factory movement. All the short-time committees were animated by a kindred spirit, and all worked harmoniously together for the same end, each seemed to feel that nothing was done while anything remained to be done. It was this spirit of self-sacrifice that animated and enabled numerous bodies of working men, as well as their representatives, which gave unity and power to the factory movement, a striking result of which was the Wibsey Low

Moor meeting. The importance of this remarkable gathering was undeniable. The ground on which the meeting was held stands high, and commands a splendid prospect from the Craven hills on the one hand, to the peak of Derbyshire on the other. Certainly one of the finest sites for such an assemblage in Yorkshire. So far as scientific knowledge could settle the question of the due limit of labour in factories, the medical evidence before the Sadler committee was decisive; the county meeting at York, and the West Riding meeting on Wibsey Low Moor, so far as popular feeling and stern resolution were concerned, were not less so. A summary of the proceedings of the latter will convey a knowledge of the facts of the factory movement as they then existed, and illustrate the nature of the out-of-doors agitation which forced attention from even the most indifferent of statesmen. Mr Oastler and his supporters based their approval of personal punishment for a third breach of the law, on the principle—" that wilful crime against the person should be punished in the person of the offender," a proposition, the justice of which, under the circumstances suggested, cannot easily be shaken. It is assuredly not to the credit of Roman jurisprudence, that Gibbon recorded : " Veratius ran through the streets striking on the face the inoffensive passengers, and his attendant purse-bearer immediately silenced their clamours by the legal tender of twenty-five pieces of copper." Honour is due to those who neutralized so gross an outrage on justice and equity. Punishment for crime is mainly defensible, as a precaution against future offences, and ought to be of that kind and degree most likely to produce the result desired.

The numbers present at the Wibsey Low Moor meeting, were estimated by the chairman at not fewer than 120,000 persons. They arrived on the ground in divisions from the different surrounding districts, headed by leaders, each division had banners and bands of music, all occupied their previously allotted places with perfect order. Among the inscriptions on banners were the following : " Sadler and the abolition of slavery at home and abroad." " No child-murder." " Proverbs, 6 c. 16 v.—These things doth the Lord hate, a proud look, a lying tongue, and hands that shed innocent blood." " Yorkshire expects every man to do his duty, to the poor factory child." " Muzzle the monster steam." " To your tents, O Israel, it is better to die by the sword than hunger." On some of the flags were painted emblematic devices. One of these represented the good Samaritan staunching the wounds of a poor man ; another exhibited an overlooker strapping a child into a factory at ten minutes past five in the morning; a third was the scene of a poor mother leading her children through the snow to a mill in the morning; another, a coat of arms; on a shield was painted a billy-roller, a time clock, a book of fines, a screw key, and a knotted strap, the whole supported by two factory cripples ; the crest portrayed an infant entwined by a serpent, which was represented as about to dart its poison into the mouth of its victim. These mottoes and emblems were the reflex of the feelings and thoughts of their bearers. The meeting was presided over by Captain Wood, of Sandal, and the speakers were Mr Oastler, Mr Bull, Mr William Stocks, chief constable of Huddersfield, Mr Busfield (Ferrand), Mr John Ayrey, of Leeds, Mr Bedford, of Keighley, Mr George Condy, of Manchester, Mr Lawrence Pitkethly, of Huddersfield, and Mr Richardson, of Leeds.

The proceedings throughout were of the most animated kind, and occupied five-and-a-half hours, Mr Oastler and Mr Doherty (the last named gentleman had been specially deputed by Lord Ashley, Mr Sadler, and Mr Wood to represent their views, and for that purpose had come down from London,) debated with much earnestness on the propriety of their adopting a resolution in support of the personal punishment of hardened offenders against factory law, Mr Oastler for, Mr Doherty against its adoption; Mr Doherty was opposed to Mr Oastler only on grounds of expediency. Mr Doherty contended, on behalf of those whom he represented, that the retention in Lord Ashley's bill of the personal punishment clause, would endanger the passing of the Ten Hours' Bill during that session; and that if this clause were withdrawn, and the Ten Hours' Bill should be passed without it, then in the next session of parliament it would be easy to add thereto the imprisonment clause. Mr Oastler asked if Mr Doherty could give to the meeting any valid guarantee that the withdrawal of the imprisonment clause would insure the passing of the ten hours' limitation clause? Mr Doherty was on that point unprepared. Mr Oastler contended that concession to opponents was at all times dangerous, and that the strength of the Ten Hours' Bill movement mainly depended upon a strict adhesion to principle. That the object of that meeting, and the other numerous meetings which had been held on that question, was not to weaken the hands of Lord Ashley, but, on the contrary, to make his lordship so strong, being backed by the united support of the people, that both the government and the millowners might perceive the folly of hoping by any stratagem to resist his just demand as already embodied in his own bill. A resolution embodying Mr Oastler's views in support of the personal punishment clause of Lord Ashley's bill, as originally introduced, was twice put to the meeting; on the first occasion two hands were held up against it, on the second three; on both occasions the number of hands raised in its support was immense, the chairman declared the resolution "all but unanimously carried." A declaration which was followed by "thunders of applause." Mr Oastler was throughout supported by the Rev. G. S. Bull, and all the representatives of the short-time committees present. The result spoke trumpet-tongued of the state of feeling then existing, as a rule, between the employers and the employed, engaged in factory labour ; the last saw no hope for improvement but through stringent restrictive enactments, supported by severe penal clauses. Mr Oastler, though deeply sympathising with the discontent of his hearers, yet directed their indignation into the channel he thought would ultimately lead to the consummation desired, as expressed in all the resolutions adopted; namely, an efficient Ten Hours' Bill. The moral effect of the Wibsey Low Moor meeting was great throughout the country ; it convinced all those who attended to public proceedings that the ardour of the Ten Hours' Bill advocates had not abated, and that, under Mr Oastler's and Mr Bull's counsel, they were opposed to all compromise, no matter by whom suggested.

These proceedings at Yorkshire and Lancashire, originally undertaken at Lord Ashley's own request, were conducted in the most spirited and efficient manner. His lordship's changed opinion proved to him a source of weakness. Not any act of Mr Sadler's life caused him greater regret than his having agreed to the temporary abandonment of the imprisonment clauses ; this regret was often expressed to his friends, Mr Oastler and Mr Bull. The decision of the Wibsey Low Moor meeting did not alter the course latterly adopted by his lordship. The subject was again under the notice of parliament on July the 18th ; when the bill was in committee, Lord Althorp, on behalf of the government, urged strenuously on " the house " the necessity of its rejection, and the adoption, in its stead, of a measure founded on the report of the factory commissioners. The principal features of the government measure were the limitation of the hours of labour to twelve per day, for five days, and nine on Saturday, for all persons above thirteen and under eighteen years of age ; children above nine and under thirteen not to be employed more than eight hours; in silk-mills, children of thirteen years of age to be allowed to work ten hours a-day.

In the course of the discussion, all the old objections against factory regulation were renewed and answered. Lord Ashley firmly resisted the efforts to change the bill from a Ten Hours' to a Twelve Hours' Bill. The supporters of the government measure contended that the eight hours' labour clause, for children from nine to thirteen, would allow of relays, or in other words, the employment of two sets of children in one day. It was maintained by the supporters of the Ten Hours' Bill that the government bill would prove impracticable and unsatisfactory. Lord Ashley asked the questions, "Where were the children to be found in numbers sufficient to render the government bill practicable?" "Was the house prepared to say that a master manufacturer might send his waggon to any part of the country for a load of children, like so many hogs, and bring them away from their natural protectors, to place them, unprotected, among strangers?"

On the amendment, naming eighteen years as the age of those to be worked twelve hours per day, under the law, the house divided—Ayes, 93; noes, 238. Majority for the government, 145. The government was successful. Lord Ashley said: "Having taken up the subject fairly and conscientiously, he found that the noble lord (Althorp) had completely defeated him. He should therefore surrender the bill into the hands of the noble lord, but having taken it up with a view to do good to the classes interested, he would only say into whatever hands it might pass, God prosper it." After this formal retirement on the part of Lord Ashley, the measure was wholly in the hands of the government.

It was finally "enacted, That, from and after the first

day of January, one thousand eight hundred and thirty-four, it shall not be lawful for any person whatsoever, to employ in any factory or mill, except in mills for the manufacture of silk, any child who shall not have completed his, or her, ninth year. That, from and after the expiration of six months after the passing of this Act, it shall not be lawful for any person whatsoever, to employ, keep, or allow to remain, in any factory, or mill, as aforesaid, for a longer time than forty-eight hours in any one week, nor for a longer time than nine hours in any one day, except as herein provided, any child who shall not have completed his, or her, eleventh year of age, or after the expiration of eighteen months from the passing of this Act, any child who shall not have completed his, or her, twelfth year of age, or after the expiration of thirty months from the passing of this Act, any child who shall have completed his, or her, thirteenth year of age: provided, nevertheless, that in mills for the manufacture of silk, children under the age of thirteen years shall be allowed to work ten hours in any one day."

The Act, therefore, was intended to come into complete operation in 1836. The government claimed great credit to itself for having, in this Act, for the first time, appointed factory inspectors, a class of officers whose official duties were to examine into, and report upon, the condition of those employed in factory labour, and enforce obedience to the law. The reports of these inspectors have often contained most valuable information; they have been unpopular among many millowners; on the whole, they have performed their duties efficiently.

The government act for the regulation of factories was condemned and disowned by all the supporters of the Ten Hours' Bill movement in and out of parliament. They affirmed that the act, so far as it could be reduced to practice, would involve the greatest cruelty, and the very worst consequences, to those whose interest it professed to promote ; that as it only afforded protection to those under fourteen years of age, all young persons above that age were without protection, subject to the possibility of labouring against two sets of those under fourteen ; that the long hours consequent would, during the period of growth, be very irksome and injurious, and would entail consequences most prejudicial to the future health and strength of those so employed. That the law could not be fully reduced to practice was seriously and repeatedly affirmed, also, that the efforts necessary for that end would cause great dissatisfaction ; that even the partial operation of the law would to the adults be a source of grievous suffering and complaint; that the evasions of the law would be frequent, and further legislation inevitable. The government, on the other hand, were quite confident of the success of their measure ; each party pointed to time as the test by which their opinions should be judged. Upon this understanding Lord Ashley resolved to desist from future efforts at legislation, and thus allow the government act a fair trial.

The strength of the government, and the weakness of Lord Ashley in opposition, strikingly illustrate the danger of concession, when made under the hope of thereby acquiring power. It was a saying of Dryden—" Politicians neither love nor hate," a maxim the philosophy of which Lord Ashley had failed to appreciate. Those who asked for concession had not any intention of supporting the Ten Hours' Bill, their object was to weaken his lordship's influence in the north, and ultimately to desert him when he had ceased to be formidable ; they were successful, but the lesson thus taught was not lost on the minds of those who were thoroughly in earnest, and were recognised as the influential leaders of the Ten Hours' Bill movement.

CHAPTER IV.

INFLUENCE OF THE OPERATION OF THE NEW POOR LAW
AMENDMENT ACT, ON THE CONDITION OF THOSE EMPLOYED
IN FACTORIES.—THE MIGRATION SYSTEM.—OPPOSITION THERETO,
BY MR OASTLER, MR FIELDEN, MR BULL, AND THE REV. JOSEPH
RAYNER STEPHENS.

IT is impossible to apprehend rightly the operation of the
government factories act, without a reference to the operation
of the New Poor Law Amendment Act of 1834. The
principle of the poor law known as the 43rd of Elizabeth,
was the localization of population, localization of authority
in the management of the poor. The principle of the
new poor law was centralization in the fullest meaning of
that word, the controlling power being vested in three
commissioners who practically, under the provisions of the
New Poor Law Amendment Act, governed the poor of
England. These commissioners had large discretionary
powers, so much so, indeed, that they, with the sanction
of one minister of the Crown, legislated for the poor as
well as administered the act of parliament. The leading
difference between the principle of the old and the new
poor law was this,—under the old poor law the right to
live in England, and while able and willing to labour, to
be supported in comfort, at home, was granted under the
constitution. By the same authority the right to a
maintenance was secured under every possible affliction
to which life was subjected, and that too in priority of

F 2

all other claims. This right of the poor was held to be anterior to the right of the proprietors of the soil to rent or the manufacturers to profit, and in the event of the income arising from the labour and land of the country being inadequate to the supply of the wants of all, each class in its own relative position, then that the poor should be the last to suffer ; thus their rights under the old poor law were justly called " sacred and inviolable." Under the new poor law property of all kinds claimed priority, and divorced the poor from constitutional right of maintenance. The first was benevolence and justice embodied in law; the second was property and power claiming *all*, under the belief that all poor laws were wrong in principle, and injurious to the interests of the commonwealth.

The new poor law received from the heads of the great parties of Whigs and Conservatives a very general support; the late Duke of Wellington and the late Sir Robert Peel, by their votes, supported the passing of the New Poor Law Bill. The change in the government of the poor was very energetically opposed by the principal supporters of the Ten Hours' Bill, Lord Ashley being an exception to the rule.

It was very soon discovered that the number of children in the factory districts were unequal to the demand under the relay system. In June 1834, a letter was addressed by Mr Edmund Ashworth, to Mr E. Chadwick, secretary to the poor-law commissioners, suggesting that the greatest possible facilities should be afforded to agricultural families, enabling them to move into the manufacturing districts. It had been customary for years on the part of Lancashire millowners to encourage rural labourers and their families to leave their parishes and become residents in the factory districts. There was thus kept up, between the English and the Irish poor, a competition for labour in factories; the object of Mr Ashworth was, to use the new poor-law commissioners, as the agents of the Lancashire millowners, for the transfer of population from the southern agricultural to the northern manufacturing counties, thereby enabling the Lancashire millowners to cheapen the price of labour. " I am most anxious," wrote Mr Ashworth to Mr Chadwick, " that every facility be given to the removal of labourers from one county to another, according to the demand for labour ; this would have a tendency to equalise wages, as well as prevent, in degree, some of the turn outs which have of late been so prevalent." Mr Robert Hyde Greg, in a letter addressed to Mr E. Chadwick, on the same subject, and bearing date, September 17, 1834, observes, " The suggestion I would make is this, that some official channel of communication should be opened in two or three of our large towns with your office, to which the overcharged parishes should transmit lists of their families. Manufacturers short of labourers, or starting new concerns, might look over the lists and select, as they might require (for the variety of our wants is great), large families or small ones, young children or grown-up men, or widows, or orphans, &c."

In a letter on the same subject, addressed to Mr E. Chadwick, by Mr Henry Ashworth, "Turton, near Bolton, Lancashire," and bearing date February 13, 1835, there are the following passages :—" I may with safety state, by way of encouragement to them (the unfortunate poor of rural districts), that there is in this neighbourhood a greater scarcity of workpeople than I have ever known, and this fact was never more universally acknowledged, not only by those engaged in manufactures, but by others also, in almost every branch of trade. . . . . I know of no better way to promote the emigration of families, than the direct transmission of them to some extensive field of manufacture ; allow them a temporary abode for a few days, and the assistance of an active trusty person, to show them and make them acquainted with the nature of the employments offering, and the rates of wages paying; and when they have selected such as appear most likely to suit them, and bargained for their wages, they will soon become regularly domiciled, and will feel better satisfied with their change, than they would otherwise have been, had they undertaken a blind bargain with a registry office."

More correspondence of a similar kind, on the same subject, will be found by reference to the poor law reports for 1835, from the appendices to which the above extracts have been copied. The poor law commissioners opened an office in Manchester, under the superintendence of Mr Muggeridge, to accelerate the transfer of labourers from the south. The spirit with which this traffic was conducted may be judged of by reading the following extracts from a letter by Mr Langston, the travelling Agent of the Ampthill and Woburn board of Guardians. "At Derby I found an opening for children, from nine to seventeen, &c. A number of persons to the amount of one hundred, sent at different periods (say ten every two or three weeks), could now be employed, and many more will be wanted early in the spring, at the different mills of Messrs Taylor, Bridgett, and More, with other silk manufacturers. . . . . . At another there is an opening for ten or fifteen children; widows with families might be sent, and homes would be provided for those without mothers, with careful people. At Stockport, two families might be sent, with as many children above ten as can be found, to Mr Robinson, of Spring Bank; and if they (the families) suit, two more; and no doubt more would follow. Messrs Marshall and Sons would be glad of a widow and family, and provided the children were numerous, a family with a father would not be objected to."—October 17th, 1835.

The period to which these dates refer was one of "commercial prosperity," which, in 1837, was followed by "commercial depression." The sufferings of the labourers, women and children, imported into the manufacturing districts, were necessarily very great, and were made known to the poor-law commissioners in London, by their Manchester agent, Mr Muggeridge.

The opposition of Mr Oastler, Mr Fielden, Mr Bull, and others, to the new poor law, had its foundation in the conviction that the old poor law was Christian and constitutional, that the new poor law was anti-Christian and unconstitutional. They said, "Cursed is he that removeth his neighbour's land-mark;" and the old parochial system in their judgment was the land-mark of the labourer. The centralizing system of the new poor law, they denounced with a solemnity and earnestness akin to the spirit of Hebrew prophets. While, allowing the factory experiment a trial, they transferred their opposition unimpaired to what they, quoting the words of the first Earl of Eldon, designated, "the most infamous law that ever was enacted in any Christian country." No doubt, this opposition was increased in intensity, because of the use made of the powers with which parliament had invested the new poor-law commissioners, as regarded the supply of the factory districts with "hands" from the agricultural counties.

The poor-law commissioners caused advertisements to be circulated in the rural districts, setting forth the advantages of migration to the manufacturing districts. In many cases these advertisements were, by the poor-law guardians, shown to the paupers, who were, if persuasion failed, told to make their choice between removal and the union workhouse, with all its horrors of separation and prison-like surveillance. Many of those who were thus driven from their native parishes, afterwards complained bitterly of their changed lot in life. Work in the mills was burdensome indeed to those who had been accustomed to the healthful labour of the fields. For workers in the mills there was no gleaning in harvest, no cottage and garden, no pig, nor a plentiful supply of milk. These unfortunate labourers had in most cases to undergo grievous disappointments; they were generally hired or rather sold for three years at fixed rates of wages; these were lower than the current wages of the neighbourhood. The glowing pictures of high wages, low-priced provisions, and family comfort, of which they had been told were deceitful promises ; the reality was the reverse of what they had been assured would be their happy fate in Lancashire and Yorkshire. Sometimes those serfs of the soil, sold to the lords of the mills, would be misdirected, carted to Halifax, when the desired destination was Leeds, and so on ; wherever left by their guide, there they would stand, enquiring of every passer-by if he could give them any information as to their future employer, until some kind Samaritan pitied their case and tried to unravel the mystery. Instances have been known of families sent into districts in which their services were not wanted, and they, in consequence, were left to get on as they best could, the deluded victims of a heartless policy. The opponents of the new poor law published accounts of many cases of the kind referred to, giving names, dates, and circumstances. These accounts were eagerly read by the factory-workers, who declared enmity against the new poor law, and renewed their pledges to continue their efforts for a ten hours' bill. Such circumstances made plain to the understandings of the factory operatives the intimate connection between the new poor law and long hours of labour in factories, and, in consequence, increased their hatred of and opposition to both.

In the opinion of Mr Oastler and his coadjutors against the new poor law, labour was by that act placed absolutely at the mercy of the capitalists ; under its operation the poor were forced to work, without any legal power of resistance, for such wages as they were offered, to starve or suffer a penal imprisonment. It was contended that the certain effects of that act would be to increase the competition of the labourers in the labour market; to crowd the manufacturing districts with a greater population than could be regularly employed; to increase the competition of employers against each other, and thereby lower prices, profits, wages; to strengthen the feeling of the employers against factory regulation, and the necessity on the part of the employed for THE TEN HOURS' BILL.

In the mind of Mr Oastler, the new poor law severed the clergy from the poor, destroyed the connection between the rate-payers and their dependants, broke up the homes of the labourers necessitated by occasional scarcity to sue for relief. separated families, and forced the virtuous and the vicious, indiscriminately, to herd together. It thus sapped the very foundation of the ancient parochial system. He was convinced that the strength of England could only be maintained by an increased application of the industry of her labourers to her fields; and he believed, he saw, in all the acts of the poor-law commissioners, a desire to build up the towns at the cost of the agriculture, and the health of the country. Strong in the energy of his will, naturally vigorous and enthusiastic, he was unsparing in his condemnation, and the migration scheme was in letters, pamphlets, and speeches, a constant object of denunciation.

Mr Oastler believed that the new poor law was the offspring of covetousness on the part of the rich, and so was the unregulated factory system. Mr Oastler had read in his Bible " Turn not your face from the poor man." He had read in the speech in which Lord Brougham introduced the Poor Law Bill that " hospitals for the support of old men and old women, may, strictly speaking, be regarded as injurious in their effects on the community. Nevertheless, their evil may be counterbalanced by the good they do. . . . . But the next species of charity to which I would refer, is one which sins grievously against all sound principle—I mean hospitals for children, whether endowed by the public, or by the charity of individuals. These, with the exception of orphan hospitals, are mere evils ; and the worst of all is a foundling hospital." To reconcile the spirit of his lordship's speech, which was also the spirit of the new poor law, with the divine precept was beyond Mr Oastler's power, and, consistently with his own principles, he believed that to resist such a law was a Christian duty. The poor-law commissioners, in keeping with the spirit of the law, issued a public notice, announcing that—" a principal object of a compulsory provision for the relief of destitution, is the prevention of almsgiving." An order which the late Sir Robert Peel, in a debate in the House of Commons in 1841, characterised in the words: " Good God! it is a complete desecration of the precepts of the divine law ! ' Give alms to the poor,' ' turn not your face from the poor man.' " Sir Robert thus proved, in 1841, the anti-Christian character of the poor law, asserted by Mr Oastler in 1834. Certainly the condemned order of the poor-law commissioners was not, in any sense, a departure from the spirit of the law, or from the openly-avowed intentions of its original promulgators. The two following extracts, the first from a speech, the second from a letter, will better than any words at our command convey Mr Oastler's impressions of the spirit and ob-ject of the new poor law : " If this starvation measure," said he, " be forced upon the country, it will produce a great deal of crime; our prisons will be filled with delin-quents, and much more serious expenses will be incurred by their prosecution, than the new poor law can save by pre-venting relief being given to the poor. The great argument for the passing of this law in the House of Commons was, that if the old law had been allowed to remain in force, it would ultimately have taken away the whole landed estates of the wealthy. The old law never took more than eight millions, and out of that amount four millions were annually spent in litigation. This was indeed a strange argument. They begrudged a little pittance which was to be paid to the poor, and determined, if they could, to prevent them having any aid. This showed them the necessity of being ready to oppose this enactment. If the people of England had done their duty to themselves before this bill was introduced into the House of Commons, there would not have been any need for such meetings as these."

" I have this moment," wrote Mr Oastler, " returned from beholding one of those awful scenes—so grand, so terrific—which force man to acknowledge the existence and the power of that being whose ' is the sea,' because he made it; a scene which feeble man can never contemplate without reverence and awe. I have been standing on the beach, when a mighty storm was raging, and the sea was troubled; roaring, as the waves in majestic grandeur, rolled upon the agitated surface, ' and beat about the dry land,' which the same God had ' prepared ' as a boundary for the safe residence of man. His voice, louder than the ocean's thunder, proclaimed: ' Hitherto shalt thou come, but no farther, here shalt thy proud waves be stayed.' The tempest cracked and howled around me. The sea in mountains of water, rolled in terrific waves, and, curling themselves together as they approached the shore, as if, in united force, to vent their rage at the interruption offered to their conquering course, they dashed themselves in fury upon the beach; thus, spending themselves in volumes of foam, covering the strand (which seemed to laugh at their menaces), with broad layers of quivering froth. The sight was truly magnificent. Thank God! no ships were nigh. No lives, as far as our eyes could reach, were endangered. As I stood listening to the howling of the wind, the roaring of the waves, and watching the raging of the ocean, I thought—just so furiously is man now raging against his fellow man—just so is infidelity now vainly daring to vent its rage and malice against Christianity—just now, embodied in the accursed new poor law, is falsehood warring against truth ; tyranny against justice; Satan against God. But as surely as these waves are stayed by this sandy beach, so surely shall it soon be said to that power infernal, which now seems to hold our destiny in his hands, ' Thus far shalt thou come, but no farther.' "

The anti-new-poor-law agitation, though separated from the Ten Hours' Bill movement, was analogous in spirit, and served to keep alive the senses of the people to what they felt to be their wrongs and believed to be their rights. The transfer of population from the rural to the manufacturing districts was loudly condemned, and the necessity for the Ten Hours' Bill was a theme of frequent conversation and reference. The passing of the New Poor Law Amendment Act did more to sour the hearts of the labouring population, than did the privations consequent on all the actual poverty of the land. Rightly, or wrongly, may be a subject of discussion, but the fact is undeniable, that the labourers of England believed that the new poor law was a law to punish poverty; and the effects of that belief were, to sap the loyalty of the working men, to make them dislike the country of their birth, to brood over their wrongs, to cherish feelings of revenge, and to hate the rich of the land. These results did not lessen the necessity of, nor the desire for, factory regulation, and its supporters awaited the trial of the government measure, with confidence in the soundness of their own judgment, and distrust in the judgment of the authors of the existing factory law. Those, old enough to remember these times of stirring political and social interest, will bear testimony to the important crisis this country has lived through, from the passing of the Reform Bill until now. Very much of the political excitement of later years had its origin in the passing of the New Poor Law Amendment Act. The leaders of the chartist movement, without an exception, made the new poor law the burden of their complaint against the government and the owners of property. They said, in the bitterness of anger, " Laws grind the poor, and rich men make the law." In the earlier stages of the chartist movement, the objects of the leaders were social; very few among their disciples cared for political power for its own sake, all looked to ulterior objects. The late Mr O'Connor, in and out of parliament, opposed the New Poor Law Amendment Act, and supported the Ten Hours' Bill. The late Mr Beaumont, Mr Hetherington, and Mr Cleve, were strenuous opponents of the new poor law. Mr Bronterre O'Brien has, throughout a lengthened political career, opposed the political economists and Malthusians on all the more important social questions of the age. It was the conviction of the late Mr Walter, of the *Times*, that chartism was the offshoot of the oppression of the poor, under the new poor law. Lord John Russell broadly stated that chartism sprang out of the " agitation got up against the Poor Law Amendment Act " The opinions of his lordship, and of Mr Walter, on this point harmonize ; they require, in our opinion, considerable qualification. They, however, fully corroborate our conclusion, that the New Poor Law Amendment Act increased to a great extent the discontent of the country ; it is also noteworthy that the chartists, in their crusade of opposition against other parties, political and social, were, at public meetings, properly so called, unanimous and overwhelming ; but they, instead of carrying out their policy of opposition, against the anti-poor-law agitation and the Ten Hours' Bill movement, invariably, without any reference to party politics, supported both—a circumstance deserving the attention of the student in political and social progress, and of statesmen. It is also a startling fact in the social and legislative history of this country, that the principle and objects of the new poor law, as originally promulgated by its authors, have been in practice very much modified, its harsher provisions have been abolished, and there has been a growing tendency towards the spirit and practice of the old poor law, as regards the treatment of the poor. The scientific " statesmen," as they were pleased to call themselves, who originated the new poor law, and, in Earl Fitzwilliam's words, supported it as " a step to no poor law at all," have thus undergone reproof at the hands of time.

It was one of the openly avowed objects of the poor-law commissioners, that they would " depauperise England by the terror of the workhouse." Mr Mott, Assistant Poor-law Commissioner, assured Mr Oastler, that if the union work-houses, then in the course of erection, should be filled, the law would be found a failure, "the object in building those union-houses being to establish therein a discipline so severe and repulsive, as to make them a terror to the poor, and prevent them from entering." " By that test," added Mr Mott, "our principles will be tried; if the union-houses should be occupied we shall have been proved in the wrong, but if they should remain empty, we shall know that we were right." England has not been depauperised, the workhouses have again and again been filled to overflowing. It is in the nature of poverty to overcome every obstacle but itself, and to permanently fear no terror that the ingenuity of man can suggest. Between 1834 and 1837, various circumstances combined to reduce poor rates; the supporters of the new poor law trumpeted the success of their measure. The illusion was of short duration: 1838 indicated the adverse change, and succeeding years have proved the principle of the new poor law to be a decided failure. So far from the new poor law having been, as its founders declared, " a step to no poor law at all," it has been the predecessor of organised poor laws for Ireland and Scotland, to the serious annoyance of the economists, and the benefit of the poor and the rich of Ireland and Scotland. Several among the more prominent of the supporters of factory regulation were opposed to Mr Oastler's views on the connection between the poor law and factory questions. We copy his ripened judgment on the course he pursued:—

" Many a time," says Mr Oastler, in a letter, bearing date July, 1856, " I have been asked, What connection can there be between the Ten Hours' Bill and the New Poor Law Bill? I answered logically. But prejudice and party feeling resisted my appeals to reason ; and even by my most valued and most beneficent friend and coadjutor, I was forsaken, and, therefore, left to my own weak resources when the progress of the Ten Hours' Bill was very expensive.

" The two questions were, are, and ever must be inseparably connected. It was in evidence that the new poor law was intended to be used to perpetuate slavery in factories. The Ten Hours' Bill was intended to destroy that slavery. It was in evidence that the new poor law was intended to decrease the wages of the factory operatives. The Ten Hours' Bill was, as I always believed and maintained, calculated to increase those wages. It was in evidence that the new poor law was, by the introduction of the families of agricultural labourers into the factory districts, intended to increase the competition for labour in factories. The Ten Hours' Bill was intended and calculated to decrease that competition. For those and for other very weighty reasons, we resolved, as I think, most wisely, and I am sure, as Ten Hours' Bill men, most consistently, to resist the passing of the New Poor Law Bill. Under my convictions it would, in myself, have been worse than cowardice, had I otherwise acted. It would have involved the sacrifice of principle and truth, and a good conscience, to the short-sightedness of others. To have been saved by the ever-watchful providence of God, from shipwreck on that rock, I account among my greatest mercies."

On July the 29th, 1835, the supporters of factory regulation endured a serious loss in the death of Mr Sadler. He had removed from Yorkshire to Belfast, at which place he died, aged fifty-five. The grave had not long closed over his remains, before his merits were acknowledged by those whose approbation was honour.

Mr Sadler's claims on the respect of posterity do not rest alone on his efforts in parliament, though these were important. His pen was the first which successfully proved the foundation of the Malthusian theory of the *super-fecundity* of the human species to be hollow and untenable—a theory no longer advocated by any statesman or author of reputation, and which the Census commissioners of 1851 have disproved by an appeal to the facts of population as made known to them through investigation. The persevering industry of Mr Sadler brought to light many circumstances in connection with population, and the means existing for its sustenance, which previous to his work, thereon, were but little known and indifferently understood. His work on Ireland was a noble contribution to the social and political literature of the century, and its merits were acknowledged by statesmen of all parties.

A monument was erected by public subscription to his memory, in the parish church of Leeds, in 1835, and in 1856 another has been raised over his body in the churchyard of Ballylesson, County Down. On both are appropriate inscriptions, and his memory as a philanthropist, an author, statesman, and friend, is fondly cherished by those whose opportunities of knowing and judging were many. His labours on behalf of the interests of the poor and the oppressed have been of real and permanent service to society, and are worthy of grateful remembrance.

CHAPTER V.

UNSATISFACTORY OPERATION OF THE GOVERNMENT FACTORIES' ACT—
EXCITEMENT IN THE MANUFACTURING DISTRICTS—EFFORTS OF
MR CHARLES HINDLEY, M.P. FOR ASHTON, TO OBTAIN A TEN
HOURS' ACT, WITH A RESTRICTION ON THE MOVING POWER—
ATTEMPT OF THE GOVERNMENT TO REPEAL PART OF THEIR OWN
ACT IN 1836—ABANDONMENT OF THEIR ENDEAVOUR.

LEGISLATIVE enactments bearing upon the practices of numerous bodies of working men, to be beneficial, require to be framed with the greatest possible regard to circumstances. Those parties most capable of forming correct opinions as to the details of such legislation, are, necessarily, those most closely connected with the actual circumstances of the parties legislated for. " It is," said Edmund Burke, " one of the finest problems in legislation, and what has often engaged my thoughts whilst I followed that profession:—' What the state ought to take upon itself to direct by the public wisdom, and what it ought to leave with as little interference as possible, to individual discretion.' Nothing, certainly, can be laid down on the subject that will not admit of exceptions, many permanent, some occasional." This is the language of practical wisdom, and, in few words, leaves the theory of universal non-interference, or the opposite, to the system-mongers, who are blind to the wants of men. It may be, under some circumstances, a grave error to endeavour to modify very strictly the practices of society by the force of positive laws, but the error is not less serious which allows positive evils to exist, injurious to body and mind, from the fear of exerting a power inherent in the very constitution of society for the wisest of purposes. The more complete the freedom allowed to the exercise of those principles of the human constitution, which in their own nature are positively good, the greater in proportion must be the virtue and happiness of mankind. On the other hand, the more thoroughly that which is in itself evil can be restrained, the less influence will it exercise over the habits of society. Of this, statesmen may rest assured, that no discoveries as to the motives of man, his interests, or duties, can lessen their responsibilities, and, that whatever they resolve to do, will require at their hands the most careful consideration in all that relates to details as well as principles; the more simple and uniform laws are in operation, the more complete the means of discovering their violation is rendered, the more uniform and satisfactory will they prove in practice.

One of the surest modes of bringing government into discredit, is to pass laws which, in practice, are easy of evasion, or from inconsiderate legislation are impracticable. Every step taken in practical legislation is surrounded by some difficulties ; these do not constitute a valid defence for legislative bungling, nor for the foolish cry of " Do nothing." So absurd was the government Factories' Act in its details, that practical men in favour of legislation on that subject were frequently heard to declare, " The law is not intended to be obeyed ; the object of those who framed it is to disgust the people with factory legislation; it is the law of the enemies of all factory legislation." Mr Steward, one of the factory commissioners, had stated that the government listened to what he designated " a bit of a parliament of millowners," who were opposed to all legislation ; but when they found that a law on the question must be passed, desired to render it as impracticable as possible, consistently with their desire to work their factories for the longest possible hours.

To the younger children employed in factories, the operation of the act was beneficial, inasmuch as it limited the hours of their labour to eight per day; even this relief from labour was paid for by the labour of the children between thirteen and eighteen years of age, who, in most cases, were required to perform not only their own tasks but those of the absent children. To the adult operatives the operation of the act was vexatious and harassing; to those spinners who themselves employed and paid children, it caused a direct loss in wages; the scarcity of the younger children caused an advance of their wages, which was not met by a corresponding advance on the part of the masters. The act having allowed the earlier employment of young children in silk than in cotton mills, caused an excess in the former and a deficiency in the latter. To the millowners and occupiers the operation of the act was unsatisfactory. It caused confusion in the conduct of extensive works, because of the difficulty of procuring an adequate supply of work-people of the various ages; this was more especially the case in fine spinning establishments in which young children were employed in greater numbers.

On the authority of the factory inspectors, the number of factories actually at work and reported on, early in the year 1835, was 1948, the number of the convictions under the factories act was 177, thus every eleventh millowner had been proved guilty of an offence against the law, or a lower number had been proved guilty of one or more offences. The number of convictions does not even indicate the number of times the law was violated; the government were energetic in their efforts to enforce the law, but many among the local magistracy, of Lancashire especially, themselves millowners or related to or influenced by millowners, made no secret of their disregard for the law. This very reprehensible conduct on the part of some among the magistrates, was subject

of complaint by the factory inspectors, and a source of
very great annoyance to the supporters of factory regulation. Assuredly such proceedings were very discreditable, and contributed to bring not only the Factory Act,
but the very principles on which law rests into disrepute. The principal among the leaders of the factory question did not interfere, the agitation of the
question out of doors had ceased, Mr Oastler and Mr
Bull, in their own words, " had resolved to give the
master's act fair play;" they, however, closely watched the
whole proceedings, and, in common with their supporters,
awaited anxiously for the next movement on the part of the
government.

In the summer of 1835, Mr Oastler addressed a series
of letters to the editors of the most popular unstamped
political periodicals of the time, and he continued in the
unstamped press to make known the whole history of
the factory movement, and his views thereon. In this
course Mr Oastler was opposed by some of his dearest
friends, who were shocked at the thought of him, a churchman and tory, writing in the pages of what they knew to
be " radical and revolutionary journals." These letters were
certainly among the ablest Mr Oastler has written, they
contained very graphic descriptions of scenes from life, as he
had witnessed them, and as they had been narrated to him
by others. In these letters, Mr Oastler avowed broadly
his opinions on infidelity and republicanism, and his
regard for the church and the constitution. On being
questioned in *The Twopenny Despatch* on behalf of the
" Manchester Radical Association," as to his opinions
on " Universal Suffrage," he answered through the same
medium. " My opinion on ' Universal Suffrage' is, that
if it were the law of the land next week, it would in a
very short time produce ' universal confusion,' and would
inevitably lead to ' despotism.' " The unstamped press had,

at the time referred to, command of the active mind of the working men. Mr Oastler had the merit of seeing that this was a source of strength, that it was desirable on his part to possess and control. As he used to say: " I have petitioned the two houses of parliament, I have endeavoured to gain the ear of the King of England; and I firmly believe his majesty would have listened had there not been a power behind the throne greater than the throne. I have addressed the church, the aristocracy; I have not been idle in public meetings. I have attended these from a Yorkshire county meeting with the High Sheriff in the chair; a city of London meeting, with the Lord Mayor in the chair, down to a country village meeting, with an operative for chairman; as yet I have not succeeded. I have tried the press, pamphlet after pamphlet have I sent forth, full of ' mourning, lamentation and woe,' but the rulers of the land have turned a deaf ear, the stamped newspapers have been witnesses of my exertions, yet ' Yorkshire slavery' still exists ! Now I will labour in another field, in it I will sow the seed, and the harvest will come in its season, I want the aid of all parties, and must work on until I succeed." The resolution was politic and far-seeing, and much of the popular feeling afterwards manifested on behalf of the Ten Hours' Bill had its foundation in the letters written by Mr Oastler in the unstamped press. " Knowing, as I do," continued Mr Oastler, " that the working men and their families do not obtain the stamped press, and that the unstamped press is universally read by them; regardless of caste or party, I have resolved to avail myself of the only medium through weekly periodicals, in which I can effectually communicate what I know and think on subjects most important to the working men."

Towards the close of 1835 very considerable excitement prevailed in the factory districts as to the course the government intended to pursue on the factory question. The law had been proved to be unsatisfactory, and when the additional restriction, limiting the employment of children under thirteen years of age to not more than forty-eight hours in any one week, or longer than nine hours in any one day, came into operation, the dissatisfaction and difficulty would increase. This change would occur early in 1836, all parties interested were, therefore, preparing for the future. Mr Charles Hindley, an extensive millowner, and member of parliament for the borough of Ashton-under-Lyne, had made known his intention to the operatives of introducing to parliament a bill for regulating the hours of labour to ten per day, with a restriction on the moving power. Mr Hindley was well known in the manufacturing districts, and the operatives felt very anxious to know his opinions on all phases of the short-time question. On December the 5th, 1835, a meeting of a very important character was held at the Albion Hotel, Manchester, consisting of delegates from the spinners of Bolton, Bury, Ashton, Preston, Oldham, Chorley, and Manchester; and Mr Phillips, M.P. for Manchester, Mr Brotherton, M.P. for Salford, Mr Fielden, M.P. for Oldham, Mr Hindley, M.P. for Ashton, Mr Potter, M.P. for Wigan, Mr Brocklehurst, M.P. for Macclesfield, Mr Walker, M.P. for Bury. The proceedings of this meeting were very important; the following facts were elicited. That many of the children, certified as being twelve years of age, were known to be under that age; that the increased speed of machinery required increased attention and labour on the part of the spinners. Mr Hindley recommended ten hours a day, and a restriction on the moving power, recommendations which met with the approval of the operatives. Mr Fielden declared himself in favour of the shortest time that could be agreed to, and supported by the assent of parliament. Mr Hindley pledged himself to divide the house on the ten hours' question, but would not pledge himself to give up his bill, provided he was in a minority. He admired Mr O'Connell, and considered him a superior statesman. It was Mr O'Connell's rule, to ask for what he should have, but to take the most that he could get, and by the strength so acquired to strive for the remainder. Mr Hindley pledged himself to introduce the question of ten hours' labour per day session after session, until that limitation constituted the limit of the factory day. This latter declaration was to the operatives very satisfactory. On the 2nd of January 1836, a delegates' meeting was held in Manchester. Ashton, Oldham, Bury, Bolton, Macclesfield, Manchester, and Preston were represented; Mr Hindley, M.P., Mr Condy, and Mr Bull were present by invitation. At this meeting resolutions were passed in favour of a Ten Hours' Bill, for sending delegates to London, for holding meetings throughout the country to propagate the views of the delegates, and thus to renew the agitation. Mr Hindley stated at length the course of policy he approved, and urged the operatives to send delegates to London, so that every member of the House of Commons should be canvassed on the question. " If the masters asked for twelve hours, let them prove to the House of Commons that this time was required by foreign competition; if the men desired ten hours, let them show that this time is the extreme limit allowed by consideration of humanity. The house must decide between them; and in order to give each party fair play, he would pledge himself to divide the house on the ten hours' clause. With regard to the decision to which the legislature might come, he could only say that, as a practical man, he could not pledge himself to throw up the bill if it did not obtain all that the operatives desired." Mr Bull was decidedly of opinion that a Ten Hours' Bill could alone be practically operative, that the responsibility of any bill, legalizing longer hours of labour, should rest with those who passed the law, to which he recommended no true Ten Hours' Bill man to be in any sense a party. Mr Bull handed in a paper containing his reasons in support of the decision he, after mature consideration, had arrived at; among these was the following:—" Because ten hours is the least limitation which affords me, as a Christian instructor, any chance of attempting the religious, moral, or literary improvement of my flock." Mr Bull's sense of his responsibilities as a Christian minister were always uppermost in his mind, and were, in themselves, the motives which propelled him to action.

The necessary preliminary arrangements having been entered into, public meetings were held throughout the manufacturing districts, to support Mr Hindley. These meetings, which were numerous and important, had features distinct from the preceding agitation. The mind of the country and the writers for the press had become more familiar with the details of the question. At a meeting in Manchester, held early in March, 1836, the Reverend Joseph Rayner Stephens thus illustrated the connection between the new poor law and the factory question. The Reverend gentleman said :—" Mr Chairman and good men of Manchester : you have this night had a nail or two well driven, and I hope before I have done to clench them. The first speaker has told you that you ought not to be slaves. The second told you that you *ought* to be slaves, though you were not. I tell you—and I hold the evidence of the fact in my hand, and will now adduce it, lest I should forget it—I tell you, in the outset, that you are slaves. I hold in my hand a bargain—a document of sale ; it is the resuscitation of slavery in the British dominions, in the sale, for thrice twelve months, of twelve human beings—the father, mother, and ten children—who this day passed through Ashton on their road to Glossop, which is to be the seat of their slavery for the above time. This, too, takes place under the powers

of the new poor law amendment act; and the tendency
of it will be to prevent you from accomplishing the object
which has called you together. Your masters talk to you
of foreign competition—they are not afraid of that. But
you ought to be afraid of home competition. Will you
allow me to read the article of contract to which I refer?
The individuals are twelve of the finest human beings that
can be seen anywhere upon earth. The young people are
healthy, lusty, and blooming ; how long they will remain
so Mr Waterhouse shall tell us. The agreement is between
Benjamin Waterhouse and James Aldis—that is the name of
the father of the family, but he says that he is no party
to it, but that the agreement is between Mr Waterhouse
and the overseer of Worlingworth, in Suffolk, which is
100 miles beyond London, from which place the family
came down in one of Pickford's fly boats, by canal, and
went to the Friendship Inn in Ashton, there to wait for
one of Mr Waterhouse's waggons to convey them to Glossop.
I will now tell you the price of a man. James Aldis has
been bought of the overseer of Worlingworth for 10s. a week
for the first year, 11s. shillings the second year, and 12s.
the third year. Here follows the price of the respective
children with their ages ; but I ought to tell that they are
all a year older than the age specified in the register.

"Eliza, aged 16 years, is to have 4s. 6d. weekly for
the first year, 5s. the second year, and 6s. the third year.

"William, aged 12, is to have 2s. 6d. weekly for the first
year, 3s. the second year, 3s. 6d. the third year.

"Lydia, aged 15, is to have 4s., 5s., and 5s. 6d. respectively
for the three years.

"Caleb, aged 13, is to have 3s., 3s. 6d., and 4s.

"Joshua, aged 11, is to have 1s. 6d., 2s., and 3s. 6d.

"Rachel, aged nine, is also to have 1s., 1s. 6d. and 2s.

"William, aged nine, is also to have 1s., 1s. 6d. and 2s.

"John, aged eleven, is to have 1s. 6d., 2s., and 3s. 6d.

" Then, on the poor wretch's paper he is told that houses may be had varying from one shilling to four shillings per week ; but if iron bedsteads are to be found with the cottages, he must pay one penny per week for each iron bedstead. This, then, is the contract entered into and signed, and it is copied from the poor wretch's paper. He was at first directed just like a bill of parcels—' To Mr Benjamin Waterhouse, Glossop ;' but before he would leave the sod—before he would leave the land of his fathers and his childhood, he insisted upon a specific engagement, that he might not be left entirely at the mercy of his *owners*, and the above contract was therefore drawn up. The contract is signed— ' Richard Muggeridge, Poor Law Commissioners' Agent for Emigration, Manchester, 9th February, 1836,' and countersigned, ' Benjamin Waterhouse, Glossop, February 2nd.' "

This statement caused very great sensation, and no doubt contributed to keep alive the hatred of the factory workers against the new poor law. Similar statements were made at other meetings. The questions of home and foreign competition were much debated, and Mr Hindley was evidently disposed to give to the question of foreign competition considerable weight. Mr Baines, M.P. for Leeds, also proprietor and senior editor of the *Leeds Mercury*, advocated a compromise for an eleven hours' bill, but this was impossible, for Mr Oastler declared, on the subject being named, that he would agitate for a ten hours' bill to death, or succeed in its accomplishment. He and Mr Bull were, in Yorkshire, all powerful, and so far as the operatives were concerned, Oastler and Bull were popular and powerful throughout every factory district in Great Britain. While the question was in this state in the north, the delegates of the employers and the employed were busy in London. The delegates from the operatives were in London in the beginning of March, every day active in canvassing for support and keeping up a correspondence between themselves, the committees, and the active leaders in the country. Mr Hindley's bill had been printed and circulated, when it was made known that Mr Poulett Thomson, on behalf of the government, intended to introduce a bill to repeal " the thirteen year old clause," thus making twelve years the limit for those to be employed for eight hours per day. The factory delegates and their influential friends resolved to oppose the government measure and to have moved, in the House of Commons, a ten hours' clause as an amendment. The excitement and anxiety in the factory districts were intense; meetings, remonstrating against the government proposition, were held ; every available means in London and the country were applied to insure the defeat of the ministry. At a meeting in Huddersfield, Mr Oastler denounced the proceedings of the government in very strong terms. " He could assure the government that the people of England had determined that their children should be free. He had the Bible, truth, and justice at his back, and in front nothing but gold and Poulett Thomson's bill." At Leeds Mr Oastler was equally decided ; he was ably supported by his constant coadjutor, the Rev. Mr Bull. Yorkshire, Lancashire, and Cheshire were unanimous against the government proposal, and in favour of a ten hours' bill. The proceedings of these meetings were remarkable for the expression of a strong sense of remonstrance against the change suggested by the government ; the principal speakers denounced the intended change in the law as " a violation of every principle of justice and humanity, as if the legislature of this country had not the common lights of moral and Christian precept to direct them; " but the petitioners to the House of Commons resolved to continue the agitation, con- vinced " that inhumanity had not generally taken possession of the bosoms of fathers and mothers, whatever might be the feelings of masters and legislators." " It is true," said the remonstrants (the petitioners had now changed their tone, and openly declared themselves "remonstrants," a marked difference, and one which parliament could not fail to have observed) "that petitions to your honourable house, from the people, seem of no avail, but to excite laughter and be rejected," yet they were resolved to persevere. In the Huddersfield remonstrance were the following paragraphs. " Your remonstrants, however, can never forget that 20,000,000*l.* have been paid, out of the labour of these children, to purchase for the black adults eight hours' labour per day, and that the friends of the negro are in motion, with a view of obtaining more power, and a new act to enforce the eight hours' act in Jamaica ; yet, strange to say, whilst the laws of humanity are enforced by the government and their friends, when the wrongs of black men require their enforcement, and an appeal (justly indeed) is made to the people of England to raise their voice for this purpose, yet, at the same time, the same government is requiring the same people to submit to the destruction of the same principles of humanity, incorporated in one of their own acts made for the protection of the most industrious, the most oppressed part of the community—the little white factory slaves. The government seem to act on these questions as though the people of England could not judge of the simple principles of right and wrong." " And your remonstrants regret to find that the right honourable the Secretary for the Home Department and the right honourable the President of the Board of Trade have brought in a bill to your honourable house, to repeal the best part of the present bill, which was agreed to by your honourable house to be absolutely necessary for the health and education of the factory children, that act having been granted on the ground of evidence drawn from repeated inquiries, begun by the first Sir Robert Peel, continued by select committee after select committee, and crowned by a royal commission of inquiry—the only reason given *now* for the withdrawal of that protection being, that it is ' expedient ' so to do; while your remonstrants, on the contrary, assert from their own knowledge that the manufacturing districts are in a much better condition than before the passing of that bill, and have been materially improved during its operation.

" Your remonstrants are as decided as ever for a Ten Hours' Bill, on the ground that such a measure would combine the greatest advantages with the least amount of evil or inconvenience, and therefore solemnly protest against any proposition above that standard as being the offspring of avarice, cruelty, and oppression.'

On Monday, May the 9th, 1836, Mr Poulett Thomson moved the second reading of the Factories' Act Amendment Bill, which was met by a motion intended to test the strength of the government on the question. Lord Ashley moved, " That the bill be read a second time this day six months." In the debate which followed, the question of factory labour in all its relations was very thoroughly discussed. The government admitted that the existing law was not obeyed. Quoting the authority of the factory inspectors, it was declared to be " almost impossible to enforce the law as it has stood since the 1st of March last." " It had been found almost impossible to procure children enough for the execution of the relay system." " Hence, therefore," said Mr Poulett Thomson, " the necessity for the bill I am now advocating." All the former arguments about the danger of foreign competition, the hardships of children not being allowed to earn their own bread, the necessity for long hours, in order that the operatives should have high wages, the danger of interference with labour and capital were restated by the speakers on behalf of the government, and answered by Lord Ashley and his supporters. The weight of fact and argument was decidedly against the government. The speeches of Lord Ashley and Mr Charles Hindley were distinct and full of facts, proving the inefficiency of the existing law, and the addi-

tional injury which would follow from declaring that all
the children above twelve years of age were free agents,
and therefore should the government bill become law, subject
to work long hours.   Mr Brotherton and Mr John
Fielden, two practical and successful manufacturers, distinguished themselves by speeches which exhausted the
subject. Both were ardent supporters of factory regulation,
and had decidedly more practical knowledge of the question
than had any other two members of the House of Commons.
The late Sir Robert Peel cast the weight of his eloquence
and vote into the ministerial scale.   The late Mr O'Connell
and his family followers voted with the ministers.   Not any
petitions had been presented in favour of the government
bill; there were many opposed thereto.   The importance of
the decision in the House of Commons may be appreciated from
the numbers voting.   There were for the second reading,
178; for the amendment, 176; majority, 2.

Some very important facts were stated during the
debate.   It was affirmed that the firm of Wood and
Walker, of Bradford, had complied with the act, and by
attention to the physical condition, education, and morals of
those in their employment, they had proved that factory
labour could be conducted under conditions not seriously
injurious to health.   Mr Brotherton stated, that on the
authority of the factory inspectors, which he, as a practical
man, approved, "that human labour, in connection with the
machinery of a cotton mill, is not free."   The late Mr
Baines, of Leeds, stated his opinion, "the result of many
years' experience," "that there is no class of children better
fed, better clad, better lodged, or more healthy, than those
of manufacturers."   Sir John Ellery, speaking from his
experience "on many recruiting parties," replied: "When
the proper officer examines the recruits, he almost invariably rejects five out of ten of the manufacturing classes,
whilst of the agricultural he scarcely rejects one out of

ten." Dr Bowring asked, "Why continue in this course of helpless legislation? Why struggle, perpetually, to maintain a state of things which the common interest overthrows? What is the use of laws to which you cannot give effect?" Mr Hindley answered, "Certain gentlemen, averse to any legislation, finding they could not prevent a law, have studiously contrived to make it ineffective, in the hope of inducing the house eventually to reject legislation on the subject." Mr John Fielden reminded the house that, on a recent occasion, the political economists had said: "It would not signify if England did not grow a bushel of wheat or barley, so prosperous were manufactures, and so completely were we independent of land; and yet, according to these same political economists, we cannot go on, in manufactures, without working those poor little children for twelve hours a day. That is our prosperity!" The government were anxious to escape from the operation of their own law: the Ten Hours' Bill men were resolved to bind the government to it, in the hope that they might ultimately consent to an efficient measure of regulation; the government having been in so small a majority, felt their success to be, in fact, equal to a defeat, and resolved that the law should take its course. This resolution was, to the opponents of the Ten Hours' Bill, unsatisfactory, and left them and the government in an unpleasant dilemma.

CHAPTER VI.

THE REV J. R. STEPHENS, HIS PRINCIPLES, ELOQUENCE, TALENT, AND GREAT POPULARITY AS " A POLITICAL PREACHER," IN 1838 AND 39.

JOSEPH RAYNER STEPHENS is a name familiar to the ears of all the working men in the manufacturing districts of Lancashire and Yorkshire. Mr Stephens is a man of small stature but of great power ; he is more than a man of talent and acquirements ; he is a man of genius, and possesses the art of reaching and quickening the hearts of others. Mr Stephens began the active duties of life as a Wesleyan Methodist minister, and was, twenty-five years ago, looked up to among his ministerial and lay brethren as " a young man of great promise." It could not be otherwise, for he was gifted with all the requisites of a popular preacher. Mr Stephens's connection with the Wesleyan body was not of long duration.

Whoever can and will, in his own active labours, unite the theologian and politician, and become, as did Mr Stephens, " a political preacher," will, in times of political excitement, increase his popularity and the means at his command for good or for evil. The phrase, " political preacher," is now a term of opprobrium. Without desiring to discuss the abstract question—" What are the proper duties of the ministry in the pulpit ? "—we are reminded that the greatest preachers the Church of England has known have made continual reference to the duties of the *rulers and the ruled.* At the head of the list stand the names of Bishop Latimer and John Wesley.

The centre of Mr Stephens's labours was Ashton-under-Line and district. In 1838 and 1839, he travelled from the Tyne to the Thames as occasion required, and preached in the open air, sometimes thrice on a Sunday, to audiences numbering from five to twenty thousand, speaking at each service from one to three hours, travelling during the week and attending public meetings, at which he was the leading orator. It was calculated by Dr Franklin, that Whitfield, the greatest out-of-doors travelling preacher of his day, might be clearly understood in the open air by 20,000 persons. Mr Stephens has been distinctly heard, on several occasions, by as great a number. The sources of his influence as a political preacher were various. He was an orator, a logician, and knew how to appeal to the affections of the poor. It was his habit to raise himself, step by step, to an altitude of reasoning which all could see ; he would then strike out in bold and homely Saxon against his opponents ; depict in thrilling words the sufferings of the oppressed, and having pointed to the victims, he would appeal to the affections of the heart, asking, " If the poor had not feelings, sympathies, and love for their kind and country ? " Mr Stephens was never more thoroughly " at home " than when talking of the gambols of children, the affections of mothers, the duties of manhood; by appealing to the innermost workings of the heart of each, he concentrated the sympathies of all. He received power from, as well as gave force to, the thousands of human beings, to whose hearts his words were welcome messengers of reproof and hope. This is the case with every really popular speaker ; hence the failure of the best possible reports of speeches to convey the electric influence which bound audience and orator. Few truer words have been penned than those of Hooker—"He that goeth about to persuade a multitude that they are not so well governed as they ought to be, shall never want attentive and favourable hearers, because they know the manifold defects whereunto every kind of regiment is subject; but the secret lets and difficulties, which in public proceedings are innumerable and inevitable, they have not ordinarily the judgment to consider. And because such as openly reprove supposed disorders of state, are taken for principal friends to the common benefit of all, and for men who carry singular freedom of mind; under this fair and plausible colour, whatsoever they utter passeth for good and current. That which wanteth in the weight of their speech is supplied by the aptness of men's minds to accept and believe it." Mr Stephens possessed the faculties which in action could not fail to give to the side he espoused increased influence; but he was, for the reason stated by Hooker, more popular than he would have been had he been the supporter of government, yet, surely, he advocated no measure for popularity's sake, for no man has greater moral courage, or knows better how to bear neglect or slander, or can laugh more heartily at the venom of personal or party sarcasm. It is due to truth to say that few men can more boldly oppose a multitude, when he believes them to be in error. The religious and political tenets of Mr Stephens were thus sketched by himself before his congregation in Ashton-under-Line, in a new year's day address in 1839— they are substantially a summary of his preaching and teaching :—" I exhort you, my brethren, again to possess your souls in patience in reference to everything that concerns you now, and that awaits you in time to come—everything, especially, that relates to your enthralled and unhappy country at this eventful crisis in her social and religious history. I know how the heart of her children heaves with the flutterings of a new-born hope, and again sinks down burdened with a dark despair. But be patient, brethren, ye have need of patience ;

for, rest assured, the year on which you have just entered will not only be the trying year, but the telling year of England's future destinies. The battle which we are now fighting, from one end of England to the other, is not the battle which most men take it to be. It goes much further— it runs much deeper than most men have yet supposed it to do. It is not a battle of party against party for the time being. It is not a struggle for power or for place among men who, for the moment, are placed in antagonistic relation to each other. Much less is it a war of words—a mere strife between unthinking men about trifling points of faith, the idle theories, the dry abstractions, or the circumstantial —secondary relations of acknowledged law when applied to practice. No. It is the question of law or no law—order or anarchy—religion or infidelity—heaven-sprung truth and peace and love ; or hell-born, withering atheism. It is the working of the mystery mentioned in the Holy Scripture —the mystery of ungodliness—the battle directly, though not ostensibly—the struggle actually, though not openly avowed—the life and death struggle of Christ in his spirit, and through his spirit in his followers, against Belial in his spirit, and through his spirit in his children. It is the battle between God and Mammon—between Christ and Beelzebub, the prince of the devils. The question is whether God shall reign in England, or whether Satan shall domineer—the question is, whether the laws of Heaven and its institutions of mercy are to be the laws of a Christian land, and the institutions of a Christian people ; or whether laws begotten below, and born here on earth, are to be the laws and institutions to which a once Christian land and a once Christian people are to be compelled to submit. It is the battle, my brethren, of this book (the Bible) against the men of the world and against hell. If this book stand, they fall. If this book fall, great will be the temporary fall of the house of God, and you will be buried in its ruins.

The lists are drawn—the battle is set—the field is pitched—
deadly will be the struggle; and who is able—who feels
himself willing to enter into that warfare? Pray God that
He would teach your hands to war and your fingers to
fight.

"I am well aware, my brethren, that I have long been
charged—indeed, have always been charged, with a devia-
tion—a positive departure from the line of duty prescribed
to the profession, of which I am an unworthy member,
though I trust an upright, a sincere and a devoted one It
is said that I have dishonoured and desecrated that holy
office, by neglecting the purely religious and exclusively
spiritual claims, which the church has made upon the
time, the talents, and the influence of her ministers—by
postponing the discussion of abstract doctrines, the tenets
of a metaphysically reasoned system of theology—or the
admitted articles of a settled and established orthodoxy—
and instead of this, or before this, or along with this,—
insisting on the obligation the whole Christian world is
under to carry into actual, visible, immediate practice the
plain precepts of that religion—whose first and last, and
only law on earth is, that we should love our neighbour
as ourself—doing unto others as we would they should do to
us. It has been my practice, and been charged upon me
as a crime—to apply the rules of God's commandments
to various institutions of the social system, in my own
immediate neighbourhood, and in the country at large—
to bring the principles and operations of the manufactures,
the commerce, and the legislation of this professedly Christian
land to the standard of God's holy word,—the law of the
Creator,—the witness-bearer of his mind and will to man.
I have asked whether merchants, senators, and statesmen
are amenable to any authority higher than themselves,
or whether they are free to do what their own thirst for
gold or lust of power may lead them to attempt to execute

upon the poor—the weak—the unfriended and defenceless portions of the community. I have asked whether all rights are not reciprocal—all duties relative—all privileges mutual—held together by all in the holy bonds of righteousness and love; whether there be not some given, acknowledged, and universally admitted standard of truth and untruth; right and wrong—good and evil;—whether the standard be not the written word of God—whether the God by whom that word was written be not the one lawgiver,—the King of kings, the Lord of lords, the only ruler of princes? If it be so—and that there is none will gainsay,—I have gone on to inquire whether the practices of the factory system, for instance, are in accordance with the precepts of our most holy religion,—whether Christian millowners are justified in pursuing a system of manufacture, which has done more to injure the health,—impair the constitution,—and demoralize the character of a vast mass of our population, than any other recorded in history,—which has made such a fearful waste of the natural, the social, and the moral life of our industrious countrymen, that it has become a question—not only whether the silken ties, that should bind society in love, can any longer hold her various members within its soft and peaceful circle; but whether the race itself,—the human breed, be not so far degenerate as to threaten imbecility, idiotcy, or actual extinction to a most extensive and alarming degree? I have asked, especially, whether the principles of our modern political economy can be made to quadrate with the statements of divine revelation,—whether it be indeed true that the earth is too small for its inhabitants,—whether the beings born into the world are indeed too many, or multiply too fast for its harvests—the production of its husbandry and the supplies that lie hidden in the mysterious storehouses of the great Creator of heaven and earth—whether to keep down the population of a Christian country be in accordance with the commandments of that Father in heaven, who made man at first in his own likeness—a being of knowledge and righteousness,—who loved him from the beginning, and sent his Son to seek the lost and raise the fallen, to whose eye all the springs of action in man were open and uncovered. who had not to learn from another what man was, and what he was not,—what he knew and what he did not know,— what he could do and what he could not do,—where and how he could settle in his wanderings,—where and how he would have to live and move, and have his being here upon earth, during his progress through the world of men and things seen to the author of beings and of things as yet unseen, I have asserted that the God and Father of mankind has in His wisdom and of His great goodness written out His will to man in this holy book, the Bible. That will makes fully known to man all he has to learn—all he has to trust in— all he has to do in the many and varied relations in which he may be placed in reference to his fellow-men. His duties all rising from one spring, flow into different channels, as the case may be. As a child the bend of duty is to father and mother—as one of other children to brethren—as husband or wife to wedded mate—as householder or master to those that are around or near him—as a son of the soil— a child of his fatherland, the drift of duty is to the over-head, the Father King, whose law of love, the image transcript and impression of the will of heaven, gives equal shelter and protection to all the members of the common-wealth—as monarch or magistrate the drift of duty is as direct and as strong towards the governed for their good and happiness as is the homage of the subject towards the liege lord,—the lawful, because the righteous sovereign of a loyal and obedient, because a happy and prosperous people. I have argued that to the holding of an even beam, the weight of reciprocal obligation must correspond in either scale. If one, no matter which of them preponderate, the equilibrium is lost—the balance of society is destroyed. This idea of the harmony subsisting between the various branches of the great national family I have found in the word of the Lord, the only book in the world that has upon its pages—and communicates to all men, everywhere alike, the immutable principles of truth and righteousness and love. Seeing this to be the truth taught us by God, I have striven to teach it to my fellow-men—for of what use are the principles of moral science, unless they be applied to the actual circumstances of the individuals, before whom they are set forth—and be morally brought out into the practice of their lives ?" This was a groundwork sufficiently broad to give good standing-room for an able and efficient preacher, who knew how to make special applications of texts against refractory and greedy millowners, and the propagators of Malthusian poor laws. What Mr Stephens' political principles were, was, for long, a matter of uncertainty; he was not prone to be explicit, and preferred, in politics, to enjoy the advantages, and bear with the disadvantages of mystery. In all speeches and sermons of Mr Stephens, factory labour and poor laws, were favourite topics; he often invoked the power of God on " the side of the oppressed, and against the oppressor." It was impossible that a public man of Stephens' mark could continue his career unchecked; he was attacked and denounced in 1838 by the radicals of several localities; to these attacks he issued an explanatory reply.

CHAPTER VII.

PLEDGE OF THE GOVERNMENT TO COMPEL OBEDIENCE TO THE FAC-
TORIES' REGULATION ACT.—REFUSAL OF MAGISTRATES TO ENFORCE
THE LAW.—DETERMINATION OF MR OASTLER TO INSURE OBEDIENCE,
HIS THREAT OF "THE LAW OR THE NEEDLE."—IMPORTANT PUB-
LIC MEETINGS FOR THE TEN HOURS' BILL.—SPEECH OF MR
STEPHENS AT OLDHAM, 1836.

THE nominal victory of the government was practically a
defeat ; they felt it to be so, and resolved to allow the
Factory Act to remain in force. On June 23rd, 1836,
Mr Charles Hindley, in the House of Commons, "moved
for leave to bring in a bill, to amend the present Factory
Act." The motion of the member for Ashton was received by the house with surprise, but it served the
useful purpose of wringing from an unwilling government,
a direct and distinct pledge that the existing law should
be enforced, with all the authority at its command, and
also an acknowledgment from the lips of Lord John
Russell, that the introduction of a new bill on the subject would render the efforts of the government, to carry
the law into effect, inoperative. None knew better than
his lordship the difficulty of enforcing the Factory Act;
in not a few instances, the same persons were millowners,
magistrates, and opponents to all factory legislation. In
the theory of the British constitution, the legislative and
executive branches are separate; the more complete the

correspondence between the theory and the practice, the better for Queen and subjects. Experience has very fully proved in the factory districts of Lancashire, that magistrates have refused to enforce the law, when opposed to their own desires and what they believed to be their own interests; the prevalence of so dangerous a procedure is highly culpable, and is, to whatever extent practised, tyrannical. The pledge of Lord John Russell that the Government Factories' Act should be enforced was very important. Mr Hindley, finding the feeling of parliament favourable to a further trial of "the experimental act," and hostile to further legislation on the subject, withdrew his motion.

The various short-time committees were pleased with their position and prospects. They had gained a victory, proved to themselves and to others their power in the legislature, now that the government had undertaken the responsibility of enforcing an Act, which operatives and millowners believed to be impracticable; the former resolved to persevere in their demands for a Ten Hours' Act, hoping to profit from the difficulties of their employers and the government. "The united delegates from the factory districts" issued an address to their constituents, setting forth in glowing terms the struggles which had been undergone, in the hope of gaining a Ten Hours' Bill. "For nearly half a century," said the united delegates, "it has been officially declared that the factory system is committing a continuous and increasing crime against mankind—inflicting sure and certain DEATH, on those who have been drawn, and are compelled to continue, within its widely-extended vortex. It has been charged with wholesale murder; with the actual, though gradual, slaughter of free-born Englishmen, women, and their children. It has been proved to occasion the death of more of our fellow-countrymen under twenty years of age, wherever its influence has prevailed, than in ordinary circumstances under forty. And more than all this, if more be necessary and must be told, it has succeeded in so far drying up the springs of natural affection, and perverting the very instincts of the human heart, that its selfish and insatiable abettors assert, with an air of confidence and triumph, that fathers and mothers are everywhere to be found in plenty, who are willing, eager, and importunate, to offer their own children to a toil of fifteen hours a day, at the price of a few paltry shillings at the end of such a week's work—as neither felon, transport, nor slave was ever known to perform. It has occasioned this awful change in the *natural* character—the change it has wrought in the moral character we cannot, dare not, trust ourselves to depict. But *you* know it—for unhappily you are first the unwary dupes, then the unwilling slaves, and at length the pitiable victims of a system, which, for the perpetration of wrong, and the infliction of misery, has no parallel in the annals of the human race. You are denounced as a dissolute and a degraded people— ignorant, dissatisfied, and refractory—not worthy to be entrusted even with the time necessary for recreation and repose, and only fit for a drudgery, which barely leaves you one hour out of the twenty-four, for all the higher duties and nobler avocations of life. Having first reduced you to the most abject condition to which man can be brought, the wealthy masters of the mill become the base calumniators of those, whose misery, wretched-ness, and crime, are chiefly chargeable upon themselves. You have bent your shoulders at their bidding, and they have not been slow to heap on the burden. But the load has grown too heavy to be borne. It must, and shall be shaken off. You can stand it no longer, and there is no reason why you should. There are many reasons, and very good reasons too, why you should *not*. Forbearance, once a virtue—and nobly you have displayed it—has now become a crime. Rise up to your work, and rouse yourselves for action. We, your delegates, have done our duty. We have listened to no overture, accepted no compromise—and made no surrender. We have told one and the same tale always, and everywhere. We have demanded in your name, and on your behalf, a good and effective Ten Hours' Bill for all your children, and, consequently, for yourselves—the restriction being laid on the moving power. We have succeeded in beating back the insidious advances of Poulett Thomson, intended only to be the prelude of a series of still further encroachments and aggressions upon the residue of your too often, and too much diminished rights. We have come back victorious in this, in spite of open foes and rotten friends—ministers, masters, tyrant tories, pretended reformers, treacherous allies, and immoderate enemies, have opposed their united strength in vain. But we have *not* got, and they say we shall never have the Ten Hours' Bill. We say we will either have *that*, or something else, a great deal *more*, and a good deal *better*—and what say *you?*" The "something better," referred to was expressed in a resolution of the central committee, asking the factory operatives to offer to their opponents the alternative of the adults ceasing to work with the children at the close of eight hours, or the parliament enacting a ten hours' factory law. An alternative clearly impracticable; anything short of law would have failed to produce uniformity in the hours of labour in factories, but the resolution and the address bear evidence to the earnestness and determination of the factory operatives.

This address was received with approval. Public and delegates' meetings were held, and the organisation for the purposes of watching the operation of the Act, and moving public opinion on the question, remained in full force.

A circumstance occurred near to this time which caused

much commotion, and has been a source of some misapprehension, in and out of parliament; it has to the principal actor, from opponents, been a cause of abuse and condemnation. The facts were as follow: Mr Oastler was, by the Short-time Committee of Blackburn, invited to that town for the purpose of addressing a meeting to be held in the theatre, on the 15th of September, 1836, on the factory question. Notwithstanding the pledge of the government that the then existing Factory Act should be enforced, on Mr Oastler's arrival in Blackburn he was informed by the Short time Committee, " that a few days ago the magistrates at Blackburn, in reply to a complaint under the factory law, had from the bench been refused a hearing. At the same time they declared, 'Oh, that is Oastler's law; we have nothing to do with it; take your complaints to him,' thus dismissing the complainants." Having ascertained the truth of that statement, Mr Oastler went to the public meeting in the theatre. It was crowded; in one of the boxes to his left sat those magistrates and several millowners known as opponents to the law; they were pointed out to Mr Oastler, who, in the course of his address, directed his observations to that portion of his audience. He told them, as above stated, what he had heard, and pointedly asked them, " Is that true? " They were silent, and laughed at the speaker. Many voices shouted, " It is true; they know it," and so forth. After these interruptions had subsided, Mr Oastler spoke to the magistrates to the following effect—"Your silence, after my public appeal to you, and after the declarations of your neighbours in your hearing, convinces me that I have not been misinformed. You say that the law is mine; I say that it is the law of the land which you have sworn to enforce. If you do not regard your oaths, and if the King of England has not the power to enforce the law, why, then, it becomes my duty to explain in your hearing how you stand before the law. You are regardless of your oaths, you are persons holding property, your only title being the law of the land. Now, if the law of the land, intended to protect the lives of the factory children, is to be disregarded, and there is to be no power to enforce it; it becomes my duty, as the guardian of the factory children, to enquire whether, in the eye of the law of England, their lives or your spindles are most entitled to the law's protection. If the King has not the power to enforce the factory law, I must and I will strive to force even you to enforce that law." Then, turning to the audience, Mr Oastler said, "If, after this, your magistrates should refuse to listen to your complaints under the factory act, and again refer you to me, bring with you your children, and tell them to ask their grandmothers for a few of their old knitting-needles, which I will instruct them how to apply to the spindles in a way which will teach these law-defying, mill-owner magistrates to have respect even to 'Oastler's law,' as they have wrongly designated the factory law."

Mr Oastler followed up this declaration with a series of observations on the necessity of obedience to the law; assuring his hearers that his threat should remain on record, and urging the magistrates and millowners to consider their own responsibilities, and beware of disobeying the law.

The Blackburn newspapers contained an imperfect condensation of Mr Oastler's address, from which the *Manchester Guardian* selected a few lines containing Mr Oastler's threat, but entirely omitted any reference to the conduct of the magistrates, of which Mr Oastler complained. The editor appended to the obnoxious paragraph a series of animadversions on the character of Mr Oastler. He replied to the remarks of the editor and defended himself. The editor inserted Mr Oastler's defence, and appended thereto the editor's own remarks, to which Mr Oastler replied—that reply having been refused insertion, Mr Oastler felt it necessary to publish the whole correspondence in a pamphlet entitled *The Law or the Needle,* which, when published, caused a great sensation. The principle maintained by Mr Oastler and plainly stated in his speech, was simply this—The lives of the factory children were as much entitled to protection under the law as the property of their employers ; if the latter defied the law passed expressly to protect the lives of the factory children, and the government failed to enforce the law, then, the question was, made by the magistrates themselves, one of power between the contending parties; and it became the duty of the factory children to use every possible and necessary agency at their command in their own defence, in support of their lives and the law, and against the law-breakers, for, as Mr Oastler pithily observed—" Where there is no law there is no property."

Towards the close of 1836, several important public meetings were held, principally to encourage the operatives to be vigilant in their efforts to secure obedience to the law, and to show the advantages of a ten hours' bill. One of the most important of these gatherings was at Oldham; the principal speakers were the late Mr John Fielden, one of the members representing that borough in parliament, Mr Charles Hindley, M.P. for Ashton, Mr Oastler, and Mr Stephens. At this meeting grave complaints were made of the conduct of certain magistrates failing to enforce the law. On the question of the improvement in machinery, Mr Fielden stated that he had recently made a calculation of the increased power of manufacturing production, and discovered that ten persons could in 1836 produce as much cloth as one hundred persons could have done in 1796, yet then they had the carding engine, the roving billy, and spinning jenny. If he were to revert to the time of carding by hand upon stocks, and spinning upon one spindle, the increase of the powers of production had no doubt been an hundred-fold. On this occasion Mr Fielden expressed his opinion

on the relations of employers and employed; he maintained that it was "the duty of employers, whether for operations on land, or with the jenny and the shuttle, to take care that the labourers were well fed, clothed, and sheltered, in consideration of moderate labour." At this meeting the question of foreign competition in its connection with the hours of labour was fully considered; the opinions of the speakers are expressed in the subjoined proposition—"Whatever contributes to lower prices between rival manufacturers at home, contributes to increase foreign competition; long hours of labour contribute to lower prices in the home market, and, for that reason, to increase foreign competition." The soundness of this proposition rested upon the fact that foreign competitors in the branches of manufacture, under the operation of factory law, adjusted their prices to the scale of those of British manufacturers. It was maintained, that foreign trade was barter, and the profit to England depended upon the relative quantity and quality of the articles exchanged; that the effect of low prices was to increase the quantity exported, without increasing, in a like proportion, the quantity imported; that long hours of labour reduced prices to the injury of the home producer, and the benefit of the foreign consumer; that to reduce and regulate the hours of labour would tend to increase the value of British produce given in exchange for foreign commodities. This argument was based upon Mr Fielden's practical experience in trade, and after mature consideration pronounced by Mr Hindley to be sound. Mr Hindley's words were :—
"The natural and necessary consequence of a limitation of hours would be to lessen the quantity of goods produced, and lead to a rise in the prices of commodities. A restriction of products advanced the prices of the most material article of our exports; a corresponding rise in the value of imports would ensue, and the effects of the higher value of commodities would fall on the whole people. On these grounds

it was just to conclude that a diminution of the time of working would be a benefit to the operatives."

The most remarkable speech was that of Mr Stephens. Alluding to Mr Hindley the speaker said :—" As the honourable member has declared that on this question he will know neither rich nor poor, neither friend nor foe, I wish to call his attention to the facts I have stated, all of which have transpired in his immediate neighbourhood. Here is a key [Mr Stephens exhibited a house-key] which the millowner compels the operative spinner to receive, so soon as he enters the millowner's employ, and for which he deducts three shillings or three shillings and sixpence a week from this operative's wages, no matter whether he be married or single, householder or lodger. If he be in lodgings, so much the better for the master, who then gives him the key of a house already tenanted, by which means he receives two and sometimes three rents at the one and the same time. Now this practice is notorious. But where is there a man of station and influence who is bold enough to expose it and denounce it as it deserves." The above extract makes known a discreditable means of acquiring riches, and one which, at the time referred to, was frequent, and well deserved the exposure it received at the hands of Mr Stephens.

Mr Oastler, in a speech delivered with much solemnity, took occasion to revert to the new phase in the movement caused by the declaration of the Blackburn magistrates, " that they would not regard the factory law," and warned those law-defying magistrates of their danger, should they persist in their illegal course. Mr Fielden said, in reference thereto,—" Mr Oastler had pointedly put the question, ' What were the people to do when the laws cease to exist?' When laws were set at nought, they might be said to have ceased to be ; and the best constitutional writers had told us, that when laws were disregarded and oppression was carried to an extent not to be endured, it was right that resistance should ensue, and resistance, at such a period, became a virtue."

The reports of the meetings on the factory question had the average circulation in newspapers, and were usually published in pamphlets or placards, and circulated in great numbers; copies were forwarded to all the more active public men of the time, without distinction of creed or party. Mr Oastler's pen was in constant use, and many letters written by him on the question were widely circulated. His talent and money were applied without reservation to what, in his own words, was then the object of his life,— "the release of the factory operatives from bondage." The constant use of the press was a powerful lever, and could not fail ultimately to produce a change.

CHAPTER VIII.

IT is said that Coleridge, whose opposition to many modern propositions was no secret, when on one occasion strongly pressed by a political economist of the Benthamite school, on the "dangerous tendencies" of the opinions the philosophical poet had maintained in conversation, answered his opponent by taking up the down of a thistle which lay by the roadside, " and holding it up, said, after observing the direction in which it was borne by the wind: the tendency of that thistle is towards China, but I know with assured certainty that it will never get there; nay, that it is more than probable that, after sundry eddyings and gyrations up and down, backwards and forwards, that it will be found somewhere near the place in which it grew." We have been frequently reminded of this interesting incident, when observing the pertinacity with which theorists maintain their favourite tenets, and enlarge with copious eloquence on the dangerous tendency of measures, which, in themselves, are by those in want of them, felt to be undeniably necessary. The necessity for further legislation for factories had been so fully demonstrated, that objectors were forced to lay aside their former pleas in opposition, and take refuge in an exposition of the dangerous tendency of such legislation. On this head they were indeed verbose and energetic, they too were, as usual, prophetic, and foretold the most calamitous results, which, on their authority, were certain to overtake the unfortunate factory workers, who, in their ignorance, had invoked the protection of the legislature. The factory workers, with what, in the eyes of their prophetic opponents, appeared to be a perverse blindness, clung to their favourite Ten Hours' Bill, and believed that it would, in practice, all tendencies notwithstanding, settle down somewhere near to where it had originated, and contribute, as intended by its promoters, towards the improvement of all practically employed in factory labour.

Dean Swift, in his imaginary travels, has been careful to impress on his readers, the folly and danger of relying too confidently on the authority of those who assume to be, beyond all others, " scientific statesmen." When Gulliver was among the practical Lilliputians, and in want of garments, by a very simple process of measurement and the help of an old shirt, they succeeded in fitting him exactly. When the renowned traveller was cast among the learned and abstruse Laputans, whose whole time was devoted to a consideration of tendencies and abstract principles, " passionately disputing every inch of a party opinion," he was again in want of the tailor's assistance. " Those," says he, " to whom the king had entrusted me, observing how ill I was clad, ordered a tailor to come next morning, and take measure for a suit of clothes. This operator did his office after a different manner from those of his trade in Europe. He first took my latitude by a quadrant, and then, with rule and compasses, described the dimensions and outlines of my whole body, all of which he entered upon paper; and in six days brought my clothes very ill made, and quite out of shape, by happening to mistake a figure in the calculation." The factory operatives were in like condition. They had been legislated for after the most approved fashion, they had been measured by

gentlemen sent from Downing street on purpose, in defiance
of all expostulations, the garments had been made, but as
even more than one figure had been mistaken in the
calculation, they were felt, in wear, to be troublesome and
vexatious. The operatives and their friends were by no
means satisfied with the alternative of " Be content with
what you have, or go naked," they believed that they
were good judges of the troubles they endured, and were
enabled to point out some of the mistakes which the
somewhat pretentious mathematical tailors had committed.

In modern politics, compromise is the order of the day.
When there exists on a public question of interest considerable dissatisfaction, and the opposing parties are strenuous
and energetic, there usually arises a party anxious for a
settlement, and prepared to recommend " a middle course."
The idea of moderation is agreeable to the minds of
many, and concession is regarded as being so amiable
and desirable, that to be stubborn is, in many circles, considered to be fitting ground for political excommunication.
The most popular statesman of the age built his reputation
on concessions; the late Sir Robert Peel, when nominally
a tory, was dearer to the liberals than to his own followers;
his concessions were so many and important that the
amiable politician recruited his party by agreeable accommodation, and conciliated his opponents by doing their work
more rapidly and efficiently than it was in their power to
do it for themselves. In all the leading questions of his
age, the late Sir Robert Peel was the highest practical
authority on both sides. Now against Catholic Emancipation,
Reform in Parliament, and Free Trade, then for Catholic Emancipation, Reform in Parliament, and Free Trade, no other captain
knew so well how to trim his sails to the wind : the merits
of concession were measured by the obstinacy of former
opposition, and the anxiety of the popular party for success.
Every successful man, no matter in what position of life,

has a host of imitators. Does a quack doctor grow rich by filling coffins, then, there is a brood of the same species busy in every village, the more talented and ambitious become *professional*, the humbler sort work on in the peddling way most congenial to their habits. Does an expert politician ruin fame and confidence by acting in the spirit of compromise, then all the smaller fry ape him in his practice. Have you an energetic Irishman, ripe and ready in eloquence and repartee, devoting respectable talents to continuous agitation, then, you will have in almost every parish a mimic orator, but possessing neither the honesty, the talent, nor singleness of purpose of the original. Does a poet of great power and striking faculties of illustration arise, then, all the little fledglings begin to chirp after the like fashion, and some among the little critics praise the imitators almost indiscriminately. Imitation is an epidemic ; once begun, it runs its course, obeys the same laws irrespective of class; it is practically the same from emperors to beggars, in the age of witchcraft and in that of steam; and knows no limit, from the search for the philosopher's stone to a sincere belief in spirit-rapping. In politics, it is apt to become extravagant and useless by flattering vanity to its bent, and encouraging the meretricious rather than the modest and useful talents of ordinary men.

On the 9th of November, 1837, a public meeting was held in the Court House, Leeds, intended, by its promoters, to settle the factory question by a compromise in favour of an eleven hours' bill. In a question so thoroughly agitated as had been factory regulation, it was by the supporters of the compromise felt to be necessary to try to win public favour, otherwise there could not be entertained any reasonable hopes for success. The meeting was called at two o'clock, a most inconvenient hour for working-men ; the only notice having been a brief advertisement in the columns of the *Leeds Mercury,* and a few small bills posted in Leeds.

Between the publication of the *Mercury* and the time of
meeting, there were four days. So alive were the factory
workers to their interests, so complete their organization,
that though the notice of meeting had been limited and
obscure, by two o'clock on Thursday the 9th, the day for
which the meeting was called, the Leeds Court House
was crowded to excess, and delegates were present from
every manufacturing town in Yorkshire and most towns
in Lancashire. The Mayor occupied the chair. Mr Wrigglesworth, of Leeds, introduced the principal proposition to
be considered, in the form of a resolution for an eleven
hours' bill. Mr Wrigglesworth stated that the existing
law was unsatisfactory, and that the interests of masters
and workmen would be promoted by an eleven hours' bill.
Mr Joshua Hobson, of Leeds, met the resolution of Mr
Wrigglesworth by an amendment, deprecating any change
in the existing law, beyond the limitation of the working
hours of young persons to ten per day. The attention of
the meeting was intense,—each man seemed to feel that an
important moment had arrived. The Rev. Mr Stephens
rose to address the meeting—he was received with approbation.
This speech is a complete study of the kind of eloquence
of which he was master. He regretted the mournful truth
that the workman and his employer had been in conflict,
which he hoped would be changed to concert. He raised
the meeting in importance, seized aptly on all the circumstances of weight, and arrayed them in their order. He
maintained that the meeting was a conference of millowers,
overlookers, and operatives to deliberate on the interests of
all, that their decision would instruct the members representing
the borough in parliament, these the legislature, and ultimately affect the law. Thus far, all was conciliation; the
astute orator hinted at the short notice calling the assembly—
"Some might have thought it advisable in those calling
this meeting, to publish their call in the leading journals

of the country; this might have been considered necessary
in ordinary cases and on ordinary subjects; but it would
appear that when the people of Leeds came to consider
the subject, it was deemed by them one of that kind that
would be communicated with the rapidity of the whirlwind
or lightning through every part of the empire; that
they thought it merely necessary to whisper in Leeds,
that the meeting would be holden, when the four
winds of heaven would carry that whisper to the remotest
part of the country, and as they carried it, would cause
it to swell like the rolling peal of thunder before it reached
its termination in the final crash. I am happy to inform
you that such has been the case. I am not complaining
of the omission, for the address has accomplished *more than
its intention!*" Mr Stephens described the effect of the
address in his own district. All felt how momentous was
the question to be decided. He then appealed to the nature
of the evidence already known on the subject of factory
labour; showed that the proposition of the promoters of
that meeting was opposed to known and oft-corroborated
evidence; and to work children to the certain injury of
their health, he denounced as being " political, social, moral,
and physical murder." He continued :—" The cause which
has brought us together, is the fact that the monster, steam
power, in the hands of its brother monster, capital, enables
the capitalist to dictate to his workman, the latter not being
a voluntary agent in the transaction—how many hours he
shall work—which enables the capitalist to dictate what
wages the workman shall take; which enables him, by a
combination with other capitalists, to depress the energies
of industry, to throw the chains of bondage around the
necks of human beings, and to bring millions of Englishmen
to accept, at their hands, just so much time for reading, and
eating, and sleeping, and recreation, and just so much wages
as they choose to allow, and all this is the result of a simple

combination of steam power, and money power, with human power. This is the question which must be met to-day in such a manner as for ever to preclude the necessity of further parliamentary interference. This we are convinced can alone be done by considering this question as one of humanity— as one which involves every principle of morality and religion —and after it has been thus considered, to base upon the premises thus laid down such a superstructure as to produce harmony and peace, reconciliation and happiness amongst all classes of the community." From this foundation Mr Stephens continued to address his hearers at great length, dexterously introducing every popular topic connected with the actual condition of the working-man, and likely to tell with effect against the Malthusian and free-trade political economists; rising with the impetuous feeling which he poured into the meeting, as from an ever-flowing spring, he impersonated their wrongs, their rights, their sympathies, and resolution, declaring that " before children eight years of age shall be allowed to go into a factory for the purpose of unnatural and killing labour, before they shall cross the threshold of a mill to be murdered, the door-posts shall come down ! Before they shall enter underneath the roof, the roof shall be untopped, and the walls themselves shall be levelled with the foundations." To talk of compromise, to men of the temper, resolution, and eloquence of Mr Stephens was absurd; they had resolved on victory, and would turn neither to the left nor the right. The amendment for a Ten Hours' Bill was declared carried by a decided majority. Mr Stephens' reputation for violence and control over the masses was enhanced among the Yorkshire millowners. Mr Baines, M.P. for Leeds, and the government were very distinctly informed that only one measure would satisfy the factory operatives ; with a continuous disregard for the ' dangerous tendency of restrictive legislation," they were resolved on obtaining from parliament a Ten Hours' Act.

In the course of the proceedings the Mayor, because of other important business, vacated the chair, which was subsequently occupied by Mr Baines, who, on behalf of the meeting, signed petitions, one to each house of parliament, and founded on the resolution in support of the Ten Hours' Bill. One hand only was held up against the adoption of these petitions, a circumstance which proved to demonstration the unanimity of the factory operatives on what, to them, was the question of all others important.

While this was the temper of the factory operatives and their acknowledged leaders, the factory inspectors were in their reports complaining of their inability to enforce the law; the government received the remonstrances of the inspectors, but failed to adopt requisite means to insure obedience. Under the factories' act magistrates had the power to mitigate penalties following conviction. To such an extent was this privilege indulged, that to violate the law was a common and a profitable practice. In the words of one of the factory inspectors, " The disreputable millowner, who is regardless of the discredit of a prosecution for violating the law, solely made for the protection of helpless children, looks only to the amount of penalty imposed on his neighbours, and on casting up the account he discovers that it is far more profitable to disobey than to observe the act,"—a statement fully borne out by the returns of the number of convictions and the fines imposed : thus between May the 1st, 1836, and January the 1st, 1837, there were 822 convictions ; the average of penalties was $2l.$ 5s. The average of penalties for 1837 was $1l.$ 10s., thus exhibiting a rapidly decreasing scale. To break the law was profitable, and to be convicted for its violation was not considered in the least disgraceful among those millowners who opposed factory legislation. The frequent and profitable violation of the Factories' Act was a circumstance used by a portion of the press, which aimed at proving, that all such legislation was absurd, and, in evidence of their proposition, pointed to the inability of the government to command obedience to the law. In the expressive words of Lord Ashley : "Was it then surprising that there should be discontent and dissatisfaction among the operatives in the manufacturing districts, when they saw that the law which had been passed for the protection of young children was daily violated, not only with impunity but also with advantage to the rich, but with tremendous consequences to the poor ? Could parliament be surprised that these men thought that it was inclined to legislate for the richer in opposition to the poorer classes, and that, as a necessary consequence, they held in equal contempt the makers of the law, the administrators of the law, and the law itself ?" Not any words could more correctly express the feelings of the operative classes of the north. It was well for the House of Commons to be thus plainly informed of the result which followed from their own negligence ; the spirit of Mr Oastler, Mr Bull, and Mr Stephens was thus re-echoed in the House of Commons, strengthened indeed and dignified by the position of the speaker, but clearly bearing towards the same end—the necessity for equal justice to all, and the danger to be apprehended from the practice of magistrates and statesmen disregarding the law of the land and the feelings of the poor. There exists at all times, in the minds of those who have no direct power in the enactment of the laws, a latent desire to complain of their partiality in operation which trifling circumstances are apt to warm into active life. A wise and a strong government is careful to prevent, on so delicate a point, unnecessary scandal. The whig government of 1837 was neither wise nor strong ; its promises were large, its performances small ; its vacillation and weakness contributed to bring into disrepute the very foundations of government, and to prepare the way for that outburst of popular discontent in 1839, which only subsided after several severe state prosecutions, the expatriation of some and the incarceration of many of "the democratic leaders of the people."

All this was opposed to the intention of ministers, but it was inseparable from their acts; they hoped to perpetuate their rule by the conciliation of capitalists rather than labourers, an effort at all times dangerous, but hazardous beyond calculation, when followed in violation of the laws of the land, and the spirit of equity. That the whig ministers of 1837 were ignorant of the fatal effects of their own trifling with the factories' act, is no doubt true, but effects follow causes without respect for the blindness of their authors; the spendthrift may in a moment of mental delusion sign away his patrimony, but the folly of the act will not save him from poverty and neglect. The whig government, by pandering to the interests of millowners in violation of the law, loosened the bonds of society, by weakening the regard in the minds of many, for the majesty of the law; the partial and timid conduct of the government in the matter of factory legislation afforded to every one disposed to use it, a ready illustration of the maxim, " The law itself follows gold." There were not wanting those willing agents who knew how to apply that maxim with effect, on the minds of the multitude.

On June the 22nd, 1838, Lord Ashley formally brought the factory question, at the request of the factory operatives, under the notice of the House of Commons, by moving the second reading of the Factories' Regulation Bill as an amendment on a government measure relating to Irish tithes. Lord Ashley charged the government with having deluded him by false promises, with having pledged themselves to bring in an effective measure, and with having failed to redeem their pledges. The government were hardly pressed, in the debate which followed, especially by Sir Robert Peel, who though "not prepared to support the ten hours' clause of his noble friend (Lord Ashley), this he most certainly was prepared to assert, that if the arguments of the right honourable gentleman opposite (Mr Poulett Thomson) were good for anything, they went to show that the factory question was the one subject with which it was the imperative duty of parliament to deal, and without a moment's delay. If the interests of humanity were at stake, then surely no one would say that there ought to be any delay. If the right honourahle gentleman were right, on that ground then did he (Sir Robert Peel) call upon the House of Commons to apply themselves to the question forthwith." The division very distinctly indicated the feeling of the house and the state of parties.

For Lord Ashley's amendment   .   .   . 111
Against it   119
_____
Majority for the Government .   .   8

This defeat of Lord Ashley was almost equivalent to success. It was clear as the sun at noon-day, that to evade the factory question was impossible. The promptitude and activity of his lordship were beyond all praise; certainly not any leader could have done more for his clients than did his lordship. The respect and attention he commanded, in the House of Commons, were outward and visible signs too marked to be misunderstood by ministers ; he renewed his assault against the government by again bringing the factory question under the attention of parliament, on July the 20th.

The speech of Lord Ashley on this occasion was one of the ablest we remember to have heard or read on the factory question. He, from public documents sanctioned by the authority of the factory inspectors, convicted the government either of an unwillingness or inability to insure obedience to the factory act of their own approval. As a masterly array of facts and arguments, his lordship's speech produced great effect in the House of Commons, which was much increased by the speaker's ability to pourtray, from observation in Manchester, the wretched social condition of the factory operatives. At this period, Lord Ashley had made the factory question thoroughly his own; he was in correspondence with millowners and operatives; in brief, men of all ranks and classes, at home and abroad, interested in the factory question, looked up to his lordship as the leader of the ten hours' bill movement; and interest in the factory question had, within a comparatively few years, spread from Fixby Hall and the West Riding of Yorkshire to the closets of thoughtful authors and the minds of enlightened statesmen throughout Europe, an apt illustration of which was brought under the attention of the House of Commons by the noble lord; he said—" The interest which this question excited was not confined to England, it had extended to France, where it had been discussed in the chamber of deputies, and had engaged the eloquent pens of some of the ablest writers of the country—M. Sismondi and others—who had not disdained to support the cause of the helpless children in France and Switzerland. He had received within the last fortnight a communication from France, requesting him to join in a general society to wipe out this blot from the civilization of Christian Europe, in the propriety of which he heartily concurred. He had hoped that this country would have been the first to set the example of such an association, and he felt ashamed that another country, possessing advantages so much inferior, should have anticipated it in setting on foot a general scheme for the amelioration of the condition of infant labourers."

As if to prevent the possibility of any hope of compromise, Lord Ashley assured the house that the question was not in any sense a party question; without regard to political parties, he, and those who supported him, were resolved on success; so flagrant were the violations of the law, so strong the sense of the country in defence

of the rights of humanity, that "if he should hold his
peace, the very stones would immediately cry out;" and
concluded a most convincing and manly speech with an
appeal to the house "to decide whether they would
amend, or repeal, or enforce the Act now in existence;
but if they would do none of these things, if they continued idly indifferent, and obstinately shut their eyes to
this great and growing evil, if they would give no heed
to the fierce and rapid cancer that was gnawing the very
vitals of the social system; if they were careless of the
growth of an immense population, plunged in ignorance
and vice, which neither feared God nor regarded man,
then he warned them that they must be prepared for
the very worst results that could befal an empire. Then
would that great and terrible prophecy have its second
completion—' Amalek was the first of the nations, but
his latter end shall be, that he perish for ever.' The
noble lord concluded by moving a resolution—"That this
house deeply regrets that the law affecting the regulation
of the labour of children in factories, having been found
imperfect, and ineffective to the purpose for which it was
passed, has been suffered to continue so long without any
amendment."

The discussion which followed did not evolve any
material point of importance; the facts of Lord Ashley
were unanswerable, and the opposition was confined to a
repetition of prophecies, resting on the danger of restricting the hours of labour. Among these gloomy prophets
was Mr O'Connell, who, amidst the cheers of the free-
trade political economists, solemnly assured the house, that
under the operation of a Ten Hours' Bill, "the Belgians,
with cheap bread and no corn laws, would undersell
British merchants in the market, Manchester would become
a place of tombs, the children would be turned out of
the factories, and the manufacturers cast on the poor laws."

On a division taking place, the numbers for going into committee of supply were, 121; for Lord Ashley's amendment, 106: majority against the amendment, 15.

The tergiversation of Mr O'Connell on the factory question was the cause of much complaint and dissatisfaction ; certainly Mr O'Connell's speech and vote were directly opposed to all he had said at the London Tavern meeting in 1833. The speech of Lord Ashley, on the contrary, was read with delight; and his words, condemnatory of the conduct of the government, were often quoted with approval, and very materially served to strengthen the disgust of many among the working-men at the discreditable faithlessness and weakness of the ministry, and their evident preference for the millowners over the operatives. His lordship's rank was to him a source of power which, united with popular support, placed him on a pedestal, and which bade fair to elevate him above most of the statesmen of the time. He had spoken in a tone so decided on the duties of government and the relation which existed between the rulers and the ruled, the rich and the poor, as to warrant the hope that at least one statesman would endeavour to identify moral principle and British law. Mr Oastler, Mr Bull, and Mr Stephens were the exponents of the doctrines in the country on law and property, which Lord Ashley communicated to the ear of the House of Commons. This agreement in principle and policy mutually increased the power of all. Mr Oastler said, " Where there is no law there is no property ;" Mr Bull, " The rich and the poor are equal in the eye of God, and ought to be in that of the law ;" Mr Stephens, " He who makes war against the labourer's rights is the enemy of man, and a rebel against the tenth commandment ;" Mr Fielden, " Laws set at nought may be said to have ceased to exist, and resistance then becomes a virtue ;" Lord Ashley, " Could parliament be surprised that the operatives of the manufacturing districts thought that it (the parliament) was inclined to legislate for the richer in opposition to the poorer classes, and that as a necessary consequence they (the operatives) held in equal contempt the makers of the law, the administrators of the law, and the law itself?"

CHAPTER IX.

PROCEEDINGS IN PARLIAMENT IN 1839 AND 1840.—POLITICAL
EXCITEMENT.—POPULAR DISCONTENT.—DISSOLUTION OF THE
HOUSE OF COMMONS.

THE determination and untiring energy of Lord Ashley
had won for him the sincere and enthusiastic approval of
the factory operatives. The whig ministry, of which Lord
Melbourne was the head, possessed, in a remarkable degree,
the unwillingness for action which distinguishes authority
in weak hands. It is reasonable to suppose that it would
be for the welfare of society, and for the honour of ministers,
that they should institute measures because they are
required for the country's good, rather than wait until
public opinion force parliament to legislate. Such, however,
is not the rule, and, consequently, the slow growth of the
ministerial mind on the factory question is not matter of
surprise. It was felt by ministers to be a necessity to make
another effort towards the adjustment of the factory question,
otherwise, Lord Ashley would probably become on that
question supreme, and the opposition would profit from
further ministerial delay.

The year 1839 will be long remembered by the active politicians of this age, and when the history of the present age
shall be faithfully written, that year will be marked as among
the most important of the first half of the present century.

The greater portion of the more active of the working classes, weary of the professions of politicians of the liberal school, and disgusted with their practices, particularly as embodied in the New Poor Law Amendment Act, had betaken themselves to political agitation. Throughout England, Scotland, and Wales public meetings were of frequent occurrence, and the agitation on behalf of *The People's Charter* was rapidly accelerated. That document was the joint production of the late Mr Hume, the late Mr O'Connell, Mr Roebuck, Mr Hindley, and others. A respect for the law has been, in the education of every Englishman, predominant, and the circumstances which could change that respect, even transiently, were not trifling. In the earlier period of the chartist agitation, it was customary to appeal to ancient authority in support of universal or manhood suffrage; latterly this ground was abandoned, and the shibboleth was: " The charter peaceably, if we can; forcibly, if we must." This was the rule, there were very many who were opposed to physical force, but the extreme party were sufficiently numerous and powerful to create very considerable alarm in the minds of ministers. The late Mr Feargus O'Connor, the acknowledged head of the chartist party, was a man of great energy, a rapid and ready speaker, he was in the strength of manhood, and possessed a commanding bearing. He was aristocratic in manner, the descendant of an ancient, honoured, and persecuted Irish family; his influence over the working men was great, and rapidly on the increase. Mr O'Connor had been reared in the school of Irish agitation, and possessed that floating recklessness, which is, in part, inseparable from a political agitator; fed by the events of the hour, he was ambitious of popularity, and not scrupulous as to the sacrifices he made for its attainment. In passing, it is but just to observe that Mr O'Connor's intellect and stores of knowledge, did not improve with his years. When first in the House of Commons he was checked by men at least his equals in talent and knowledge; and he had regard for his standing as a politician and a gentleman. When he became the popular leader of working-men, his popularity gave him the choice of his colleagues, who were, with rare exceptions, subservient to his desires, and to none was his absolutism more injurious than to himself, for not any man stood more thoroughly in need of that kind of training which conflict with equals and superiors can alone give. When Mr O'Connor entered on English agitation, he was far from being a vulgar demagogue; he was among the last of that class of Irish orators who made agitation a business and hatred of the English government a profession; he possessed that kind of oratorical talent necessary for successful platform speech-making, and he seemed to rely on it to serve him on all occasions, and for all purposes; as a writer he was irregular and diffuse, but strong in denunciation, which, with his readers, was the principal commodity in demand. He was frank and bold, and under better training than an anti-tithe agitation in Ireland, and a desultory political warfare in England, might have been, in parliament, a man of mark; to consider-able talent and fine physical power, he inherited from his father, a manly generosity of heart. In 1839, that political agitation of which Mr O'Connor was the head, was the terror of the Melbourne administration, and the absorbent of a deeply-seated discontent. The leaders of the Ten Hours' Bill movement, satisfied with past labours, and deter-mined that their object should stand apart from the political commotion of the time, made no public effort, but continued, with unabated attention, to watch with interest the diffi-culties of the government, so far as factory regulation was concerned. It is noteworthy that at the public meetings in support of *The People's Charter*, the speakers were wont to allude to the New Poor Law, as one of their greatest grievances; they marked the Ten Hours' Bill with their special approbation.

On February 15th, 1839, a Factories' Act Amendment Bill, prepared by the government, was brought under the notice of the House of Commons. On February the 29th, Mr Fox Maule (now Lord Panmure), then Home Secretary, moved the second reading. The proposed alterations were, that no child should work in more than one factory in any one day, additional powers to factory inspectors in checking certificates of age, and increased stringency in granting them ; "any regular surgeon would still be allowed to grant a certificate, but a certificate granted by any other than the regular certifying surgeon, would be of no avail until countersigned by a magistrate, not being a millowner, who should further ascertain the truth of the certificate, and the identity of the child brought before him. The certificate should be given at the factory where the child, or young person, was employed, that the inspector, or sub-inspector, should have the power to annul any certificate, where they had reason to believe that the real age of the child was less than the age specified." It was proposed to abolish the right, on the part of mill-occupiers, to recover lost time, "except where the machinery was moved by water-power, nor even then, except when the loss should arise from the total stoppage of the water-wheel from the want of water." Mr Fox Maule admitted that "the existing schooling clauses were not only inconvenient, but almost entirely useless ;" in the proposed bill, it was suggested that "two hours of each day should be devoted to education."

In the debate which followed, Lord Ashley claimed the measure as a justification of his past efforts. Not any petitions were presented from either masters or work-men, a circumstance so unprecedented in the factory question, as to be subject of remark. On July 1st, Mr Fox Maule moved, " That the house resolve itself into a committee on the Factories' Regulation Bill." In the debate which then followed, some important facts were elicited. The population employed in factories, under the factory law, numbered 419,590, of which, 242,296, or $57\frac{3}{4}$ per cent., were females. The penalties paid under the Act, were stated by the late Mr Brotherton to have been, for the year 1838, 8,300l., and it was notorious that the inspectors could not prevent young children from being overworked. In the government bill, the limit of the age to which its clauses applied, was eighteen; and Mr Brotherton proposed twenty-one, on which amend-ment the ayes were 49; noes, 55. Lord Ashley pro-posed to strike out the words in the bill which excepted silk-mills from its operation : ayes, 69; noes, 58: majority for the amendment, 11. These minorities and majorities show the state of the question in the house. On July 26th, the order of the day for the further consideration of the report on the Factories' Bill having been read, Lord John Russell informed the house, " that in consequence of Lord Ashley having declared his intention of opposing the bill, if it were not extended to silk mills, he, Lord John Russell, had determined to withdraw the bill." This withdrawal of a government measure was an acknowledg-ment of ministerial weakness, and of Lord Ashley's strength in opposition. Lord Ashley had been the leader of the factory question when public meetings in the country, factory dele-gates in London, and numerous petitions to parliament, gave to his efforts encouragement and prestige; he was equally vigilant when there was not a petition in his favour.

The Melbourne administration appeared willing that Lord

Ashley should, to some extent, take the management of the measure. His lordship, without opposition, on March 3rd, 1840, moved—"That a select committee be appointed to inquire into the operation of the act for the regulation of mills and factories, and to report thereon to the house." Mr Hindley seconded the motion, which was agreed to. On August the 4th, Lord Ashley moved—" That an humble address be presented to her Majesty, praying that her Majesty will be graciously pleased to direct an inquiry to be made into the employment of the children of the poorer classes in mines and collieries, and in the various branches of trade and manufacture in which numbers of children work together, not being included in the provisions of the Act for regulating the employment of children and young persons in mills and factories, and to collect information as to the ages at which they are employed, the number of hours they are engaged in work, the time allowed each day for meals, and as to the actual state, condition, and treatment of such children, and as to the effects of such employment, both with regard to their morals and their bodily health." The late Mr Brotherton seconded the motion, which was agreed to.

This resolution is evidence of the advancing influence of Lord Ashley on questions of social importance. While others were busy with a discussion on the forms of government, his lordship was alive to its duties, and was taking the preparatory steps necessary for showing to statesmen the condition of the labouring classes; and practically asking the former, to consider what they could do for the welfare of the multitude. The wisdom of this course was sanctioned by the experience of the times; for, while society was con-. vulsed with political agitation, the facts and arguments used to illustrate what were called "political evils," were, in most cases, connected with the production and distribution of riches; and the questions were constantly asked, "What has civilization done for working men ? What share have they in the improvements of which the talking philosophers are so proud ?" And appeals to the multitude were made in words expressing the sense condensed in the lines :

> "Art thou so bare, and full of wretchedness,
> And fearest to die ? famine is in thy cheeks,
> Need and oppression starveth in thy eyes,
> Upon thy back hangs ragged misery ;
> The world is not thy friend, nor the world's law :
> The world affords no law to make thee rich ;
> Then be not poor, but break it, and take this."

A will, begotten by poverty, yielded a qualified but yet ominous approval. While the mind of the country was in this discontented and unsatisfactory mood, the Factory Act remained unchanged, and the parliamentary efforts of all parties were brought to a close by a dissolution of the House of Commons; the whig party having sunk in reputation and lost much of the popular respect which they had formerly commanded. It would have been impossible for any intelligent thinker to have surveyed, at this period, the social condition of England, without arriving at a judgment somewhat unfavourable to the character of British statesmen, or the theory of government. It is on the conditions under which the wealth of a nation is produced and distributed, that the comfort of a population directly depends ; and forms of government ought to be considered in connection with their bearing on the wants of men. A government may be good in its constitution, and statesmen, from ignorance, may sanction laws injurious to the interests of the many, or from indolence and ignorance, fail to enact the laws required. A government bad in its constitution, because of a wise and prudent policy, conducted by wise statesmen, may rule over a happy and prosperous population. The

extreme section of political reformers argued, that the enactment of *The People's Charter* would lead to the most desirable
social results. The excitement consequent on the agitation
for that end, forced on the attention of men of all parties,
the necessity of attending to the condition of the people,
a consideration which had occupied the minds of the leaders
of the Ten Hours' Bill movement for years, and the general
neglect of which was a principal source of governmental
difficulty.

CHAPTER X.

MR OASTLER'S DEPARTURE FROM FIXBY—IMPRISONMENT OF MR OASTLER
AT THE INSTANCE OF THE LATE MR THORNHILL, OF RIDDLES-
WORTH, NORFOLK ; THE EFFECT THEREOF ON THE PROGRESS OF
THE FACTORY MOVEMENT.

THE factory movement lost much in Mr Oastler's imprisonment for debt, at the instance of his former employer,
Thomas Thornhill, Esq., of Riddlesworth, in Norfolk, proprietor of the Fixby and other large estates in Yorkshire.
Respect for Mr Oastler among rich and poor was increased
by this circumstance, but his power of travel and talk was
at an end. Public speaking is as necessary for success in
agitation, as is the breeze to the mariner; and a movement
can no more command an orator at will, than can a sailor
the wind. " Imprisonment for debt," and " respect among
rich and poor increased," are sentences which, at first sight,
seem discordant,—in this case they were reconcileable.

The circumstances which led to Mr Oastler's appointment
to a stewardship, the duties of which his father had faithfully discharged for nearly twenty years, and which were
fulfilled by the son for a like period, are minutely detailed
by Mr Oastler in *The Fleet Papers*. Without encumbering
these pages with a recapitulation, it is enough that we remark
that Mr Thornhill's estimation of the father's services induced
him, unsolicited, to offer Mr Oastler the stewardship of the
Yorkshire estates. This act on the part of Mr Thornhill

was conveyed in expressions relating to both father and
son, which, to Mr Oastler's mind, increased the worth of
the act manifold, and gave a weight to one declaration therein
which made an impression that has never been obliterated.
In allusion to Mr Thornhill's self-imposed absence from his
Yorkshire estates (which continued during the whole period
of Mr Oastler's stewardship), Mr Thornhill said—" I am,
in some measure, compelled to leave my name, as well as
my property, in the hands of my Yorkshire steward." To
guard and improve that property, to sustain and increase
respect and reverence for the name of Thornhill, in Yorkshire,
were duties thus imposed and afterwards faithfully performed.
During the period of Mr Oastler's connection with Mr
Thornhill, there was manifested, on both sides, the strongest
regard ; and though Mr Oastler's public exertions were
obnoxious to many persons in Yorkshire, who thought it
desirable to make representations thereon to Mr Thornhill,
these representations rather strengthened than diminished Mr
Thornhill's respect for his steward. Mr Thornhill approved
of Mr Oastler's private and public proceedings in the ten
hours' movement, and, on one occasion, Mr Thornhill contributed 20*l.* to the funds of the operatives' Short Time Committee.
Mr Oastler's knowledge and opinions, on questions of public
interest, were so highly estimated by Mr Thornhill, that
he felt anxious they should have influence in high quarters,
and for that purpose, introduced Mr Oastler to the late
Duke of Wellington, and the late Earl Grey (then Prime
Minister), and other important aristocratic and political
personages. With the late Duke of Wellington, Mr Oastler
had many interviews, and was honoured by his grace with
a request to " call at Apsley House when convenient." Mr
Oastler corresponded with the late duke (at his own request)
for several years, and his grace highly valued, and with
punctuality replied to, the letters of his Yorkshire correspondent. The question of the new poor law was an exception

to the customary concordance in opinion between Mr Thornhill and Mr Oastler. On that question, Mr Oastler faithfully communicated his views to Mr Thornhill. For several years Mr Oastler's communications, by letter and conversation, were kindly received, and the discussions on the new poor law were continued in a most friendly manner. Mr Thornhill, while differing from Mr Oastler in opinion, did not attempt to dissuade him from the course he, on the poor-law question, was pursuing. Until, in 1838, the Poor Law Commissioners having resolved to introduce the new poor law into the Huddersfield and Halifax districts, and having found that Mr Oastler's influence was a barrier against their success, the late Mr Frankland Lewis, then the chief Poor Law Commissioner, wrote to Mr Thornhill, requesting his support to aid the commissioners to enforce the new poor law. He promised that aid, corresponded with Mr Oastler thereon, and having found him inexorable, on May the 29th, 1838, Mr Thornhill wrote to Mr Oastler, as follows. " I am sorry to say that I cannot employ you any longer as my steward, therefore, we must part. I wish you well for your own sake, and doubly so for that of your father."

Mr Oastler had not long entered upon the stewardship, before he discovered that the expenses attendant upon the faithful discharge of his duties, were much greater than the amount of his salary, that being 300*l.* a year, without a single perquisite. Mr Oastler was received by the gentry, and others, who were more or less connected with the estates, in the most hospitable manner, and when they called upon him, like hospitality was returned. In affairs relating to the church, turnpike roads, and other public works, in parochial as well as in county questions, Mr Thornhill, through Mr Oastler, was constantly advised with ; on such matters many were the guests at Mr Oastler's table. The tenants were invariably received at Fixby Hall with hospitality, the poor were not sent empty away. Mr Oastler had regard to Mr Thornhill's name, and thus it was that name was honoured. Mr Oastler received some legacies, and became possessed of other property, all of which he devoted in the above-named services. To make up his yearly balance with Mr Thornhill, Mr Oastler borrowed money from his friends; at length, he felt it to be his duty to explain these facts to Mr Thornhill, and to relinquish a situation, the necessary duties of which were involving him year by year in an increasing debt. On the 5th of June, 1834, Mr Oastler, by letter, communicated, in detail, the circumstances above referred to, assuring Mr Thornhill that so long as he (Mr Oastler) remained steward, he must reciprocate hospitality, and show kindness to the poor, and that "he could not live to be a simple money-getting, money-scraping, money-hoarding earthworm," and declared his inability any longer to bear the burden. Mr Oastler's resignation was not accepted; on December 13th, 1834, he settled his yearly accounts with Mr Thornhill, at Riddles-worth, and instead of borrowing money, as usual, to make up the balance, he left the accounts in their actual state. In fourteen years, the balance against Mr Oastler, had accumulated to 2,709l. 11s. 4½d. Mr Thornhill was convinced that Mr Oastler's salary had been inadequate, the offered resignation was not accepted, and Mr Thornhill, in the kindest possible manner, proposed an additional 200l. a year to his steward's salary. The balance due to Mr Thornhill was agreed to be taken in Mr Oastler's promissory note, with an understanding that the debt should be annually reduced, which agreement was adhered to by Mr Oastler, and recorded by Mr Thornhill on the back of the promissory note. The arrangement was throughout satisfactory to Mr Thornhill. That Mr Oastler had endeared himself to Mr Thornhill's tenantry, was proved by their having presented to him, on the day of his departure from

Fixby, a handsome silver salver, on which was engraved
the following inscription:—"This piece of plate is presented
by the tenants of Thomas Thornhill, Esquire, who are
resident in the township of Fixby, to Richard Oastler; and
is intended as a feeble expression of their sincere respect,
and heartfelt affection, both towards himself, and his late
revered father, who, together, have for thirty-eight years
discharged, with unblemished integrity, genuine kindness,
and unsuspected disinterestedness, the office of stewards
upon Mr Thornhill's Yorkshire estates: and who will both
live, at whatever distance of time, in the best feelings
of their hearts.—Fixby, the 25th of August, 1838."

The character which Mr Oastler earned for himself, in
the neighbourhood in which he lived, was reflected by a
demonstration in his honour, on his departure from Fixby
Hall, August the 25th, 1838.

The morning of that day was, in Huddersfield and neighbourhood, a time of stirring interest; the roads leading to
Fixby were crowded with travellers bent on paying their
respect to a man whom they honoured, and whom they
believed "to be persecuted for righteousness' sake." The
Hall was thronged with friendly visitors; on the spacious lawn,
in front, were assembled groups of warm and anxious admirers;
the coach road through the park to the lodge was lined by
crowds of people, waiting to greet the "discharged steward"
as he passed. In this assemblage were many of the most
influential inhabitants of the neighbourhood; numbers of
the tenants were there, in whose faces was depicted a
strong sense of decorous sorrow. Vast numbers of the poor
had that day congregated; all felt that they were losing a
counsellor and friend. The poor seemed especially desirous
of showing their attachment to one, whose ear had always
been open to their complaints, and whose feeling heart,
had oftentimes prompted him to minister to their wants.

The tenants were evidently loath to part with a steward whom they loved, and with whom, for nearly twenty years, they had consulted as with a brother. The neighbouring gentry, too, evinced their sorrow at parting with one whose society had habitually cheered their family circles. Fixby was never dearer to Mr Oastler than on that morning; in his own words, " Fixby is twice dear to me, from the memory of my father and the remembrances of my early years; it was there I spent my school-boy holidays."

Mr Oastler was escorted into Huddersfield with a long procession of friends, accompanied by bands of music and banners; all the way to Huddersfield the road was lined with an enthusiastic throng. As the open carriage in which Mr and Mrs Oastler and their adopted and affectionate daughter, Miss Tatham, with their faithful friend, Mr Wm. Stocks, passed along the road, they were cheered and blessed by young and old, by rich and poor. Mothers held their babes uplifted, and asked them, to look on the "factory child's benefactor." When the procession reached Huddersfield, it was welcomed by a vast number of factory children, who sung their song, "We will have the Ten Hours' Bill," &c. The streets of Huddersfield were filled with human beings, who made way for the procession, and cheered most lustily. The windows of the houses were occupied, and, in many instances, the house-tops were covered with anxious spectators. Commodious hustings had been erected in a spacious plot of ground near St Paul's Church, where the business of the day closed with the presentation of addresses to Mr Oastler, and the delivery of speeches in favour of the Ten Hours' Bill and against the new poor law. That was a day of triumph to those principles of which Mr Oastler was the exponent. It was estimated that at least one hundred thousand persons had thus openly expressed their attachment to Mr Oastler's principles and character. Not a few had come from Lancashire to take part in these proceedings.

We know of nothing in our experience, or reading, which has equalled this expression of sympathy. From what had that sympathy arisen? No man had ever despised riches, for their own sake, more thoroughly than had Mr Oastler. That fact was known and appreciated. In the expressive words of a working man, who, when questioned as to the reasons of his sympathy, answered, " He is a gentleman, sir, and honest; is not that enough"?

These proceedings were reported very fully in the press, the strangers present, who were numerous, carried back with them to their homes an account of what they had that day heard and seen. The effect in favour of the Ten Hours' Bill movement was widely spread, and decisive.

The enthusiasm of Mr Oastler's friends led them into error, they, without having consulted him, published a placard which was very offensive to Mr Thornhill. Mr Oastler was deeply grieved at this ill-judged proceeding of his own friends. Mr Thornhill, erroneously, conceived that Mr Oastler was the author of that placard, and replied to it by a letter in the newspapers, in terms not friendly towards his former steward, which letter was followed by a rejoinder. This was the first indication of an unkindly feeling on either side. By a portion of the press, which hoped to destroy Mr Oastler's influence, that circumstance was seized upon with avidity, and political rancour wreaked its revenge on the " discharged steward " with much asperity. An amicable settlement was thereby prevented. On the 25th of October 1838, Mr Oastler was served with a copy of a writ at the suit of Mr Thornhill. On the 10th July, 1840, the cause was tried. Mr Oastler appeared in person to defend; for what reason the following extracts from the *Times*, July 11, 1840, will explain:—

"COURT OF COMMON PLEAS; FRIDAY, JULY 10.

"Sittings in London before Lord Chief Justice Tindal and a Special Jury.

THORNHILL v. OASTLER.

"Mr Kelly (now Sir Fitzroy Kelly, M.P.) with whom was Mr Peacock, stated, that the plaintiff was a gentleman of fortune, possessed of extensive estates in Yorkshire. The defendant, who was, no doubt, well known to the jury, and whose talents and abilities were such as to entitle him to their consideration, had been for many years land steward and agent to the plaintiff, which situation had been previously filled by his father, whom, on his death, his son, the present defendant, had succeeded . . . . In order to show, beyond all doubt, that the plaintiff was entitled to what he sought to recover, he would proceed to read some letters which had passed between the parties, from which it would appear, upon the defendant's own acknowledgment, that the balance in question was clearly due. The learned counsel then read some portion of the correspondence, which so far was couched in friendly terms on both sides; and he observed that he would refrain from introducing any other matter, not bearing on the precise question before the jury—a course of proceeding in which he hoped that he should be followed by the defendant, who appeared in person to defend the cause.

"Mr Oastler interposed, and observed, that he had no wish to waste the time of the court. If the plaintiff's counsel were sincere in the sentiments he expressed, and was now satisfied to acknowledge, on the part of his client, that he intended only to treat the sum here claimed as a debt, he would give him no further trouble, but submit to a verdict at once, and place himself in Mr Thornhill's hands. He had merely resisted the action, because he understood that it had been imputed to him that he had fraudulently detained the money; whereas it now appeared to be acknowledged that it was a simple matter of debt.

" The Lord Chief Justice observed, that there was no imputation whatever on Mr Oastler's character here.

" Mr Oastler said, that that was all he ever wished to be settled.

*　　*　　*　　*　　*

"Mr Kelly said he felt great pleasure at this unpleasant affair being thus satisfactorily settled.

" Lord Chief Justice Tindal : ' I am very glad, Mr Oastler, that this action is brought to such a satisfactory settlement.'

" Mr Oastler bowed to his lordship.

" A verdict, for the plaintiff, was then entered."

By a private arrangement with Mr Kelly, it was agreed that the verdict then given should be, " Without prejudice to a claim of the defendant against the plaintiff for 500l."

These proceedings were watched with much interest by the supporters of the Ten Hours' Bill, who appeared to identify their cause with the circumstances and character of their friend, and to increase their devotion to him and the short-time question, because of his misfortune.

" I am," wrote Mr Oastler to a friend, November 21st, 1840, " now in my third year of unprofitable and expensive wandering and legal proceedings ; and I may tell you that I do not know by whom I am supported. It is a fact, that the only money I have, comes by letters—sometimes a five-pound note, sometimes a ten, sometimes a twenty— but from whom, except in two instances, I know no more than you." The debt due from Mr Oastler to Mr Thornhill having been demanded, Mr Oastler not having the means to discharge it, was, on December 9th, 1840, lodged in *The Fleet Prison.*

The period between Mr Oastler's departure from Fixby and his arrival in *The Fleet Prison,* was necessarily one of anxiety and expense ; he was throughout, very active in propagating his opinions on the poor-law and factory questions.

Idleness in health was with Mr Oastler an impossibility, and, therefore, he established *The Fleet Papers*, a weekly journal devoted, chiefly to a discussion of the factory and poor-law questions. These papers won their author a wider reputation than he had hitherto enjoyed. Passages from their pages were frequently copied into the columns of the *Times* and other journals, in England and on the continent. Men of all ranks and parties visited Mr Oastler in prison. He very seldom failed to impress visitors with a sense of the importance of the subjects nearest his heart—foremost among these was factory regulation; and thus it was that the means adopted to destroy his influence contributed towards its increase.

Moore, in his witty lampoon, the *Literary Advertisement*, has acknowledged the reputation of that city of refuge, the Fleet prison, for men of letters:—

> "If in gaol, all the better for out-o'-door topics ;
> Your gaol is for trav'llers a charming retreat ;
> They can take a day's rule for a trip to the tropics,
> And sail round the world, at their ease, in the Fleet."

These lines, though full of satire, are not void of truth. Sometimes the imprisonment in a gaol does not unfit a politician for "out-o'-door topics." Mr Oastler, by many agencies, was kept constantly informed of the proceedings of all parties in the state, and the table of few London editors was covered, every morning, with more important or interesting letters, than were delivered daily into the hands of the discarded and imprisoned steward of an English squire. That the prison hours of Mr Oastler were not without sunshine, the following picture, from the pen of a visitor, will show; it appeared, originally, in the *Leeds Intelligencer*, May 22, 1841, under the heading, "Life in the Fleet!" "I found Mr Oastler," said his visitor, "in good health and high spirits, but he looks thin; for what with his 'Fleet Papers,' his correspondence, his hard reading, and constant succession of visitors, 'from early morn to dewy eve,' he sadly overleaps his favourite and salutary doctrine of ten hours a day! I met in his room, all in the short compass of a few hours, a member of parliament; the son of a peer, not a public man; an LL.D. of great literary renown; a Polish count, eminent as a linguist; and an author in various walks of literature; another Polish count, who greatly distinguished himself in the recent attempt to liberate his country from the grasp of Russia, and whose father served with distinction in the armies of Napoleon; the author of one of the best books ever published on the social economy and true policy of the British empire; the editor of a daily journal; the editor of a London weekly journal; a gallant and most amiable French captain of horse, who left his country on account of his attachment to Charles the Tenth; the editors of several country journals; several distinguished mechanists; and a long train of casual and almost daily callers, ladies included, who all crowd around the imprisoned champion of humanity, attracted by his fame, or led thither by personal attachment. Men of all parties flock hither. On Monday morning I breakfasted with his 'Majesty.' The party consisted of eight, namely, two Polish counts, the French captain, an author, two editors of public journals, a gentleman from Huddersfield, and your humble servant. Though the beverage consisted of tea and coffee, there was so much sprightliness and *bonhommie,* that one might have supposed that care finds no entrance within the walls (not 'wooden') of the 'Fleet.' The apartment is not large. The Monarch for once made his bed his 'throne;' I was honoured with the chair of state; the friend from Huddersfield attended to the tea-kettle, and the tea and coffee-pots; the gallant

captain took command of the egg department; and there
was an appointed purveyor of ham and bread and butter,
all of the best quality. I have seen many a 'public breakfast;' but none wherein I found more enjoyment, none near
so much intellect or animation of conversation." Such
society was to be met with in few places, and it could
not fail to exercise a desirable influence on the mind of Mr
Oastler.

As proverbial wisdom hath justly said, " Every medal has
its reverse." Imprisoment, under favourable circumstances, is
still a severe punishment. The caged starling of Sterne, that
cried, " I can't get out—I can't get out," forced from the
sentimental traveller words which have found an echo in
every prisoner's heart—" Grant me but health, thou great
Bestower of it, and give me but this fair goddess [Liberty]
as my companion—and shower down thy mitres, if it
seems good unto thy Divine Providence, upon those heads
which are aching for them."

The following extract, from an unpublished letter, de-
scriptive of " prison experience," is graphic and interesting.
It has been generously communicated for publication in
these pages ; a favour which the author gratefully acknowledges:—

" Although," writes Mr Oastler, " many deprivations
are necessarily consequent on imprisonment, by this time
you will have learned that, compared with that of many
others, mine was indeed a season of sunshine. It was
truly so. Yet, as every one knows, even in sunshine
gnats will sting. So it was in my case. Surrounded by
so many friends, daily enjoying so many comforts, I
had one 'thorn in the flesh,' that, humanly speaking,
could not be extracted. There were, in my own neighbourhood, a few self-seeking men, whom I had nourished as
friends, who (hoping thereby to better their condition, by
obtaining favour with Mr Thornhill), among their associates,

my old neighbours, whispered dark insinuations, intended tc produce a suspicion that 'all was not exactly as it should be between Oastler and his late master;' by such disreputable conduct, they hoped to create an impression adverse to my honesty and honour, and thus to justify their own treachery.

" I had not any power to shield myself from the secret workings of these slanderers. I was conscious that they were moved by selfishness, thus to injure the absent, who, they knew, was guiltless—that, in the hope of their own advancement, they were endeavouring to degrade one who had often been their friend. It was annoying, thus, in prison, to be assailed, without the power to reply. I was obliged to endure those stings with patience, hoping my friends would remember, that I had, in person, appeared in the Court of Common Pleas, to answer any charge or insinuation that might there be brought against me. Resignation was soon followed by an antidote to the venom. It pleased GOD, in his own way, entirely to remove the annoyance caused by those ungrateful slanderers. When I tell you how, you will marvel; and, at the same time, receive an answer to your question. 'I perceive in the second volume, number seven, of the *Fleet Papers* (in your rent-roll) the following notice: " June 13th, 1841.—Fitzroy Kelly, Esquire, Q.C., brought me six bottles of wine, and such wine as would have done honour to a royal cellar. I could say much about my feelings when that gentleman visited me, but I refrain." I do not perceive any farther notice in the *Fleet Papers* of that visit. It must have been very interesting; have you any objection to favour me with an account thereof, for publication?' Indeed I have not. I rejoice that you favour me with an opportunity to make known an act, so thoroughly generous. I should be glad, publicly, to express my gratitude to that friend, whose visit to me, in prison, was so unexpected, and so opportune; to record my thanks to Almighty God, who, by his own messenger, sent to me the deliverance, so much desired, from the net which my ungrateful slanderers had laid.

"I cannot hope, that any words of mine will convey to others, even a faint idea of the gratitude inspired in my bosom, when the learned and eminent *leader* against me in the trial 'Thornhill *versus* Oastler,' entered my cell, and told me his errand. I will relate to you the circumstances. "Before you hear my tale, be pleased to place yourself in thought, where I then was—in prison, with a loved wife and daughter 'outside,' tortured under that calamity,— their wounded feelings being most sensitive to every breath of slander against him they loved more than life, being unable to grapple with insinuations which, to them, were very annoying,—nay, being sometimes obliged to meet the slanderers, who, then, assumed the grasp and smile of friend-ship and condolence! Remember, too, that I was a prisoner for a debt incurred in upholding the name and character of him, who thus repaid ; whose charges against my honesty (if he had any to make), I had appeared in open court to answer. Under these impressions, your mind will be able to under-stand the full force of the following truth asserted by the editor of the *Times* (Jan. 31st, 1857):—'A malicious word may do more certain wrong than a lie graven on the base of a column. If a man be an honourable man, he would wish that if an imputation be made against him, it should not be whispered in a corner, or passed along from mouth to ear, but made publicly in print, where he could recognise it and destroy it.' Such being the feeling of an honourable man, at large, you may be able to imagine, though I cannot describe, with what feelings of gratitude I listened to the kind offer of one who knew every fact in the case,—Mr Thornhill's leading counsel, when he so unexpectedly visited me in prison.

"I had, once before, met Mr Fitzroy Kelly,—and then, in court, opposed to me. Now, in my cell, he came to offer his unsolicited, unpaid, and powerful influence with his client, my detainer, to obtain my release ! After this preface, you will, I am sure, read with attention and interest the sequel.

' "On Sunday, June 13, 1841, after my return from church, being seated in my cell, engaged in conversation with a fellow-prisoner (a respectable London solicitor), a knock at the door announced a visitor. A servant in livery entered, the bearer of a hamper and a card. He informed, me that his master was at 'the gate,' having been refused admission because at that hour on Sundays ' the gate' was closed ; but that the turnkey had allowed him to bring in the hamper. On looking at the card, I said, ' You must be mistaken, Mr Fitzroy Kelly cannot wish to see me.' " Is not your name Oastler, Sir?' ' Yes, certainly.' ' The hamper is directed for you, sir.' There could not now be any mistake. I ran to the lobby, desired the turnkey to see the warden, and ask permission that Mr Fitzroy Kelly might be admitted. That request was instantly granted. When Mr Fitzroy Kelly entered my cell, he saw and instantly recognised my prison companion, whom he kindly accosted. In a few minutes, the London solicitor withdrew. Mr Fitzroy Kelly, in the kindest terms, then informed me, that he sincerely regretted my imprisonment; that, when we parted in the Court of Common Pleas, he thought the dispute was so arranged, that not any unpleasant consequences would follow. Since it had proved otherwise, he having been engaged in the suit for Mr Thornhill, felt, that so far, he was a party, and thought that he was the most likely person to interpose as a mediator, to obtain my release from prison, where, he was sure, I ought not to be. ' If you will accept of my services as your adviser and friend,' said Mr Fitzroy Kelly, and will communicate to me the particulars of your own case, as you would have explained to the court, had you not stopped me, and consented to a verdict; I will, to the best

of my ability, endeavour to persuade Mr Thornhill to grant
your release. ¶ 'I am already fully acquainted with Mr Thornhill's case, and am 'sure, there is not any reason why you
should 'suffer imprisonment.' Gratefully, I accepted that
most generous offer. From that moment, I felt that the
venom was extracted from the slanderers' sting!

"Before Mr Fitzroy Kelly withdrew, it was arranged, that
I should prepare to lay before him the particulars of my case,
especially, with regard to the 'set offs,' which I had
pleaded, when he would return to hear me, and examine
my documents. With a light heart I accompanied my kind
benefactor to 'the gate,' returned to my cell, and thanked God
for this so great manifestation of his goodness.

"My gratitude to my kind and influential friend was
much increased, by the conviction, that the leading counsel
of Mr Thornhill was the only person whose good offices
could have completely vindicated my character, from the
secret and slanderous whisperings of my ungrateful traducers.

"Mr Fitzroy Kelly was punctual to his appointment. I was
prepared to receive him. He listened with attention to my
explanation, fully apprehended my arguments, requested that
he might take with him the documents to which I had
referred, to peruse and consider them, before he applied to Mr
Thornhill for my release.

"Mr Kelly assured me that he would exert himself to the
utmost on my behalf; and asked me, if I would consent that
he should make such proposals to Mr Thornhill as, on a full
consideration of the case, might to him seem best? I assured
Mr Fitzroy Kelly that I gratefully accepted his kind offer,
with full confidence, confiding my honour to his keeping.
If Mr Thornhill insisted on his *legal* claim, and would give
me the opportunity, I would endeavour to earn the money
and pay him, but, denying his *moral* claim, and having
incurred the debt in his service and for his benefit, I would
not ask any person to give him security for the payment

of such debt. I added, 'If Mr Thornhill should ask for an apology from me, I cannot gratify him. I do not owe him an apology. I have served him with zeal and fidelity, and that he knows.'

" After perusing the documents, and considering the whole case, Mr Fitzroy Kelly wrote to Mr Thornhill. That letter was read by Mr Thornhill to several deputations of gentlemen, who waited upon him at Fixby Hall to ask him to release 'his old steward' from imprisonment. The particulars of one of those interviews are briefly recorded in the *Leeds Intelligencer*, and the *Halifax Guardian* of September the 25th, 1841. I extract the following :

" 'Mr Oastler and Thomas Thornhill, Esq.

" 'At a meeting of the friends of Mr Oastler, held at the New Inn, in Bradford, on Friday, September 17th, convened to take into consideration the propriety of addressing Thomas Thornhill, Esq., on the subject of Mr Oastler's liberation, a deputation, composed of Messrs Auty, Balme, and Clarkson, was appointed to wait upon Mr Thornhill, at Fixby Hall, which mansion he was expected to visit, in the early part of the ensuing week.

" ' Agreeable to the above directions, the deputation having received information on Monday noon, that Mr Thornhill was at Fixby, took an early conveyance and arrived at Fixby Hall at three o'clock, previous to which, two deputations had already had interviews with Mr Thornhill, viz., from Huddersfield and Dewsbury, on the same subject. The Bradford deputation, however, soon found themselves in the presence of Mr Thornhill, when the object of their mission was briefly stated, viz., that they had been deputed by a meeting of the friends of Mr Oastler, in the town and neighbourhood of Bradford, to wait upon him for the purpose of inducing him to liberate Mr Oastler from the Fleet, believing, as they did, that his services in Yorkshire at the present time, would be of essential benefit to his country ; and they feared, that if Mr Oastler was confined much longer his health would be materially injured and his life shortened, and that they trusted Mr Thornhill had no desire to shorten the days or injure the health of his old steward. They also assured Mr Thornhill, that he could not bestow upon the working class, as well as his own order, the aristocracy, a greater benefit than by allowing Mr Oastler free action in their defence.

" ' Mr Thornhill, in reply, stated that he had no ill-will towards Mr Oastler whatever ; that he had no wish to shorten his life or injure his health ; that he had no doubt but that Mr Oastler might be of use to the country were he at large ; that he should be glad to see him liberated ; but that he felt that he would not be doing his duty to himself and to his family were he to consent to Mr Oastler's liberation without security for the debt.

" The deputation discussed the subject with Mr Thornhill for upwards of an hour and a-half, urging Mr Oastler's claims upon him, believing as they did that Mr Oastler had sacrificed his all for his country's welfare ; all of which Mr Thornhill listened to with the greatest courtesy, and stated, that an influential gentleman in London (the late John Walter, Esq., M.P.), had called upon him a short time since on the same subject, and to whom he had returned the same answer. He also showed the deputation a letter which he had lately received from one of his own counsel (Sir Fitzroy Kelly, Q.C.) in the late action (Thornhill v. Oastler), interceding in Mr Oastler's behalf, but to which he had not yet been able to reply.

" ' The deputation expressed their gratitude for the interest which that learned gentleman had exhibited in Mr Oastler's behalf, and hoped that that, together with the wishes and interests of the thousands which had, that day, been represented, would be taken into serious consideration, and, that whatever proposition might be made for Mr Oastler's release, they entreated Mr Thornhill to be as lenient as possible ; when Mr Thornhill assured the deputation that their visit would not prejudice him against Mr Oastler, but the contrary.

" ' The deputation retired, regretting that Mr Thornhill could not consent to liberate Mr Oastler, but was glad to hear him express himself ready to enter into an amicable arrangement for that purpose ; and they would hope that the time is not far distant, when Mr Oastler will be again restored to his family and friends.'—*Leeds Intelligencer* and *Halifax Guardian*, September 25th, 1841.

" One of the gentlemen then present told me that he had never heard anything so eloquent and so affecting as that appeal from Mr Fitzroy Kelly to Mr Thornhill, adding, ' When the squire read that letter there was not a dry eye in the room, the reader himself being moved to tears.' I have not seen that letter, and, consequently, cannot full apprehend how much I am in debt to the writer!

" My gratitude to Mr Fitzroy Kelly is not less, because his eloquence, so affecting and persuasive ; his exertions, so great and disinterested, were unavailing. Daily I pray my Heavenly Father to bless him ; while memory lasts, when this transitory scene has vanished away (surely gratitude is not confined to earth) I shall, to him, be grateful.

" True, I know full well, from a very long experience, that gentlemen of the legal profession, as a rule, are very generous. I have often, in private and in public, been honoured with proof thereof.

" I cannot forget that memorable instance of their disinterested friendship, when (before the Lord Chief Justice Denman, and a special jury) I was at York, defending myself against the charge of libel, so many of the learned gentlemen (some of them have since then become judges), rendered me most useful and unsolicited aid,—thus essentially contributing to the glorious victory obtained that day. I have, indeed, good cause to be very grateful to the lawyers—they have ever been kind to me; but I do not remember to have heard of any instance of their generous solicitude to rescue the persecuted from undeserved punishment so striking, as that shown to myself, by Mr Fitzroy Kelly.

" To this hour I gratefully number among my regular benefactors some honoured members of that learned body. I should be wanting in gratitude were I to omit stating that since my release from prison I have found in Sir Fitzroy Kelly, M.P., a constant, faithful friend and benefactor— one who is ever accessible, ever willing to advise and aid.

I have, my good friend, in thus complying with your request, gratified my own feelings, though I have failed to do justice to the noble act of generosity which I have endeavoured to describe."

Mr Oastler's imprisonment no doubt deepened his experience of life, and increased his influence on national politics. The mind is influenced by associations, and, like the dyer's hand, it is coloured by that with which it comes in contact. It was the saying of a baronet—a scholar and an M.P.—that " the most instructive society in London was to be met in Mr Oastler's room in the Fleet." It must in some respects have been advantageous to the gentleman who was the centre of attraction. Many as were the services rendered to the factory movement by the imprisoned editor of the Fleet Papers, they were much more than balanced by the loss sustained in the absence of his fiery and inspiring oratory over the masses in the north. Mr Oastler's imprisonment very materially retarded the progress and delayed the final triumph of the short-time movement, with which his name and fame are indissolubly connected.

CHAPTER XI.

LORD ASHLEY'S REFUSAL OF OFFICE IN 1841; BECAUSE OF THE UN-
DECIDED VIEWS OF THE LATE SIR ROBERT PEEL ON THE FACTORY
QUESTION.—MR FERRAND, HIS POSITION AND PRINCIPLES EX-
PLAINED.—THE LATE MR WALTER, OF THE 'TIMES:' HIS SERVICES
IN THE TEN-HOURS' BILL MOVEMENT.

LORD MELBOURNE dissolved parliament in 1841, and the
country returned a majority of 100 against him; the position
of parties was, consequently, changed, and the late Sir Robert
Peel became the head of a conservative ministry. Not any
circumstance could have proved more decidedly the dissatisfaction of the country with the effete and temporising
policy of the whig administration, than the weight of property and numbers which, at that time, called the late Sir
Robert Peel to power. He offered to Lord Ashley an
office, which was refused, and why, the following note will
show:

"London, September 4, 1841.

"Mr Crabtree,—In answer to your inquiry on behalf of
the operatives of the West Riding of Yorkshire, I have to
reply that an office was tendered to me by Sir Robert Peel.
Having, however, ascertained from him that his opinions on
the factory question were not matured, and that he required
further time for deliberation, I declined the acceptance of
any place, under circumstances which would impede, or
even limit, my full and free action in the advancement of

that measure, which I consider to be vital both to the welfare of the working classes and the real interests of the country.

"In taking this course, however, I neither express nor feel despair. It will be your duty and mine, not only to persevere, but to redouble our efforts ; and I still entertain a hope that her Majesty's advisers, after an investigation, conducted with sympathy and candour, will, under God's good providence, give to us all an answer of happiness and peace.

"I remain your most obedient humble servant,
"(Signed)   ASHLEY.
"Mr Mark Crabtree, Bradford, Yorkshire."

The refusal of Lord Ashley to accept of a place under the leader of the conservative party, was evidence of his lordship's determination to succeed with the measure he had taken in hand, and an announcement to all parties, that he had resolved against compromise; the supporters of the Ten Hours' Bill had thus in parliament a recognized leader, who had made known to the two rival parties, his resolution to continue in opposition to both, and on the ground chosen by Sadler to fight successfully to victory. The position of parties in the parliament of 1841 did not materially change the numbers of pledged supporters to the Ten Hours' Bill cause, but, it gave to them an advantage in having the whig party in opposition : it may be accepted, as a phase in the constitutional history of England, that the whigs are most disposed to vote for popular measures, when on the bleak side of the Speaker's chair. Lord Ashley's refusal of office gave great satisfaction to his clients in the factory districts, and contributed to strengthen their hopes of success.

Among the new members of the House of Commons was one well known to the working men of the north, and from whom much was hoped ; he had been long conspicuous in his own district as a supporter of the principles of the

British constitution, as understood by politicians of the Sadler and Oastler School, and William Busfeild Ferrand was a name closely associated in the minds of working men in Yorkshire with that of Richard Oastler, and of what, the working men believed to be, in their own words, "the rights of labour." We embrace this opportunity of stating summarily our estimate of his views and character.

Mr Ferrand has been for many years a decided supporter of the Ten Hours' Bill; his first public effort was in that movement, a speech at the great Wibsey Low Moor meeting. The circumstance which directed his attention to the condition of the factory children was interesting and remarkable, and is thus related in one of a series of public letters, addressed by him to the Duke of Newcastle, in 1852. " It was soon after Sadler and Oastler unfurled the banner of protection, that I became a public man. At the hour of five on a winter's morning, I left my home to shoot wild fowl. On my road, I had to pass along a deep and narrow lane, which led from a rural village to a distant factory. The wind howled furiously —the snow fell heavily, and drifted before the bitter blast. I indistinctly traced three children's footsteps. Soon, I heard a piteous cry of distress. Hurrying on, again I listened, but all was silent except the distant tolling of the factory bell. Again, I tracked their footmarks, and saw that one had lagged behind; I returned, and found the little factory slave half buried in a snow-drift, fast asleep. I dragged it from its winding-sheet; the icy hand of death had congealed its blood and paralysed its limbs. In a few minutes it would have been ' where the wicked cease from troubling and the weary are at rest.' I aroused it from its stupor and saved its life. From that hour I became a ' Ten Hours' Bill man,' and the unflinching advocate of ' protection to native industry !' "

Mr Ferrand's life has been spent in the heart of a manufacturing district, he has consequently witnessed some of the changes which have operated on the condition of the working classes; his fine property, Harden Grange, is close to Bingley, and in the centre of the West Riding. The hand-loom weavers and wool-combers of former days stood high as regarded wages, comfort, and morals. It is universally admitted, that the first effects of the rapid improvement and unregulated introduction of machinery are injurious to the interests of those classes whose labour is thereby supplanted. Mr Ferrand has witnessed the demoralisation of two numerous divisions of the army of industry, who, in the language of modern statesmen, have been engaged " in a hopeless competition against machinery;" so impressed was his mind with the results, that when a member of the House of Commons, he begged of the legislature to institute an inquiry into the effects of the unregulated introduction and use of machinery on the condition of the working men.

He has been, all his public life, in antagonism against a very energetic and powerful body in the state, namely, the free-trade political economists. It has been his habit, in and out of parliament, to denounce the frauds of manufacturers, and he has the honour of giving to the press of the age a new phrase; he was the first, in parliament, to designate that kind of woven fabric, made of old rags, separated by a machine, remade into cloth and sold as new, " devil's-dust cloth," the name of the tearing machine being " the devil." His denunciations of dishonest trading have been fierce and full-spoken, and made him many enemies; had these denunciations received the attention they deserved in 1844, England would, in 1854, have been spared the shame and sorrow of her soldiers having been in rags in the Crimea, and their having had tools useless for the purposes of war, grievously for their own and their country's loss, and notoriously for the gain of the enemy. Mr Ferrand has enjoyed at various periods of his political career the support of vast numbers of working men. In parliament he was too decided in his views to be an obedient partizan; and his error, in a partizan sense, and in no other, seems to have been that he loved plain speaking, "not wisely, but too well." It has been said, that "men should speak the truth with moderation, that they may speak it the longer"—a maxim profound in worldly experience, but to speak the truth boldly is noble even if uttered in excitement, and without regard to quantity or circumstances; it is more creditable to err in the anxiety of being right, than to live in mental indolence, or to become a mere pawn in the fingers of a political chess-player. In Mr Ferrand's opinion, agriculture is the foundation of all lasting national greatness. We once heard him say, "man deals alone in earth, and all manufacture is a modification of the earth's produce. Now, I say, the more we grow at home the better. Tell me not, Englishmen can't or won't eat home-grown corn—grow enough to feed them all, and try them. Tell me not, that we can have no great home manufacture—look to our woollens, see what flax might be grown. I dare pledge my life, that Englishmen could do very well with linen shirts. I say, everything you import, which you can grow at home or find a substitute for, so long as you have men who beg 'a brother of the earth to give them leave to toil,' is a national loss. Then, to boast of your imports is folly; and if all have not a reasonable share of their own produce, that which they themselves have helped to bring into existence, to brag of your exports is madness. It is our duty to look at home first." These opinions may or may not meet with popular approval, but they are sincerely entertained by Mr Ferrand, and in keeping therewith, he is an improving agriculturist. He has, on many occasions, rendered to the Ten Hours' Bill movement very effective services. He is a man of natural talent, an apt, ready, and powerful speaker; his speeches have been, by a portion of the press, subjected to much adverse criticism, yet, so far as we know, his leading principles remain unchanged, and he is now, as of old, " A church and king tory, and proud of being by birth an Englishman." The centralization and increase of manufacture in a district, is a certain cause of an increase in the rental of land. The rapid communication of steam power has equalized, or nearly so, the market prices of the principal produce ; the ready market afforded for milk and butter where there is a crowded factory population, raises the value of land in the immediate neighbourhood. Had Mr Ferrand encouraged the building of factories on his own estate, he would, beyond doubt, have vastly increased his own income : he prefers keeping up the old mansion and its wide-spread grounds in a thoroughly rural state. It is a saying of his own— " Factories in brisk times spring up like mushrooms, no extra encouragement is required—in dull times, they are too numerous to be useful." Few land-owners in England could gain more by the local growth of manufacture, than Mr Ferrand. His unwillingness to encourage the building of mills on his property has been frequently urged against him: it is an evidence of his consistency, for which he foregoes large yearly advantage, and one, for which he deserves the respect due to an act of duty, as appreciated in his own understanding ; he has for many years been an advocate for a parochial allotment system suited to the wants of a manufacturing population, under the impression that the employment of spare hours in garden culture was necessary for health and desirable for morals, a practice he approved of as "a check against the evils of the mill system," and which he has advocated, in and out of parliament, with all the energy of his nature. Like Sadler, Oastler, Fielden, Bull, Walter, Mr Ferrand has, from first to last, opposed the principle of the New Poor Law Amendment Act.

Mr Ferrand has endeavoured to reduce his views on public

questions to practice, by letting land in small allotments to working men in Bingley and its neighbourhood. He has let above a hundred acres to working men, the average is one quarter of an acre to each allottee. The experiment has been in operation for fifteen years. The landlord has not lost one sixpence of rent ; the effect, socially and morally, has been most beneficial. During the whole of that period, there have not been more than two or three applications to the poor-law guardians, from these small land occupiers, for relief, and these were cases of severe family sickness. Mr Ferrand recently expressed his satisfaction on the result of his attempt at practical improvement in the following terms :—" Confirmed drunkards have been completely reformed, idlers have been changed to busy operatives, families, formerly steeped in poverty, have been raised to comfort and independence ; their meals supplied with wholesome vegetables, both in summer and winter; and I have solid reasons for believing, that a happy and satisfied contentment pervades the minds of the occupiers.

" As a magistrate, I am not aware of an allotment occupier having ever been brought before the bench for any infringement of the law."

It is to be regretted, that a public question of so much importance as manual labour, in its relation to machinery and national strength, did not receive, as Mr Ferrand desired, the attention of parliament; majorities can out-vote minorities, and writers declare that " the whole question is settled," but it is always desirable to give to an important and disputed subject, the most complete possible investigation. The working-men are not now satisfied that machinery is to them invariably advantageous, and among their leaders, the subject is one of constant discussion. Mr Ferrand's failure in commanding the attention of the legislature, on this great social question, was one of those unsuccessful efforts, which can only be named to be deplored. Truth

M 2

never loses by investigation, and those who opposed Mr Ferrand's opinions would have honoured themselves, had they manifested a willingness for enquiry; his efforts to suppress "the truck system" were energetic and useful. Mr Ferrand has for some time past ceased to take a leading part in the local politics of the West Riding. His occasional letters in the press show that he is not an inattentive spectator of the events of the age, and that he, as formerly, keeps a keen eye on those signs which form the index of the social condition of England.

Another important acquisition to the supporters of the Ten Hours' Bill movement in parliament, was the late Mr Walter, who, in 1841, represented for a brief period the important town of Nottingham. The late Mr Walter belonged to a class of men truly valuable, but frequently unappreciated, those active and practical men, who work themselves, and find useful employment for others. Mr Walter had a mind well proportioned and balanced, he was mentally strong, rather than great. In any sphere of life requiring industry, and only solid working talent, he would have been successful, he knew well how to appreciate and reward merit, how to combine and apply agencies to produce the desired result, under a settled contempt for all counterfeit humanity; there was in him, a genuine and generous love of mankind; he was eminently the friend of the working man, so far as his social interests were understood. The *Times* is, in an industrial sense, Mr Walter's monument, and who in England could desire a greater. Mr Walter gave to the Ten Hours' Bill a constant and powerful support, and for many years, on fitting occasions, it was in the columns of the *Times* a leading subject; the value of such aid cannot be estimated. It is astonishing how men, having kindred sympathies, will sometimes allow their antipathies to direct them in opposition; a remarkable instance of this kind of angular antagonism existed for a considerable period, between Mr Walter and Mr Cobbett,—each had said strong things against the other ; on the most practical questions of their age they were agreed. Mr Oastler and Mr Walter were cordial friends, a concordance of opinions in politics, caused a sympathy and respect, which became personal and lasting. Mr Walter, when in London, was a regular visitor at *the Fleet*, and *the Queen's Bench*, and, for years, kept up with Mr Oastler a correspondence on subjects of public interest. The following extract from one of Mr Walter's letters to Mr Oastler, written on the evening of the day on which the poll, in favour of Mr Walter, had closed at the Nottingham election of 1841, will illustrate the influence exercised by the editor of the *Fleet Papers*, on " out-o'-door topics." " I hope," wrote Mr Walter, " to make to you in person my acknowledgments for the kind interest you have taken in the affair throughout, and for your propounding originally the important measure which has been crowned with such success." Mr Walter's introduction to the constituency of Nottingham, was under the following circumstances: a vacancy in the representation of that borough having occurred, an influential tory, and an influential chartist, without having communicated with each other, wrote on the same day, to ask Mr Oastler if he could recommend a candidate, in favour of the Ten Hours' Bill, and opposed to the New Poor Law. On the day Mr Oastler received these letters, his friend Mr Walter called at the Fleet, and asked if he, Mr Oastler, had any influence at Nottingham, there being a vacancy in the representation of that borough, and he, Mr Walter, being wishful to have a seat in parliament for the purpose of obtaining the repeal of the New Poor Law. Mr Oastler replied (at the same time handing to Mr Walter the two letters that morning received from Nottingham), " I was just about sending those letters to you, and to ask you, if you would allow me to give to my two friends your name."

After enquiring as to the influence of Mr Oastler's correspondents, it was resolved that Mr Oastler should communicate Mr Walter's name, advising each of his, Mr Oastler's, friends to meet the other, and mutually consult on the subject. Mr Oastler did so, and strongly recommended Mr Walter to his, Mr Oastler's, correspondents; they met, and forwarded to Mr Walter a requisition, signed by influential electors of the tory and chartist parties, requesting him to become a candidate.

Mr Walter entertained a decided conviction, that the average talent and honesty of the House of Commons reached a comparatively low standard; he was very anxious to discharge faithfully the duties of the representative of the people; within the walls of parliament, his efforts on their behalf did not meet with the support requisite for success, and it is not surprising to read, as we have done, expressions of his disregard concerning the decision of the election committee, appointed by the House of Commons, to try the validity of his claim to represent Nottingham, and which committee unseated him on petition. His ejection from parliament was a loss to the supporters of the Ten Hours' Bill; which measure he approved to the close of life, and the principle of which continues, when necessary, to receive the influential support of "the leading journal," a position, which the *Times* newspaper acquired under the control of Mr Walter, and which it continues successfully to retain.

Why Mr Walter supported the movement for factory regulation, we can answer from his own lips, his words explain the foundation of his politics. Addressing a public meeting in the Corn Exchange, Manchester, on April 17th, 1844, he said, "What is the object of domestic legislation? It is not to improve the condition of the rich: they can sustain themselves. The laws may restrain the improper indulgence of their passions, indeed, and they have a right to look for protection under them from external violence; but the great object of home legislation is, or should be, to improve the condition, and strengthen the foundation of the great basis of society, the industrious, the operatives, upon whom the whole structure of human society rests; for if this be disturbed and unsettled, there can be no tranquillity or security above." "It is not likely that I should seek to degrade my humble brethren by an unseemly comparison; but let us take that noble animal the horse, man's companion and fellow labourer. Whence is it that so many are crushed down to an early death,—whence is it that we see so many with tottering knees, broken wind, and premature infirmities? Is not the universal answer, "They have been worked too young—they have been made to toil too long, and are now, when they should be in the vigour of their days, worth nothing; the sand cart, and soon after the dog-kennel, are their doom; and that remark which applies to this noble animal, may, but with too much truth, be applied also to a large portion of our labouring fellow subjects in the manufactories. They are worked too young, and too hard; and hence they drop into a premature grave; or, which they dread almost as much, an union workhouse. Domestic legislation, I say, should prevent, not sanction, such barbarity." These are words of clear, practical common sense, flowing from an honest heart, and will commend themselves to the hearts of those who can feel for the least fortunate, but not the least useful portion of society.

Mr Wm. Walker, and Mr William Rand, of Bradford, impressed with a deep sense of duty, resolved to wait personally on every member of Sir Robert Peel's cabinet, in the hope of convincing, at least, some among them of the propriety of supporting the Ten Hours' Bill. This self-imposed task was promptly executed; it is not too much to say, that two gentlemen practically conversant with factory labour, were capable of imparting the fullest information on the subject. The Hon. John Stuart Wortley, M.P., Wm. Beckett, Esq., M.P., George Strickland, Esq., M.P., John Hardy, Esq., M.P., Charles Hindley, Esq., M.P., and John Fielden, Esq., M.P., at the request of Messrs Walker and Rand, signed their names to a circular requesting a meeting of members of parliament for Yorkshire, Lancashire, and Cheshire, and desired them to invite such of their constituents, being millowners, as should be likely to attend a meeting in London. A numerous and influentially attended conference was, consequently, held in the British Hotel, in Cockspur street, to discuss the merits of the Ten Hours' Bill. The Hon. John Stuart Wortley, M.P. for the West Riding, occupied the chair; the discussion which ensued was of the highest importance, and occupied the greater part of two days : the most bitter opponent to interference by law with the hours of labour in factories, was Mr John Bright, who was supported by the disciples of " the Manchester school," they scorned the very thought of interference as utopian and unnecessary, and claimed " the right to do with their own as they liked; " they, however, were not generally supported, and a resolution in favour of an eleven hours' bill was approved of by a considerable majority. This was, by all the promoters of the Ten Hours' Bill present, considered as an attempt at compromise, to which they at once refused to concede. These proceedings, in London, were brought before a public meeting in Bradford; the conduct of those who adhered to the Ten Hours' limitation, was highly approved. Messrs Walker and Rand were thanked for their spirited efforts on behalf of a cause they had so generously espoused and steadfastly maintained.

CHAPTER XII.

RENEWED AGITATION IN THE FACTORY DISTRICTS—EFFORTS OF SIR
JAMES GRAHAM TO INSURE A SETTLEMENT OF THE QUESTION—
PROCEEDINGS IN PARLIAMENT.

IN the autumn of 1841, Lord Ashley visited the manufacturing districts of Lancashire and Yorkshire, and was received with enthusiasm; his lordship's object was to acquire such information, relative to the wants and interests of the manufacturing population, as was required to enable him, with effect, to pursue his labours in parliament. The visit of Lord Ashley aroused the dormant energies of the supporters of the factory movement, and steps were immediately taken to strengthen his efforts in the House of Commons. The political excitement of 1839 had died away, leaving behind it much angry feeling and disappointment among the remnant of its supporters. It was a saying of one of the leaders of the first French revolution—"Those who make half revolutions, dig their own graves." This saying was the result of a penetrating insight into the nature of events; its spirit has been reproduced, after the lapse of three quarters of a century, by so impartial an observer as M. Guizot, who in his *Life of Richard Cromwell*, declares that to watch the escape of power from the hands of men who have failed in using it, "is a melancholy but most instructive study." The failure of the attempted insurrection at Newport, in 1839, though supported only by a section of those who avowed themselves, the " advocates of the *People's Charter*," was most injurious to the reputation of the whole. A result which did not in any way affect the worth of principles, but which was most material as to popular power in a state. In passing, we venture to observe, that a contributing but minor cause of the extraordinary emigration of late years, was the dissatisfaction which followed the failure at Newport. Very many of the young men, of high spirit and resolution, left England with a strong feeling of repulsion, and settled in the *United States*; in many cases, the remaining portions of their friends followed in after years.

Not any parliamentary leader of an important social question, could have manifested greater devotion and industry than was, in 1841, practised by Lord Ashley. In the course of his speech at Leeds, in August of that year, his lordship narrated the following circumstance :—" At Stockport, a young woman, twenty years of age, was caught by the machinery in a mill in which she worked, and, after being whirled round, was dashed to the ground with her ankles dislocated and her thighs broken. He would not say all that he had heard about her employer, though it might be well enough known; but this he would state, that her wages were due on the Wednesday, and the accident happened on Tuesday. It might be supposed that he paid her wages, and several weeks in advance, to support her under her distressing circumstances; but did he do so? No; he calculated what the time would come to from the accident to her wages being due, and deducted eighteenpence from her earnings. He (Lord Ashley) knew that the principle of the law was favourable to the workman, and, determined to show that it was so, he instituted a prosecution against the factory owner, and had the pleasure of recovering for that poor girl, 100*l.* damages, besides which, the man who refused 4s. to box his machinery off, had all the expenses on both sides to pay, amounting in all to nearly 600*l.*" The factory operatives thoroughly appreciated the worth of the facts stated. These impressed them with a sense of the value of law, and helped to destroy the popular belief that the law was opposed, in principle, to the interests of the working man. His lordship acknowledged the assistance he had received from Mr Sadler, Mr Oastler, the Rev. G. S. Bull, Mr John Wood, and Mr Wm. Walker, of Bradford; in parliament, from Mr John Fielden, of Oldham, Mr Brotherton, of Salford, and Mr Hindley, of Ashton, names known to and honoured by the factory operatives. When in Yorkshire, his lordship was the guest of Wm. Walker, Esq., of Bolling Hall, Bradford. They devoted their days to waiting on influential opponents of factory regulation, in the hope of making converts or weakening the virulence of opposition; and their nights in addressing public meetings. These efforts were pursued with untiring energy, and his lordship esteemed no labour too arduous on behalf of his unfortunate clients, whose hopes of redress he increased by sympathy, and whose confidence he sustained by frankness, energy, and perseverance on their behalf.

While Lord Ashley, in his speeches at this period of factory agitation, was careful to express his sense of the importance of the particular measure he advocated, he was specially watchful to guard against being misunderstood, as believing that a Ten Hours' Bill, alone, would prove a panacea for the social evils of the manufacturing districts. He looked on it as " a prelude to other healing and beneficent measures." This statement, alike candid and creditable to his lordship, was, by his opponents, frequently, in the bitterness of party-feeling, urged against making any concession to the " Ten Hours' Bill men," who were charged with aiming at more than they avowed.

The members of Sir Robert Peel's administration were not unobservant spectators of the events of the time : they had driven the whigs from power, because of doubts and delays on questions of national moment, and with Sir James Graham at the Home Office, were not likely to be unmindful of the proceedings of parties in the manufacturing districts. Lord Ashley's refusal of office had forewarned them that, so far as he was concerned, not any compromise was probable. On February 7th, 1841, Sir James Graham, in answer to a question put by Mr Stuart Wortley, then one of the members for the West Riding, made known the intentions of the government, which were limited to the introduction of a bill, found in the Home Office, having been prepared by Sir James's predecessor, Mr Fox Maule. This announcement was accompanied by the significant declaration that "It was not intended to propose any such regulation, as in some quarters had been strongly recommended, as to the limitation of the time of labour in factories of young persons between the ages of thirteen and eighteen, as some persons hoped, to ten hours a day." This declaration was fully appreciated by the advocates of the Ten Hours' Bill, who now understood their true position, and, as of old, resolved to oppose the government by moving amendments in favour of their adopted measure.

Public feeling on the question of factory labour, was kept alive by public speaking and writing. Mr Oastler was writing, week by week, in *The Fleet Papers* on the subject, and kept up a constant correspondence with his many friends in the north—his letters were very influential; the delegates, when in London, consulted with him regularly and profited by his advice. Among the humbler but telling efforts was the publication of "A narrative of the experience and sufferings of William Dodd, a factory cripple, written by himself." This narrative corroborated the evidence of many witnesses on the factory question. It possessed all the force of individual experience, and the unaffected simplicity of its style had a charm for every reader, while the past sufferings of "the cripple," the past circumstances of his life considered, and his intellectual power, awakened pity and admiration. One of the best, because clearest and most practical, pamphlets of that time, was "A Letter, addressed to the Right Honourable Sir James Graham, Bart., M.P.,"—the production of two influential and successful Yorkshire manufacturers, Mr William Walker and Mr William Rand, of Bradford. These gentlemen, after having waited on the principal members of Her Majesty's government, published their answer to objections in the form stated. We have hitherto omitted some facts of moment, because they were contained in the subjoined letter of Messrs Walker and Rand :—

" To the Right Hon. Sir James Graham, Bart., M.P., Her Majesty's Principal Secretary of State for the Home Department, &c., &c.

"Bradford, Yorkshire, Nov. 16, 1841.

" Sir,

" Availing ourselves of the permission with which you have favoured us, we now endeavour to lay before you answers to some of the leading objections which have been advanced against the proposal, that the hours of labour in mills and factories for all young persons, between thirteen and twenty-one years of age, be restricted to Ten per day. They can now be legally worked twelve, which is two hours a day longer than those work who are otherwise employed.

" The first objection to which we advert is, that ' interference with labour is improper.'

" Our answer is, that parliament decided this objection forty years ago ; and that every subsequent alteration in the law has been a still more positive interference, the justice of which is apparent; for there is no maxim clearer, than that it is the bounden duty of the legislature to interfere with labour, when the oppressed parties are too weak and helpless to make proper terms for themselves, and cannot, by an appeal to their employers, obtain a remedy.

"The case of the negroes in Great Britain's West India possessions is one in point. Their claims were found so unquestionable, that parliament interfered even to the extent of manumitting purchased slaves—adults as well as children. And the Commons of England scrupled not to vote twenty millions sterling to satisfy the slaveholders, because the state had become implicated by sanctioning that species of property.

"A second objection frequently urged is, that 'parents are the natural protectors of their children.'

"We readily admit that parents will, for the most part, protect their children from imminent and apparent danger; but all experience shows, that few can resist the temptation to derive advantage from the labour of their children, even when its duration may be carried to a length which must eventually prove destructive to their health, and incompatible with their moral improvement. It is also well known, that the parents of many of the children who work in factories, are unable to obtain the means of their support in any other way, and therefore cannot be considered in a condition to refuse to let their children work the long hours therein required and allowed.

"The English factory inspectors, over and over again, have drawn attention to the fact, that the parents in these districts are not to be relied upon as protectors of their children, but are often ready to go all lengths in getting them false certificates of age. We might refer to many instances which have occurred under our own eyes; but we prefer presenting you with the opinion of the Rev. Walter Fletcher, chancellor of the diocese of Carlisle; a venerable man, who had been in the commission of the peace for many years. That gentleman told a friend of ours, a year or two ago, that his 'experience had convinced him, that while the masters and surgeons were often much to blame in the matter of certificates of age, the parents themselves were decidedly most of all to blame: that from their own parents especially, the children needed protection. He had been so much pressed by parents to countersign certificates of ' thirteen' for children, whom he knew (having their baptismal registers in his own possession) to be under the age specified, and had found so much ill-feeling created by his conscientious refusals, that he did not re-qualify as a justice of the peace, for that and no other reason.'

" A third objection, to which we take this opportunity of alluding, is, that ' factory labour is not more injurious to health than agricultural employment.'

" When those who make this assertion select their cases (and that is too often their course), there can be no approximation to truth. The averages of both pursuits must be taken, and the results are then obvious to all. The official returns of mortality decide this question. The tables calculated upon the showing of those returns in 1832, and appended to the report of Mr Sadler's committee, established the fact—that taking a given number of deaths in the great spinning and power-loom weaving towns, and the same number in ordinary towns; and comparing them with those in agricultural districts of unhealthy, as well as healthy counties, as many deaths in the former (the spinning and power-loom weaving towns), occur under twenty years of age, as in the latter, under forty! An attempt indeed was made to invalidate these deductions, but it signally failed. The late Mr Sadler, in a pamphlet of great labour and research, entitled ' Factory Statistics,' and published after his death, refuted every objection raised; and the arguments and calculations employed by the several parties who had engaged in the controversy, were finally submitted, by Lord Ashley, to the impartial investigation of Mr Woolhouse, an eminent actuary, well known by his labours on the ' Nautical Almanack,' and esteemed by the late Dr Greggory, of Woolwich, to be the second mathematician of his day. Mr Woolhouse corroborated the original statement. And it is a curious fact, that the excessive mortality of the manufacturing districts, long the subject of vehement dispute and contradiction, has so entirely ceased to be so, that Dr Bowring, the member for Bolton, in a recent debate in the House of Commons, availed himself of the undue rate of mortality which notoriously exists in the spinning and manufacturing towns, as an argument for the repeal of the corn laws !

" The annual reports of the registrar-general give further incontrovertible evidence on this head. But they do not give all the evidence they might. If that public officer would take townships instead of what he calls districts, which are generally poor-law unions, where an agricultural population is often classed with a manufacturing one, the information afforded would be far more valuable than it is.

" The ex-registrar of Birmingham, Mr Paer, instituted a compasison between that town and Manchester a year or two ago. There is, doubtless, much that is wrong going on in Birmingham in reference to the maternal care of children; but Mr Paer, notwithstanding, could state that, in the same aggregate of deaths, the number in Birmingham under sixteen years of age, did not exceed those in Manchester under three years of age!

" A fourth objection often insisted upon is, that ' if parliament should interfere as we propose, the English manufacturer would be unable to compete with foreigners.'

" We hold this argument to be a most fallacious one. Great Britain is, after all that can be said, the great regulator of prices in most manufactured articles. The foreign manufacturer would gladly get better prices, if England were not perpetually lowering the continental markets, in spite of their prohibitory duties. Their tariffs, altered as they are from time to time, to meet emergencies, sufficiently show in what dread they are of English goods.

"The British manufacturer possesses many local and natural advantages, but there is one which is too often lost sight of, though it surpasses all others—he employs the most skilful and industrious people on the face of the globe. No race of people, of whom we have any knowledge, will work with the steadiness and expertness which so generally characterize the natives of Great Britain. We may also offer the decisive fact on this head, that the cost of cotton goods in France is thirty to forty per cent. more than the cost of similar goods in this country. This has been stated by Dr Bowring, but other respectable authorities have affirmed the difference to be much greater. Next to Great Britain, France consumes more cotton than any other nation. The same remarks apply in a great degree to the United States of America, which country, next to France, rivals Great Britain. In America we learn that wages are higher than in England—that machinery costs double the price—that fuel is much dearer —and the interest of money greater. But if (passing over the question of right and justice, which ought to be paramount) we must argue this subject on the ground of political economy, and we are able to show that the limitation of labour in factories to ten hours a day would make no material difference in the cost of production, the argument about foreign competition must fall to the ground.

"Now, it is universally admitted, that the term of twelve hours' labour cannot be maintained for any lengthened period. If it were constantly persisted in, the redundancy of goods in the market would be so great, that they would be sold at ruinous prices. All profit would be annihilated. It is also our conviction, that the daily hours of working in mills have not exceeded ten, on the average, for the last seven years. Moreover, the usual amount of orders could be executed with ten hours' daily labour, even without additions to the existing machinery. The markets would thereby be kept more regular, and, as a matter of course, employment and wages would not be subject to so many vicissitudes. There are persons who think, that the cost of production would not be at all increased by a reduction of the hours of labour from twelve to ten. We are of a different opinion; but we are persuaded that the extent of its influence upon the price of the manufactured article would not exceed what is often effected by the fluctuations of a single market-day. It, therefore, cannot be right that a consideration so trivial as this, should delay the settlement of a great question, involving the highest interests of an immense population.

"These objections failing, another of an opposite kind might be urged, namely, that 'wages would be reduced' by lessening the hours of labour, and that thus much misery would be occasioned. The government may be told, that the operatives would have their wages reduced to the full extent of the reduction of the time of labour. We by no means believe that such would be the case, and for the following reasons.

"The twelve hours' term of labour, as we have already said, cannot be maintained throughout the year. The attempt causes a constant recurrence of gluts. The glut is taken advantage of to force a reduction of wages, and reductions of wages are generally followed by a shortening of work. The operative has thus two evils to contend with at once. It is not an uncommon thing for even partial work to be refused in some mills, and that for months together. The cotton districts, especially, are greatly harassed by these changes. The more frequent the recurrence of these alternations in the quantum of labour, the more readily does one abatement follow another; and we believe, that the enactment of a ten hours' term of labour would greatly check this downward tendency of wages, which is creating wide-spread misery and discontent amongst the working people.

" But to take the very lowest view of the subject of wages,—for the sake of the argument, we will admit that wages might possibly be reduced to the same extent as the hours of labour. Still, with a ten hours' restriction, as much work can be performed in the aggregate, as is now performed, taking the whole year round, under a twelve hours' limit; and should it be performed, and at only the existing rates per pound, or per yard, or per hour, there would, at the end of the year, have been the same amount of capital distributed in wages as before.

" Again, the value of labour must always be influenced by the extent of redundant labour in the market ; and the tendency of the ten hours' restriction would be, to diminish the number of the unemployed. This could not fail to have a beneficial influence on wages. The great causes of distress amongst the operatives are, the irregular supply of work, and irregular wages. For want of a system of education, which can never be carried into effect until a Ten Hours' Factory Act is passed, there is undoubtedly great improvidence in the factory districts; that improvidence never can be checked while the working classes are exposed to such perpetual changes in their circumstances, and while the demand for labour itself is so often interrupted. No system of education alone, could meet and cure the evil, while those causes remain in operation.

" There is another view of the subject which is too important to be passed over. At the present time, a considerable number of unemployed persons are to be found in the manufacturing districts. We do not attempt to touch upon the causes of this, further than is absolutely necessary for our immediate purpose; but if the legitimate trade of the country should (under the auspices of a conservative government) extend, and more of our products be called for after the enactment of a ten hours' term of daily labour, many who are now standing idle in the market-places, because 'no man hath hired them,' would find profitable employment far more readily and generally than they can under the present long hours' system. Thus there would be less 'complaining in our streets.'

"Again, under a limitation of factory labour such as we advocate, there would also be less necessity for the population to be crowded into large towns. They might live more in the neighbouring villages; whereas now they must need be near the mills.

"Before we bring our remarks to a close, we feel it incumbent upon us to remind you of the medical evidence which parliament, from time to time, has taken on this subject ; and, especially, we would draw your attention to that which was given before the select committee of the Commons in 1832. One of those professional gentlemen, Dr Bisset Hawkins, in his published report, inserted a very remarkable passage to this effect,—'that he had less difficulty in stating it as his opinion, that the labour of young persons working in mills and factories should be limited to ten hours a day, because his opinion was corroborated by that of a great majority of all the respectable practitioners in Lancashire.' We may add that the same sentiments have been expressed by nearly all the medical practitioners in the factory districts of Yorkshire.

"A most important part of the case still remains to be noticed. The present factory hours of labour prevent young persons from learning domestic, moral, and religious duties. They have no time before six in the morning, nor after eight in the evening, to acquire any useful knowledge. How then can we wonder that they grow up in ignorance, and become a prey to vicious habits ? When we recollect that the great majority are females, it is truly awful to contemplate the result of continuing to absorb and enslave their energies of body and mind in factory labour.

" Some most interesting facts in connection with factory legislation may now be mentioned; which ought, we think, to settle the question in the minds of those who are afraid of foreign competition.

" The late King of Prussia, having had his attention drawn to the fact that the manufacturing districts under his dominion could not supply their contingents to the army, and that the agricultural districts had, in part, to make up the deficiency, made a law, bearing date March 9th, 1839, which decrees that no young person under sixteen, employed ' in daily labour in any manufactory, or in the works attached to mines,' should be worked for a longer time than ten hours in any one day. The regulations allow no child to be admitted to work before nine years of age, and are very stringent with regard to education.

" The unsatisfactory state of factory legislation in our own country, may account for the delay that has occurred in France, in reference to it. But the difficulty of obtaining recruits for the army in the manufacturing districts of France, in a due proportion to the population, has forced the legislature to pay great attention to the subject ; and though some delay has arisen, we cannot doubt that something will be speedily done in France, to place the factory system upon a proper footing. The French minister presented a factory bill to the Chamber of Peers on the 11th of January, 1840. The bill was referred to a committee, and Baron Charles Dupin, in the name of the committee, drew up and presented a report, in which he makes such honourable mention of England, that we cannot resist quoting a sentence or two.

" ' Great Britain, while she was the first to set the example of a protecting law for children and young persons, and took this step without waiting until rival countries would unite in such a measure, far from finding that it has checked the progress of those branches of industry to which the restrictions were successively applied, has, on the contrary, seen them flourish and increase with a rapidity four times as great as all her other manufactures.'

" ' More recently, similar laws have been passed,' continues the report, 'by two of the principal European powers, Prussia and Russia; and Austria has fixed a limit below which children cannot be employed in factories. With these great facts before us, of four great nations having anticipated us in the generous purpose of coming forward in aid of injured youths and children, we cannot, without dishonour, turn a deaf ear to those demands that have been made upon us on behalf of the young persons in our manufactories.'

" Alluding to the sordid considerations which are too often urged, the report contains this remarkable passage,— ' But so far from being stopped in her humane course by them, Prussia, which placed herself at the head of the Commercial Union of Germany, did not fear to establish a duration of labour, even two hours a day less than the highest limit fixed by the English law.'

" The French factory bill passed the Chamber of Peers, after discussions, in which unusual eloquence and ability were exhibited, ninety-one voting for its adoption, and only thirty-five for its rejection. It was presented to the Chamber of Deputies on the 11th of the following April. So much of powerful argument was used in the discussion and advocacy of the measure, that it is certain the subject will not be suffered to slumber long. We attribute the interval chiefly to the repeated postponements which the English amended bills have experienced. There is too much talent and high character enlisted on the side of factory legislation in France, not to bring the question there to a successful issue.

"In these facts we see the strongest inducement for the British parliament to mature the good work which it has commenced ; and we confidently hope, that the ensuing session will not be suffered to pass without a satisfactory and final measure being brought forward, by Her Majesty's ministers, with all the strength of the government. Certain we are, that nothing short of a ten hours' limitation can be a settlement of the question ; because nothing less can prevent an overwhelming mass of ignorance, pauperism, and misery from accumulating. The extent of suffering has repeatedly been such, that the local authorities have not known how to deal with it ; a crisis every now and then arises which is checked (not the misery, but the outbreak) by the military being called in, and thus our manufacturing towns, one after another, and in quick succession, become garrisoned towns. The coercive system takes the place of paternal government and ancient institutions; and men learn to look upon those among whom their lot is cast, no longer as friends and neighbours, but as enemies. It is an exorbitant price which a government pays for attending only to the wishes of the few, and disregarding the just claims of the many.

"The factory system is fast superseding domestic employment. The daughters of the working classes are now required to leave their home occupations, and enter the factories. Many of these formerly possessed the means of profitable industry at home as hand-loom weavers, but by the power looms they are either deprived of work altogether, or have their wages reduced to a mere pittance. Immense numbers of hand-loom weavers are brought into the pitiable condition of being unable to get work for themselves, and at the same time of having their daughters employed in the factories for such long hours as are quite inconsistent with female strength, and the performance of cottage duties.

" To a conservative government, the factory workers are looking for the redress of their wrongs, and we earnestly hope they may not be disappointed.

" Allow us to apologize for the length at which we have taken the liberty to address you (a length, however, which has far from exhausted all the points we could have urged, as intimately bearing upon this most important question), and in conclusion to intreat you to relieve the oppressed youths and maidens of our factory districts ; to give them time to learn to fear God, and honour the Queen ; to understand their domestic duties, and to fit them for the character they have to sustain in the world. We would implore you to afford the clergy and other ministers of religion, opportunity to exercise amongst these greatly neglected masses of population, the pastoral office. Then may we hope to see paternal and filial ties strengthened by family intercourse and Christian principle—then may we expect the blessing of Almighty God upon Her Majesty and Her Majesty's government.

" It is now full five-and-twenty years since the first Sir Robert Peel himself proposed a ten hours' bill, and on the 13th of June, 1815, a committee of the Commons fixed upon ten hours and a half, as the daily period of labour for all between nine and eighteen. In the following year, the same or a similar bill was referred to a select committee, on which occasion the first Sir Robert Peel thus recorded his deliberate opinion of a state of things which, in many respects, might be advantageously compared with that which now exists.

" 'Such indiscriminate and unlimited employment of the poor, consisting of a great proportion of the inhabitants of trading districts, will be attended with effects to the rising generation so serious and alarming, that I cannot contemplate them without dismay; and thus that great effort of British ingenuity, whereby the machinery of our manufactures have been brought to such perfection, instead of being a blessing to the nation, will be converted into the bitterest curse.' Mr William Rathbone Greg, in a pamphlet, published in 1831, and Mr Sheriff Alison, in his evidence given before the select committee on the combination of trades, about three years ago, have uttered similar predictions.

" If we did not know that interests of the highest importance would be hazarded by any further procrastination of this question, we should not press it as we do ; but we feel confident that there can be no subject more urgently demanding the attention of Her Majesty's government.

" We have the honour to be, Sir,

" Your most obedient and very humble servants,

" WILLIAM WALKER.

" WILLIAM RAND."

A deputation from the Ten Hours' Bill committees of the West Riding of Yorkshire was appointed in 1842, to wait on the second Sir Robert Peel, to state generally the condition of the working classes of the West Riding, and to urge on Sir Robert the necessity for remedial measures, and principally the Ten Hours' Bill. The deputation were received cordially by Sir Robert; they had also interviews with Sir James Graham, Lord Wharncliffe, the Right Hon. W. E. Gladstone, with the Duke of Buckingham, and Lord Lyndhurst, then Lord Chancellor. The deputation consisted of Mr George A. Fleming, Mr Joshua Hobson, Mr John Leech, Mr Mark Crabtree, and Mr Titus S. Brooke, than whom no men were more familiar with the condition of the West Riding, and none better able to state their views as to remedial measures. The report of the deputation is a very able document, and well deserves the attention of those who desire to understand the social condition of the manufacturing districts in 1842. The conversation of such men must have had weight on the minds of statesmen; it brought the question of the social condition of the labouring population to the ears of ministers from the lips of those who, from observation and much study, had made the past and present condition of those whom they represented integral parts of their own knowledge. Copies of the report of the deputation were widely and numerously circulated; the mind of England was during this period in much trouble as to what could be done by way of relief for the distress in the northern counties, and a document which at any time, because of its own merits, would have commanded attention from those who study the condition of the people, received, in consequence of the difficulties of the times, a more than usual share of attention. It is at all times desirable that statesmen should attend to the representatives of working men, they have often information of the greatest moment to convey, information frequently of a kind not to be had from other organs; and those who listen to their statements will seldom fail to reap a reward. Nature is not a bigot in the distribution of her gifts, and it sometimes happens that men of the highest order of genius are labourers, who, amidst many trials, have preserved the true dignity of manhood, and with whom to come in contact is instructive and refreshing. The members of this deputation, with the exceptions of Mr Titus Brooke and Mr John Leech, had earned their bread by manual labour; in the advance of others in the social scale their sympathies for their own order have been kept keenly alive. Mr Fleming and Mr Hobson, as members of "the fourth estate," have, on many occasions, proved how thoroughly versed they are in that knowledge of "common things," which is never so well understood as by those superior minds whose early training has been in "labour's rugged school."

The opinion of the supporters of factory regulation, as to the seriously injurious effects of factory labour on health, received a very remarkable corroboration in the general report of the sanitary condition of the labouring population of Great Britain, 1842, prepared from documents supplied by the sanitary commission, to Mr E. Chadwick:

"In the evidence of recruiting officers, collected under the factory commission of inquiry," wrote Mr Chadwick, "it was shown that fewer recruits of the proper strength and stature for military purposes are attainable now than heretofore from Manchester. I have been informed that of those labourers now employed in the most important manufactories, whether natives or emigrants to that town, the sons who are employed at the same work are generally inferior in stature to their parents. Sir James M'Grigor, the Director-General of the Army Medical Board, stated to me the fact, that a corps levied from the agricultural districts in Wales, or the northern counties in England, will last longer than one recruited from the manufacturing towns, from Birmingham, Manchester, or near the metropolis. Indeed, so great and permanent is the deterioration, that out of 613 men enlisted, almost all of whom came from Birmingham and five neighbouring towns, only 238 were approved for service."

On March the 7th, 1843, the long-desired government measure was introduced by Sir James Graham :—"The age of children," said the honourable baronet, "employed in factories was, at present, limited from nine to thirteen. He proposed to reduce the number of hours from eight to half-past six, and also proposed that six and a half hours' labour must take place either in the forenoon, or in the afternoon, wholly, and not in both. He was disposed to believe that the lowest age at which children might begin to work could be safely reduced from nine to eight, so that a child from eight to thirteen might work from six and a half to eight hours, either in the forenoon or in the afternoon, wholly, and not in both. The committee had recommended that the maximum age for females should be altered from eighteen to twenty-one. Young persons were not now permitted to work more than twelve hours a day. He proposed to alter the age at which females should be permitted to labour ; in the case of males coming under the denomination of 'young persons,' he did not propose to make any alteration. . . . With respect to Saturday, he proposed that the hours of work should be limited to nine, so that young persons would be worked twelve hours on the other days, and nine on the Saturdays. He proposed to limit those modes of making up lost time to those factories where water labour is used, and to provide for the fencing of machinery. The bill would include within the scope of its operation all children employed in silk factories ; and he hoped still further by a separate bill, brought in with the sanction of Her Majesty's government, to include the lace factories, and the children engaged in print works." Thus far the contemplated measure had the merit of extending the application of the principle of regulation, and was, on the whole, a decided concession to the claims urged by Lord Ashley, but did not meet the views of his lordship as to a limitation of the hours of labour.

The bill was read a second time on March 24th, and on this occasion the educational clauses of the bill, which were very important, were subjected to severe animadversion. The educational part of the ministerial measure aimed at uniting the church and the dissenting bodies with the " Committee of Privy Council on Education." All parties admitted that education under the factory act had, with rare exceptions, been a failure, and that a necessary provision was required for the education of factory operatives. Sir James Graham, in his attempt to reconcile the heads of the various religious parties in a general measure of education, succeeded in offending all. On May the 1st, the bill was read *pro forma*, and we find Sir James declaring that—" The petitions which have been presented against the educational clauses of the Factories' Bill, to which I am about to advert, have been numerous almost without a parallel;" and he proposed, in consequence, important modifications. "Coming events cast their shadows before." These educational discussions, remarkable as they were for calm deliberation, notwithstanding, foreshadowed the difficulties since realized by every statesman who has endeavoured to solve the educational problem; then, as now, the difficulties necessary to be overcome were greater without than within the walls of parliament. On June the 15th, Sir James explained to the House of Commons, that his efforts to conciliate the dissenters had been fruitless, and that he had resolved not to press the educational clauses of the bill. On the 19th the bill passed through committee with amendments, and was ordered to be printed, and on the 30th Sir James Graham explained the proposed alterations in the law; those that referred to education were as follow:—" In five days out of the seven the children should be educated for three hours, either in the forenoon or in the afternoon. By the existing law, no notice was taken as to the place where the education was given, or as to the system of instruction that was adopted. Now it was proposed by the present bill that the Privy Council should have the power to appoint inspectors to visit the schools to which certificates were granted; and on receiving a report from the inspectors as to the inconvenience of the place, or as to any objection in the method of education pursued, the Privy Council were empowered to notify to the schoolmaster the defect so reported, and unless within three months that defect should be remedied, the Privy Council would have the power of stopping the grant made

to the school." These proceedings in parliament awakened
an additional interest, beyond that at all times existing, on
the question of factory legislation. This increased interest
was educational, and had its roots deeply buried in the party
and sectarian influences of the age, no doubt representing
much that was sincere and excellent in character, but
also much that was pretentious and intolerant; the government having been repulsed and obliged to amend their
own measure, not from a conviction of the propriety of
amendment, but from the force of a variously expressed and
clamorous opposition, were not very energetic in urging
the amended measure on the renewed attention of parliament. On July the 31st, the late Sir Robert Peel, in reply
to a question put by Lord Ashley, said: " The postponement of the factories' bill which had been before the house,
to a future session, had not arisen from any doubt on the
part of the government of its importance or propriety, but
only from the desire expressed by hon. gentlemen on both
sides of the house, that it should be fully discussed. He was
prepared to give his noble friend an assurance that a bill
would be introduced at a very early period of next session,
for the purpose of amending the law on this subject."

Mr Charles Hindley, the member for Ashton-under-Line,
on the same evening moved for leave to bring in a bill to
amend the Factory Act. At the request of Sir James
Graham the motion was withdrawn.

Mr Hindley, himself a millowner, had often expressed his
conviction that the workers in factories were not free agents,
and that the simplest and most efficient means of enforcing
obedience to the Factories' Act, was by placing a restriction
on the moving power. Beyond doubt, this course, if adopted,
would have facilitated the discovery of the violation of the
law, and thereby have contributed to certainty in punishment.
The honourable member for Ashton-under-Line had a

standing maxim, namely, " man in a factory is not free," it was opposed to the current opinion of the legislature; its soundness, however, was apparent to the mind of the factory operatives, who in this instance entirely agreed with Mr Hindley, and would have rejoiced to have had this view of the question fully discussed in the House of Commons. It has been often repeated by Mr Hindley, no doubt from a consciousness of its truth and importance.

CHAPTER XIII.

MR OASTLER'S RELEASE FROM PRISON—PUBLIC ENTRY INTO
HUDDERSFIELD.

IF to bear misfortune and imprisonment with fortitude and
without complaint be an evidence of greatness, to Mr Oastler
must be conceded that merit. True, he had during his
imprisonment many friends and enjoyed some comforts, but,
to be confined within prison walls for three years and two
months was not a trifling trial to even a man of a sound
and strong body and mind, and it is not remarkable that
after so long a confinement, Mr Oastler's health began to
give way. Among Mr Oastler's prison friends was Mr
William Atkinson, author of a very ably written book on
The Principles of Political Economy and of *The Church.*
Both works are remarkable for a close analysis of the
principles maintained by others, and contain full expositions
of the author's views on the Christian theory of government.
The substance of the first appeared in a series of letters in
The Fleet Papers. Mr Atkinson suggested the possibility
of Mr Oastler's release by public subscription.

Mr Oastler had not a more constant, indefatigable, and
affectionate friend than Mr Lawrence Pitkethly, of Huddersfield. That gentleman, from the first to the last, throughout
the factory contest, had been to Mr Oastler as a right arm.
Not any one felt the absence of Mr Oastler more keenly;
and it was Mr Pitkethly who adopted the first practical

step towards the accomplishment of Mr Atkinson's object.
Knowing the ardent friendship which subsisted in the mind
of Mr Ferrand towards Mr Oastler, Mr Pitkethly resolved
to consult with Mr Ferrand as to the propriety of adopting
the means necessary for gaining the desired end. Mr Ferrand
immediately tendered his services, adding, " Call your meetings, and for a month I shall be at your service."

The trustees for " The Oastler Liberation Fund" were—
the Right Honourable Lord Feversham, John Walter, Esq.,
Sir George Sinclair, Bart., John Fielden, Esq., M.P., William
Busfield Ferrand, Esq., M.P. The treasurer was Matthias
Attwood, Esq., M.P. The central committee, meeting in
London, was composed of gentlemen of the highest standing ;
the committees in the country were not less respectable.

The late Matthias Attwood was well known as an influential banker, and was, on mercantile questions, justly
esteemed as a very high authority, and acknowledged to
be the most influential opponent of the second Sir Robert
Peel on the currency question. Mr Attwood had been a
member of the Sadler committee in 1832, and continued
to be a constant supporter of factory regulation in and out
of parliament; integrity and benevolence were the leading
traits of his character. He was the active coadjutor of
Mr Sadler, and his personal friendship for Mr Oastler was
manifested in many a kindly act. The name of Matthias
Attwood had great influence; he was for thirty years a
member of the House of Commons, and was invariably
admired for his clear practical common sense, his urbane
and manly bearing. His death, in 1851, was the subject
of regret to all who knew him.

The chairman of the London central committee was Lord
Feversham. No man knew Mr Oastler better than did his
lordship, and it was an act worthy of a British peer, to be
faithful to an old friend in the hour of trial. Mr Ferrand was
the active spirit of the Oastler liberation movement. In all
the arrangements for meetings throughout the country, Mr

Ferrand was assisted by Mr Squire Auty, of Bradford, Yorkshire. For many years Mr Auty has been the supporter of factory regulation ; in politics he may be briefly designated " an Oastlerite ;" he is an active politician in his own neighbourhood, and is remarkable for perseveringly maintaining what he believes to be the truth, without regard to opposition ; he was personally attached to Mr Oastler, a circumstance which gave additional zeal to his labours, and fitted him to be the useful ally of Mr Ferrand in their labour of love.

We are unable to recall, by the aid of memory, a more pleasing instance of how thoroughly the spirit of party may at times become paralyzed, and the nobler sympathies of the heart of man rule predominant, than by remembering the circumstances attendant on Mr Oastler's release from prison.

The press was unusually unanimous in its support of the Oastler liberation movement ; party feeling (with a few exceptions, which only served to make the rule conspicuous), was forgotten ; London and provincial editors united in urging freedom for the captive. Few men, in the heat of political conflict, had said stronger or less pleasant things of each other than had Mr Oastler and the late Mr Baines, M.P. for Leeds. Forgetting the annoyances of the past, and remembering only Mr Oastler's many virtues, which Mr Baines had recognized early in life, he, when solicited, generously cast his mite into the common treasury, and heartily desired to shake hands with his early friend, as a free man. This was very creditable to Mr Baines, and we record the circumstance as a just tribute to the memory of a public man. Many members of the press and others, while helping forward the desires of Mr Oastler's more immediate friends, were very decided in expressing dissent from some of his views, and naming what they conceived to be his failings; but the substance of all such dissent and criticism referred, in most cases, rather to manner than to objects; and all agreed that a very heavy compensating penalty had been paid for what had, when viewed in the severest possible light, been an act of indiscretion. In the words of the editor of the *Times*—" Without taking into account many special pleas in favour of Mr Oastler, and which appear on the face of this unfortunate affair, the worst his case amounts to is this—that he discharged too liberally and too hospitably the delicate office of resident representative of a wealthy absentee—an office in which he succeeded his father; that he did not sufficiently number and weigh his own outlays and services in this situation; that in the course of many years he suffered a large debt thus to accumulate, which, however, for many years, his employer even made a ground of increased liberality; and, lastly, that he suffered his public labours to draw too largely on his time and means."

There were exceptions—a ministerial journal, a Liverpool newspaper, and *The League* (the official organ of the free-trade party), had the unenviable notoriety of making some bitter observations ; these exceptions served to make the rule more conspicuous.

The meetings which were held in the principal towns of Yorkshire and Lancashire, to aid in Mr Oastler's liberation, were enthusiastic and unanimous ; the subscriptions paid were varied in amount, and manifested an extended sympathy. These meetings were attended by Mr Ferrand, who travelled and talked incessantly; resolute in his purpose, and sparing neither time nor money in its consummation. Persons of all ranks addressed these public meetings ; clergymen, noblemen, magistrates, and working men, bore a willing testimony to Mr Oastler's high character, and valuable services. The first public meeting was in Huddersfield, a town in which Mr Oastler was thoroughly known. At this meeting, the Rev. Wyndham Madden, incumbent of Woodhouse, near Hudders-field, said, that " his feelings of personal regard for Mr Oastler had brought him to that meeting. Had his presence implied a concurrence in all the sentiments, all the sayings and doings of Mr Oastler, he would not have been present. He differed from Mr Oastler upon many points, and had expressed his difference to him at various times, when he had the pleasure of meeting him; but had always ventured to express himself as Mr Oastler's friend. The object of the meeting was, simply to express sympathy for Mr Oastler, contrive means to effect his liberation, and to put forth a helping hand here and elsewhere, in the accomplishment of that object. He was fully persuaded there was not a kinder-hearted man, nor one more desirous for the welfare of his fellow creatures, than Mr Oastler. He had been his pastor for many years, and ought to know him, and he could bear witness to his private character. He never applied to him on behalf of any religious or charitable object, but his heart and his hand were immediately opened more freely and largely than he anticipated, for the cause he advocated, and even to give, in the cause of distress, sometimes, more than he could afford. He considered that Oastler, with all his faults, had been a great benefactor to his country. This had been the result of his own personal observations as a minister. He had been in Yorkshire about nineteen years, and he had seen a marked difference in the condition and character of the operatives, which he could trace to the exertions of Oastler. He could remember, in 1825, seeing from his residence, being on a hill that overlooked Huddersfield, the factories of Huddersfield illuminated all night; and he could adduce an instance which had come under his own observation, of the hardships inflicted upon the working classes, during a period of supposed prosperity in 1825:—in many of the mills 'the hands' were kept at work through the whole night. He would relate an instance connected with the horrid system, to show the necessity of Mr Oastler's exertions on behalf of the mill operatives, and which also showed the cupidity of the masters; one which showed the necessity of legislative interference between the avarice and cupidity of the

millowners, and the weakness and impotence, he might say, of
the working classes, who were *compelled* to work those long
and inhuman hours, or *starve*. He had visited one of his poor
people, and saw a girl in bed; he asked what was the matter,
and if she was sick? The answer was, no; she was tired, and
had been worked too hard. This was before the passing of
Lord Althorp's Eight Hours' Act, when the masters sought to
make as much as they possibly could of human flesh and
sinews; which system had destroyed many lives. He asked
for the particulars of the case, of which he would give them
the substance. That child had been in the factory from six
o'clock in the morning on Monday, until six o'clock on
Tuesday night. On Wednesday morning, she again went to
work till Thursday night; Thursday night she came home,
and slept that night if she could. She went on Friday, and
remained until five o'clock on Saturday night. He observed,
' that this was cruel.' She replied, 'If I don't go, they
will get another, and some must do it.' He said, ' It was impossible, and that they could not subsist thus ; ' but they said,
' The men and the children worked and got rest at different
times, beneath the machines.' He asked the mother, ' Why
she did not send another girl (for he saw she had one) to
relieve this overworked child,' and the mother answered, ' that
the factory masters would not let her send her sister to help
her; and they told her, if she would not work the hours required, others were ready to do so.' At that time, he knew
it was not uncommon for children to sleep in the mill, under
the machines that they worked at; such treatment it was impossible for nature to stand. That such a case as he had
mentioned, should have been one that could not be punished
by the law, showed the necessity for interference between the
cupidity of the masters and the weakness of the persons
employed. He considered that Mr Oastler had, under God,
been primarily instrumental in putting a stop to this
abominable system, having first directed public attention to

the evils of the system, and to the misery that was inflicted
on young children, and others, by excessive labour in those
dens of unhealthiness. And he also considered, that to Mr
Oastler, under God, with the assistance of others, they were
indebted for the Eight Hours' Act, which was certainly an
improvement on the former state of things. As a clergyman,
who had received a commission from his Master to look after
the lambs of his flock, he felt that Oastler had thus conferred
a benefit, by rescuing these lambs from the cruelties to which
they have been subjected, and by allowing the children, not
only time for recreation, but for education, and also for allowing them time to attend to the concerns of their souls. He
utterly condemned that system, which, whilst it destroyed
their bodies, rendered them unable to attend a Sabbath school,
or the house of God, and led to the destruction of their souls
also. He could bear testimony to the effects of Oastler's
labours in this neighbourhood; and he could only say that he
should truly rejoice if the effect of that meeting stirred up a
determined spirit in that neighbourhood in favour of Oastler.
He considered he was only doing his duty in bearing testimony
to the benefit accruing from the exertions of Oastler, and he
would bear testimony to those exertions. Human nature was
selfish at its root, and when a man was shut up in prison,
people were apt to forget their benefactor. But they ought to
feel for the prisoner; and he hoped that the voice of that
meeting would awaken the dormant feeling of sympathy
towards a man, who had been a benefactor to the operative
classes, and that those friends of Oastler, who had the means,
would contribute towards his liberation."

This kind of testimony, as to character and usefulness,
was unimpeachable, and of it there was an abundance.
It was felt by those who knew Mr Oastler to be a reproach,
that a man who had so disinterestedly and eminently served
the interests of humanity, should continue to live within
the walls of a debtor's prison. To no man was time of

more value than to the late Mr Walter, of the *Times*; he, notwithstanding, travelled specially to Huddersfield, in order by his presence and words to give effect to the first meeting for the liberation of his imprisoned friend. Mr Walter's speech was excellent; his anxiety to convey to Mr Oastler the result was creditable in the highest degree. "On the 23rd of November, 1843," said Mr Oastler, "after the prison gates were closed, late in the evening, I was sitting in my solitary apartment. A turnkey entered.—'A gentleman wants to see you, sir, in the outer lobby.'—'Who is he?'—'He did not give his name; he said he wished to see you, sir.'—'Is he old or young?'—'I cannot tell, I scarcely noticed him; but came directly to inform you.'—The prisoner entered the outer lobby—there stood the gentleman in travelling attire. He was indeed a friend!—'How are you, my friend?'—'Quite well,' I thank you.'—'I have just returned from Huddersfield;—I came direct from the station, before I went home. We had a public meeting last night, in order to effect your liberation.'—What followed need not be told, save, when I declared my inability to express my gratitude, the visitor, taking me by the hand, said,—'Don't say a word, my friend. Had I refused to go, I never could have seen your face again. It was my duty, and I am delighted that we have succeeded so well.' That friend was Mr Walter." There was in this act, on Mr Walter's part, a generous manliness, deserving to be remembered. Such friendship ennobles character, and conscience, yields an ample satisfaction in return for the gifts of *duty*.

These public meetings served the twofold purpose of aiding Mr Ferrand's benevolent object, and, because of his advocacy of Mr Oastler's claims to public sympathy, they forwarded very materially the Ten Hours' Bill movement, for the merits of that measure, and Mr Oastler's exertions on its behalf, were ever uppermost in Mr Ferrand's mind, and constant themes of approbation from his lips.

In addition to the meetings held in the manufacturing districts of England, there was one in Ireland which, because of some specialities, deserves attention. Mr Oastler's ultra-protestantism has been a feature in his public life, and the protestants of Dublin felt the desirableness of assisting in the liberation of one who from principle, and at the sacrifice of high personal position, had proved his adhesion to the church, and the constitution as by law established. In 1837, when Mr Oastler contested, for the second time, the borough of Huddersfield, he was in a minority of twenty-one. On that occasion, on the hustings, he was asked, "If you are returned to parliament, and a bill should be brought in to repeal the Roman Catholic Emancipation Act, would you vote for that bill ?"—Mr Oastler replied, " Yes, I would." In the afternoon of that day a number of voters, more than sufficient to have turned the scale at the election, waited upon Mr Oastler, to ask him to withdraw that declaration, or in some way to lessen its effect, else, they would not be able to vote for him, which on other grounds they very much wished to do. Mr Oastler thanked them for their friendly feeling, and added, " If I enter the House of Commons, it shall not be by equivocation; what I stated on the hustings I shall perform, if returned." The consequence was the loss of a seat in the legislature.

The Dublin meeting was thoroughly protestant, and was addressed by the Rev. T. D. Gregg (now Dr Gregg), and other distinguished Irish protestant leaders. In addition to the local protestant talent of Dublin, there were Mr Ferrand, Mr Squire Auty, and Dr Gifford, editor of the London *Standard,* whose long-tried and able advocacy of protestantism, gave to his words, in such an assembly, great weight. Dr Gifford said:—" He owed to Richard Oastler, to say, that he

(Dr Gifford) had observed him for many years, and a nobler specimen of that noblest work of the creation—an honest Englishman—he had never seen. He was a man of truth, a man of courage, a man of power, a man of honour and religious feeling ; and if he had done wrong (and who had not done wrong ?) his wrong had been the excess of right; his errors, if he had errors, were those of a noble mind, and it belonged to a noble mind, not only to forgive such errors, but to support such a man as Richard Oastler. It was such men as Oastler who protected the integrity of the British empire." These were the words of a generous heart, which, when spoken by so high an authority, could not fail to serve the end desired; they reflect honour on Dr Gifford, who was anxious to serve a persecuted and much misunderstood man.

Mr Ferrand was present at from thirty to forty meetings, and the result of his labours, with those of other friends, was, at the close of 1843, the realisation of nearly 2,500*l.* Early in January, 1844, the central committee resolved to take immediate steps for Mr Oastler's liberation.

Mr Oastler's friends being anxious for his release, Jonathan Schofield, W. Walker, W. B. Ferrand, John Milner, Joshua Pollard, Isaac Milnes, J. Walter, Wm. Underwood, Lord Feversham, John Fielden, L. Pitkethly, and Samuel Glendenning resolved to guarantee what remaining sum was required ; and on Monday, February 12th, 1844, Mr Walker and Mr Pollard, both magistrates in the West Riding of Yorkshire, paid to Mr Thomas (Mr Thornhill's attorney), for debt, interest, costs, and sheriff's expenses, 3,243*l.* 15s. 10d. In this sum was included the 500*l.* claimed by Mr Oastler, which claim was not prejudiced in the arrangement made in the Court of Common Pleas, between Mr Kelly and Mr Oastler. That sum was demanded in deduction from the above-named amount. Mr Thomas replied, that his instructions were positive to receive the whole sum, but on behalf of Mr

Thornhill he promised that the 500*l.* should be returned. Messrs Walker and Pollard, desirous that not any further delay should take place in Mr Oastler's release, accepted that promise, and paid the sum demanded. Mr Thornhill died a few weeks after the payment of Mr Oastler's debt, his daughter inherited the entailed Yorkshire estates ; his son, Mr Thomas Thornhill, possessed the Norfolk estates, purchased by his father. Mr Oastler desired his friends not to press for the payment of the 500*l.*, the return of which had been promised, he was confident of Mr Thornhill's honour, and believed the promised payment would be made. A considerable delay ensued; a full statement of the facts was made to Mr Thomas Thornhill,—no answer was received ; subsequently application was made to his solicitors in London, to whom a full detail of the circumstances was forwarded. They readily undertook to make the required representation to Mr Thornhill; the applications were repeated from time to time. He continued to treat these with silence; a solicitor on behalf of Messrs Walker and Pollard demanded payment; the agents of Mr Thornhill intimated, on behalf of their client, his intention to plead the statute of limitations. Mr Thomas Thornhill thus retains 500*l.*, which his father's solicitor was pledged to return.

Mr Oastler was conducted from the prison to the British Coffee House, Cockspur street, by Mr Ferrand and Mr Rashleigh, then members of the House of Commons ; he was welcomed by a body of friends, presided over by Lord Feversham. In the proceedings which followed, the noble lord congratulated Mr Oastler on his release, and avowed that the principles of both on all leading questions were identical. Mr Walter declared, that in his efforts against the New Poor Law Amendment Act, he had never received so much assistance from any man as he had from Mr Oastler. All felt that an honourable Englishman had been liberated ; the expression of his gratitude, as best befitted the occasion, was dignified and manly. Mr Oastler possessed the affectionate regards of many among the working classes, who felt truly grateful to Lord Feversham, Mr Ferrand, Mr Rashleigh, and others for their exertions on behalf of " the king of the factory children."

On the question of principles, Mr Oastler was as usual distinct. He said :—" I believe the country will prosper when the church assumes its proper place in the state, and is considered, not as the political engine of any government, but as the mother teacher of principles of religion. I believe, also, that there is another essential principle of the constitution of England, without which it cannot stand, and that is the principle of self or parochial government. I believe the principles which have lately been introduced into this country, under the name of centralization, to be at eternal war with the principles of liberty incorporated in the constitution. I believe, too, that the principles of our constitution demand, that every man that is born in the country should have a home in the country ; and it is because of the maintenance of that principle, that I have been so much hated, and so much maligned, by those who profess to be the friends of the poor ; but, who in works, belie their professions. I believe, also, that the rights of the Crown, the rights of the peerage, and the aristocracy, are as sacred in the eye of the constitution as all other rights." This was plain speaking, and easy of comprehension.

Mrs Oastler was a gifted, pious woman, whose whole desires were concentrated in the welfare and labours of her husband. It is more easy to conceive than express the emotions which moved the heart of her liberated husband, when addressing his benefactors, he said :— " Permit me to offer you the thanks of my dear wife. I have it in charge from her,—'The first time you meet your friends, tell them, if you can, how much I feel obliged to them.'"

On Shrove Tuesday, February 20th, 1844, Mr Oastler
made a public entry into Huddersfield; his old friends and
neighbours welcomed him back among them, with a right
hearty Yorkshire greeting. The circumstances of that day
are fresh in our memory ; it was to thousands a day of
heartfelt rejoicing. The roads leading to Huddersfield,
from towns and villages miles distant, were enlivened by
groups of men, women, and children, travelling thitherward
to manifest their affection for him whom they designated
" the poor man's friend." The morning was fine, the sun
brilliant, and nature joyous with the hopes of spring. About
eleven o'clock in the forenoon, crowds gathered at the
railway hotel, Brighouse ; all was contentment and rejoicing,
and from many lips passed the words, " God bless the old
King." An address was presented to Mr Oastler from his
supporters in Yorkshire. We shall never forget the attendant
circumstances. There stood a venerable Englishman, released
from prison, surrounded by old and loved neighbours and
friends; the eyes of all were moistened with tears. The
words spoken by Mr Tweedale, a dear and valued friend
of Mr Oastler, and one whose labours for factory regulation
had been constant and influential, on presenting the address,
were few; the reply was brief, but full of meaning : the
declaration—" our aim has been to divorce labour from
poverty, and to wed labour with plenty," met with a ready
response. There are times when thought and feeling discard
the copious use of words ; this was one of these occasions.
The scene closed, and preparations were made for mustering
the procession; soon, all were in motion, preceded by bands
of music. The distance from Brighouse to Huddersfield
is about four miles, through a hilly and romantic part of
Yorkshire. At every turning of the road the numbers
augmented; as the crowd increased, so did the musicians,—
for Yorkshiremen, like the inhabitants of all lands of hill
and glen, are lovers of music. The cheering was repeated

loud and long, and the sound echoed from hill to hill, human voices and soul-stirring strains mingling together. As the procession approached Huddersfield, it was marshalled in the following order :—A body of horsemen. Band. Banner inscribed, " Oastler, our defender"—" Oastler and native industry." Band. Flag—" Oastler and no Bastille." A group of small flags—Union Jack. Band. Several carriages. Band. Banner inscribed, " Lindley—welcome," and on the reverse, " The Ten Hours' Bill." Band. Mr Oastler, in an open carriage, accompanied by the Rev. G. S. Bull, Mr Jonathan Schofield, of Raistrick, and Mr Wm. Stocks; Mr W. Hulke was upon the box-seat with a splendid Union Jack. Numerous other carriages. Band.

Mr Oastler addressed from 12,000 to 15,000 persons in public meeting, assembled in the open space of ground in front of the Druid's Hotel, on the Halifax Road. The anxiety of that vast crowd to hear the words which fell from the lips of their venerated friend, was extraordinary, and the calm attention of all was not the least remarkable feature of that day's proceedings.

Mr Oastler was a changed man ; the energy of former years had been mellowed by experience and reflection, and chastened by imprisonment. The same principles were enunciated, but there was a gravity and weight in the manner, a mildness yet strength in the expression, unknown in the earlier stages of the factory and anti-new-poor-law movement. The press (metropolitan and provincial) reported the proceedings, and the event contributed its share of influence to the growing force of public opinion in favour of an efficient ten hours' bill.

Mr Jonathan Schofield, of Raistrick, who presided over the Huddersfield meeting, was the oldest of the tenants of the late Mr Thornhill, on his Yorkshire estates. Mr Schofield is in all senses " a representative man." He is a York-shire manufacturer of the old school, whose principal pride has been to make the best goods, and pay the highest wages in his district. He believes it to be his duty to find regular employment for his workmen, at all times, and has occasionally paid a heavy penalty in consequence. He has, throughout a long life, been remarkable for his attention to the old and the young; he has not moved with the times. On all occasions he talks the Yorkshire dialect, makes no pretensions to being " the fine gentleman," but carries everywhere with him the politeness of the heart, and is welcomed alike by rich and poor, is esteemed among his neighbours as a " father and friend," and is justly valued by the Thornhills, as an excellent tenant, as a man of probity and honour. Mr Schofield had witnessed the whole progress of the change from domestic industry to the introduction and development of the unregulated factory system, and its improvement by act of parliament, and has, from first to last, been the friend of the oppressed. The judgment of such a man, on what he has observed in his own experience, is worth much more than the rhapsody of innumerable theorists, no matter how eloquently penned. Mr Schofield entirely agreed with Mr Oastler, as to the effects of unregulated factory labour, and the deterioration during its operation on the social condition of numerous bodies of working men in the West Riding; both zealously worked together throughout the factory agitation. It was spirited and becoming of Mr Schofield cordially to receive his old friend and neighbour on his return to Huddersfield, and to preside over the first public meeting which welcomed him home again, among those to whom he was so well known, and by whom he was so sincerely beloved.

CHAPTER XIV.

PROCEEDINGS IN PARLIAMENT IN 1844.—IMPORTANT PUBLIC MEETINGS
IN THE COUNTRY.—CONFLICTING DECISIONS IN THE HOUSE OF
COMMONS.—MRS OASTLER.

IT has been a feature of modern times, for the speeches in
parliament to increase in length, to such an extent, indeed,
as to have become, in the opinion of some persons, unneces-
sarily lengthy. Every attentive observer of parliamentary
history, must have perceived the great change in the time
consumed in parliamentary debates now and formerly. When
the first Sir Robert Peel introduced the factory question to
the attention of parliament, debates were conversational;
speech-making, except by a few orators of the highest mark,
was then an unknown art. Parliamentary oratory, like some
others of the products of modern industry, has been remarkable for increase in the quantity rather than the quality. Beyond doubt, the influence of the debates in parliament is greater
now than at any former period; the improvement in reporting,
and the vastly extended circulation of the press, give to
orators an influence which their predecessors did not possess,
and one which it will be to their credit and usefulness not to
abuse. The great length of the debates on the factory
question, precludes the possibility, in consideration of time
and space, of presenting to the reader more than a summary
of the facts necessary for an understanding of the position of
the opposing parties in the legislature. In these debates, no

new facts were stated; the more important phase of the
question, was the. influence marshalled, by the leaders of the
factory movement, at public meetings, and the efforts made
to induce parliament to adopt the Ten Hours' Bill.

On February the 6th, 1844, Sir James Graham introduced
to the notice of the House of Commons the promised
measure on factories; the following were the principal
points of his speech: " As the law now stands, the word
' child' applies to children who are admitted between the
ages of nine and thirteen. I propose in the present bill
that the age shall be altered, and the term ' child' be applied
between the ages of eight and thirteen, instead of nine and
thirteen, and that such children shall not be employed in
the forenoon and the afternoon of the same day. By the
existing law ' young persons' are defined to be those who
are between the ages of thirteen and eighteen. I do not
propose to make any alteration in that part of the act,
but I propose that such young persons shall not ' be employed
in any silk, cotton, wool, or flax manufactory for any
portion of the twenty-four hours longer than from half-
past five o'clock in the morning, till seven o'clock in the
evening in summer, and from half-past six o'clock in the
morning till eight o'clock in the evening in winter; thus
making thirteen and-a-half hours each day,—of which one
hour-and-a-half is to be set apart for meals and rest, so
that their actual labour will be limited to twelve hours.
By the law, as it now stands, all persons above the age
of eighteen, without distinction of sex, are considered to
be adults, and to their hours of labour there is no limitation
whatever. Under this state of the law, female adults are wholly
unfitted for the tasks to which they are subjected. I propose
to limit their hours of labour. No time to be made up,
excepting where the power is water exclusively, and that
lost time shall be made up within three months ; that 'young
persons' shall not labour more than thirteen hours in any

one day, and that there shall be a cessation of all labour between the hours of twelve at night and half-past five in the morning; silk mills to be brought under the operation of the act. In allowing full time for education, and in not permitting any child to be employed who does not produce a certificate of attendance at some school, government does all that it can under the present circumstances. I much fear that the enactments already existing are almost illusory. . . . . Even the stoker of the furnace is occasionally to be found acting the part of a factory schoolmaster. Up to this time, it has been confinement in a school-room, not education." Sir James's opinions were very much modified, not as regarded the desirableness of education, but as to the ability of the state to provide the required means, and he founded his hope of improvement, on the belief, that " the most flagrant abuses were fast giving way under the force of public opinion."

The discussions at various times, on the factory question, had evolved many striking and, comparatively, unknown facts.

Mr Oastler's re-entrance into public life, contemporaneously with the desire of the government to effect a settlement of the factory question, was an interesting and important event. The Ten Hours' Bill committees, in Yorkshire, naturally looked to their old friend for counsel, and he naturally desired to express his opinions, on the position of the factory movement, in and out of parliament. On February 26th, 1844, Mr Oastler was invited to address a body of his own friends in Leeds. Mr Summers occupied the chair. In the course of his address, Mr Oastler made the following special allusion to his own position and that of the ministry on the factory question : " There does want something doing. Yes, my friends, I rejoice that I have come out at such a time. The government, too, confess that some-thing must be done. We, therefore, of the old Ten Hours' Bill school are still in our places—to tell them, that if they will not adopt some measure or other to regulate machinery: machinery which, being unregulated in its operations, has already destroyed its tens of thousands, nay, its millions of the operative classes; which has destroyed its tens of thousands of the middle classes, and which is now destroying its hundreds even of the higher classes of manufacturers, must go on, if unrestricted and unregulated, until one successful manufacturer shall possess himself of the whole; and when he has acquired his accumulated millions, we can tell him, that he will find no happiness in his wealth, but he will be more miserable in the possession of his millions, than he was when he only possessed a few thousands. Well, then, my friends, we stand upon the same ground we ever did ; and we offer to the country the Ten Hours' Bill —the simple, plain, efficient Ten Hours' Bill, unaccompanied by inspectors, superintendents, or any other government officers, who, let me tell you, are always the spies of the government. Let the stoppage of the moving power be enacted, or let the clauses for personal punishment to the millowners who shall wilfully break the law be adopted, and we can do without inspectors." Mr Oastler stated many reasons why a Ten Hours' Bill should be adopted. The voice of Sir James Graham in the House of Commons, and that of Richard Oastler in Yorkshire, sounded very differently : the latter did not at this time contemplate a renewal of factory agitation, but, with Lord Ashley, Mr Fielden, and Mr Ferrand, in parliament, a discussion of the merits of the Ten Hours' Bill was a certainty. Lord Ashley's intention of moving an amendment in favour of the Ten Hours' Bill, was speedily made known throughout the manufacturing districts, and met with the enthusiastic approval of the factory operatives.

On March the 5th, a meeting of millowners, overlookers, and others was convened in the Temperance Hall of Bradford, in Yorkshire. The proceedings at this meeting, because of the high social standing of the principal speakers, commanded much attention. Joshua Pollard, Esq., a West Riding magistrate, occupied the chair. Mr Pollard unites in his own person many of the elements of influence in England. He is the representative of an ancient and influential Yorkshire family ; as a magistrate, a very impartial and strict administrator of the law; a shareholder and manager of the Bowling Iron Works, and, consequently, a large employer of labour. Mr Pollard is a thorough Yorkshireman, proud of his own country, careful of family honour, very hospitable to his poorer neighbours, by whom he is much beloved. He is a churchman and tory; socially, he is very tolerant, but devoted to principle, and, in political conflicts, proclaims fearlessly his own convictions. These are ingredients of character and position which, in the West Riding, give to their possessor a high moral influence. Mr Pollard has often presided over Ten Hours' Bill meetings. " That it is the duty of a government to watch with a father's eye over the moral and physical interests of its labouring classes," is, with him, a standing maxim. He, as chairman of the Bradford meetings, strenuously recommended adhesion to the Ten Hours' Bill, and, assured his hearers, that Mr Oastler's release from prison was an "augury of success." " I cannot but believe," said Mr Pollard, " that he who, side by side with the venerated Sadler, fought the battles of the poor factory child, in years long gone by, released at this important crisis, will be the instrument in the hands of a merciful Providence to carry out a triumphant success in the achievement of a Ten Hours' Factory Bill; and I sincerely pray that such may be the result."

Mr Wm. Walker and Mr Wm. Rand, both manufacturers of influence, urged on the meeting the necessity for a Ten Hours' Bill. The Rev. Dr Scoresby, the vicar of Bradford, supported by the Rev. J. Cooper, the Rev. W. Sherwood, and the Rev. W. Morgan, addressed the meeting in favour of a Ten Hours' Bill. Dr Scoresby maintained "that the great evil of this country, was the vast exertions of individuals to get wealth; that the injury done to our population was great, and that, consequently, the real blessings of wealth were not enjoyed to an extent consistent with the welfare of all; he approved of the factory regulation as a remedial measure." Not any man was better able to judge of the evils of the factory system than was the Rev. Doctor; he had investigated these evils closely, and was anxious for their removal. The Rev. J. Cooper affirmed, from his own experience, "that long hours of labour seriously affected all the domestic relations of life, and left the labourers so worn out, both bodily and mentally, that they had not the power, nor had they the time, for moral and religious improvement. The Sabbath day was much neglected through this system of long hours in the factories. The factory labourers now, to a considerable extent, instead of making Sunday a day of rest, made it one for bodily rest only, and the soul was left to starve altogether ; and there should certainly be a restriction on the labour of at least all young persons, in order that this evil system should be put an end to." Similar sentiments were expressed by the other clergymen present, which were very heartily approved, and responded to, by the working men. This union of Christian ministers, county magistrates, influential millowners, and oppressed factory operatives, for one common object, was significant, and proved how successfully the teachings of the earlier advocates of factory regulation had impregnated the public mind.

The meeting at Bradford was followed by similar meetings at Leeds and Manchester. On March the 9th, the Leeds meeting was convened in the music hall, presided over by Mr Joshua Hobson, and was addressed by some of the principal clergymen and medical men of the borough. The Rev. Dr Hook, the vicar of Leeds, seconded a resolution in support of a Ten Hours' Bill, in a speech of much ability;—his observations on the connection between reasonable and regular hours of labour, and the mental and moral elevation of working men, are deserving of special attention. The Rev. Vicar said :—" I have turned my mind more especially to the mental question. Now we hear on all sides much talk about the education of the people; but where is the use of teaching people to read and write and think, unless you give them time also for mental cultivation ? I, for one, shall always be desirous of contending for leisure time for the rational enjoyment of the working classes. We see the middle classes toiling hard, working very hard, but even they always find time for recreation and for enjoyment ; and why should not all of us labour to obtain this right, this privilege, for the working classes also? I think we ought never to rest contented until, in every business where it is practicable, in every mill where it is practicable, we should supply the place of children and females by men capable of doing the work. It is impossible to train children in the way they ought to go, unless we have more time to train them ; and it is demoralising to witness the system which now prevails in most of the manufacturing districts. It is contrary to nature that children should be the bread-winners of the family. Fathers ought to support their families ; and it is a monstrous thing to find families supported by the labour of little children, the parents being, perhaps, all the while idle. Children who have supported their parents for a time, soon cease to have any regard for that commandment which requires them to honour their parents; they soon assert their own independence, and take their own course, and, from being disobedient children, they soon became disloyal members of the state. There is another thing that we cannot insist upon too much, namely, that wherever it is practicable (and I say wherever practicable, because I am told that there are some places where it is not practicable), we ought to have men to suppl the place of women. Let me ask, *how* is the process of civilisation to go on if men have not happy homes? Why is it that men so often resort to the alehouse rather than to their own homes? Because, their wives being otherwise engaged, there is no home prepared to receive them. The business of woman, is to make home comfortable and happy for man, after he has earned sufficient for the support of his family; not by over-working, but with such a moderate amount of labour as will enable him to prepare his mind to give instruction to his children. Those are the objects which I think we now have in view. We are come here for the purpose of advancing one step, if we can, in the furtherance of those great ends. Our desire, our object, is to have the men of the working-classes not over-worked; to emancipate the children and females. We are assembled, therefore, to assist human nature under its most helpless and most lovely form ; and I think that, engaged in such a cause, we are labouring not only for the promotion of man's happiness, but for the promotion also of God's glory."

This comprehensive and reasonable view of the working-man's interests was ably supported by the Rev. T. Nunns, incumbent of St Paul's, Leeds, who also maintained that the Ten Hours' Bill was a wise and humane suggestion, and would, in practice, be found beneficial for the rich and the poor. " He asserted that it would benefit the millowners, because it would contribute towards making them humane, and not avaricious. The Ten Hours' Bill system was calculated to make men love each other. It would make the millowners feel more than at present for their fellow-creatures, instead of having their hearts steeled by the love of filthy lucre—a love, which God had declared to be idolatry."

The Manchester meeting, as reported in the *Manchester Courier* of March the 16th, and other newspapers, had features in common with those of Bradford and Leeds. It was held in the Corn Exchange, and presided over by a faithful and long-tried friend of the Ten Hours' Bill movement, Mr J. Gregory, who was supported by the Rev. C. D. Wray, the sub-dean of Manchester; by the Rev. W. Huntington, rector of St John's; the Rev. T. R. Bentley, incumbent of St Matthew's, and one or two dissenting ministers. The Rev. C. D. Wray, on moving the first resolution, said:—" With respect to the object of the meeting, so important to all the working classes, not only of this country, but wherever the factory system was known, no one who had a human heart, and could feel at all for human suffering, could refuse to support it; certainly when he called to mind the numbers of poor children who, at such a tender age, were working in the heated atmosphere of factories, and who, on coming out, with the snow perhaps on the ground, themselves but scantily clad, were exposed to the most trying alternations. The physical strength of these children was exhausted long before they came to manhood ; and, therefore, even in a political sense, it would be for the national benefit that these children should not be put to work so early. The effect of this system on females was, frequently, to incapacitate them for the duties of after life ; if they became wives and mothers, they were frequently worn out before they were forty years of age. In visiting a Sunday school child, a week or two ago, he found her one of the most diminutive objects of her age he had ever seen, and absolutely in a consumption. She worked in a factory, and on his expostulating with the mother against her being sent so young, the answer was: ' Unless we send them at a certain age, they will not take them at all; and we cannot live without their labour.' This he had himself seen in Salford. He had frequently lamented that any persons should work more than twelve hours a day,—the period assigned by Scripture, and out of this, proper intervals for meals should be allowed. He did not blame the masters, the whole system was bad. . . . .

When children were taken into the factories at so tender an age, how were they to be educated ? If men were designed for this world alone, and had to do nothing but work, this would be all very well; but mankind needed to be instructed in their duty to God and each other; and *how* could children be taught, if they were made to work twelve hours a day?"

Among the speakers at these meetings, in Leeds and Manchester, was Mr B. Jowett, the personal friend of Mr Sadler, and the intimate fellow-labourer of Lord Ashley. Mr Jowett's knowledge of the progress of the factory question was very great, and his devotion to the interests of humanity was intense. When addressing the Manchester meeting, he said:—

"The first mover of a Ten Hours' Bill was the first Sir R. Peel. It will be found, by a reference to *Hansard's Debates*, that when he first mentioned this measure, he spoke of it as a Ten Hours' Bill. He subsequently brought in what was called a Twelve and a Half Hours' Bill, intending that there should be ten and a half hours for labour, one and a half hours for meals, and half an hour for education. That bill he prosecuted with all the energy of his powerful mind ; and so much had he it at heart, that after giving evidence before a select committee of the House of Commons, not content with the oral testimony he had given, he presented a memorial to that committee, in which he left on record his opinion that if the factory system was not duly regulated, it would become the bitterest curse of the country. That bill, unfortunately, was so materially altered in its progress through parliament that instead of a Ten and a Half Hours', it became a Twelve Hours' Bill ; but for ten and a half hours Sir R. Peel asked, and I will ask you, whether a Ten Hours' Bill would now give you the relief that a Ten and a Half Hours' Bill would have done then? What has been the progress with regard to the spinner? How many spindles had he to attend to in the time of the first Sir R. Peel, in 1815 for instance, and how has that number since increased? How was the speed of the machinery increased? Do the children travel more or less than they did at that time? It was stated by the spinners of Manchester some years ago, and the subject was afterwards discussed in the House of Commons, that the children in the mills at Manchester, working twelve hours a day, in spinning what you would call from 36's to 40's, were liable to walk in the mill, traversing backwards and forwards, from twenty to twenty-four miles in the day. That statement was disputed, and several members of parliament connected with the factory system corroborated it. Still those facts remained upon the mind of Lord Ashley, as so important, that he requested a very eminent actuary, Mr Woolhouse, to come down into the manufacturing districts, and make the calculation. That gentleman, who had been introduced to Lord Ashley as the second mathematician in the country, came down into Lancashire; and with his watch in his hand, accurately measured the distances, he calculated the ground over which those young persons had to travel, he not only corroborated the statement of the spinners of Manchester, but proved that the distance was greater than they had stated—namely, from fourteen to thirty-two miles, according to the fineness of the thread they were employed upon. There was another investigation which Mr Woolhouse made for Lord Ashley. A great deal had been said about the tables of mortality attached to the report of the select committee, of which Mr Sadler was chairman; and Mr Drinkwater had attempted to call them in question. The late Michael Thomas Sadler employed some of the last months of his life in corroborating and confirming those tables. And the pamphlet was published after his death, in which he completely vindicated them. Still, Lord Ashley never made any use of those tables till Mr Woolhouse had investigated the subject, wishing that it should be investigated by an unprejudiced person; and he came to the conclusion that the opinion Mr Sadler had formed was correct, and that the mortality of Leeds (the town in which Mr Sadler had lived) was such, according to the census of 1831, that it required two thousand fresh inhabitants to Leeds, annually, to keep up the numbers. Mr Drinkwater had felt that the rate of mortality, according to the tables, was enormous, and had spoken of it in the strongest terms; but he had denied the correctness of Mr Sadler's tables, which was subsequently established by Mr Woolhouse. Well, then, you are asking nothing but what is reasonable, and if you only go on with the same unanimity that there has been in Yorkshire, you will carry the question.

"I am happy to see the progress it is making. In Yorkshire, two years ago, a petition for a Ten Hours' Bill was signed by 294 manufacturers. In Lancashire it is notorious that this question is advancing, even among the millowners themselves, and I am confident that their interests are most deeply involved in it. This first resolution which I am called upon to support is for a plain Ten Hours' Bill. Now, it is to be remembered, that the relay system is not the system Mr Sadler recommended, nor the system that the first Sir R. Peel recommended. Sir Robert was decidedly of opinion that such a system would not operate well, and this resolution says it has been found impracticable in many parts of the country. I will give you an idea of the extent to which it has been found impracticable. The relay system has hardly been acted upon in Scotland at all; and the certificate system, which has been hitherto adopted, for ascertaining whether young persons were thirteen years of age, has been so very lax, that Mr Horner, the inspector for this district, has stated, in his report, that full one-half of the children who were working as thirteen years of age were only eleven. Thus the children of eleven have not been protected; the law has said that they shall be protected, by their labour being limited to eight hours a day, but many of them have been working the full period of twelve hours. The interests of both millowners and workpeople are most deeply interested in having a more equal distribution of labour over the whole of the year."

Both these meetings were addressed at great length by Mr Oastler, who, though in shattered health, was anxious to urge the question onward to a final settlement. The speakers at those meetings, and especially Mr Oastler, thanked the government for the manifest progress shown in their own bill, which was decidedly in advance of any previously proposed governmental measure. He and others contended, however, that there could not be any satisfactory settlement except by the passing of a Ten Hours' Bill. The public mind, for obvious reasons, apprehends much more clearly a defined object than a series of details ; in a public movement, the reiteration of one " cry" exercises a wonderful influence, a circumstance which " the king of the factory children " very thoroughly appreciated. It was hoped that these meetings would have weight with parliament. The factory question was understood to be an open one in the cabinet, it was, therefore, thought possible that the pressure of public opinion would, probably, have influence with some of the cabinet ministers.

The Government Factories' Bill, which, in the House of Commons, had, on the 12th of February, been read a second time, was expected to be again under discussion. The supporters and opponents of the Ten Hours' Bill were unusually active, and the future proceedings in parliament were awaited with much anxiety by all the parties interested.

The subjects of factory labour and factory regulation were under the consideration of the House of Commons, on March the 15th and 18th; the debates which ensued, called forth much practical talent on both sides, and the regulation of factory labour was evidently understood by all parties, as being of the highest importance, and the question at stake, not only one of detail but of principle. Lord Ashley moved, that in the second clause of the bill, the word " night " shall be taken to mean from six o'clock in the evening to six o'clock in the following morning. The intention of which motion was practically to limit the working hours of factory labour to ten per day. The word "night," in the government bill, was defined to mean from eight o'clock in the evening to six in the morning; the object of which definition was to limit the working hours of factory labour to twelve per day.

The committee divided on the question that the word " eight " stand part of the clause, Lord Ashley having moved, that it be struck out, in order to substitute the word "six:"—ayes, 170 ; noes, 179 : majority 9.

The word " eight " having been struck out, the committee again divided on the question, that the word " six " be inserted —ayes, 161 ; noes, 153: majority, 8. This decision was, in effect, and was considered by the government to be, " a virtual adoption of a Ten Hours' Bill."

On March the 22nd, the subject was renewed, and a discussion of great excitement and interest followed. The committee divided on the question that the blank in the bill be filled with the word " twelve," relating to the hours of labour—ayes, 183; noes, 186: being a majority of three in favour of a Ten Hours' Bill.

The committee again divided on the question, that the blank be filled up with the word " ten "—ayes, 181; noes, 188: majority of seven against the Ten Hours' Bill. This neutralising result was produced by Mr W. Aldam, Captain M. Archdall, Mr W. Ewart, and Mr G. Palmer, having voted with the " noes " on both divisions.

The House of Commons, having thus decided against a

Ten Hours' and a Twelve Hours' Bill, Sir James Graham suggested a postponement of all further proceedings, until Monday, and Lord Ashley, after having assured the House of Commons of the respect he entertained for its deliberative judgment, used the expressive words:—" But, though defeated now, I have a right, which I shall endeavour to exert on every legitimate occasion. I shall persevere to the last hour of my existence, and I have not the slightest doubt, that with the blessing of Heaven, I shall have a complete triumph."

On March the 25th, Sir James Graham explained to the House of Commons, at considerable length, his views, and those of his colleagues, on the critical position of the factory question. The subject and the circumstances were of interest. Sir James reviewed the state of the question, as regarded the interests of the country, and the position of ministers and Lord Ashley, and concluded by moving: " That the order of the day for the house resolving itself into committee on the Factories' Bill be now read," which, after a protracted debate, ended in a postponement until Friday. On the 29th March, the question was again under the reconsideration of the house, and after a debate, and explanations on both sides, the government bill was withdrawn, on the understanding that another should be substituted in its place. On the same evening, Sir James Graham moved for leave to bring in the new Factories' Bill, the objects of which he explained at length. Leave having been given, the bill was brought in, and read a first time.

In the course of these discussions in the House of Commons, Sir Charles Wood, the member for Halifax, and an opponent of all factory regulation, made a statement to the effect, that the manufacturing operatives were not really in favour of the Ten Hours' Bill; an assertion which ministers made much of, but one which was not likely to remain long unanswered. On April the 8th,

1844, Mr Oastler, addressing a public meeting in Leeds, said: ‘ There are individuals in the House of Commons who, after the sanction which a majority gave to the Ten Hours' Bill, have dared to assert, that parliament has been taken by surprise, and, also that the factory operatives are not for the Ten Hours' Bill. Why, I have been, during the last fourteen or fifteen years of my life, in every factory town of Yorkshire and Lancashire, year after year, asking the assembled thousands and tens of thousands, and in one case 150,000 of these poor operatives, whether they were for the Ten Hours' Bill or not, and the Ten Hours' Bill has been enthusiastically passed, and unanimously too, save on two occasions—once I remember to have seen three hands held up against it, and once two. Yet, we are to be told by persons who pretend to represent the manufacturing operatives in parliament, that the manufacturing operatives are not in favour of the Ten Hours' Bill. And ministers, too ready to lay hold of any straw by which they can adhere to the oppressive measure of twelve hours, gave more credence to the assertions of those persons than to the loud petitions and urgent requests of the hosts of friends whom we have in and out that house. Well, hearing that the decision of the House of Commons had been unconstitutionally rescinded—for, I maintain, let others assert what they may, that it is unconstitutional in any minister, after a decision had been taken in the House of Commons, to attempt forthwith to reverse that decision—hearing that such an unconstitutional mode had been taken to destroy the effect of the vote in our favour, I was waited upon by a deputation of the Short Time Committee, and asked to tell them what I thought should be done in this emergency. I was glad when they came to see me; I was sorry for the cause. I knew that there was, as Sir James Graham has said, ‘ inextricable confusion’ in the House of Commons. I knew that the government had got themselves into inextricable difficulties, and that the best way of unravelling all those intricacies would be, as I had always done, to go to the people who were most interested, and ask them what they thought about it; and therefore I suggested that, instead of going through the manufacturing districts, and attending the *soirees* which were projected in my honour, I should throw my own individuality overboard, and that we should hold public meetings in every factory town of Yorkshire and Lancashire, and let the operatives speak for themselves. That, my friends, is the reason why you to-night are called together to speak for the town of Leeds." The Leeds meeting was presided over by the Rev. Dr Hook. The Bradford meeting was held on the 9th; the Huddersfield meeting on the 10th, and in rapid succession meetings were held in the more important towns of Yorkshire and Lancashire, at each of which was asked the question: "Are you in favour of the Ten Hours' Bill?" The answer was in the affirmative. Through the medium of the press Sir Charles Wood was challenged to make good his parliamentary assertion; Mr Fielden specially challenged Sir Charles to meet him at Halifax,—the former was present according to promise; the Hon. Baronet was absent. Those meetings were adjudged to be of the highest importance, and special reports thereof appeared day after day in the columns of the *Times*, which reports were read with attention in the manufacturing districts, and by those who watched public proceedings; for the moment, the national mind was concentrated on the factory question. At those meetings Mr Oastler was the principal speaker; a perusal of the speeches then delivered by him would convince even the most sceptical as to his ability. The *Times* reporter, a gentleman of education and of great professional experience, said : " I have never before known such an extraordinary exhibition of versatility on one subject." One effect of Mr

Oastler's imprisonment was an improvement in mind, which, united with the increased responsibility now attached to his words, caused him to be careful in expression, while it detracted nothing from mental energy, and very much elevated the tone of his discourse. The speeches made in parliament against the Ten Hours' Bill were closely examined at these meetings, and the parliament and the people were kept, through the columns of the press, face to face, on the factory question.

The impressive character of the agitation was increased by the important part taken by the clergy. Dr Hook, of Leeds, Dr Scoresby, of Bradford, the Rev. Mr Nunns, of St Paul's, Leeds, the Rev. C. D. Wray, sub-dean of Manchester, Rev. Mr Albutt, the vicar of Dewsbury, set before their brethren in the church a noble example, which, was well followed up; medical men, tradesmen, operatives, *all* told their experience, and all united in one common verdict against the government, and in favour of the Ten Hours' Bill. Mr Ferrand, Mr Walter, and Mr Fielden, gave to the movement the benefit of their labours, and, by common consent, it was agreed that there should not be " permanent peace until the Ten Hours' Bill was law." The editor of the *Times* wrote with decision on the question, and gave to the operatives' view of their own case, the influence of his authority, and opposed the government with much power. This agitation enlightened the public mind, and concentrated it on a fixed purpose.

The government watched these proceedings closely, changed its tone, and strengthened itself in the House of Commons, by considering the factory question as a party one, and making it known that defeat would be considered just ground for resignation ; a stroke of policy which had due effect on the minds of many members. The second reading of the Government Factories' Bill was taken on April the 22nd, a brief discussion followed; it was understood by both parties that the question should be tested in its future stages through parliament.

The government was strengthened by the policy of Mr Roebuck, who having at all times bitterly opposed factory regulation, very consistently raised the question of the wisdom of parliament interfering with adult labour, by moving for a resolution of the whole house before going into committee on the Factories Bill :—

" That it is the opinion of this house, that no interference with the power of adult labourers in factories, to. make contracts respecting the hours for which they shall be employed, be sanctioned with this house." In the debate which followed, all the old arguments for and against government interference were reproduced, and the discussion, although conducted on both sides with great ability, did not evoke any novel features, nor change the opinion of the house as to the desirableness of factory regulation; the question had, in fact, ceased to be, with the majority of the members of both houses, one of principle, and was considered, in fact, as one of degree.

On May the 6th, some clauses of the bill were considered in committee.

On May the 10th, the bill having been read a third time, Lord Ashley closed an elaborate speech by moving the following clause :—

" And be it enacted, that from and after the 1st day of October in the present year, no young person shall be employed in any factory more than eleven hours in any one day, or more than sixty-four hours in any one week ; and that, from and after the 1st day of October, 1847, no young person shall be employed in any factory more than ten hours in any one day, or more than fifty-eight hours in any one week : and that any person who shall be convicted of employing a young person for any longer time than is in and by this clause permitted, shall for every such offence be adjudged to pay a penalty of not less than   *l.*, and not more than   *l.*"

In the above clause the word "young person" refers to all between the ages of thirteen and eighteen.

The debate which followed was sustained with great ability, and adjourned. It was resumed on the 13th; the house had from habit become familiar with the question, every phase of which was considered, and opinions of the most conflicting kind urged with confidence by opposing speakers.

The house divided—ayes, 159; noes, 297 : majority for the government, 138.

Among the names of the minority were Lord John Russell and the Right Hon. T. B. Macaulay; the former supported the Ten Hours' Bill clause of Lord Ashley, by a speech in which he frankly confessed that his opinions had undergone a change. The conversion of these two important leaders of the great whig party was important.

On the question that the bill do pass the house divided —ayes, 136 ; noes, 7 : majority, 129.

The bill was read a second time in the House of Lords on May the 20th, was discussed in committee on May 31st, and read a third time on June the 3rd. The principal opponent being Lord Brougham, who protested against the principle of the measure with all the energy for which the noble and learned lord is remarkable.

The perseverance and steadfastness of the leaders of the factory movement was bearing legitimate fruit. The position of rival sections in the House of Commons no doubt contributed to increase the force of the Ten Hours' Bill party ; the two rival chiefs in the House of Commons, Sir Robert Peel and Lord John Russell, had used the factory question to injure each other in turn, but the speech and vote of Lord John Russell were too important easily or readily, on any future occasion, to admit of retraction. Lord John Russell was now pledged to Ten Hours per day, as the limit to which factory labour might be advantageously reduced. The vote of Mr Macaulay was equally marked, and not less important; former opponents felt that after these examples, to make a concession, notwithstanding past declarations, was not discreditable. It would be uncharitable to suppose that the serious effects which had followed the vacillating policy of the whigs, on the factory question, were without effect on the mind of Lord John Russell, and could not fail to be appreciated by Mr Macaulay. These effects, the persevering efforts and ability of the leaders of the factory question, and the changed position of parties in the House of Commons, are circumstances sufficient in themselves to account for the progress of the question in parliament.

The House of Commons had yielded an undignified assent to the demand of the ministers, and this, too, in opposition to a repeated vote in favour of a Ten Hours' Bill. The conscience and judgment of the house were opposed to those of Sir Robert Peel and Sir James Graham, who, on the factory question, led the cabinet. This palpable contradiction between the opinions and votes of the House of Commons was a twofold testimony; it was evidence of the growth of public opinion, and of the power of ministers over the House of Commons. The strenuous opponents of the factory question became forthwith the opponents of the Peel administration, who, on the other hand, were supported with additional ardour by the ultra-section of political economists. The importance of the numerous and influential meetings held in the country in support of the Ten Hours' Bill, it was impossible to deny; the moral certainty of final success was, to many minds, equally apparent. The policy of Sir Robert Peel's cabinet was evidently to conciliate " the Manchester men," who were known to be in the ascendant on the question of free trade. A change in the ministry was therefore desired by the advocates of the Ten Hours' Bill, a desire consistent with their position, and founded upon an acute knowledge of the motives of politicians. This result accomplished, it was anticipated that another renewed and spirited effort might prove successful.

Among the many friends of the factory children, there was not one who supported the cause more earnestly, and whose influence was more felt, than Mr Richard Oastler. In his conflict for the emancipation of the factory children, Mr Oastler, whose chief happiness was in the enjoyment of pure domestic pleasures, always found in his wife a true helpmate. He even boasts that in that strife, Mrs Oastler was his mainstay; but for her, he declares he could not have withstood the powerful and malignant opposition from his opponents—the more painful separation from friends. From first to last, in the wife of his youth he found a ready, an efficient helper. When the storm of persecution raged most furiously—when best friends forsook—her calmness and fortitude, her constancy and self-sacrifice, her never-tiring solicitude, and never-failing affection—her unbounded reliance on the Arm unseen, joined with her entire disregard of consequences to herself —never failed to inspire her husband with hope—always restored his confidence.

Mrs Oastler was of delicate frame—her manners were gentle, unassuming, and retiring—but, in the cause of truth, she was bold and unflinching, entirely divested of self-seeking ; she was affectionately devoted to relieving the despised and neglected poor. She secured the love of all who knew her.

For twenty-eight years, Mrs Oastler was a sharer of her husband's joys and sorrows. Deceit, malice, or jealousy, had not any place in her breast. She was frank, generous, sincere, and confiding; never so happy, as when, at any sacrifice to herself, she could increase the happiness of others. Her religion was unostentatious—" pure and undefiled:" and so, her faith and trust in God never failed.

Next to her God, she loved "her own Richard,"—on her he could always rely. Their happiness was unbroken—whatever storms outside might rage.

In his labours for the poor factory children, she more than sympathised. Night and day, cheering, helping, and comforting him in the prosecution of his overwhelming labours. Writing for him, sometimes through the night—and day by day, when he was weary, exhausted, absent, or, on the bed of sickness, Mrs Oastler never allowed the great work to stand still. She would take up his pen, and continue his public and private correspondence, where he had left off; she would read back a few sentences, ascertain his thoughts, and then finish his argument or directions, none being able to detect that another mind or hand had been engaged, so entirely, as in all other things, were their style and handwriting one.

Returning home late at night, or at early morn, wearied and exhausted by his "factory labours," Mr Oastler was sure to find his wife attending with every comfort and kindness—and when refreshed, she would listen with anxious attention to his report of proceedings; they were as deeply interesting to herself as to her husband.

Mrs Oastler always welcomed to Fixby Hall the friends of the Ten Hours' Bill, differing on many other subjects from some—*that* was their bond of union. Sometimes, with meekness and softened affection, she would warn her husband to be guarded—being fearful, lest his strong devotion to " the great question " might cause him to associate too freely with those whom, she thought, were not " God-fearing men."

With the people, especially with those nearest home,

Mrs Oastler was a great favourite. They daily saw her "going about doing good."

Bashful and timorous as, by nature, Mrs Oastler was, when she believed her presence could rebut the slanders of his foes (among other reports they told, that, "Mrs Oastler's life was made miserable by her husband"), she would appear, side by side, with him, in public processions, or on the hustings—then, the sincere devotion of the people to "the Queen," was manifested, in such terms as Yorkshiremen, women, and children, are wont to greet their best beloved! Happy was the working man whom Mr Oastler requested, "to take charge of his wife from the hustings—through the crowd,"—eager was every one to cheer and make way for "the Queen."

When forsaken by his chiefest friend—whom they both loved most ardently—it was thus that Mrs Oastler addressed her almost despairing husband; "Never mind, Richard! It is God's work! Only stand firm yourself, though all forsake! God will provide." And, when his character was assailed, Mrs Oastler would smile and say, "Poor things—they do not know you. They can never change my opinion of my own Richard! Go on, my love—trusting in God! He will take care of your character." When poverty seemed to be the certain consequence of Mr Oastler's proceedings, Mrs Oastler would say, "Poverty, with God's blessing, will be our greatest riches. Let us be poor and despised, rather than that you, for my sake, should slacken your efforts in the great work which I am sure God has put into your hands. Come what may—God will be our friend, while we strive to do his work, trusting in him." Yes, Mrs Oastler was, indeed, Mr Oastler's mainstay!

The faithful wife, followed her persecuted husband to prison—she consoled, helped, and nourished him *there!*

She lived to witness his release, and to express her gratitude to his deliverers. She died in peace, at Headingley, near Leeds, July 12, 1845—just when the sun of prosperity seemed to be rising on her husband—to set upon her grave !

Mrs Oastler's remains were buried in Kirkstal churchyard. The bodies of their infants, Sarah and Robert (having been buried in Leeds), were, at the same time, placed in the same grave ; where "the old king" has been heard to say, he hoped his bones may rest.

CHAPTER XV.

PROCEEDINGS IN THE HOUSE OF COMMONS IN 1846.—OPINIONS OF
THE OPPONENTS OF THE TEN HOURS' BILL.—MR MACAULAY'S
OPINION IN SUPPORT THEREOF.

ONE of the effects of the extraordinary exertions of the
Anti-Corn Law League was a conviction on the
minds of many leading statesmen, and among these
Sir James Graham, that England had passed that
state of national existence in which her prosperity
mainly depended on agriculture; so rooted was this
opinion in the mind of some among the free-trade party,
that they ventured to declare that, were the whole surface
of these islands covered with lava, no real national loss
would be sustained, they anticipating that more than a
compensation would be found in the increase of our
foreign trade, consequent on the opening of British ports
to foreign grain, duty free, and the application of the
scientific, chemical, mechanical, and manual powers of the
country to purposes of manufacture and commerce. The
experience of late years has thoroughly dissipated this
opinion; under the operation of high prices during the war
with Russia, agriculture has made such decided progress,
that its importance is at a premium, and now, as of old,
" speed the plough," is a popular sentiment. A reference
to the past is necessary to explain the proceedings of some
among the opponents of the Ten Hours' Bill in parliament;

these refused all further concession, under the belief that a further reduction in the hours of factory labour would endanger our national interests. Among other supporters of the free-trade party were those who pledged themselves to vote for a Ten Hours' Bill, so soon as free trade in corn was established; these assumed that the reduced price of bread, and the increase of foreign exchange, would fully warrant a reduction of the hours of factory labour; others of the free-trade party were of opinion that, were the corn laws once repealed, the demand for labour would be so great " that three masters would bid for two men, and no Ten Hours' Bill would be demanded, because it would not be required." Every great popular movement begets a mental activity in a free state, and whether right or wrong in its object, brings into collision opposing intellectual forces; the successful and the unsuccessful party are alike apt to hazard decided prophecies, which time in most cases proves to have been not well-founded. The repeal of the corn laws was a source of high gratification to the commercial classes generally, and was, on the part of the late Sir Robert Peel, a concession to the expressed will of the nation. The immediate satisfaction resulting therefrom, and also the state of parties, were favourable to the renewal of popular and parliamentary efforts on the factory question, and the opportunity was not likely to pass unimproved with Oastler in the provinces, Ashley, Fielden, and Ferrand in the House of Commons.

On Jan. 29, 1846, Lord Ashley consequently reintroduced, to the notice of the House of Commons, the Ten Hours' Bill; circumstances, in addition to those already named, contributed in some respects to favour the noble lord's intentions. The mind of the country and of parliament had been expressed in favour of Ten Hours a day, as the limit of the labour of women and young persons in factories ; experiments had been made by Mr Gardiner, of Preston, and others, of working factories eleven hours per day, being one hour less than the law specified; the results were in all respects favourable to a further reduction of the hours of factory labour. Mr Gardiner wrote: " I am quite satisfied that both as much yarn and power-loom cloth may be produced, at quite as low a cost, in eleven as in twelve hours a day." . . . . " All the arguments I have heard in favour of long time appear based on an arithmetical question; if eleven hours produce so much, what will twelve, thirteen, or even fifteen hours produce ? This is correct so far as the steam engine is concerned; whatever it will produce in eleven hours, it will produce double the quantity in twenty-two; but try this on the animal—horse—and you will soon find he cannot compete with the engine, as he requires time both to rest and feed. It is, I believe, a fact not to be questioned, that there is more bad work made the last one or two hours, than the whole of the first nine or ten hours." All experience from those countries in which the hours of labour in factories had been reduced, united in showing considerable improvement in the character and habits of those under its operation. Lord Ashley collected, with a persevering industry, the important facts favourable to his own proposition; he was promptly and ably supported by Lord John Manners, Mr Wakley, Mr Fielden, and others. Sir James Graham met the motion with all the interest of the Peel administration, and urged strongly " that to carry interference further in its application to capital and labour, was a dangerous experiment in a country dependent, for much of its prosperity, on its commercial and manufacturing resources." Sir James was supported by the late Mr Joseph Hume, who, throughout a long parliamentary career, consistently opposed all interference with labour by law, as being wrong in principle; Mr John Bright acted in concert with Mr Hume and Mr Roebuck; Sir James Graham, as an act of courtesy to the motives and high position of Lord Ashley, as, on this question, representing a very numerous body of his fellow countrymen, agreed to the introduction and first reading of the bill.

Lord Ashley having retired from parliament, because of his support of Sir Robert Peel's free-trade measures, the future conduct of the factory question in the House of Commons devolved on Mr Fielden. His lordship having been returned for Dorsetshire as a protectionist, and having voted for the repeal of the corn laws, gave to the electors an opportunity of expressing a judgment on his parliamentary conduct; the decision was adverse to his lordship —he was not re-elected.

On April 29th, Mr Fielden having presented twenty-six petitions in favour of the bill, moved its second reading; so important had the question become, that the clergy generally of England and Scotland were petitioning in its support. The Free Church presbytery, in the town of Dundee, having petitioned in favour of the measure, a body of the millowners, members of the free church, remonstrated with the clergy, who answered the complainants in words worthy of record :—"While resolved," said the Free Church ministers, "as opportunity affords, to multiply the means of education, and render more available those already existing, we must be permitted to remind you, that no school education, however protracted, or however excellent, can ever compensate to the female factory operatives between the ages of thirteen and eighteen, for the want of that home education which forms the future housewife and mother. This, we believe, is at the root of most of the social evils of Dundee; and what, but more time at home can provide the cure?" The Free Church clergy of Scotland, then the representatives of the feeling of the country, and popularly esteemed for their secession from the national establishment on a question of conscience, had resolved, with few exceptions, to give to the Ten

Hours' Bill movement their support. Mr Fielden directed his speech to a consideration of the arguments of opponents which he endeavoured to answer, and declared his conviction that the manufacturing supremacy of England would not be endangered by further restriction of the hours of labour in factories. Mr Fielden's position as a successful cotton-spinner stamped every word he uttered with the respect inseparable from high commercial authority.

Mr Hume, while admitting that the sense of the country was against him, "thought it his duty, and the duty of every one who believed the working classes to be in error in holding this opinion [in favour of a Ten Hours' Bill], to stand forward and resist that which, if adopted, would ultimately ruin the best interests of the country. . . . . There ought to be no compromise upon it; they should act upon principle, and that would require them to reject the bill." Sir James Graham, in an elaborate speech, in which he urged the importance of the interests at stake, the consequent danger of a false step in legislation, appealed to the house to remember their adoption of free trade, their having resolved to allow the free export of coal and machinery, and cautioned the house to beware of prejudicing the interests of the manufacturers, and avowed the decision of himself and colleagues in the following words :—" There ought to be no hesitation on the part of the executive government, in a question of this kind, and I announce our firm determination to resist the further progress of this bill."

The debate was adjourned.

On Wednesday, May the 13th, the question was again under consideration. In the debate thereon, the principal speakers in support of the measure were Mr Colquhoun, Mr Cowper, Lord John Manners, Sir Robert Inglis, Mr Sharman Crawford, and Mr Brotherton: against the measure, Mr Labouchere, Mr Dennistoun, Mr Trelawny, and Mr Cardwell. The hour having arrived for the house to break up, no vote was taken.

The adjourned debate on the second reading of the Factories' Bill was resumed on May the 22nd. The speakers on this occasion were Mr Bankes, Mr Ward, Lord G. Bentinck, Viscount Morpeth, Mr Macaulay, Sir J. Hanmer, Mr Bright, Mr B. Denison, the second Sir Robert Peel, Lord John Russell, Mr Cobden, and Mr Muntz—names representing the highest practical talent, and the various parties in the House of Commons. Mr Macaulay and Lord John Russell maintained (the former in a brilliant speech) that it was the duty of the legislature to protect health and morals by restrictive legislation. Mr Macaulay said :

" He was as firmly attached to the principle of free trade as any gentleman in that house, and he admitted that it was not desirable that the state should interfere with the contracts of persons of ripe age and sound mind touching matters purely commercial, but they would fall into error if they applied that rule to matters which were not purely commercial. Take, for instance, one of the questions of police, namely, the regulation of cabs on a stand. If on a very wet day there were but few cabs on a stand, and many persons requiring them, why should not the driver of a cab ask a high price for the accommodation he could afford when persons were willing and glad to give it ? Where the health of the community was concerned, the principle of non-interference did not apply. He had read a report issued by the Duke of Buccleuch and the noble earl, the present Secretary for Ireland (the Earl of Lincoln), upon which that noble earl brought in a bill with respect to sanatory regulations, and which, as it applied to the principle of free trade, was a most monstrous production. He found by the act to which he referred, that no person was to build a street unless it was of a certain width, or to erect a house without giving notice to a commissioner ;

he must also have a drain, or they would make one for him, and send in the bill. Moreover, if he refused to white-wash his house, they would do it for him, and at his own expense. On the principle of free trade, why should not a man run up a house as cheaply as he could, and let it for as much as he could possibly obtain? He defied them to defend such an act on the principle of free trade, and non-interference. But he had no doubt the noble lord would say, ' there are other interests which are higher than mere commercial interests, and which concern the public weal.' The great masses of the people shall not live in a way that will abridge life, that will make it wretched and feeble while it lasts, and send them to untimely graves, leaving behind them a more miserable progeny than themselves. And who would contend, where the public morality was concerned, that the principle of non-interference should be affirmed. He hoped to carry the house with him thus far—that the principle of non-interference was one that must have great restrictions. Was not the public health, then, concerned in the question of labour? Was not twelve hours a day more than was desirable for a youth or a female to labour? Was not education necessary, and did they believe that after twelve hours' work enough time would remain for that amount of education which they believed the whole of the population ought to possess? The principle on which they interfered to protect public morality justified an interference in matters of this sort.

*   *   *   *   *   *

" If we consider man simply in a commercial point of view, simply as a machine for productive labour, let us not forget what a piece of mechanism he is,—'how fear-fully and wonderfully made !' If we have a fine horse, we do not use him exactly as a steam-engine, and still less should we treat man so, more especially in his earlier years. The depressing labour that begins early in life, and is continued too long every day, enfeebles his body, enervates his mind, weakens his spirits, overpowers his understanding, and is incompatible with any good and useful result. A state of society in which such a system prevails, will inevitably, and in no long space of time, feel its baneful effects. It will find that the corporal and mental culture of the population cannot be neglected, without producing results detrimental to its best interests, even in regard to accumulation and creation of property. On the other hand, a day of rest regularly recurring every week, and hours of exercise, of leisure, of intellectual improvement, recurring in every day, elevate the whole man—elevate him physically—elevate him intellectually—elevate him morally ; and his elevation—physical, moral, and intellectual, again falls on the commercial prosperity of the country, which is advanced with it."

This truly enlightened and philosophical view of the interests of a nation was worthy of an English historian. It is, in substance, a reproduction of the sentiments expressed by Mr Sadler, on introducing the factory question to the attention of parliament. Homage to the memory of Sadler, from so high an authority as Macaulay, was, indeed, honour. The propriety and justness of Mr Macaulay's observations were generally admitted. He was faithful to free trade, as a general principle, but admitted the necessity for so many exceptions, that the force of the rule was much shaken. Well, and wisely, did Mr Macaulay ask, " What is it on which, more than on anything else, the wealth of a nation depends? What is it which makes one community prosperous and flourishing more than another ? You will not say that it is the soil—you will not say that it is its climate—you will not say that it is its mineral wealth, or its natural advantages, its ports, or its great rivers. These are things which are very valuable, indeed, when human intelligence and energy use them well ; but human intelligence and energy can do much

without them ; whereas, without human intelligence and
energy they are as nothing. You see countries, that in
the highest degree possess all these advantages, with a
miserable population—with men having hardly a rag to
cover them ; while, on the other hand, in the most sterile
soils, the greatest human industry and prosperity are to
be found. Is it anything in the earth, or in the air, that
makes Scotland a richer country than Egypt,—or Batavia,
with its marshes, more prosperous than Sicily ? No; but
Scotchmen make Scotland what she is; and Dutchmen
raised their marshes to such eminence. Look to America.
Two centuries ago it was a wilderness of buffaloes and
wolves. What has caused the change ? Is it her rich
mould ? Is it her mighty rivers? Is it her broad
waters ? No; her plains were then as fertile as they are
now; her rivers were as numerous." Mr Macaulay, tread-
ing in the footsteps of Locke, concluded that this mighty
revolution had been effected by the labour and energy of
man. "The great instrument that produces wealth," continued the orator, " is man; and the vast difference
between the climates and natural advantages of Campagna
and Spitzbergen, is not to be compared to the difference
between a country inhabited by a population in a condition
of full physical, moral, and intellectual health, and a country
whose inhabitants are in a state of physical, moral, and
intellectual degeneracy. These, I believe, are the reasons
which explain why the wealth of this country has not been
diminished by the observance, century after century, of one
day of rest in the week, when your industry seems to be
suspended, when your machinery is not at work, but when
the machine of machines, man—upon whom everything else
depends—is winding up and repairing, so that he returns to
his work and labour on the Monday with renovated spirits,
with clearer intellect, and with restored physical power. Am
I to believe that a change, which would clearly be found to

improve the moral, physical, and intellectual character of the people, could possibly make them poorer?" The answer was in the negative, and Mr Macaulay judiciously concluded, that, to grant, under certain circumstances, protection to public health and morality, was one of the legitimate duties of the British parliament.

Mr Bright was, on principle, opposed to all interference, and prognosticated that the bill, if passed, "would cause, in the first place, an extraordinary delusion, and, in the second place, a fatal disappointment." Mr Cobden spoke of Mr Oastler as "the originator of this agitation ;" quoted his evidence, given before the committee of 1832, on the probable result of the bill on wages, to the effect "that it would tend to increase rather than lower wages," an opinion which Mr Cobden thought erroneous. He complained of the leaders amongst the operatives, of the short-time question, having opposed the *League* in the manufacturing districts. "If we found it proved that in this country great numbers of infants were being worked to death, he would step in by law to take them out of the hands of their parents." Beyond this limit Mr Cobden was opposed to regulation by law. He expressed his anxiety that the House of Commons "should not fall into a measure for which the working classes would not thank them, and which might procure them very great unpopularity." Sir Robert Peel was of opinion "that the principles of free trade ought not to control our legislation, provided that, by our interference, we can promote the social comforts, the health, and the morality of the community." He was also of opinion that further interference was, under existing circumstances, undesirable, and begged of the house to refuse its assent to the bill. Lord George Bentinck and his political adherents supported the bill on principle— thought it necessary and desirable. Lord Morpeth was doubtful as to what should be done, but thought delay advisable.

On a division having been taken, the votes for proceeding with Mr Fielden's bill were 193 ; against, 203: majority, against the bill, 10. The second reading was formally postponed for six months.

During the course of these proceedings in parliament, the political excitement of the country was great. The House of Lords had not formally approved of the free-trade measures of the government, but the conviction was decided that free trade was equal to a fact already accomplished. The factory operatives watched the conduct of parliament on the short-time question, with unabated interest, and thoroughly distrusted the prophecies of those who foretold that the change in the commercial policy of the country would render factory legislation unnecessary. The Peel administration and the " Manchester men," were united against Mr Fielden and the principal leaders of the whig party in the House of Commons. The discussion of the question in the Press had proved very advantageous to the supporters of the Ten Hours' Bill ; and the speech of Mr Macaulay was acknowledged, by the opponents of the bill, as having been seriously injurious to their view of the case. Mr Macaulay had, at the first election of members to represent the borough of Leeds in parliament under the Reform Act, been successful against Mr Sadler; a principal cause of this success was Mr Sadler's determined support of a Ten Hours' Bill, a measure to which Mr Macaulay was, in 1846, a convert, and which he supported by arguments akin in substance with those used by Mr Sadler in 1832, and with an aptness of illustration greater and more forcible than at the command of any other member of the legislature. Mr Macaulay's conversion had been gradual and complete, and in the capacity of a practical statesman he had fully refuted his early opinions as an *Edinburgh Reviewer.*

CHAPTER XVI.

CHANGE IN THE MINISTRY.—RENEWAL OF FACTORY AGITATION.—
PROCEEDINGS IN PARLIAMENT UNDER THE LEADERSHIP OF MR
FIELDEN.—ADOPTION OF THE TEN HOURS' BILL BY PARLIAMENT.—
MESSRS WOOD AND WALKER, OF BRADFORD.—MANIFESTATIONS OF
JOY ON THE PART OF THE OPERATIVES.—ACCEPTANCE OF A GOLD
MEDAL BY THE QUEEN.

THE place in the history of his country, which the second
Sir Robert Peel may occupy, in the judgment of coming
ages, is a problem which time alone can solve; his enthusiastic
admirers, and his not less energetic opponents, have expressed their opinions freely; the majority of his own
age have pronounced a favourable verdict; his reputation,
however, has depended upon concessions; his laurels have
been won by yielding rather than by teaching; his mind
was a mirror, and it reflected the substance of that which
was fullest and strongest for the time being. The second
Sir Robert Peel (in this respect honourably distinguished
from some among his rivals), while conscious of the responsibility and honour of office, was not disposed to retain
these, under the ódium of parliamentary defeat.

On the 26th of June, 1846, the Corn and Customs' Bill
received the Royal assent, and the free-trade measures of
the cabinet became law. On the same day, the motion for
the second reading of the Irish Coercion Bill was defeated,
by a majority of seventy-three, upon which Sir Robert re-

signed, and the whigs, with Lord John Russell at their head, again possessed the reins of office. In anticipation of the change, Sir Robert said (and his words are worthy of remembrance):—"With the sense of public duties, I am ready to bear its toils and to confront its responsible dangers; but I will not continue to hold this position with mutilated power, or shackled independence. . . . I must reserve to myself to do that unfettered which I believe to be right." The House of Commons, therefore, knew the responsibility of a decision against ministers, and the manly words of Sir Robert Peel gave dignity to his colleagues in their retirement. On the factory question, Sir Robert had taken sides with the opponents of the measure, and Mr Fielden's defeat was the result of ministerial influence. The change in the position of parties was favourable to the success of the Ten Hours' Bill, the premier, Lord John Russell, being pledged to its support.

Mr Fielden was an untiring man, his position as parliamentary leader of the Ten Hours' Bill increased his own sense of his powers, and he and Mr Oastler resolved that there should not be any further delay, — that they should profit by the circumstances of the time, and push forward to victory. In this resolve they were strenuously supported by all the usual leaders of the Ten Hours' Bill party in the country. The one course open was a renewed appeal to public opinion.

Mr Oastler, having been applied to by the central committee for his judgment, as to what ought to be done, suggested a plan of operations, the first condition of which was, "no compromise;" the next, a recommendation for the convening of weekly meetings in every manufacturing town and village;—those to prepare for monthly meetings, and these to be preparatory to public meetings and demonstrations throughout the country. This plan of operations was, in all its main features, adopted. A general election was anticipated, members of parliament and candidates for parliamentary honours, were on the alert. Wherever these appeared in the factory districts, they were closely questioned on the Ten Hours' Bill. By way of example, Dr Bowring, an opponent of the bill, addressed his constituents at Bolton on October the 21st. He was asked to state his reasons for opposing the Ten Hours' Bill. So far were these from being satisfactory, that, the opinion of the meeting having been taken on the question, only three hands were held up against the Ten Hours' Bill; the dissentients were Mr G. Ashworth, Mr John Dean, and Mr P. R. Arrowsmith, gentlemen who, with Dr Bowring, believed that all interference with labour was unsound in principle. The majority opposed to them proved how decidedly public opinion was against their views. Mr Bright was then canvassing Manchester, and was very popular with the free-trade and liberal electors ; he was questioned, on all fitting occasions, about the Ten Hours' Bill, and having expressed opinions depreciating Mr Oastler's judgment on the question, in common with those of Mr Fielden and Mr Ferrand—Mr Bright having expressed a willingness to discuss the question—Mr Oastler challenged Mr Bright to debate, "in the spirit of calmness and friendship," in the Free-trade Hall, Manchester,—Mr Oastler to maintain the affirmative of the following propositions:—

" 1st. That it is a delusion to suppose that the factory children can be educated under the present system of twelve hours' daily labour.

" 2nd. That it is a fallacy to suppose that a reduction of the hours of labour from twelve to ten per day will cause a reduction of ' one-sixth or one-seventh' in the wages of persons whose labour is thus reduced."

The mode of arrangement, as regards these propositions, originated in a statement made by Mr Bright, at a meeting of electors of the Chorlton-upon-Medlock district, Manchester.

Mr Bright declined meeting Mr Oastler, " not from any feeling of disrespect for him," but, because he considered that Mr Oastler's opinions were represented in parliament by Mr Fielden and Mr Ferrand, in which place Mr Bright was prepared for controversy. These circumstances serve to illustrate the kind of warfare, in one of its phases, then common between the supporters and opponents of the Ten Hours' Bill. The meetings convened in Lancashire and Yorkshire were numerous, enthusiastic, and unanimous in their decision; Mr Fielden, Mr Oastler, and Mr Ferrand were the principal speakers, the clergy and medical profession gave most influential and powerful assistance; the subject was re-discussed in all its bearings, and the columns of the daily newspapers, morning after morning, contained reports of speeches, and *leaders* on the restriction of labour in factories, the *Times*, *Standard*, *Morning Herald*, and *Morning Post*, taking the lead in favour of the measure, they were supported by the talent and circulation of the weekly journals, with but few exceptions. There was published in Manchester a weekly periodical—*The Ten Hours' Advocate*, edited with much tact by Mr Philip Grant, who had for many years interested himself in the factory question, and who, in early life, had suffered from the evils the supporters of factory regulation desired to remedy. In this weekly periodical was condensed the important public events of the week, connected with factory labour and factory regulation; it, therefore, served the useful purpose of bringing under the notice of its readers the most interesting facts bearing on the question. Mr Grant acted, under the direction of Lord Ashley, with much zeal and ability, and contributed by his energy and talent very materially to further the Ten Hours' Bill cause. Mr Oastler, who has the habit of writing essays in the form of letters to the editors of newspapers, was constantly at work, and his pen did good service.

The firm of John Edwards and Sons, of Halifax, set the country the spirited example of working a large factory ten hours a day. The Edwardses of Halifax had been long conspicuous for their support of the Ten Hours' Bill movement. Mr Henry Edwards (better known as Major Edwards, and who, from 1847 to 1852, represented Halifax in the House of Commons) had often contributed most generously towards the funds of the short-time committee of his own district, and had perseveringly advocated regulation by law. This union of precept and example was most important; Halifax had long been a stronghold of the influential opponents of the Ten Hours' Bill movement, and they had often; exercised undue weight in cabinet councils, through the instrumentality of Sir Charles Wood. The right honourable baronet had, on one notable occasion, *mis*represented the public opinion of Halifax in parliament; his principal supporters were strenuous opponents to the interference of government with the operations of labour and capital, and in their contact with Sir Charles, probably helped to confirm his prejudices and mislead his judgment, as to popular feeling on the question. The prominent example of John Edwards and Sons was specially significant, and served to destroy the genius of evil prophecy, by the opposing practice. " Counsel," says Blackstone, " is only matter of persuasion, law is matter of injunction; counsel acts upon the willing, law upon the unwilling also." " Counsel," supported by such an example—which manifested the fullest possible confidence of the soundness of the ten hours' a day theory, and this too, in the stronghold of opposition, contributed very powerfully to check the force of long-cherished adverse opinion. The act was in keeping with the reputation of the actors, who have richly earned a high character as just, benevolent, and large employers of labour; it was viewed with much satisfaction by Mr Fielden and his. principal supporters.

Lord Ashley strengthened the movement by making a tour in Lancashire ; his lordship was everywhere received with enthusiasm, and urged his hearers to action; his lordship reminded them, that his opponents were wont to taunt him about the corn laws, and argue that they formed the obstacle which prevented the passing of a Ten Hours' Bill. " With respect to myself," said his lordship, at a public meeting in Manchester, " I know the arguments I used to encounter, while the corn law was yet in force—how often it was said, ' You are the cause of the long-time vexation ; it is you who are to blame, because, for your own exclusive interest, you keep up the price of bread, and prevent us entering into competition with foreign manufacturers.' I recollect perfectly well one of your present members saying, ' If I vote with the noble lord for the Ten Hours' Bill, will he follow me into the lobby on a division upon a motion for a repeal of the corn laws ? ' " His lordship having voted for their repeal, asked for concession in return. This course of reasoning had force on many minds. The noble lord, referring to past labours, said on the same occasion :— " For nearly fourteen years he had had the honour, and, notwithstanding the intense labour and anxiety which it had cost him, he felt great satisfaction in that position to be their representative in parliament, for the attainment of this great and mighty question." Acknowledging the satisfaction he would have had in leading the question in parliament, he counselled his hearers not to relax their efforts, but to give to Mr Fielden all the aid in their power, until he had acquired for them final success. His lordship had undergone severe training and some trials; his words were valued on the Ten Hours' Bill question, and his name was reverenced in the mills and workshops of the north. Mr Fielden was anxious to test the public opinion of Scotland, some of the Scotch members having strenuously opposed the bill, and a belief being current, that Scotland was more thoroughly pledged to absolute non-interference than England. Scotland has a reputation for an adherence to the free-trade school of political economy, principally from the facts that Adam Smith was born in Kirkaldy; that the *Edinburgh Review* was the organ of his disciples; and that the late Mr Cobbett used to write of the Scotch as "philosophers" and "economists;" he had a gift in giving names, and that they were retained was an evidence of his power. Mr Oastler having been invited by very many working men, of Edinburgh, Dundee, Glasgow, and Paisley, undertook, with the special approbation of Mr Fielden, a mission to Scotland. No man could have been better adapted for the work; Mr Oastler's strong religious feeling and bold oratory were in keeping with the Scottish character; though apt to calculate consequences, the Scotch are capable of great enthusiasm, and are eminently alive to the bearings of a question argued on religious and moral grounds. Mr Oastler's visit to Scotland was a tour of triumph; he addressed crowded meetings in Glasgow, Paisley, Dundee, and Edinburgh. In the last-named city two meetings were held, and after a full explanation of his mission and objects, the feeling expressed was unanimous in favour of the Ten Hours' Bill. In these meetings the clergy and gentry took part, or supported them by their presence.

Sir John Maxwell, when M.P. for Lanarkshire, had given to every question bearing on the social interests of the working classes his consideration and support. He has for many years maintained, with much ability, the proposition—" The capital of the working man is his labour; the higher the selling price of labour, the better for the interests of society." He endeavoured, when a member of the House of Commons, to establish local boards for the settlement of disputes between the employers and the employed, and assured the legislature that he considered its direct interference, under certain circumstances, a duty.

Factory regulation received Sir John's sincere and hearty support, he therefore willingly presided over the Glasgow meeting. The Paisley meeting was presided over by Mr Ker, an influential manufacturer. Sir James Forrest presided over the Edinburgh meeting. Mr Ferrand was in Edinburgh with Mr Oastler at both meetings. Their speeches were replete with fact and argument, and very efficiently served the interests of the Ten Hours' Bill movement. The opponents of the bill deemed prudence a necessity. The late Dr Chalmers was waited on by Mr Oastler, having been introduced, by letter, from the Rev Mr Lewis, of Dundee. An interesting conversation followed, a portion of which Mr Oastler subsequently published, during which the Doctor used the words—" I am a Christian—free trade must yield to Christianity; I will give my support to the Ten Hours' Bill, although its principle is opposed to that of free trade;" and, immediately thereon, wrote the following letter :—

                                " Burnside, December 23rd, 1846.
  " MY DEAR SIR,

        "I have great pleasure in introducing to you Richard Oastler, Esq., the coadjutor of Lord Ashley, and himself a very devoted philanthropist. I should rejoice if he hath a good meeting tomorrow night.

    " Please return this letter to him, as it may serve for introducing Mr Oastler to others.

            " I ever am, my dear Sir,
                    " Yours very truly,
                        "THOMAS CHALMERS.
  " To John Hamilton, Esq."

  Among the Doctor's friends were some of the most influential citizens of Edinburgh; his name in Scotland, was "a tower of strength ; " his adhesion, therefore, to the Ten Hours' Bill cause was justly esteemed an event of importance. Scotland was evidently as unanimous in support of factory regulation as England. As a fair illustration of the spirit which pervaded the mind of Scotland on the question, we copy from the newspapers of the time a speech of one of its ablest exponents. The Rev. Dr Grey, at the Edinburgh meeting, on December 28th, 1846, said :— " The facts which had been brought before the meeting were indeed most interesting and affecting. They had responded to them by the expression of their sympathy. It had been impossible, to listen to the narration without deep sorrow and distress of mind, and without a feeling of indignation. The circumstances in which the poor, the labouring poor, the operatives, had been reduced, were peculiar. England was considered the richest country in the world, and yet nowhere, he believed, in the world was there so much abject poverty to be found. Lately, when travelling on the continent, he no doubt saw much poverty; but he never witnessed such degrading poverty as might be found even in that town; and, from the account given by Mr Ferrand, the state of things was still worse in the manufacturing districts. Again, England was considered, he believed justly, as the most intelligent country in the world; and yet nowhere did they find the human mind reduced to such a shrivelled state of ignorance. And this, again, was to be attributed to the impossibility of affording education to those poor children who, at the age of seven, were introduced to factory work. England also presented many of the noblest specimens of Christian character ; and yet nowhere did they find vice so rampant, and exhibiting such revolting features. Surely there must be something wrong in the constitution of things, or at least in the arrangements of society. He could not but express a sympathy of feeling with those who regretted the immense differences found, not in rank, not in honours, but in property—the immense disparity in respect of property to be discovered in the different classes of the community—some loaded with immoderate wealth, while the great mass—the myriads

—were sunk in the deepest destitution. He was happy to find that in that meeting the obligations of religion had been so distinctly acknowledged ; and on looking to the institutions of the Great Ruler of the world—on looking at the arrangements prescribed by Infinite Wisdom for the government of that nation, which, in former ages, it pleased God specially to distinguish with his favour, he observed that provisions were made to prevent the excessive accumulation of property, and, again, for preventing the test of destitution. He would just refer to that remarkable arrangement by which, at the commencement of every fiftieth, the year of jubilee, he who had been compelled by the pressure of circumstances to sell his inheritance, was again put in possession. This law at once prevented a great accumulation at least of landed property, and provided relief for the destitution of the distressed. And agrarian laws they knew were continually aimed at by the people of Rome. He spoke not now in praise of such an arrangement—the thing was impossible. Property must, of necessity, be dispensed in very different allotments; still, they could not but regret, not the comfort and happiness of the rich, but the degradation and misery of the poor. He had listened with the deepest interest to the speeches of their friends from England who had addressed them, and of the very affecting speech delivered by Mr Oastler ; no portions were more refreshing than those which cast some little light on his personal character and history. He, like others, he supposed, had been led on some occasions to suspect that Mr Oastler was an agitator, and, perhaps, something worse; but he was delighted to find him a witness for the truth, and almost a martyr for it. It gave him the greatest pleasure, if he might judge from the whole tenor of his communication, to welcome him among them, not only as a man of humanity, but a Christian—one who recognized the obligations of religion, the authority of the Saviour ; and who appeared to be actuated by that spirit of love which was, indeed, the great distinction of the gospel. He could not but express a hope, that as the abolition of West Indian negro slavery was, as he believed, to be attributed pre-eminently to the influence of Christian principle, so the abolition of home slavery, of factory slavery, would be won by the operation of the same great principle. The feelings of humanity were the work of God and the gift of God, and ought to be cherished by us ; still they all knew there were higher principles summoned forth by the Gospel by the word of God. He was persuaded that the victory they aimed at would be won, not merely by feelings of humanity, but by the principles, the operative principles, of Christianity."

There was complete agreement between the ministers of the Gospel in Scotland and those of England. The speeches, at the various meetings in Scotland, were very fully reported in the columns of the *Times*, and in the columns of the local newspapers in the cities and towns in which they were spoken. While these public proceedings, through the agency of the press, were commanding universal attention, the signing of petitions, praying parliament to enact the Ten Hours' Bill, was rapidly in progress, committee and delegate meetings in all manufacturing districts were frequently held and numerously attended; for the time being, the whole attention of the workers in factories, and that of the majority of others, who were interested in public questions, was concentrated on the one subject of factory regulation.

The proceedings in parliament were looked forward to with anxiety. The opponents of the measure, and its more timid supporters, were heard to talk of a compromise in the form of an Eleven Hours' Bill. Mr Oastler everywhere proclaimed " no compromise;" Mr Fielden, and all the leading promoters, eschewed all concession; every one was certain that " no proposition in favour of any measure beyond ten hours a day would be listened to." On January the 26th, 1847, Mr Fielden moved the first reading of the Ten Hours' Bill, which was read a first time without opposition; in the ministry, it was an open question, and many members of the House closely watched the progress of events. The subject had been so thoroughly discussed that it did not admit of any novel feature; it was now a question depending upon petitions and votes. All the more active among the leaders of the Ten Hours' Bill movement were in London, canvassing members of both houses of parliament, and using every practicable effort to insure success. There seemed to be no limit to petitions in support of the measure; those against were comparatively few. The bill was read a second time on February 10th; Mr Hume led the opposition, and was supported by the usual opponents of factory regulation, prominently, by Mr Bright, Dr Bowring, and Mr Mark Phillips. The debate was adjourned, and again resumed on February 17th, on which occasion the principal speakers against the bill were Mr Roebuck and Sir A. L. Hay. The speakers in support of the bill, during these debates, were Mr Fielden, Mr Ferrand, Lord John Manners, Mr Newdegate, Mr G. Banks, the Hon. Mr Howard, Mr Muntz, Mr Bernal, Mr Sharman Crawford, Sir Robert Inglis, Sir George Strickland, and Mr T. S. Duncombe. The second Sir Robert Peel, in a motion for adjournment, made by Mr Escott, stated that he (Sir Robert) was opposed to the passing of the bill; and referring to a complaint that he and others had not spoken, observed :—" After the time that had been wasted, and when their opinions were perfectly well known—when the subject had been completely exhausted —and when no new arguments had been introduced, he really thought that they had better consulted the public convenience, and deferred to public opinion, by remaining silent on the occasion."

A division was taken, and the numbers were—for

the second reading, 195 ; against the second reading, 87: majority for the second reading, 108.

In the House of Commons the result was received with " loud cheers;" the news was rapidly communicated throughout the manufacturing districts; the excitement and satisfaction of the operatives were great; many committee meetings were held, resolutions and memorials passed, thanking Lord John Russell for past support, and praying him to be faithful to the cause of the factory workers, and to aid their friends in parliament on the third reading of the bill. Resolutions expressing gratitude were also passed, embodying the names of those members of parliament who had distinguished themselves by their support of the Ten Hours' Bill; the efforts on behalf of the measure were not relaxed, while the enthusiasm of the operatives was increased.

On March the 17th the subject was again under discussion in the House of Commons, and on a division, which tested the supporters and opponents of the measure, the numbers were, 144 against 66; being a majority of 78 in support of the bill. The number of firms, of factory masters, which forwarded petitions in support of ten hours' labour per day in factories, in 1847, was 922—they represented much wealth and influence. The opposition was influential, but inadequate any longer to prevent the enactment of the Ten Hours' Bill; it received the assent of the House of Commons. All the efforts made to divide its supporters on eleven hours were thus proved to have signally failed.

In the House of Lords the bill under the charge of the Earl of Ellesmere and Lord Feversham made rapid progress. In the debate on the second reading the economical, religious, and moral bearings of the question were considered. The speeches of the Earl of Ellesmere and of Lord Feversham contained a recapitulation of the principal facts and arguments of the case, and a summary of those urged in opposition. The speech of the Earl of Ellesmere was a masterly piece of reasoning, and all but exhausted the subject. Considered in connection with political economy and the duties of government. His lordship said:—

"My Lords,—The measures now proposed for your acceptance have originated in far different quarters than in the mind of one so little entitled to your lordships' attention as myself. They have originated in the crowded receptacles of human labour ; they have been elaborated in the factory and the alley, amid the whirl of machinery, and in those long rows of lodging-houses which grow up around the giant chimneys of Lancashire and Yorkshire. This bill has its root in the stern experience of the husband and the father. From this humble, but, I am sure, in your lordships' view, not contemptible seed, the idea has mounted upwards in the shape of such petitions as those which have encumbered your lordships' table. Men of higher education —men whose lives are one professional and practical exercise of philanthropy, have assisted the progress of the measure to the ears of the legislature by their sanction and their advocacy ; medical men in every branch of practice, clergymen of every religious persuasion. Springing from such a source, founded on such a basis of feeling and opinion, it has made its way through much difficulty against powerful opposition, till it has obtained the sanction of an influential portion of the cabinet, of a conclusive majority in the House of Commons, and, so supported and recommended, has reached the table of your lordships' house. I state these things, my lords, not for the purpose of inducing any one of your lordships to abdicate your privilege of free discussion or of deliberate judgment. Latest and least of the accessions to your lordships' house, I should be sorry to signalize my first endeavour at addressing your lordships by proposing any surrender of your independence, any infraction of your privileges. Considering, however, the nature of the question at issue — considering that in the majorities which have sanctioned this measure elsewhere—considering that every debatable point has been argued elsewhere by men who have stood on their own weary feet at the mule, and pieced the thread with their own hands, and who, by the strong exercise of that strong intelligence which appears to me an indigenous plant of the manufacturing districts of England, by their perseverance in honest industry, have raised themselves to the House of Commons ;—I ask you this at least ;—I ask you to receive this bill with something of that *prima facie* deference with which, some months ago, I, as a member of the House of Commons, should have received some measure of equity law perchance, which had come down to that house, having passed through the ordeal of those legal minds which adorn and instruct, and, in such measures, greatly govern your lordships' deliberations. My lords, the principle of this bill has been impugned, as involving legislative interterference with the rights of capital and labour. I might slur over this objection on the ground of repeated precedent. In the House of Commons I would do so ; but addressing your lordships, who have been less engaged with the subject, I think it more respectful, briefly to attempt my own vindication on this head. I am not one of those who presume, out of their own ignorance or idleness, to cast reflections on the acute and laborious men who have devoted themselves to the science of political economy, nor am I a sceptic as to the general validity of the main tenets of that school, nor an impugner of the truth which it professes to have demonstrated. I am prepared, however, if necessary, to contend that I am advocating nothing inconsistent with the doctrines of political economy. I do not wish to enter at length on such debatable ground, but I would much rather refer your lordships to an argument which you would find in the debates, delivered by a noble earl, now on the Ministerial bench, who drew the just distinction between restrictions on labour and capital devised to increase wealth, and those intended for other purposes—to guard against want and physical evils. My lords, I dislike a meddling government. I believe with him, that for the creation of the greatest producible wealth in any given community, and, therefore, for the widest diffusion of that material wellbeing which attends the production of wealth, the policy of abstinence from legislative meddling is the surest policy, and, therefore, I think it incumbent on any one who departs from that policy, to assign distinct grounds for his justification. The master manufacturer and the operative have both a right, I admit it, to say to me— you are interfering with my free action, you are selecting mine from a crowd of other occupations, to make it the subject of experimental legislation. I claim an explanation, I demand an exceptional reason for your conduct. My lords, I find that justification, as most of your lordships will anticipate, in the inherent, inalienable tendencies of that agent which Watt forced into the service of man, as applied to the four great branches of our textile industry, which come under the provisions of this bill ; I mean the tendency, in the first instance, to attract to its ministration the labour of those whom in respect to age or sex, or both, nature never intended for hard and continuous labour, and next, in its tendency to make that labour continuous and unceasing, and protracted to a limit of physical and mental endurance which, in my opinion, no Christian legislature can see its subjects approach without acknowledging the duty of interfering, if it can interfere, for their relief and protection. It is on this ground, my lords, that find- ing, as I do, with regard to these branches of industry, the means and opportunity of interference, I claim the right to exercise them. I say, my lords, finding the means and opportunity, for this also is an essential element of practical interference, and is my reply to an argument which, though often used, is I think singularly inconclusive—to a course of reasoning very commonly adopted towards any man who is hunting down a particular grievance, and which endeavours to divert his attention by pointing out fifty other objects in pursuit. My lords, there is doubtless enough of abuse and misery and oppression in the world, to make a sentimental or flighty philanthropist fold his arms in despair. My lords, I invite your lordships to interfere with these large collective aggregations of labour, because theory and experience tell me, you can do so with effect—because they are open to inspection and capable of control—because you can do much to prevent abuse, and, if the hard necessity arise, to punish it. I am aware that this very feature of the case has been alleged as a reason for non-interference; it has been said, that the factory system is the very department of our industry in which abuse and oppression are most discoverable and can least escape detection. We have been repeatedly told, that we take an unphilosophical view of the effects of the use of machinery; that it is the great diminisher of the sum of mental and physical labour, the fertile source of leisure and contentment, and that we should be cautious how we meddle with its operations. I admit these facts; but I demand your lordships' attention to some further facts connected with the employment of that fixed and expansive capital, into the scope and effect of which it becomes a duty from which, as a legislator, I cannot shrink from inquiring. There is, in my opinion, no grander result of human intelligence than a large cotton mill; but I say this of it, that from the moment its engine is started, raised by the capital and governed by the will of the acute and enterprising individual who sits in its office, it becomes the direct interest of that presiding genius, that its motions should be as unceasing and continuous as human contrivance can make them, that there is no part of that vast system of wheels and levers which can rest without

s 2

loss, or in the ordinary and average course of commercial prosperity, pursue its motions without gain. The human labour attached hand and foot to that system, for the most part, admits not of relays. What is the natural, the inevitable consequence of this? Why, that which has resulted—that with which, step by step, gradually, cautiously, effectually and successfully, you have been endeavouring for thirty years to moderate and curtail, in wise defiance of the stated principles of political economy. That the strong impulse of gain is placed in direct and dangerous antagonism with the claims of humanity—that it almost invariably prevails in the struggle, as for a time it was left, and if left to itself, unchecked and uncontrolled, it reduces a part of your population to the condition of slavery, unmitigated by that interest in the physical well-being of the party which does operate on the slave-owner of Carolina. My lords, such things have been ; to prevent them you have repeatedly interfered, and your exertions have not been in vain. Now, my lords, does the same reason hold good with other departments of human industry in which machinery of human contrivance is less complicated ? I say machinery of human contrivance, for I hold that, in some sense, the earth itself is a machine—that the clod of the valley in which you drop the germ of future vegetation, is as much a machine as that in which you deposit your portions of raw cotton. In another place, my lords, I took the liberty of telling the lords of the soil, that in this point of view I considered them as monster manufacturers, and I re-assert that opinion here. Your lordships, in the management of hereditary estates, which have descended to you from the Conquest, are connected with machinery as well as Mr Gregg ; but, my lords, there is a difference between the machinery of God's contrivance and that of his creatures. Now, I will pass to the practical consideration of the degree to which we shall extend our interference in this matter.

My lords, after long discussion, after repeated consideration, the House of Commons has decided, so far as that branch of the legislature can decide, that the labour of women and young persons under eighteen years of age, shall be limited to ten hours of work, exclusive of the two which are necessary for refreshment. I am bound to state, though no one of your lordships can be ignorant of the fact, that from the necessary intermixture of the hands of different ages and sexes, in the operations of the manufacture, this promise will include, in its direct operation, those whom it does not directly affect. Adult man is not affected directly by it, but I can by no means avail myself of that circumstance, in argument, as to the evil effect of the measure ; well knowing this, the adult population of the manufacturing districts, so far from shrinking from the consequence, is to an enormous extent interested in its acceptance by your lordships. I believe that an overwhelming majority of it is at this moment trembling with expectation, perhaps, with just apprehension, that the cause they support may suffer prejudice from my own incapacity as an advocate. I do not state this as an argument to your lordships, I admit it, as a subordinate consideration to myself. I think it an unquestionable collateral advantage that its acceptance will realize hopes which have been entertained and fostered since the attempt of the first Sir Robert Peel, in 1815, whose measure, which was on the verge of completion, was nearly a fac-simile of the present. I think it a vast advantage that it will put a close to a peaceful and orderly, but an intense and peculiar agitation, but I do not state this as a reason for influencing your lordships' better judgments. I think a bill supported by such Ministers in the House of Commons entitled to much respect; but I am not here to register the decisions of that house, or, to induce your lordships to do so. I accept this measure because we find, after some hesitation—after listening much, and thinking much, and speaking a little, I think it a beneficial bargain, by which the parties to be affected will obtain certain advantages of incalculable importance to them, at a risk of certain sacrifices, which it is not possible precisely to calculate, but, which will leave at the least the balance of advantage largely in favour of those who have to make them. Two main objections have been taken to the measures, two principal and inevitable consequences have been held out as certain to ensue. It is said that, by striking off a twelfth from the time during which, when employment is rife, you are at present able to labour, you will either diminish wages or cause defeat from foreign competition. I am not bound, throughout, to argue with those who predict both these consequences, because I think the one consequence lost in connexion with the other. For the first of these consequences I have always advised those with whom I had been in communication, to be prepared, and I have certainly always received the advice that, to the best of their ability, they had counted the cost and were prepared, on behalf of themselves and their families, to encounter it. I am not fond of prophecying in matters of this description, if, on the one hand I am not prepared to risk my reputation for accuracy in a calculation of the exact effect upon wages ; on the other, I ask any man to favour me with a calculation of the amount of actual domestic economy which may be effected by the mother of three children who returns to her home two hours sooner than at present. I cannot calculate this, because I cannot see —I cannot hear—I cannot wish—I cannot ask—still less can I calculate the evanescent quantities, the social effects of leisure and repose to the mind, or lay down in advance statistical results on bodily health or longevity. I have no doubt whatever that the average sum total of these elements, if they could be calculated, would show a set-off to any probable diminution of money wages, which will, one day, be satisfactory to those who have co-operated in passing this measure. On this subject I must also call your lordships' attention to another circumstance—the deductions are made, when the article is brought in by the operative, for 'waste' and 'spoil.' My lords, from such information as I can obtain, it is my firm belief that nine-tenths of that spoiled will arise in the task-weary hours of the operative's present average toil. I have never met with any man of any class, conversant with the subject, who has not laid much stress on this circumstance. I pass, my lords, to the question of foreign competition. I do not profess to receive with indifference, from men for whose station, acquirements, and abilities, I have profound respect, their ideas on this subject, but, I am consoled by the reflection, that no step has been taken in this matter which has not been preceded by similar warnings of ruin, and similar threats of emigration by them, which I doubt not have assailed many of your lordships as they have assailed me. And yet, my lords, I hold in my hands a paper which shows that England has yet held her own against the competition of the world, and which leads me to think that if she is allowed to suffer decay, it will originate rather in a diminished supply of the raw material than in any legislation which, for the sake of the highest interests of humanity, we may have consented to adopt. My lords, I must say that the language of some of these parties has varied very much with circumstances, in a very short space of time. I am addressing many now who retain, through evil report and good, the opinions which they have uniformly expressed in favour of restrictions on the free importation of corn, but I doubt whether the sternest adherent to that system would not admit that, whilst those restrictions existed, the case of the worsted manufacturer, as an opponent to this bill, did not present a difficulty in the way of limiting the hours of labour. My lords, I speak for myself at least,

and say, I had no occasion to broach what was then urged
by the millowner. From what I have lately heard, I can
hardly believe that the old corn law and the duty on raw
cotton are not still on the statute book. I look for them
there in vain, but I also listen in vain for a repetition of
language which was used at the period when a struggle
was going on for their removal. Then the grievance and
the evil of long hours were admitted, then the factory
delegates were told,—' It is true that overwork is decreasing
your stature, but do not agitate for the immediate alteration
of those laws. Join us in agitating to remove the real
obstacle to that measure, and that removed, you shall gain
your object, at least with his employer's consent, if not with
that active co-operation which might be too much to expect.
My lords, such was the nature of the language, and I
have proofs of it, used by some gentlemen, who, doubtless,
in the heat of the moment, in the ardour of pursuit of
a great political object, thought, and intended what they
said, but who were deceived, that free trade and relief
from duty is no guarantee against the danger, and is not
to be spoken of as a palliation of the effects of foreign
competition. My lords, I believe that from a concourse of
circumstances, peculiar to the character of this nation, England
is in a condition to set an example to the world in this
matter, as she has done in others ; and that she is able
to do right and fear not; and more than this, that her
example. will be followed, and that foreign statesmen, who
may not be disposed to follow it, will be pressed by that
influence of public feeling and opinion which is acting upon
ourselves. . . . .
My lords, these and such as these are considerations
which divest me of any serious apprehension for the result
of the measure I propose; which inspire in my mind a stern
hope that its advantages will not be purchased at the price
which some predict. It is said sometimes that, after all,

these advantages will be small—that we overrate the opportunities which a reduction of ten hours will afford to the artisan, and it would almost appear as if some supposed, that his time may be as profitably employed, in an honest and respectable occupation, as it will be when at his own command. There may, there probably will, be cases in which these hours may be mis-spent; the factory may be exchanged for the gin-shop. I am not of opinion that the hours so torn from the mill and the loom will be sufficient to raise materially the standard of education or mental culture. I am not caring to enquiré where or how the man, woman, or child who has worked hard for ten hours, employs the remainder. I do not think, on the average, that the population of Manchester is the least disqualified for exercising its own judgment and following its own tastes in this particular, or in the least requires any meddling supervision of mine. My lords, in the course I have taken, in accepting the conduct of this bill, I have undertaken a given responsibility for its eventual consequences. Should it prosper to the extent of my hopes and expectations, and should I live to see that result, I reserve to myself, as my sole but all-sufficient reward, the gratification of that spectacle. Popularity I have not sought, and utterly disdain. If that reward should eventually fall due, it is impossible that the intelligence and justice of the people should not place the saddle on the right horse. It will be due to my noble friend [Lord Ashley]—it will be due to the master manufacturer, who has not allowed himself to be swayed by circumstances which would insure his own interests, in securing, as I believe, completed contracts with others. It will be due to those who have worked through the long hours of this bill in the workshop of the legislature, and not to the labourer of the eleventh hour, who now begs your lordships' pardon for so long trespassing on your lordships' attention." The noble earl concluded by moving the second reading of the bill.

Lord Feversham spoke with special reference to the progress and history of the factory movement. A subject on which his lordship was a high authority. He had known the factory movement from the first letter written, on *White Slavery*, by Mr Oastler, in the *Leeds Mercury*. His lordship had, at all times, been ready of access to the factory delegates ; he had communed with them freely, contributed generously towards their funds, and watched the progress of their movement with the closest possible attention ; the experience of years had deepened his conviction of the importance of the measure ; he had advocated it in the Castle Yard of York, side by side with Sadler, Oastler, and Bull. The audience and the circumstances in the Castle Yard of York, in 1832, and in the House of Lords, in 1847, were widely different ; then, the struggle was but begun, now, it was drawing towards a close; then, the voice of prophecy was loud against the measure, now, reason and experience were on its side—the voice of Lord Feversham was unchanged. Addressing the peers of England, he said:—"That this measure was one of great importance in reference to the moral and social welfare of the operative classes employed in factories of the United Kingdom, as well as to the national honour and character, no one who had paid the least attention to the subject would for one moment doubt. It was now some years since parliament had been addressed in favour of a Ten Hours' Bill, and the manner in which those who sought the boon had conducted themselves, was well worthy of their lordships' consideration. They had never had recourse to violence, to unscrupulous agitation, to combinations against employers, although suggestions were not wanting to prompt them to such a course. Never, in one single instance, so far as he was aware, had they committed a breach of the peace at any of the great meetings in the manufacturing districts, although thousands, and tens of thousands, were congregated in furtherance of their common object. On the contrary, their assemblages had been distinguished by unequivocal manifestations of loyalty to the institutions of the country. The advocates of the bill were the industrious and well-disposed; its opponents, the idle and evil-disposed, who cared not how their families toiled, whilst they themselves spent their time at a public-house. The question of wages was undoubtedly one of the greatest importance, and this point had been invariably discussed in the meetings which had been held in the manufacturing districts. The operatives were invariably asked, ' Are you prepared to submit to a reduction of wages, in case such should be the effect of the passing of the Ten Hours' Bill.' And the answer to that question had always been in the affirmative. For his own part, he was convinced that the effect of the bill, would be to cause more regular employment, without the fluctuations experienced under the existing system. The average of mills do not work ten hours a day; and he did not think that, on an average of five or seven years, there would, in fact, be any diminution in the rate of wages. Whenever the subject had been brought forward in parliament, it had always been met by the same anticipations of evil, and, yet, he had not seen one single instance in which these predictions had been verified. Was it likely, if such were the probable result, that so large a number of master manufacturers would be found amongst its supporters ? Who was the individual that had introduced it, in the other house of parliament ? The hon. member for Oldham, Mr Fielden, a gentleman who had been engaged during his whole life-time—and that not a short one—in manufacture, and is now bringing up his sons to the same occupation. Was it reasonable, or likely, that such men as Mr Fielden, for he was representative of others, would support a measure which in practice would inflict injury on themselves and their children." [The noble lord related the history of the various legislative measures connected with factory labour.]

His lordship continued: — " It appeared from the evidence taken before Mr Sadler's committee, that the highest authorities in such matters, anticipated the most beneficial results from the limitation of the hours of labour in factories. The measures heretofore passed, for limiting those hours of labour, had proved in no way injurious to our manufacturing industry. He found that between the years 1819 and 1845 the consumption of cotton in this country had increased 400 per cent. Many clergymen and other persons in different parts of the country, well acquainted with the wants and interests of the working classess, had expressed their belief that the present arrangements for the employment of operatives in factories had the unhappy effect of leaving them no time for attending to religion and education; under these circumstances, he hoped that their lordships would not refuse to give their assent to the second reading of the bill then under their consideration. He hoped, that the members of her Majesty's government in that house would be unanimous in favour of the measure. The noble lord at the head of the government [Lord John Russell] had, in the other house, fully redeemed the pledge which he had given to the electors of the City of London last autumn, when he had told them that Her Majesty's government would be prepared to take into their consideration the important subject of the moral and social condition of the great masses of the people, with a view to the improvement of their condition, and the elevation of the character of those masses. The bill before their lordships was but a part, although by no means an unimportant part, of the measures bearing upon that great question. The noble lord at the

head of the government had honourably redeemed the
pledge he had given; for, although he would have preferred
an eleven hours' clause to a ten hours' clause, he had given
his vote in the House of Commons in favour of the third
reading of the bill as it then stood. He trusted that the
noble earl at the head of the Board of Trade [the Earl of
Clarendon] would pursue a similar course, and he earnestly
hoped that their lordships, generally, would extend, on that
occasion, to the operative classes the benefits of their legislation. They had, of late, passed several measures calculated
to promote the interests of master-manufacturers; they
had, last year, repealed the duty on foreign corn; and they
had, in a preceding year, removed the duties on foreign
cotton and wool. A promise had been given to the working
classes that, after the corn laws were repealed, they should
have a Ten Hours' Bill, or, at all events, there had been a
general understanding to that effect in the manufacturing
districts. It might, however, be said that the principles
of political economy were opposed to that measure. Now,
he could not enter into that question, but he should observe,
that they had, at least, on the other side, the principles of
justice, of humanity, of religion, and of Christianity. He
trusted their lordships would give their cordial, their zealous,
and, he would add, their unanimous support to the bill;
and sure he was, that even those who had been its most determined opponents would, after having witnessed the beneficial effects of its operation, admit that it was a measure
which had conferred incalculable benefits on the working
classes of this country, and which had ensured the triumph
of justice, benevolence, and patriotism over injustice, inhumanity, and oppression."

The Bishop of London observed:—" That he thought that
a great part of the question concerned that very numerous
and unprotected class—the children who were employed in
factories, and it was with reference to them, particularly, that

he wished to ask for their lordships' attention to the observations he had to offer. The factory workmen, acting
under the consideration of that necessity which was produced
by the peculiar state of the labour market in the manufacturing districts, seemed to regard their children as mere instruments for making money; and, here again, he thought the
parental functions of the state came into play, and ought
to interpose to relieve those children from that necessity.
If the cupidity of their employers, or the ignorance of their
parents, compelled them to extend their labour far beyond
those limits of exertion which their bodily constitution was
suited for, and, therefore, he might say, beyond that point
which their benevolent Creator designed for them, he thought
it became the sacred duty of the legislature to interfere
and afford them that protection which their natural guardians
were not inclined, or in a condition, to give them. If they
desired that the evil should not be perpetuated or aggravated, and that some chance should be given to the rising
generation of growing up in habits of religion and morality,
their lordships must interpose to save them from their
ceaseless round of exhausting toil, and leave them more
time for improvement. Their intellectual faculties were
contracted by the monotonous and wearisome labour to
which they were subjected, and that formed no unimportant
consideration in the question then before their lordships.
The agricultural labourer, notwithstanding the eloquent
description of his noble and learned friend of the effect
which the toil of that labourer produced on his health
and spirits, was in a much more favourable condition for
carrying out the great object of his being than the factory
workman. His work was carried on in the open field, where
he was inhaling pure air, and saw the pure light of heaven,
and, at any moment, he might suspend his toil to prevent
exhaustion to his strength and spirits. It was not so with
the factory workman. His loom must move on with unceas-

ing motion for the appointed number of hours, to complete the proper quantity of work, and it admitted of no suppression in the labour of those children, who were deputed to carry on and watch its ceaseless process. But that imprisonment, as it were, of a large class of our fellow creatures, was not a case in which the legislature ought to interfere, unless the evils which were shown to be wrought in an opposite direction could be shown to be greater than those which would be produced by their interference. The evils, however, of the present system were so great, that they could hardly be contemplated by any humane man without shuddering. The debility of frame, the shattered strength, the exhausted spirit, the early death, were various and lamentable evils; but they were not the worst. Before, however, he proceeded to the consideration of the latter point, he would advert to the mortality of the manufacturing districts. It might be argued that the diminished average of human life in those districts was to be ascribed to the unhealthy condition of large towns; but that was completely refuted by certain facts which had been ascertained. It appeared from a statement which had been made by a most able and benevolent individual, Mr Fletcher, a medical man, who had made a close investigation of this subject, that the average duration of life of the factory operative was something less than one-half that of other operatives in the same districts. He would now advert, to what he considered the worst consequences of the present system—namely, that it entirely disqualified the children from receiving the benefits of education after a certain age, when, perhaps, it is not going too far to say education was more important to them than before. He would admit, that up to the age of thirteen years, those children were comparatively well provided for, as the hours of labour, up to that age, were limited to six hours; but the moment they attained that age their work was doubled, and they very soon lost all they had learned before, because, after twelve hours of exhausting labour, they had no spirit or strength left to attend school or to profit by it. Their lordships must also consider, that in addition to those twelve hours for which they are obliged to work in the factory, two more were reckoned in going to and from the mills, and in the necessary cleansing and refreshment; so that, even if this bill passed, and the hours of labour were restricted to ten hours, there would be still twelve hours of the day no portion of which could be devoted to school for the purpose of deriving sound and wholesome instruction. Under these circumstances, it was no wonder that the clergy and medical men of the manufacturing districts were all but unanimous in favour of this bill, which, they believed, would at least diminish, if not altogether cure, the evils that existed. But the bill was also supported by a large portion of those whose interests would be most deeply affected by it, not merely by factory workmen, but, by many of the great millowners, who, according to the opinions of the opponents of the measure, would be great losers by it. It was said they would lose one-sixth of the factory labour of the country, and to that extent our manufacturers would be destroyed. But, on the other side, he placed the great gain the measure would produce to morality and humanity."

The Bishop of Oxford:—" Begged to remind their lordships of the bill passed two years ago to prevent women working in mines. Every argument, employed at the present time against this measure, had been used then. They were told, it was impossible to legislate safely upon subjects which involved labour and wages; that the result of interference would be that the mines would be ruined, and miners driven abroad. The legislature did, however, pass that measure, and what had been the consequence? The miners had become better workmen, and the women good mothers. The principle had, in fact, been given up, or rather, this was no exception to the general rule. This was an attempt to fix the rate of wages; this was a different subject-matter; it was wrong to create wealth by sacrificing the souls and bodies of men. The law interfered to prevent the creation of wealth by working on the seventh day. Why not work on the seventh day? It was considered no infraction of the principles of political economy to rest on the seventh day. The only question for the legislature in such cases was, when and how it should interfere, and here moral and religious considerations exacted interference at its hands. The legislature did not suffer a man to build a house where he liked, if it should be a nuisance to others, or was unsafe; and, although in such a case it interfered with natural liberty, it did so in order to protect others from injury; and so here, they were called upon to protect those who could not protect themselves—against what? Why against being forced, contrary to their desire, so to work that their bodies and souls were liable to be sacrificed by labour. And what would they be reduced to if this measure was refused? He did not say that their lordships would drive those people to take the law into their own hands, though it would be well if this matter were seriously considered by their lordships. Nothing was more dangerous than to refuse the petitions of a great body of the people, to leave their desires unsatisfied, to put them off with cold rejection, or even with needless delay. Let their lordships consider the position of these people. The capitalists and great manufacturers could make their own terms; the working classes had only the option of working at the wages offered, or not working at all. The capitalists could exert a complete power over the working classes. How could these men resist?—only by combination. Were their lordships prepared to make them see that the only way to resist was by combination against their masters? He (the Bishop of Oxford) had asked the factory delegates about this matter, and their answer was that there were combinations, and that it was their (the delegates') great endeavour to prevent such combinations. But, if this measure was rejected, it would be difficult to prevent illegal combinations, to which the men would consider they were driven, in order to obtain their just rights. Depend upon it, there would be attempts made to force from a reluctant legislature, what they considered to be their due, and therefore he warned their lordships to weigh well what they were doing, before they rejected a measure which so deeply affected the interests of all classes in this country. What gave the manufacturers their present superiority? It was the security of all property in England; but if they were bringing up in the manufacturing districts a population altogether strange to legislative matters, in the belief that legislation was unconnected with moral considerations, they would go on unsettling the very basis of the security of property. Nothing was so likely to deprive the manufacturers of this security as to expose it to the risk of conflict with the physical strength of the people. The acquisition of wealth was based upon moral principles. There could be no political wrong, which was politically expedient, or that could tend to the production of wealth. Depend upon it, that if they neglected the people, in order to make the nation rich, they would in the end make the nation poor, by debasing the people."

Successful opposition was impossible, but Lord Brougham, on what he believed to be sound economical grounds, felt bound to argue and vote against the bill. The Bishops, as the guardians of the interests of the church, gave to the Ten Hours' Bill their unanimous and influential support; those of London and Oxford replied to the objections of opponents, and pressed the claims of the measure earnestly on the attention of their lordships. For the second reading, the Contents were 53; the Non-contents, 11: majority, 42.

A protest against the third reading was entered on record, signed "Monteagle, Brandon, Ashburton, Radnor, Foley, Wrottesly;" this document was a recapitulation, in a condensed form, of the principal objections which had been urged against a limitation of the hours of factory labour by law, from the opening of the controversy. It must be some satisfaction to the noble lords, whose names it bears, that the serious and evil results they predicated have not been realized.

In the House of Lords, the details of the bill did not undergo any change, it passed through its last stage on June the 1st, and received the royal assent on June the 8th, 1847. A few bold and persevering men, after a struggle of many years, were successful in their efforts to protect the weak ; they, on behalf of the interests of humanity, had stamped the impress of their minds on the statute-book of their country, and by their efforts they had directly and practically benefited many of their fellow beings, and proved that, under certain circumstances, the state may beneficially interfere to protect the health and morals of the people.

The words of the Speaker of the House of Commons, when addressing the Queen and the House of Lords, on July the 23rd, 1847, deserve preservation: " We have found it necessary to place a further limitation on the hours of labour of young persons employed in factories; and by giving more time and opportunity for their religious and moral instruction, for healthful recreation, and the exercise of their domestic duties, we have elevated the character and conditions of a large and industrious class engaged in manufacturing operations."

Among those who have been least conspicuous but most helpful in the accomplishment of this great and good work, must be ranked the names of " Wood and Walker," the eminent worsted spinners of Bradford, in Yorkshire; their aid has been continuous, their labours incessant, and of the kinds most required. In public efforts for social and political ends, it may be truly said, " money is power, and good example a wholesome external influence," and of both, have this firm been liberal; their character and services demand a fuller notice than they have hitherto received, apart from their claims to attention, in a work devoted to a narrative of events in which they were influential agents: facts in the lives of men of industry, are, at all times, instructive, and form the kernel of the history of the age.

In the year 1812, Mr John Wood, of Bradford, having obtained a knowledge of the worsted business with one of the millowners of that town, which, at that time did not contain more than half a dozen of the same class, induced his father to erect for him a small mill, with steam engine of 20 horse-power, and began his career as a worsted spinner. He very soon effected great improvements in the machinery then employed, which enabled him to introduce new and superior yarns, and thus to acquire an important position. The profits of the trade were so large, that very few years passed over before he began to make an extension of his operations by the erection of additional buildings.

As a man of education and Christian principle, Mr Wood was not long in perceiving that the hours of labour, in the mills, were incompatible with the health and well-being of the children and young persons whose fingers were absolutely requisite in piecing or uniting the threads broken in the spinning, and who performed the other light work of the mill; he began at an early period, to grant ameliorations, and to adopt a course of liberality towards his workpeople, so that by the time he had been in business ten or twelve years, he had carried out an improved system. The great profits which were realized, led the millowners generally to exact an excessive length of toil, and contributed to cause the gross abuses, which, for many years, were practised in that department of labour.

The extension of the factory system, brought on a more glaring amount of suffering and injury to the children and young persons working therein, and, about the year 1830, the evil became so great, that Mr Wood felt impelled, by a sense of duty, to make efforts for their deliverance. No law then existed, in the woollen and worsted mills, to restrain millowners from enforcing lengthened hours of working, and some of them exacted from those juveniles of both sexes, fourteen, sixteen, and even eighteen hours of daily toil, the year round! Although Mr Wood never worked his mill so long as any of the hours, per day, above mentioned, he felt that even from twelve to thirteen hours a day were far too protracted for human endurance ; he determined to adopt a plan whereby ten hours working per day was the rule for the younger, and eleven hours for the elder branches of those employed at his works; he also then established a school on the premises with a master and mistress, the latter to instruct the girls in needle-work. When the parents did not furnish their children with materials for sewing, calico and other cloth were provided by Mr Wood, and the articles, made up by the children, were sold to the parents at the cost of the cloth. In these arrangements Mr Wood was greatly assisted by the Rev. George Stringer Bull, then incumbent of Bierley, near Bradford, whose zeal and success, in promoting the education and physical improvement of the poor, have been surpassed by none.

Mr Wood not only deemed it right to place his own work-people in an improved position; but also to engage in arduous efforts to obtain parliamentary powers for enforcing proper hours and other regulations upon the whole factory system of the United Kingdom. He opened his mind and heart— as has been previously related—to his friend Mr Richard

Oastler. The result of Mr Wood's conference with Mr Oastler was, that the latter, at once entered upon the work, with a stern resolve to succeed, and, although in the course of the ensuing eventful agitation, of seventeen years duration, which terminated in the passing of the Ten Hours' Bill, very strong expressions were occasionally used, there was in no instance any breach of the peace, nor was there in Mr Oastler's conduct any features so prominent as those of disinterestedness and patriotism.

From 1832 to 1847, during which period the establishment of Mr Wood had been changed to the firm of Wood and Walker, and afterwards Walkers and Co., no more than eleven hours a day were worked, and the reason why ten hours was not the restriction, arose from the fact that the sacrifice annually made by working eleven hours, instead of those longer hours practised by their competitors, was as large as could be prudently made.

Mr Wood's anxiety for the physical and mental improvement of those in his employment was very great. We have heard Mr Oastler narrate, how he and Mr Wood have stood on the steps of the counting-house, facing the mill-yard, and watched the hungry children rush in to their previously prepared and well-arranged dining-room (a luxury known then to few factory children). They had watched the children's return, after dinner, in groups of twos, threes, fours, and fives, in animated conversation. Some running and romping, others shouting and singing, until suddenly, in joyous expectation of the "better time a coming," they would unite in their chorus:—

> "We will have the Ten Hours' Bill,
> That we will, that we will."

There was, then, in Mr Wood's face an expression of satisfaction and enjoyment, which "stores of gold" could not have awarded. Mr Wood embarked in the Ten Hours' Bill movement under a strong sense of religious duty; over him, neither commercial, personal, nor political influences, had any longer control. He knew that he was rich, but his enjoyment of wealth was tainted by the impression, that many had endured grievous wrongs during its acquisition, and he most heroically resolved that, come what **might**, all factory children should, for the future, be protected by the law; for the attainment of that end, he was prepared to make every sacrifice. Though a man of most retiring habits, when the factory children required his presence, he was in the busiest of the throng. Public speaking was to him abhorrent; when his voice could serve the cause, no matter how numerous the assembly, that voice was heard. Disputes in newspapers were obnoxious to his habits, but when a millowner's opinion was required, in defence of the interests of factory children, his pen was used in their service. Mr Wood cherished a lively attachment to his friends, Lord Ashley, Messrs Oastler and Sadler, and the Rev. G. S. Bull, who, on all important occasions, received his counsel and support. When the Ten Hours' Bill was before parliament, Mr Wood was in London, advising and instructing members of both houses on the merits of the question. It was his habit to attend, when asked, all the more important of the committee meetings in Yorkshire and Lancashire. Mr Wood was honoured by a circle of admiring friends; their friendship he highly appreciated, but, on behalf of the factory children, he risked their approval and intimacy. With a generous heart, and liberal hand, he opened widely his well-filled purse, and made its contents tributary in every place to the requirements of the factory movement. His house was open at all times to the active friends of the Ten Hours' Bill, who, on their journies in furtherance of that cause, required rest and refreshment.

He continued faithful to the question of factory regulation, until his originally contemplated object was realised. We have trustworthy authority for asserting, that, uniting the sacrifices consequent on the practice of working shorter hours

than other capitalists in the neighbourhood, to the actual money
spent by him in the furtherance of the Ten Hours' Bill
movement in connection with the firm of Wood and Walker,
and Walkers and Co., the total would amount to 50,000*l.*

Having realised a large fortune, Mr Wood retired from
business some years back, and is gratefully remembered by
his friends and old neighbours of the town of Bradford. His
wealth was honourably acquired, not by sordid accumulation,
but by steady commercial efforts, during the progress of which
he lived as became an English gentleman, and liberally
benefited all around him. When in possession of riches
sufficient to enable him to change from an active Yorkshire
manufacturer to the position of a country squire (which
change, sanctioned by usage, is the natural desire of many
enterprising Englishmen) he built, in his native town, a
substantial and handsome church, parsonage, and schools, the
former of which he endowed with an annual stipend of 350*l.*
He now resides on his own large estate, Thedden Grange, in
Hampshire. Mr Wood, though often pressed by the burgesses
of his native town—Bradford, to become its representative in
parliament, uniformly refused ; this circumstance is in keeping
with his character ; he has courted privacy, except when
impelled to appear in public by a keen sense of duty—and has
at all times preferred the unostentatious exercise of charity
and benevolence to external, worldly distinction. The tem-
perament of some men unfits them for active conflict in the
senate, but the wants of society are so varied that all may be
useful. Mr Wood has been eminently serviceable to mankind,
and the appreciation of his talents and virtues by his fellow
townsmen, cannot have failed to have been gratifying to him,
as it certainly was creditable to them.

Mr William Walker, for many years the active head, and,
after Mr Wood's retirement, the principal of the firm of Wood
and Walker (now Walkers and Co.) has, from 1830, been an
unswerving supporter of the Ten Hours' Bill movement, and

not any man has rendered thereto more efficient service. Mr Walker is an excellent illustration of the benefits arising from probity, activity, and order; he knows, thoroughly, the value of minutes, and, in consequence, is enabled, without injury to himself or others, to devote hours to the fulfilment of the social duties of his position, as one of the chiefs of an industrial community, and a magistrate of the West Riding. In the capacities of proprietor and manager of a manufacturing firm, he has been essentially " the right man in the right place," and few places can be more important. Any one who has a knowledge of what Yorkshire woollen and worsted factories were thirty years ago, and is desirous of seeing the many advantages arising from judicious arrangement in manufacturing industry, should visit the factories of Walkers and Co. Everything necessary for the health and comfort of the factory workers, so far as the nature of wool-spinning allows, is done, and this, too, consistently with the profit of the employer, and necessarily for the welfare of the employed; these facts present a striking contrast with the unregulated factories in the town of Bradford thirty years back, and the change reflects high credit upon their spirited and benevolent proprietors.

Good example is not without effect; there are among Mr Walker's neighbours those who emulate him in the care he manifests for the lives and limbs of those he employs: and their merits ought not to pass unappreciated. Mr Walker is a tory and churchman, he is also what is called " a no-popery man," contending that every gain acquired by the pope is a loss to the British crown and constitution. As a clear-headed man of business, and a practical improver of the condition of working men, a useful Englishman, and an upright magistrate, his reputation is deservedly high. He is possessed of superior talent, efficient rather than showy; like most men of enlarged commercial experience, he is more apt to affirm conclusions, than to state the reasonings by which he arrives at them, but is very capable of doing both, when necessary. Though a warm and active politician, he is tolerant to those who conscientiously differ from him in opinion, always taking care to state boldly his own convictions.

A keen apprehension of responsibility is the primary requisite for the fulfilment of duty. Mr Walker, in the management of his factories, carries his sense of duty into the particular circumstances of the lives of others, showing that the factory system need not necessarily be a national reproach. Should a person of immoral character find employment at " Walkers and Co." Mr Walker endeavours, in the first place, to impress the individual with a conviction of the evil and danger to himself and others of the practice complained of ; if amendment does not promptly follow, dismissal invariably takes place. It is the rule at " Walkers and Co.," and at some other firms, to pay the wages of those in their employment about the middle of the week ; the object is to enable operatives to expend their weekly earnings with full time for deliberation. This is a matter of importance ; the payment of wages on a Saturday, very frequently leads to the practice of hurried and unprofitable marketing, with the attendant evils of temptation to irregular habits, and trenching on the rest and quiet of the Sabbath-day. Mr Walker rigidly maintains that home is the proper sphere of duty for married women, and therefore objects to employ them. It is well understood by females, on being married, that they are expected to remain at home, which causes greater care in the choice of husbands. Mr Walker has often said—" The practice of husbands depending on the wages of their wives, is an inversion of family order, and ought to be put down by every means reasonably available for that end." A declaration to which all right-minded men must subscribe. The payment of wages for work done, is not, in itself, a fulfilment of the obligation of an employer. A large amount of good would be the result to the country, if capitalists and employers of labour would admit and act upon the necessity of this sense of enlarged responsibility; and thereby show that the health, morals, education, and general thrift of those in their employment were, at least, as much deserving of attention as the state of the markets, or the payment of accounts. The congregation of workers might by such means be made a practical advantage to society.

Messrs Wood and Walker, in addition to personal services and sacrifices, have been the centre of a spirited and influential circle of friends, who have indirectly, but powerfully, helped onward the common cause. In no country in the world does social position exercise so much influence on public opinion, as in England. Some among our gentry can count back a long line of ancestry, who have been recognised as the resident leaders of society, in their own neighbourhood, and to whom land and honours have been hereditary. The direct and indirect influence of such men is, at all times, very great. In the West Riding, there were several such among the friends of Messrs Wood and Walker, and to whom they were united by ties of friendship, and by a concord in principle and practice on public questions. Colonel Tempest, of Tong Hall, has at all times been ready to support the factory movement. He is a landowner of ancient family, a magistrate in the counties of York and Lancaster; a gentleman of sterling intergrity, he never yields on a question of principle. He maintains that it is the duty of the church to christianize the state; that it is the primary business of the state to care for the church; that the poor have prior rights of maintenance to all others. He viewed with horror, the cruelties practised in some factories, and affirmed that the church, state, and the law were disgraced by the very existence of the evils of the unregulated factory system. Were one asked to define the character of Colonel Tempest in a few words, the safe definition would be—"He is an English gentleman of George the Third's time." Colonel Tempest has only once spoken at a Ten Hours' Bill meeting, in the Castle yard of York; but his known support of that cause, and friendship for its public advocates, were of much importance, and he, unitedly with others of similar influence, constituted a powerful lever for the elevation of the oppressed. He is representative of others, not a few of whom, have been personally attached to Mr John Wood, or to Mr William Walker, or to both.

The joy of the factory operatives at the final success of their much and long-desired measure was great, and expressed in various ways; but invariably combining promise and exhortation for future improvement. The factory movement had been the means of training considerable numbers of working men to a high sense of responsibility and moral duty; they felt, that from them much was hoped, and they were anxious to guard against disappointment. Every great movement quickens the national intellect, and brings prominently forward those who would, otherwise, have remained in obscurity. Many among the working men, distinguished as leaders in the factory agitation, were of the rarest moral worth. The teachings of those more elevated in the social scale, who were also principals in that movement, from Gould to Oastler, directly tended to develope the devotional and moral properties of their humbler, but not less honourable coadjutors. The salutary results of this training were very apparent, in the modes adopted by the operatives to express their gratitude and joy. Many festivals were held in honour of the auspicious event. The most important of these was in the Free-trade Hall, Manchester, on June the 7th, 1848; it was a most imposing gathering. The addresses then delivered were of a truly ennobling kind. Lord Ashley condensed and expressed the feelings and desires of all when he said :—" I especially rejoice that we are here to testify, in the words of this important resolution, our thanks to Almighty God, who has blessed us with so happy an issue to all our efforts." "This great victory is, of all the victories I have ever known or heard of, the finest proof of moral triumph that has ever been exhibited to the admiration of a free people." "This we can promise, we who are in parliament, and we who are out of it, that if you will only be vigorous in the assertion of your own rights, we never will be wanting at any moment, in any circumstances, at any expense of time, trouble, aye, and of money too—we will, by the blessing of God, be ever ready at your call; and sure am I of victory ! And should it be necessary (to use a common phrase), ' we are all ready to die in the last ditch.' "

In commemoration of the event medals were struck. The Queen was pleased to mark her approbation by receiving from the factory operatives, at the hands of Lord Ashley, a gold medal.

Much labour and anxiety had brought on Mr Oastler a severe and dangerous illness. "The King of the factory children " was stretched on a bed of sickness, when his " subjects" were jubilant in the excess of joy. His absence only served to render his name the more impressive ; all acknowledged his services, all were anxious for his recovery.

The movement which had rendered principle triumphant, which had been successful against opposition, and many attempts at compromise, invariably rejected ; which had been the ally of humanity, and maintained directly on behalf of the oppressed, was worthy of being thus signally solemnized. A struggle of many years' duration, of unexampled perseverance, and aimed at the noblest of ends, had been brought to a successful issue. A national reproach had been blotted out; it could not any longer with truth be said, that the law allowed the flagrant sacrifice of the lives and health of factory operatives, in open defiance of physiological science, and the proved experience of thousands of sufferers. An important and indispensable preliminary step had been taken towards the physical and moral improvement of those whose lives, from infancy to death, are devoted to the maintenance of important branches of national industry. The spirit of mercy, by the authority of parliament, had been made consonant with national interests, and the lives and limbs of human beings, unable to protect themselves, shielded from unnatural and excessive risk and suffering by a judicious application of the beneficent principles of the constitutional law of these realms—a result alike worthy of the approval of the Queen and her subjects.

Mr Wm. Walker resolved to have a public rejoicing, and treated the whole of the workpeople of the firm of Walkers and Co., numbering at least 3,000, to a feast in the grounds of Bolling Hall; the men lunched in hospitable Yorkshire fashion, the children and women were amply supplied with tea and cakes—all enjoyed a substantial repast. The scene was one to make the heart glad, and none were more gratified than Mr Walker and his family, whose sympathies had been long keenly alive to the necessity of an improvement in the condition of the factory operatives. After the entertainment, several of Mr Walker's friends, among whom was Mr Ferrand, addressed the people. Suitable addresses were delivered by tried and known friends of factory regulation, and the proceedings were conducted throughout with much spirit and harmony. The following address was presented to Messrs Walkers and Co., "by their workpeople:"—

"Gentlemen—We, the workpeople in your employ, avail

ourselves of this opportunity of expressing the deep debt of gratitude we owe to you for the distinguished part you have taken, and the unwearied interest you have evinced, by your long-continued efforts in behalf of that measure, the accomplishment of which we are this day celebrating— 'The passing of the Ten Hours' Bill.'

" For a great number of years we and our children have been enjoying many of the advantages which must necessarily flow from the universal adoption of a reduction in the hours of labour in factories. Sixteen years have elapsed since you first joined us in the glorious cause, during the whole of which time we have been practically receiving some of the fruits which must arise from the Ten Hours' Factory Bill, you having, from that period to the present day, been working shorter hours than other manufacturers in the same branch of trade, and for which we now beg to offer you our most grateful acknowledgments.

" The improvement which we have witnessed in the minds and morals of our children and the younger branches of our fellow workers, is of such infinite magnitude that for their sakes and for the sake of society at large, we are, if possible, more highly grateful.

" We are sure, that you will not consider it any deprecia- tion of our sense of our obligation to you as a firm, if we make special mention of Mr Wood, and, separately, thank him for the princely munificence with which he has supported the Ten Hours' Bill. When that measure was first pressed upon the attention of parliament, and when it was uncommon for men of wealth and influence to stand up in defence of the factory children, he was found in the front ranks of their advocates, and was, we believe, the first manufacturer in Yorkshire who came forward boldly in their cause. It is, therefore, because he was thus early in the field that we deem it right specially to express out most grateful thanks to him for the benefits which he then conferred upon us.

" Whilst we have been receiving the fruits of your generosity, we trust that our conduct as servants has, in some
measure, merited your esteem and confidence, which it shall
ever be our most anxious wish to deserve.

" And now, that the object of our most anxious wishes
and solicitude is obtained, by the passing of the Ten Hours'
Bill, we beg to offer you our most grateful congratulations,
and, also our thanks to all the champions of this sacred
cause, whether in or out of parliament, who have, with such
indomitable zeal and perseverance, pursued this object to
its final accomplishment, an object so desirable, and one
which will be so beneficial to us and all the operative manufacturing classes.

" With every wish for your health and prosperity, and
that the same unity of sentiment and good feeling may
ever exist between us, we beg to subscribe ourselves, on
behalf of the operatives in the various departments we
represent,

"Your faithful and obliged servants,

"MATTHEW BALME, schoolmaster.

"THOMAS WALMSLEY, for the overlookers.

"JOSHUA LONGFIELD, for the mechanics.

"HENRY LUPTON, for the woolcombers.

"JOSEPH BEST, for the woolsorters."

Mr John Rawson, of Bradford, was, for many years,
chairman of the Short-time Committee, and took a conspicuous part in all the proceedings connected with the
factory movement. Mr Rawson was originally a factory
operative, and was then active in efforts to promote factory
legislation. On becoming a master, his zeal did not in the
least relax; he and Mr Matthew Balme, the energetic
secretary of the Bradford Short-time Committee, rendered
valuable services to the cause in which they were engaged.

It was thus that master and servant acted in "unity,"
as became those mutually dependent on each other.

On the following day Mr Walker received fifty guests at dinner, which included many of the supporters of the Ten Hours' Bill.

Thus ended one of the most extraordinary social movements on record, uniting within itself much of the energetic and philanthropic mind of the country, directed towards the accomplishment of a most important object. The labours of its advocates were not only crowned with success; to them belongs the honour of having pointed out to statesmen and philanthropists the importance of the consideration of the physical health, the moral welfare, and the education of the working classes. The factory movement was the precursor of the regulation in coal mines, sanatory, educational, and early-closing movements of later years. The enquiries and discussions, consequent on the investigation of the unregulated factory system, instructed and improved the understandings of vast numbers of men and women of all classes, and awakened them to a sense of the duties they owed to others as well as to themselves. Many who, in 1830, were startled at the novelty and the extreme nature of a remedial measure, regulating the hours of labour in all factories to ten per day, sanctioned by the legislature, were, in 1847, astonished, that opposition should have been offered, to a proposition so reasonable and humane. It is thus that public opinion undergoes, imperceptibly, changes of a most decided character, and, in its advancement, is apt to forget the point from which it has been moved by the intelligence and energy of the few. Factory regulation is, in the social economy of this country, an important fact, and the experience acquired thereby, serves the useful purpose of showing, which is the safe course to be followed by those who desire the permanent improvement of overworked and helpless children, women, and men.

Among the clergy, conspicuous for their services in the factory movement, must be prominently ranked the Rev.

James Bardsley, of Manchester, formerly of Burnley ; Rev. D. Jenkins (late) of Pudsey ; Rev. Wm. Heald, vicar of Birstal; Rev. James Cooper, Rev. J. Manning, of Huddersfield; Rev. J. Bateman, vicar of Huddersfield ; Rev. Joseph Loxdale Frost, of Bowling, near Bradford, Yorkshire ; Rev. George Smith, of Birkinshaw.

The Rev. Dr Aldis, a Baptist minister, formerly of Manchester, and now of London, was anxious in his efforts to make the Christian religion the practical rule of trade; consistently with this view of his duty, as a follower of Christ, the doctor was zealous in support of the Ten Hours' Bill. One effect was, that he gave offence to some among the principal members of his congregation ; he continued faithful to duty, without regard to personal consequences. Were he now to visit Manchester, he would find that good has followed from the measure he supported, and it is very probable, that some among those who thought him mistaken would acknowledge their former error. To Dr Aldis, and such as he, the factory operatives owe much ; their condition has been improved, through the assistance of such benefactors.

The Rev. Philip Garrett, Wesleyan minister, was very energetic in his efforts to impress on the minds of all the necessity for factory regulation.

A well-known name, among the Wesleyan Methodists, was William Dawson ; popularly and endearingly spoken of as "Billy Dawson." This gifted lay-preacher was a great favourite wherever known. Among the Wesleyan Methodists in Yorkshire and Lancashire "Billy" was "a power in the State;" the homely force and real eloquence of his preaching are, among Wesleyans and others, a frequent theme of conversation. From a close connection with the labouring portions of the population in the factory districts, he was well able to judge of the effects of the factory system, physically, morally, and mentally.

William Dawson joined Mr Sadler and Mr Oastler early, in their efforts for factory improvement. When the grave closed over this Christian and devoted man, tens of thousands mourned over his departure from earth; and the helpless factory children lost a kind, faithful, and powerful advocate of their cause. William Dawson frequently corresponded with Mr Sadler on the factory question; the published letters of the former breathe a spirit of devotion and earnestness which awakened in the breasts of many a desire to be useful; and induced them to become supporters of factory regulation. William Dawson was learned only in the Scriptures, and the vigorous writings of John Wesley; but these he applied with point and force, to every public question which commanded his attention. His denunciations of covetousness and fraud, wherever known, and without respect to persons, were proofs of the manliness and sincerity of his character. "Godliness," in William Dawson's sense of the word, was an eminently practical power; spiritual in its origin, but temporal, as well as spiritual, in its application; and especially to be tested by the fulfilment of the daily duties of life; a standard by which he measured the professions of factory owners, sometimes, to their annoyance, and, frequently, to their improvement. William Dawson was a sincere promoter of, and a powerful auxiliary to, the factory movement.

"Father Hearne," a Roman Catholic priest, who officiated in Manchester during the earlier efforts of Sadler and Oastler, was, in many respects, a remarkable man. The holding up of his hand had more weight in a street disturbance or riot, on the Irish present, than the authority of the magistrates backed by the police. The "Father," from his priestly office, exercised much influence; this was vastly increased by the natural force of his character and high moral principle. Often did

"Father Hearne" declare "that the misery of Ireland was physical and moral health, compared to what he had witnessed under the unregulated factory system in England;" and that he was "heart and soul" on the side of "Ten Hours a day, and no surrender." He was a *father* to all who sought his counsel and aid ; his name is seldom pronounced by a Roman Catholic in Manchester, but with devotional reverence, and rarely by a Protestant, but with respect. "Father Hearne" was a leader on the side of factory regulation, and considered no efforts too great in that cause ; this good man suffered considerable persecution, because of his support of Oastler and Sadler, without complaint ; and continued, in defiance of remonstrance, often urged, to wish success to their efforts.

John Brooke, Esq., of the firm of John Brooke and Sons, Armitage Bridge, near Huddersfield ; John Whitacre, Esq., of Woodhouse, near Huddersfield ; Thomas Cook, Esq., of the firm of Hagues, Cook, and Wormald, of Dewsbury ; the late John Halliley, Esq., of Dewsbury ; John Rand and Sons, of Bradford, Yorkshire ; and J. R. Kay, Esq., Bury, Lancashire, gave to the efforts of the more active promoters of the factory movement their approval. These names represent much respectability and wealth, and the sanction of their authority had weight on the minds of many others.

Among the working men who distinguished themselves by their persevering and anxious labours, were Samuel Glendenning, Joseph Hawkyard, Thomas Hutton, John O'Rourke, Henry Barker, Benjamin Copley, Thomas Walmsley, Joseph Firth, Isaac Bottomly, Wm. Gibson, Charles Howard, Samuel Walker, John Spencer, Abraham Wildman, William Rouse, Benjamin Wood, James Thornton, George Adams, James Gallimore, David Howgate, John Abbey, James Glendenning, James Hustler, James Mills, John Mills, Ralph Taylor, Robert Pounder.

Joseph Firth, in early life, suffered from the cruelties of

the unregulated factory system; his simple, methodical statements, before the Sadler committee, in 1832, and at many public meetings, were influential in producing the change he so earnestly desired. For many years he has been out of the factory, and is well known, in Keighley and neighbourhood, as a public-spirited and useful citizen. He now resides in a small cottage, his own property, situated on a Yorkshire moor edge; the scene and circumstances constitute a striking contrast with life in a factory, as formerly known to him.

James Mills, of Oldham, died about three years since, and was followed to his grave by a procession of those who honoured him when living.

The late Earl of Ellesmere, who, in the House of Commons, as Lord Francis Egerton, represented a manufacturing district, was widely known as a Christian nobleman of enlarged benevolence and benignant manners. His lordship's acute and unbiassed mind, readily apprehended the importance of factory regulation. The door of his princely mansion in London was, at all times, open to the factory delegates; his ear was ever ready to listen to their statements, and, for the benefit of their clients, his counsel was cheerfully given. When opposed by theoretical reasoners, or by those who designated themselves "practical men," he listened attentively, but usually answered, "What is best for the weak, will, in time, be proved to be also best for the strong." This justly lamented nobleman exercised great social influence in the cotton factory districts; in his own character were embodied, to a considerable extent, literature, art, philosophy, industrial, social, and moral progress; he was eminently the representative of the virtues and graces of the English nobility, and was withal, "great in his humility." The services which his lordship rendered to the factory movement were many and important; in his capacity of statesman, he advocated the Ten Hours' Bill, and his name gave influence to the cause he espoused. The working men of England have never had for their " friend," one of a kindlier heart. The late Earl of Ellesmere understood and reduced to practice the wisdom and philosophy of Shakespeare, as expressed in the words :

> " To thine ownself be true ;
> And it must follow as the night the day,
> Thou can'st not then be false to any man."

Hence it was, that he became the constant supporter of the claims of the workers in factories to legislative protection.

It was said, by Richard Brinsley Sheridan in 1810, when an influential member of the House of Commons deprecated the publication of parliamentary debates: " Give me but the liberty of the press, and I will give to the minister a venal House of Peers—I will give him a corrupt and servile House of Commons—I will give him the full swing of the patronage of office—I will give him the whole host of ministerial influence—I will give him all the power that place can confer upon him, to purchase up submission, and overawe resistance; and yet, armed with the liberty of the press, I will go forth to meet him undismayed; I will attack, with that mightier engine, the mighty fabric he has raised. I will shake down from its height corruption, and bury it beneath the ruin of the abuses it was meant to shelter."

This noble declaration, worthy the Augustan age of parliamentary eloquence, was prophetic in spirit. It was a glance by the soul of genius, beyond the historical letter of its time, but true of the future, and never more conspicuously verified than in the history of the factory movement. It was by the agency of the press, that the insolence of wealth had been subdued, and the lust of avarice made ashamed. Every debate in parliament was a tolling of the knell of factory despotism, and a precursor of its fall ; nobly as the newspaper press had done its duty, it was not alone ; —the *Quarterly Review, Blackwood's Magazine, Fraser's*

Magazine, distinguished themselves by an unreserved condemnation of factory cruelties, and a defence of the necessity for regulation by law; the able writing in the pages of these representative and directory organs of public opinion, was of inestimable value. The independent thinkers of the age were represented by Walter Landor, Robert Southey, and William Wordsworth, three stars in the literary hemisphere, which have shed more pure light below, than any other three we can name. Landor's *Imaginary Conversation between Romilly and Wilberforce*, is a complete digest of arguments in support of factory regulation. The striking delineation of, and reasoning upon, the evils of unregulated manufacturing industry, in the eighth and ninth books of Wordsworth's *Excursion*, will retain its place in our literature. Southey's more diffuse expositions on the same subject have out-lived much adverse criticism. There are others who have done good service.

James Montgomery, of Sheffield, a poet whose verses have been sung by many factory children, was anxious for the passing of a Ten Hours' Bill; he was an early and a faithful supporter of the cause. Montgomery had a sympathy for the oppressed and helpless, wherever known; and, while anxious for the emancipation of the " blacks," did not forget, for a moment, the claims of the " whites.' No poet, in the capacity of a citizen, ever more thoroughly reduced to practice the sentiments of humanity, as breathed forth by the inspiration of genius; his pity for the sufferings of the factory children was in keeping with the character of the man, and the spirit of the poet.

Mrs Trollope's novel, *Michael Armstrong*, has been much abused; it has, however, been useful, and so, also, has been *Helen Fleetwood*, by Charlotte Elizabeth.

The press has been powerful for good in the progress of the factory movement, and none can acknowledge its services more heartily than have the factory operatives. Seldom has any question enlisted so much talent, united to humanity, and strengthened by a consciousness of right; its supporters in literature and in law, have applied their influence to a desirable end, and, before their powers, ministers have yielded, and mammon has been cast prostrate. The circumstances of the country have contributed to increase the extent of the advantages of factory regulation; this result has been inseparable from the growth of British manufacture, and was forecast by those most zealous for the passing of the Ten Hours' Bill, and frequently urged by talented writers in the periodical press—" the fourth estate " was a principal propelling power in moving the other three; to it, in consequence, much honour is due. " Give me," said Mr Oastler, at the commencement of his labours, " Give me but this fact, that infants of seven years of age, in the mills of Bradford, positively work thirteen hours per day, with an intermission of half-an-hour for dinner, and you furnish me with a *fulcrum*, on which I will place the lever of truth, and, by the force of public opinion, obtain the Ten Hours' Bill."

Many among the former opponents of factory regulation have avowed their approval of the Act in operation; its supporters have good reasons for contentment with their labours. How that feeling is enjoyed, the following extract from a letter by Lord Feversham, to his friend, Mr Oastler, will exemplify:—" Time has confirmed most cordially and satisfactorily the views we entertained as to the beneficial effects of the measure, as it has completely set at naught the predictions of our opponents, who cannot now deny the improvement evinced in the condition of the operatives since the passing of the Act : to the humble, but sincere, and zealous part I had in the meetings, discussions, and parliamentary debates, I look back with a satisfaction unsurpassed on any other occasions or subjects whatever—the victory we at length achieved, was one of the greatest triumphs of the nineteenth century.—January 12th, 1857."

Lasting attachment is one of the rarest boons of life. Lord Feversham is known, as a nobleman of delicate sensibility, and of high honour. His unceasing friendship for Mr Oastler is creditable to his lordship: it has been, to the former, a source of confidence and consolation through many varied and trying troubles. His lordship's sympathy with his venerable coadjutor, has not been of the evanescent and easy kind, frequently awarded to public men, it has been solid and substantial, and is referred to in the most kindly way, by his lordship, in the following letter:—

"25 Belgrave square, May 23rd, 1857.

"Dear Sir,—I duly received your letter of the 20th, and am sincerely obliged. You are, it is superfluous to say, extremely welcome to any benefit you have received from me, and I truly hope your health will improve as the summer advances.

"We were, for years, fellow-labourers in a righteous cause, which it pleased God to prosper, and most important are the results, as regards the condition of those for whom we, or rather you, worked. Twenty-five years have elapsed since the County Meeting, at York. You headed the people from the West—I represented those in the North—from such a meeting we can date the victory we at length achieved, a hard-fought, but peaceful contest, because we were resolved not to violate the law or the constitution.

"Of all the measures I supported, whilst a representative of Yorkshire, I look upon the Ten Hours' Bill as the best, and most fraught with beneficial effects—it was a measure of justice, philanthropy, patriotism, and policy.

You see, I consider you, and write to you, as an old— one of my oldest friends !

" Had I been at home the day you called, it would have gratified me to have seen you.

                         " Ever yours truly,
                                   " FEVERSHAM.

" To Mr Oastler, Guildford, Surrey."

His lordship's expressions of satisfaction are reciprocated by all those of influence from their social position, who were the active promoters of the measure. Mr Fielden did not long survive the final success of his great parliamentary effort. His sons and relatives, " the Fieldens of Todmorden," who shared with him the labour and trouble attendant on his great exertions, have worthily and honourably guarded the boon won at so much cost, labour, and talent, and, through the hands of the late Mr John Fielden, of Todmorden, at length conferred upon the factory operatives.

The part sustained throughout the factory movement by Mr Oastler, the preceding pages have unfolded. His labours have not brought to him the honours which most men covet ; but, they have earned for him the affections of many whose love cannot fail to impart enjoyment. " The noblest of all martyrdoms is that of an old age impoverished by the generous sacrifices of youth ; and dependent on the gratitude or ingratitude of a world for whose good it has relinquished its all."—(The *Times*, March 16th, 1847.)

It was the working men of Huddersfield, who first united with Mr Oastler in active efforts, to instruct and direct public opinion, on the factory question. It was their conjoint agreement, to lay aside party politics, and apply their united energies in one common cause and for one common end, that constituted the " purchase power," which, in its application, led to such desirable social results. In all the vicissitudes of life,—and, during more than a quarter of a century, they have been many,—the friendship between Mr Oastler and the Huddersfield factory operatives has remained undisturbed. He now enjoys the tranquillity of an old age,—impoverished, in a worldly sense, it is true, by the generous sacrifice of manhood; but, hallowed and enriched, by a consciousness of much good having been done in earlier years, and gladdened by the contemplation of the benefits conferred on others. The reader who has accompanied us thus far, will not fail to appreciate the sincerity of the sympathy existing between Mr Oastler and his old friends, as unfolded in the following correspondence; a sympathy, rendered the more touching and creditable by the minute details and humble circumstances it reveals, and which, better than any words at our command, will convey to the reader the appreciation, on behalf of the operative classes, of a sense of benefits enjoyed. This correspondence is copied from the *Huddersfield Chronicle* of August 19, 1856, and is alike creditable to both the parties concerned.

" To Richard Oastler, King of the Factory Children.

" Dear Old Friend,—You are not forgotten. The factory operatives of Huddersfield never cease to remember you, their friend—the " King of the Factory Children." We know that your labours on our behalf, though profitable to us, have, in a money sense, made you poor; and knowing that, we feel persuaded you will not reject the accompanying present of a suit of cloths, top coat, and hat—all of the very best manufacture and workmanship, paid for by hundreds who have little to spare, but who thus wish to express their gratitude and hearty good-will. It is a small instalment of the great debt they and their children owe to you, for your long and devoted services in the great war against oppression and wrong, fought under the banners of the ' Ten Hours' Bill,' and for the restoration of the ' 43rd of Elizabeth.' The sacrifices you so nobly made, regardless of reproach, calumny,

and persecution—while battling for the weak against the
strong, for truth against error—for principle against expediency—although they have deprived you of many worldly
comforts, we doubt not in their results, and in their now
pleasing remembrance, fail not to yield you more real comfort, more solid satisfaction, than money can buy. We know
you feel, that you have not lived in vain. Of that fact we are
the evidences. We rejoice to tell you, because we know it will
gladden your heart—one of the results of the factory legislation in this part of Yorkshire, is, as you always said it
would be, the best of good feeling generally between masters
and workmen—the few exceptions being among those who,
in spite of God and man, are resolved to have their own
way. We heartily wish for the continuance and increase of
that good understanding. We are happy also to inform you,
that many who formerly opposed, now cordially approve the
' Bill.' One pleasing incident connected with our present
to you is, we intended to purchase the top coat cloth from
John Brooke and Sons, of Armitage Bridge; and when our
secretary, John Leech, called upon Mr Brooke, and informed
him what was on foot, Mr Brooke said, ' We do not cut
ends;' but, turning round, he further said, ' What length do
you require ? ' and on being told, went into the warehouse
and brought the required length of a super-Oxford broad,
observing, ' There now, tell the " old king," that is a present
from John Brooke and Sons, of Armitage Bridge, who wish
him health to wear it.' When Mr Brooke was told that the
operatives had subscribed the money to pay for it, he said,
' I am glad to hear you have not forgotten your old friend,
if you have any money to spare, send it to him, I dare
say he will find good use for it.' We know that the above
little incident will not be taken amiss.

" We most cordially beg your acceptance of our small
token of respect, with wishes for your health and strength
to wear it, knowing you will not like it the worse, because

it is given to you by the factory workers. To ensure a 'good fit,' we have had the suit made by your old tailor, Mr John Scott. When you write to us, we shall be glad to hear how you get on in your old age; and we assure you, your opinion and advice, on any subject, will be read with delight.

"Yours faithfully, (for the committee of operatives,)

"JOHN LEECH, Sec.

"P.S.—In one of the waistcoat pockets you will find two sovereigns which we had collected, but which, in consequence of the kindness of John Brooke and Sons, was not wanted.

"Huddersfield, July 20th, 1856."

Mr Oastler replied to his Huddersfield correspondents in a letter, bearing address and date; "South Hill Cottage, Guildford, Surrey, February 26th, 1856," reviewing their united exertions in the past, and expressing his opinions on some current questions of interest ; the concluding portions we quote, because they refer to the present position and habits of their author :—

"See, my friends, what a long letter I have written to you. Did not I tell you that your kindness had caused my heartstrings to vibrate ? You cannot wonder that, after a silence so long, being aroused by your striking token of affectionate remembrance, I who, for many years, in the strength of my manhood, watched and toiled with you, should, when thus refreshed by your love in my retired old age, in this, may be, my last letter to you, talk to you of things new and old. Your love will blot out all that is worthless ; it will cause you to treasure up what may be note-worthy. Here, I might conclude, had you not kindly said, ' We shall be glad to hear how you get on in your old age ?'

"Fancy an old man, satisfied with the share he has taken in the turmoil of life, with pleasing recollections of the past, and hopeful expectations for the future ; in the enjoy-

ment of moderate health, always in good spirits, his mind
being as elastic as in youth, retired to a neat, clean, comfortable cottage, standing in a very pretty walled-in garden,
half way up a hill as high as Fixby, overlooking an old
castle in ruins, and a fine old agricultural county town,
from which his cottage is separated by gardens and a
bowling-green ; the square lines of buildings being beautifully
broken by ivy and the rich foliage of forest and fruit trees.
That town is never darkened by a cloud of smoke. The
old man often sits in his rustic chair, at his cottage door,
gazing on the fine old ruin, and the lovely view of fields
and lanes, and woods, and heaths, and farm-houses and
cottages, spreading far beyond the town. The passing of
the railway trains reminds him of the busy trafficking of
the world; but he prefers the rural sounds and scenes by
which his prospect is enlivened. He is thankful that the
music of his charming songsters is near, and that the whirl
and whistle of the trains are at a distance. He spends
much of his time in his garden, delighting to watch the
progress of nature, and having a double relish for the
flowers, fruit, and vegetables ' grown in his own garden.'

" The old man's household is small, but as happy as
the day is long. A loved, a long-tried friend, in sickness,
his ever-watchful nurse ; in health, the lively companion
of his hearth and rambles; that faithful friend and a good
servant, who knows and loves and does her duty, form his
' establishment.' A little sweet-tempered black and white
spaniel (Phillis) adds to the pleasures of the three.

" The old man, in winter as in summer, rises early—
delighted with rambling in the fields, and lanes, and woods,
but chiefly rejoicing in his 'before-breakfast ramble,' the
air being then, as he says, 'most refreshing, most invigorating,
and the early song of the lark welcoming the great orb of
day, being more soul-stirring than his after notes.' The
sweet melodies of the cheerful songsters of the woods, fields,

and gardens, are, in his ear, the sweetest concerts. Nor does he fail to relish the rural music that most charms the shepherd's boy. The tinkling of the sheep's bells, the bleating of the lambs and sheep, the lowing of cattle, the neighing of horses, with many other rural sounds of cheerfulness, serve to banish gloom and foster joy.

"Though not an enemy to any real improvement in agriculture, the old man is not 'disgusted' when he sees a yoke of oxen ploughing or conveying manure to the field There may not be any 'profit' in the sweet peals of bells overhanging the fine teams of horses, when leading corn to market; but those bells impart cheerfulness to labour, both to man and horses. On the morning of the market-day, many such teams congregate in the High street, forming groups of men and horses, cheerfully and usefully employed, in storing the market-house with the richest produce of the fields, 'the staff of life.' There, many a time, he strays to feast his eyes and ears. 'Were I a farmer,' says he, 'I would aim at having the sweetest peal of bells; for it is becoming, that nature's bounty should be marketed with sounds of joy.' There is, however, one rural sight, above all others, which yields him pure delight—the old shepherd, with his crook in hand, leading (not driving) his flock. Delighted, the old man sits upon the grassy bank to see them pass. When any loiter or stray, the well-known voice allures them; they follow obedient to its call, but 'they know not the voice of strangers.' Then, the old man thinks of 'the Great Shepherd of the sheep, who, when He putteth forth His own sheep, He goeth before them, and the sheep follow Him; for they know His voice,' and who has graciously thus revealed himself to man—'I am the good shepherd, and know my sheep, and am known of Mine.' Oftentimes, the old man wanders among such sounds and scenes, accompanied only by his faithful Phillis, whose gambols always add to his delight. Frequently, his joy is increased when his beloved Maria is his companion, and when 'young students' honour him with their society. His cup of joy is full, when the group of ramblers is swelled by 'old friends from the north,' to whom he loves to exhibit his rich rural treasures, and point out the beauty-spots in the scenery, with a zest increased by repetition. He never seeks for new acquaintances; he cherishes old friendships, having a host of tried and faithful friends, who, with himself, bore the burden and heat of the day of struggle. Many such, and, not unfrequently, their children who have learned to love him, honour and refresh him by their visits. It is not easy to measure his delight on such greetings. He knows not that he has one enemy. His correspondence is as varied as it is extensive. Young and old, rich and poor, noble and plebian, are among his correspondents. He has many books, but the Holy Bible may now be said to constitute his library. On his intercourse with God, I may not dwell. He is full of faith and hope. In every day's blessing, realizing the truthfulness of Almighty God; and, sometimes, obtaining a glimpse of that glorious purchased inheritance, into which many of his friends and fellow-labourers have entered. Relying upon the mercy of God in Christ Jesus, he waits his turn in patience. When he looks backward, at every step he traces the hand and the goodness of God; if forward, his reliance is still upon that hand.

"In the eye of the mere merchant trader, the old man may be counted poor, but having long since placed his 'capital' in the 'Bank' that never fails, he is rich. In faith he cast his bread upon the waters, and now, after many days, he finds it. His God provides. The means of his sustenance come from the hands of generous clergymen, nobles, members of parliament, landowners, farmers, lawyers, bankers, merchants, factory masters, and (as your gift bears witness) the little fingers of grateful factory children. Say, then, my kind old friends, is not that old man rich? He has discovered the true secret of happiness, and thus, from year to year, he lives in contentedness and peace; sometimes receiving from those who know him best the consoling assurance, ' You have not lived in vain; of that fact we are the evidences.'

" I say, my friends, fancy an old man like that, and you will be able to answer your question, as to ' How I get on in my old age.'

" Fare ye well. Receive this letter as it is written—in love. God bless you all.

" I remain,

" My old and faithful friends,

" Yours, in truth and love,

" RICHARD OASTLER."

In the commencement, and throughout the progress of this unparalleled movement, many were found working effectively in the struggle, whose names were not so prominent, as were the names of others, but who contributed most valuable assistance to the great result.

Among these, and foremost, was Mr Charles Walker, whose brother William, and himself, were in intimate business connection with Mr Wood.

The talent of Mr Charles Walker was much appreciated in the Ten Hours' Bill committees. His counsel in difficulties, his firm adherence to the right, where some were disposed to waver—his logical power to unravel the sophistries of cunning opponents, on many occasions of deep interest; his manly, intelligent, and effective advocacy of the cause upon the platform and in the press, were rightly appreciated.

Mixing much in business transactions with all ranks of manufacturers, Mr Charles Walker had many valuable opportunities of silencing, if not convincing those adverse to his opinions, which he seldom failed to employ; and it would be unjust not to count him among the most valued friends of his great and successful effort.

Mr Lawrence Pitkethly, whose name has been frequently mentioned in the foregoing pages, has rendered services which it is not easy to acknowledge in fitting terms. He has been constant " in season, and out of season;" a man of remarkable physical and mental activity, of lively and enlarged benevolence. He has a reward for the many sacrifices he has made for the factory operatives in a consciousness of good done. Mr John Leech, of Huddersfield, was the constant coadjutor of Mr Pitkethly; Mr Leech's sterling honesty of purpose, untiring activity, and urgent earnestness, were oftentimes of great utility.

Few men have a kindlier, or a more generous disposition, than Mr David Weatherhead, of Keighley. As a tradesman and citizen, his reputation for honour and probity stands deservedly high. He, like Mr Pitkethly, and many others, is, in politics, a radical, but on the poor-law and factory questions, worked heartily with Sadler and Oastler. From 1829 to 1847, Mr Weatherhead supported, with much energy, the Ten Hours' Bill movement; and has witnessed, with satisfaction, the good effects which have followed the labours of himself and others. He has been often heard to say: " Whatever is really good for others, as a public measure, cannot be injurious to me; no man ought to allow his fear of results to prevent him from being faithful to what is in itself right." This may, or may not, be esteemed a wise maxim; it assuredly bears the stamp of a mind singularly free from prejudice and a contracted selfishness. At the great county meeting at York, at the Wibsey Low Moor meeting, and on many other occasions, Mr Weatherhead has rendered efficient service. In the township of Keighley, and neighbourhood, he has, at all times, advocated what he believed would, in practice, be most beneficial to working men, conspicuously so—the Ten Hours' Bill.

Robert Owen has been spared, by the hand of time, to a venerable old age. Mr Hindley is still in active public life; Mr Bull is rector of St Matthew's, Birmingham; Mr Stephens resides in Staleybridge; Mr Brotherton has paid the debt of nature; but few of the active spirits of the Ten Hours' Bill movement remain. " Lord Ashley" is now the Earl of Shaftesbury. Robert Blincoe, whose sufferings, in early life, must have, in the breast of every reader, awakened feelings of pity mingled with shame, is, in Manchester, a comparatively prosperous man. The good effects flowing from the labours of the dead and living advocates of factory regulation, are becoming every day more and more manifest, in the improved physical, educational, and moral condition of those engaged in factory labour. The factory districts are still capable and much in need of amendment, but no one who knew them, even ten years back, and has eyes to see, can doubt the improvement which has taken place. It is very satisfactory to be able to record, that not a few factory owners, formerly the opponents of all regulation, are now firm friends and willing witnesses of its good results. A few there are who still remain in stern opposition.

The increase of demand for cotton, beyond the existing means of supply, and which, at this time, is a subject of great and growing public interest, has caused some of those interested in manufacture, to think of the propriety of a further reduction in the hours of labour, and many to acknowledge, with renewed earnestness, the salutary influence of the Ten Hours' Act. The increase of machinery having surpassed the supply of cotton and raised the price of the raw material, to an extent incompatible with reasonable profits in manufacture, is a striking fulfilment of what John

Fielden, and others among the Ten Hours' Bill advocates, thought probable, and which, among other reasons, induced them to advocate regulation and restriction by law. It is very well known, and generally acknowledged, that with the present supply of cotton and the existing consuming power of machinery in manufacture, the working hours in factories are quite long enough to be profitable to manufacturers ; in fact, not a few mills are working shorter hours than fixed by the Factories' Act, for the reasons stated.

The events of the time, as regards the supply of cotton and its manufacture, prove, very decidedly, the advantages arising from the Ten Hours' Act; in the absence of such a law, cotton would have been higher in price, and the embarrassment of manufacturers from that cause, consequently, greater; this view of the case is now very well understood by many Lancashire cotton manufacturers, some among these were formerly opponents of all factory laws ; with a frankness that does them credit, they acknowledge their former mistake. Not any provincial town has a newspaper press conducted with greater talent than that existing in the city of Manchester ; its columns have recently contained correspondence of high value on the supply, demand, and price of cotton; from such correspondence, from personal inquiries, and other sources of information, it is pleasing to be enabled to record that the economical bearings of the short-time question gain in the estimation of public opinion by experience and discussion.

The whole tone and character of the factory system has, of late years, been elevated. Factory regulation, with other agencies, has operated to produce this desirable change; it has been the principal. There is now a much higher sense of the responsibilities of their position maintained among the millowners as a body, than was formerly common. Cruelties, such as those detailed in previous pages, could not now occur; all parties concerned would be ashamed of their existence;

a wholesome fear of public censure would, alone, be sufficient to deter many from the commission of gross outrages on humanity and decency. Some, among the owners of factories, where shameful cruelties were frequent, under the unregulated system, were guilty of a neglect of duty, rather than of positive cruelty ; they ignorantly allowed over-lookers and others to abuse the trust reposed in them. In the evidence given before parliamentary committees, and in speeches made at public meetings, the names of the principals of firms were necessarily conspicuous. It some-times happened that facts thus made known, awakened enquiry, which was followed by amendment. It is fortunate, most fortunate, that after trial, trouble, and tribulation to many, the whole system has undergone a decided improve-ment.

For the sake of example, such an incident as that so feelingly described in the evidence of Gillet Sharpe, of Keighley, before the Sadler committee of 1832, could not, from existing facts, be readily conceived. The circumstance formed the foundation of the following pathetic lines by Mr Sadler ; they contributed very influentially to bring about "a better time" for factory children :—

THE FACTORY CHILD'S LAST DAY.

"'Twas on a winter's morning,
    The weather wet and wild,
Three hours before the dawning
    The father roused his child ;
Her daily morsel bringing,
    The darksome room he paced,
And cried, 'The bell is ringing,
    My hapless darling, haste !'

"Father, I'm up, but weary,
    I scarce can reach the door,
And long the way, and dreary—
    O carry me once more !

To help us we've no mother,
   And you have no employ :
They kill'd my little brother—
   Like him I'll work and die !

" Her wasted form seem'd nothing,
   The load was at his heart :
The sufferer he kept soothing,
   Till at the mill they part.
The overlooker met her,
   As to her ' frame ' she crept,
And with his thong he beat her,
   And cursed her as she wept.

" Alas ! what hours of horror
   Made up her latest day ;
In toil, and pain, and sorrow,
   They slowly passed away :
It seemed as she grew weaker,
   The threads the oft'ner broke,
The rapid wheels ran quicker,
   And heavier fell the stroke.

" The sun had long descended,
   But night brought no repose ;
Her day began and ended
   As cruel tyrants chose.
At length a little neighbour,
   Her halfpenny she paid,
To take her last hour's labour ;
   While by her ' frame' she laid.

" At last the engine ceasing,
   The captives homeward rush'd ;
She thought her strength increasing—
   'T was hope her spirits flush'd :
She left, but oft she tarried ;
   She fell and rose no more,
Till by her comrades carried,
   She reached her father's door.

" All night, with tortured feelings,
   He watched his speechless child ;
While close, beside her kneeling,
   She knew him not—nor smil'd.

Again the factory's ringing,
　Her last perceptions tried ;
When from her straw bed springing,
　' 'Tis time !' she shrieked, and died !

" That night a chariot pass'd her,
　While on the ground she lay,
The daughters of her master
　An evening visit pay ;
Their tender hearts were sighing,
　As negro wrongs were told,
While the white slave was dying,
　Who gained their father's gold ! "

There is now, happily, no such " Factory Child's last day."

The home humanity of England is not, by any means, so great as her home wants require, to render the lot of the majority of her children desirable, but, as regards those employed in factory labour, there has been a marked and a necessary change. The light of experience and experiment cannot be wholly lost ; the empiricism of many pretenders to superior knowledge, and who opposed factory regulation as " a mischievous delusion," has been demonstrated; the theory of universal non-interference, even when clothed in the garb of " perfect liberty," has lost much of its power over the minds of the working men; they feel that they are not " perfectly free agents." Let sophists write and orators declaim to the contrary as much as they may, the error of the past has not been in the principle of interference; it is the foundation of all government, The error has been, that the physical and moral existence of the major part of British society—the working classes—has, in too many instances, been made subservient to the mere acquisition of riches. In a country avowedly Christian, mammon has been raised above man in the eye of the legislature. The passing of the Ten Hours' Act, in 1847, has proved a decided check to a dangerous delusion, and opened out the way for further improvements. What these ought to be, and how they may be accomplished, are questions demanding the attention of every thoughtful citizen. The business of those who assume to lead society in its course, is, to discover, what are the right objects towards which the combined action of public opinion should be directed. In the application of the necessary means for the realization of these objects, it is necessary to possess the most perfect possible knowledge of *all* the interests concerned, fully to weigh their equitable claims, and, on the balance of these, establish a practical rule of action. Man is both the instrument and subject of all human legislation, and is apt to fall into serious errors; when under the control of pure motives and an informed judgment, these will not be of frequent occurrence, and, when existing, will serve, like the sailor casting the lead, to indicate where, with safety, the vessel may be navigated.

And what were the characteristics of the ardent supporters of factory regulation? Consciousness of a just cause, and faith in its ultimate success. A small band of men united together, for a common purpose, pledged their word that they should succeed, and they, by force of conviction, dragged public and parliamentary opinion in their wake. No great object can be accomplished without confidence; it is, to the human mind, a lever of power. Does Chat Moss sink under the weight cast on its surface, and men stand aghast, and prophesy failure? What, under these circumstances, sustained the simple-minded George Stephenson? Confidence in the soundness of his own judgment. This is one of the latest, and most striking proofs of the power of faith, founded on knowledge. The result of such knowledge and confidence, as applied in the material world, and manifested in railway communication, is travelling at numbers of miles per hour, which, even men of scientific reputation declared to be irreconcilable with human existence. Theory has been disproved by fact, and every bar of iron laid down for railway purposes, is a rebuke to the pretentious ignorance that prophesied "Impossible." History has many illustrations of the potent power of faith in the future; one of the most remarkable, was the confidence of Columbus in the existence of "a new world;" he, of all his companions, had faith, and "the new world" is now the rival of the old. Physical facts come home to the senses of men; they are visible to the eye. Results in the region of mind and morals, though less distinct, are not less real. As a physical fact, factory regulation may be seen; its real and effective power on mind and morals, can only be understood by a contemplation of what must have been, had the evils forenamed in these pages, not been checked. The propelling power to action, on the part of the principal leaders in the Ten Hours' Bill movement, was a union of knowledge and faith ; many were called to rest with their fathers, before the object desired was realised ; yet, the labours of such were not lost. History, offers her tribute of testimony to the truth, tersely expressed by a gifted poet:—"They never fail, who die in a great cause."

THE END.